The Urbana Free Library

To renew materials call
217-367-4057

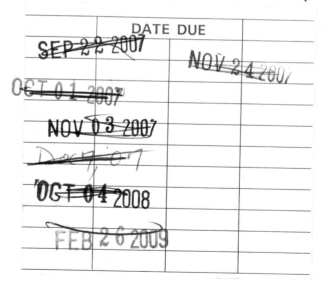

FOUNDED BY BURNS MANTLE

THE BEST PLAYS THEATER YEARBOOK 2005–2006

JEFFREY ERIC JENKINS
Editor

EDITORIAL BOARD
ROBERT BRUSTEIN
TISH DACE
CHRISTINE DOLEN
ROBERT HURWITT
JOHN ISTEL
CHRIS JONES
JULIUS NOVICK
MICHAEL PHILLIPS
CHRISTOPHER RAWSON
ALISA SOLOMON
JEFFREY SWEET
LINDA WINER
CHARLES WRIGHT

PAST EDITORS
(1919-2000)
BURNS MANTLE
JOHN CHAPMAN
LOUIS KRONENBERGER
HENRY HEWES
OTIS L. GUERNSEY JR.

CONSULTING EDITOR
HENRY HEWES

PHOTO EDITOR
ROBERT KAMP

ASSISTANT EDITORS
RUE E. CANVIN, PAUL HARDT, VIVIAN CARY JENKINS

THE BEST PLAYS
THEATER YEARBOOK

Editorial research and data compilation
for *The Best Plays Theater Yearbook 2005–2006*
has been partly underwritten by a generous grant from
the Harold and Mimi Steinberg Charitable Trust.

Carole A. Krumland, James D. Steinberg, Michael A. Steinberg,
Seth M. Weingarten, William D. Zabel
Directors

○ ○ ○ ○ ○ ○ ○ ○ ○ ○ ○ ○ ○ ○ ○ ○

THE BEST PLAYS
THEATER YEARBOOK
2005–2006

○ ○ ○ ○ ○ ○ ○ ○ ○ ○ ○ ○ ○ ○ ○ ○

EDITED BY

JEFFREY ERIC JENKINS

Illustrated with production photographs

○○○○○

LIMELIGHT EDITIONS
An Imprint of Hal Leonard Corporation
New York

Published in 2007 by
Limelight Editions
An Imprint of Hal Leonard Corporation
19 West 21st Street, New York, New York 10010
www.limelighteditions.com

INTRODUCTION

THE 2005–2006 SEASON had barely begun when summer rumors began to circulate that the health of playwright August Wilson was in jeopardy. As journalists in Wilson's adopted hometown of Seattle investigated reports of intensive treatment for liver cancer, the daily newpaper in Pittsburgh, city of his birth and the locus of his 10-play cycle on the African-American experience in the 20th century, published news that his illness was fatal. Speaking to *Pittsburgh Post-Gazette* theater editor Christopher Rawson—a *Best Plays* editorial board member and frequent contributor to the series—Wilson said, "I've lived a blessed life. I'm ready." The news broke in the Pittsburgh paper and in Seattle newspapers August 26, 2005, a week before the Labor Day holiday whose end marks the traditional beginning of the theater season. (For purposes of record keeping, *Best Plays* marks the season from June 1 through May 31.) To say that the news cast a pall on those late summer days is the height of understatement. But there it was: confirmation that one of our greatest playwrights had been given a death sentence from which there would be no reprieve. How could it be that, as late as 2005, a national treasure—who surely had more plays to share with his audience—could not be saved by medical technology or miracle? What would Aunt Ester do?

Aunt Ester, Wilson aficionados will recall, is the sage, seer and healer who figures in several plays of the cycle. But Aunt Ester dies in *King Hedley II*, set in 1985, creating a spiritual dislocation that plays out in *Hedley* and informs *Radio Golf* (honored herein with a Steinberg Citation)—the final play of the cycle, set in the 1990s. One suspects, though, that Aunt Ester, who is, after all, a product of the playwright's experience and consciousness, might herself have said, "I'm ready." A poignant irony also haunted many in the community: as Wilson battled his own illness *American Theatre* published the playwright's eulogy for his friend and frequent collaborator, producer Benjamin Mordecai, who died a few months earlier (May 8) at the same age as Wilson and of a similarly debilitating illness. Soon after it was learned that the masterly dramatic poet—only 60 years old—had been given a terminal diagnosis, Jujamcyn Theaters, which housed and/or produced six of the cycle plays on Broadway announced that it would rename the Virginia Theatre in honor of the playwright. The name-change ceremony at the August Wilson Theatre occurred October 16, 2005, exactly two weeks after the playwright succumbed to his illness.

For the *Best Plays* series, the loss is both institutional and personal. Each of Wilson's plays in the cycle has been honored in these pages as either a Best Play in New York or through the American Theatre Critics Association's New Play Awards and Citations, now known as the Steinberg/ATCA New Play Award and Citations. Wilson was never anything but generous toward the editors of the series—although he was, admirably, a stickler for making sure that whatever was quoted from a play of his was from the correct version (a sometimes tricky task as his plays evolved from production to production). A few years ago, Wilson showed his appreciation for *Best Plays* by writing, in part, that the series "is an indispensible compendium of theater fact and lore, a much-needed chronicle of the season that has proven to be a boon for theater historians. I can't imagine the theater world without it." We were so moved by his thoughts and feelings that we asked to include them on the book's jacket and did so until his death. Now, it is we who cannot imagine the theater world without him.

A week after the christening of the August Wilson Theatre, Wendy Wasserstein's new play, *Third*, opened Off Broadway at Lincoln Center. Here was reason for celebration: Wasserstein's new play mined, in especially lively fashion, issues surrounding privilege and what they mean in contemporary America. It was the playwright's best play in years and certainly one of her finest to date. Yet the exultation was muted as it became known in New York's tight-knit theater community that Wasserstein was gravely ill. As Anne Cattaneo relates in her essay in this volume, by the time *Third* closed December 18, 2005, Wasserstein was in a coma. She died of lymphoma January 30, 2006.

Ten days after Wasserstein's death, playwright John Belluso was found dead of a heart attack in his New York hotel room. Only 36, Belluso had begun to make a name for himself as a writer of plays that confronted conventional notions about disability and the disabled. Belluso had an intimate understanding of these issues due to the rare bone disorder that kept him confined to a wheelchair. As Robert Simonson reported for Playbill.com:

> many of his plays featured a disabled character. In *Henry Flamethrowa*, seen Off Broadway at Studio Dante in May 2005, a

teenager reveals his plans to disconnect his comatose younger sister Lilja from her breathing ventilator and allow her to die. *Pyretown*, staged by the Keen Company Off Broadway in January 2005, concerned an unlikely love affair between a young man in a wheelchair and a middle-aged single mom.

What, one was provoked to ask, is happening to our playwrights this season? Three prominent and promising voices were stilled, and despite the fact that theater programming is done well in advance, there was more than a hint of darkness hovering everywhere this season.

II

WHY CAST THESE DARK portents to introduce a celebration of the year in theater? As in western theater's ancient roots, which mark the life cycle of humanity—birth, life, death and rebirth (literal and figurative)—the end of life and what we make of it has for centuries been the mark of our most powerful drama. In this brief span of a few months, three bright lights of our national stage were dimmed too soon.

When is it ever the right time to lose someone we value or love? These are, to some extent, concerns of the quotidian, of melodrama; and still, they bear consideration. As the 2005–06 season ended and the next one began, three giants of the theater died: producer and composer Cy Feuer, director Lloyd Richards and theater advocate Henry Hewes. Each of these men had long and successful lives in the theater—Richards and Hewes were especially close to *Best Plays* (one as the great director and teacher, the other as the very active consulting editor to *Best Plays* until just a few days before his death)—and yet their loss is no less intense than that of the playwrights taken from us.

This darkness, this sense of loss fits somehow as we consider the 10 Best Plays of 2005–06. Two years ago (2003–04) the themes of the Best Plays, as it happened, centered largely on issues related to female subjectivity and the authors represented were women by a wide margin. In the edition prior to this one (2004–05), the chosen plays were judged to have explored "what it means to be human in a world where borderlines between public and private have become increasingly blurred." In the choices made by the editor and editorial board for 2005–06 edition, melancholic themes abounded: Even comically oriented works center on a dark emotional core.

The musical *Grey Gardens* by Doug Wright, Scott Frankel and Michael Korie takes as its inspiration the 1975 cult documentary film about two women—a mother and her daughter—who were once near the center of high society. Relatives of Jacqueline Kennedy Onassis and Lee Radziwill,

Edith Bouvier Beale and her daughter were ultimately abandoned by all of their male relatives and forced to fend for themselves in a large Hamptons home that fell into decrepitude, as did the women themselves. Wright's second Best Play (a first for Frankel and Korie), it is a sad tale given greater poignancy by the creators' employment of a first act showing better days. In Alan Bennett's *The History Boys*, a roguish teacher and polymath—whose behavior borders on pedophilia—struggles for the intellectual souls of his students against a young tutor who turns learning into a commodity that can be packaged for easy consumption by admissions directors of colleges (and by the masses). In Bennett's dramatic paradigm, which represents his third Best Play, education has become merely a means for the creation of capital (economic, political, cultural)—which is essentially an argument Tocqueville made about American education nearly 180 years ago.

We welcome Danai Gurira and Nikkole Salter to the ranks of Best Plays authors for *In the Continuum*, their haunting vision of African and African-American women mired in the global AIDS crisis and disenfranchised by their respective cultures. Rolin Jones's *The Intelligent Design of Jenny Chow* brings another promising young writer into the Best Plays fold with his rollicking comedy about a brilliant (and agoraphobic) young Asian woman who was adopted as a baby by an American couple. An array of kooky computer geniuses and supersecret defense contractors help Jennifer Marcus build a flying robot (Jenny Chow) that will find the adopted girl's natural parents. As counterpoint to Jones's wacky humor, however, the play unearths an unrelentingly modern sense of dislocation: a girl searches for a sense of authentic identity, a career-driven mother marvels over mobile telephone communications as her daughter makes (highly illegal) deals for guidance systems to power a flying robot, a father wonders when his family unit disintegrated and the Asian family who gave their daughter for adoption lives in a simple, rural home of low means.

Martin McDonagh returns with his third Best Play, *The Lieutenant of Inishmore*, a blackhearted and gruesome comedy lampooning the excesses of people who cry for rebellion in the name of humanity. David Lindsay-Abaire's *Rabbit Hole* is his first work to be celebrated by *Best Plays*. The play, which received the 2007 Pulitzer Prize just as we were going to press, chronicles the challenges of a couple and their extended family after the death of a beloved little boy. *Red Light Winter* is a dark vision of a distinctly different sort. In Adam Rapp's third Best Play, a finalist for the 2006 Pulitzer Prize, a depressed, poetic soul finds himself emotionally swept away after a sexual encounter with a prostitute with whom the writer—playwright Rapp says that he is not the poet depicted—becomes obsessed. Unfortunately for the writer, the lady is enamored with the writer's friend forming an unseemly triangle of pain. Conor McPherson's second Best Play, *Shining City*, engages a form familiar to the playwright and his audience—that of the ghost story—but he infuses his tale with a love triangle filled with guilt and recrimination.

In *Stuff Happens*, David Hare's third Best Play, the author constructs (or reconstructs) from the published record, and from interviews he conducted, dialogues in the US and in England that led to the 2003 military invasion in Iraq. With commentaries provided by characters who were outside the negotiations (such as they were), Hare raises questions about how the current debacle sets dangerous precedents for future governments and for future antigovernment radicals. Finally, we return to Wasserstein's *Third*, her third Best Play, in which a college professor, endowed with all of the privileges of a senior tenured academic, assumes that a young man with a preppy nickname must be overprivileged—she gets some of this attitude by watching too many news stories about a certain President of the United States. But the professor also finds herself, at the pinnacle of her working life, suffering loss after loss: intimacy in her marriage declines, her father dissipates before her eyes and her daughter views her with contempt. It is the sad completion of a dramatic cycle of baby-boom women that began in Wasserstein's *Uncommon Women and Others*. In that play, one character is convinced that things will soon be better, that she will get her "head together," that the women of the title will be "amazing." In the final speech Rita says, "If I make it to forty I can be pretty amazing. [. . .] Holly, when we're forty we can be pretty amazing. You too Muffy and Samantha, when we're [. . .] *forty-five* we can be pretty fucking amazing."

In *Third*, Wasserstein's lead character, Laurie Jameson, seems to reach that moment of "amazing" only to be faced with the decline we all experience if we are lucky and live long enough. In this regard, Jameson is not unlike Willy Loman who tells his brother in a recalled conversation that "I still feel—kind of temporary about myself." Jameson, as with Loman, is disconnected from the identity she has carefully constructed (and not, it seems, in such very different ways from Arthur Miller's "common man").

In addition to the plays celebrated in these essays, we also hope that readers enjoy the volume's expanded statistics and index. Whenever possible we track all Broadway and Off Broadway revivals back to their original presentations in New York, around the country and abroad. In the case of William Shakespeare and others of his ilk, we employ George C.D. Odell's *Annals of the New York Stage*—which links with the *Best Plays Theater*

Yearbook series to chronicle New York theater back to the 18th century. We also use the archives of *The New York Times* and other major publications as we attempt to locate plays in their original contexts.

With our colleagues in the American Theatre Critics Association, we also keep close tabs on new plays developing in theaters across the US. Through the Harold and Mimi Steinberg Charitable Trust, we recognize the honorees of the Steinberg/ATCA New Play Award and Citations. The Steinberg Charitable Trust, which has supported the *Best Plays Theater Yearbook* series since 2001, recently demonstrated its support of our mission by refocusing its commitment to our work. We extend our deepest thanks to the Trust and its board (William D. Zabel, Carole A. Krumland, James D. Steinberg, Michael A. Steinberg and Seth M. Weingarten) for making *Best Plays Theater Yearbook* a priority for their support.

Honorees for the 2006 Steinberg/ATCA New Play Award and Citations are Lee Blessing's *A Body of Water*, which won the Steinberg top prize ($25,000). Blessing's play is discussed by Dominic P. Papatola. The 2006 Steinberg/ATCA New Play Citations (along with $7,500 each) went to Adam Rapp's Best Play (and Pulitzer Prize finalist) *Red Light Winter* (detailed here by Chris Jones), and to August Wilson for *Radio Golf* (essay by Christopher Rawson).

III

AS WE MOVE FORWARD with the 87th volume of this chronicle of theater in the United States, we celebrate our ongoing partnership with Limelight Editions, now under the management of John Cerullo.

The collection of data for a volume such as this relies on the labors of many people. Our thanks to Paul Hardt for his efforts on the Cast Replacements and Touring Productions section, and to John Istel for his essay on Off Off Broadway theater. Istel has for this edition and for its immediate predecessor sparked *Best Plays*'s process of rethinking OOB and how this series covers it. Rue E. Canvin, who has worked on the *Best Plays* series for more than 40 years, continues to make the USA section a "must-read" for those interested in theater around the country. Jonathan Dodd, the longtime publisher of the *Best Plays* series, continues to provide important background information and good advice.

We are also deeply indebted to all of the press representatives who assisted in the gathering of information for this volume, but we particularly acknowledge Adrian Bryan-Brown and Chris Boneau of Boneau/Bryan-Brown for their unflagging support of the series and its editors.

Thanks also are due to the members of the *Best Plays Theater Yearbook's* editorial board, who give their imprimatur to our work by their presence on the masthead. We are grateful as well to those who have offered and provided extra support and assistance to this edition: Charles Wright, Christopher Rawson (Theater Hall of Fame Awards), Caldwell Titcomb (Elliot Norton Awards), David A. Rosenberg (Connecticut Critics' Circle Awards), Elizabeth Maupin (Steinberg/ATCA New Play Award and Citations), Edwin Wilson and Mimi Kilgore (Susan Smith Blackburn Prize) and Michael Kuchwara (New York Drama Critics' Circle Awards). Given the volume and broad spectrum of theater books and plays now published each year—a very good trend, it seems, we no longer publish a list of books published during the season under review.

We especially note the ongoing joint efforts of the *Best Plays* editorial team and the research department of the League of American Theatres and Producers over the past several years. First with Stephen Greer and now with Neal Freeman, we have worked since 2002 to correct the records of the Internet Broadway Database (www.ibdb.com) as well as past errors made in the pages of *Best Plays*. During the past year, we have brought the records of IBDB and *Best Plays* into line with corrections to the following past productions: *Desire Under the Elms* (1924–25), *Awake and Sing!* (1935), *The Threepenny Opera* (1954; 1955–61), *A Hatful of Rain* (1955–56), *The Odd Couple* (1965–67), *Two Gentlemen of Verona* (1971–73) and *Seascape* (1975). Some of these corrections, it may be noted, are not included elsewhere in this book; that is due, in general, to those productions not being chosen as Best Plays in an earlier production or not reaching the level of 500 performances, which is required for inclusion on our Long Runs lists. Our thanks and compliments to our friends at the League for their cooperation in this long-term project of correcting the historical record.

We congratulate and thank all of the Best Plays honorees who made the 2005–06 season so invigorating to contemplate. Alan Bennett, Scott Frankel, Danai Gurira, David Hare, Rolin Jones, Michael Korie, David Lindsay-Abaire, Martin McDonagh, Conor McPherson, Adam Rapp, Nikkole Salter, Wendy Wasserstein and Doug Wright all enriched our lives during the season under review. The photographers who capture theatrical images on film and help keep those ephemeral moments alive for historical perspective are also due thanks for their generous contributions to the greater body of theatrical work. Building on our work from past years, we have included credits with each photograph and indexed the photographers' names for easier reference. Similarly, we continue offering biographical information about each of this volume's essayists and editors.

A personal note: In addition to serving as editor of this series, I teach full-time in the Drama Department at New York University's Tisch School of the Arts. I am blessed with superb students who inspire me to strive for excellence in my teaching, research, editing and writing, I also have the support and friendship of as fine a faculty of artists and scholars as I have had the honor to know. Each member of the faculty has provided the kind of encouragement one needs to keep in print an annual compendium of critical perspective and historical reference that runs more than 500 pages. Thanks to all of my colleagues for their advocacy, especially to the senior academic faculty: Awam Amkpa, Una Chaudhuri, Jan Cohen-Cruz, Laura Levine, Carol Martin and Robert Vorlicky. For the season under review, I especially thank our department chair, Kevin Kuhlke, and our director of theater studies, Edward Ziter, for their continuing support of my work as a teacher, researcher and writer.

My wife, Vivian Cary Jenkins, continues to serve the theater and *Best Plays Theater Yearbook* as a tracker of what's happening in the New York theater. Despite facing challenges that would utterly stymie someone made of lesser stuff, she continues to contribute in ways large and small to the success of the series. Although I repeat these thanks each year, one thing remains true: It is largely through her consistent efforts that this series continues to appear.

JEFFREY ERIC JENKINS
NEW YORK

Contents

THE SEASON
ON AND OFF
BROADWAY

THE SEASON:
BROADWAY AND OFF BROADWAY

○ ○ ○ ○ ○ *By Jeffrey Eric Jenkins* ○ ○ ○ ○ ○

BEFORE THE TELEVISION LIGHTS had begun to cool in Radio City Music Hall at the end of the 2006 Tony Awards telecast, Times Square touts clogged the aisles on their way to late-night parties and shook their heads as they made their way through the well-dressed throng. The jukebox musical dedicated to the careers of Frankie Valli and the Four Seasons, *Jersey Boys*, had just won the best new musical Tony Award after awards for best book (Bob Martin and Don McKellar) and score (Lisa Lambert and Greg Morrison) had gone to *The Drowsy Chaperone*, the loving sendup of 1920s musicals that made its way to Broadway from Canada.

"How," one piqued young man asked another, "can a show win best book and best score, but not best musical?" He was clearly upset at the result. It was tempting to lean over and say, "You know this happened as recently as 2002 when *Urinetown* received awards for best book (Greg Kotis), best score (Mark Hollman and Greg Kotis) and best director (John Rando), but *Thoroughly Modern Millie* won best musical." In fact, however, 2002 saw the musical spoils divided a bit unequally between *Urinetown* and *Millie*. In addition to best musical, *Millie* also won awards for best actress in a musical (Sutton Foster), featured actress in a musical (Harriet Harris), orchestrations (Doug Besterman and Ralph Burns), choreography (Rob Ashford) and costumes (Martin Pakledinaz). In the battle between *Jersey Boys* and *Drowsy Chaperone*, the playing field was more level with *Jersey Boys* receiving awards for best actor, best featured actor and best lighting design of a musical. Besides the book and score awards, *Drowsy Chaperone* also won best featured actress, best scenic design and best costume design of a musical. (Since the 2005 Tony Awards, musicals and plays have separate sets of design awards so they no longer compete across theatrical forms.) The other musical awards were divided between two revivals: *The Pajama Game* (best musical revival to Roundabout Theatre Company and best choreography to Kathleen Marshall) and *Sweeney Todd* (best direction to John Doyle and best orchestrations to Sarah Travis).

BROADWAY SEASON 2005–2006

Productions in a continuing run on May 31, 2006 in bold

Plays honored as Best Plays selections in italics

Best Plays from prior seasons are noted with a date in parentheses

NEW PLAYS (8)

After the Night and the Music
(Manhattan Theatre Club)
A Naked Girl on the Appian Way
(Roundabout Theatre Company)
Souvenir
Rabbit Hole (MTC)
Festen
The History Boys
The Lieutenant of Inishmore
Shining City (MTC)

NEW MUSICALS (11)

Lennon
In My Life
Jersey Boys
The Woman in White
The Color Purple
Chita Rivera: The Dancer's Life
Lestat
The Wedding Singer
Hot Feet
The Drowsy Chaperone
Tarzan

PLAY REVIVALS (11)

The Constant Wife (26–27) (RTC)
Absurd Person Singular (MTC)

PLAY REVIVALS *(cont'd)*

The Odd Couple *(64–65)*
Seascape (74–75)
(Lincoln Center Theater)
A Touch of the Poet (58–59) (RTC)
Barefoot in the Park (63–64)
Well (03–04)
Awake and Sing! *(34–35)* (LCT)
Three Days of Rain
Faith Healer
The Caine Mutiny
Court-Martial (53–54)

MUSICAL REVIVALS (3)

Sweeney Todd *(78–79)*
The Pajama Game (RTC)
The Threepenny Opera
(75–76 Special Citation) (RTC)

SOLO PERFORMANCES (4)

Mark Twain Tonight!
Primo
The Blonde in the Thunderbird
Bridge and Tunnel

SPECIALTIES (2)

Latinologues
Ring of Fire

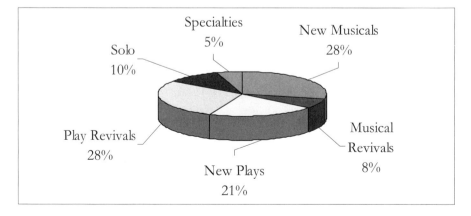

Specialties 5%
New Musicals 28%
Solo 10%
Musical Revivals 8%
Play Revivals 28%
New Plays 21%

The annoyed young men, however, seemed to have Canadian accents—we slipped around them and into the crowd. After enjoying a couple of seasons of *Slings and Arrows*, the brilliant Canadian television program about an often-mad theater company, we knew better that to mess with Canadian theater folk. (And, by the way, the creative forces behind *Drowsy Chaperone* are also the talents behind that television show.)

The big news of the 2006 Tony Awards, though, was the utter dominance in the play category by the British import, *The History Boys*. With six awards, it seemed to have set a new record for Tony Awards in its category: "seemed to" because some believe that Arthur Miller's 1949 *Death of a Salesman* also won six awards. In the case of *Salesman*, however, those six include separate awards for best play, best dramatic author and best dramatic producer. This raises questions: Were those really three separate awards? How does one separate best play and best author? (Contemporaneous news accounts are not definitive and the American Theatre Wing is researching the issue.) For the record, the best musical of the 1949 season, *Kiss Me Kate*, also won what appears to be a separate prize for best musical authors (Bella and Samuel Spewack), best composer (Cole Porter) and best musical producers. Another issue from those 1949 awards is that the great scene designer Jo Mielziner was honored for five shows he designed that year, not only *Salesman*. So while it is unclear if *History Boys* actually set a record, it certainly demonstrated a dominance unseen in more than 50 years—some of which was aided by the addition of the aforementioned second set of design awards: *History Boys* received awards in scenic and lighting design.

Variety's Gordon Cox wrote that *History Boys* author Alan Bennett seemed to feel a bit guilty about his play winning so many awards. In remarks backstage, the playwright said, "It almost seems unfair to be given prizes for something we've had such a good time doing." Bennett needn't have worried, though, he was merely part of the trend of the evening. Of the 24 competitive categories, 13 of the awards were won by works that began outside the US. Furthermore, of the four new pieces nominated for the best play Tony, three were Anglo-Irish imports; the play-revival category was a 50-50 split: an American entry (*Awake and Sing!*) received the well-deserved honor. It was clear for the 60th anniversary of the Tony Awards that excellence on Broadway was a transatlantic, if not global concept.

One person very present in his absence was the larger-than-life producer and director Harold Prince, who had been voted a special lifetime achievement Tony Award. Prince, who already had special Tony Awards given to him in 1972 and 1974, had also received 18 Tonys as a producer and director in competitive categories since 1955—he was a producer of the original version of *The Pajama Game*. He could not attend the Tony ceremony because he was readying the Las Vegas production of *The Phantom of the Opera*, now the longest running show on Broadway. According to the London *Guardian*, more than $75 million had been spent to get to the first performance at the Venetian Hotel—including a $40 million, 1800-seat replica of the Paris Opera House and a $5 million chandelier effect. With that much money riding on a production scheduled to open only a couple of weeks after the Tony Awards, it is no wonder the great impresario skipped the trip to the Radio City stage.

In one sense, the 2005–06 season had Las Vegas productions of Broadway product as an interwoven subplot throughout. *Best Plays* readers may recall the controversy sparked following the 2004 Tony Awards when producers of *Avenue Q* elected to forgo a national tour—after presumably receiving a substantial number of Tony Award votes from road presenters—because they were offered a "sitdown" run at Steve Wynn's Las Vegas resort. *Avenue Q* producer Kevin McCollum told Jesse McKinley of *The New York Times* that staying in Las Vegas "could save more than $2 million a year in touring expenses." Despite the feelings of betrayal evoked in road presenters by the deal, other shows began looking to the desert playground as a new source of audience (and revenue). *Phantom* was announced for Las Vegas in July 2004—to begin a run in 2006—though tour presenters could hardly have felt snubbed after the Andrew Lloyd Webber show's nearly continuous tours since the late 1980s. Then *Hairspray* made a deal in January 2005 for a streamlined production—Las Vegas shows almost never run longer than 90 minutes or have intermissions—to play at the Luxor Hotel.

By the fall of 2005, Chris Jones wrote in *Variety*, "Producers are blabbing everywhere about sweetheart desert deals and $100 million, custom-designed theaters as playgrounds. Hotel owners are happy to declare Vegas the new Broadway." It was enough to send a chill through the Broadway theater landlords and to make road presenters, particularly in the southwest, worry about the future. In October 2005, *The New York Times* ran a Sunday Arts and Leisure piece by Jesse Green on theater in Las Vegas titled, "Live on the Strip: Broadway's Second City." The article was filled with verbal swipes from Las Vegas hotel personnel and from producers who had done well on Broadway. As the Luxor's Felix Rappaport told Green, "The financial model here is much better. Broadway, which arguably has the greatest concentration of live entertainment in the country, also has a failure rate of 90 percent."

Avenue Q's McCollum extolled Las Vegas work rules that offered greater creative freedom. Green recounted this story:

> There is, for instance, the case of the ceiling fan: a little visual joke [director Jason] Moore wanted to add to the set in New York. Mr. McCollum, the producer, said that because of what he called "idiotic" union work rules on Broadway, "it would have cost $100,000 in labor. Here it costs $28, the price of the fan. New York has some things to learn from Las Vegas."

Las Vegas *Hairspray* co-producer Michael Gill told Green,

> Broadway theaters are lacking because they're landlocked and landmarked[. . . .] They have no space to grow or accommodate innovations. Here in Las Vegas we have nothing but space. There are no landmark laws: we can go up and out or anywhere we need. And to the casinos, the cost of a theater is, relatively, nothing.

As it happens, though, Broadway on the Vegas Strip is not the sure thing that some thought. In a town where "the house" always wins, what could go wrong? After five months at the Wynn Las Vegas, *Avenue Q*'s 1200-seat theater was only selling at about 65 percent capacity and announced it would close May 28, 2006. Its replacement, *Spamalot*, would have an exclusivity deal similar to *Avenue Q*'s, except that Arizona and California would be the only excluded states. Ironically, the announcement of the *Avenue Q* closing appeared in *The New York Times* the morning after *Hairspray* opened February 15 at the Luxor—that show lasted less than four months, closing the night of the Tony Awards (June 11). Although more Broadway productions are destined for the desert—and *Mamma Mia!* continues to sell well there—it may yet prove that visions of Las Vegas bonanzas are little more than mirages.

Broadway Beginnings

THE BROADWAY SEASON usually begins in earnest after the Labor Day holiday, with the technical beginning—June 1 for *Best Plays*'s record-keeping purposes—marked by closings of disappointed awards aspirants, productions that haven't much hope of attracting summer tourists and other shows that have run their course. (In an odd symmetry, there were 39 openings and 39 closings on Broadway during the 2005–06 season.) But before the closings got underway, Manhattan Theatre Club (MTC) got the new season rolling June 1 with a collection of vignettes by Elaine May under the title *After the Night and the Music*. Opening in MTC's Biltmore Theatre, the production, even under the expert direction of Daniel Sullivan, never rose above its

1970s romantic aesthetic despite a cast that included J. Smith-Cameron, Brian Kerwin, Jere Burns, Eddie Korbich and the playwright's daughter, Jeannie Berlin. *USA Today*'s Elysa Gardner wrote that "the writer's insights" into her characters were "seldom fresh or funny." Michael Kuchwara of the Associated Press saw things a bit differently when he wrote that Korbich managed to be "touching and hilarious at the same time." Kuchwara, though, agreed in principle with Gardner's assessment of the work calling it "minor stuff" and arguing that the "sitcom sketches" were "far too long." David Rooney's tone in *Variety* was even sharper, "It takes either audacity or lunacy to bill your work 'about life in the new millennium' when your comic engine appears to have stalled in the 1970s." The first to open in the new season, *After the Night* was soon to close (July 3), dimming its lights after only 38 performances.

The estimable Hal Holbrook returned to the Main Stem with his classic re-creation of Mark Twain's 19th-century platform performances (June 9). *Mark Twain Tonight!* might have been retitled *Mark Twain's Fortnight* because the production was withdrawn June 26 after 15 performances, which meant that many in the theater community—who may have been too young to see its earlier Broadway iterations in 1966 and 1977—did not get a chance to see this revival. The reviews were respectful, if less than enthusiastic, noting Twain's topicality in his curmudgeonly approach to politics and politicians. The final opening of June was the fourth Broadway revival of W. Somerset Maugham's *The Constant Wife* with the effervescent Kate Burton in the title role (June 16). Michael Cumpsty played her philandering husband with Lynn Redgrave as her mother. Burton deservedly received a Tony Award nomination for her performance, but the Roundabout Theatre Company production ended its run August 21 after 77 performances—long before the awards season—making it unlikely that most Tony voters had a chance to see her sparkling performance.

There were only three more openings before October, each of which had fewer than 50 performances but for very different reasons. The extraordinary Antony Sher performed the solo piece *Primo* at the Music Box for 35 performances beginning July 11. Based on Holocaust survivor Primo Levi's *If This Is a Man*, the work was a harrowing exploration of the ends to which a human being may go in order to survive. Although the production was heralded by the critics, it was only scheduled for a limited engagement. Ticket demand required that it extend for a week to August 14. Suzanne Somers's *The Blonde in the Thunderbird* was an onstage confessional with music chased from Broadway by the critics and an unsympathetic theater community after only nine performances (July 17–23).

The final opening of summer was the Yoko Ono-approved musical *Lennon*, which centered on telling the story of songwriter John Lennon's life through a chronology of his music—although very little of it related to his work with the Beatles. The songwriter was portrayed by a diverse cast of men and women who represented Lennon at different moments (or moods) in his life. As Marilyn Stasio wrote in *Variety*, "as righteous as that [concept] sounds, the notion doesn't quite pan out, because membership in the universal brotherhood of man seems not to extend to Paul, George and Ringo." *The Village Voice*'s Michael Feingold concurred, noting that "the

Excellence on Broadway was a transatlantic, if not global concept.

show is barely complete enough to be called perfunctory" and "close to contextless." Feingold admitted, however, that he "got all teary when they sang 'Imagine.'" Nicola Christie, in *The Daily Telegraph* (UK), resisted the production's charms, writing that there was "no excuse for the syrupy fare that's served up here" and blasting the "Imagine" number as "cringeworthy as it is predictable." *Lennon* eked out an existence for a little more than six weeks, but never rose above 54 percent capacity. It closed September 24 after 49 performances.

There were 10 other closings in the summer weeks leading to (and including) Labor Day weekend. Billy Crystal's sentimental solo piece about losing his father at a relatively early age, *700 Sundays*, closed June 12 (163 performances). It had extended numerous times, done sellout business for its entire run and won a Tony Award for Crystal. Daniel Sullivan's production of *Julius Caesar* with Denzel Washington as Brutus was not rapturously received by almost anyone—except for the audiences who made nearly every performance a sellout before it too closed June 12 (81 performances). Three holdover productions shuttered June 26: *Brooklyn* (284 performances), *La Cage aux Folles* (229) and *On Golden Pond* (93). The two Tennessee Williams dramas from the previous season dimmed their lights as one July 3. *The Glass Menagerie* finished with 120 performances and *A Streetcar Named Desire* ended with 73. *Steel Magnolias* held on against the inevitable until July 31 (136 performances), but even the Tony Award-winning revival of *Glengarry Glen Ross* could not make it through the dog days of summer; it succumbed August 28 (137 performances). The final closings of the summer season came September 4 when two diametrically opposed productions closed shop: *Who's Afraid of Virginia Woolf?* (177 performances) and *Jackie Mason: Freshly Squeezed* (172).

As the season got fully underway, five more holdover productions closed between September and January. *The Pillowman* (185 performances) released its gruesome grip on its audiences as of September 18. A week later the Elvis Presley musical, *All Shook Up* removed its blue suede shoes (September 25; 213 performances). The long-running Twyla Tharp and Billy Joel musical, *Movin' Out*, departed December 11 after 1,303 performances—making it 58th on the Long Runs on Broadway list as of May 31, 2006. *Chitty Chitty Bang Bang* (285 performances) and *Sweet Charity* (279), which opened a few days apart at the end of the previous season, sipped bitter champagne New Year's Eve with their December 31 closings. The final holdover production to close this season was the fourth Broadway revival of *Fiddler on the Roof*, which provoked controversy for its "lack of Jewishness" when it opened with Alfred Molina as Tevye. When Molina was replaced by Harvey Fierstein last season the critics were gentle to the new star—if not sold on his singing voice—as they were to Andrea Martin who joined him as Golde. When Martin left in September 2005, she was replaced by Rosie O'Donnell, the talk-show host, comic, actor, producer and theater advocate. The critics were no longer kind. Peter Marks in *The Washington Post* wrote, "her rudimentary acting skills and his grating vocals put thick walls between you and *Fiddler*'s warming, effervescent spirit." Others felt more or less the same, but *Variety*'s Rooney took note of an interesting cultural development: "what's most significant about this latest cast overhaul is less her performance than her pairing with Fierstein, which underlines the uniqueness of commercial theater in America as a mainstream artistic arena in which an actor's offscreen sexuality is irrelevant." Rooney was referring, of course, to the fact that Fierstein and O'Donnell are both homosexual and open about it, yet can be cast as a married couple in a Broadway show. It may also be true, however, that theater is simply marginal to mainstream American culture, a very different kind of irrelevance. It's a sad thought, perhaps, but all too possible in this era of digital primacy. *Fiddler* closed January 8 after 781 performances.

Broadway by the Numbers

OF THE 39 NEW productions to open on Broadway this season, 23 of them (59 percent) did not survive to May 31. Some of those closures, it should be noted, were preplanned by nonprofit Broadway entities. Compared with the previous season, the total number of productions in 2005–06 was identical with the only variance coming in the areas of new plays and solo performance (see list and chart on page 4). There were two additional new plays this season (an increase to 8 from 6) and two fewer solo shows (a decrease from 6 to 4). Over the past five years new Broadway production has held fairly steady with an average of 37 productions per year. These years take into account the season of the September 11, 2001, terrorist attacks when Broadway business suffered losses, but during that season of 2001–02 new production was up by 7 productions (a 25 percent increase). New production, of course, may also be explained by a rising number of failures, which create openings for new shows; it stands to reason that most producers would prefer to have a show humming along than to face all of the issues attendant to opening a new production.

Another measure, then, for the financial health of Broadway is a combination of attendance and ticket prices—issues of creative health will be covered throughout this narrative. According to the League of American Theatres and Producers, attendance in Broadway theaters topped 12 million for the first time and ticket prices increased as they have each year for at least the past 20 years. In its executive summary, the League claims that Broadway in 2005–06 outdrew all 10 of the professional sports teams in the New York area, which our research disputes for both 2005 and 2006. But the difference is close and Broadway certainly outdraws the New York Yankees, Mets, Giants, Jets, Knicks and New Jersey Nets combined. The attendance increase over the past five years is 1.048 million admissions in the aggregate (9.6 percent). The average ticket price is up to $71.79, an increase of more than $13 (or 22 percent) over those same five years. As ticket prices rise at more than double the rate of attendance increases, it will be interesting to see how long this growth rate can continue to rise. Given the demographics of the baby-boom audience, the "echo" generation of the boomers' children and the nearly 20 percent of tickets that are unsold in any given year, it would seem that Broadway could continue to be a growth industry despite its "landmark limitations."

When comparing the charts for Broadway (page 4) and Off Broadway (pages 14 and 15) with charts from the League or *Variety*, the reader must be aware that we use a slightly different rubric to determine into which category a given work falls. For instance, the two productions from this season that we have listed as specialties might be carried as a play (*Latinologues*) or as a musical (*Ring of Fire*). From our perspective, a collection of monologues and dialogues that are only loosely linked do not qualify as a play. *Latinologues*'s (October 13; 93 performances) reliance on simplistic stereotypes went far beyond the merely politically incorrect, but it raised an interesting question: Can Latinos legitimately employ stereotypes that degrade Latinos? Of course they can, but it would help if there were some new insight into the human condition on display, some artistic seed instead of "wetback" jokes well past their expiration dates. Similarly, *Ring of Fire*'s (March 12; 57 performances) songbook of music that was once performed by Johnny Cash does not a musical make—it would be going too far even to call it a revue: it is a Johnny Cash concert without the crucial "man in black." The one other production that might count in other models as a play was Sarah Jones's solo performance piece, *Bridge and Tunnel* (January 26; 140 performances as of May 31). In the 2003–04 edition of this narrative it was said about the Off Broadway version of this work that it

> was a tour-de-force of powerful performance and witty observation. Framed as a "poetry slam" in a borough of New York City, Jones unearthed personal stories that reflected an international culture of aspiration. It was a poignant demonstration of what Mayor David Dinkins used to call the "gorgeous mosaic" of our great metropolis.

In Jones's Broadway stand this season her performance was more powerful, more sharply observed than ever, which led to her receiving a special Tony Award for her excellent work.

What Is a Best Play?

FOR THE PAST THREE seasons, we have tracked the number of former Best Plays that arrive as revivals on and Off Broadway. In yet another parallel with last season, this Broadway season saw 8 of 11 play revivals and 2 of 3 musical revivals that were former Best Plays. Off Broadway play revivals and specialties such as the New York City Center Encores! series generally include only one or two Best Plays from a past season. Play revivals Off Broadway tend to privilege classics that antedate the *Best Plays* series and about half of Off Broadway musical revivals are Gilbert and Sullivan operettas. But on Broadway, the total number of former Best Plays in revivals of plays or musicals over the past three seasons equals 29 of those 43 productions (67 percent). These numbers certainly support John Istel's contention in this volume's Off Off Broadway essay that "Broadway and large nonprofit theaters are museums of theater, where producer-curators display anything that has bubbled to the top and may draw large audiences." It is an argument that editors of this series (and many others) have been making for years. We ersatz visionaries type away in our closets, Chekhovian characters muttering about "new forms," while producers struggle to offer programming that demonstrates the human condition *and* attracts an audience.

Setting aside the former Best Plays for now, we must consider the 2005–06 models. This season 4 of the 10 Best Plays played Broadway, although Martin McDonagh's dark and gruesomely funny *The Lieutenant of Inishmore* (May 3 on Broadway; 33 performances as of May 31) began its New York life at the superb Atlantic Theater Company (February 27; 48 performances). A satire on the brutality of those who would rescue humanity, it transferred to the Lyceum Theatre under the leadership of Randall L. Wreghitt, the talented commercial producer, and his partners. As with the McDonagh play, other Broadway Best Plays hopped the pond to be honored by the American theater. *The History Boys* by Alan Bennett (April 23; 44 performances as of May 31) was a history-making entry to the season when it snagged six Tony Awards on its way back home. There is some question, as noted above, whether this collection of Tony Awards ties or breaks the record set by *Death of a Salesman* in 1949, but there can be no question that *History Boys*'s whirlwind dominance of Broadway was breathtaking. Bennett's thoughtful and funny excoriation of the ways education has been turned into bite-size pieces of a bourgeois commodity had many heads nodding in agreement (when they weren't bobbing with laughter). Conor McPherson's *Shining City* (May 9; 27 performances as of May 31) is a haunting—literally, it happens—tale about a defrocked priest who practices psychotherapy even as he struggles with his own conflicted feelings of sexual preference and familial responsibility. McPherson's fondness for spectral stories weaves through the play from beginning to end, leaving the audience with a (literal, again) glimpse of the burden the therapist carries into his unseen future.

Only one of the Broadway Best Plays was written by an American playwright, David Lindsay-Abaire's domestic drama about a family coping with the death of a child, *Rabbit Hole* (February 2; 77 performances). It was also the only Best Play to have its world premiere on Broadway, although it was commissioned by South Coast Repertory in Costa Mesa, California. As this book was going to press *Rabbit Hole* was announced as the 2007 Pulitzer Prize honoree in Drama. (It is worth noting here that there was no Pulitzer Prize in Drama during the season under consideration in this volume, although any of the three finalists named—*Red Light Winter*, *The Intelligent Design of Jenny Chow* and *Miss Witherspoon*—would have been worthy of the honor. It was the 15th time that the Pulitzer board has declined to honor recommended work.) Both *Shining City* and *Rabbit Hole* were Broadway projects at the Manhattan Theatre Club's Biltmore Theatre.

OFF BROADWAY SEASON 2005–2006

Productions in a continuing run on May 31, 2006 in bold
Productions honored as Best Plays selections in italics
Best Plays from prior seasons are noted with a date in parentheses

NEW PLAYS (41)

Manuscript
The Paris Letter
  (Roundabout Theatre Company)
Private Fears in Public Places
  (Brits Off Broadway)
Birdie Blue (Second Stage Theatre)
Fatal Attraction: A Greek Tragedy
Oedipus at Palm Springs
  (New York Theatre Workshop)
Joy
Sides: The Fear Is Real
Spirit (NYTW)
Fran's Bed (Playwrights Horizons)
In the Wings
Cycling Past the Matterhorn
Third (Lincoln Center Theater)
Manic Flight Reaction (Playwrights)
A Mother, a Daughter and a Gun
Bach at Leipzig (NYTW)
Hilda
The Ruby Sunrise
  (The Public Theater)
Mr. Marmalade (Roundabout)
Miss Witherspoon (Playwrights)
Apparition
The Other Side
  (Manhattan Theatre Club)
Dog Sees God: Confessions
  of a Teenage Blockhead
The Little Dog Laughed
  (Second Stage)
Beauty of the Father (Manhattan)
Almost, Maine
Red Light Winter
Indoor/Outdoor
The Lieutenant of Inishmore
  (Atlantic Theater Company)
Defiance (Manhattan)
Measure for Pleasure (Public)
The Property Known as Garland

NEW PLAYS (*cont'd*)

The God Committee
Pen (Playwrights)
Show People (Second Stage)
Tryst
Based on a Totally True Story
  (Manhattan)
On the Line
Stuff Happens (Public)
All Dolled Up
columbinus (NYTW)

PLAY REVIVALS (8)

Hecuba
  (Brooklyn Academy of Music)
As You Like It (Public)
A Soldier's Play (81–82)
  (Second Stage)
Rope
Hedda Gabler (BAM)
Entertaining Mr. Sloane (Roundabout)
Peer Gynt (BAM)
The Importance of Being Earnest
  (BAM)

NEW MUSICALS (16)

Once Around the Sun
Dr. Sex
The Great American
  Trailer Park Musical
Slut
Five Course Love
See What I Wanna See (Public)
Captain Louie
Bingo
The Ark
The Seven (NYTW)
Fanny Hill (York Theatre Company)
I Love You Because
Bernarda Alba (Lincoln Center)
Grey Gardens (Playwrights)
Sidd

NEW MUSICALS (*cont'd*)
A Fine and Private Place (York)

MUSICAL REVIVALS (4)
Two Gentlemen of Verona (Public)
Peter Pan
HMS Pinafore (G&S Players)
The Mikado (G&S Players)

REVUES (2)
Almost Heaven:
  Songs of John Denver
**Jacques Brel Is Alive and Well
  and Living in Paris** (Revival)

SOLO (12)
Border/Clash: A Litany of Desires
  (The Culture Project)
The One-Man Star Wars Trilogy
A Woman of Will
RFK (Culture Project)

SOLO (*cont'd*)
Lenny Bruce: In His Own Words
Confessions of a Mormon Boy
Family Secrets (Revival)
George M. Cohan Tonight!
  (Irish Repertory Theatre)
A Safe Harbor for Elizabeth Bishop
  (Primary Stages)
**Sandra Bernhard:
  Everything Bad and Beautiful**
Los Big Names
Annulla (Revival)

SPECIALTIES (5)
Lazer Vaudeville
Drumstruck
Kismet (Encores!)
70, Girls, 70 (Encores!)
Of Thee I Sing (31-32) (Encores!)

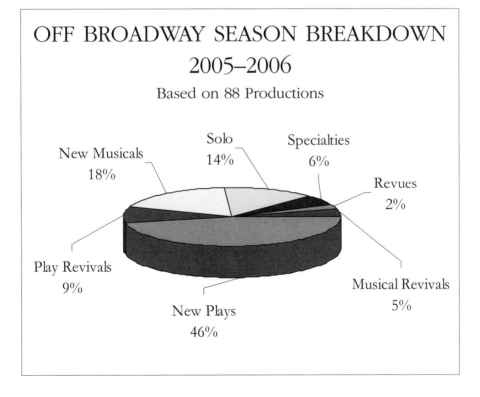

OFF BROADWAY SEASON BREAKDOWN
2005–2006
Based on 88 Productions

New Musicals 18%
Solo 14%
Specialties 6%
Revues 2%
Play Revivals 9%
New Plays 46%
Musical Revivals 5%

Five of the Best Plays appeared Off Broadway—including Atlantic Theater Company's *Inishmore*, which transferred to Broadway—with all except one opening in nonprofit productions. Wendy Wasserstein's *Third* (October 24; 64 performances) opened at Lincoln Center Theater's Mitzi Newhouse Theater as the playwright underwent treatment for lymphoma. Smart, funny and wide-ranging in its approaches to what it means to be privileged in America, the play echoed the playwright's own incipient mortality in a supporting character who, battling a deadly cancer, stopped caring about the quotidian battles of politics in academia or anywhere else. But it was her central character of Laurie Jameson (as poignantly played by Dianne Wiest), who seemed to symbolize a position where many baby boomers may feel stuck in late middle age: in a muddle partly of her own making with a deteriorating father who needs her support. One of her best works in years, the play closed before its time due to Wasserstein's ill health. (It was sadly reminiscent of Lorraine Hansberry's death a day or two after the final performance of the 1964–65 *The Sign in Sidney Brustein's Window*. During that production's run, Hansberry—who died at the much-younger age of 34—had been quite ill.) *Stuff Happens* (April 13; 56 performances as of May 31) at the Public Theater may appear to be an odd Best Plays choice, given that it was based on documented history and interviews with principals. (*Guantánamo: Honor Bound to Defend Freedom* was a similarly constructed work—and Best Play—from last season.) Even though there was little new information to come from the production, its reconstruction of the path the US government took into Iraq in 2003—and the fact that the play's message was never effectively repudiated—will allow future cultural and political historians to use the play to help create a living historical context. Both *Third* and *Stuff Happens* were guided by the steady directorial hand of Daniel Sullivan.

Although Adam Rapp's *Red Light Winter* (February 9; 128 performances as of May 31) was the only commercial Off Broadway play honored as a Best Play, the production began at Chicago's Steppenwolf Theatre Company and was essentially a transfer under the auspices of significant backers such as Scott Rudin, Robyn Goodman and Roger Berlind. After creating a stir in Chicago, Rapp's gaze into the abyss of obsession—as manifest by a pathetic love triangle involving an AIDS-infected prostitute, a depressed poetic soul and his unscrupulous best friend—considerably enlivened the theater season. Once again demonstrating keen insight into the dark underbelly of the American dream, Rapp's play was nominated for the Pulitzer Prize, but it would be hard to imagine the board of that organization rewarding so desolate a work—and they did not.

The final Off Broadway Best Play honor to be noted here is the musical *Grey Gardens* by Doug Wright, Scott Frankel and Michael Korie (March 7; 63 performances). Based on the cult-hit 1975 documentary of the same title by the Maysles brothers, the musical juxtaposes the lives of a mother and daughter before (in the 1940s) and after (in the 1970s) they were abandoned by the men in their lives. The first act shows the women, both of whom are more than a little eccentric, before their world unwinds. (*Grey Gardens* and *Third* have more than a little in common in their exploration of issues that arise between aging parents and children.) The daughter, Little Edie, is promised to Joseph P. Kennedy Jr. and the mother, Edith, rehearses a repertoire of songs she will perform at the girl's engagement party. When it is announced that Little Edie's father has left the family for another woman, Kennedy quits the premises and his relationship with Little Edie. The opening act is a product of the imagination's of the musical's creators, though young Ms. Beale was purported to have been involved with Kennedy. The second act follows the contours of the Maysles documentary, with Christine Ebersole and Mary Louise Wilson giving performances that were astonishingly similar to the genuine article in the film. Although 1970s interest in the two women turned on their relationship to Jacqueline Kennedy Onassis—she was a cousin and niece to them—and the decrepitude into which they had fallen, the musical itself is another potent example from the 2005–06 season of the myriad ways in which an American dream can metamorphose into a nightmare. By the season's end, *Grey Gardens* had closed but looked forward to a possible Broadway run.

There are two works from Off Off Broadway honored herein—*The Intelligent Design of Jenny Chow* and *In the Continuum*—which prompt a further explanation of a *Best Plays* rubric. For purposes of the listings and consideration of the Best Plays honorees, Off Broadway and Off Off Broadway are divided by two crucial elements: the venue's size and the number of performances per week. Although some productions of fine groups such as Signature Theatre Company, Atlantic Theater Company and others of their ilk operate on a modified Off Broadway contract, we require a full eight-performance schedule in a theater substantially larger than a 99-seat house. Our preferred venue size for Off Broadway ranges from 199 to 499 seats, but we make allowances to include companies working in theaters with as few as 120 to 130 seats—although the eight-performance rule remains, except for solo shows and some limited engagements. When we err, we attempt to do so on the side of inclusion. Over the past six seasons, 10 of the 60 Best Plays chosen by the editor and editorial board have been produced in an Off Off Broadway environment.

The Intelligent Design of Jenny Chow by Rolin Jones (September 19; 28 performances) is a lively comedy with a provocative title that has very little to do with the current religious debate over the teaching of evolution. In the play, Jones seriously considers the dislocated identity of a young Asian woman adopted as a baby by Caucasian parents. The girl, Jennifer Marcus, is a computing genius whose prowess is prized by the Defense Department, but who argues with her mother about taking out the trash: Jennifer is agoraphobic and that trip outside is just too much for her. She builds a flying robot to find her Asian birth-mother in an attempt to make a connection that she feels is missing. After making a vicarious journey, she begins to realize inner peace may be found at home. Danai Gurira and Nikkole Salter's *In the Continuum* features a pair of monologues interwoven into a narrative about AIDS-infected women of African and African-American descent. After opening at Primary Stages (October 2; 9 performances at Primary Stages), the play enjoyed a run at the Perry Street Theatre (December 1; 81 performances) before embarking on a tour. The manner in which the authors—who also performed the piece—were able to evoke the lack of agency experienced by women who become pariahs in their own homes and communities was as disheartening as it was searingly honest.

Broadway Plays: Something Old, Something New

A QUICK GLANCE at the table and chart on page 4 shows that play revivals were a significant force in new Broadway productions again this season. Since we began tracking these percentages six years ago, play revivals either have been the dominant category on Broadway (2001–02, 2002–03, 2003–04) or have been tied with new musicals (this season, last season and the 2000–01 season). Although the nonprofit Broadway entities—Roundabout Theatre Company, Manhattan Theatre Club and Lincoln Center Theater—account for a significant number of revivals, most of the play revivals this season were staged under commercial auspices. Only four of the 11 play revivals made it through the end of the season and all had a closing date planned when May 31 arrived. Despite the note in the section above that three of the play revivals were not Best Plays from past seasons, the authors of those three plays (Alan Ayckbourn, Richard Greenberg and Brian Friel) had 16 former Best Plays among them—they were not in any way unknown quantities.

After the Roundabout's production of *The Constant Wife*, mentioned above, the next play revived was Ayckbourn's *Absurd Person Singular* at MTC's Biltmore Theatre (October 18; 56 performances). *Variety*'s Rooney referred to its 1970s dissection of British social class as "a mummified romp." Gardner in *USA Today* saw it differently, "there is pathos underlying all these wacky shenanigans" that left "a bittersweet aftertaste." Linda Winer in *Newsday* was more nuanced in her appraisal, finding the production "deftly performed," if only "mildly amusing." Winer also wished that MTC would focus its resources on the playwright's "darker, richer human studies," noting that the stylish scenery of John Lee Beatty and costumes of Jane Greenwood "often say more about character than the script does."

The revival of the year was to have been the reunion of Nathan Lane and Matthew Broderick in Neil Simon's *The Odd Couple* at the Brooks Atkinson Theatre (October 27; 244 performance as of May 31). Although the play sold extremely well—in its first 34 weeks, including previews, it generally sold between 98 and 101 percent with very rare exceptions—it was beset by stories from the rehearsal hall that all was not well. Whatever one thinks of backstage gossip, these stories were coming from inside the studio where director Joe Mantello was reportedly unhappy and Broderick was having a difficult time learning his lines (something for which he is apparently known). Lane, on the other hand, is always fully prepared and colleagues say he usually knows whatever he is working on well enough to perform almost any role in it. *Newsday*'s Winer had heard the rumors, but her review attempted to lay them to rest: "Fear not," she wrote, Broderick and Lane were "as symbiotically inspired as they were in *The Producers*." Ben Brantley in *The New York Times* called it a "bland, mechanical new revival" that at times summoned "so exactly the stars' performances in *The Producers* that you wonder where the songs have gone." *USA Today*'s Gardner declared that it was the "rapport between them that truly delights." Due to the extraordinarily good ticket sales to see the comic power-duo, most of the critics noted a version of what Michael Kuchwara wrote for the Associated Press, "it doesn't matter what any critic thinks." And that is music to any producer's ears.

Although there was no Pulitzer winner for this season, the 1975 honoree was in evidence with the Lincoln Center Theater revival of Edward Albee's *Seascape* at the Booth Theatre (November 21; 55 performances). The production, in which a married couple in their 70s encounter a pair of "evolving" lizards on the beach one day, received warm, positive notices. Even *The New York Times*, in the person of Ben Brantley, found much to admire. Brantley, however, also believed that the revival—a term Albee dislikes, favoring instead "new production"—was "perfectly likable and, to be honest, forgettable." Contrary to Brantley's assertion, it was not at all forgettable, but those who marked *Seascape*'s uniqueness within the body of Albee's work were onto something. The play—in a fine production directed by Mark Lamos with Frances Sternhagen, George Grizzard, Elizabeth Marvel and Frederick Weller—unearths some of the most delicate, loving language in any Albee work. It also ends on a note of hope that provokes a desire in its audience to see what happens next. Since Albee has written a prequel to *The Zoo Story* titled *Homelife*, perhaps he can be prevailed upon to create an Act III for *Seascape*.

Gabriel Byrne returned to Broadway in yet another Eugene O'Neill play, *A Touch of the Poet* at Roundabout's Studio 54 (December 8; 50 performances). His last venture in this realm was in the quasi-biographical role of James Tyrone Jr. in *A Moon for the Misbegotten* opposite Cherry Jones as Josie Hogan at the Walter Kerr Theatre (3/19–7/2/2000; 120 performances). In the latest O'Neill production, Byrne played the preening Irish immigrant Con Melody, who regales others with stories of his glory days in the British army. He's been taken down a peg or two by his American immigrant experience, however, and in the play finds himself proprietor of a rundown tavern near Boston in 1828. Although the notices were generally positive, the all-important review from *The New York Times* complained of a lackluster production—directed by Doug Hughes—and supporting cast, particularly in the first act. *Times*man Brantley, however, found much to admire in Byrne's work in the second half of the performance.

Although Neil Simon's *Barefoot in the Park* (February 16; 109 performances) was a Best Play for the 1963–64 season, it is hard to credit it today as a work of anything much more than nostalgia. People who can recall a time when the wife stayed home and dealt with domestic issues while the husband was out in the world earning a living are today referred to either as "senior citizens" or "the rich"—and the rich aren't recalling it, they're still living it. There are, of course, certain inexorable truths (and laughs) about love and relationships between two people that arise in the play, but even given its 1964 vintage it seems a bit dated. Then again, playwright Simon didn't get to his lofty status by working at the cutting edge of culture. Scott Elliott directed a cast that included Patrick Wilson, Amanda Peet, Tony Roberts and the ubiquitous (of late) Jill Clayburgh. Coming as the second Simon play this season, *Variety*'s Rooney seemed to get it right when he began his review, "Strike two."

Lisa Kron's *Well* at the Longacre Theatre (March 30; 52 performances) might almost have been considered a transfer from the Public Theater (3/28–5/16/2004; 57 performances). But the original Off Broadway production, for which the work was named a Best Play of 2003–04, closed nearly two years before the 2005–06 production opened. Kron and co-star

Jayne Houdyshell were nominated for 2006 Tony Awards based on their performances in the play, which cleverly examines the impact of emotional well-being on physical health. The piece employs a cast of six actors operating in a metatheatrical framework with Kron performing herself as Houdyshell performs Kron's mother. The playwright's narrative is continually disrupted by competing narratives from characters in the play. Not unlike Luigi Pirandello's *Six Characters in Search of an Author* in its form, the play itself felt a bit too intimate for a Broadway house. That said, producer Elizabeth Ireland McCann should be given a medal for pushing *Well* (and its creator) into the mainstream.

Bartlett Sher's production of *Awake and Sing!* under the auspices of Lincoln Center Theater at the Belasco Theatre revealed the Clifford Odets play in thrilling ways (April 17; 43 performances as of May 31). It is hard to imagine Harold Clurman's original production rising to the levels that Sher inspired his cast, which included Zoë Wanamaker, Ben Gazzara, Mark Ruffalo, Lauren Ambrose and Pablo Schreiber. Michael Yeargan's scenery, Catherine Zuber's costumes and Christopher Akerlind's lighting added a nearly vertiginous theatrical excitement. That the production won the 2006 Tony Award for best revival was just; that Sher saw the best director award go to Nicholas Hytner was not. (See the Plays Produced on Broadway section for other details on the 1935 production.)

One of the big stories of the year was the Broadway debut of Julia Roberts in the revival of Richard Greenberg's *Three Days of Rain* at the Bernard B. Jacobs Theatre (April 19; 49 performances as of May 31). It was nearly impossible to move on West 45th Street in the hour before and after the play because tourists and—could it be?—New Yorkers clogged the sidewalks and street making it impassable for pedestrians or motorists. Under these circumstances, exiting the theater after the show was more tension-filled than the performance itself. Greenberg's low-key play centers on a pair of siblings and their friend who plumb an odd diary entry in an attempt to understand their famous, troubled parents. It was a strange (and brave) choice for Roberts because the play is a balanced, ensemble piece in which the woman plays two characters—as do the men—who are mere pieces within the overall puzzle. The critics were underwhelmed by Roberts's somewhat stiff performance, which might have been alleviated, one suspects, by director Joe Mantello (having an off season). Roberts ultimately won over the community and cemented her role as a member of it when she agreed to present a 2006 Tony Award even though she had not been nominated. Denzel Washington, in a similar position in 2005, had declined to participate. Before giving the award for best actor in a play, Roberts told the 6,000 people at Radio City that they were "insanely talented." The theater community has a long memory, and a happy one of Roberts.

Ralph Fiennes and Cherry Jones returned to Broadway in Irish playwright Brian Friel's *Faith Healer* at the Booth Theatre (May 4; 32 performances as of May 31). The original production of the play had its 1979 world premiere in the US. (See the Plays Produced on Broadway section for details.) In *Faith Healer*, four monologues tell a story of love, art, passion and death from three perspectives. Some of the speeches were delivered in a haunting, incantatory fashion, lulling the audience into a state of near somnolence, as one does a child being read a bedtime story; others enlivened the proceedings, especially Ian McDiarmid's Tony Award-winning turn as the Cockney manager of the faith healer.

Herman Wouk's 1954 play, *The Caine Mutiny Court-Martial*, opened at the Gerald Schoenfeld Theatre and quickly closed (May 7; 17 performances). Critics slammed David Schwimmer as lacking in subtlety and similarly appraised Jerry Zaks's production, although Zeljko Ivanek was lauded for his nuanced portrayal of Captain Queeg. Ivanek was nominated for a Tony Award for his performance, but it is difficult to imagine that many Tony voters saw the show, which closed quickly. In fairness to Schwimmer, however, it should be noted that the story—about a possibly crazy, incompetent leader in time of war (Queeg) who first disintegrates on the witness stand and then is defended by Schwimmer's character in a ringingly patriotic speech—had a peculiar disconnect with US culture when many here were asking competency questions about their own war leaders. The production never played to more than 43 percent attendance after the opening, but even in previews its best week was only 52 percent.

Of the eight new plays on Broadway this season, only three were running at the end of the season and those were all late entries opening April 23 and after. The first new play of the fall season was Richard Greenberg's comedy, *A Naked Girl on the Appian Way* at Roundabout's American Airlines Theatre (October 6; 69 performances). Directed by Doug Hughes, the cast featured Jill Clayburgh and Richard Thomas as a married couple with adopted children of different races. Set in a gorgeous Hamptons home designed by John Lee Beatty, Clayburgh and Thomas's characters were the epitome of wealthy—and highly literate—New York liberals. The core situation centered on an adopted heterosexual son and daughter deciding to marry and a bisexual Asian son feeling excluded with kooky neighbors of a radical bent tossed into the mix. While the production was not without its pleasures, critical complaints that it leaned too much on its situational comedy were not completely unwarranted.

The transfer of Stephen Temperley's *Souvenir* to the Lyceum Theatre (November 10; 68 performances) from Off Broadway brought the estimable Judy Kaye back to Broadway as the legendarily bad singer Florence Foster Jenkins. After two hours of listening to the character's excruciating caterwauling, her pianist and foil, played with a light touch by Donald Corren, brought the character onstage at the end to sing "Ave Maria" as she "hears" it in her own head. Kaye, of course, rendered the song beautifully. But why bother with all of the rest? *Souvenir* is a dispiriting example of nostalgia for the schadenfreude of an earlier era. What is it about certain kinds of humans that makes them want to encourage (and then sneer at) the delusions of another? *Souvenir* neither asks nor answers this question.

Festen, adapted by David Eldridge from a 1998 film and play by Thomas Vinterberg, opened at the Music Box (April 9; 49 performances) after successful runs at London's Almeida and on the West End. The starry American cast included a mix of stage, film and television veterans: Michael Hayden, Jeremy Sisto, Stephen Kunken, Julianna Margulies, Ali MacGraw, Larry Bryggman, Christopher Evan Welch and others. During a special celebration, the dark secrets of an austere, aristocratic family cause it to become thoroughly unhinged. Due in part to several unwise casting decisions, the production landed few powerful emotional blows.

The Sound of Musicals

NEW MUSICAL PRODUCTION remained level on Broadway this season. Although the same number of new musicals opened on Broadway this season as last (11), the average for each of the past six seasons is just under eight. The 11 this year, then, would be good news if the new musicals were significant quality, but that was not the case. In addition to *Lennon, Jersey Boys* and *The Drowsy Chaperone*, mentioned above, there were eight other new musicals that each attempted to connect to some element of pop culture or prior success. *In My Life*, a goofy musical about a boy with Tourette syndrome and a girl with obsessive-compulsive disorder whose lives are touched by angels, played longer than expected at the Music Box after being trounced by critics as "an overblown soap opera . . . dripping with mawkish sentiment," as *Variety*'s Rooney wrote (October 20; 61 performances). The attempt by creator Joseph Brooks, a successful songwriter, to capitalize on his pop-music success desperately needed someone who understood musical-theater structure to guide the process.

Andrew Lloyd Webber returned to Broadway with an odd, romantic confection titled *The Woman in White* at the Marquis Theatre (November

17; 109 performances). Beset by ill health, leading actress Maria Friedman labored mightily to carry the operatic adaptation of the 1860s Willkie Collins novel. In an interesting culture clash, the production designs of Victorian-era scenery were almost completely created via video projections. The attempt to illuminate Victoriana with 21st century technology was oddly disjunctive and did little to strengthen the production. Its London counterpart, however, enjoyed an 18-month run at the Palace Theatre; here the production barely managed three months.

An American novel came to Broadway under the auspices of Oprah Winfrey and her partners when *The Color Purple* opened at the Broadway Theatre (December 1; 207 performances as of May 31). Adapted from the captivating 1982 Alice Walker novel and the competent 1985 Steven Spielberg film, the musical attempted to inject as much story into the production as possible creating a narrative checklist that was heavy with exposition. That point made, one of the high points of the season was the gooseflesh induced by the ringing musical finale, led by 2006 Tony Award-winner, LaChanze.

Two more musicals made from novels came to Broadway this season when *Lestat* and *Tarzan* opened. Compiled from Anne Rice's The Vampire Chronicles series by book writer Linda Woolverton, *Lestat* featured music and lyrics by the team of Elton John and Bernie Taupin. After a dicey tryout in San Francisco that included a battle with San Jose theater critic Karen D'Souza over audience web-postings, the musical went into overhaul mode: Choreographer Jonathan Butterell was hired and the Palace Theatre opening date was moved back 12 days (April 25; 39 performances). The result was a lugubrious production that was creepy (in unintended ways) and featured whiny vampires complaining about eternal "life." Producer Warner Bros. Theatre Ventures didn't take long to drive a stake into its heart, but not before some noticed an almost antigay subtext here and there. Disney's musical version of *Tarzan* credits Edgar Rice Burroughs's book *Tarzan of the Apes* in addition to Disney's 1999 film. Given the participation of composer Phil Collins—who wrote five songs for that film—this production at the Richard Rodgers Theatre was Disney through and through (May 10; 25 performances as of May 31). Relying heavily on flying primates and less focused on a well-honed narrative (whether spoken or sung), the family friendly show received only one 2006 Tony Award nomination (for Natasha Katz's lighting). Before the *Tarzan* "remake," another new Broadway musical based on a film opened near the season's end: *The Wedding Singer* at the Al Hirschfeld Theatre (April 27; 40 performances as of May 31). Adapted from the charming Adam Sandler and Drew Barrymore romantic comedy set in spiky-haired 1980s New Jersey—who says Broadway does not know its audience?—the musical's two strongest songs were taken from the film (and had been co-written by Sandler). An agglomeration of tired New Jersey stereotypes—more winningly done by *Jersey Boys*—fashion nightmares best forgotten and casting errors, the show surprised Times Square touts by continuing to run into the next season.

There were two new musicals focused on dance during the 2005–06 season: *Chita Rivera: The Dancer's Life* at the Gerald Schoenfeld Theatre (December 11; 72 performances) and *Hot Feet* at the Hilton Theatre (April 30; 36 performances as of May 31). Although neither production was particularly successful, it was for very different reasons. Rivera's celebration of her career as a "gypsy" dancer and, later, as a star opened not long before her 73rd birthday, but she still managed to be the main attraction in the production. Beginning in her childhood and moving through time, Rivera replayed roles she performed onstage and off. *The Dancer's Life* invited comparison with Elaine Stritch's 2001–02 one-woman show, *At Liberty*, but Rivera's story lacked the colorful, cantankerous quality of Stritch's. The production never rose above 76 percent attendance and mostly played to half-empty theaters. *Hot Feet* is a dance musical created by Maurice Hines—brother of the late Gregory Hines—who had his first Broadway credit at about age 11 and later appeared with Rivera in 1981's short-lived *Bring Back Birdie*. Set to the music of the power group Earth, Wind and Fire, this adaptation (and updating) of *The Red Shoes* explores the Faustian bargains dancers often make to live through their work. Hines's glitzy dance numbers, which punctuated the action, were athletic and fun to watch but they did little to enhance the narrative.

With only three musical revivals on Broadway this season, it made for an intimate Tony Award category. All three productions—*Sweeney Todd*, *The Pajama Game* and *The Threepenny Opera*—were nominated and *Sweeney Todd* was the odds-on favorite to win. John Doyle, who received the Tony Award for his direction of *Sweeney Todd* at the Eugene O'Neill Theatre (November 3; 240 performances as of May 31), constructed a production in which the actors played all of the musical instruments but were also patients in a mental hospital. Many of the same folks who were outraged at the split of the new musical awards mentioned at the beginning of this narrative, were sure that Patti LuPone would win for best actress in a musical. LuPone was quite something to see, her Mrs. Lovett strutting about the stage, occasionally puffing on a tuba with gusto and gobbling the scenery. With every facial twitch, every leering grin, every cackled syllable, Sondheim fans nearby (or were they LuPone fans?) howled with appreciative laughter—even, it seemed, when scenes were meant to be darker in tone.

Similarly dark was Scott Elliott's production of Kurt Weill and Bertolt Brecht's *The Threepenny Opera*, in a new translation by Wallace Shawn, for Roundabout Theatre Company at Studio 54 (April 20; 48 performances as of May 31). *Threepenny* is meant to be dark, of course, because every character in it is in some way corrupt. Unfortunately, however, director Elliott's vision of the play seemed to combine the aesthetics of the musical revival of *Cabaret*—which played in the same theater a few years ago (actor Alan Cumming was central to both productions)—with an after-hours party in San Francisco's Castro District in the late 1970s. But even if the recurrent ethos of switch-partners-and-have-sex was a bit overdone, one wondered what Brecht (the eternal polygynist) might have thought. The critics, for their part, called it "puerile," "self-defeating" and "anemic." As an aside, it is nearly always amusing to read the critical explanations of Brecht that reviewers insist on foisting upon their readers. Nearly every technique that Brecht advocated is now (and has been) consistently employed in every mainstream area of performance: Bob Fosse was a Brechtian director, Harold Prince has been for many years. Tony Kushner is the quintessential Brechtian writer. Even the Academy Award-winning film *American Beauty*, directed by Sam Mendes of the *Cabaret* revival mentioned above, employs Brechtian technique. It may be time now for drama critics to retire their explications of the so-called "alienation effect."

It was Kathleen Marshall's lively, entertaining production of *The Pajama Game* at Roundabout's other Broadway theatre, the American Airlines (February 23; 111 performances as of May 31), that snatched the best musical revival Tony Award. Marshall also received the award for best choreography in a production that made the most of Harry Connick Jr.'s ability to play a piano during a dance number and showed Kelli O'Hara to her best advantage. Still, with two of the three musical revivals running in their houses, Roundabout had pretty good odds on Tony night—and they paid off.

Off Broadway Commerce

NEW OFF BROADWAY production in 2005–06 decreased to 88 from the 2004–05 total of 93. This marked the second annual drop in the new production totals. As a percentage of the total, this season's decrease was more than double that of last year's, but the result may not be too dire. The reduced number of play revivals alone account for more than the entire decrease. Declining from 14 play revivals to 8, it may be that Off Broadway was healthier in 2005–06 given the increasing number of new works to appear. New-play and new-musical production were both on the upswing this season. It is worth noting, however, that Off Broadway producers told *Variety*'s Gordon Cox a darker tale. Marc Routh, president of the League of Off Broadway Theatres and Producers, said "The economics at this point don't make sense. We have trouble hitting the numbers we need to keep a show running and to recoup." Even *Altar Boyz*, which had 521 performances by the end of this season, had a difficult time in the fall of 2005. Producer Robyn Goodman told Cox, "We're just barely making it. We make $8,000 one week, we lose $3,000 the next." Two points must be made here: The most obvious is that using Goodman's figures, her show seemed to be turning a profit. The second part is that some version of this story runs in *Variety* almost every season. Producers are rarely happy about the financial state of the theater.

New-play production Off Broadway increased for a fourth straight year in 2005–06 to a total of 41 productions. Of the total, 18 productions (44 percent) were generated as commercial entities—although many of the commercial partnerships were not developing new works but optioning plays honed in nonprofit settings (see *Red Light Winter*, above). Paul Grellong's *Manuscript* opened the new season at the Daryl Roth Theatre (June 12; 73 performances) in a crisp production directed by Bob Balaban that featured Jeffrey Carlson, Pablo Schreiber and Marin Ireland. In the play, three college students engage in a round-robin of literary competition that ends with the female character betrayed by her own ambition. Although the playwright constructs a labyrinthine moral study, the lack of accountability in today's celebrity culture makes his ending something less than plausible. *Fatal Attraction: A Greek Tragedy* opened a month later and managed a seven-week run at the East 13th Street Theatre (July 10; 56 performances). A campy spoof of the 1987 Michael Douglas and Glenn Close film about an affair gone horribly wrong, the show's cultural referents, Greek chorus and the presence of Corey Feldman as "Michael Douglas" kept audiences entertained for the run.

Fully half of the commercial new plays Off Broadway were comedies clearly aimed at the entertaining the clientele. Only three of the nine commercial comedies ran more than 50 performances—*Fatal Attraction*, *Sides: The Fear Is Real* and *Dog Sees God: Confessions of a Teenage Blockhead*. *Sides* (August 25; 72 performances) and *Dog Sees God* (December 15; 86 performances) were both transfers from nonprofit runs. A fourth comedy, *Joy*—a San Francisco transplant formerly titled *The Joy of Gay Sex*—just missed the 50-performance cut (August 14; 49 performances). *Sides*, which started at P.S. 122 under the auspices of the Ma-Yi Theater Company, focuses on the trials and tribulations of casting (especially typecasting) faced by Asian-American actors. *Dog Sees God*, which premiered at the 2004 New York International Fringe Festival, examines the neuroses of the *Peanuts* comic-strip characters as they grow into adolescence. The other commercial comedies—*In the Wings*, *Cycling Past the Matterhorn* (comedy-drama), *A Mother, a Daughter and a Gun*, *Indoor/Outdoor*—all came and went within a few weeks of opening. *All Dolled Up*, produced by comedian Colin Quinn, was a late comic entry into the season. *Dolled*, about a cross-dressing mobster, continued its run at the end of the season, but was destined to close soon.

Of the commercial new dramas Off Broadway, only *Red Light Winter* would break 100 performances during 2005–06 (128), with its run continuing into the next season. *Manuscript* had the second longest run of the commercial new plays (73), with a Judy Garland biodrama *The Property Known as Garland* starring Adrienne Barbeau at Actor's Playhouse placing third (March 23; 68 performances). *Tryst*, a romance at the Promenade Theatre (April 6; 63 performances as of May 31)—and the final production to play there before the theater was slated to close permanently on June 11, 2006—finished fourth in new-play runs. None of the other commercial dramas—*Hilda*, *Apparition*, *Almost, Maine*, *The God Committee* or *On the Line*—managed as many as 50 performances.

Elsewhere in the Off Broadway theater, there was a sharp increase in the number of new musicals over the previous season; most were commercial works. Ten of the 16 new musicals this season were either commercial transfers or new productions. The Off Broadway new-musical season began with *Once Around the Sun* at the Zipper Theater (August 11; 66 performances). The musical focuses on a musician's conflicts as he pursues career aims: Is success worth the cost of losing one's true self? According to Playbill.com, the musical's producers announced a month-long extension (to October 16) a few days after the opening. A few weeks later, a fall 2006 Broadway run was announced, but the production closed nine days early and the Broadway move seemed to be abandoned. *Dr. Sex*, at the Peter Norton Space (September 21; 23 performances), rode into New York from Chicago on a crest of good notices and seven Joseph Jefferson citations. A comedy about the life of sex researcher Alfred C. Kinsey, the musical suffered growth pains that included early talk of a Broadway run and, later, the firing of director Pamela Hunt (who was reportedly replaced by the uncredited Ethan McSweeney). The reviews were not especially unkind—Jason Zinoman in *The New York Times* wrote that it was "a small, silly musical in the guise of a big, silly one"—but the show did not find its audience and disappeared October 9.

After a week-long run at the 2004 New York Musical Theatre Festival, *The Great American Trailer Park Musical* found backers in Jean Doumanian, Jeffrey Richards and others for a run at Dodger Stages (September 27; 80 performances). The production did not stint on performance talent hiring Tony Award-winner Shuler Hensley and talented veterans such as Kaitlin Hopkins, Linda Hart and Orfeh. The sketch-driven celebration of white-trash lifestyle seemed unlikely to be the sort of thing people look for in a night at the theater and the 10-week run probably exhausted most of the interested audience. If trailer-park humor was not appealing in 2005–06, there was always—for a few weeks anyway—*Slut* at the American Theatre of Actors (October 1; 51 performances). First presented at the 2003 New York International Fringe Festival, the musical centered on the sexual misadventures of a pair of heterosexual men causing *Variety*'s Rooney to ask, ironically, "A frothy musical about horny straight dudes chasing tail? Is that marriage of form and content even legal?" In general, the critical reaction leaned to terms such as "sophomoric," "frat boy" and "crass."

The longest run among the commercial new musicals this season had a staged reading in July 2005 before its presentation at the festival of the National Alliance for Musical Theatre in September. Ryan Cunningham and Joshua Salzman's *I Love You Because* at the Village Theatre, an updated gender-reversal of Jane Austen's *Pride and Prejudice*, found an audience for its brand of romantic comedy (February 14; 111 performances). Although it was, "slight, modest, and flawed," as Feingold put it in *The Village Voice*, "its charm is simply that it's too busy being young in the big city to bother about anything more serious." And it probably didn't hurt to open on Valentine's Day, when even critics may be susceptible to the prick of Cupid's arrow.

Other commercial new musicals included *Five Course Love*, in which vignettes about love played out over plates of diverse ethnic foods at the Minetta Lane Theatre (October 16; 70 performances); *Captain Louie*, a family-oriented transfer from York Theatre Company that departed quickly from the Little Shubert Theatre (October 31; 16 performances); *Bingo*, which covered the pleasures of and conflicts over the popular game, at St. Luke's Theatre (November 7; 92 performances); *The Ark*, a musical about Noah and the Flood at 37 Arts (November 14; 8 performances); and *Sidd*, based on Hermann Hesse's *Siddhartha*, at Dodger Stages (March 15; 13 performances). A quick glance at the titles and brief descriptions of the commercial new musicals, gives a sense of what "works" in the Off Broadway environment. Those quotation marks are in place because 111 performances is no way to run a business. But it seems clear that, in general, producers are looking for the next *I Love You, You're Perfect, Now Change*, which opened in 1996 and finished the 2005–06 season with 4,089 performances—although it is not so clear how the stories of Noah and Siddhartha were envisioned as theatrical ATMs. There was, however, more commercial courage in the 2005–06 season than in the prior year. Commercial production Off Broadway equaled 48 percent of all new productions (a 10 percent increase). In 2005–06, there were a third more commercial productions of new plays and nearly twice as many new musicals.

Although solo performance is one of the areas that experienced a decline in new production during the 2005–06 season—the others were revues and specialties—there were notable successes in the solo form. Charles Ross brought his 2002 Toronto Fringe Festival hit, *The One-Man Star Wars Trilogy*, to the Lamb's Theatre (August 9; 122 performances). Ross demonstrated his facility as an actor and mimic by performing an extremely abbreviated form of *Star Wars*'s "greatest hits." Sandra Bernhard returned to New York with *Sandra Bernhard: Everything Bad and Beautiful*, at the Daryl Roth Theatre, in which the pioneer of ironic pop-culture affectation skewered her targets in song and story while backed by musicians called the Rebellious Jezebels (April 5; 57 performances as of May 31).

The remainder of the solo works succeeded to varying degrees with Amanda McBroom's *A Woman of Will*—about a woman struggling with her songwriting talent—succumbing quickly at the Daryl Roth Theatre (October 2; 9 performances). Likewise, *Lenny Bruce: In His Own Words* at the Zipper Theater failed to find an audience for the observations of the late comedian (February 1; 26 performances). Steven Fales's *Confessions of a Mormon Boy* at the Soho Playhouse was a stop on the gay actor's tour in which he tells of growing up in Utah, getting married and beginning a family before coming to terms with his sexuality (February 5; 81 performances). Sherry Glaser returned with *Family Secrets* to 37 Arts (March 8; 39 performances). The show first played Off Broadway for nearly 15 months beginning in October 1993 at the Westside Theatre (458 performances). Marga Gomez arrived at the 47th Street Theatre with the touring *Los Big Names* about Gomez's life as the daughter of Latino performers (April 9; 41 performances). Edmund Gaynes presented Eileen De Felitta, as a Jew who pretended to be Aryan in order to survive the Holocaust, in a revival of Emily Mann's *Annulla* at St. Luke's Theatre (May 14; 14 performances as of May 31).

Forbidden Broadway: Special Victims Unit continued in June 2005, but did not open a new show this season, making the new-revue list shorter than usual. *Almost Heaven: Songs of John Denver*, based on the songs and autobiography of the popular singer, played at the Promenade Theatre

(November 9; 61 performances). *Jacques Brel Is Alive and Well and Living in Paris* returned to New York after a 30-year absence and played at the Zipper Theater (March 27; 74 performances as of May 31). The original revue, which ran for more than four years at the Village Gate (1968–72; 1,847 performances), was inspired by Brel's withdrawal from concert performing when he and his work were still relevant and popular. Specialties, those odd theatricals that defy easy categorization, also declined by four this season. *Lazer Vaudeville*'s run at the Lamb's Theatre (June 9; 86 performances) was little more than a transfer from the John Houseman forced by that space's demolition. The show centered on juggling, rope spinning and other acts of theatrical magic. Three of the specialties were staged readings of "lost" Broadway musicals in the nonprofit New York City Center Encores! series: *Kismet, 70, Girls, 70* and *Of Thee I Sing*. The big hit of the specialty (and Off Broadway) season, however, was a performance of percussion titled *Drumstruck* at Dodger Stages (June 16; 400 performances as of May 31). The show, which began in a Johannesburg café belonging to producer Warren Lieberman, gave every audience member a drum and all were expected (or encouraged) to participate in the performance.

There was one commercial revival of a play and one of a musical during the 2005–06 season. Patrick Hamilton's *Rope* became *Rope's End* when Lee Shubert transferred the 1929 London production to the Theatre Masque (now the John Golden). Based on the Leopold and Loeb thrill-killers story, the play begins in complete darkness with two young men dropping a dead body into a trunk and then proceeding to throw a party in the same room. It was later made into the classic 1948 Alfred Hitchcock film—adapted by Hume Cronyn with a screenplay by Arthur Laurents and uncredited assistance from Ben Hecht—starring James Stewart, Farley Granger and Cedric Hardwicke. In recent years, scholars have written extensively about the homoerotic content in the film, which revival director David Warren took care to clarify. The lead producer on *Rope* was the Drama Dept., a nonprofit group, but a four-entity partnership presented it at the Zipper Theater (December 4; 24 performances).

Cathy Rigby returned to New York with her production of *Peter Pan* in the Theater at Madison Square Garden. The iconic musical first became a Broadway hit in 1954 after tryouts in San Francisco and Los Angeles. Although the original production was slated for a limited-run before a national tour, NBC television broadcast that production, starring Mary Martin, in March 1955. It was viewed in an estimated 20 million homes by a record 65 million persons. Rigby has played the title role in four (of five) Broadway revivals of the musical, and she was nominated for a 1990 Tony Award for her performance. Rigby's company also was nominated for a best musical revival Tony Award for a 1999 production.

Ars Gratia Artis?

DESPITE THE ATTENTION paid here to commercial Off Broadway, it is the nonprofit arena that dominates Off Broadway year in and year out. It isn't merely in terms of the number of productions that the nonprofits outshine the commercial producers, it is also—with a few exceptions—in the quality of the work presented. If numbers of performances and productions were our only guides, of course, then *Drumstruck* and *Peter Pan*, or any of the long-running shows, would be the standard to which everyone would aspire. Before we explore new plays in the nonprofit arena, which accounted for more than a quarter of all Off Broadway production in the 2005–06 season, we should turn to play revivals presented by the nonprofits in limited engagements. The Brooklyn Academy of Music's presentation of the Royal Shakespeare Company's *Hecuba* returned Vanessa Redgrave to New York in the title role (June 18; 10 performances). After the London stand of this production, director Laurence Boswell was removed and adapter Tony Harrison was credited as the developer for "its US engagements." The point of the change may have been to counter negative reviews from London where it was called a "monumental fiasco" and a "crying shame" by Charles Spencer in *The Daily Telegraph*. Other London critics were equally dismissive. In New York, where reviewers regularly genuflect before all things Anglo, the response was not much better. *Variety*'s Rooney, for example, found *Hecuba,* "rendered for much of its duration as academic diatribe."

Mark Lamos, lauded here for Broadway productions of *Seascape* and last season's *The Rivals* at Lincoln Center Theater, directed *As You Like It* for the New York Shakespeare Festival (now rebranded as the Public Theater) in Central Park with James Waterston, Lynn Collins, Herb Foster, Richard Thomas and Brian Bedford. Even though it was the 50th anniversary celebration of the festival, critics aligned with the dour Jaques (Bedford), finding fault with the production. *The Village Voice*'s Feingold plaintively argued for a rewrite of the work, while others laid problems at the feet of the director. *A Soldier's Play*, the 1982 Pulitzer Prize-winning play by Charles Fuller—also a 1981–82 Best Play—came to Second Stage Theatre this season (October 17; 48 performances). The original production, which ran 468 performances at the Lucille Lortel Theatre (1981–83), featured such talents as Adolph Caesar, Charles Brown, Denzel Washington, Samuel L. Jackson and Peter Friedman. The 2005–06 production, directed by Jo Bonney, featured Taye Diggs in the central role of Captain Davenport with excellent supporting help from Teagle F. Bougere, James McDaniel, Anthony Mackie and others.

Play revivals elsewhere Off Broadway allowed stars to shine, if only for brief runs. BAM continued to present classic works of interest in productions of *Hedda Gabler, Peer Gynt* and *The Importance of Being Earnest*—all of which were planned as limited engagements. Ibsen's *Hedda* was adapted by Andrew Upton in the Sydney Theatre Company production starring Cate Blanchett (March 1; 26 performances). Blanchett's was a superb performance of the title role, making the audience long to see the gifted actor essay more of the great female roles. The star of *Peer Gynt*—presented in association with the National Theatre of Bergen and the Norwegian Theatre of Oslo, Ibsen's native theaters—was its director, the uniquely talented Robert Wilson who modeled the morality tale along his customary imagistic lines (April 11; 5 performances). The last of BAM's presentations in its spring theater season was Peter Hall's production of *The Importance of Being Earnest* by Oscar Wilde (April 18; 28 performances). But director Hall was not the only star of his production: The estimable Lynn Redgrave appeared as Lady Bracknell with James Waterston as Jack Worthing. With this performance, Redgrave bracketed the season in charmingly comic performances of two different women of a certain age—as noted above, she played Mrs. Culver in *The Constant Wife* on Broadway.

Roundabout Theatre Company's final production for 2005–06 at the Harold and Miriam Steinberg Center for Theatre was an interesting idea that came to fruition in unexpected ways. Joe Orton's 1964 play *Entertaining Mr. Sloane*, a dark comedy about a middle-age brother and sister who compete for the affections of a sociopathic young man, joined film star Alec Baldwin and television actor Chris Carmack with stage veterans Jan Maxwell and Richard Easton (March 16; 77 performances). Carmack was well cast as the hunky boy pursued by the siblings and Easton carried his weight as the crotchety father who has an unfortunate "accident." But the preternaturally sexy Maxwell, whose svelte figure and facial features are the types that drive other women to plastic surgeons, seemed ill-suited to the supposedly dowdy Kath. If the sociopathic title character swings whichever way the wind blows, Baldwin's Ed would have been in for a real battle against this seductive Kath. In Scott Ellis's staging, however, there was never much struggle as Ed dominated the boy's attentions from the moment they met. What makes the play interesting (and funny) is Sloane's sociopathy, not his penchant for older men. The play's run was further marred by friction between Baldwin and Maxwell, however, with the latter leaving the show several weeks early and the *New York Post* reporting that she had feared for her safety.

Nonprofit Bits and Pieces

NONPROFIT THEATER COMPANIES accounted for 23 new play offerings, six new musicals, three musical revivals and four solo performance pieces Off Broadway this season. Of the solo works, *RFK* by Jack Holmes made its way to the Culture Project's 45 Bleecker Street space after a 2004 run at the Court Theatre in Los Angeles under the title *The Awful Grace of God: A Portrait of Robert F. Kennedy* (November 15; 117 performances). Earlier in the season, Staceyann Chin had returned to 45 Bleecker Street with *Border/ Clash: A Litany of Desires*, which chronicled her life as a "lesbian activist slam poet from Jamaica who was born to a black mother and Chinese father" (June 16; 54 performances). The Irish Repertory Theatre provided a home for Chip Deffaa's *George M. Cohan Tonight!*, a tribute to the great Broadway figure as rendered by Jon Peterson (March 9; 77 performances). Amy Irving performed *A Safe Harbor for Elizabeth Bishop*, a dramatic portrait of the American poet, for Primary Stages at 59E59 Theaters (March 30; 33 performances).

The musical revivals in the nonprofits included two productions by the New York Gilbert and Sullivan Players—*HMS Pinafore* and *The Mikado*—and the first revival of the groundbreaking 1971 musical version of Shakespeare's *The Two Gentlemen of Verona*, which was part of the New York Shakespeare Festival's 50th anniversary celebration. The musical adaptation by John Guare, Mel Shapiro and Galt MacDermot caused a stir in its initial incarnation, transferred to Broadway, won two Tony Awards in 1972 and ran for 614 performances. The musical's allure in the early 1970s was two-fold: the significance of "love" in the culture at the time and the multiracial cast, which was far ahead of the multicultural curve. Despite Kathleen Marshall's direction and choreography, the production at the Delacorte Theater had a museum quality that it never fully transcended—a rarity in Guare's work (August 28; 13 performances).

Michael John LaChiusa was a prominent figure both onstage and off this season. In the August 2005 edition of *Opera News*, the composer argued strongly that the American musical was "dead" in the first sentence of a piece titled the "The Great Gray Way," which LaChiusa later told Playbill.com was not his title of choice. He described his concerns in the essay:

> Everywhere you look in Times Square, you see the advertisements for what seem to be musicals. *The Producers*! *The Lion King*! *Mamma*

Mia! *The Phantom of the Opera*! *Hairspray*! *Movin' Out*! Musicals appear to be everywhere; many are box-office hits. But are they really musicals? I'm old-school about what makes a musical a musical. Lyric, music, libretto, choreography—all work in equal parts to spin out the drama. And the best of craftsmanship is employed, craftsmanship that nods to the past and leans to the future: a great song is something we *think* we've heard before but haven't. A real musical makes perfect symmetry out of the muck of diverse and eclectic sources, and transcends those sources. A real musical is organic in all its parts. It's equal parts intelligence and heart. It can never be realistic theater, only realistic in its humanity. But who wants that in 2005? We're into reality programming, after all—which is hardly real at all. It's post-America America: we want *faux*!

Faux-musicals are just that—*faux*. *The Producers* is an example; so is *Hairspray*. If that label sounds disparaging, it's not meant to be. The creators of these shows set out to make musicals based on formulae, and they delivered. Neither transcends its source material (both are based on wonderful cult films), but as facsimiles of the real thing, they do very nicely—and the box-office receipts prove that. In no way do these two shows aspire to be the next *West Side Story* or *Sunday in the Park with George*. There's not even an attempt to deliver an old-fashioned, knock-'em-dead, lodge-like-bullet-hook number à la Jerry Herman. All sense of invention and craft is abandoned in favor of delivering what the audience thinks a musical should deliver. Everyone involved, from the usher to the stage manager to the producer to the landlord to the critic, is satisfied. There is no challenge, no confrontation, no art—and everyone sighs with relief.

Marc Shaiman, composer of *Hairspray*, took notable exception to LaChiusa's comments in a widely publicized online posting, which led to a report by Robert Simonson in *The New York Times*. There was no shortage of annoyance from the members of the *Hairspray* team including lead producer Margo Lion and co-librettist Thomas Meehan (who performed the same function on *The Producers*). Meehan told the *Times*, "It's almost an unwritten thing that you don't knock other people. It's a tough business. Everybody who's anybody in the theater has had failures, up to and including Stephen Sondheim." Meehan knows, one imagines, that theater people routinely are harshly critical of the work of others—but to put those thoughts into print is something that just isn't done.

When the tempest erupted LaChiusa was in rehearsal for a Los Angeles production of *The Wild Party* and unavailable for comment, except in a prepared statement that said he was "pleased the essay served its purpose, which was to generate discussion." With musicals scheduled for Off

Broadway production at the Public Theater and Lincoln Center Theater, LaChiusa seemed to have painted a large target on his back. *See What I Wanna See* in the Public's Anspacher Theater managed to elicit a fair amount of respectable comment for LaChiusa's emotional writing and storytelling if not for technical control of his craft (October 30; 41 performances). The *Times*'s Brantley noted that the "second act throbs with both communal feelings of hope and anxiety and a specific sense of character." In describing what he called the work's "second-act letdown," the *Voice*'s Feingold countered that LaChiusa's "tremendous fecundity of invention often runs way ahead of his ability to ground his work in reality." Although *Variety*'s Rooney thought the composer's aspiration merited respect, he found it "overall a dull, distancing experience." In March, LaChiusa's *Bernarda Alba*—based on Federico Garcia Lorca's *The House of Bernarda Alba*—in Lincoln Center's Mitzi Newhouse Theater (March 6; 40 performances) caused the critical daggers to be more fully unsheathed. Even the usually even-handed Kuchwara of the Associated Press, wrote that star Phylicia Rashad was "miscast" and that the musical itself was "claustrophobic." Targeted for scorn or not, LaChiusa's work this season brought to mind Steven Adler's comment regarding serious musicals, from his book *On Broadway: Art and Commerce on the Great White Way* (2004), that "the perception of a work as challenging does not mean, however, that it is artistically engaging." And just because the critics are unsupportive does not mean that the work is *not* (engaging, that is).

The other nonprofit new musicals included the aforementioned *Grey Gardens* at Playwrights Horizons, the York Theatre Company's *Fanny Hill* and *A Fine and Private Place* and New York Theatre Workshop's *The Seven*. The York's two productions began their journeys to New York 10 years apart at Goodspeed Musicals in Chester, Connecticut. *Fanny Hill*, whose pornographic literary pedigree dates back to the 18th century, started at Goodspeed in 1999 in this adaptation by Ed Dixon. Although *Fanny* is pretty tame stuff by today's standards of decency, it made a lively, clever showing at the York's home in St. Peter's church. *A Fine and Private Place*—based on a 1960 novel about how the dead (and the living) cope with their state of being—tested the waters at Goodspeed almost exactly 10 years earlier in 1989. A few months later the musical was staged in New Jersey, but apparently not resurrected again until the York production this season, which was found generally to be of only moderate interest. Will Power's *The Seven*, however, at New York Theatre Workshop garnered enthusiastic support and was honored with a Lucille Lortel Award for best musical. Adapted from Aeschylus's *Seven Against Thebes*, Power crafted, according to Mark Blankenship in *Variety*, "two hours of impressive flow, letting his rhymes change their meter and rhythm to signal differences in character and emotion." The production was widely seen as a new high point in the convergence of hip-hop music and conventional theater.

The Play's the Thing

OPENINGS OF NEW PLAYS in the nonprofit arena Off Broadway began early in the new season and continued until almost the final moment. Nine different companies produced a total of 23 new plays on topics ranging from the lies we tell ourselves to the many ways violence dominates modern life. Among these plays (and companies), of course, are the Best Plays already addressed above: *Third* at Lincoln Center Theater, *The Lieutenant of Inishmore* at Atlantic Theater Company and *Stuff Happens* at the Public Theater. Roundabout Theatre Company continued to present new works at the Harold and Miriam Steinberg Center for Theatre with Jon Robin Baitz's *The Paris Letter* in the Laura Pels Theatre (June 12; 65 performances). Baitz's play about the choices made by a homosexual financier who hides his true nature featured a powerful cast of Ron Rifkin, John Glover, Michele Pawk, Jason Butler Harner and Daniel Eric Gold in key roles. Critics were intrigued by the tale and praised director Doug Hughes. The intricate plotting of the piece, however, seemed to prevent their full embrace. Several months later, the company staged the New York premiere of Noah Haidle's *Mr. Marmalade* (November 20; 79 performances). A dark comedy about the overexposure of young children to adult issues, Roundabout's proclivity for hiring "name" actors kept the play's essence under wraps in a one-note performance by Mamie Gummer that vitiated the sweetness and innocence of the central character. The 2004 premiere production at South Coast Repertory in Costa Mesa, California, was funny and wrenching to witness. But the New York production never captured the naiveté at the play's core.

Brits Off Broadway continued its run at 59E59 Theaters with a production of *Private Fears in Public Places* by Alan Ayckbourn (June 14; 23 performances). It was a positive beginning to the season for Ayckbourn, whose later entry on Broadway (*Absurd Person Singular*) is addressed above. Charles Isherwood wrote in *The New York Times*, "a minor-key comedy about six Londoners leading lives of quiet desperation, it is rueful, funny, touching and altogether wonderful." Noting that Ayckbourn had brought his company from the UK's Stephen Joseph Theatre to perform the work, *Variety*'s Rooney wrote, "even without such an unexpectedly satisfying play, this fine company's brief New York stint would be something to celebrate." Given the reception Ayckbourn's production at the Biltmore Theatre would later receive, it was ultimately puzzling that *Private Fears* came and went so quickly.

In addition to the warmly received revival of *A Soldier's Play* at Second Stage Theatre, three new plays made their Off Broadway bows there: *Birdie Blue*, *The Little Dog Laughed* and *Show People*. The superb S. Epatha Merkerson led the cast of Cheryl L. West's *Birdie Blue*, a character study about an African-American woman who carries the burdens of her life with upbeat faith and vigor (June 23; 29 performances). Another powerful leading lady strutted her stuff when the incomparable Julie White appeared as a "dragon lady" of an agent in Douglas Carter Beane's delicious comedy, *The Little Dog Laughed* (January 9; 56 performances). When her film-star client's homosexuality threatens to become public, White's Diane constructs an elaborate ruse that centers on a sham marriage of her client to a pregnant woman—which reminded more than a few audience members of a splashy Hollywood-marriage-and-child story of recent vintage. Paul Weitz returned to Off Broadway with a wink-and-nudge valentine to theater folk in *Show People* (April 6; 29 performances). Debra Monk and Lawrence Pressman played a pair of hard-pressed actors in middle age who are asked to "perform" as the parents of Tom (Ty Burrell) because he wants them to impress his girlfriend. As the comedy unfolds, nothing is as it seems (including Tom or his girlfriend)—except, perhaps, the transforming power of performance.

Oedipus at Palm Springs marked the beginning of an eventful season for New York Theatre Workshop (August 3; 31 performances). The production by the Five Lesbian Brothers focused on the ennui that settles over relationships—in these cases, lesbian—and how people try to rekindle sparks of romance and connection. Both members of one couple, however, happen to carry secrets known and, ironically, unknown to themselves. Any half-sentient audience member—who can, say, read the title—figures out the secret long before the characters, but the play's lively humor kept the action engrossing. *Spirit* was first given as a production in Glasgow by the group Improbable. By the time of its NYTW presentation, the group clearly understood the dynamics of *Spirit's* nonlinear narrative, which explored the nature of conflict with the inventive use of live actors, puppetry and miniature models (September 15; 29 performances). Itamar Moses's *Bach at Leipzig* comically enacted a competition for the organist position in St. Thomas's Church in Leipzig (November 14; 38 performances). With an extraordinarily talented cast in Boyd Gaines, Reg Rogers, Michael Emerson, Jeffrey Carlson, Richard Easton and others, the play itself was a bit of a comic fugue interweaving elaborate plot points into something of a muddle.

Still running at the end of the season was *columbinus* (May 22; 10 performances as of May 31). As its title suggests, the work was a meditation on the incidents surrounding the 1999 mass killings at a high school in Colorado. Developed by the United States Theatre Project, which included such sharp young talents as Will Rogers, Karl Miller, Anna Camp, Nicole Lowrance, Keith Nobbs and others, the play focused not only on social situations that helped exacerbate the antisocial behavior of the killers but also explored the thoughts and feelings recorded in their private writings.

This was also the season, however, when NYTW made arguably its largest blunder to date and lost credibility as a path-blazing presenter of new work. The decision in question was to postpone production of *My Name Is Rachel Corrie*, scheduled to begin performances March 22, 2006, just a few weeks before the first performance. Artistic director James C. Nicola told *The New York Times* that he polled local Jewish religious and community leaders as to their feelings about the work. "The uniform answer we got," said Nicola, "was that the fantasy that we could present the work of this writer simply as a work of art without appearing to take a position was just that, a fantasy." He cited recent Palestinian elections and the illness of Ariel Sharon as making "this [Jewish] community very defensive and very edgy." The response to Nicola's decision prompted outrage from Alan Rickman and Katherine Viner, authors of the true story about a young American woman who was killed by an Israeli vehicle while trying to stop the bulldozing of a Palestinian home. Others who joined in the protest over the presumed censorship included Vanessa Redgrave, Harold Pinter, Gillian Slovo, Stephen Fry, John Weidman, Gloria Steinem and Eve Ensler. Managing director Lynn Moffat said, "The charge of censorship is what's really distressing to us. We didn't take the word postponement to mean censorship." Editorial writers and theater critics voiced their disagreement with the decision throughout the English-speaking world and the play moved to a West End theater in London for a run. Although decidedly not the kind of attention a cutting-edge theater in New York seeks, Nicola may have a reservoir of goodwill in reserve to help weather the storm.

Things were calmer at Playwrights Horizons where plays focused on women as central characters. *Fran's Bed* by James Lapine arrived six months or so after legal (and political) battles over end-of-life issues surrounding Terri Schiavo, who existed in a vegetative state for 15 years until she was allowed to die—or killed, depending on one's perspective (September 25; 17 performances). Lapine's play, which he also directed, was freighted with possibly unintended concerns as it explored the consciousness of a woman in middle age who has failed in an attempt to take her own life.

Mia Farrow played the comatose Fran, who exists for the audience in a half-light of consciousness, skipping from scene to scene in her once-active but seemingly unfulfilling life. The play also examined what happens to family members when their linchpin is incapacitated and they are forced to make unpleasant decisions. In Sarah Schulman's *Manic Flight Reaction*, a scatterbrained, freespirited academic finds herself sexually involved with a male graduate student, who is near the age of her own daughter, when a former female lover (now the wife of a Republican politico) arrives and attempts to quash a brewing scandal (October 30; 25 performances). Schulman's play satirizes the incessant chase in American culture for celebrity and scandal, but undermines its comic power with sermons on the importance of love and forgiveness. Deirdre O'Connell as Marge, the academic, made her character's contradictory behavior work in an encompassing performance, but the other pieces of the dramatic puzzle never quite fit. Christopher Durang returned to Playwrights with *Miss Witherspoon* a comic (and cosmic) exploration of the anxieties we face in life after life after life. When a chunk of Skylab lands in her backyard, Veronica (Kristine Nielsen) commits suicide, which leads to a series of reincarnations that are humorous and dark partly because the central character keeps trying to obliterate herself (November 29; 40 performances). Perfectly capturing the anxieties that afflict many post-September 11 Americans, Durang's play was a finalist for the Pulitzer Prize this season. The award, as noted above, was given to no one. In David Marshall Grant's *Pen*, divorced parents in 1969 use their teenage son to bludgeon one another emotionally (April 2; 16 performances). Disabled and in a wheelchair, the mother (J. Smith-Cameron) does everything she can to keep the son under her control. The father encourages the boy to attend school in California, where the father is moving with his pregnant new wife. The boy shoplifts. Along the way, the playwright employs a mystical device that allows the mother to rise from her wheelchair, although the son is disabled by her action. The mother eventually returns to her prison on wheels, recognizing that she must stay and the son must go. For Grant, clearly, no one completely escapes the dysfunction of family.

When Rinne Groff's *The Ruby Sunrise* arose at the Public Theater (November 16; 20 performances), it was another revelation of Oskar Eustis's talent in working with a playwright to develop a work—which may lie in asking the right questions and getting out of the writer's way. First seen in Louisville at the 2004 Humana Festival of New American Plays, the work seemed to have solved problems from its earliest incarnation. The critics disagreed with that assessment, by the way, generally finding Groff's politics too baldly stated and the acting lacking in nuance. It is unfortunate that critics seem forever wed to some version of the "well-made play" structure and to whatever passes for naturalist-realist acting today. Groff's tale of a young Indiana farm woman's aspiration to invent in 1927 what became the technology of television—only to be beaten to the punch—is set against a backdrop of progressive politics that drive Ruby to envision the communitarian possibilities of television. The second act shows Ruby's daughter attempting in 1952 to get her mother's story told through the medium of television, which was then in the throes of anything but progressive values. What eventually appears in the television-show-within-a-play would be familiar to anyone who can recall the creaky dramatic frameworks of early television—often remembered with reverent nostalgia as quality work. Groff, Eustis and company delivered the goods, even if the critics were blind to them. *Measure for Pleasure* by David Grimm, on the other hand, with its bawdy jokes and licentious characters always ready for a sexy romp had no such difficulty with the reviewers (March 8; 23 performances). A comedy that is Restoration-ish in its spirit (with a few other periods included), Stasio of *Variety* called it an "extremely stylish (and exuberantly filthy) sex farce that's just the thing to get us through the dark days of Lent." Just so.

As we draw to the end of this narrative, we must consider Manhattan Theatre Club's four Off Broadway plays in its City Center home. Ariel Dorfman's *The Other Side* featured the remarkable talents of John Cullum and Rosemary Harris as a couple whose difficult life together is made worse when a negotiated peace between two countries causes their house (even the bed) to be divided in the middle (December 6; 48 performances). A black comedy with many contemporary resonances, it echoes works in the absurdist mold but does not maintain its comic edge throughout. Pulitzer Prize-winning playwright Nilo Cruz's *Beauty of the Father* carried forward the MTC season (January 10; 48 performances). Cruz's lyric drama centers on the reunion of a father and his adult daughter, with whom the father later competes for the affections of a young man. The poetry of the piece, which also featured Federico Garcia Lorca as a spirit guide, had a tendency to hold the play's passions at a distance and ultimately kept the piece from soaring completely. John Patrick Shanley's *Defiance* was the second part of a projected trilogy (February 28; 107 performances as of May 31). The first part was Shanley's Pulitzer Prize-winning *Doubt*, which continued to run on Broadway throughout this season. In *Defiance*, a Marine officer runs headlong into conflicts faced by the military in the waning days of the Vietnam War. Issues of morality, free will and reason are woven throughout the play as a gung-ho senior officer destroys his career by fraternizing with the wife of a man in his command. But it isn't only the senior officer's defiance of military rules that drives the action, there is also a man of God, a chaplain, who forces issues that might otherwise stay buried. The 90-minute play has the dramatic tension of a full-length study of the issue at hand. As a result, when the play came to an end one could feel the audience longing to know more. The final MTC production of the season was Roberto Aguirre-Sacasa's comedy, *Based on a Totally True Story* (April 11; 56 performances). The play focuses on the life of a comic-book writer whose family is unraveling just as he is getting involved with a new boyfriend and Hollywood has come calling. An amusing, if self-indulgent tale of a 20-something's burgeoning career success, the play was aided by lively performances from Carson Elrod in the central role with Kristine Nielsen and Michael Tucker adding memorable supporting performances.

So there they were: 127 new productions opened on and Off Broadway during the 2005–06 season. Of this total, only 26 continued to run at the end of the season and most of these holdovers were destined to close within a few weeks. Producers bemoaned the state of the business (see page 27) and critics found much to dismiss as they documented the "decline" of the theater—an annual journalistic exercise. But each spring as the season staggers to the finish line, winded and in need of refreshment, thousands of young people exit theater-training programs ready to create new work. It is the paradox of live theater that it is ever dying to be reborn; and that shows open to close. Even *The Fantasticks*, which ran for 17,162 performances through 10 presidential administrations (1960–2002) was marked for ending. And still producers mount new shows, critics march into theaters night after night looking for the next bit of clarity: an unusual story, perhaps, with heart or humor. Alexander Pope seems to have unwittingly described this dilemma of theater and its makers, audiences and critics, when he wrote in another context, "Hope springs eternal in the human breast: Man never is, but always to be blest."

Take a breath, it's a new season.

THE BEST PLAYS
OF 2005–2006

2005–2006 Best Play

GREY GARDENS

By Doug Wright, Scott Frankel and Michael Korie

○ ○ ○ ○ ○

Essay by Michael Feingold

EDIE: Sometimes I think I have the saddest life.

MUSICALS HAVE BEEN INSPIRED by movies since the days when the two forms first took leading positions in American popular culture, but until *Grey Gardens*, virtually none of the theater's film-inspired musicals was based on a documentary film. Historical figures aplenty have appeared in musicals but the preferred subjects of documentary filmmakers are not people who loom large in history, or in the body of folk myth that surrounds it. Annie Oakley (*Annie Get Your Gun*) and Thomas Jefferson (*1776*) have attained a certain significance in the archive of world events. But the people in documentary films, for the most part, are those whose stature is embodied in their curiosity value: What they do or say on film—not what they did in life—is the source of their hold on the public imagination.

That fact makes the achievement of *Grey Gardens* all the more astonishing. The musical's three creators—book writer Doug Wright, lyricist Michael Korie and composer Scott Frankel—have mined the Maysles's Brothers 1975 film for a wealth of details. But what they have created is an entirely different object, in which documentary facts are mined for mythic meaning rather than left to testify on their own. In 1975, the world discovered Edith Bouvier Beale and her daughter Edith ("Big Edie" and "Little Edie") still living in the 28-room East Hampton mansion where, decades earlier, they were notable figures in an elite society of wealth and privilege. That they happened to be the aunt and first cousin, respectively, of JacquelineKennedy Onassis and her sister, Lee Radziwill, only heightened the shock of their condition. Subsisting on meager savings and handouts from relatives, the two women had become semi-recluses, their once-elegant house now a wreck with a leaky roof, crumbling walls, barely functional plumbing and floors covered in the fecal debris of more than 50 stray cats that the Beales had taken in—as well as several raccoons said to be rabid. The *Grey Gardens* documentary records this nightmarish life, varied by an

Musicale: Christine Ebersole and company in Grey Gardens. *Photo: Joan Marcus*

occasional visitor, an occasional attempt at mitigation, with quiet objectivity. The effect, which has given it an extensive cult following, is like that of a particularly messy two-car collision: Horrible and grotesquely funny, its images are unbearable to look at and impossible not to watch with fascination. The last thing you could ever expect it to become is a piece of musical theater.

Wright and his colleagues solved the problem by granting the Beale ladies something the film frequently alludes to but couldn't possibly show: their earlier life. *Grey Gardens*, the musical, is in a sense two musicals, which interpenetrate but also oppose each other, a diptych contrasting before and after. The first act, after a brief prologue showing the house as it was in 1973, takes place in the summer of 1941. The mansion is in spotless condition. Mrs. Beale, still married to her stockbroker husband, is preparing to throw a lavish garden party at which Little Edie's engagement to Joseph Kennedy Jr., elder brother of the still-immature Jack and Bobby, will be announced. Giddy with pre-party bustle and gossipy information, this act has the swanky tone and pace of a 1940s musical about the rich—with a cheeky parodic sense that evokes Cole Porter or Rodgers and Hart of the era. Cannily, the action is strung along a series of pastiche songs, evoking the pop tunes of the period and earlier. The nominal excuse for these is that Mrs. Beale and her live-in accompanist, GeorgeGould Strong, are rehearsing the concert they expect to give for the party guests.

THIS CUNNING LEAP backward allows the writers to show us something other than the squalor and decrepitude that the film has primed theatergoers to expect. The two women are seen in a more positive light, at the height of their social glory, as the writers simultaneously hint at the causes that will bring them misery later. And the authors get what must be the secret

---

The action of the first act is strung along a series of pastiche songs.

---

wish of many contemporary writers for the musical theater—the chance to create, on a miniature scale, an old-fashioned musical, with no need for apologies or attempts to cover what would today seem lapses in tone.

By including in Mrs. Beale's repertoire a kind of ethnic-stereotype pop song that she almost certainly did not sing in real life, they open a window for the audience on the prejudices of the period, and the obliviousness of its "respectable" white elite to the sensitivities of others—elements that, as things turn out, will play a strong role in the fate of the two characters. Listening to Mrs. Beale rehearse songs about an "itty bitty geisha [. . .] hobbling on her poor bound feet," or about a black plantation woman cooking hominy grits because, "dem's de bestest vittles / us colored folk gits," we may laugh at the absurdity of the ethnic condescension, but we may also see it as a double mirror. Isolated in a large house that requires endless maintenance, with an unloving husband who prefers to stay in New York—where he keeps a mistress—and whose disapproval prevents her from having a fulfilling concert career, Mrs. Beale is more comfortably situated than a geisha or a Southern mammy, but she is no less trapped in an inferior position. Her absent spouse's disapproval has an onstage agent in the equally disapproving presence of her ultraconservative, elderly father, "Major" Bouvier, whose martial-music injunctions to his granddaughters add another nostalgic element to the musical mix. In a constant state of thwarted rebellion against the homemaker-hostess role the men demand that she play, Mrs. Beale is equally conflicted as a parent, alternately desperate ensue for her once the fledgling has left the nest.

Gould, her accompanist and semi-permanent house guest, would be a possible source of support, except that he himself is in a similarly equivocal situation: A socially "presentable" composer manqué, he is depicted in the musical as an obvious homosexual whose sexually ambiguous connection to Mrs. Beale is dependent on the tenuous financial support she receives from her husband and father. Made to feel unwelcome during the confrontations that arise over the plans for the party, Gould shrewdly realizes that his days at Grey Gardens are numbered; the authors give him a solo that evokes the dreamy jazz-influenced ballads of the 1940s, with hints of morbidity to foreshadow the suicide they hypothesize for him, mentioned in passing by Little Edie during one of her Act II tirades against her mother.

In another canny stroke, the authors make Mrs. Beale's recital repertoire serve not only as the first act's structural principle but as the source of its central conflict: The issue of whether she will or will not sing at Edie's engagement fete becomes a bone of contention between mother and daughter, then between mother and grandfather, which leads to the disinheritance threat that will abet the Beale women's economic downslide. In this sense, despite the jaunty 1940s tone, *Grey Gardens* is a classic

Pod persons: Sara Gettelfinger and Christine Ebersole in Grey Gardens. *Photo: Joan Marcus*

specimen of today's musicals in its self-aware use of music: Its songs are its subject matter. And if music is a source of the two women's conflict, it is also the medium through which they bond: Edie repairs the quarrel with her mother by luring her into a duet version of "Two Peas in a Pod," which she describes as "the first song you ever taught me." The quarrel over songs for the engagement party is echoed in the second act by a quarrel over allowing Jerry, a visitor to the house, to search for the record player on which Mrs. Beale can hear her old recordings. "Two Peas in a Pod," which temporarily heals the breach in Act I, also serves as a summation of the women's troubled but loving kinship in its Act II reprise.

As in his words for other consciously pastiche numbers, Korie's lyrics for "Two Peas in a Pod" serve simultaneously to enhance the period tone and to puncture it with distancing effects. Steeped in references to the late 1930s and early 1940s, the song can't possibly have existed long enough to be the first one Edie was taught; its eerily veiled hints of a sexual connection between its two participants ("physically a few discreet disparities") make it the "wrong" sort of song to teach a child, and a work that both does and does not mirror the women's tangled relationship. Couched in a diction that shifts recklessly from high to low and past to present—often alternating line by line with snippets of dialogue that make aggressively dramatic contrasts to them—*Grey Gardens*'s lyrics convey an eccentric sensibility wholly their own, mirroring the two heroines' eccentricity.

"The 5:15," named for the commuter train on which Edie's father is expected to arrive, is the key point on which the first act's dramatic suspense hangs. From the fraught state in which everyone behaves throughout the act, it is easy to predict that—despite the song's repeated assertions—Mr. Beale will not be "arriving on the 5:15," that something will happen to blight Edie and Joe's engagement and that the mother-daughter conflict over the concert will be resolved in a way that makes neither woman particularly happy. The dialectic between respectability, as preached by Major Bouvier, and the more nonconformist gospel of art, as exemplified in Mrs. Beale's concertizing, is the real conflict in which the characters are caught. Joe Kennedy's sudden cold feet about the engagement come partly from his desire to avoid scandal—which has already begun to dog his family. The only characters aloof from the struggle between these two forces are Brooks, the African-American butler, who employs the impassive discretion expected by the rich from domestic servants, and Edie's two little-girl cousins, Jackie and Lee, the visiting daughters of Mrs. Beale's brother, "Black Jack" Bouvier. While these children watch, in wide-eyed consternation, as the conflict burgeons, the text is dotted with clues about their own future careers, including Jackie's own marriage to a handsome Kennedy scion.

INSTEAD OF MR. BEALE, what arrives at the climax of Act I is a telegram, wishing Edie luck and announcing that he and "Linda" are in Mexico, where he is obtaining a divorce. As the Bouviers and Beales—like the Kennedys—are Catholic, this torpedoes all possibility of the engagement. Joe Jr. rushes out to head off his parents; Little Edie, devastated, declares her determination to escape Grey Gardens and never come back. As her mother steels herself to welcome the arriving guests from the French windows overlooking the gardens, we see Edie, suitcase in hand, slipping out to escape the impending social disaster. The act's closing song, warbled from her window by Mrs. Beale, is a plaintive song of the classic turn-of-the-century type beloved by parlor sopranos, titled, "Will You?" Announced by Mrs. Beale as "our tribute to young love," its lyric contains a variety of jarring and ominous notes, as if some innocent Victorian wordsmith had not quite been able to make his sentiments coherent:

> EDITH: [. . .] When wild geese in autumn fly
> Will you?
> When hearth fires of winter die
> Will you? [. . .]

These little verbal grenades give the music's deliberately arch sugariness—after the bickering and repudiations we've just seen—a bitter undertone that, paradoxically, makes its sweet tune seem all the sweeter, because everything around it evokes or conveys so much pain.

> EDITH: [. . .] Time rushes by
> Memories fade
> Dreams never do. [. . .]

The second act will display the truth of those statements in most unexpected ways.

Thanks to a subtle use of projections and shadows, the house is already beginning to decay as the first act closes. When we return for Act II, the sagging wreck of the prologue appears, shadowy shapes abound and we hear the screech of older women's voices. Their conversation—about cats escaping through a hole in the wall and about not answering the phone—is conducted shrilly and at cross purposes; we are clearly in a different world from that of Act I.

Revolutionary costume: Christine Ebersole in
Grey Gardens. *Photo: Joan Marcus*

WHEN LITTLE EDIE enters, coming onto the porch through the front door, we see that the characters, like the house, have metamorphosed. Little Edie is now a middle-age woman, played by Christine Ebersole, who played Mrs. Beale in Act I. Mrs. Beale, whom we will see in subsequent scenes, elderly and bedridden, is now played by MaryLouise Wilson. Edie is now more eccentric and more disturbingly cartoonish, talking to people who may or may not actually be present—directly to us, that is—instead of addressing people we know to be present onstage with her. And she expounds to us her ideas—astonishing ideas. This number, "The Revolutionary Costume," dazzlingly performed by Ebersole provides a detailed view of the complex mosaic that is Little Edie's mind. Scattered spoken fragments reassemble into a tidy overall picture, rather like the outlandish, yet innovative, clothing she wears.

Edie's description of her outfit is motivated by her new relation to her surroundings: Grey Gardens has now been ruled a public health hazard. The town of Easthampton, which once viewed the Beales as an ornament of its social elegance, now see them as a menace; Edie regards her neighbors, with their constant complaints about the house's condition, as enemies and spies. Rich with the political jargon of the 1960s and 1970s, her speech is as radical as her attire. Her costume is "revolutionary," both in its unexpected use of its materials—skirts worn upside down as capes, bedding articles and wall hangings adapted for wear—and in the political stance it represents:

> EDIE: [. . .] You fight City Hall
>
> With a Persian shawl
>
> That used to hang on the bedroom wall
>
> [. . .]
>
> The full-length velvet glove
>
> Hides the fist. [. . .]

In addition to itemizing the outfit Edie's wearing and stating her political position, the lyric supplies images of the community she now lives to battle:

> EDIE: [. . . T]o show those polo riders
>
> in khakis and topsiders
>
> just what a revolutionary costume has to say.
>
> [. . . .]
>
> Honestly! They can get you in Easthampton for wearing red shoes on a Thursday[. . . .] They can get you for almost anything. It's a mean, nasty, Republican town. [. . .]

In the scenes that follow the drop-dead brilliance of "The Revolutionary Costume," we observe the elaborate dialectic the Beales have developed in their semi-isolation. It offers alternative readings—often supplying two versions from each of the two women—of their past as we viewed it in Act I, of the intervening decades, of how they cope with the present and what motivates them. We see, too, what might be called their support staff, which includes innumerable cats, ghosts and memories, two local handymen—one of whom is the son of Act I's African-American butler, played by the same actor—and Mrs. Beale's favorite spirit-strengthener, the radio preacher NormanVincent Peale.

The dialectic, in a sense, is going on in Edie's head. Raised in an era when ladies were trained to look past anything unpleasant, Mrs. Beale is a classic embodiment of denial (it's no wonder that she loves Dr. Peale's doctrine of "positive thinking"). Her song, "The Cake I Had," which follows "The Revolutionary Costume" in the second act's succession of remarkable numbers, sums up her philosophy. Now crippled by gout and chair-bound, she sits on the upstairs sundeck, beaming placidly while Edie, prone next to her, sunbathes and frets about gaining weight, about roads not taken, about all the good things in life she has missed. Mrs. Beale, in contrast, asserts that she has had everything she wanted. She rewrites history, describing her marriage as "terribly successful" and her sons (who have disowned her) as "perfect." And although she concedes that,

> EDITH: [. . .] The days are gone
>
> When money grew on trees.
>
> The money trees
>
> Came down with elm disease.
>
> At my age, ducks,
>
> For my two bucks
>
> I'll eat the cake I have[. . . .]

In dialogue intrusions between her mother's warbled stanzas, Edie pours out her regret over having stayed at Grey Gardens to care for her mother, at not having made herself a life in New York and most of all at never having married. Humorously and bluntly, Mrs. Beale declines to accept the blame, telling Edie:

> EDITH: Enough with all
>
> Your celebrated loves.
>
> You had two hands.
>
> You could have modeled gloves. [. . .]

THE CONFLICT BETWEEN Mrs. Beale and Edie is intensified by the presence of their most constant visitor, Jerry. A handsome local boy just out of his teens, his Greek-god looks have caused literary Edie to christen him "The Marble Faun" (after the sculpture at the center of Nathaniel Hawthorne's novel). Seemingly concerned with helping the two distressed women, Jerry is a figure of troubling ambiguity, an easygoing, semi-educated fellow who apparently wants only to rescue the women from the worst of their plumbing and sanitation disasters, but whom Edie suspects of stealing—when he takes money from Mrs. Beale's purse for purchases, he makes an ostentatious show of the amount—and for whom Mrs. Beale accuses Edie of harboring sexual cravings. Squatting patiently by the elder lady's bed, flea collars around his pants cuffs to ward off the house's profuse insect life, he seems thoroughly benign as she boils corn on the cob for him on her bedside hotplate. Her tender tribute to their relationship, "Jerry Likes My Corn," shows a gentler aspect of Mrs. Beale's gift for coping with whatever life brings—but the number itself contains a furious argument between mother and daughter over the alleged motives for Jerry's presence. Later, in her own room, Edie alternately consoles herself with souvenir trinkets and fantasies of faraway places, and gives vent to bursts of rage at her mother's insistence on running the house her way and cultivating her own choice of companions. Jerry, in effect, is the alternate Edie, a docile but self-assured child on whom the mother can dote, which precipitates ferocious seizures of sibling rivalry.

"Around the World," the huge, aria-like song in which Edie alternately rages and consoles herself, is *Grey Gardens*'s dramatic core, a musicalized essence of the ambiguities that make up the two women's eerie codependency. Edie's struggle to be independent, to make a life of her own, to leave Grey Gardens for the big city, is balanced and ultimately cut short by her fears, her little-girlish sense of helplessness without her mother, her worry—as time brings increasing confusions to her memory—that she may be mentally unstable. Edie appears at the end dressed for travel, with a suitcase. But she puts the suitcase down in the hall, and does not leave. Her fear and resentment of the outside world, coupled with the sense of affection and camaraderie so strongly built into her contorted connection to her mother, are too much for her.

At the end, "Mother darling," as Edie calls her, gets her way—not without resistance—but she gets her way nonetheless. Setting out such an extreme case, *Grey Gardens* is pitched to leave us wondering about the extent to which any of us can escape the emotional bond we share with our parents. Freud said that we all carry them around with us. Mrs. Beale, not being so easily transportable, Edie stayed home with her instead. Whether that made the burden easier or harder for her to bear is left to the audience to puzzle for themselves.

2005–2006 Best Play

THE HISTORY BOYS

By Alan Bennett

○ ○ ○ ○ ○

Essay by Charles McNulty

IRWIN: History nowadays is not a matter of conviction. It's a performance. It's entertainment. And if it isn't, make it so.

NO ONE COULD HAVE PREDICTED the stunning Broadway success of Alan Bennett's *The History Boys*. Though the play and Nicholas Hytner's production racked up prizes when it premiered at the Royal National Theatre of Great Britain, the story of eight high school boys preparing for their entrance exams to Oxford and Cambridge sounded a bit remote (not to say twee) for American audiences. Hailed as a "national treasure" in England, Bennett possesses a gift for tea-kettle drollery that isn't a natural fit for the Great White Way, which explains perhaps why none of his plays—not even the recent smashes, *The Lady in the Van* and *The Madness of George III*—have found welcome there.

The impression has been that Bennett doesn't travel well, that his irony, like kidney pie, is better enjoyed within the UK or in specialty houses abroad. It is not that he has been ignored in the US. *Beyond the Fringe*, the 1964 comic revue he wrote and performed with Peter Cook, Dudley Moore and Jonathan Miller, won a Tony for its creators. The Brooklyn Academy of Music presented *The Madness of George III* as part of a national tour, which preceded the release of the critically praised film. And *Talking Heads*, his series of dramatic monologues originally written for television (and shown on PBS), enjoyed a lengthy commercial run at Greenwich Village's Minetta Lane Theatre. But his celebrity is largely a British phenomenon.

The outré charms of *The History Boys* could hardly be described as universal. Imagine someone blindly pitching the play to one of the Shuberts: "Okay, so we have this honors class of history students from an industrial town in North England. All of them are super-smart, but they're not the usual upper-crust Oxbridge types (think Harvard and Yale, only snootier). Plus they have this eccentric, bow-tie wearing teacher (ideally played by the corpulent Uncle Vernon-guy from the *Harry Potter* movies) who doesn't

Boys' life: Jamie Parker, Andrew Knott, Dominic Cooper and James Corden in The History Boys. *Photo: Joan Marcus*

think that higher learning should be about brand names. He has them memorize Thomas Hardy poems and act out scenes in French using only the subjunctive or conditional tenses. (He's a real hoot!) But their ambitious headmaster wants to raise the school's stature. He's convinced these kids have a genuine shot at the big leagues, so he hires another teacher who's all about slick packaging. The conflict is between the new guy and the old-timer, who by the way has this bad habit (call it a tragic flaw) of groping the boys on his motorcycle."

Even the most prescient of producers would have a hard time accepting that such a work was destined to be a blockbuster. Yet *The History Boys* provides a legitimate opportunity to borrow the term "boffo" from *Variety*'s lexicon. There's no better way to sum up a critical and commercial triumph that includes virtually every major theater award, including six Tony Awards (tying *Death of a Salesman*'s 1949 record for drama), and a film adaptation that features—miracle of miracles—the original no-name cast.

How to explain the magic? Elegantly composed though the play is, one could hardly call it a masterpiece of dramatic structure. Sui generis, it neither conforms to existing genres nor challenges them. Basically, it just ignores them. Bennett's too busy pursuing his thematic quarry to worry about breaking new formal ground, which is another way of saying that he allows his content to dictate his form rather than the other way around.

TOO SINGULAR TO SERVE as an example, *The History Boys* isn't likely to become a staple of playwriting workshops, and when it appears on undergraduate modern drama syllabi it will no doubt be to spark students' engagement with its ideas. One can already see the paper titles: "Alan Bennett's Education and its Discontents," "The End of History: A Theatrical Teach-In."

Bennett doesn't allow his ideological bent to eclipse his observations.

In terms of storytelling, *The History Boys* seems oblivious to the value of rising suspense. Aristotle would have to deduct points for the intermixing of narrative telling with dramatic enactment, never mind the complete absence of inevitability. Events transpire less in an organic fashion than in a randomly imposed one, which has a kind of realism if you agree with one of the students' definitions of history as "just one fucking thing after another."

Yet realism isn't Bennett's cup of tea either. Though the drama takes place in the Thacherite 1980s, many of the details of secondary school education are pulled from the playwright's own outdated past. "When I was writing *The History Boys* I didn't pay much heed to when it was supposed to be set," Bennett acknowledges in the play's introduction. He subsequently learned, for example, that the scholarship exams his titular characters are studying for the kind that the author himself successfully sat in the early 1950s to win his place at Oxford, are no longer given. Bennett ponders this dilemma in his diaries and sides in favor of poetic license: "Take a poll of all the playwrights at the National and you wouldn't find one whose lover had shredded their masterpiece, fed it into the stove and gone out and shot themselves. But that doesn't rule out *Hedda Gabler.*"

Still, Bennett remained mindful of the challenge before him: "[O]nce the audience starts thinking, 'But school isn't like that,' they're off the hook." Plausibility rather than realism is the ultimate goal. Interestingly, the area in which this is most strained has little to do with college prep. It concerns the sexual mores of the play—more precisely, the handling of gay character and themes. The casual attitude toward homosexuality among a group of teenage boys (only one of whom is gay) requires a leap of faith, at least for American audiences with a knowledge of the virulence of high school homophobia. Bennett conjures a Freudian world in which bisexuality is, if not the norm, at least nothing to get too worked up about. It's a fantasy, in other words, in which desire is allowed to manifest itself without much fear of persecution, a stretch for the most aristocratic of public school lads, never mind a class of socially unglamorous Sheffield sixth-formers. Even when Hector, the charismatic teacher with the lecherous paws, is exposed for fondling the boy's privates, he's more upset at having to retire early than humiliated for his actions. As he explains to his fellow teacher Mrs. Lintott, "It was a laying-on of hands, I don't deny that, but more in benediction than gratification or anything else."

There's a darker side to Bennett's placidly perverse universe, which is crystallized in Posner, the queer, Cambridge-bound student, whose future will be marked by unrequited romantic attachments and catastrophic nervous breakdowns. By the end of the play, he seems more like a psychiatric

Sad sacks: Samuel Barnett and Richard Griffiths in The History Boys. *Photo: Joan Marcus*

object lesson, a throwback to the way gays were often depicted in the moviemaking days before Stonewall ignited the liberation movement. But one shouldn't read *The History Boys* as though it were an installment in the *7 Up* documentary series keeping tabs on the lives of a group of Brits at regular intervals. Posner's spectral presence reminds us of the gap between promise and fulfillment that is the fate of even the most spectacularly gifted among us—a central theme in Bennett's dramatic design.

Inspired by life, though not naturalistic, the play creates its own theatrical reality. One can quarrel with superficial facts (such as college application protocol) and question fundamental choices (the nature of Hector's proclivities or Posner's punishingly lonely demise), but taken as a whole the vision has an incontestable poetic truthfulness. In "Four Elizabethan Dramatists," T.S. Eliot discusses the challenge of evaluating work that is at a remove from the dominant convention of realism. The model he holds up is Aeschylus, which may strike us as unduly archaic, yet who better to demonstrate the majestic way realism can be subordinated to a more revelatory aesthetic pattern? Recognizing the difference between art and life, Eliot argues that critics should spend less time faulting a play for its lapses in verisimilitude and more time assessing how well the various parts relate to the whole:

> It is essential that a work of art be self-consistent, that an artist should consciously or unconsciously draw a circle beyond which he does not trespass: on the one hand actual life is always the material, and on the other hand an abstraction from actual life is a necessary condition to the creation of a work of art.

The test of greatness for the Greeks had nothing to do with how well the quotidian was copied. Instead, it was judged by how effectively a work's animating idea or set of ideas gave rise to a complex theatrical journey. Aristotle famously defined tragedy as the mimesis of a praxis, the representation of an action, which in its fullest sense can be understood as thematic thought in motion. This may seem like oddly rarefied background for a discussion of Bennett, a writer who specializes in miscellany—sketch comedy, extended prose anecdotes, literary diary, dramatic monologues and other uncategorizable theatrical offerings. But the signal beauty of *The History Boys* is as intellectual as it is anything else. The work invites us to ponder the connections between education and society, history and politics, literature and life. It is, in short, that rare thing—a play of ideas, one that finds expression in heightened character, witty dialogue, and stirring song. The informality of its style may have no precedent in *The Poetics*, but the integrity of Bennett's vision has a classical integrity.

THE HISTORY BOYS BEGINS not at the beginning but far into its story's future. Irwin, the teacher who had been hired to give the promising sixth-form boys an edge, is now a Member of Parliament. He addresses a small group of MPs about a bill that will do away with trial by jury and the presumption of innocence in a large percentage of cases. The strategy he proposes to his political allies is similar to the one he gave to his former students: A sensational inversion of conventional wisdom, conveyed with the assurance that the desired ends more than justify the radical means.

> IRWIN: I would try not to be shrill or earnest. An amused tolerance always comes over best, particularly on television. Paradox works well and mists up the windows, which is handy. "The loss of liberty is the price we pay for freedom" type of thing.

Straight away, Bennett announces that what's to follow isn't merely a tale of provincial lads hellbent on Oxford and Cambridge, but an examination of a widespread social malady. Just as Alexander Payne's film *Election*, which satirized America's victory-at-any-cost mentality, went beyond its high school setting, *The History Boys* targets more than the college admission process in its consideration of the way spin has come to trump substance. The word "sophistry" ineluctably springs to mind. Webster's definition ("unsound or misleading but clever, plausible, and subtle argument of reasoning") implies the manipulative bending of logic to achieve a dubious outcome. The play sees this kind of fraudulent rationalizing as increasingly rampant in public life. And just as the sophists were roundly criticized for precipitating the moral degeneration of ancient Athens, their contemporary descendents in education, journalism and politics seem to be threatening, in Bennett's view, an equally devastating breakdown in the fabric of society.

Hector, the General Studies teacher, stands in stark opposition to these trends. Early on, the headmaster characterizes his teaching style:

> HEADMASTER: [. . .] There is passion there. Or, as I prefer to call it, commitment. But not curriculum-directed. Not curriculum-directed at all.

Indeed, Hector's pedagogy values process over outcome. He espouses a living relationship to literature and culture. The poetry that he teaches in his classroom isn't meant to be glibly parroted but rather deeply felt. He wants to cultivate responsive, independent-minded young men who recognize Auden's verse as something more than a self-aggrandizing accessory. Hector's not against academic success per se, but he's after something truer, less exploitative, more autonomous. As he says to his

Fancy this: Stephen Campbell Moore and Dominic Cooper in The History Boys. *Photo: Joan Marcus*

esteemed colleague Mrs. Lintott, who has given the boys their solid academic foundation:

> HECTOR: You give them an education. I give them the wherewithal to resist it. We are that entity beloved of our Headmaster, a "team."

The rankings-obsessed headmaster, however, is tired of languishing in the bottom tier.

> HEADMASTER: [. . .] I want to see us up there with Manchester Grammar School, Haberdashers' Aske's. Leighton Park. Or is that an open prison? No matter.

His manner may be farcical, but his determination is ruthless.

> HEADMASTER: [. . .] Mr. Hector has an old-fashioned faith in the redemptive power of words. In my experience, Oxbridge examiners are on the lookout for something altogether snappier.
>
> After all, it's not how much literature that they know. What matters is how much they know about literature.

Irwin couldn't be more in agreement, as makes clear when later coaching the boys:

> IRWIN: [. . .] History nowadays is not a matter of conviction. It's a performance. It's entertainment. And if it isn't, make it so.

What's more, he wants the students to flaunt the "gobbets" of wisdom that they've gained from their General Studies course. Aghast at the idea of ransacking literature and history for "handy little quotes," Hector argues that what his boys have learned by heart should stay there and not be "defiled by being trotted out to order." In a speech provoked by the realization that his teaching career is coming to a premature close, he describes the inward-directed path he has sought to impress by example:

> HECTOR: The best moments in reading are when you come across something—a thought, a feeling, a way of looking at things—which you had thought special and particular to you. Now here it is, set down by someone else, a person you have never met, someone even who is long dead. And it is as if a hand has come out and taken yours.

The educational quarrel at the heart of *The History Boys* would seem to be fairly clear cut—Irwin's ambitious flash versus Hector's beleaguered authenticity. But Bennett's treatment is far from schematic. Irwin's manner is diffident to the point of lonesome. Not long out of university himself, he's searching to make his way in the world. Played with wounded hesitancy by Stephen Campbell Moore, Irwin seemed like a shrinking violet next to Hector, who holds forth in great self-dramatizing gusts. As forcefully embodied by the incomparable Richard Griffiths, Hector dominated the stage physically as well as theatrically. A Falstaffian-proportioned man, Griffiths was virtually impossible to eclipse, which made the mountainous shadow he cast over his class that much more troubling.

> HEADMASTER: [. . .] Your teaching, however effective it may or may not have been, has always seemed to me to be selfish, less to do with the interests of the boys than some cockeyed notion you have about culture. [. . .]

Now that Hector's sexual misconduct has been exposed (a misdemeanor, it should be underscored, in Bennett's accounting, as his journalistic remarks stressing the boys' adult status as 17- and 18-year-olds makes clear, the school can finally be done with his quaintly outmoded pedagogy. Mrs. Lintott (brought to life with expert drollery by Frances de la Tour) refers to her Headmaster with that favored British expletive, "cunt," but she doesn't idealize Hector's professional effectiveness either:

> MRS. LINTOTT: [. . .] When I was teaching in London in the seventies there was a consoling myth that not very bright children could always

become artists. Droves of the half-educated left school with the notion that art or some form of self-realization was a viable option[. . . .] And love him though I do I feel there's a touch of that to Hector . . . or what's all this learning by heart for, except as some sort of insurance against the boys' ultimate failure?

For their part, the boys are less worried about the neurotic origins of Hector's teaching than in using it to get ahead. Dakin, who's both the class genius and Casanova, wants to score high marks with his teachers, with the Oxbridge examiners and, most especially, with the headmaster's secretary. Learning for him is first and foremost a tool for advancement. In fact, the more he reads, the more he sees that "literature is about losers," a "consolation" for those whose lives, like Hector's, are lacking in some fundamental way. Why else would an old bloke try to cop an innocuous feel at high speed on a village roadway?

HOWEVER POLITICALLY DUBIOUS Bennett may personally find the divergent perspectives in his play, he give them their due. *The History Boys* unfolds as an evolving question, posed by the most charmingly open-minded of questioners. At once progressively committed and skeptical of his own convictions, the playwright doesn't allow his ideological bent to eclipse his observations of the human comedy. Writing in the *Sunday Telegraph*, Hytner suggest this may be the secret to the playwright's success:

> His plays glow with the authenticity that comes from an entirely unsentimental identification with everyone he writes about. There's some of him in each of the eight history boys and in all three of their teachers: even the self-regarding Lothario, Dakin, shares Alan's wit. Alan's ideas are often subversive and his politics are radical even as they dally regretfully with nostalgia for an imagined golden age. But they are subsumed, always, in a consuming sympathy for the way people actually are.

There's no arguing with the results of this method. The *New York Times*'s Ben Brantley described Bennett's "madly enjoyable" play as teeming with "idiosyncratic life." He especially praised the classroom theatrics orchestrated by Hector and the production's ability to keep you "always aware of the complex emotional currents of doubt, perplexity and eroticism that throbs among practically everyone onstage." Certainly, Hytner's staging, pulsating with intermittent bursts of new wave music and featuring snatches of video to lend the tale a reality beyond its proscenium confines, heightened the play's thrilling grip on its audience. More impressive still was the acting ensemble, which under Hytner's nuanced direction, bucked stereotypes at every turn. The secret? The cast shaded its characterizations with psychology too supple and well-observed to be reductively doctrinaire.

The conflicts, in other words, weren't theatrically cheapened. Satire was softened into comedy, and melodrama was kept safely at bay. In the spirit of Bennett's dramaturgy, the production asked us to make our own judgments, and then revise them, and revise them again. *The History Boys* may have made for one of the more unexpected Broadway sensations, but in the unsettled quality of its moral inquiry, it stands nobly in the tradition of virtuosic drama.

2005–2006 Best Play

IN THE CONTINUUM

By Danai Gurira and Nikkole Salter

○ ○ ○ ○ ○

Essay by Anne Marie Welsh

NIA: You trying say I'm Ho' do I look like a junkie do it look like I'm gay do I look like I'm from Africa.

[. . . .]

NURSE MUGOBO: I know it can be dangerous to tell him; many women are scared he will beat them and take the children—

IN THE EARLIEST PLAYS about the continuing pandemic, the theatrical face of AIDS was male, gay and usually, white. Twenty-one years after Ned Weeks in Larry Kramer's *The Normal Heart* broke the silence about the mysterious illness then ravaging his community, the interlocking monologues of *In the Continuum* revealed with passion, humor and heart, a different face of AIDS, a black, female face. A pair of young writers, Nikkole Salter and Danai Gurira, created and enacted the roles of two women, a middle-class African journalist and a rudderless African-American teenager. Their lives are turned upside down when each is diagnosed HIV positive. For Salter and Gurira, growing up in disparate cultures that shrouded women with HIV/AIDS in shame and stigma, merely creating the characters of Nia James and Abigail Murambe was a political act. Yet their writing and skilled performances possessed such expressive vitality that the play, like the best of earlier AIDS dramas, has moved and entertained audiences in an unlikely range of settings. Their drama, like the pandemic, swiftly became global in reach.

In the Continuum revisits emotions of panic and isolation that fueled such AIDS plays as Kramer's and William Hoffman's *As Is*, scripts written before life-prolonging protease inhibitors and other drugs became available. But in the new millennium, despite those scientific advances, and for different cultural reasons, women such as Nia and Abigail may find themselves without access to treatment. Female and black, these women are also as likely to be social outcasts as were their gay, male forbearers.

Handy attitude: Nikkole Salter in In the Continuum. *Photo: James Leynse*

Black women have the highest rate of new HIV infection in the United States and throughout Africa; and AIDS remains the leading cause of death among black American females, ages 25 to 34. These compelling statistics motivated Salter and Gurira to treat the subject in their final graduate projects at New York University's Tisch School of the Arts in 2004, although no such numbers and few hard medical facts are cited in the play they eventually co-wrote. As writers and actors, they instead conjure two flesh-and-blood women living at opposite ends of the world and seen during the same intense 48 hours during which each learns that she is pregnant and HIV positive.

Primary Stages produced the first commercial run of *In the Continuum* in New York; directed by Robert O'Hara, it opened on October 2, 2005, with Salter and Gurira initially performing two nights a week at 59E59 Theaters. When critics from the leading newspapers and other city media strongly praised the unusual diptych, Primary Stages executive producer Casey Childs joined with three independent producers to move the work to the larger Perry Street Theatre in Greenwich Village. *In the Continuum* opened there on December 1, 2005, and had an extended run through February 18, 2006. Wherever they have taken *In the Continuum*—at press time it was 10 venues and counting—Salter and Gurira have performed on a bare stage with very few props and costume pieces. Yet their vivid portrayals, energetic dialogue and sharply detailed descriptions populate the space with contrasting, yet ominously similar, societies.

LIKE THE BEST of the 1980s and 1990s plays representing the toll of HIV/AIDS on gay men, their partners, caregivers and families, *In the Continuum* defines its central characters and creates a mosaic of their

---

The play is unflinching in its depiction of irresponsibility and complicity.

---

often-hostile cultural contexts—social, medical and, indirectly, political. With virtually no issue-laden discussion or agitprop, the play cuts through widespread denial about patterns of abuse, sexual exploitation and poverty that have contributed to the rapid spread of the HIV/AIDS among black women. Yet for all its robust humor, *In the Continuum* is unflinching in its depiction of irresponsibility among black men and complicity in the black women who enable their selfishness.

A prologue establishes the characters' parallel lives and their subtextual bond. The athletic Salter becomes a Los Angeles ghetto girl playing hopscotch, while the quicksilver Gurira plays an African child singing jump-rope songs, one of which they chant together:

> NIA and ABIGAIL: Cousin's on the corner in the welfare line
>
> Brother's on in the slammer, he committed a crime
>
> Preacher's in the club on the down low creep
>
> And yo' mama's in the gutter screamin' HIV

After a blackout we meet Abigail, a newsreader on the state-owned television station in Harare, Zimbabwe. Her script conjures a nation in denial and attacks Western news media for reporting the truth: that the country is beset by famine. With a shift of lighting, we move to Nia and her world. In the bathroom of a club, the tough-talking teen is huddled over a toilet vomiting and talking to her friend Trina in the next stall. Nia's most recent five-finger-discount at Nordstrom has cost her her job. Out of work and "aged out" of the social welfare system, she has won $500 in a poetry contest and she's passionate enough about writing to teach Trina the metrical basis of haiku. Her gangsta rap language cuts comically against the austerity of the poetic form:

> NIA: Bright Ass sunny day—5 syllables
>
> Burning the shit outta me—7
>
> I wish it was cold—5
>
> You try. It's like flowin', you can flow. Look:

Nia's second improvised poem attacks a "skank hoe" rival "wit yo'crunchy baby hair": the girl's been messing with her boyfriend Darnell. Nia's dreams center on a local basketball star, a kid her cousin thinks is sure to get a college scholarship, then make millions playing for the NBA. Director O'Hara smoothly intercuts these brief glimpses of the women. As Salter and Gurira shuffle the two voices, they contrast physically and vocally; Salter's Nia speaks and lives to the percussive beat of hip-hop while Gurira's melodious speech suggests the tuneful lilt of South African song.

Collateral damage: Nikkole Salter and Danai Gurira in In the Continuum. *Photo: James Leynse*

Educated and ambitious, Abigail married an equally upwardly mobile African, Stamford. She dreams of being a real journalist with a better job in South African television or on CNN, any news outlet other than the propagandistic and bureaucratic state-run operation, ZBC. She dreams, too, that her young son Simbi, celebrating his seventh birthday this weekend, might grow up to become the next Kofi Annan or Bill Gates. She wants to move out of the Harare suburb of Hatfield where too many rural types still have chickens or goats in their yards. In their tonier new place, she and her husband will have a swimming pool. She'll "drive the benz."

BOTH WOMEN ARE SPIRITED and bristling with potential. But each soon reveals her dependence upon an unreliable man who, as an individual and a representative of his culture, takes little or no responsibility for her. Abigail's husband, Stamford Murambe, is already disappearing too many nights. Instead of upbraiding him and risk losing him to "a hure," Abigail will seduce him back with a new baby.

> ABIGAIL: Granny always said showing the husband you're a good
> and fertile wife will keep him indoors[. . . .] He'll come around, he
> just needs another boy, that will help.

When one of her unseen co-workers suggests she might have a girl, she replies: "a girl?! What am I going to do with a girl in this world?" Girls in Abigail's universe are worthless.

Nia discovers she's pregnant at the hospital where she's gone to get her friend Trina treated; they've both been wounded by flying glass during a shooting at the club. Nia tells her friend that she'll tell Darnell about the baby and he'll be thrilled to hear she's carrying his child, again assumed to be a boy:

> NIA: Then he gon' get on his knees and put his ear against my belly
> and listen. Then he gon' look up at me and say, "my son in there?"
> And I'ma say, "umm-humm." And he gon' look up at me and smile.
> Just like that, watch. I'ma call him now.

Like Abigail, Nia wants to believe that a baby can cure a man of his philandering. But when Nia calls Darnell from her cell phone, it's clear from the message she leaves that he's already lost interest in her. "Why haven't you called me?" she asks before settling down to wait for a ride from him that never comes.

The women's stories run on these parallel tracks through most of the brisk 90-minute evening, their tales mirroring and counterpointing one another's. Sometimes the stories interweave or briefly intersect. Between them, the actors play eight other characters, the first of whom emerges in the pivotal third scene titled "The Diagnosis."

So fluent is O'Hara's direction of this overlapping scene in which both women are present that we don't notice right away the source of its devastating impact. Gurira now plays an unsympathetic and overworked nurse offhandedly giving Abigail the news that she has tested positive for HIV. But instead of Abigail's reaction, we see Nia's tough-gal façade melt away as she absorbs the same news from an unseen nurse at the hospital where she and Trina are still waiting after the shooting at the club. Furiously, she shouts,

> NIA: Everytime we come in here ya'll try to make us feel like we're dirty. You don't know what the fuck you're talking about, s'cuse you—S'CUSE YOU!

In Salter's fierce performance, Nia's rage is palpable. But the focus immediately shifts to the impassive African nurse. She carries on like an automaton giving Abigail instructions. Twice the stage direction signals that the nurse's "eyes wander." In Robert Mugabe's corrupt and mismanaged Zimbabwe, the social network and certainly the medical system have frayed past the breaking point. The nurse offers Abigail three condoms, with the merest apology: "sorry we have run out."

The women's problems have intensified and multiplied, and their separate searches for solutions and support take up the remainder of the play. During these brief, telling encounters, the spine of the action follow the stages of grief delineated by Elisabeth Kübler-Ross and popularized during the first wave of AIDS consciousness in the US. More aptly for *In the Continuum*, these stages apply to the initial shock of receiving catastrophic news: denial, anger, bargaining, depression and acceptance.

> NIA: These doctors is crazy. I seen this shit on Sally Jesse—Nothin's wrong, I'm fine! C'mon.

Nia tells her friend she's pregnant but not about the HIV. Abigail's denial is shorter lived. She appears on the street, attempting to hail a commuter bus:

> ABIGAIL: No, Mawari, no Jesus, no—please God, no, no, God, no.

Her armor is soon pierced by a cellphone call from her son. He needs her and wants to know if she's found a drawing of the family that he hid in her purse. In this potent scene, the distraught Abigail's conversation gets interrupted by street kids who gather round her while she tries to talk.

Sales pitch: Danai Gurira in In the Continuum. *Photo: James Leynse*

ABIGAIL: Where are your parents? [. . .] They died of what?

She stops, looking horrified, for she's answered her own question. The parents no longer exist. Gurira and Salter do not introduce the alarming truth that may be rippling just below consciousness in their audience: more than three million children in sub-Saharan Africa have been orphaned by AIDS.

AT THIS POINT, Nia and Abigail disappear and the actor-writers create a medley of voices and viewpoints that delineate the roles of women in their respective cultures—and the challenges each faces. Several of these characters are drawn in such sharp relief they seem intentionally comic; the writers even title the sixth scene "Chatter Heads," referring to Nia's optimistic probation officer Patti (played by Salter) and Abigail's high school friend Petronella (played by Gurira). Well-intentioned, liberal and proud of their respective accomplishments, each of these women natters on in intercut speeches that employ jargon from social services and self-empowerment seminars. Both do-gooders approach the particular dilemmas of women such as Nia and Abigail in the abstract; the more each talks, the more confused and contradictory her voice becomes. Petronella wants to be on a ZBC show, *Breaking New Ground*, even as she believes traditional healers (aka witch doctors) might have something to offer. Patti tells Nia "There's no place for you to go but up—well, you could spiral down." What Patti offers, in the end, is a hug.

Salter's most memorable scene and vivid character emerge when the desperate Nia comes to her mother's place in South Central Los Angeles to borrow money. In a lengthy monologue, the mother shouts through an imaginary window shooing kids away before berating her daughter for asking for $400.

> MAMA: [. . .] I'm tired of comin' second to ya'll. I can't remember the last time I had me some lotion or some new panties. Besides, you grown, remember? Us grown folks pay for our own shit.

We learn indirectly that this mother had her first child at Nia's age of 19, that she's still desperately clinging to a man and that all her nagging of Nia about postponing sex or at least using a condom has done little to counter her own bad example. Spirited and funny as she is, she's also paranoid about whites "trying to get rid of us since the Emancipation." Unaware of her daughter's diagnosis, she tells her "three minutes of slappin' bellies ain't worth death." She calls the disease, which she won't name, a government experiment engineered by "monkey fuckers" who brought it from Africa to America. She gives the girl $60 and, most painfully, mirrors her daughter's anxieties over Darnell when she says of her own boyfriend, Marvin:

> MAMA: I ain't gonna let you scare this man away. [. . .]

From this rejection, Nia turns to her exuberant cousin Keysha who's just as male-dependent and wrong-headed as Nia's mother; Keysha's voice alternates with that of another enthusiast, the Witchdoctor, to whom the distraught Abigail has now turned. As Salter and Gurira create these boisterous, comical characters, the tone of their piece grows more buoyant. Yet the misinformation these characters give underscores each woman's dependence upon the whims of the man who has infected her. As the scene develops, unspoken questions center upon the possibility of abortion, the unnamed reason for Nia's trek to her mother for money. Keysha tells Nia she should have the baby.

> KEYSHA: [. . . This is] not some ole, dirty, jerry curl juicy, gold-tooth pimp, but this is Darnell Smith. Dar-nell Smith. The crem de la crem. You know how many girls pokin' needles in condoms tryin'ta have his baby. [. . .]

Onstage nearby, Gurira's witch doctor, still in his tourist-pleasing traditional outfit complete with fly-whisk, at least acknowledges his client's problem. Abigail will get "The Sickness" he cannot cure; but the remedies he offers are proof she's lost control of her life. One vial contains medicine to kill the baby before it's born. The other contains a love potion; rubbed on her husband's penis, it will make him faithful. The Sex Worker Abigail visits will have none of that. She speaks more realistically than either Keysha or the witch doctor—and in a distinctive staccato rhythm. Like Keysha in L.A., she's all for keeping any baby:

> SEX WORKER: It's important to be a mother, it's the one thing we can do that these bastards can't. [. . .]

The whore thinks Abigail should find a rich man to keep her, help protect the child and pay for the expensive medicine. Both Keysha and the Sex Worker see babies as blessings. But in a moment of clarity, Keysha also admits that she's talking about a middle-class man's baby as an instrument of social mobility, not about a real infant.

> KEYSHA: [. . . W]e already live in hell. Don't make it so you have to spend eternity there too. God gave you that baby. That baby is yo' ticket out. [. . .]

AS IN THE SOLO docudramas of Anna Deavere Smith, the accumulation of voices becomes a collage of the worlds in which these women are trapped. The men in both worlds are selfish and irresponsible. Still, the last of the outside voices belongs to Darnell's calculating mother, Gail. *In the Continuum* indicts her as the classic overprotective enabler. Cruel and self-deluded, if not so powerful as the closeted red-baiting lawyer Roy Cohn in the first part of Tony Kushner's *Angels in America*, Gail fights for her son's public image by denying his illness and blaming his sexual escapades upon the girls who find him irresistible.

> GAIL: My baby worked hard. Look at these trophies. Look at them! Does that look like AIDS to you?

After telling Nia a threatening fairy tale, Gail hands her an envelope; it's $5000 meant to silence her.

The play's penultimate scenes involve bargaining with God. Nia, drunk, improvises another haiku, and discovers enough self-respect to tear up Gail's check and create a rap-prayer in which she promises her God:

> NIA: [. . .] If you help me out, this one last time
> I won't let you down.

I'll give up sex, weed, and wine
Plant my feet on solid ground.

Abigail's prayer takes her back to her high school dreams of becoming the very model of a postcolonial, modernizing New African Woman; she questions how God could want her to die like a prostitute. Her bargain: She'll tell her husband and the families about her diagnosis if God can guarantee they won't blame her, will stand by her and Stamford will stay put.

THE STORIES CONVERGE one final time, on what *New York Times* theater critic Charles Isherwood noted is a "slightly contrived note of symmetry, with each facing a chance to confront the man who has infected her, and to bring to light the anguish each has been grappling with alone." Nia and Abigail separately rehearse the planned revelation; in the event, however, each is intimidated into silence by shame and her unequal relationship to her man. Fearing the isolation she knows may result from breaking the silence, each puts on a happy face and does what's expected of her: Abigail joins Simbi's birthday party and announces that she and Stamford are going to have another baby; Nia congratulates Darnell and asks if he can get her a ticket to his next game.

As *In the Continuum* closes, neither woman has resolved her conflict between loneliness and belonging; each still fears violating the taboo against discussing sexual practices and HIV/AIDS openly. Neither has spoken to the man who infected her. Neither has found emotional support or access to treatment. Yet by individualizing these likable and resilient women, Gurira and Salter have themselves broken the silence that stymies their characters. In the vivid particularity of their performances, the talented young writers have employed artistic representation to counteract the invisibility of the AIDS crisis among black women. They have made us empathize in the special way that theater can with the millions of women now confronting the challenges of Nia James and Abigail Murambe.

2005–2006 Best Play

THE INTELLIGENT DESIGN OF JENNY CHOW

By Rolin Jones

○ ○ ○ ○ ○

Essay by Charles Wright

JENNIFER MARCUS: [. . .] The world, the whole world, you know, can pass right through your house. You don't have to even move. And it's beautiful, you know?

NOT EVEN TWO YEARS out of Yale Drama School, playwright Rolin Jones (MFA, 2004) was buffeted this season by a tempest in the teacup of American theater. A committee of three arts journalists, an actor-playwright and an academic chose Jones's *The Intelligent Design of Jenny Chow* as one of three finalists for the Pulitzer Prize, which supposedly goes annually to "a distinguished play by an American author, preferably original in its source and dealing with American life." Complying with the rules of the prizes, the committee sent its recommendations to the Pulitzer Board at the Columbia University Graduate School of Journalism, the body that administers the awards and has final say regarding who may win. After reviewing the proposed plays—Christopher Durang's *Miss Witherspoon* and Adam Rapp's *Red Light Winter*, as well as *Jenny Chow*—the Board declined to grant any award for drama in 2006.

In the *Pittsburgh Post-Gazette*, Christopher Rawson lamented that, while "[i]nformed opinion may differ" as to a theater season's superlatives, the idea of "sponsor[ing] an award" and "authoriz[ing] jurors to search out the best and then [. . .] announc[ing] that none of their recommendations measure up to some hypothetical benchmark, is a slap in the face not only to their work but to the art they represent." Other writers shared the Pittsburgher's dismay, though none outstripped him in high dudgeon. Rawson implied that the Pulitzer Board, parochial in its frame of reference, is reluctant to consider plays beyond the intellectually limited, strictly commercial realm of Broadway. He asserted that, "if your theater experience is defined by Broadway, you have no business pretending to hand out an award for the best American play, since so few plays make it to Broadway at all."

Girl genius: Julienne Hanzelka Kim, Linda Gehringer and Ryan King in The Intelligent Design of Jenny Chow. *Photo: Carol Rosegg*

With its Marvel Comics sensibility, sci-fi trappings and in-jokes about New Haven, *The Intelligent Design of Jenny Chow* would be an unlikely candidate for the theme park of revivals and movie-to-stage adaptations that Broadway has become. Subtitled *An Instant Message with Excitable Music*, Jones's comic drama caught the attention of the Pulitzer committee in Chelsea, 20 blocks south of the Broadway district, where it ran for two months in a refurbished church that is the Atlantic Theater's cozy, well-equipped mainstage. Jones's use of that hot-button phrase—"intelligent design"—is prankishly misleading since he isn't writing about the theory that posits divine action in evolutionary processes or the tension between fundamentalist Christian education and scientific research. Jones's intelligent designer is a 22-year-old Asian-American, suffering from agoraphobia, an eating disorder and Tourette Syndrome, who trumps all wonders of modern technology by devising a robotic alter ego to traverse the globe on a mission she is psychologically incapable of undertaking herself.

Jones's play offers variations on coming-of-age themes familiar in O'Neill, Williams, Inge, and Salinger (as well as more recent writers such as

Richard Nelson, Craig Lucas and David Lindsay-Abaire). For all that's familiar in it, though, *Jenny Chow* is fresh and surprising—a live-action, sci-fi comic book with 14 vivid, idiosyncratic characters (performed by six actors), who are entirely believable within the confines of the dramatist's kooky universe. Under Jackson Gay's direction, the New York production was so fast-moving and whimsical that the spectator never questioned the wonderland logic of the characters' world. Though the entire cast was admirable, Remy Auberjonois's intense, high-energy shenanigans in five roles, each an ingeniously performed cameo, proved a high point of the 2005–06 season. (As Dr. Yakunin, Auberjonois delivered a monologue—"aria" would be a

The hot-button phrase "intelligent design" is prankishly misleading.

more apt description—that elicited an ovation worthy of the 11 o'clock number in a hit Broadway musical.) The play's designers—Takeshi Kata (scenery), Jenny Mannis (costumes) and Tyler Micoleau (lighting)—managed to evoke an atmosphere of Southern California and the cluttered aesthetic of graphic novels. Matthew Suttor composed the "excitable music" of the play's subtitle, and Daniel Baker's sound design lent a high-tech edginess to the proceedings.

JENNY CHOW TAKES PLACE in the San Fernando Valley, where the dramatist grew up. Jones's protagonist, Jennifer Marcus (Julienne Hanzeika Kim), adopted from China as an infant, lives with her parents in a gated community in Calabasas. Jennifer solves Rubik's Cube in a trice, hacks into government satellites and analyzes the Book of Mormon with the sophistication of a divinity-school professor. Yet the mindless rituals of obsessive-compulsive disorder make her robot-like; and agoraphobia prevents her stepping outside her family's home. To her mother's dismay, Jennifer is unable even to carry a garbage can to the edge of the property for weekly pickup.

In Act I, Jones establishes the toxic environment in which Jennifer's psychological handicaps have blossomed. Todd (Ryan King), Jennifer's only confidant, is a Valley slacker, lame-brained but loyal, who's as terrified of the world, in his own way, as is she. Jennifer's father (Michael Cullen)—an injured, unemployed fireman—indulges her neuroses. Adele, the mother (Linda Gehringer), is a thwarted businesswoman whose instinct for controlling others spills over from the office to her relationship with Jennifer, whom she tries to nag and cajole in the direction of "normal" behavior.

As the play begins, Jennifer is barricaded in her bedroom, communicating via computer with an offstage character—a "freelance bounty hunter"—whom she hopes will track down her android dopplegänger. As Jennifer recounts how her robot has gone missing, other actors materialize and events unfold in flashback.

Though physically isolated by her compulsive rituals, Jennifer is in touch with people around the world through various forms of network-based communications, plus telephone, fax and overnight courier service. In the chat room of a genealogy website, she encounters an American Mormon named Terrence (reminiscent, in his neediness and repression, of Tony Kushner's Mormon, Joe Pitt). Terrence (Auberjonois) is surfing the internet for a correspondent to jazz up his autoerotic fantasies with explicit messages. Discovering that Terrence is doing missionary work in China, Jennifer proffers "a little cyberaction" in exchange for help locating her birth mother. Their online phone sex dramatizes, in a sourly funny way, the alienation of sensitive souls in the midst of modernity.

Dr. Wizard: Remy Auberjonois in The Intelligent Design of Jenny Chow. *Photo: Carol Rosegg*

Terrence procures Jennifer's birth certificate, which identifies her biological mother as Su Yang. When the birth certificate arrives by snail mail, Adele intercepts it. As she reads Terrence's letter, the audience hears it recited by its author.

> TERRENCE: Dear Jennifer. Thank you for spending all this time online with me lately. I don't think I really understand your reading of the Angel Moroni, but I appreciate it. [. . .]
>
> JENNIFER MARCUS: (*To the audience.*) I'd been laying out a litany of inconsistencies found in the Mormon bible. He's a secular humanist now.
>
> TERRENCE: I wrote to my elders back home and they say I should stop talking to you because they say you're dangerous. [. . .] And I do think you rely on swears way too much, but I think you're smart and well . . . don't say this to anyone but I do like it when we talk about sex. [. . .] See you online. Your brother in the celestial kingdom, Terrence.

Taken aback at this glimpse of Jennifer's yearning for a lost Chinese mother, as well as her adult sexuality, Adele lashes out.

> ADELE HARTWICK: They make names up, Jennifer. [. . .] There's probably a thousand birth certificates with her name on it. And that silly scarf you wear around . . . probably the nurse's. The truth? That woman abandoned you. And your father and I took two years filling out paperwork, getting signatures and mortgaging our lives into the stratosphere so we could get on a plane, to a scary country where we knew *no one!* So we could save your life.

Jennifer turns for counsel—via electronic communication—to Dr. Yakunin (Auberjonois again), a wild and woolly professor who, years before, spotted genius in one of Jennifer's student projects and who describes her (in out-of-kilter English) as a "shooting star who starts revolution in cognitive artificial intelligence at give me break, high school science fair." Jennifer confides in Yakunin that she dreams of finding her Chinese mother but can't leave home to do so.

> JENNIFER MARCUS: [. . .] So, I guess I thought, if I could figure out how to build a propulsion system requiring a basic but stable energy source and attach it to an android simulation of myself, one that would be capable of self-navigation, conceptual thinking and language comprehension, that I could in a sorta-kinda way, go and be with my mother.

Yakunin encourages Jennifer's dream and arranges a top-secret assignment—"reengineering obsolete missile components" for the US

Department of Defense in exchange for robotics equipment. "[T]he Department of Defense has some policies when it comes to bartering," an Army colonel—Auberjonois, of course—advises Jennifer when they meet by telephone; but that impediment is circumvented by "working through a subcontractor at Raytheon."

Jennifer assembles a robot capable of long-distance flight (Eunice Wong, in an endearing, athletic performance), manipulated with virtual reality gloves and shoes via computer-controlled satellite connection. Her humanoid is equipped with computer voice-translator to permit communication in Chinese (it also allows Jennifer to understand Chinese speakers). Near the end of the first act, the robot intones in a "wonderfully human-sounding" voice:

> JENNY CHOW: My name is Jenny Chow. [. . .] I was born in a mud
> hut in China and my mother loved me so much she gave me away.
> [. . .]

THE NARRATIVE OF JONES'S first act is so ambitious and unruly that the playwright is hard-pressed to resolve things neatly in the time allotted for Act II. At moments, this clever young playwright—too clever, perhaps—lets his exuberant imagination overpower his craft (much as Jennifer loses control of her android alter ego). The material throughout is such a feast for actors, though, that it's easy to understand why neither dramatist nor director was inclined to wield a red pencil.

In a comic montage at the top of the second act (maniacally choreographed by Gay), Jennifer and Todd subject Jenny to a rigorous test flight and, when Terrence locates Su Yang, the robot—"curious, excitable, [. . .] beginning to make her own decisions"—is ready to embark on her mission. Terrence announces he's returning to Utah "to reestablish [his] relationship with God" and, presumably, evade carnality.

> TERRENCE: You changed my life forever and I don't know if that's a
> good thing. [. . .]

Jennifer's farewell email is Jones at his poignant best, yet true to his comedy's Gen Y quirkiness:

> JENNIFER MARCUS: Dear Terrence, I'm glad to hear about your
> decision. I think it's the right one, okay. I don't believe in your God,
> you know that. But I think if He did exist, He'd be really pleased
> with you. Thank you so much Terrence, and in case you're really
> serious about never talking to me again, I just wanted to say, you're

Teen Frankenstein: Eunice Wong and Julienne Hanzelka Kim in The Intelligent Design of Jenny Chow. *Photo: Carol Rosegg*

like, the sexiest Mormon I've ever known. Smiley face. (*She smiles.*) Your sister in the celestial kingdom, Jennifer. [. . .]

Jennifer gives Jenny the scarf that is the Marcuses' only relic of Jennifer's infancy in China.

> JENNIFER MARCUS: You wear it around your neck. [. . .] The last time you saw your mother, she left this with you. It's very special to her. She asked for it back. That's why I built . . . That's why you're going tonight. To give Su Yang something she lost a long time ago.

After Jenny is launched and barreling toward China—"up the Coast of California and then up through the stratosphere, reentering above North Korea"—Jennifer ponders what she has previously screened out: "Like what was I going to say? What did I want to hear? [. . .] I mean, I had been so caught up in doing it, I hadn't like even asked, why?"

Adele, calling from an airplane, attempts to salve the injuries of mother-daughter conflict, admitting that the name on the birth certificate might be accurate. (As indication of the distance between the generations, Adele asks the techno-savvy Jennifer, "Isn't it incredible they can make a phone that works from the plane?") She confides in Jennifer that, in China, the officials in charge of foreign adoption "just hand you a baby and that's it." The potential rapprochement is interrupted by the news that Jenny has reached her destination.

Through virtual-reality goggles, Jennifer sees what Jenny sees. When Su Yang (doubled by Gehringer) responds to Jenny's knock, she recognizes the scarf and, "weeping uncontrollably," touches Jenny as if to reclaim the infant she relinquished 22 years before. As directed by Gay, this scene—the apotheosis of Jones's theme of the individual's quest for identity apart from family, nation and race—became an andante cadenza, far slower and more lyrical than the rest of the play's scherzo proceedings. After a moment, Su Yang's cognizance that her husband and son are nearby stanches the flow of her emotion. She inquires about Jenny's adoptive mother, and Jennifer prompts the robot via satellite: "She loves me very much." When Jennifer (through Jenny) asks for the identity of her father, Su Yang implies she was raped. As a gesture of regret and desire, Su Yang fetches dumplings for Jenny from the family table, telling her, in parting, that she is "very beautiful."

Later, in Calabasas, Adele demands that Jennifer take the garbage to the street. Unable to comply, Jennifer storms upstairs, abandoning herself to wild discharges of obsessive-compulsive energy. When Jenny returns, Jennifer spills her residuary anger and frustration on the android. She berates Jenny as a failure, telling her that Su Yang "heard you talk like an idiot and you scared her away." In a swift volte-face, though, Jennifer turns the blame on herself: "Your design sucks," she screams. Jennifer rants about her own "accelerated education," her overscheduled childhood, and the adults who were responsible:

> JENNIFER MARCUS: See it starts when they see you get nothing but straight A's, that's the fucking problem. [. . .] I mean God forbid, Mr. and Mrs. Marcus, we just leave Jennifer out there on the playground. [. . .] How could we do that? She has to come inside. [. . .]

When Jenny Chow responds with human emotion, Jennifer replicates her parents' insensitivity, forcing her robot to intone phrases of self-loathing, spraying her with disinfectant, urging her out of the house.

> JENNIFER MARCUS: [. . .] I do not want you in my room. [. . .] I have to stay inside. You have to go outside. [. . .] You are flawed. You have to go. [. . .]

In a gesture both greedy and Eucharistic, Jennifer devours Su Yang's dumplings, which the robot has left behind. Later, lamenting her sorry treatment of the android, Jennifer tells the bounty hunter that Jenny is her "perfect girl":

> JENNIFER MARCUS: [. . .] She won't cause anyone harm but she's infinitely more complex than anything out there. And she's very afraid. I can feel her. [. . .]

It is a bleak, uncertain ending, with the robotic protagonist still unable to leave her home and the sensitive robot fleeing human brutality. What's most striking in the text of *Jenny Chow* is the Swiftian motif of humans hellbent for tragic miscommunication. Jones's characters are able to convey information quickly, even instantaneously, across vast distances; but they cannot connect in a meaningful way with those nearest them. Jones nonetheless sounds a note of hope when, moments before the play's conclusion, Todd—accustomed to being useless—is emboldened by having been useful to Jennifer and takes off to test his mettle outside Calabasas.

In Gay's hands, Jones's comedic science-fiction almost eclipsed the near-naturalism of his family drama, except in the beautiful exchange between Jenny and Su Yang. Oddly, though, this imbalance proved beneficial, creating a buoyancy of tone that sent the audience back to the real world with a modicum of good cheer, despite the playwright's absurdist vision.

JONES WROTE *JENNY CHOW* for a 2002 student workshop. David Chambers, a member of the Yale faculty, staged the script at the South Coast Repertory Theatre in Costa Mesa, California, while the playwright was still enrolled at the drama school. On the strength of that presentation, the American Theatre Critics Association in 2004 gave Jones the M. Elizabeth Osborn Award, in recognition of noteworthy work by a new dramatist. *Jenny Chow* was subsequently produced by San Diego's Old Globe Theatre, Yale Repertory Theatre and the Studio Theatre in Washington, D.C., before premiering in New York.

While *Jenny Chow* was being presented around the country, Jones graduated from Yale, became playwright-in-residence at Yale Rep, won a Fringe First Award at the 2004 Edinburgh Festival—for his play *The Jammer*—sold a pilot to Fox and established himself as a staff writer for the Showtime series *Weeds*. The playwright received an Obie Award for *Jenny Chow* but, because no commercial producer stepped forward, the Atlantic production did not get the second wind it deserved. Late in 2005, the dramatist was selected for the Screenwriters' Lab of the Sundance Institute where, in January 2006, he began developing an "intelligent design" for Jenny Chow's future life on film.

The controversy surrounding the 2006 Pulitzer Prize speaks volumes about the conditions that playwrights accept in order to see their work on professional stages. In light of what awaits most dramatists—negligible (if any) financial compensation, ignorant responses from a surprising proportion of the so-called "critical community" and startling instances of enmity such as the Pulitzer Board's refusal to award a prize this year—it is phenomenal that American writers bother with what *Variety*, amusingly, still calls "legit." The dramatic instinct, it seems, is inextinguishable; and the theater's siren song remains seductive enough for young talents such as Jones to elect drama school over academic programs that could lead to consistent employment and far greater financial rewards.

2005–2006 Best Play

THE LIEUTENANT OF INISHMORE

By Martin McDonagh

○ ○ ○ ○ ○

Essay by John Istel

Dead black cat

Live black cat

Ginger cat

Dead ginger cat

Telephone

Cat's collar and name tag

3 guns

Wooden cross

Cat basket

Dismembered corpses

NO SINGLE LINE of Martin McDonagh's typically loopy Irish dialogue in *The Lieutenant of Inishmore* can convey the play's dark comic tone better than the prop list, quoted above. Every item serves a hyperactive plot with enough "well-made play" hallmarks to make Scribe or Sardou blush: Secrets are withheld from the main character; neck-breaking reversals lead to a pivotal "recognition scene"; and stage props become crucial devices used to drive the bloody plot into further paroxysms of violence.

Chekhov famously maintained that a gun that appears onstage must be fired by the end of the play. McDonagh multiplies the fun by including a small arsenal. In addition to the three handguns listed above, there are three more not included in the list above that are "personal properties" handled by actors. One is an air rifle owned by the 16-year-old town revolutionary Mairead, the only female character of the eight who populate the play; another two weapons are Padraic's—he likes to use both at once. By the play's end, every character has had a gun held to his or her temple or been threatened with some serious bodily harm. Each time a firearm is triggered, the plot grows thicker and sicker.

Dragged in: Peter Gerety and Domhnall Gleeson in The Lieutenant of Inishmore. *Photo: Monique Carboni*

In this satire there's absurdity in the tension between sadism and sentimentality. Padraic is a lieutenant in his own IRA splinter group who relishes causing pain to other humans—yet can't abide the slightest thought of ill when it comes to his longtime feline companion, Wee Thomas. The viciousness of this splatter-fest (five gallons of fake blood are used at each performance) could be taken as a political comment on terrorists who, in their patriotic fervor, commit the most heinous acts. But considering McDonagh's devotion to the gruesome in all of his plays, I'd argue that he has no specific political agenda at work here. The playwright himself, if his rare interviews are to be trusted, suggests that critics shouldn't get their knickers all twisted: he's just telling a story. The filmmakers McDonagh is most often compared to—Sam Peckinpah, Quentin Tarantino, John Woo—often get the same treatment in the press when their movies are portrayed as having sociopolitical messages that their creators didn't necessarily intend. In *Lieutenant of Inishmore*, McDonagh mixes the narrative violence of these *cinéastes* with the nihilism of Samuel Beckett—while retracing the satiric path J.M. Synge blazed through the west of Ireland.

Originally produced in 2001 by the Royal Shakespeare Company at Stratford-Upon-Avon before moving to its London home, *Lieutenant of Inishmore* doesn't have the obsessions of *The Pillowman*. If that play was McDonagh's most philosophical work, *Lieutenant of Inishmore* is pure entertainment. The Broadway production was nominated for five Tony Awards, including best new play. The dark comedy's nine scenes were played with an intermission between the penultimate and last scene. The action takes place "circa 1993" primarily in and around a rustic Inishmore cottage on an island off the coast of western Ireland. In McDonagh's view

---

McDonagh multiples the fun by including a small arsenal.

---

of this fabled land, life is a 50-50 proposition. By the final curtain, of the eight characters and three cats we meet, four humans and a cat survive.

THE LIGHTS RISE to find Donny (Peter Gerety) and a neighborhood teenager, Davey (Domhnall Gleeson), inspecting the body of a dead black cat they fear belongs to Donny's son, Padraic. The animal's guts slither around the kitchen as the two men belittle and blame each other. Donny, who was catsitting the creature, insists the pet's death is the fault of the doltish Davey when he ran over the animal on his bicycle. Davey says he found the animal by the side of the road and only brought him inside to save him. One fact is clear: there is a lot at stake because its owner will seek revenge.

> DONNY: Why else would I be upset? I don't get upset over cats!
>
> DAVEY: Not your Padraic?! [. . .] Was he fond of him?
>
> DONNY: Of course he was fond of him.
>
> DAVEY: Oh he'll be mad.
>
> DONNY: He *will* be mad.
>
> DAVEY: As if he wasn't mad enough already. Padraic's mad enough for seven people. Don't they call him "Mad Padraic"?

This scene sets up the next, in which we witness the madness of Padraic. The lights rise to find a small-time pot dealer dangling upside down from a chain. Padraic (David Wilmot)has already pulled the toenails from one of James's feet. The scene is made more harrowing by the lightness of Padraic's banter as he chastises James (Jeff Binder) for corrupting children with marijuana. To teach him a lesson, Padraic prepares to slice one of the nipples from James's chest. In what he sees as an act of generosity, however, he allows James to choose the left or the right. Padraic's phone rings just as he's about to apply knife to chest. It's his father calling with news of Wee Thomas's ill health. Padraic leaves James dangling:

> PADRAIC: [. . .] I haven't been up to much else, really. I put bombs in a couple of chip shops, but they didn't go off. (*Pause.*) Because chip shops aren't as well guarded as army barracks. Do I need your advice on planting bombs? (*Pause.*) I was pissed off, anyways. The fella who makes our bombs, he's fecking useless. I think he does drink. Either they go off before you're ready or they don't go off at all. One thing about the IRA anyways, as much as I hate the bastards, you've got to hand it to them, they know how to make a decent bomb. [. . .]

McDonagh's offhanded treatment of terrorism, demonstrating Padraic's sentiment and savagery, makes for uneasy laughter. In Scene 4, Davey, an innocent horrified by the violence around him, returns from a fruitless

Close shave: Jeff Binder and David Wilmot in The Lieutenant of Inishmore. *Photo: Monique Carboni*

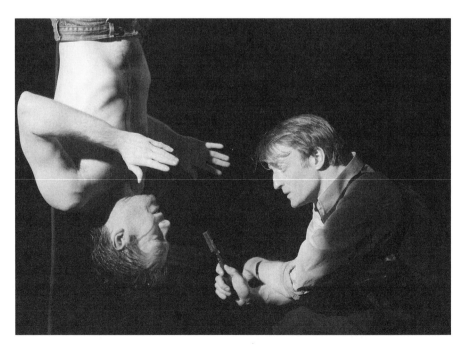

search for a black cat to replace Wee Thomas. The only cats Davey saw were "being played with by children," and, as he says, "I am no man to be pinching cats off of children" or their mothers. The ensuing dialogue reveals a clue to Padraic's sadistic streak:

> DAVEY: I'm no man to go trampling on mams. Not for the sake of a cat anyways. Would you've liked your mam trampled on when she was alive?
>
> DONNY: Many's the time I trampled on my mam when she was alive. After she'd died I stopped. There seemed no sense.
>
> DAVEY: What did you go trampling on your mam for?
>
> DONNY: Ah, she'd get on me nerves.
>
> DAVEY: I can see where your Padraic does get his outlook on life now.

MCDONAGH INTERRUPTS THE DESPERATE shenanigans in the cottage to thicken the plot. The fifth scene takes place beside a village road where we meet three INLA colleagues of Padraic's. We learn that they have murdered the black cat to lure Padraic home for assassination. Apparently, Padraic has gone too mad even for their IRA splinter group. He doesn't understand, for instance, that "it isn't only for the school kids and the oul fellas and the babes unborn we're out to free Ireland," according to INLA ringleader Christy (Andrew Connolly), who wears a black eye patch. "No. It's for the junkies, the thieves, and the drug pushers too!" Padraic's torturing of pot dealers goes beyond the call of duty.

The whole scene, from its discussion of whether Marx was the one who said the "end justifies the means" to Joey's bereaved state about killing a cat is a satire on misguided violence in the name of a cause. "I'd've never joined the INLA in the first place if I'd known the battering of cats was to be on the agenda," Joey (Dashiell Eaves) complains. "The INLA has gone down in my estimation today." Christy defends their actions by giving an impassioned speech about their mission and the place for sentiment in it:

> CHRISTY: [. . .] I was near crying meself, even as I brought me gun swinging down the fourth and fifth times, and the blood spraying out of him. But hasn't it worked? Haven't we lured the Madman of Aran home to where never once will he be looking behind him for that bolt from the blue he knows is some day coming? [. . .]

Soon, McDonagh uses an action film cliché: the firearm standoff. Joey's compatriots, Christy and Brendan (Brian d'Arcy James), get fed up with his wailing about the cat and draw their weapons on him. He also pulls his revolver out. The threat of a shootout hangs in the air until Joey apologizes for his "fondness for cats" and agrees half-heartedly that "an Ireland free" and not "happy cats" is their goal.

The same standoff occurs in the next scene, but the effect is a surprise. Mairead (Alison Pill), Davey's tomboy sister (and wannabe freedom fighter) has overheard the three INLA stooges' plan and waits by the road to warn Padraic. She's already used her BB gun in the third scene, when she shot her brother in the cheek. We also know she is a sharpshooter with a reputation for shooting cows in the eyes from a distance, rendering them useless for the meat market. Scene 6 opens with her singing "The Patriot Game," whose words satirically serve as McDonagh's recurring theme: "Come all ye young rebels and list while I sing. The love of one's land is a terrible thing." Mairead hopes to trade her information for membership in Padraic's splinter group. He thinks her message has to do with Wee Thomas, so when she refuses to say anything about it, he pulls out both guns and aims one at each of her temples. The stage directions convey the lass's reaction:

> [. . .] *Poised, disgusted and superior, Mairead picks up her air rifle, cocks it, and, while Padraic still has his guns to her head, points the rifle towards one of his eyes, so that the barrel is almost resting against it.* [. . .]

It's a gutsy enough move to make even Padraic blink and, as he sizes up the young woman before him, he lowers his weapon. But it is not enough for him to agree to allow Mairead entrée into the INLA. McDonagh twists the plot further by having her lie and tell him his cat is just fine. He's so ecstatic at the news, he kisses Mairead and marks the beginning of a strange romance.

Padraic's elation is short-lived. He arrives home at noon the next day to find his father and Davey asleep in drunken stupors. They're covered in black shoe polish and they've left a wooden cross to mark Wee Thomas's grave face down in the middle of the floor. Padraic finds what he thinks is his cat asleep as well, but when he pets it, his fingers become black. He becomes confused and suspicious; picking up the cross confirms his worst fears. In the blink of an eye, Padraic becomes enraged, shoots the imposter cat and wakes the sleeping men. He soon has Davey and Donny on their knees facing the audience, hands tied behind their back, a gun at each head. As Padraic prepares to shoot his father and Davey, he gives a comic farewell speech:

> PADRAIC: I will plod on, I know, but no sense to it will there be
> with Thomas gone. No longer will his smiling eyes be there in the

Irish standoff: David Wilmot and Alison Pill in The Lieutenant of Inishmore. *Photo: Monique Carboni*

back of me head, eggin me on, saying, "This is for me and for Ireland, Padraic. Remember that," as I'd lob a bomb at a pub or be shooting a builder. Me whole world's gone, and he'll never be coming back to me. (*Pause.*) What I want ye to remember, as the bullets come out through yere foreheads, is that this is all a fella can be expecting for being so bad to an innocent Irish cat. [. . .]

Just as Padraic gets set to pull the trigger, there's a knock at the door. The three INLA boys have arrived, hiding guns behind their backs. Padraic greets them genially: "Come on in ahead for yourselves. I'm just in the middle of shooting me dad." As he turns his back on them and levels the pistols at Davey and Donny's heads, he hears the clicks of three guns cocking. What a stage tableau appears: two men kneeling side-by-side with Padraic holding guns to the back of each head to form one triangle; and three men with guns at Padraic's head, one on either side and one in back, forming a second triangle: it's like a preposterous anti-pieta.

Tension builds as Padraic convinces the trio to take him out back so it'll be easier to bury him. He also claims he wants to spare his father having to watch a son killed—even though Donny doesn't care, having been on the brink of death himself. As Padraic is dragged out, Davey taunts him about his dead cat. The crazed killer swears he'll be back in 10 minutes to kill Davey and Donny: "Something'll turn up! I can feel it!" But no one— onstage or off—believes him. After the group exits, Davey says understandingly to Donny, "after your son tries to execute you, your opinions do change about him." Suddenly, they hear Mairead's air rifle, followed by the screams of the gunmen who stumble, blinded, into the house. They start shooting wildly as Padraic and Mairead glide inside. Padraic grabs his guns and, as Mairead massages his neck and shoulders, he executes Brendan and Joey at close range, sending geysers of blood all over the cottage. When Christy stops to reload, he doesn't hear any other firing. He pleads not to be shot in the head "for me mother's sake." Padraic shoots him twice in the chest and turns lovingly to Mairead.

> DONNY: That was some gutsy shooting, Padraic!
>
> DAVEY: What's he kissing me fecking sister for?

That question breaks the spell and Padraic returns his attention to his execution victims. He offers to spare Mairead's brother but she takes a gun and puts it to her brother's head. "If I'm to be traveling back up North with you, I suppose I'll have to be getting used to proper guns some time." Once again, the guns are cocked, with son ready to kill father and sister aiming at her brother. Once again they're saved by Christy—this time when with his last breaths he apologizes for killing Padraic's cat. But his confession so infuriates Padraic that he tells Mairead to bring him some preferred instruments of torture: a cheese grate, a razor, a knife, an iron. "Yes, Lieutenant," she replies. The eighth scene ends with Christy's screams and blood splattering as Padraic makes sure his last moments on earth won't be peaceful ones.

WHEN THE LIGHTS RISE after intermission, the last prop on the list dominates the stage: the dismembered corpses. The cottage is littered with limbs, torsos and body parts. Donny and Davey saw away at the cadavers in order to make them more disposable. Meanwhile, Padraic sits on Christy's corpse, stroking the dead, dirt-covered cat that he exhumed. Mairead enters wearing a dress—unusual, for her—and carrying a backpack, ready to leave with Padraic. Davey asks what their mother said at the news of her departure. "She said good luck and try not to go blowing up kids," replies the teenager, now an "officer." "I'm a second-lieutenant," she says proudly.

Once the groans and moans from the audience have died away at the initial sight of the bodies being hacked, McDonagh's plot whirls into its final frenzy of recognitions and reversals. As Donny and Davey are urged to hammer away at the corpses, especially the teeth that can identify them, Padraic and Mairead begin making plans for their futures together as lover-terrorists.

> MAIREAD: We should make a list of valid targets. From one to twenty. Like *Top of the Pops.*
>
> PADRAIC: I used to have a list of valid targets but I lost it on a bus. Who would be top of your list?
>
> MAIREAD: People who brain cats for no reason.

That's when Padraic remembers he himself "brained" a cat—the "ginger cat" covered in shoe polish—although he claims there was a valid reason: it was unhygienic. That causes Mairead to realize she hasn't had a chance to say goodbye to her cat, Sir Roger Casement.

Mairead goes into the bathroom to wash blood from her dress and discovers her "brained" cat, Sir Roger. Padraic laughs that they both have dead cats in their arms. But Mairead doesn't seem amused. She blankly kisses Padraic to distract him, reaches for his pistols and blows his brains out. Donny and Danny have another body to chop up. Now the 16-year-old hellcat becomes the new Lieutenant of Inishmore and she exits promising a thorough investigation about her shoe polish-covered cat.

A moment later, in the most dramatic entrance of the night—if not the entire theater season—a black cat saunters through a gap in the kitchen wall: It's Wee Thomas. The dead black cat in the street was a stray, the bloodshed all for naught. Donny and Davey are so furious they grab Padraic's guns and prepare to blast the cat. This time, however, McDonagh lets the cat live. Donny asks, "Hasn't there been enough killing done in this house for one day?" The lights fall as they pet Thomas and feed him.

IF THERE'S ANY MESSAGE to be had from the gallons of gore, it is that some humans have a propensity to love pets more than members of their own species. Mairead, a paramilitary soldier in training, embraces the black-and-white world of all fundamentalist thinkers: either you're for them or against. No matter how absurd the distinction, the treatment must be the same: No mercy for the other side. It's one reason why teens make great foot soldiers in armed conflicts. The only shade of gray in the whole play occurs with the last line of the printed script, for which McDonagh offers two options depending on whether the live cat eats or doesn't eat the Frosties that have been poured for it. As with Padraic and Mairead, who value their pets more than family, McDonagh the playwright, offers the cat not only a great entrance but more mercy than any of his characters.

2005–2006 Best Play

RABBIT HOLE

By David Lindsay-Abaire

○ ○ ○ ○ ○

Essay by Michael Sommers

BECCA: [. . .] But let me just say, Howie, that I am mourning as much as you are. And my grief is just as real and awful as yours.

HOWIE: I know that.

BECCA: You're not in a better place than I am, you're just in a different place. And that sucks that we can't be there for each other right now, but that's just the way it is.

ENTERING THE HANDSOME Biltmore Theatre for the premiere of *Rabbit Hole*, Manhattan Theatre Club's subscribers probably expected to enjoy yet one more quirky comedy from David Lindsay-Abaire. They certainly had every reason to anticipate funny business. In recent seasons, MTC had premiered three of the playwright's oddball yet touching comedies.

Fuddy Meers (1999) was a dark farce regarding a woman who nightly suffers complete memory loss and awakens every day to cope with strangers insisting they're her relatives. *Wonder of the World* (2001) offered a screwball trek to Niagara Falls with a runaway wife seeking romantic adventure who winds up bobbing in a barrel toward the cataract. *Kimberly Akimbo* (2003) saw a New Jersey teen resourcefully deal with neglectful parents, an ex-convict aunt's scam and most significantly a rare disease rapidly aging her into an elderly woman.

For anyone acquainted with Lindsay-Abaire's comedies, a play with a title such as *Rabbit Hole* promised a weird wonderland of fun, probably centered on a heroine enjoying mad escapades. But no. This particular Alice has fallen into a deep, dark hole of grief and doesn't appear to be escaping it any time soon.

Rabbit Hole represents a sharp, significant change in style and mood for Lindsay-Abaire. His contemporary drama about the lingering aftermath of death in a suburban family is anything but a laugh riot. Subdued in its everyday sorrow, understated in conversation, the play is composed in a completely naturalistic manner. Unlike the free-wheeling action of its

Family plan: Tyne Daly, Cynthia Nixon, John Slattery and Mary Catherine Garrison in Rabbit Hole. *Photo: Joan Marcus*

predecessors, *Rabbit Hole* remains confined to the tastefully decorated rooms of a home in Westchester.

AS WITH SO MANY American plays before it, *Rabbit Hole* begins in a kitchen. Oh, so quietly. And in such a beautiful Martha Stewart vision of an eat-in kitchen. There, on a sunny afternoon in February, Becca Corbett is methodically folding a basket of freshly-washed clothes—the tiny shirts and pants for a child—while listening to her sister, Izzy, describe a rambunctious encounter in a local bar.

It is evident these 30-something siblings differ in nature. Rarely ceasing her chores—wiping counters, stacking laundry, dishing snacks—Becca appears quiet and composed; perhaps judgmental toward her dizzy sister. Lolling around the highly polished table, the chattering Izzy is vaguely justifying why she slugged a woman at that tavern.

As Becca probes into the brawl's circumstances, she discovers that the guy in question has been sleeping with Izzy. In fact, Izzy is pregnant. That's probably why his former girlfriend was so annoyed. Becca herself looks none too pleased by the news. She hears Izzy has already informed their mother, Nat. And that Izzy has lost yet another waitressing job. Believing that a child will give her life clarity, Izzy remarks how the pregnancy may be difficult for Becca to deal with right now but she'd like her sister to at least pretend to be happy. After a moment, Becca warms to the idea. They hug.

Glancing over the folded clothes, Becca suggests that instead of making a drop-off at Goodwill she will store them in the event the baby is a boy. Izzy resists the offer, believing it "weird" to see her kid running around in Danny's clothes. Besides, Izzy predicts a girl. Before heading off, Izzy

This play represents a significant change in style and mood for Lindsay-Abaire.

apologizes for any unfortunate timing of her pregnancy. After some hesitation, Becca shrugs with affectionate resignation.

Later, after supper, Becca and her husband Howie are finishing crème caramels in the living room. They look like a perfect well-off couple. He's in risk management. She left her post at Sotheby's to be a mom. Urging another glass of wine on Becca, Howie lowers the lights. They chitchat about Izzy as well as their friends Rick and Debbie, whom they haven't seen lately. Apparently there's awkwardness. Debbie hasn't called for a while. Becca refuses to phone her. Howie recalls how his own brother spent most of Danny's funeral talking about the Mets.

SO THERE IT IS: Their little boy is dead. All along the playwright has eased into viewers' awareness through vague references that sorrow dwells in this glossy house. Finally the couple's tragedy crystallizes, although specifics about Danny's accidental death nearly eight months before will continue to trickle in as the play progresses.

While Al Green's voice seductively croons on the stereo, Howie kisses Becca's neck until she playfully pushes him away. She has chores to do. When Howie remarks it's been months since they've been intimate, Becca stiffens and declares she's not ready yet. Howie suggests they visit a therapist together. Or maybe she should again try those group sessions for bereaved parents that he attends. Becca responds that the best thing for them to do would be to sell their house.

BECCA: He's everywhere, Howie. Everywhere I look, I still see Danny. [. . .] I can't move without—I mean, Jesus, look at this. (*Grabs a spiky toy dinosaur from nearby.*) Everywhere. Do you even know? (*Grabs a kid's book from a stack of magazines.*) Here: *Runaway Bunny* for godsake. The puzzles. The smudgy fingerprints on the door-jambs.

HOWIE: I like seeing his fingerprints.

When Howie hints that maybe they could have another child, Becca ends the discussion and goes upstairs. Turning off the lights, Howie pops a video into the VCR. The volume is low but the voices of Danny and Howie are heard at play with their barking dog, Taz. Somehow Howie manages not to cry while he views his keepsake of sweeter times. Becca's shadow hovers at the top of the stairs and disappears. Howie watches the video as the lights fade.

A week later, Becca, her mom, Nat, and Howie celebrate Izzy's birthday around the kitchen table. No one is having a particularly good time. Izzy isn't pleased with her practical gift from Becca. Howie thinks Nat is not properly feeding Taz, whom she's now keeping. Drinking more wine than she ought, Nat blabs sporadically about fatalities cursing the Kennedy and Onassis clans. For awhile, Becca busies herself passing out the elegant cake she's made but eventually challenges her mother to come to the point.

Worst nightmare: Cynthia Nixon in Rabbit Hole. *Photo: Joan Marcus*

So Nat urges Becca to return to the support group. Becca explains she doesn't care for the crowd.

> NAT: What's wrong with the people? They've lost children too. They understand what you're going through.
>
> BECCA: No they don't. They understand what they're going through.

Nat argues she found comfort in just such a group when her son Arthur died. Her faith in God helped, too. Becca's mood darkens and she savagely declares disbelief in God. When Nat brings up Arthur again, Becca loses her temper.

> BECCA: [. . .] I wish you would stop comparing Danny to Arthur! Danny was a four-year-old boy who chased his dog into the street. Arthur was a thirty-year-old heroin addict who hung himself. Frankly I resent how you keep lumping them together.
>
> (*Silence.*)
>
> NAT: He was still my son.
>
> BECCA: And I don't recall anyone giving you instructions on how best to grieve for him.

After Becca leaves, Howie tells the others she was upset by a letter they recently received.

Later that night, Becca enters Danny's room, which still looks as it did when her son was alive. Sitting on the bed, she re-reads a letter. Nerdy 17-year-old Jason materializes to voice his words. He expresses his ongoing regret about the traffic accident that killed Danny. Jason encloses a short story he has written for his school literary magazine he'd like to dedicate to Danny. It is a science fiction piece he thinks Danny might like if he were Jason's age. He also asks to meet Becca and Howie in-person some time.

Becca looks around the room as the lights fade on Jason to reveal Howie downstairs in front of the TV. When Howie plays another home video of Danny, he discovers Becca has taped over it with a tornado documentary. Summoned to the living room by her husband's frantic calls, Becca insists the erasure was accidental. Furious at losing the most recent momento of their son, Howie wonders aloud whether Becca subconsciously—or deliberately—made it happen. Near tears, Howie points out Becca has been systematically removing reminders of Danny from the house. His drawings, clothes, shoes—even the dog.

> HOWIE: You're trying to get rid of him. I'm sorry, but that's how it feels to me sometimes. Every day, it's something else. It feels like you're trying to get rid of any evidence he was ever here.

The couple's confrontation twists into mutual recriminations about the day Danny died. The phone call distracting Becca's attention. The gate Howie left unlatched. Losing control, Howie yells that Becca needs to stop erasing their son from their existence. Denying his accusations, Becca counters how their conflict probably comes from being in different stages of mourning. Neither is in an emotional place to comfort the other. Howie responds that something has to change because he can't continue living this way. And he wants the dog back.

THE SECOND ACT BEGINS two months later, in early May. Izzy's pregnancy is starting to show. Howie has just finished conducting potential buyers through the house. Izzy thinks it might be smart to redecorate Danny's room as an office or some other space. When strangers discover robot-cartoon sheets on the bed, the topic of kids arises and Howie talks about Danny, which Izzy believes freaks them out.

> IZZY: [. . .] You wanna tell total strangers all about Danny and how he died, it's none of my business. God knows it's something you enjoy doing, so you go ahead. But don't be surprised if nobody wants to buy your house [. . .]

With Becca and Nat away at the supermarket, Izzy vents about her sister's chronic irritability. Then she gets down to cases with Howie. One of Izzy's friends, a waitress in a restaurant a few towns away, recently saw Howie holding hands there with somebody who wasn't Becca. Howie claims the woman was just a bereaved parent from his support group. Declaring she knows the couple is "having troubles," Izzy seems none too confident about Howie's assertions of fidelity.

Returning from shopping, Becca and her mom recount an incident that blew up in a supermarket aisle. It seems a little boy wanted his mother to buy a treat but she deliberately ignored him. Troubled by the woman's cold attitude, Becca intervened but was told to mind her own business. So Becca smacked the woman. Hard. (Izzy gets a kick out of that news.) Nat managed to smooth over matters with the startled lady, which scarcely improves Becca's touchy sensitivities.

The sudden barking of a dog outside—Taz is back in residence—makes everyone aware that a teenager is standing tentatively in the doorway. It's Jason, who saw the open house sign on the lawn and ventured in for a hello. They are startled by his unexpected appearance. Becca seems receptive to this intrusion but Howie dismissively tries to hustle the teenager out. When Jason insists he wants to have a conversation with them sometime

At a loss: Tyne Daly and Cynthia Nixon in
Rabbit Hole. *Photo: Joan Marcus*

soon, Howie's temper flares. Apologizing, Jason goes away. Howie is still
fuming after Becca leaves the room.

> HOWIE: That was the last thing she needed. That kid showing up.
>
> IZZY: She seemed fine with it. You were the one who got upset.

Another week goes by and Nat is helping Becca clean Danny's room.
Toys and other possessions are tossed into a garbage bag or placed in a
keep-box. According to Becca, it was Howie's idea to redo the room to
make the house more salable. Coming across a pair of Danny's little sneakers
brings Nat up short.

> BECCA: Don't do that. (*Takes the sneakers.*) Quick and clean, like a
> band-aid. (*Places the sneakers in a garbage bag.*) Otherwise we'll
> never get through it.

Handing her mother a tissue, Becca mentions a continuing ed. class in
literature she's been taking. They're reading *Bleak House*, she notes with
some irony. Becca likes going to school in a town where nobody knows
her story. She doesn't encounter "the face" she gets from their pitying

neighbors. Nat recalls how one friend practically made a hobby out of consoling her after Arthur died 11 years earlier.

Discovering Jason's sci-fi story, Becca outlines for Nat its tale of a boy seeking his dead father through a network of rabbit holes leading to parallel universes. Then Becca mentions her intention to see Jason—without Howie. Their conversation drifts into recalling a funny incident when Danny consumed a bowl of chocolate-covered expresso beans that made him buzz around the house for hours. They smile over the memory.

Then Becca asks Nat whether "this feeling" of sorrow ever goes away. Nat doesn't believe so but observes how it changes:

> NAT: [. . .] The weight of it, I guess. At some point it becomes bearable. It turns into something you can crawl out from under. And carry around—like a brick in your pocket[. . . .] It's what you have instead of your son, so you don't wanna let go of it either. So you carry it around. And it doesn't go away, which is . . .
>
> BECCA: What.
>
> NAT: Fine . . . actually.

SEVERAL DAYS LATER, Jason is eating homemade lemon squares with Becca. After some careful small talk, Jason hesitatingly confesses that at the time of the accident he may have been driving a few miles above the speed limit. Becca chooses to pass over his admission. Soon, Jason is talking about attending college in the fall and enjoying last week's prom. And suddenly Becca is crying. Jason doesn't know what to do. After a minute or so she recovers.

Becca remarks how she liked Jason's story. It reminds her a little of the myth of Orpheus and Eurydice. She's taken with the idea of everybody having variations of their lives unfolding in parallel universes. Jason believes it to be a probable phenomenon.

> BECCA: And so this is just the sad version of us.

When Howie walks into their kitchen later that afternoon, Becca is surprised to see him home so early. Howie decided to skip his group session and thinks he is finished going for good. They talk about perhaps keeping the house. Becca mentions that their friends Rick and Debbie—she called them—have extended an invitation for a cookout with their children. It'll probably be hard for everyone, but they'll go.

> HOWIE: [. . .] And then we'll wait for Rick and/or Debbie to bring up Danny while the kids are playing in the rec-room. And maybe that'll go on for a little while. And after that we'll come home.

BECCA: And then what?

HOWIE: I don't know. Something though. We'll figure it out.

BECCA: Will we?

HOWIE: I think so. I think we will.

Perhaps they're getting on with their lives. They scarcely can look at each other. Becca takes Howie's hand. The play ends.

PULITZER PRIZE-WINNER Marsha Norman ('night, Mother) reportedly advised Lindsay-Abaire, her former student in Juilliard's playwriting program, to write about something that frightened him. The father of a young boy, Lindsay-Abaire had come across several stories about children dying unexpectedly. The notion developed into Rabbit Hole.

A beautifully crafted study in the day-to-day aches of loss, the sensitive drama scrupulously avoids television-movie style bathetics. Not all of my colleagues agreed on the play's merits, however. A Variety poll of 16 metropolitan critics registered eight negative, six positive and two mixed reactions. "The real disappointment of the play—of so many plays—is how little advantage it takes of all the peculiar, wonderful things the stage can do," noted Jeremy McCarter in New York magazine. "There's neither poetry nor spectacle here, nothing to engage the audience's imagination or to involve us in the action." Among the favorable notices was Ben Brantley's New York Times assessment, which admired the play's accessibility. "This anatomy of grief doesn't so much jerk tears as tap them from a reservoir of feelings common to anyone who has experienced the landscape-shifting vacuum left by a death in the family," he observed.

Embedded beneath these mundane routines and conversation typical of suburban American life, a strong emotional undertow lurks in the play's subtext: the words these characters cannot say, the pauses freighted with hurt. Yet Lindsay-Abaire's plaintive, perceptive story of this household is scarcely without humor as these otherwise functional characters go about grieving in different ways. Self-centered Izzy and blundering Nat sometimes register as seriocomic foils to the damaged Becca and Howie whose marriage is coming unglued by the bleak middle of the play. Gradually the uncoordinated evolution of their sorrow into some kind of equilibrium provides the drama with momentum and at last a sense of emotional deliverance.

Director Daniel Sullivan's delicate staging and the nuanced acting of his sterling ensemble could not be bettered. Partnered by John Slattery's wounded Howie, the quiet poignance of Cynthia Nixon's performance as

Becca deservedly won a Tony Award. Tyne Daly's warm, gauche humanity as Nat and Mary Catherine Garrison's wiser-than-she-knows Izzy were richly observed portraits. John Gallagher Jr. imbued Jason with just the right degree of awkwardness.

Another significant player was designer John Lee Beatty's scrupulously furnished setting of a side-hall colonial house in the suburbs. Mounted on two revolves, rooms came and went with dramatic urgency, animating the story's relatively static action. Christopher Akerlind's subtle lighting design and Jennifer von Mayrhauser's insightful way with characters' clothing also contributed much to the production's effect.

A compassionate play drawn with great skill and meticulously produced by Manhattan Theatre Club, *Rabbit Hole* charts bereavement with devastating restraint. Although the play marks a significant breakthrough in style for Lindsay-Abaire, the story is clearly rooted in his fanciful earlier works regarding people trying to make sense of a world turned upside down.

2005–2006 Best Play
2006 Steinberg/ATCA Citation

RED LIGHT WINTER

By Adam Rapp

○ ○ ○ ○ ○

Essay by Chris Jones

DAVIS: (*To Christina.*) Matt's what we in the world of letters call a wordsmith. A lover of language. He's a bit of a pedant too, but we'll talk about that at our next cultural enrichment seminar. The truth is he's a damn good playwright. Outside of a small, vaguely attended, week-long showcase at this place called La Mama that feel more like a community center for recovering glue huffers than a theater, he hasn't had a single production, bless his heart. But he keeps plugging away. Old Sisyphus himself. Pushin' that rock.

But there is light at the end of the old Hershey Highway as he recently got this award for being burgeoning or something. What was it called again?

IF ADAM RAPP were an emerging baby instead of an emerging playwright, he'd have long ago panicked both his mother and his obstetrician. For years, the 37-year-old Rapp has plugged away on the scruffy edges of the American theater, writing for storefronts and second stages, and suffering through more readings and workshops than a Broadway jukebox musical in perpetual crisis. To some degree, he has himself to blame.

The polar opposite of a commercial playwright, Rapp has always written dangerously. Its bucolic title notwithstanding, his play *Blackbird* (the tale of a pair of drug addicts) went out of its way to shock with the scatological, the sexual and the narcotic. The depressing *Gompers* evoked a dead, ex-urban town (not unlike Joliet, Illinois, where Rapp was raised) wherein nothing happens for a long time. In *Finer Noble Gases* (a play fully intended to be wrenchingly painful for an audience to watch) a naked actor both throws up and urinates on stage—for what feels like several minutes.

And *Nocturne*, a devastating play about the consequences of an automobile accident, begins with the less-than-cheering line, "fifteen years ago, I killed my sister." Even in the circles that recognize his talents as a

Door Matt: Christopher Denham in Red Light Winter. *Photo: Paul Kolnik*

writer, Rapp had become known for minimal plotting, maximum potential for offense and a tendency to stick odious, dysfunctional characters before an audience for a couple of hours, and just let everyone hang out together.

Red Light Winter, which burst onto the scene at Chicago's Steppenwolf Theatre in June 2005 in a fresh, edgy production directed with care by the author, has changed those perceptions about Rapp. The play a huge hit in Chicago—where the performance of newcomer, Lisa Joyce, caused a critical sensation. The following February, the Steppenwolf production moved Off Broadway to the Barrow Street Theatre with Christopher Denham reprising his role as the playwright, Matt, and Gary Wilmes returning as Matt's best friend, the sleazy publisher Davis. The New York production enjoyed a successful commercial run—in Off Broadway terms, at least—and became a finalist for the Pulitzer Prize in Drama (as it turned out, no 2006 award was made). It has since appeared frequently on the regional circuit.

In some ways, the play was a departure for Rapp. The piece oozes sexual mystery and has far more narrative tension than his prior works. It also comes with a clever plot twist late in the second act—something different for a writer who has tended to put most emphasis on style and character development and been largely uninterested in careful plotting. But in many ways, *Red Light Winter* wasn't so much a radical departure for Rapp as a refocusing of his favorite themes. This was by no means the first Adam Rapp play to include characters who are young and alienated and capable of advanced forms of self-destruction. Like most of his other plays, *Red Light Winter* includes Rapp's signature cocktail of dreamy romanticism and slice-of-life existentialism. It also features intensely lyrical writing, a perverse

---

Somehow, this play touched audiences more deeply than Rapp's past work.

---

but palpable sweetness and genuine concern for the human soul. Somehow, though, *Red Light Winter* touched audiences more deeply than Rapp's past work.

THE PLAY OPENS in a "nondescript, inexpensive" hostel room in the red light district of Amsterdam where Matt, a 30-ish nerd of a playwright, is trying unsuccessfully to hang himself with his own belt. His suicide is interrupted by the arrival of his suave former college roommate from Brown—and fellow American—Davis, who has shown up with a beautiful young hooker known as Christina. She is a Parisian cabaret singer, Davis says, and intended for Matt's enjoyment. It's Davis's treat—although he tells his sad-sack pal that he has already sampled the goods.

With the trio all smoking pot, Matt struggles with the approaching sexual moment, babbling on about his intestinal difficulties and the like. We learn that while Matt lurches from one crisis to another, Davis is a highly successful charmer—and a powerful publisher who hit it big after pulling a bestseller out of his company's reject pile. He pushes Matt into sexual action:

> DAVIS: You sure you're okay?
>
> MATT: Yes.
>
> DAVIS: Because she's not gonna want to even touch you if you're blubbering all over yourself. Frog chicks don't like that.
>
> MATT: Stop calling her a Frog.

DAVIS: She knows I'm kidding. She likes it.

(*MATT almost loses it again.*)

DAVIS: If you start crying again, I'm gonna kick your ass.

Davis leaves—with Christina asking for his address in New York as he does so (it appears she was smitten during their brief prior encounter). After he leaves, Matt tells Christina that he's figured out she's a fake.

MATT: You're not French, are you? I mean you might be, right? But I'm almost totally sure that you're like this very talented imposter.

So you can like stop the routine. I won't tell anybody. I mean your accent is spot-on perfect, and the slight lack of knowledge of English vocabulary is very subtle and authentic . . . but you sort of blew it when you sang. I mean, you have this totally, like, melliferous voice or whatever, and your song is really affecting—it's just that there was a verse or two there where you suddenly sounded really Midwestern. I'm from Illinois, so I have these like Des Plaines River Valley superpowers.

(*Awkward pause*)

I mean if you like want to continue in character or whatever, it's fine with me.

Hustlers: Lisa Joyce and Gary Wilmes in Red Light Winter. *Photo: Paul Kolnik*

Christina drops the accent—and also reveals that she is an American married to a gay Parisian. The marriage is a unconsummated sham—she spends six months of the year putting on a show for her husband's colleagues and the rest of her year turning tricks on her own in Amsterdam. Matt begins to open up, telling Christina of his old girlfriend Sarah—who left him for Davis—and his attempted suicide. Christina initiates the explicit sexual encounter that closes the first act. It is a raw, tender, impassioned affair. "It is brief," Rapp writes in the stage directions, "but something real passes between them."

By the second act, the action has moved to Matt's tiny apartment in the East Village. It is a year later. Matt, alone, is writing on his computer, when Christina arrives at the door looking for Davis. It seems that when she asked for his address a year earlier, Davis actually furnished Matt's address. She comes in for a mug of tea. Revelations ensue—Christina (who now calls herself Christine) is on her way to see her family in Baltimore. She's returned to the US because she has AIDS. She is broke.

Matt, it turns out, has been obsessed with their encounter a year ago—even to the point of keeping in his bathroom the dress that Christina was wearing. Davis's voice is heard on the answering machine, saying he's going to come over and pick up a cellphone he'd left there the previous night. Matt calls to try and dissuade him from coming. Meanwhile, Matt and Christina share moments of domestic tenderness—she takes a shower down the hall, he cries on the bed.

He tells her of his new play, entitled *Red Light Winter*—a piece about two friends who go to Amsterdam and end up sleeping with the same hooker.

> CHRISTINA: I was actually going to ask if she was in love with one of them.
>
> MATT: Oh, she is. But not with the right one. One of them is a bit quiet and nerdy and the other one is sort of dickish and macho. The quiet, nerdy one is in love with her but he isn't really her type. And the dickish macho one is her type. But he's not interested in her.

This, of course, is the scenario in Rapp's play that, as in Matt's play, has yet to have an ending. It seems that Christina and Matt will come together in their mutual neediness—until Matt goes for food and Davis conveniently arrives to look for his phone.

Davis doesn't recognize Christina at first. But after poking fun at Matt's squalid apartment, he reads part of his play, finding himself an unsympathetic character. He becomes angry. And then he turns Christina's needy attempts at affection into a horribly violent sexual encounter. "They both get lost in it," Rapp writes. "It might be the best and worst thing they've ever felt." By the time Matt returns, Davis and Christina are gone. He is, once again, alone with his emerging play.

ON SOME LEVELS, of course, *Red Light Winter* is little more than a simply and familiarly structured love-triangle. Its heritage is a combination of male, buddy-comedy movies such as *Sideways*—which it slightly recalls—and the shocking macho diabolism found in the plays and films of Neil LaBute. You could also argue—with validity—that the play is Rapp's cri de coeur for his own career. The playwright cannot resist jabbing at the nonprofit theater and the hopeless lot of the struggling serious author, and Matt is clearly a version of the playwright.

For sure, the fictional writer, Matt, and his real-life counterpart share some of the same obsessions—bodily fluids, dysfunctional sex and a kind of hyper-articulate abnormality that makes life almost unlivable. Both are perpetually close to recognition ("He's like the Olympic Gold Medalist for emerging playwrights," Davis says of Matt), and both clearly see themselves as opposite and oppositional to the world of mainstream success.

Some critics noted that the idea of a man falling in love with a prostitute hardly is unique. But as conceived by Rapp, Christina became no hooker with a conventional heart of gold. She's a much darker creation—a woman who is far from what she seems. And, as played by Joyce in Chicago, she came with such a haunting vulnerability that the play seemed also to get beyond its vivid obsession with the men on the stage. Christina seemed real and vulnerable too. This wasn't just a boys' play.

The Steppenwolf production came with a peculiarly amped-up intensity—which partially accounts for its success. Evoking the grand (but recently moribund) Steppenwolf tradition, Rapp somehow persuaded his actors not only to shed their clothing but to engage in such explicit sexual scenes that the air became thick with the complexities of passion. Since he was directing the play himself, Rapp didn't have to worry about whether or not his director was simpatico with his vision. Instead, he staged his own stage directions in astonishingly precise detail. In the original production, minutes would go by without any dialogue as Rapp concentrated on mood and intention. He also made the shrewd design decision (in collaboration with scene designer Todd Rosenthal) to create two simultaneous box-like rooms on the stage.

In other words, the second act setting (Matt's New York hovel) was visible as the first act played out in the Amsterdam hostel. And vice-versa.

Tabula rasa: Lisa Joyce in Red Light Winter.
Photo: Paul Kolnik

Built as three-dimensional boxes with a side missing, the two playing areas were tiny and crammed with properties. This gave them the overtly theatricalized feel of a Joseph Cornell collage, intensifying voyeuristic elements of the script. Moreover, the constant presence of both settings meant that the events in the script gained an almost tragic sense of inevitability.

RED LIGHT WINTER may be a buddy comedy, but *Sideways* never probed so deep. The ambiance of Rapp's play was so guttural that audiences never seemed to move so much as a digit, even though the running time in Chicago was pushing three hours (the play was slightly shortened for New York). The play succeeded because of the way it continued Rapp's longtime obsession with characters stuck at the margins of society and because it tapped into the peculiar but ubiquitous way in which male friendships are often built on the most primal kinds of rivalry. Especially when youthful relationships turn into adult friendships pockmarked by a massive imbalance of power.

Matt and Davis are rarely nice to each other, even when they are doing each other favors. They seem to hate each other, even though they're tied at the hip. And although their mutual need for each other is palpable, they cannot articulate it—as men usually cannot. Rapp may be the opposite of, say, Tom Stoppard, in style or form. But *Red Light Winter* is also very much about the Stoppardian theme of the difficulty of maintaining artistic purity in a crude, for-profit world.

The character of Davis is emblematic of the artistic type who has sold out to the marketplace—or, depending upon your political perspective, wisely tailored his own creative juices to the appetites of the hungry masses with money to pay for them. Davis is mercurial, detestable, practical and enviable all at once. One imagines that in Rapp's psyche, Davis represents a kind of Faustus. If Rapp were to set down his depressing little scripts and write pap for NBC prime time instead, he likely imagines he'd turn into Davis.

Matt may be a truer artist, but the play suggests that he's thus hopelessly condemned to a lifetime of impoverished dysfunction. One of the problems of being an uncompromising artist, the play suggests, is that you never get the kind of feedback that can let you know whether you were actually any good in the first place. And it's entirely possible that you're not any good now—thus condemned never to emerge. This is surely one of Rapp's insecurities—as is the case with most writers who plug away on the theatrical fringe—and it throbs throughout this play.

Then again, you really don't have to be a playwright to get this point. Most fields and persuasions have their purists and sellouts, idealists and pragmatists, misogynists and Messrs. Geniality. Without question, the dichotomy in Rapp's play is one of which audiences took ownership. There is also the little matter of love and sex. In *Red Light Winter*, of course, the object of all the play's gobs of male desire falls in love with the unfeeling jerk, not the delicate soul who will love her with all his tattered heart. There is some irony here, of course. In their final (and perhaps mutually retributive) sexual encounter, Davis seemingly puts himself at risk for AIDS. Matt, on the other hand, loses both the love of his life and the risks that come from loving her.

Still, you could almost sense the messy, dysfunctional, nervous, loving men in the audience recognizing and bemoaning the tragedy of their own life experience. Women pick the wrong men. Confound them! And yet Rapp was also shrewd enough to ensure that preferring the rich jerk also made sense. It's one thing to fall in love with a gentle soul, but who the hell wants to be stuck with a neurotic for life?

2005–2006 Best Play

SHINING CITY

By Conor McPherson

○ ○ ○ ○ ○

Essay by David Cote

JOHN: Do you believe what I'm saying to you? That this is happening to me?

(*Pause.*)

IAN: I believe you . . . that . . . I believe something is . . . I believe you, in that I don't think you're making it up.

JOHN: I'm not making it up.

IAN: Yes but . . . I believe you're telling me you saw something, but if you're asking me if I believe in ghosts, I . . .

JOHN: Yeah but can you help me with this? [. . .]

THERE ARE ANGELS, there are devils and then there are ghosts. The latter class of apparition occupies a shadowy nook in the pantheon of supernatural beings: In art, ghosts aren't advocates of good or evil, emissaries from heaven or hell—they're mirrors or mnemonics, reminders of moral duty. A ghost haunts to warn us, shame us, drives us away or scare us silly, but its exact purpose can also be cryptic. Ambiguity is part of the ghost's scare arsenal. In Shakespeare, unquiet spirits are often goads to revenge; in Dickens, catalysts for ethical reform; in Strindberg and Ibsen, metaphors for moral or social rot; in Coward, farcical devices; and in Kushner, mystical-satirical mouthpieces. But what's the mission of the ghost in *Shining City*, mentioned in the first scene, forgotten for a while, then shockingly manifested in the final seconds of the play? Conor McPherson's 90-minute work offers no pat solutions, but it prompts a walk down a hall of mirrors in which psychoanalysis and metaphysics converge to shivery effect as a playwright wrestles with his demons in the cold light of a sober dawn.

The 35-year-old Dublin dramatist has trafficked in otherworldly creatures before, but never so literally. In *St. Nicholas* (1997), he cast Brian Cox as a bastardly theater critic who falls in with a pack of vampires (though we never see them); and in his 1999 Broadway debut, *The Weir*, the action was driven by a series of increasingly grim ghost stories told by Irish pub

Ghost story: Oliver Platt and Brían F. O'Byrne in Shining City. *Photo: Joan Marcus*

mates trying to impress a woman from Dublin. But generally, McPherson's dramaturgy concerns lonely, regretful alcoholics (*Rum and Vodka*, *Dublin Carol*) or young men adrift in a morally indifferent world (*The Good Thief*). The playwright's pet mode is the monologue. When his characters aren't pure storytellers, on a bare stage with a yarn to spin, he contrives for them to dilate on a topic between stretches of connective dialogue. *Shining City* belongs to a small subset of his work in which the aria alternates organically with the duet. It is also a departure for the playwright, in that the ghosts aren't just metaphorical, they get stage time.

Lately, in fact, McPherson seems to be incorporating supernatural elements in his plays. In his newest work, *The Seafarers*, scheduled to open at London's National Theatre in September 2006. Satan himself plays poker with a group of down-and-out Dubliners to win one of their souls. Why this turn from the loamy but realistic landscape of drunks, old men and garrulous duffers to dark fantasy and metaphysical elements? The answer may have to do with McPherson's brush with death a few years ago, a result of years of alcoholism that left him comatose for weeks. *Shining City* was the newly detoxed writer's first work after his season among the dead.

SHINING CITY BEGINS in the mode of closely studied conventional realism: Ian (Brían F. O'Byrne) is a newly licensed therapist who left the priesthood a year earlier. According to McPherson's notes, Ian has hung his shingle on the third floor of a massive building in a neighborhood "around Phibsboro maybe, or Berkeley Road, an old part of the city which, while it retains a sense of history, is not a salubrious area." The unhealthiness of the surroundings extends to the faulty door buzzer in Ian's office, which rings at the top of the play and serves as a minor running gag: Ian can barely

Paranormal elements in his work attest to a refreshing lack of certainty.

hear who's at the front door, and he can never buzz them in. The detail is not just narrative garnish; communication, access and threshold-crossing, are central themes in the play. Also, two spires are visible from the office's windows, reminders that the Church still looms over Ian's life.

His first patient is John (Oliver Platt), a middle-age sales representative who has never been to a psychologist. Nevertheless, within seconds of settling on Ian's couch, John breaks into quiet sobs, explaining that his wife died a few months ago in a car accident. The basic facts dribble out, which Ian dutifully records on a pad: John and his deceased wife, Mari, never had children. Before her death, the spouses had grown apart—and recently, John has been seeing her ghost in the house.

Naturally, the last detail jolts the therapist, who composes himself and coaxes more information out of John. The patient relates the first haunting, which took place one evening after he met with his estranged brother for a pint. John returned home, noticing nothing unusual, except for the distant sound of an ice-cream van's jingle.

> JOHN: [. . .] I was just going into the living room and I put the lights on, and . . . when I turned around I could see that she was standing there behind the door looking at me.
>
> (*Pause.*)
>
> IAN: Your wife?
>
> JOHN: Yeah. She . . . I could only see half of her, behind the door, looking out at me. Eh . . . but I could see that . . . her hair was soaking wet, and all plastered to her face. And her mouth was open like she was trying to . . . And I, I fucking jumped, you know? And I

> fucking stood there, I froze, it was terrifying. And I mean she was as
> real as . . . you know if you've ever seen a dead body? How strange
> it is, but . . . it's . . . real! [. . .]

The terrified John rushes past his wife's apparition, out the door and spends
the night in a bed and breakfast. He then tells of a second incident. Having
summoned the courage to return a couple of days later, John is soaking in
the bathtub, listening to the radio. Suddenly, he has the sensation of someone
in the house. There's a rapping at the bathroom door. Alarmed, John jumps
up, slips in the tub and finally wrenches the door open to find no one
there. McPherson ends this strange, unnerving little scene as Ian falteringly
comforts John: "You're not on your own, now. We'll sort it out."

The next scene, the second of five, takes place weeks later. (McPherson
indicates that about two months elapse between each scene.) Rather than a
continuation of John's ghost story or his therapeutic process, the playwright
plunks us down in the middle of Ian's messy personal life. The scene
opens mid-argument with Ian and Neasa (Martha Plimpton), his girlfriend.
Neasa has come to Ian's office to confront him about his absence from her
and their child. Here we learn that Ian is an ex-priest and Neasa, with

Spooked: Oliver Platt in Shining City. *Photo: Joan Marcus*

whom he's had a baby out of wedlock, helped him to leave the clergy. Ian arduously tries to break things off with Neasa, but cannot articulate the root cause. He has stowed her and their child, Aisling, at his brother's house but hasn't visited for four days. Neasa is uncomfortable with the housing situation, and she's alternately incensed and concerned about her lover, who seems to struggling with some terrible inner pain.

> NEASA: An ex-priest? Forget it. [My father] said anyone who goes next or near the priests is a fucking headcase to begin with. But I wouldn't listen to him!

Ian feels like he's still in the middle of a massive life change.

> IAN: [. . .] I had to make that big decision—and it was a *huge* thing for me—(*As though he has accomplished something completely unthinkable.*)—to turn my back on the Church?!—that was a *huge* thing for me. You were there for me, and I couldn't have come through it without you[. . . .] But . . . the fucking huge mistake I made was thinking that that was the end of the journey for me—and it wasn't.

This stuttering, agonized scene ends with Neasa confessing a past, minor infidelity to Ian, restating her love for him—to which he can only numbly reply "I'm sorry"—and gathering her things to go.

The next scene centers on a session between John and Ian. The patient, now about four months into therapy, seems to be benefiting from the "talking cure." He is taking daily walks and his speech flows, no longer perforated by ellipses and pauses. Even so, this will be one of those difficult "breakthrough" sessions in which a patient unburdens feelings that festered for years. John talks a bit about how his inability to have children with Mari inspired regret about the marriage. "[M]aybe I felt that the whole thing should be different," he muses. "[N]ot that we should adopt some kid or something—but that I should change the whole . . . the whole fucking thing you know?"

This desire to run away leads into an embarassing affair that John attempted with a married woman. John's speeches here are some of the best writing in the play, as he narrates the first flush of illicit communication through text messages and the unbearable anticipation of a new lover. McPherson's flair for storytelling serves him well, as we become deeply involved with the charming, self-deprecating Dubliner's romantic pursuit of a woman he describes as painfully glamorous. But the affair ends in awkward pathos, since John rushes things and discovers that he and the woman actually have no chemistry. From there, lust and self-loathing drive him to a brothel, where, again, he finds no satisfaction. John returns home to his wife overflowing with guilt and disgust—the miserable Mari tries to get him to open up—and he erupts:

> JOHN: I just turned on her, Ian, you know? I just . . . exploded. And I ate the head off her. I was like an animal. And it was just so . . . sudden. She looked so frightened[. . . .] And I . . . grabbed her by the shoulders and I shook her. I shook her so hard. I could feel how small and helpless she was. It was a terrible thing. And I said to her, "Don't fucking speak to me anymore. Don't you dare fucking speak to me." And she just cowered down on the floor[. . . .]

John hits rock-bottom in his loneliness, reaching a profound sense that life has been wasted. Here, most of McPherson's characters would retreat into a world of booze and solitude with no hope of salvation, but John's admission has the purifying force of a confession to a priest. As the sessions winds down, he wonders if his wife's ghost is trying to save him.

Complicating matters further, in the fourth scene, Ian brings a male prostitute, Laurence (Peter Scanavino) into his office. Laurence is a scruffy, homeless hustler with a bandaged hand who regards his john with mingled suspicion and pity. Ian is deeply nervous about this encounter, his first time with a man. They exchange details about their lives. Laurence is married with a child, but must trade sex for money. Ian pays him, they drink some wine between bursts of small talk, and the scene ends with an awkward embrace. Obviously this raises basic questions about the therapist: Is he a closeted homosexual? Or is this merely a pitiful fumble for human contact? Again, McPherson provides only fragmentary snapshots here, telling his characters' stories—and the development of their inner lives—between the scenes.

By the final scene—roughly a year after the play began—Ian's office is full of moving boxes; he's packing. John, now no longer in therapy, visits bearing the gift of an antique lamp and reporting that life is good: a new girlfriend, plans to sell the house, no more sightings of ghosts, good health. The therapist's life also seems to have improved. He is relocating to Limerick with his fiancée and their baby to start over there. We appear to be at the end of a slight, optimistic slice-of-life about grief and recovery:

> IAN: So, no ghosts.
>
> JOHN: No. No ghosts. (*He exhales.*) But, I'll tell you, you know, even if I saw one, Ian, it's not . . . I mean, seeing something is one thing but . . . it's how it makes you *feel*, isn't it? It's how that makes you feel. That's what's important. Someone could see something and it

Fond farewell: Oliver Platt and Brían F. O'Byrne in Shining City. *Photo: Joan Marcus*

doesn't really matter. Someone else'll see it and . . . it's the end of the world, you know?

IAN: (*Affirmative.*) Mmm.

JOHN: That's the reality, you know? What it *does* to you is the reality.

IAN: I know.

JOHN: But you don't believe in ghosts anyway, Ian. You've got it sussed.

(*They are moving toward the door.*)

IAN: John, there was a time I would've given anything to see one. Just to know that there was . . . something else. Do you know what I mean?

JOHN: Sure.

IAN: Just something else, besides all the . . . you know . . . the pain and the confusion. Just something that gave everything . . . *some* meaning, you know? I'm talking about God, really, you know?

On his way out the door, John laughs: "I'll tell you, the mind, it's mad, isn't it?" To which Ian replies amiably, "John, we know nothing. We just know nothing really." John leaves, and now, without warning, the action lifts to the level of the uncanny. McPherson's stage directions continue:

> *Ian throws one of the two books in a box near the door. He shuts the door and crosses the room to throw the other book in a different box.*
>
> *In the darkening gloom of the afternoon, we see that Mari's ghost has appeared behind the door. She is looking at Ian, just as John described her; she wears her red coat, which is filthy, her hair is wet. She looks beaten up. She looks terrifying.*
>
> *Ian has his back to her at his desk, going through some old mail. But he seems to sense something and turns.*
>
> *Lights down.*

In the darkened Biltmore Theatre, the audience's astonished confusion was palpable. Was that *really* a ghost? Why was she haunting the therapist? *That's* the ending? Is this what they call transference in psychoanalysis?

MOREOVER, WHAT ARE we dealing with: a ghost story or a tale of psychic healing? And who's story is this, John's, or Ian's? It's worth pausing to bring up McPherson's biography. *Shining City* was his first play after a near-fatal 2001 collapse from pancreatitis that rendered him unconscious for three weeks. At 29, the writer was a young, successful, but intensely self-destructive drunk. He'd been a high-functioning alcoholic for years. When he left the hospital, McPherson entered Alcoholics Anonymous and got sober. So *Shining City*, in this reading, is the writer is taking stock of his life, the past and his newfound clarity.

As McPherson noted in a *New York Times* interview when *Shining City* opened: "You look at all those plays back before I stopped drinking, and I think there's a certain monolithic quality. *Shining City* feels completely split in two, in all kinds of ways, like two mirrors reflecting [. . .] until infinity." The last comment is telling. Ian and John *are* mirrors of each other, in terms of action and general life-circumstance; even their names are twinned. *Ian* is the Scottish-Gaelic version of *John*. How fitting: two men fleeing their pasts, burdened by guilt, lust, self-loathing, each trying to begin life again. In McPherson's echoic structuring of "John" scenes and "Ian" scenes, there emerges a dual portrait, two men who may be the same man: one unintentionally fathered a child, the other is unhappily childless, each is part of a dysfunctional couple, both reach out to a sexual surrogate. These small, understated coincidences parallel fates that neither man seems to recognize.

On a basic level, *Shining City* is a play about connection and communication. There is the running joke about the wonky intercom buzzer at Ian's office. And John saw Mari's ghost halfway in a door frame. The concept of liminality, of crossing over and shifting perceptions, has ghostly connotations. And what is psychoanalysis, ultimately, but the act of telling ghost stories in a room with the help of a medium?

Robert Falls's low-key, naturalistic staging and his keen ear for the text's halting, elliptical rhythms resulted in a rich, engrossing production. Two fine character actors—Platt and O'Byrne—also had the chance to stretch their acting muscles. In his stage and television work, the chubby, baby-faced Platt was known for comic relief. But here, while he certainly had laugh lines, Platt was able to show more colors, particularly as a man with a short temper who alienated loved ones. O'Byrne, who distinguished himself on Broadway as a psychotic child-killer (*Frozen*) and a possible child molester (*Doubt*) finally got the chance to play a decent fellow, albeit one with skeletons in his closet. Plimpton and Scanavino shone briefly but memorably in their supporting roles.

As far as mainstream culture goes, *Shining City* has more in common with the recent wave of Japanese horror movies (*The Ring*, *The Grudge*) than with standard drama. While J-Horror is comparatively cruder—more interested in shocks and gross-out imagery than in psychological nuance— it taps into the same well of guilt, terror and rising tension that McPherson probes through Irish-Catholic folkways. *Shining City* is the sort of play that electrifies the playgoer looking for more than representational reality onstage, who hungers for escapism, surprise and shock.

Unfortunately, not all critics were so receptive. Michael Feingold deplored the twist ending, arguing that it cheapened what he pedantically termed McPherson's first real play. But other reviewers welcomed it, including *The New York Times*'s Ben Brantley. "In terms of construction," he wrote, "*Shining City* is as close to perfection as contemporary playwriting gets." *Shining City* earned a Tony Award nomination for best new play, taking its place alongside two other Irish dramas—Martin McDonagh's *The Lieutenant of Inishmore* and a revival of Brian Friel's monologue-driven *Faith Healer*. For this critic, the weird, partly opaque drama was a welcome change from the living-room mediocrities that dominated the Biltmore Theatre through Manhattan Theatre Club's conservative subscriber-friendly programming. *Shining City*'s predecessor at the Biltmore, for example, couldn't have been more different: the conventional, inert, ready-for-television *Rabbit Hole* by David Lindsay-Abaire. As in *Shining City*, *Rabbit*

Hole examined grief and recovery. It just did nothing to stimulate the imagination or leave the spectator abuzz with metaphysical questions.

Despite Brantley's claim that the play *Shining City* is flawless (and it is well-constructed), the play is not a carefully reasoned psychodrama or an exploration of ghosting as an occult phenomenon. McPherson says in interviews that he writes instinctively, from an impulsive, emotional place. The inexplicable, paranormal elements in his work attest to a refreshing lack of certainty about human nature or the natural world. Thus the play is ultimately a mood piece that depends more on intuition and subtlety than logical consistency. It appeals to the submerged, superstitious part of our brain that longs for redemption but fears damnation.

2005–2006 Best Play

STUFF HAPPENS

By David Hare

○ ○ ○ ○ ○

Essay by Misha Berson

RUMSFELD: I've seen those pictures. I could take pictures in any city in America. Think what's happened in our cities when we've had riots, and problems, and looting. Stuff happens.

SINCE THE UNITED STATES and its "coalition of the willing" invaded Iraq in 2003, dozens of books have appeared analyzing the escalation to war. Countless debates over the rationale for the conflict have raged in the global media. So far, however, prominent British dramatist David Hare's *Stuff Happens* is the only play to translate the chain of geopolitical maneuvers and compromises, deals and betrayals that preceded the war into the "stuff" of riveting popular drama.

The prolific Hare has often addressed topical concerns in his plays. But with *Stuff Happens* he struck an especially raw, trans-Atlantic bundle of nerves. Raiding the public record and taking full artistic license, Hare reconstructed (and imagined) how US and British leaders plotted and parried over a major "pre-emptive war." In a near-seamless melding of fictional speculation and on-the-record speeches, memos and other documents, *Stuff Happens* boasts a cast of characters familiar to news junkies—from UN weapons inspector Hans Blix and French diplomat Dominique de Villepin, to US President George W. Bush and British Prime Minister Tony Blair.

In a 2005 *Los Angeles Times* essay, Hare admitted that his play was a "work of the imagination" about who might have said what behind closed doors at the White House, 10 Downing Street and other bastions of power. But he has always insisted that his speculations were often fueled by information from (anonymous) reliable sources in high places. *Stuff Happens*, however, was never intended by its author simply to rewind recent history. Using the paradigmatic historical dramas of Shakespeare as his model, Hare has crafted an absorbing rumination on the dynamics and manipulations of power—a subject as timeless as war itself. Hare acknowledged that "any play on how and why we went to war was bound to be superfluous, or

Bermuda triangle: Peter Francis James, Gloria Reuben and Jay O. Sanders in Stuff Happens. *Photo: Michal Daniel*

already outdated, because journalism had already done such a thorough job of covering a process of which we were by now heartily sick."

But theater affects people in ways the news media do not—or will not admit. In the best hands, theater can compress, humanize and impose a cogent narrative on an unwieldy, ambiguous snarl of events, personalities and viewpoints—while making it clear this isn't "the whole truth." A play such as *Stuff Happens* also invites us to ponder this narrative collectively, in a shared space and with a heightened intensity. Hare sincerely taps a common desire among us to learn how fateful decisions were (and are) made in our name. The play is a chess match of motives and tactics, and without glossing their own roles in the debacle evokes empathy for Tony Blair and US Secretary of State Colin Powell, two well-respected public figures who staked their integrity on a violent course of action—and had their reputations irreparably tarnished as a consequence.

The rhetoric in *Stuff Happens* mostly comes from composite characters representing dialectical viewpoints not otherwise covered: an Iraqi who supported "regime change" to his later regret; a conservative journalist who believes spreading democracy in the Arab world is a moral duty. More engrossing are the realpolitik portraits of top global players, as Hare paints them. President Bush gets particularly nuanced treatment, emerging not as the inarticulate bumbler many imagine him to be, but as a shrewd, sometimes inscrutable commander in chief who relishes his authority.

THE PLAY CALLS for more than a dozen actors in multiple roles, and zigzags across time. The format is a fast-moving, neo-Brechtian montage of short scenes—snippets of speeches and press conferences—introduced in concise narrative footnotes spoken by different cast members in turn. As the play opens on a sparely dressed stage, Donald Rumsfeld comments to the press about the pillaging of Baghdad after US forces "liberated" the Iraqi capital.

Hare's revised script highlighted the plight of Colin Powell.

RUMSFELD: [. . .] And it's untidy, and freedom's untidy, and free people are free to make mistakes and commit crimes and do bad things. They're also free to live their lives and do wonderful things, and that's going to happen there. [. . .]

Hare has several major players describe what they were doing in the 1970s—only Powell served in Vietnam. Other context follows, as George W. Bush describes his Christian faith and God's plan for him to lead. Once elected president, Bush revels in not owing "anybody an explanation" for anything he says or does. It is during the first 2001 meeting of Bush's National Security Council that Condoleezza Rice "expresses what the president is feeling" with regard to disengagement in issues concerning Israel and the Palestinians, saying that President Clinton's failed Mideast negotiations "took up a huge amount of time" and left the US "looking weak." Although Powell counters this position, Bush argues for allowing "a real show of strength" by the Israelis. The conversation then shifts to Iraq—to Powell's surprise—as CIA director George Tenet shows intelligence photos purported to depict an Iraqi chemical or biological weapons factory. Bush orders more investigation.

Flash forward to September 11, 2001, and the deadly terrorist attacks on the World Trade Center and the Pentagon. Soon after the attacks Bush declares "a war on terrorism" and a White House "war cabinet" briefing convenes. The president's advisors agree that the US must strike Afghanistan to drive out the Taliban regime sheltering the al-Qaeda terrorist group led by Osama bin Laden. Some suggest Afghanistan will serve as "demonstration model" of regime change. Paul Wolfowitz guesses there's a "10 to 50" percent chance that Iraq dictator Saddam Hussein was "directly involved" in the September 11 attacks.

After lunch, the Secretary of State promotes building a coalition to strike Afghanistan only:

> POWELL: [. . .] Since Tuesday we have the support of the whole world. People don't want to go for one thing, and then find they've signed up for another. Nobody likes bait and switch. Who we go against is going to decide who goes with us.

To which the president responds:

> BUSH: You know, Colin, finally this is a war on terror. And at some point we may be the only ones left. That's fine with me.

Bush authorizes military action against Afghanistan. In England, Tony Blair commits Great Britain to the campaign "to re-order the world around us." After the Taliban are driven from Kabul, Blair calls Bush to complain that British special forces briefly located Osama bin Laden in Afghanistan, but were ordered by the US military not to capture him.

Front man: Peter Francis James and company in Stuff Happens. *Photo: Michal Daniel*

In Bush's 2002 State of the Union address, he starts making the case for toppling Saddam Hussein as antiwar sentiment builds in Britain. An anxious Blair arrives at Bush's Texas ranch and he tells the president to urge Israel to soften its treatment of the Palestinians, or risk alienating much of the Arab world. When Bush mentions Iraq, Blair says he's been advised an invasion without UN sanction would violate international law:

> BLAIR: If Britain is involved, we will need evidence that Iraq can and will launch a nuclear, biological or chemical attack on a Western country. We can't go to war because of what we fear. Only because of what we know.

Blair argues for more weapons inspections, diplomacy and UN resolutions vis-à-vis Iraq—he fears without them his political clout at home will erode. Bush assures Blair that "no war plan is on the table." But in a press briefing soon after, Blair is visibly stunned to hear Bush call for "the removal of Saddam." Later, Blair tells an advisor:

> BLAIR: He is tricky, isn't he? You don't know exactly what's been agreed. You don't know where you are.

Blair orders British intelligence to search for proof that Iraq has weapons of mass destruction.

Meanwhile, Powell complains bitterly to Bush that he's being "left out of the loop" on Iraq. He stresses the need to avoid an ill-advised war that could destabilize the Mideast, a war designed by "armchair generals" and "intellectuals":

> POWELL: [. . .] If you go into Iraq you're going to be the proud owner of 25 million people. Their lives. All their hopes and aspirations. All their problems. Has anyone begun to think about that?

Bush hears him out, and says he hasn't made a decision yet. Later Rice speaks privately with Powell, complimenting him on his forceful exchanges with the president. But an unspoken gulf seems to have opened between the two African-American colleagues. The act ends with Powell standing isolated and alone on a darkened stage.

AT THE TOP of Act II, in one of several monologues by fictive characters who express different views of the Iraq War, a female Palestinian academic decries Bush's disinterest in helping her people. Back in the White House, Cheney and Rumsfeld object to seeking a new UN resolution for more Iraq weapons inspections. Cheney dismisses the UN as "an East River chattering factory." He suggests by talking up the UN's shortcomings to the press, an Iraq invasion would no longer be perceived as a "question of foreign policy," but as proof of the UN's impotence. Publicly, Cheney links the September 11 attacks to Saddam for the first time. Rice backs him up with her famous warning:

> RICE: There will always be some uncertainty about how quickly [Saddam] will acquire nuclear weapons. But we don't want the smoking gun to be a mushroom cloud.

September 12, 2002, Bush delivers what some call "the most important speech of his life" to the UN General Assembly, urging a resolution that gives Iraq an ultimatum to disarm:

> BUSH: The history, the logic and the facts lead to one conclusion: Saddam Hussein's regime is a grave and gathering danger. [. . .]

To his dismay, Powell realizes Cheney has cut a pledge from Bush's speech that would have tied the use of force against Saddam to a second UN resolution. Powell meets privately with European and Russian diplomats to thrash out a UN resolution agreeable to all. France's de Villepin is skeptical:

> DE VILLEPIN: I think the world outside America has felt a little like a rejected lover these past two years. Now it's one o'clock in the morning and you're coming to our door with a bunch of flowers and whisky on your breath. You can see some of us are feeling just a little bit cautious.

There is sharp verbal sparring between the diplomats, with Powell insisting the US views its allies as "equal partners," and seeks 15 "freely given votes" for an Iraq resolution. De Villepin lobbies for a second resolution, to sanction military action if Iraq doesn't comply with the first—and a fragile agreement is struck.

As the US Senate debates the Iraq weapons "crisis," President Bush summons the chief UN weapons inspector Hans Blix.

> BUSH: [. . .] They say I'm a mad Texan bent on war. That's not so. That's what I wanted to say to you. I want to go through the UN and see [Saddam] disarmed. [. . .]

Wolfowitz takes Blix aside to suggest that an Iraqi weapons scientist be served with an international subpoena, taken out of Iraq, and grilled to "get what we need" to prove Saddam has the feared weapons. Blix responds:

> BLIX: Forgive me, but somehow I've never seen the U.N. as being in the kidnapping business.

Press briefing: Members of the company in Stuff Happens. *Photo: Michal Daniel*

AFTER THE UN Security Council votes down the first resolution drafted by the US, Powell talks with Rice about devising a new resolution more likely to pass:

> POWELL: I'm trying to avoid war.
>
> RICE: We're all trying to avoid war.
>
> POWELL: Are we?

The unspoken tension between the two intensifies, as Powell complains he is still not in the White House's Iraq "loop":

> POWELL: It's hard to negotiate the importance of a course of action if another course of action has already been decided. The person who does that looks like a fool.

In November 2002, the UN passes a compromise Iraq resolution, and Saddam releases a rambling, 12,000 page document to "prove" Iraq has no weapons of mass destruction. In England, Blair tells his advisors the UK must stay loyal to the US:

> BLAIR: [. . .] If for a moment, if even for a moment, we come adrift from Washington, our influence is gone. It's gone! [. . .]

Powell meets again with Bush, who tells him the UN inspections are a "distraction" that "weaken" the US, and he's come to a decision about Iraq—implying he favors military action. Asked by Bush if he disagrees, Powell says he does not.

De Villepin suddenly announces that, for France, "nothing justifies military intervention" in Iraq. Americans respond with a frenzy of "France bashing," and Powell privately rages that he's dealing with "a bunch of right-wing nut cases in the White House" on one hand, and "the treacherous French" on the other. Powell meets with Bush, Cheney and Rumsfeld about the second UN resolution he promised Blair. During an intense, extended debate, Rumsfeld says the US should "maybe stop listening to Europe":

> RUMSFELD: I know why we're going to war. And so do you, Colin. Because [Saddam] is a lunatic and we can't afford the risk that one day he might team up with terrorists.

Powell argues Blair has been loyal, and must be consulted, but Cheney and Rumsfeld mock the English leader's global idealism, and Powell's ambivalence. Says Cheney:

> CHENEY: [. . . Y]ou like it both ways, don't you Colin? Being one of us and one of the good guys as well. Don't you think one day you're going to have to make a choice?

Bush forces the choice, by asking Powell to address the UN about Iraq's "imminent threat" to the world. Privately, Powell rejects much of the intelligence information available to back up this claim as "garbage." But at the UN, he follows orders and states Iraq may well have mobile labs to make biological weapons. Blix reports he has found no such weapons in Iraq, and in February 2003 massive antiwar protests erupt around the world. Later that month, the US, Britain and Spain try to get support for a second UN resolution to sanction military force against Iraq. But when the French vow to vote against such a resolution, under any circumstances, that gives Bush's advisors an excuse to withdraw it, and embark on their own course of action.

The "shock and awe" bombing of Iraq by coalition forces led by the US and UK begins March 20, 2003. A week later, Wolfowitz tells Congress:

> WOLFOWITZ: We're dealing with a country that can really finance its own reconstruction and relatively soon.

In April, Bush flies a plane onto a Naval aircraft carrier, and in front of a "Mission Accomplished" banner gives a victory speech:

> BUSH: [. . .] No terrorist network will gain weapons of mass destruction
> from inside the Iraq regime, because that regime is no more. [. . .]

The scene shifts to 2005 and Rumsfeld is asked by the press if the US is winning the war.

> RUMSFELD: Winning or losing is not the issue for "we," in my view,
> in the traditional, conventional context of using the words "winning"
> and "losing" in a war.

We learn that Cheney's stock options in Halliburton—a company given no-bid contracts to supply the war effort—have risen in value to $8 million from about $242,000. In November 2004, Powell resigns and Rice becomes Secretary of State. A British television interviewer later asks Powell if he'll apologize for misleading the world about weapons in Iraq.

> POWELL: I did not mislead the world. You can't mislead when you
> are presenting what you believe are the facts.

The play ends with an anguished monologue by an Iraqi exile:

> IRAQI EXILE: [. . .] A vacuum was created. Was it created deliberately?
> I cannot comprehend. They came to save us, but they had no plans[.
> . . .] We opposed Saddam Hussein, many of us, because he harmed
> people, and anybody who harms innocent Iraqis, I feel equally
> passionately and strongly about and I will oppose them. And I will.

LAUDED IN ITS 2004 premiere as staged by Nicholas Hytner at London's National Theatre, *Stuff Happens* received a cooler reception in its 2005 US premiere at Los Angeles's Mark Taper Forum. Some reviews of Gordon Davidson's production echoed American distaste for political art—and for any perceived "Yank-bashing" by Brits. In *Time*, Richard Schickel described Hare as "a British twit of the tiresomely superior leftist kind[. . . .] We have no doubt of his pip-pip contempt for the primitive politics of his slightly dim-witted American cousins."

Fewer cavils, and more raves, greeted *Stuff Happens* in its hit 2005–06 New York run at the Public Theater. Hare's revised script highlighted the plight of Powell, a troubled pragmatist among ideologues, and added more shades of gray throughout—and director Daniel Sullivan expertly re-scaled the play for the intimate confines of the Public's Newman Theater. Patrons sat on opposite sides of a runway-style staging area, able to observe one another as well as the actors. *New York Times* critic Ben Brantley likened the arrangement to a "town meeting." And he found the retooled script "less an arrogant, animated history book with a fixed agenda, than a fluid public speculation[. . . .]"

Will *Stuff Happens* change hearts and minds? Or just "preach to the converted"? Will it be relevant to future viewers, or just collect dust with other epochal relics? We don't know, and we don't need to know. Let it be enough that *Stuff Happens* offers a bracing notion of how we are governed now—which might help us better debate and define who we are.

2005–2006 Best Play

THIRD

By Wendy Wasserstein

○ ○ ○ ○ ○

Essay by Anne Cattaneo

LAURIE: But as Stephen walked me home, he suddenly took my hand and said, "Dearest, loveliest Elizabeth! By you, I was properly humbled." Of course I recognized the quote from the film, [of *Pride and Prejudice*] and I responded appropriately: "Now be sincere; did you admire me for my impertinence?" And he responded still quoting, "No, for the liveliness of your mind." Then he turned my face to him. He dropped the Jane Austen and whispered, "Most of all, I admire the openness of your heart."

CONTEMPLATING WENDY WASSERSTEIN'S *Third* almost a year after its October 24, 2005, opening at Lincoln Center Theater's Mitzi Newhouse Theater marks a bleak anniversary. Stephen, the offstage husband of *Third*'s central character Laurie Jameson, is describing both the central character and the playwright—an author whose work merged the personal and the political in a wide, popular arena on the American stage for nearly thirty years. Wasserstein's heart, impertinence and liveliness of mind shine through her plays, from her earliest successes, *Uncommon Women and Others* and *Isn't It Romantic*, through her prize-winning and highly influential *The Heidi Chronicles* and *The Sisters Rosensweig*, to her more direct and disturbingly insightful later works, *An American Daughter* and *Third*. Wasserstein was in a coma by the time *Third* closed at Lincoln Center, and she died of lymphoma at the age of 55 in early 2006.

As in many of her plays, *Third* is structured around the friendship of two plain-speaking women, grappling with a time in their own lives, and a time in the life of their country. *Third* begins in September 2002 and in its second scene, Laurie Jameson is in her kitchen watching President Bush's address to the United Nations, in which he accuses Saddam Hussein of possessing weapons of mass destruction. As the scene progresses, she awaits the results of the vote in Congress to authorize the use of force in Iraq. Jameson's home is a small, prestigious New England college, which in Wasserstein's plays is always a location akin to paradise. The character is a

Professorial privilege: Dianne Wiest in Third. *Photo: Joan Marcus*

professor of English, the first woman to be tenured in the department. She is a renowned and fearless activist who has helped to transform the college from a bastion of privilege to an open-minded and inclusive place of learning where many kinds of ideas and people are tolerated—or so she believes as the play opens.

In *Third*'s first scene, Jameson, memorably portrayed by veteran stage and screen actress Dianne Wiest, delivers a charming and politically correct lecture on Shakespeare's *King Lear* and meets the title character. He is a student and "legacy" admission—Woodson Bull, nicknamed Third—who wants to be a sports agent. The young actor Jason Ritter made his New York stage debut in this role, following in the footsteps of his father and grandfather, veteran stage and television actor John Ritter and the legendary singing film-cowboy, actor Tex Ritter. Jason Ritter's fresh, nuanced and low-keyed performance earned him both the 2006 Clarence Derwent Award for the season's Most Promising Male Performer and Lincoln Center's Martin E. Segal Award.

Jameson's increasingly fraught relationship with Third, whose primary interest is wrestling, is chronicled in the play. As she seeks to understand her feelings about Third, she comes into conflict with her friend Nancy, Jameson's colleague in the English department whose area of expertise is

Jane Austen. By the time the bombing of Baghdad appears as background on television at the top of *Third*'s second act, much has fallen apart in Jameson's world, and we see this to be true in the formerly (to her) Eden-like world of the Ivy League as well as the world at large.

THE FRIENDSHIP OF Laurie Jameson and Nancy Gordon mirrors the close bonds of Wasserstein's *Uncommon Women* at college, worrying whether they will still be incredible when they turn forty. It harkens to the insecurities of Janie and Harriet in *Isn't It Romantic* as they seek to come to terms with their lives as women with or without romantic relationships. A more complex

---

Wasserstein's heart, impertinence and liveliness of mind shine through her plays.

---

palette of mortality, both within a family and, with AIDS, across a community, enters the worlds of Wasserstein's *The Heidi Chronicles* and *The Sisters Rosensweig*. These plays depict the roads taken and not taken as choices are made in adult life. Wasserstein widened her focus both in *The Heidi Chronicles* and in *An American Daughter* to take in the arena of national politics and feminism, always a central concern, and by *An American Daughter*, the friends Lyssa Dent Hughes and Judith Kaufman are battered by the truths revealed to them in their defeats.

Third opens in an even darker world. While the wit and humor that always made her plays so appealing are still in evidence, they glimmer only fleetingly in Wasserstein and Jameson's middle age. Jameson's husband, a political science professor of lesser renown at the same college, remains offstage in his own midlife crisis. Jameson's daughter Emily, played by newcomer Gaby Hoffman, visits from Swarthmore and expresses her growing disenchantment with her mother's world. Jameson is a sympathetic and concerned mother, but she is more taken with her elder daughter who lives in Vermont with her lover: a prize-winning lesbian poet. Emily, in contrast, has just gone to college and is dating a bank teller who dropped out of Trenton State College. To Jameson, Emily's life is going in the wrong direction and she is unable to recognize Emily's worth without the validation of brand-name awards and institutions.

As Jameson and Emily spar, Jameson's adored father Jack appears, visiting from his nearby assisted-living community. Jack is suffering from Alzheimer's disease, and Jameson has brought him to live near her. She is responsible for him and much of her time is taken with his care. In a remarkable performance, Charles Durning gave the increasingly bewildered but ever-charming Jack Jameson a quiet power that brought home the situation faced by Wasserstein's generation as it deals with aging parents. As in all her earlier work, Wasserstein is smack-dab in the middle of her generation's lives, exploring in *Third* the concerns of the final third of life.

This is most notably brought home in the character of Jameson's colleague and friend Nancy who has breast cancer; as Jameson struggles to help her friend, Nancy pushes her away. Amy Aquino portrayed Nancy in the Lincoln Center Theater production in a haunting, brittle and dryly humorous performance. Looking back, knowing only later that Wasserstein herself was struggling with disease, makes the scenes almost unbearable to read. Nonetheless, as Nancy wolfs down Kit-Kat bars to keep her chemotherapy side-effects at bay, she shares with Jameson her knowledge that Robert Frost's poem "Stopping by Woods on a Snowy Evening" scans exactly to the old tune "Hernando's Hideaway." The two friends harmonize ruefully.

Object of disaffection: Jason Ritter in Third.
Photo: Joan Marcus

MOST DISTURBING AS the play begins are Jameson's own actions, which precipitate the evening's main event. Jameson reacts strongly and irrationally to her student, Third. Upon reading his first paper of the semester, on *King Lear*, she accuses him of plagiarism. Wasserstein took the central conceit of the play from a real incident: she heard the story of an undergraduate athlete accused of plagiarism and created her play around this resonant idea.

> LAURIE: Mr. Bull, anyone who is capable of quoting Reggie Jackson and *The Wretched of the Earth* in one speech did not write this paper on *King Lear*.
>
> THIRD: Professor Jameson, I did not plagiarize.
>
> LAURIE: No one with your verbal facility and interests would write this. This paper is not just intelligent. It is a comprehensive, intellectual reading of this play. I personally don't agree with it, but it's the work of an advanced scholar, not a wrestler, even from Groton.
>
> THIRD: Are you accusing me of stealing based on socio-economic profiling?

Jameson files a formal complaint with the college's Committee of Academic Standards and as the date of the hearing approaches, in a series of swift scenes that bring Act I to its conclusion, she and Third both seek to understand where this action has brought them.

"I have no idea why I can't exorcise this kid from my psyche," Jameson confesses in a scene with her analyst, when her worries about the war in Iraq, her father's condition, her daughter leaving home and her increasing distance from her husband should by rights be her first preoccupations.

Third brings his paper to Nancy (who sits on the Academic Standards Committee) for another opinion and we learn that the afternoon of the hearing Nancy is scheduled to have a bone marrow transplant:

> NANCY: Please try to understand that for me right now, it would be a luxury to just worry about you and your *King Lear* paper.

The end-of-the-semester hearing itself is the climactic scene in Act I. Third defends his paper and reveals a surprisingly nuanced understanding of Shakespeare, and he presents a heartfelt defense of his own honesty. Jameson's emotions, by contrast, are as irrational as everything in the larger world outside academia that she despises. In a brief and brutally honest fantasy interlude during the hearing, Wasserstein has Jameson stand, sweating through her hot flashes, remove her shirt, and cry out,

> LAURIE: If we permit this kind of unethical behavior within these gates, then inevitably it will proliferate outside them. And this man's

> type of easygoing, insidious charm and a-moral intelligence will
> continue to be rewarded with the most powerful positions in this
> country. That's why I need to be vigilant. I want to bang my fist on
> his head and say, "I know who you are, goddamn it! You're a walking
> red state!" And if I can't bang the President on the head, or the
> Vice-President on the head [. . .] why can't I hold Woodson Bull the
> Third accountable?

Following the hearing, Nancy rebukes Jameson for projecting onto one
innocent young man all that is wrong with the country and with her own
life. Jameson stands firm—and totally alone—as the act ends.

THIRD'S SECOND ACT moves off-campus to a nearby bar, where in a
lovely, low-keyed and insightful scene that takes place during spring break
the following semester, Jameson's twenty-year-old daughter Emily,
encounters Third, a stranger to her, tending bar. It is the night of "Shock
and Awe" as the US invades Baghdad, and the bar is empty. The Committee
of Academic Standards has decided the case in Third's favor, but because
of the plagiarism charges, he has been placed on academic probation and
he has lost his wrestling scholarship. His father, an alum of the college from
the Midwest, prone to depression and of surprisingly modest means, has
had a setback.

> EMILY: What did they accuse you of?
>
> THIRD: Let's start with I exist. [. . .] I'm a living dead white man. Just
> ask Laurie Jameson. She said I plagiarized my paper on *King Lear*
> because I'm a wrestler.

Third and Emily, two young people with a great deal in common, find
a powerful moment of mutual empathy, which is artfully crafted by
Wasserstein as they discover they share a favorite play, Thornton Wilder's
Our Town. The audience realizes they have much in common with George
and Emily from the earlier play. But in their more complex contemporary
circumstances, these decent young adults are wounded by the expectations
and passions of their parents and their parents' generation. At the end of
the play, they will both, independently, seek to make lives of their own by
leaving the orbit of the older generation that has made so many assumptions
about them.

Emily returns home from the bar towards midnight to confront her
mother. Jameson is awake late, unable to sleep, watching television and
remembering simpler times: Frankie Avalon, Bobbie Vinton and the pop
stars she loved in high school. She's tired and aware of her age. Emily has

Life, contextualized: Dianne Wiest and Amy Aquino in Third. *Photo: Joan Marcus*

run out of patience with her mother, and inflamed by her recent meeting with Third, she upbraids her,

> EMILY: You categorized him and you got it totally wrong. [. . .] You almost ruined that kid's life. [. . .] You decided he plagiarized because you needed that to be true. Just like they decided there were weapons of mass destruction because they needed that to be true.

Emily goes on to accuse her mother of neglecting her husband, a lesser light in academia, and driving him away from the family. She resents how her mother favors her older sister and her sister's lover, the Guggenheim prize-winning poet, even though the poet is cheating on her sister. And finally she tells Jameson how much she hates her interference in her own nascent love life. The audience understands both of the characters' points of view: Jameson is right to want more for her daughter and Emily is reacting to the strength with which her mother has expressed her own desires for Emily—desires that are, as always, linked to brand-names of intellectual and social achievement. As the argument escalates to its climax, Emily tells Jameson she is moving in with her boyfriend:

> EMILY: I want out of your world. [. . .] This is my chance not to be you.

At this moment, a beeper goes off. It is the police, alerting Jameson that her father is missing and Jameson pulls on her coat and runs into the night.

THE FINAL SCENES of the play move swiftly to the conclusion of the school year. Third takes the open microphone in his dormitory dining hall to confront his politically-correct classmates who are busy agitating for nude dorms, and demonstrating on campus against the Patriot Act. It's the first time he has spoken up in public about something that concerns him and he speaks movingly about the discrimination faced by student athletes, stigmatized as "jocks" and placed on academic probation or suspended at twice the rate of other students. Third links this grievance to a larger one,

> THIRD: I hear you guys saying all the time that you don't understand what's going on west of here, you know, in those states that show up red on Election Day in the heartland. Well, I can tell you that when someone like me, a Midwesterner, and athlete, on the fence politically, comes looking to you for answers, I am dismissed, even before I ask the goddamn question. And from my point of view, that's how you lost this country.

Jameson ends the semester finishing the class on Jane Austen she has agreed to teach for Nancy, who has been in chemotherapy. It is here that she recalls her courtship in the quote cited at the beginning of this essay, and we see how much her life has changed from these earlier, more optimistic times. As she ends the class, Nancy herself appears, her hair beginning to grow in after her treatments, and with a new view of life. She is looking forward to the future, she wants to reconnect with Jameson, and she tells her that, against all odds, she is starting a new phase of her life. During her cancer treatments, Nancy has met a rabbi—while on the chemo drip—fallen in love and accepted his proposal of marriage. She has come to Jameson because she recalls their shared, youthful mission to reform academia and the optimism she recalls from their youth. She wants to reconnect and start the third part of her life in a new mode, even in an unoptimistic historical time. Jameson understands and expresses her admiration for Nancy, but she herself isn't able to share Nancy's views or her feelings.

Third's penultimate scene lightly brushes against the *Lear* theme that Wasserstein has woven throughout the play, as Jameson comes to the campus on a stormy night to collect her father, who has wandered away from his home into the night. It is clearly the end of his life, and he begs Jameson to accept an apology for all the trouble he has caused her. Charles Durning and Dianne Wiest, deftly guided by director Daniel Sullivan, Wasserstein's long-time collaborator, played the scene lightly and it ends in a nostalgic dance, rather than the madness of Shakespeare's play. But the subtle emotions and power of the scene contributed to both Durning and Wiest receiving Lucille Lortel Award nominations. Wiest also received as 2006 Drama League Nomination for Distinguished Performance and Durning was honored as well by the organization as a "Previous Recipient." At the scene's end, Jameson takes her father home and we realize this is the last time we will see him.

IN THE FINAL SCENE, Jameson tells us her father has died. She has come to Third's dorm room after the college's graduation ceremony. She has finished the academic year. He is packing and leaving for a new life at Ohio State. Jameson has come, following her father's example, to apologize to him. She is leaving academia, going west to attend Nancy's wedding and she will stay there to start a new, unknown life. She gives Third her academic gown and confers on him her own blessing and honorary degree. He accepts her apology. As the play ends, Jameson bids him farewell and she leaves New England, the paradise she has lived in for her entire life.

As Wasserstein was working with Sullivan and the cast in final rehearsals, her own health was failing. Jameson's farewell at the end of the play echoes eerily and disconcertingly what was happening in her own life.

Wasserstein's ability to "have sympathy for everyone's point of view" has been much lauded and appreciated. In her final play, she questions the core beliefs that she embraced for so long in her work and in *Third* she found much in her former worldview to be wanting. There is a rueful and bleak tone to this last play, which, although leavened with some humor, gives the play its strong emotional resonance and connection with the disturbing contemporary events in the United States. For this work, Wasserstein was awarded a Lucille Lortel Lifetime Achievement Award, which in light of her quick decline, came as an appreciated but sad finale to her many awards, including her 1989 Pulitzer Prize. *Third's* three-month run at Lincoln Center Theater was warmly received by the New York press and was sold out almost as soon at it was announced. Although the play was extended for a week to try to accommodate the demand for tickets, the company was emotionally unable to continue, given Wasserstein's own circumstances. Her memorial, attended by more than 1,600 people, was held at Lincoln Center Theater in March 2006.

PLAYS PRODUCED IN
NEW YORK

PLAYS PRODUCED ON BROADWAY

○ ○ ○ ○ ○

FIGURES IN PARENTHESES following a play's title give the number of performances from the press-opening date. These figures do not include previews or extra nonprofit performances. In the case of a transfer, the prior run is noted but not added to the figure in parentheses.

Plays marked with an asterisk (*) were still in a projected run June 1, 2006. Their number of performances is figured through May 31, 2006.

In a listing of a show's numbers—dances, sketches, musical scenes, etc.—the titles of songs are identified wherever possible by their appearance in quotation marks (").

HOLDOVERS FROM PREVIOUS SEASONS

BROADWAY SHOWS THAT were running on June 1, 2005 are listed below. More detailed information about them appears in previous *Best Plays* volumes of the years in which they opened. Important cast changes since opening night are recorded in the Cast Replacements section in this volume.

*The Phantom of the Opera (7,649). Musical with book by Richard Stilgoe and Andrew Lloyd Webber; music by Andrew Lloyd Webber; lyrics by Charles Hart; additional lyrics by Richard Stilgoe; adapted from the novel by Gaston Leroux. Opened January 26, 1988.

*Beauty and the Beast (4,975). Musical with book by Linda Woolverton; music by Alan Menken; lyrics by Howard Ashman and Tim Rice. Opened April 18, 1994.

*Rent (4,195). Transfer from Off Broadway of the musical with book, music and lyrics by Jonathan Larson. Opened Off Off Broadway January 26, 1996 and Off Broadway February 13, 1996 where it played 56 performances through March 31, 1996; transferred to Broadway April 29, 1996.

*Chicago (3,973). Revival of the musical based on the play by Maurine Dallas Watkins; book by Fred Ebb and Bob Fosse; music by John Kander; lyrics by Fred Ebb; original production directed and choreographed by Bob Fosse. Opened November 14, 1996.

*The Lion King (3,566). Musical adapted from the screenplay by Irene Mecchi, Jonathan Roberts and Linda Woolverton; book by Roger Allers and Irene Mecchi; music by Elton John; lyrics by Tim Rice; additional music and lyrics by Lebo M, Mark Mancina, Jay Rifkin, Julie Taymor and Hans Zimmer. Opened November 13, 1997.

*The Producers (2,129). Musical with book by Mel Brooks and Thomas Meehan; music and lyrics by Mel Brooks. Opened April 19, 2001.

***Mamma Mia!** (1,920). Musical with book by Catherine Johnson; music and lyrics by Benny Andersson and Björn Ulvaeus, some songs with Stig Anderson. Opened October 18, 2001.

***Hairspray** (1,578). Musical with book by Mark O'Donnell and Thomas Meehan; music by Marc Shaiman; lyrics by Marc Shaiman and Scott Wittman; based on the film by John Waters. Opened August 15, 2002.

Movin' Out (1,303). Dance musical based on the songs of Billy Joel; with music and lyrics by Mr. Joel; conceived by Twyla Tharp. Opened October 24, 2002. (Closed December 11, 2005)

***Avenue Q** (1,182). Transfer from Off Off Broadway of the musical with book by Jeff Whitty; music and lyrics by Robert Lopez and Jeff Marx. Opened July 31, 2003.

***Wicked** (1,079). Musical with book by Winnie Holzman; music and lyrics by Stephen Schwartz; based on a novel by Gregory Maguire. Opened October 30, 2003.

Fiddler on the Roof (781). Revival of the musical with book by Joseph Stein; music by Jerry Bock; lyrics by Sheldon Harnick; based on stories by Sholom Aleichem. Opened February 26, 2004. (Closed January 8, 2006)

Brooklyn: The Musical (284). Musical with book, music and lyrics by Mark Schoenfeld and Barri McPherson. Opened October 21, 2004. (Closed June 26, 2005)

700 Sundays (163). Solo performance piece by Billy Crystal; additional material Alan Zweibel. Opened December 5, 2004. Production on hiatus March 14–20, 2005 and April 18–24, 2005. (Closed June 12, 2005)

La Cage aux Folles (229). Revival of the musical with book by Harvey Fierstein; music and lyrics by Jerry Herman; based on the play *La Cage aux Folles* by Jean Poiret. Opened December 9, 2004. (Closed June 26, 2005)

***Dirty Rotten Scoundrels** (518). Musical with book by Jeffrey Lane; music and lyrics by David Yazbek; based on the film by Dale Launer, Stanley Shapiro and Paul Henning. Opened March 3, 2005.

***Spamalot** (504). Musical with book and lyrics by Eric Idle; music by John Du Prez and Mr. Idle; based on the motion picture *Monty Python and the Holy Grail.* Opened March 17, 2005.

Who's Afraid of Virginia Woolf? (177). Revival of the play by Edward Albee. Opened March 20, 2005. (Closed September 4, 2005)

The Glass Menagerie (120). Revival of the play by Tennessee Williams. Opened March 22, 2005. (Closed July 3, 2005)

Jackie Mason: Freshly Squeezed (172). Solo performance piece by Mr. Mason. Opened March 23, 2005. (Closed September 4, 2005)

All Shook Up (213). Musical with book by Joe DiPietro; music and lyrics by various artists; inspired by the songs of Elvis Presley. Opened March 24, 2005. (Closed September 25, 2005)

***Doubt, a Parable** (488). Transfer of the Off Broadway play by John Patrick Shanley. Opened March 31, 2005.

Julius Caesar (81). Revival of the play by William Shakespeare. Opened April 3, 2005. (Closed June 12, 2005)

Steel Magnolias (136). Revival of the play by Robert Harling. Opened April 4, 2005. (Closed July 31, 2005)

On Golden Pond (93). Revival of the play by Ernest Thompson. Opened April 7, 2005. (Closed June 26, 2005)

The Pillowman (185). By Martin McDonagh. Opened April 10, 2005. (Closed September 18, 2005)

*Lincoln Center Theater production of **The Light in the Piazza** (467). Musical with book by Craig Lucas; music and lyrics by Adam Guettel; based on the novella by Elizabeth Spencer. Opened April 18, 2005.

Roundabout Theatre Company production of **A Streetcar Named Desire** (73). Revival of the play by Tennessee Williams. Opened April 26, 2005. (Closed July 3, 2005)

Chitty Chitty Bang Bang (285). Musical with book by Ian Fleming, adapted for the stage by Jeremy Sams; music and lyrics by Richard M. Sherman and Robert B. Sherman; based on the MGM/United Artists film. Opened April 28, 2005. (Closed December 31, 2005)

Glengarry Glen Ross (137). Revival of the play by David Mamet. Opened May 1, 2005. (Closed August 28, 2005)

*The 25th Annual Putnam County Spelling Bee (450). Transfer of the musical with book by Rachel Sheinkin; music and lyrics by William Finn; conceived by Rebecca Feldman; additional material by Jay Reiss. Opened May 2, 2005.

Sweet Charity (279). Revival of the musical with book by Neil Simon; music by Cy Coleman; lyrics by Dorothy Fields. Opened May 4, 2005. (Closed December 31, 2005)

PLAYS PRODUCED JUNE 1, 2005–MAY 31, 2006

Manhattan Theatre Club production of **After the Night and the Music** (38). By Elaine May. Lynne Meadow artistic director, Barry Grove executive producer, in association with Julian Schlossberg and Roy Furman, at the Biltmore Theatre. Opened June 1, 2005. (Closed July 3, 2005)

Curtain Raiser

Gloria	J. Smith-Cameron	Bartender	Jere Burns
Keith	Eddie Korbich	Another Man	Brian Kerwin
Brittany	Deirdre Madigan	Another Woman	Joanna Glushak

Giving Up Smoking

Joanne	Jeannie Berlin	Mel	Brian Kerwin
Sherman	Jere Burns	Kathleen	J. Smith-Cameron

Swing Time

Mitzi Grade	J. Smith-Cameron	Gail	Jeannie Berlin
Darryl Grade	Jere Burns	Ron	Brian Kerwin

Understudies: Mr. Korbich—Joel Blum; Mses. Madigan, Berlin (Gail)—Joanna Glushak; Mses. Smith-Cameron, Berlin—Deirdre Madigan; Messrs. Burns, Kerwin—Peter Marx.

Directed by Daniel Sullivan; choreography, Randy Skinner; scenery, John Lee Beatty; costumes, Michael Krass; lighting, Peter Kaczorowski; sound and music, John Gromada; wigs and hair, Paul

Swingers? Brian Kerwin, J. Smith-Cameron and Jeannie Berlin in After the Night and the Music. *Photo: Joan Marcus*

Huntley; casting, Nancy Piccione and David Caparelliotis; press, Boneau/Bryan-Brown, Chris Boneau, Jim Byk, Aaron Meier, Erika Creagh.

Presented in two parts.

Comic tales of urban love and disaffection.

Mark Twain Tonight! (15). Revival of the solo performance piece by Hal Holbrook; based on the writings of Mark Twain. Produced by Ira Pittelman, Jeffrey Sine, Scott Rudin, Max Cooper, Ben Sprecher, William P. Miller, Michael Moore, Elliott Martin, Eve Holbrook, Emanuel Azenberg, at the Brooks Atkinson Theatre. Opened June 9, 2005. (Closed June 26, 2005)

Mark Twain .... Hal Holbrook

Press, Bill Evans and Associates.

Presented in two parts.

Recreates Mr. Twain's platform performances of the late 19th century. First New York presentation of record was given at the Lambs (10/30/1955). First Off Broadway presentation of record was given at the 41st Street Theatre (4/6–9/6/1959; 176 performances). First Broadway presentation of record was given at the Longacre Theatre (3/23/66–6/11/66; 85 performances). Mr. Holbrook received the 1966 Tony Award for best actor in a play. The 2005–06 production was the second Broadway revival.

Roundabout Theatre Company production of **The Constant Wife** (77). Revival of the play by W. Somerset Maugham. Todd Haimes artistic director, Harold Wolpert managing director, Julia C. Levy executive director, at the American Airlines Theatre. Opened June 16, 2005. (Closed August 21, 2005)

Sage talk: Hal Holbrook in Mark Twain Tonight! *Photo: Chuck Stewart*

Mrs. Culver .... Lynn Redgrave
Bentley .... Denis Holmes
Martha .... Enid Graham
Barbara Fawcett .... Kathleen McNenny
Constance Middleton .... Kate Burton

Marie-Louise .... Kathryn Meisle
John Middleton .... Michael Cumpsty
Bernard Kersal .... John Dossett
Mortimer Durham .... John Ellison Conlee

Understudies: Ms. Burton—Kathleen McNenny; Mses. Graham, Meisle—Tara Falk; Mses. Redgrave, McNenny—Lucy Martin; Messrs. Cumpsty, Dossett—Tony Carlin; Messrs. Conlee, Holmes—Bob Ari.

Directed by Mark Brokaw; scenery, Allen Moyer; costumes, Michael Krass; lighting, Mary Louise Geiger; sound, David Van Tieghem and Jill BC DuBoff; music, Mr. Van Tieghem; wigs and hair, Paul Huntley; production stage manager, Lisa Buxbaum; press, Boneau/Bryan-Brown, Adrian Bryan-Brown, Matt Polk, Jessica Johnson, Joe Perrotta.

Time: 1926–27. Place: The Middleton's home in London. Presented in two parts.

Domestic comedy on the social mores of privileged Londoners. First presentation of record was given in Cleveland (11/1/1926). A 1926–27 *Best Plays* choice, the original Broadway production opened at Maxine Elliott's Theatre (11/29/1926–8/13/1927; 296 performances) with Ethel Barrymore. The 2005–06 production was the fourth Broadway revival.

Primo (35). Solo performance piece by Antony Sher; adapted from *If This Is a Man* by Primo Levi. Produced by Bill Kenwright and Thelma Holt, in association with the National Theatre (UK), at the Music Box. Opened July 11, 2005. (Closed August 14, 2005)

Primo Levi .... Antony Sher

Directed by Richard Wilson; scenery and costumes, Hildegard Bechtler; lighting, Paul Pyant and David Howe; sound, Rich Walsh; music, Jonathan Goldstein; stage managers, David Hyslop and Thomas Vowles; press, Philip Rinaldi Publicity, Philip Rinaldi, Barbara Carroll.

Happy family: Lynn Redgrave, Michael Cumpsty and Kate Burton in The Constant Wife. *Photo: Joan Marcus*

Presented without intermission.

Solo performance piece recounting Mr. Levi's survival in a World War II concentration camp. First presentation of record was given at the National Theatre's Cottesloe Theatre (9/30–12/1/2004) before a run at London's Hampstead Theatre (2/23–3/19/2005).

The Blonde in the Thunderbird (9). Solo performance piece by Mitzie Welch and Ken Welch; based on *Keeping Secrets* and *After the Fall* by Suzanne Somers. Produced by Alan Hamel at the Brooks Atkinson Theatre. Opened July 17, 2005. (Closed July 23, 2005)

Performed by Ms. Somers.

Directed by the Welches; scenery and lighting, Roger Ball; sound, Robert Ludwig; orchestrations, Doug Walter; music direction, Mr. Walter; music coordination, John Miller; production stage manager, Robert Bennett; press, the Publicity Office.

Presented without intermission.

The roller-coaster existence of a television star in the confessional of a legitimate theater. First presentation of record was given in Cincinnati, Ohio at the Taft Theatre (8/30/2003).

MUSICAL NUMBERS
"The Blonde in the Thunderbird"
(Ken Welch and Mitzie Welch)
"Fifty Percent"
(Alan Bergman, Marilyn Bergman and Billy Goldenberg)
"How Do I Say I Love You"
(Ken Welch and Mitzie Welch)
"If I Could Live It All Over Again"
(Ken Welch and Mitzie Welch)

"Inventory"
(Ken Welch and Mitzie Welch)
"No More Secrets"
(Ken Welch and Mitzie Welch)
"If I Only Had a Brain"
(E.Y. Harburg and Harold Arlen)
"Take Back Your Mink"
(Frank Loesser)
"Pick Yourself Up"
(Dorothy Fields, Jerome Kern, and Ken Welch and Mitzie Welch)
"That Face"
(Alan Bergman and Lew Spence)
"If You Knew Susie"
(Joe Meyer and B.G. DeSylva)
"Johnny's Theme" (from *The Tonight Show Starring Johnny Carson*)
(Paul Anka and Johnny Carson)
"Laington's Reel"
(Celtic Fiddle Festival)
"Repartee" (from *Underground Sounds of Holland*)
(Kenneth Doekhie and Jaimy)
"Self-Portrait"
(Edward Kleban)
"She Loves Me"
(Jerry Bock and Sheldon Harnick)
"The Phil Donahue Show Theme"
(Frank Vincent Malfa)
"Wake Up Little Susie"
(Boudleaux Bryant and Felice Bryant)

Wheeee: Suzanne Somers in The Blonde in the Thunderbird. *Photo: Paul Parks*

Lennon (49). Musical with book by Don Scardino; music and lyrics by John Lennon. Produced by Allan McKeown, Edgar Lansbury, Clear Channel Entertainment, Jeffrey A. Sine, in association with Yoko Ono Lennon, at the Broadhurst Theatre. Opened August 14, 2005. (Closed September 24, 2005)

Performed by Will Chase, Chuck Cooper, Julie Danao-Salkin, Mandy Gonzalez, Marcy Harriell, Chad Kimball, Terrence Mann, Julia Murney, Michael Potts.

Orchestra: Jeffrey Klitz music director, keyboards; Dave Keyes associate music director, keyboards; John Benthal, Jack Cavari guitar; David Anderson bass; Tom Murray reeds; Tony Kadleck trumpet; Larry Farrell trombone; Dave Yee percussion; Warren Odze drums.

Standbys: Mses. Danao-Salkin, Gonzalez—Rona Figueroa; Messrs. Cooper, Mann, Potts—Mark Richard Ford; Mses. Harriell, Murney—Nicole Lewis; Messrs. Chase, Kimball, Mann—Darin Murphy.

Directed by Mr. Scardino; choreography, Joseph Malone; scenery and projections, John Arnone; costumes, Jane Greenwood; lighting, Natasha Katz; sound, Bobby Aitken; orchestrations, Harold Wheeler; music supervision and arrangements, Lon Hoyt; music coordination, John Miller; executive producer, Nina Lannan; associate producer, Louise Forlenza; casting, Janet Foster; production stage manager, Arthur Gaffin; stage manager, Laurie Goldfeder; press, Boneau/Bryan-Brown, Chris Boneau, Susanne Tighe, Juliana Hannett.

Presented in two parts.

Celebration of the life and music of John Lennon. First presentation of record was given at the Orpheum Theatre in San Francisco (4/19–5/14/2005).

ACT I

"New York City" .... Will, Company
"Mother" .... Chad, Will, Julie, Company
"Look at Me" .... Company
"Money" .... Mandy, Marcy, Julia, Julie
"Twist and Shout" .... Mandy, Marcy, Julia, Julie
"Instant Karma" .... Chuck, Company

Peace sign: The company of Lennon. *Photo: Joan Marcus*

Loving family: Jill Clayburgh, Susan Kelechi Watson, Richard Thomas and Matthew Morrison in A Naked Girl on the Appian Way. *Photo: Joan Marcus*

"India, India" .... Julie, Mandy, Will, Company
"Real Love (Boys and Girls)" .... Chuck, Will
"Mind Games" .... Chad, Julie, Company
"The Ballad of John and Yoko" .... Company
"How Do You Sleep?" .... Mandy
"God" .... Michael, Company
"Give Peace a Chance" .... Terrence, Company

ACT II

"Power to the People" .... Company
"Woman Is the Nigger of the World" .... Marcy, Women
"Attica State" .... Michael, Julie
"Gimme Some Truth" .... Will, Company
"I'm Losing You"/"I'm Moving On" .... Chad, Julie
"I'm Stepping Out" .... Will, Chuck, Company
"I Don't Want to Lose You" .... Terrence, Julie, Chad
"Whatever Gets You Through the Night" .... Marcy, Will
"Woman" .... Will, Company
"Beautiful Boy" .... Julia, Company
"Watching the Wheels" .... Will, Chad, Michael, Terrence
"(Just Like) Starting Over" .... Chuck, Company
"Grow Old with Me" .... Julie
"Imagine" .... John, Company

Roundabout Theatre Company production of **A Naked Girl on the Appian Way** (69). By Richard Greenberg. Todd Haimes artistic director, Harold Wolpert managing director, Julia C. Levy executive director, at the American Airlines Theatre. Opened October 6, 2005. (Closed December 4, 2005)

Bess Lapin ....Jill Clayburgh
Jeffrey Lapin .... Richard Thomas
Sadie ....Ann Guilbert
Elaine ....Leslie Ayvazian

Juliet Lapin.................... Susan Kelechi Watson
Thad Lapin ....Matthew Morrison
Bill Lapin .... James Yaegashi

Understudies: Ms. Clayburgh—Charlotte Maier; Mr. Thomas—Ray Virta; Ms. Watson—Phyllis Johnson; Mr. Morrison—Terrence Riordan; Mr. Yaegashi—James Seol; Ms. Guilbert—Nancy Franklin; Ms. Ayvazian—Charlotte Maier.

Directed by Doug Hughes; scenery, John Lee Beatty; costumes, Catherine Zuber; lighting, Peter Kaczorowski; sound and music, David Van Tieghem; casting, Jim Carnahan, Mele Nagler and Joanne DeNaut; production stage manager, Leslie C. Lyter; press, Boneau/Bryan-Brown, Adrian Bryan-Brown, Matt Polk, Jessica Johnson, Joe Perrotta.

Time: Early June. Place: A beautiful house in the Hamptons. Presented without intermission.

A happy, prosperous family has its serenity disturbed when adopted siblings fall in love in this domestic comedy. First presentation of record was given at the South Coast Repertory in Costa Mesa, California (4/8–5/8/2005).

Trafficking: Eugenio Derbez in Latinologues.
Photo: Joan Marcus

Latinologues (93). By Rick Najera. Produced by Tate Entertainment Group, in association with Juan Carlos Zapata, Rick Najera, AEG Live, Rene Lavan, Icon Entertainment, TATI Incorporated, Richard Martini Entertainment and Alan Spivak, at the Helen Hayes Theatre. Opened October 13, 2005. (Closed December 31, 2005)

Performed by Eugenio Derbez, Rene Lavan, Mr. Najera, Shirley A. Rumierk.

Understudies: Carlo D'Amore, Ivette Sosa.

Directed by Cheech Marin; costumes, Santiago; lighting, Kevin Adams; sound, T. Richard Fitzgerald; video, Dennis Diamond; associate producer, Kevin Benson; casting, Elsie Stark/Stark

Naked Productions; production stage manager, Arabella Powell; press, Bill Evans and Associates, Jim Randolph, Susie Albin, Trina Bardusco.

Presented without intermission.

Comic spoof of Latino and Latina stereotypes performed in brief sketches. First presentation of record was given at the South Coast Repertory's third annual Festival Latino (8/9/1997).

Manhattan Theatre Club production of **Absurd Person Singular** (56). Revival of the play by Alan Ayckbourn. Lynne Meadow artistic director, Barry Grove executive director, at the Biltmore Theatre. Opened October 18, 2005. (Closed December 4, 2005)

Jane	Clea Lewis	Marion	Deborah Rush
Sidney	Alan Ruck	Eva	Mireille Enos
Ronald	Paxton Whitehead	Geoffrey	Sam Robards

Understudies: Mses. Lewis, Enos—Crista Moore.

Directed by John Tillinger; scenery, John Lee Beatty; costumes, Jane Greenwood; lighting, Brian MacDevitt; sound, Bruce Ellman; casting, Nancy Piccione and David Caparelliotis; production stage manager, Diane DiVita; press, Boneau/Bryan-Brown, Chris Boneau, Jim Byk, Aaron Meier.

Time: Last Christmas; this Christmas; next Christmas. Place: The kitchens of Sidney and Jane, Geoffrey and Eva, and Ronald and Marion. Presented in three parts.

Three couples interact over three consecutive Christmases as their social roles undergo gradual reversals. First presentation of record was given at the Criterion Theatre in London (7/3/1973). The first Broadway presentation of record was given at the Music Box (10/8/1974–3/6/1976; 591 performances) with Sandy Dennis, Richard Kiley, Geraldine Page, Tony Roberts, Carole Shelley and Larry Blyden. The 2005–06 production was the first Broadway revival.

Christmas cheer: Sam Robards and Mireille Enos in Absurd Person Singular. *Photo: Joan Marcus*

In My Life (61). Musical with book, music and lyrics by Joseph Brooks. Produced by Watch Hill Productions and TBF Music Corporation at the Music Box. Opened October 20, 2005. (Closed December 11, 2005)

Vera	Chiara Navarra	Al	Michael J. Farina
J.T.	Christopher J. Hanke	Samantha	Laura Jordan
Jenny	Jessica Boevers	Liz	Roberta Gumbel
Winston	David Turner	Nick	Michael Halling

Ensemble: Courtney Balan, Carmen Keels, Kilty Reidy, Brynn Williams.

Orchestra: Henry Aronson conductor; Greg Dlugos associate conductor, keyboards; Ted Kooshian, Maggie Torres, Fran Minarik keyboards; Bruce Uchitel, JJ McGeehan guitar; Randy Landau bass; Brian Brake drums.

Understudies: Ms. Navarra—Brynn Williams; Mr. Hanke—Michael Halling, Jonathan Groff; Ms. Boevers—Laura Jordan, Courtney Balan; Mr. Turner—Kilty Reidy; Ms. Gumbel—Carmen Keels; Mr. Farina—Kilty Reidy; Mr. Halling—Jonathan Groff, Kilty Reidy; Ms. Jordan—Courtney Balan, Carmen Keels.

Swing: Jonathan Groff.

Directed by Mr. Brooks; choreography, Richard Stafford; scenery, Allen Moyer; costumes, Catherine Zuber; lighting, Christopher Akerlind; sound, John H. Shivers; projections, Wendall K. Harrington; wigs and hair, Tom Watson; orchestrations, Kinny Landrum; music direction, Henry Aronson; music coordination, Michael Keller; casting, Dave Clemmons Casting; production stage manager, Jane Grey; press, Richard Kornberg and Associates, Richard Kornberg, Don Summa, Laura Kaplow-Goldman.

Presented without intermission.

Boy with Tourette syndrome meets girl with obsessive-compulsive disorder and complications ensue in a musical love story.

MUSICAL NUMBERS

"Life Turns on a Dime"	Vera, J.T., Jenny
"It Almost Feels Like Love"	J.T., Jenny
"Perfect for an Opera"	Winston
"What a Strange Life We Live"	Jenny
"Doomed"	Winston, Nick, Company
"What a Strange Life We Live"	Vera
"Sempre Mio Rimani"	Liz
"I Am My Mother's Son"	J.T.
"Life Turns on a Dime" (Reprise)	Jenny
"In this World"	Al
"What a Strange Life We Live"	Nick
"Headaches"	Winston, Nick, Vera, Liz, Company
"When I Sing"	J.T.
"Secrets"	Winston, Company
"In My Life"	Jenny, J.T
"A Ride on the Wheel"	Nick, Samantha, J.T., Company
"Perfect for an Opera" (Reprise)	Winston, Liz, Nick, Vera
"Didn't Have to Love You"	Jenny, J.T
"Listen to Your Mouth"	Winston, Al
"When She Danced"	Vera, Liz
"In This World" (Reprise)	Al
"Not This Day"	Al
"Floating on Air"	J.T.
"Not This Day"	J.T, Jenny, Liz, Nick, Vera, Al, Company

*The Odd Couple (244). Revival of the play by Neil Simon. Produced by Ira Pittelman, Jeffrey Sine, Ben Sprecher, Max Cooper, Scott E. Nederlander and Emanuel Azenberg at the Brooks Atkinson Theatre. Opened October 27, 2005.

Odd sextet: Nathan Lane, Lee Wilkof, Rob Bartlett, Matthew Broderick, Brad Garrett and Peter Frechette in The Odd Couple. *Photo: Carol Rosegg*

Speed	Rob Bartlett	Oscar Madison	Nathan Lane
Murray	Brad Garrett	Felix Ungar	Matthew Broderick
Roy	Peter Frechette	Gwendolyn Pigeon	Olivia d'Abo
Vinnie	Lee Wilkof	Cecily Pigeon	Jessica Stone

Understudies: Mr. Broderick—Peter Frechette; Messrs. Lane, Garrett, Bartlett, Frechette, Wilkof—Gene Gabriel; Messrs. Broderick, Garrett, Bartlett, Frechette, Wilkof—Marc Grapey; Mses. d'Abo, Stone—Christy Pusz.

Directed by Joe Mantello; scenery, John Lee Beatty; costumes, Ann Roth; lighting, Kenneth Posner; sound, Peter Fitzgerald; music, Marc Shaiman; wigs and hair, David Brian Brown; associate producer, Roy Furman and Jay Binder; casting, Bernard Telsey Casting; production stage manager, William Joseph Barnes; press, Bill Evans and Associates, Jim Randolph.

Time: Summer, 1965. Place: Oscar Madison's Riverside Drive apartment. Presented in two parts.

A mismatched pair of divorced men attempt cohabitation in swinging New York City. A 1964–65 *Best Plays* choice, the original Broadway production opened at the Plymouth Theatre (3/10/65–7/2/67; 966 performances). The production received 1965 Tony Awards for best author, best actor (Walter Matthau), best scenic design (Oliver Smith) and best direction of a play (Mike Nichols). First presentation of record was given at Boston's Colonial Theatre (2/3/1965) before another pre-Broadway run at the National Theatre in Washington, DC (2/22/1965). The 2005–06 production was the second Broadway revival.

*Sweeney Todd, the Demon Barber of Fleet Street (240). Revival of the musical with book by Hugh Wheeler; music and lyrics by Stephen Sondheim; from an adaptation by Christopher Bond. Produced by Tom Viertel, Steven Baruch, Marc Routh, Richard Frankel, Ambassador Theatre Group, Adam Kenwright, Tulchin/Bartner/Bagert, at the Eugene O'Neill Theatre. Opened November 3, 2005.

Baker, butcher: Patti LuPone and Michael Cerveris in Sweeney Todd. *Photo: Paul Kolnik*

Mrs. Lovett .... Patti LuPone
(tuba, orchestra bells, percussion)
Sweeney Todd .... Michael Cerveris
(guitar, orchestra bells, percussion)
Judge Turpin .... Mark Jacoby
(trumpet, orchestra bells, percussion)
Pirelli .... Donna Lynne Champlin
(accordion, keyboard, flute)
Tobias .... Manoel Felciano
(violin, clarinet, keyboard)

The Beadle .... Alexander Gemignani
(keyboard, trumpet)
Jonas Fogg .... John Arbo
(bass)
Beggar Woman .... Diana DiMarzio
(clarinet)
Anthony .... Benjamin Magnuson
(cello, keyboard)
Johanna .... Lauren Molina
(cello)

Standbys: Messrs. Cerveris, Jacoby—Merwin Foard (orchestra bells, percussion); Mses. Lupone, Champlin—Dorothy Stanley (violin, keyboard, orchestra bells, percussion); Messrs. Magnuson, Felciano, Gemignani—Benjamin Eakeley (keyboard, clarinet); Mses. Molina, DiMarzio—Elisa Winter (cello, accordion, keyboard, guitar); Messrs. Cerveris, Jacoby, Gemignani, Arbo—David Hess (trumpet, orchestra bells, percussion); Mr. Arbo—Stephen McIntyre (bass, cello); Mses. DiMarzio, Champlin—Jessica Wright (flute, clarinet, violin).

Directed by John Doyle; scenery and costumes, Mr. Doyle; lighting, Richard G. Jones; sound, Dan Moses Schreier; wigs and hair, Paul Huntley; orchestrations and music supervision, Sarah Travis; music coordination, John Miller; casting, Bernard Telsey Casting; production stage manager, Adam John Hunter; press, Barlow-Hartman Public Relations, John Barlow, Michael Hartman, Rick Miramontez, Leslie Baden.

Presented in two parts.

A wronged barber wreaks bloody revenge on his enemies as his female partner profits from her new source of meat for pies. A 1978–79 *Best Plays* choice, the original Broadway production opened at the Uris (now Gershwin) Theatre (3/1/1979–6/29/1980; 557 performances). That production received 1979 Tony Awards for best musical, best book, best original score, best actor in a musical (Len Cariou), best actress in a musical (Angela Lansbury), best scenic design (Eugene Lee), best costume design (Franne Lee), best direction of a musical (Harold Prince). The 2005–06 production was the second Broadway revival. It received 2006 Tony Awards for best direction of a musical (Mr. Doyle) and best orchestrations (Ms. Travis). The original play by George Dibdin Pitt was first presented at London's Britannia Theatre in 1842. The 2005–06 production originated at the Watermill Theatre (UK).

ACT I

"The Ballad of Sweeney Todd" .... Company
"No Place Like London" .... Anthony, Sweeney, Beggar Woman
"The Barber and His Wife" .... Sweeney
"The Worst Pies in London" .... Mrs. Lovett
"Poor Thing" .... Mrs. Lovett
"My Friends" .... Sweeney, Mrs. Lovett
"Green Finch and Linnet Bird" .... Johanna
"Ah, Miss" .... Anthony, Beggar Woman
"Johanna" .... Anthony
"Pirelli's Miracle Elixir" .... Tobias, Sweeney, Mrs. Lovett, Company
"The Contest" .... Pirelli
"Johanna" .... Judge Turpin
"Wait" .... Mrs. Lovett
"Kiss Me" .... Johanna, Anthony
"Ladies in Their Sensitivities" .... The Beadle
"Quartet" .... Johanna, Anthony, Johanna,
Anthony, The Beadle, Judge Turpin
"Pretty Women" .... Sweeney, Judge Turpin
"Epiphany" .... Sweeney
"A Little Priest" .... Sweeney, Mrs. Lovett

ACT II

"God, That's Good!" .... Tobias, Mrs. Lovett, Sweeney, Company
"Johanna" .... Anthony, Sweeney, Johanna, Beggar Woman
"By the Sea" .... Mrs. Lovett
"Not While I'm Around" .... Tobias, Mrs. Lovett
"Parlor Songs" .... The Beadle, Mrs. Lovett
"City on Fire!" .... Tobias, Johanna, Anthony, Company
"Final Sequence" .... Anthony, Beggar Woman, Sweeney,
Judge Turpin, Mrs. Lovett, Johanna, Tobias
"The Ballad of Sweeney Todd" .... Company

*Jersey Boys: The Story of Frankie Valli and the Four Seasons (236). Musical with book by Marshall Brickman and Rick Elice; music by Bob Gaudio; lyrics by Bob Crewe. Produced by Dodger Theatricals, Joseph J. Grano, Pelican Group, Tamara and Kevin Kinsella, in association with Latitude Link, Rick Steiner/Osher/Staton/Bell/Mayerson Group, at the August Wilson Theatre. Opened November 6, 2005.

Hal Miller; others	Tituss Burgess	Mary Delgado; others	Jennifer Naimo
Hank Majewski; others	Steve Gouveia	Miss Frankie Nolan; others	Erica Piccininni
Bob Crewe; others	Peter Gregus	Bob Gaudio	Daniel Reichard
Tommy DeVito	Christian Hoff	Frankie's Mother; others	Sara Schmidt
Nick DeVito; others	Donnie Kehr	Nick Massi	J. Robert Spencer
Joey; others	Michael Longoria	Frankie Valli	John Lloyd Young
Gyp DeCarlo; others	Mark Lotito	Thugs	Ken Dow, Joe Payne

Orchestra: Ron Melrose conductor, keyboard; Deborah N. Hurwitz associate conductor, keyboard; Stephen "Hoops" Snyder keyboard; Joe Payne guitar; Ken Dow bass; Matt Hong, Ben Kono reeds; David Spier trumpet; Kevin Dow drums.

Understudies: Mr. Hoff—Donnie Kehr, John Leone, Matthew Scott; Mr. Spencer—Steve Gouveia, John Leone; Mr. Young—Michael Longoria, Dominic Nolfi, Matthew Scott; Mr. Reichard—Steve

No angels: J. Robert Spencer, John Lloyd Young, Daniel Reichard and Christian Hoff in Jersey Boys. *Photo: Joan Marcus*

Gouveia, Dominic Nolfi, Matthew Scott; Mr. Lotito—Donnie Kehr, John Leone; Mr. Gregus—Donnie Kehr, John Leone.

Swings: Heather Ferguson, John Leone, Dominic Nolfi, Matthew Scott.

Directed by Des McAnuff; choreography, Sergio Trujillo; scenery, Klara Zieglerova; costumes, Jess Goldstein; lighting, Howell Binkley; sound, Steve Canyon Kennedy; projections, Michael Clark; wigs and hair, Charles G. LaPointe; fight direction, Steve Rankin; orchestrations, Steve Orich; music direction, Ron Melrose; executive producer, Sally Campbell Morse; associate producer, Lauren Mitchell, Rhoda Mayerson and Stage Entertainment; production stage manager, Richard Hester; press, Boneau/Bryan-Brown, Adrian Bryan-Brown, Susanne Tighe, Heath Schwartz.

Presented in two parts.

A musical celebration of the members of a singing group and the vicissitudes of their lives and careers. First presentation of record was given at the La Jolla Playhouse (10/19–11/21/2004). The Broadway production received 2006 Tony Awards for best musical, best actor in a musical (Mr. Young), best featured actor in a musical (Mr. Hoff) and best lighting design of a musical (Mr. Binkley).

ACT I

"Ces Soirées-La (Oh What a Night)" .... French Rap Star, Backup Group
"Silhouettes" .... Tommy DeVito, Nick Massi,
Nick DeVito, Frankie Castelluccio
"You're the Apple of My Eye" .... Tommy DeVito, Nick Massi, Nick DeVito
"I Can't Give You Anything But Love" .... Frankie Castelluccio
"Earth Angel" .... Tommy DeVito, Company
"Sunday Kind of Love" .... Frankie Valli, Tommy DeVito,
Nick Massi, Nick's Date
"My Mother's Eyes" .... Frankie Valli
"I Go Ape" .... The Four Lovers

"(Who Wears) Short Shorts" .... Royal Teens
"I'm in the Mood for Love"/"Moody's Mood for Love" .... Frankie Valli
"Cry for Me" .... Bob Gaudio, Frankie Valli,
Tommy DeVito, Nick Massi
"An Angel Cried" .... Hal Miller, Rays
"I Still Care" .... Frankie Nolan, Romans
"Trance" .... Billy Dixon, Topix
"Sherry" .... Four Seasons
"Big Girls Don't Cry" .... Four Seasons
"Walk Like a Man" .... Four Seasons
"December, 1963 (Oh What a Night)" .... Bob Gaudio, Company
"My Boyfriend's Back" .... Angels
"My Eyes Adored You" .... Frankie Valli, Mary Delgado, Four Seasons
"Dawn (Go Away)" .... Four Seasons
"Walk Like a Man" (Reprise) .... Company

ACT II

"Big Man in Town" .... Four Seasons
"Beggin'" .... Four Seasons
"Stay" .... Bob Gaudio, Frankie Valli, Nick Massi
"Let's Hang on (to What We've Got)" .... Bob Gaudio, Frankie Valli
"Opus 17 (Don't You Worry 'bout Me)" .... Bob Gaudio, Frankie Valli, Four Seasons
"Bye Bye Baby" .... Frankie Valli, Four Seasons
"C'mon Marianne" .... Frankie Valli, Four Seasons
"Can't Take My Eyes Off You" .... Frankie Valli
"Working My Way Back to You" .... Frankie Valli, Four Seasons
"Fallen Angel" .... Frankie Valli
"Rag Doll" .... Four Seasons
"Who Loves You" .... Four Seasons, Company

Souvenir (68). Transfer of the Off Broadway play with music by Stephen Temperley. Produced by Ted Snowdon, in association with Janice Montana and the York Theatre Company, at the Lyceum Theatre. Opened November 10, 2005. (Closed January 8, 2006)

Florence Foster Jenkins .... Judy Kaye   Cosme McMoon .... Donald Corren

Standbys: Ms. Kaye—Meg Bussert; Mr. Corren—Bob Stillman.

Directed by Vivian Matalon; scenery, R. Michael Miller; costumes, Tracy Christensen; lighting, Ann G. Wrightson; sound, David Budries; music supervision, Tom Helm; casting, Barry Moss, Bob Kale; production stage manager, Jack Gianino; press, Richard Kornberg and Associates, Tom D'Ambrosio, Laura Kaplow-Goldman.

Time: 1964. Place: A supper club in Greenwich Village, New York. Presented in two parts.

True tale of notoriously bad singer who was wealthy enough to arrange her own concerts. First presentation of record was given Off Broadway by the York Theatre Company (12/1/2004–1/16/2005; 52 performances).

The Woman in White (109). Musical with book by Charlotte Jones; music by Andrew Lloyd Webber; lyrics by David Zippel. Produced by Boyett Ostar Productions, Nederlander Presentations, Inc., Sonia Friedman Productions, Ltd., the Really Useful White Company, Inc., Lawrence Horowitz/Jon Avnet, Ralph Guild/Bill Rollnick, Clear Channel Entertainment/PIA, Thomas L. Miller, at the Marquis Theatre. Opened November 17, 2005. (Closed February 19, 2006)

Walter Hartright	Adam Brazier	Mr. Fairlie	Walter Charles
Signalman	Norman Large	Mr Fairlie's Servant	John Dewar
Anne Catherick	Angela Christian	Laura Fairlie	Jill Paice
Coachman	Greg Mills	Village Girl	Justis Bolding
Marian Halcombe	Maria Friedman	Sir Percival Glyde	Ron Bohmer

Count Fosco .... Michael Ball	Con Man .... Richard Todd Adams
Priest... Daniel Marcus	Prostitute .... Lisa Brescia
Pawnbroker .... Norman Large	Warden .... Patty Goble

Company: Richard Todd Adams, Justis Bolding, Lisa Brescia, John Dewar, Courtney Glass, Patty Goble, Norman Large, Michael Shawn Lewis, Elizabeth Loyacano, Daniel Marcus, Greg Mills, Elena Shaddow, Daniel Torres.

Orchestra: Kristen Blodgette conductor; Milton Granger associate conductor, keyboard; Mat Eisenstein assistant conductor, keyboard; Ann Gerschefski keyboard; David Blinn, Debra Shufelt-Dine viola; Sarah Seiver, Dorothy Lawson cello; Jeff Cooper acoustic bass, electric bass; Kathleen Nester flute, piccolo, alto flute, bass flute; Paul Garment clarinet, bass clarinet; Michael Green bassoon; David Young oboe, English horn; Russ Rizner, Shelagh Abate horn; Daniel Haskins percussion.

Understudies: Mr. Brazier—Michael Shawn Lewis, Daniel Torres; Ms. Christian—Courtney Glass, Elizabeth Loyacano; Ms. Friedman—Lisa Brescia, Leah Horowitz; Mr. Charles—John Dewar, Roger E. DeWitt; Ms. Paice—Laura Dekkers, Elena Shaddow; Mr. Bohmer—Richard Todd Adams, Greg Mills; Mr. Ball—Norman Large, Daniel Marcus; Mr. Large—John Dewar, Roger E. DeWitt.

Swings: Laura Dekkers, Roger E. DeWitt, Leah Horowitz, Sean MacLaughlin.

Directed by Trevor Nunn; choreography, Wayne McGregor; scenery, costumes and video, William Dudley; lighting, Paul Pyant; sound, Mick Potter; orchestrations, David Cullen; music supervision, Simon Lee; music direction, Ms. Blodgette; music coordination, David Lai; associate producer, Stage Entertainment BV; casting, Jim Carnahan; production stage manager, Rick Steiger; press, Barlow-Hartman Public Relations, John Barlow, Michael Hartman, Dennis Crowley, Ryan Ratelle.

Presented in two parts.

Musical tale of romance and thwarted passions in 19th century England; based on the Willkie Collins novel from the 1860s. First presentation of record was given at London's Palace Theatre (9/15/2004–2/25/2006).

PROLOGUE

A railway cutting near Limmeridge, Cumberland

ACT I	ACT II
Limmeridge, Cumberland	Blackwater House, Hampshire
"I Hope You'll Like It Here"	"If I Could Only Dream This World Away"
"Perspective"	"The Nightmare"
"Trying Not to Notice"	"All for Laura" (Reprise)
"I Believe My Heart"	London
"Lammastide"	"Evermore Without You"
"You See I Am No Ghost"	"Lost Souls"
"A Gift for Living Well"	"You Can Get Away With Anything"
"The Holly and the Ivy"	"The Seduction"
Blackwater House, Hampshire	Cumberland
"All for Laura"	
"The Document"	
"Act I Finale"	

EPILOGUE

A railway cutting near Limmeridge, Cumberland

Lincoln Center Theater production of **Seascape** (55). Revival of the play by Edward Albee. André Bishop artistic director, Bernard Gersten executive producer, at the Booth Theatre. Opened November 21, 2005. (Closed January 8, 2006)

Nancy .... Frances Sternhagen	Leslie .... Frederick Weller
Charlie .... George Grizzard	Sarah .... Elizabeth Marvel

Understudies: Mr. Grizzard—Jack Davidson; Ms. Sternhagen—Jennifer Harmon; Mr. Weller—Steve Kazee; Ms. Marvel—Jennifer Ikeda.

Directed by Mark Lamos; scenery, Michael Yeargan; costumes, Catherine Zuber; lighting, Peter Kaczorowski; sound, Aural Fixation; movement direction, Rick Sordelet; casting, Daniel Swee; stage manager, Michael McGoff; press, Philip Rinaldi, Barbara Carroll.

Presented in two parts.

A couple in late middle-age encounter a pair of amphibious missing links in a meditation on the nature of existence. A 1974–75 *Best Plays* choice, the original Broadway production opened at the Shubert Theatre (1/26–3/22/1975; 65 performances). Frank Langella received a 1975 Tony Award for best featured actor in a play and Mr. Albee received the 1975 Pulitzer Prize in Drama. First presentation of record was given in Washington, DC, at the Kennedy Center's Eisenhower Theater (12/3/1974).

*The Color Purple (207). Musical with book by Marsha Norman; music and lyrics by Brenda Russell, Allee Willis, Stephen Bray; adapted from the novel by Alice Walker and the Warner Bros./Amblin Entertainment film. Produced by Oprah Winfrey, Scott Sanders, Roy Furman, Quincy Jones, Creative Battery, Anna Fantaci and Cheryl Lachowicz, Independent Presenters Network, David Lowy, Stephanie P. McClelland, Gary Winnick, Jan Kallish, Nederlander Presentations, Inc., Bob and Harvey Weinstein, Andrew Asnes and Adam Zotovich, Todd Johnson, at the Broadway Theatre. Opened December 1, 2005.

Young Nettie;	Celie .... LaChanze
Mister Daughter .... Chantylla Johnson	Mister .... Kingsley Leggs
Young Celie; others .... Zipporah G. Gatling	Young Harpo;
Church Soloist .... Carol Dennis	Young Adam .... Leon G. Thomas III
Church Lady	Harpo .... Brandon Victor Dixon
Doris .... Kimberly Ann Harris	Sofia .... Felicia P. Fields
Church Lady	Squeak .... Krisha Marcano
Darlene .... Virginia Ann Woodruff	Shug Avery .... Elisabeth Withers-Mendes
Church Lady Jarene;	Ol' Mister .... Lou Myers
Daisy .... Maia Nkenge Wilson	Buster; Chief .... Nathaniel Stampley
Preacher;	Grady .... JC Montgomery
Prison Guard .... Doug Eskew	Bobby .... James Brown III
Pa .... JC Montgomery	Older Olivia .... Bahiyah Sayyed Gaines
Nettie .... Darlesia Cearcy	Older Adam .... Grasan Kingsberry

Ensemble: James Brown III, LaTrisa A. Coleman, Carol Dennis, Anika Ellis, Doug Eskew, Bahiyah Sayyed Gaines, Zipporah G. Gatling, Charles Gray, James Harkness, Francesca Harper, Kimberly Ann Harris, Chantylla Johnson, Grasan Kingsberry, JC Montgomery, Angela Robinson, Nathaniel Stampley, Jamal Story, Maia Nkenge Wilson, Virginia Ann Woodruff.

Orchestra: Linda Twine conductor; Joseph Joubert associate conductor, keyboard; Paul Woodiel, Mineko Yajima violin; David Creswell viola; Clay Ruede cello; Benjamin Franklin Brown bass; Les Scott, Lawrence Feldman, Jay Brandford woodwinds; Barry Danielian, Brian O'Flaherty, Kamau Adilifu trumpet; Larry Farrell, Jason Jackson trombone; Sheldon Becton keyboard; Steve Bargonetti guitar, harmonica; Buddy Williams, Damien Bassman drums; percussion.

Understudies: Ms. LaChanze—Jeannette I. Bayardelle, Kenita R. Miller; Ms. Withers-Mendes—Anika Ellis, Angela Robinson; Ms. Fields—Carol Dennis, Kimberly Ann Harris; Ms. Cearcy—Jeannette I. Bayardelle, Kenita R. Miller; Mr. Leggs—Charles Gray, JC Montgomery; Mr. Dixon—James Brown III, Nathaniel Stampley; Ms. Marcano—LaTrisa A. Coleman, Francesca Harper; Mr. Myers—Doug Eskew, Charles Gray; Mr. Thomas—Corinne McFarlane.

Swings: Jeannette I. Bayardelle, Eric L. Christian, Bobby Daye, Stephanie Guiland-Brown, Corinne McFarlane.

Directed by Gary Griffin; choreography, Donald Byrd; scenery, John Lee Beatty; costumes, Paul Tazewell; lighting, Brian MacDevitt; sound, Jon Weston; hair, Charles G. LaPointe; orchestrations, Jonathan Tunick; music supervision, Kevin Stites; dance music arrangements, Daryl Waters; music direction, Ms. Twine; music coordination, Seymour Red Press; casting, Bernard Telsey Casting; production stage manager, Kristen Harris; press, Carol Fineman/Barlow-Hartman Public Relations, Michael Hartman, John Barlow, Carol Fineman, Leslie Baden.

Girlfriends: LaChanze and Elisabeth Withers-Mendes in The Color Purple. *Photo: Paul Kolnik*

Time: 1909–49. Place: Rural Georgia. Presented in two parts.

Musical celebration of an African-American woman's journey from oppression to success and relative liberation in the South of the pre-Civil Rights era. Ms. LaChanze received the 2006 Tony Award for best actress in a musical. The story is based on Ms. Walker's 1983 Pulitzer Prize-winning novel. First presentation of record was given at Atlanta's Alliance Theatre Company (9/17–10/17/2004).

ACT I

Overture	Orchestra
"Huckleberry Pie"	Young Celia, Nettie
"Mysterious Ways"	Church Soloist, Church Ladies, Company
"Somebody Gonna Love You"	Celie
"Our Prayer"	Nettie, Celie, Mister
"Big Dog"	Mister, Field Hands
"Hell No!"	Sofia, Sisters
"Brown Betty"	Harpo, Men, Squeak
"Shug Avery Comin' to Town"	Mister, Celie, Company
"Too Beautiful for Words"	Shug
"Push Da Button"	Shug, Company
"Uh Oh!"	Church Ladies, Sofia, Squeak
"What About Love?"	Celie, Shug

ACT II

"African Homeland"	Nettie, Celie, Olivia, Adam, Villagers
"The Color Purple"	Shug
"Celie's Curse"	Mister
"Miss Celie's Pants"	Celie, Shug, Sofia, Women
"Any Little Thing"	Harpo, Sofia

"I'm Here" .... Celie
"The Color Purple" (Reprise) .... Celie, Nettie, Company

Roundabout Theatre Company production of **A Touch of the Poet** (50). Revival of the play by Eugene O'Neill. Todd Haimes artistic director, Harold Wolpert managing director, Julia C. Levy executive director, at Studio 54. Opened December 8, 2005. (Closed January 29, 2006)

Mickey Maloy	Daniel Stewart Sherman	Dan Roche	Ciarán O'Reilly
Jamie Cregan	Byron Jennings	Paddy O'Dowd	Randall Newsome
Sara Melody	Emily Bergl	Deborah Harford	Kathryn Meisle
Nora Melody	Dearbhla Molloy	Nicholas Gadsby	John Horton
Cornelius Melody	Gabriel Byrne	Uilleann pipes	David Power

Understudies: Ms. Bergl—Kristen Bush; Mr. Byrne—Colin Lane; Messrs. O'Reilly, Newsome—Kevin McHugh; Messrs. Jennings, Sherman—Randall Newsome; Mses. Malloy, Meisle—Elizabeth Norment.

Directed by Doug Hughes; scenery and costumes, Santo Loquasto; lighting, Christopher Akerlind; sound and music, David Van Tieghem; wigs and hair, Tom Watson; casting, Jim Carnahan; production stage manager, Peter Hanson; press, Boneau/Bryan-Brown, Adrian Bryan-Brown, Jessica Johnson, Joe Perrotta, Matt Polk.

Time: July 27, 1828. Place: Melody's Tavern, near Boston. Presented in two parts.

A grandiose Irish immigrant sees the veil of his constructed identity destroyed in one long summer night. A 1958–59 *Best Plays* choice, the original Broadway production opened at the Helen Hayes Theatre (10/2/1958–6/13/1959; 284 performances) with Helen Hayes as Con Melody's wife, Nora. First presentation of record was given at Stockholm's Royal Dramatic Theatre (3/29/1957). The 2005–06 production was the third Broadway revival.

Chita Rivera: The Dancer's Life (72). Musical with book by Terrence McNally; original songs by Lynn Ahrens and Stephen Flaherty. Produced by Marty Bell, Aldo Scrofani, Martin Richards, Chase Mishkin, Bernard Abrams/Michael Speyer, Tracy Aron, Joe McGinnis, in association with Stefany Bergson, Scott Prisand/Jennifer Maloney, G. Marilyne Sexton, Judith Ann Abrams/Jamie deRoy, Addiss/Rittereiser/Carragher, at the Gerald Schoenfeld Theatre. Opened December 11, 2005. (Closed February 19, 2006)

Chita Rivera	Chita Rivera	Little Chita Rivera; Lisa	Liana Ortiz

Ensemble: Richard Amaro, Lloyd Culbreath, Malinda Farrington, Edgard Gallardo, Deidre Goodwin, Richard Montoya, Lainie Sakakura, Alex Sanchez, Allyson Tucker.

Understudy: Ms. Ortiz—Jasmine Perri.

Swings: Cleve Asbury, Madeleine Kelly.

Orchestra: Mark Hummel conductor, piano; Gary Adler associate conductor, keyboard 2; Entcho Todorov violin; Wolfram Koessel cello; Ted Nash, Mark Phaneuf reeds; Jeff Kievit lead trumpet; John Chudoba trumpet; Randy Andos trombone, tuba; Jim Donica bass; Bill Hayes percussion; Michael Croiter drums.

Directed and choreographed by Graciela Daniele; Bob Fosse's choreography, Tony Stevens; Jerome Robbins's choreography, Alan Johnson; scenery, Loy Arcenas; costumes, Toni-Leslie James; lighting, Jules Fisher and Peggy Eisenhauer; sound, Scott Lehrer; hair, David Brian Brown; orchestrations, Danny Troob; music direction, Mr. Hummel; music coordination, Michael Keller; additional orchestrations, Larry Hochman; executive producer, Marty Bell and Aldo Scrofani; associate producer, Dan Gallagher and Michael Milton; casting, Mark Simon; production stage manager, Arturo E. Porazzi; press, Barlow-Hartman Public Relations, Michael Hartman, John Barlow, Rick Miramontez, Jon Dimond.

Presented in two parts.

Celebration of the long "gypsy" life and career of Ms. Rivera. First presentation of record was given at San Diego's Old Globe Theatre (9/22/2005).

ACT I

Prologue
"Perfida" .... Liana Ortiz, Richard Amaro
The White House
"Secret o' Life" .... Chita
Mi Familia Loca
"Dancing on the Kitchen Table" .... Chita, Richard Montoya,
Edgard Gallardo, Allyson Tucker,
Lainie Sakakura, Malinda Farrington,
Richard Amaro
Ballet Class .... Malinda Farrington, Deidre Goodwin,
Lainie Sakakura, Allyson Tucker, Liana Ortiz
The Gypsy Life
"Something to Dance About" (*Call Me Madam*) .... Chita, Richard Montoya
"I'm Available" (*Mr. Wonderful*) .... Chita
"Camille, Colette, Fifi" (*Seventh Heaven*) .... Chita, Deidre Goodwin, Allyson Tucker
"Garbage" (*The Shoestring Review*) .... Chita
"Can-Can" (*Can-Can*) .... Chita, Allyson Tucker, Malinda Farrington,
Lainie Sakakura, Deidre Goodwin
"Mr. Wonderful" (*Mr. Wonderful*) .... Chita
West Side Story
"A Boy Like That" .... Chita
"Dance at the Gym" (*Mambo*).. Chita, Edgard Gallardo, Company
"Somewhere" .... Chita, Company
Co-Stars
"Put on a Happy Face" (*Bye Bye Birdie*) .... Chita, Lloyd Culbreath
"Rosie" (*Bye Bye Birdie*) .... Chita, Lloyd Culbreath
"Don't 'Ah Ma' Me" (*The Rink*) .... Chita
"Big Spender" (*Sweet Charity*) .... Chita, Deidre Goodwin
"Nowadays" (*Chicago*) .... Chita

ACT II

Entr'acte
The Audition .... Chita, Lloyd Culbreath, Company
The Men
"Adios Noñino," "Detresse," "Calambre"............................... Chita, Richard Amaro, Liana Ortiz
"More Than You Know" .... Chita, Company
Choreographers .... Chita, Company
The Shows
"A Woman the World Has Never Seen" .... Chita
"Class" (*Chicago*) .... Chita
"Chief Cook and Bottlewasher" (*The Rink*) .... Chita
"Kiss of the Spider Woman" (*Kiss of the Spider Woman*) .... Chita
"Where You Are" (*Kiss of the Spider Woman*) .... Chita, Company Men
The White House
"All That Jazz" (*Chicago*) .... Chita, Liana Ortiz, Company

*Bridge and Tunnel (140). Solo performance piece by Sarah Jones. Produced by Eric Falkenstein, Michael Aiden, Boyett Ostar Productions at the Helen Hayes Theatre. Opened January 26, 2006.

Performed by Ms. Jones

Directed by Tony Taccone; scenery, David Korins; lighting, Howell Binkley; sound, Christopher Cronin; associate producer, Tom Wirtshafter; production stage manager, Laurie Goldfeder; press, Pete Sanders Group, Pete Sanders, Shane Marshall Brown, Glenna Freedman.

Presented without intermission.

A pluralistic collection of 21st century American immigrant stories set against the backdrop of a poetry slam in a Queens bar. First presentation of record was given at the Culture Project in

New York (2/19/2004; 180 performances). Ms. Jones received a 2006 Special Tony Award for excellence.

Manhattan Theatre Club production of **Rabbit Hole** (77). Lynne Meadow artistic director, Barry Grove executive producer, at the Biltmore Theatre. Opened February 2, 2006. (Closed April 9, 2006)

Becca	Cynthia Nixon	Nat	Tyne Daly
Izzy	Mary Catherine Garrison	Jason	John Gallagher Jr.
Howie	John Slattery		

Understudies: Ms. Daly—Cynthia Darlow; Mr. Gallagher—Troy Deutsch; Mses. Nixon, Garrison—Erika Rolfsrud.

Directed by Daniel Sullivan; scenery, John Lee Beatty; costumes, Jennifer von Mayrhauser; lighting, Christopher Akerlind; sound and music, John Gromada; casting, Nancy Piccione and David Caparelliotis; production stage manager, Roy Harris; press, Boneau/Bryan-Brown, Chris Boneau, Jim Byk, Aaron Meier, Heath Schwartz.

Presented in two parts.

A family confronts the tragic loss of a child killed by automobile driven by a teenage boy. A 2005–06 *Best Plays* choice (see essay by Michael Sommers in this volume). Ms. Nixon received the 2006 Tony Award for best actress in a play. The play was commissioned by South Coast Repertory in Costa Mesa, California, where it was given a staged reading directed by Carolyn Cantor during the Pacific Playwrights Festival (5/6–8/2005). As this volume was going to press, it was announced that the play would receive the 2007 Pulitzer Prize in Drama.

Barefoot in the Park (109). Revival of the play by Neil Simon. Produced by Robyn Goodman, Roy Gabay, Walt Grossman, Geoff Rich, Danzansky Partners, Ergo Entertainment, Ruth Hendel, in association with Paramount Pictures, at the Cort Theatre. Opened February 16, 2006. (Closed May 21, 2006).

Corie Bratter	Amanda Peet	Paul Bratter	Patrick Wilson
Telephone Repairman	Adam Sietz	Mrs. Banks, Corie's Mother	Jill Clayburgh
Deliveryman	Sullivan Walker	Victor Velasco	Tony Roberts

Understudies: Messrs. Wilson, Sietz, Walker—Benim Foster; Ms. Peet—Erin Fritch; Ms. Clayburgh—Jennifer Harmon; Mr. Roberts—Sullivan Walker.

Directed by Scott Elliott; scenery, Derek McLane; costumes, Isaac Mizrahi; lighting, Jason Lyons; sound, Ken Travis; associate producers, Leah and Ed Frankel, Oliver Dow, CJ Entertainment/URL Productions, Stephen Kocis; casting, Judy Henderson; production stage manager, Valerie A. Peterson; press, Richard Kornberg and Associates, Richard Kornberg, Tom D'Ambrosio, Don Summa, Carrie Friedman, Laura Kaplow-Goldman.

Presented in two parts.

A young married couple finds the road to marital bliss filled with bumps and potholes. A 1963–64 *Best Plays* choice, the first Broadway production opened at the Biltmore Theatre (10/23/1963–6/25/1967; 1,530 performances). Mike Nichols received a 1964 Tony Award for best dramatic director. First presentation of record was given at New Hope, Pennsylvania under the title *Nobody Loves Me* (4/27/1963). First presentation of record under the eventual title was given at New Haven, Connecticut, (9/25/1963) before a pre-Broadway run at the National Theatre in Washington, DC, (9/30/1963). The 2005–06 production is the first Broadway revival.

*Roundabout Theatre Company production of **The Pajama Game** (111). Revival of the musical with book by George Abbott and Richard Bissell; music and lyrics by Richard Adler and Jerry Ross; based on Mr. Bissell's novel *7½ Cents*; book revisions by Peter Ackerman. Todd Haimes artistic director, Harold Wolpert managing director, Julia C. Levy executive director, in association with Jeffrey Richards, James Fuld Jr. and Scott Landis, at the American Airlines Theatre. Opened February 23, 2006.

Prez	Peter Benson	Mae	Joyce Chittick

Singing solidarity: The company of The Pajama Game. *Photo: Joan Marcus*

Virginia	Bridget Berger	Ralph	Jeffrey Schecter
Charlie	Stephen Berger	Shirley	Debra Walton
Martha	Kate Chapman	Hines	Michael McKean
Brenda	Paula Leggett Chase	Mr. Hasler	Richard Poe
Poopsie	Jennifer Cody	Gladys	Megan Lawrence
Lewie	David Eggers	Mabel	Roz Ryan
Cyrus	Michael Halling	Ganzenlicker; Pop	Michael McCormick
Carmen	Bianca Marroquin	Sid Sorokin	Harry Connick Jr.
Jake	Vince Pesce	Babe Williams	Kelli O'Hara
Joe	Devin Richards		

Orchestra: Rob Berman conductor; Chris Fenwick associate conductor, piano; Marilyn Reynolds violin; Beth Sturdevant cello; Neal Chase bass; Jim Hershman guitar; Steve Kenyon, John Winder reeds; Roger Ingram, Christian Jaudes trumpet; John Allred, Joe Barati trombone; Paul Pizzuti drums, percussion.

Understudies: Ms. O'Hara—Bridget Berger; Messrs. Poe, McCormick—Stephen Berger; Ms. Ryan—Kate Chapman; Ms. Lawrence—Jennifer Cody; Mr. Connick—Michael Halling; Mr. McKean—Michael McCormick; Mr. Benson—Jeffrey Schecter; Ms. Chittick—Debra Walton.

Swings: Michael O'Donnell, Amber Stone.

Directed and choreographed by Kathleen Marshall; scenery, Derek McLane; costumes, Martin Pakledinaz; lighting, Peter Kaczorowski; sound, Brian Ronan; wigs and hair, Paul Huntley; orchestrations, Dick Lieb and Danny Troob; music supervision, David Chase; music direction, Mr. Berman; music coordination, Seymour Red Press; casting, Jim Carnahan; production stage manager, David O'Brien; press, Boneau/Bryan-Brown, Adrian Bryan-Brown, Matt Polk, Jessica Johnson.

Time: 1954. Place: Cedar Rapids, Iowa. Presented in two parts.

Battles over wages and cost-cutting efficiencies lead to labor troubles and the spark of musical romance. First presentation of record was given at the Shubert Theatre in New Haven, Connecticut (4/20/1954). The original Broadway production opened at the St. James Theatre (5/13/1954–11/24/1956; 1,063 performances) with John Raitt, Janis Paige, Carol Haney, Eddie Foy Jr. and Shirley MacLaine—who was a dancer in the chorus. The final two weeks of the production were presented at the Shubert Theatre. It received 1955 Tony Awards for best musical, best featured actress in a musical (Carol Haney) and best choreography (Bob Fosse). The 2005–06 production was the second Broadway revival. It received 2006 Tony Awards for best revival of a musical and best choreography (Ms. Marshall).

ACT I

Overture	Orchestra
"Racing with the Clock"	Workers
"A New Town Is a Blue Town"	Sid
"I'm Not at All in Love'	Babe, Girls
"I'll Never Be Jealous Again"	Hines, Mabel
"Hey There"	Sid
"Racing with the Clock" (Reprise)	Workers
"Sleep Tite"	Joe, Brenda, Martha, Cyrus
"Her Is"	Prez, Gladys
"Once-a-Year Day"	Sid, Babe, Company
"Her Is" (Reprise)	Prez, Mae
"Small Talk"	Sid, Babe
"There Once Was a Man"	Sid, Babe
"Hey There" (Reprise)	Sid

ACT II

"Steam Heat"	Mae, Lewie, Jake
"The World Around Us"	Sid
"Hey There" (Reprise)/"If You Win, You Lose"	Babe, Sid

("If You Win, You Lose" by Richard Adler)

"Think of the Time I Save"	Hines, Girls
"Hernando's Hideaway"	Gladys, Sid, Company
"The Three of Us"	Hines, Gladys

(Richard Adler)

"Seven and a Half Cents"	Prez, Babe, Workers
"There Once Was a Man" (Reprise)	Babe, Sid
"The Pajama Game"	Company

Ring of Fire: The Johnny Cash Musical Show (57). By Richard Maltby Jr.; based on the life and work of Johnny Cash. Produced by William Meade, CTM Productions, Bob Cuillo, GFour Productions and James B. Freydberg at the Ethel Barrymore Theatre. Opened March 12, 2006. (Closed April 30, 2006)

Performed by Jeb Brown, Jason Edwards, Jarrod Emick, Beth Malone, Cass Morgan, Lari White.

Orchestra: Jeff Lisenby conductor, accordion, keyboard; David M. Lutken banjo, dobro, evoharp, guitar, harmonica, mandolin; Randy Redd keyboard, mandolin; Eric Anthony electric guitar, mandolin; Laurie Canaan fiddle, mandolin; Dan Immel bass, cello; Brent Moyer guitar, cornet; Ron Krasinski drums.

Understudies: Mr. Brown—Rob Weber, Jim Price; Mr. Edwards—Scott Wakefield, Jim Price; Mr. Emick—Mark Luna, Rod Weber; Ms. Malone—Sherrié Austin; Ms. Morgan—Melanie Vaughan, Gail Bliss; Ms. White—Gail Bliss, Sherrié Austin; Mr. Lutken—Scott Wakefield, Jim Price; Mr. Lisenby—August Eriksmoen; Mr. Redd—Eric Anthony, Miles Aubrey, August Eriksmoen; Messrs. Anthony, Moyer—Miles Aubrey; Ms. Canaan—DeAnn Whalen; Mr. Immel—Eric Anthony; Mr. Krasinski—Steve Bartosik.

Directed by Richard Maltby Jr.; choreography, Lisa Shriver; scenery, Neil Patel; costumes, David C. Woolard; lighting, Ken Billington; sound, Peter Fitzgerald and Carl Casella; projections, music direction, Mr. Lisenby; executive producer, Mr. Freydberg; associate producers, IDT Entertainment, Tamlyn Freund Yerkes, David Maltby; casting, Dave Clemmons Casting; production stage manager, Mark Dobrow; press, Boneau/Bryan-Brown, Chris Boneau, Matt Polk, Jessica Johnson.

Presented in two parts.

Pickin' 'n' grinnin': Jeb Brown, Jarrod Emick and Jason Edwards in Ring of Fire. *Joan Marcus*

A musical celebration of the life and work of Johnny Cash. First presentation of record was given at Buffalo's Studio Arena Theatre (9/9/2005).

ACT I
Dates indicate year of Johnny Cash recording or release.

"Hurt" (2002) ....Jason, Company
(Michael Trent Reznor)
"Country Boy" (1957) .... Company
(John R. Cash)
"Thing Called Love" (1972) .... Jarrod, Beth, Company
(Jerry Hubbard)
"There You Go" (1956) .... Beth, Company
(John R. Cash)
"While I've Got It on My Mind" (1974)..Jeb, Lari
(John R. Cash)
"My Old Faded Rose" (1964) .... Jason, Cass, Ron, David, Randy, Dan
(John R. Cash, June Carter Cash)
"Daddy Sang Bass" (1969) .... Company
(John R. Cash, Carl L. Perkins)
"Straight A's in Love" (1959) .... Jarrod
(John R. Cash)
"Big River" (1957) .... Jason, Jarrod, Jed, Dan
(John R. Cash)
"I Still Miss Someone" (1959) .... Beth
(John R. Cash, Roy Cash Jr.)
"Five Feet High and Rising" (1959) .... Jason, Jarrod, Lari, Beth, Jeb, Cass
(John R. Cash)

"Flesh and Blood" (1970) .... Lari, Jeb, Cass, Jason
(John R. Cash)

"Look at Them Beans" (1975) .... Jarrod, Beth, Cass, Lari
(Joseph Arrington Jr.)

"Get Rhythm" (1956) .... Company
(John R. Cash)

"Flushed" (1968) .... Cass
(Jack H. Clement)

"Dirty Old . . . Dog" (1966) .... Randy, Brent, David
(Jack H. Clement)

"Angel Band" (1979) .... Company
(John R. Cash)

"If I Were a Carpenter" (1970) .... Jarrod, Beth
(James Timothy Hardin)

"Ring of Fire" (1963) .... Jarrod, Beth
(June Carter, Merle Kilgore)

"Jackson" (1967) .... Jarrod, Beth, Jeb, Lari, Jason, Cass
(Jerry Leiber, Billy Edd Wheeler)

ACT II

Prologue: "Big River" (Reprise) .... Company

"I've Been Everywhere" (1996) .... Company
(Geoff Mack)

"Sunday Mornin' Comin' Down" (1970) .... Jeb
(Kris Kristofferson)

"Temptation" (2003) .... Lari, Jeb
(Arthur Freed, Nacio Herb Brown)

"I Feel Better All Over" (1960) .... Jeb, Lari
(Ken Rogers, Ferlin Husky)

"A Boy Named Sue" (1969) .... Jeb, Jarrod, Jason
(Shel Silverstein)

"Going to Memphis" (1960) .... Men
(John R. Cash)

"Delia's Gone" (1962) .... David
(John R. Cash, Karl M. Silbersdorf, Richard Toops)

"Austin Prison" (1966) .... Randy, Company
(John R. Cash)

"Orleans Parish Prison" (1974) .... Cass, Lari, Beth, Company
(Dick Feller)

"Folsom Prison Blues" (1955) .... Jarrod
(John R. Cash)

"Man in Black" (1971) .... Jeb
(John R. Cash)

"All Over Again" (1958) .... Lari
(John R. Cash)

"I Walk the Line" (1956) .... Jeb, Lari, Jason, Cass, Jarrod, Beth
(John R. Cash)

"The Man Comes Around" (2002) .... Jason, Beth, Cass, Jarrod, Jeb, Lari
(John R. Cash)

"Waiting on the Far Side Banks of Jordan" (1976) .... Cass, Jason
(Terry Smith)

"Why Me" (1994) .... Jason, Company
(Kris Kristofferson)

"Hey Porter" (1955) .... Company
(John R. Cash)

Well (52). Revival of the play by Lisa Kron. Produced by Elizabeth Ireland McCann, Scott Rudin, Boyett Ostar Productions, True Love Productions, Terry Allen Kramer, Roger Berlind, Carole Shorenstein Hays, John Dias, Joey Parnes, in association with Larry Hirschhorn, the Public Theater and the American Conservatory Theater, at the Longacre Theatre. Opened March 30, 2006. (Closed May 14, 2006)

Lisa .... Lisa Kron	Kay; others .... Saidah Arrika Ekulona
Ann ....Jayne Houdyshell	Jim; others .... Daniel Breaker
Nurse; others ....John Hoffman	Joy; others .... Christina Kirk

Standbys: Ms. Kron—Cindy Katz; Mses. Houdyshell, Kirk—Randy Danson.

Understudies: Ms. Ekulona—Donnetta Lavinia Grays; Mr. Breaker—Colman Domingo; Ms. Hoffman—Joel Van Liew.

Directed by Leigh Silverman; scenery, Tony Walton; costumes, Miranda Hoffman; lighting, Christopher Akerlind; sound and music, John Gromada; wigs and hair, Tom Watson; casting, Jay Binder and Jack Bowdan; production stage manager, Susie Cordon; press, Boneau/Bryan-Brown, Chris Boneau, Jackie Green, Susanne Tighe, Matt Ross.

Presented without intermission.

A woman examines the impact of emotional well-being on physical health in a performance piece that shifts between competing narratives. A 2003–04 *Best Plays* choice, its first New York presentation of record was given at the Public Theater (3/28–5/16/2004; 57 performances). First presentation of record was given as a staged reading at the Hartford Stage Company in Connecticut (5/19/2002).

Festen (49). By David Eldridge; based on the play by Thomas Vinterberg, Mogens Rukov and Bo HR. Hansen and the Dogme film. Produced by Bill Kenwright and Marla Rubin, in association with Almeida Theatre, at the Music Box. Opened April 9, 2006 (Closed May 20, 2006)

Siren song: Mark Ruffalo and Lauren Ambrose in Awake and Sing! *Photo: Paul Kolnik*

Christian	Michael Hayden	Helge	Larry Bryggman
Michael	Jeremy Sisto	Pia	Diane Davis
Little Girl	Meredith Lipson;	Helmut	Christopher Evan Welch
	Ryan Simpkins	Grandfather	John Carter
Mette	Carrie Preston	Poul	David Patrick Kelly
Lars	Stephen Kunken	Kim	C.J. Wilson
Helene	Julianna Margulies	Gbatokai	Keith Davis
Else	Ali MacGraw		

Understudies: Messrs. Hayden, Sisto, Welch, Wilson—Michael Bakkensen; Mses. Margulies, MacGraw, Davis, Preston—Natalie Gold; Messrs. Bryggman, Carter, Kelly, Kunken—Ezra Knight.

Directed by Rufus Norris; scenery, Ian MacNeil; costumes, Joan Wadge; lighting, Jean Kalman; sound, Paul Arditti; music, Orlando Gough; fight direction, Terry King; casting, Jim Carnahan; production stage manager, Michael McGoff; press, the Publicity Office, Bob Fennell, Marc Thibodeau, Candi Adams, Michael S. Borowski.

Presented in two parts.

A seemingly staid patriarch's 60th birthday party evolves into a circus of family accusations and recriminations. Based on a 1998 arthouse film by Mr. Vinterberg, the first presentation of record was given at London's Almeida Theatre (3/25–5/1/2004) before a transfer to the Lyric Theatre (9/23/2004–4/16/2005).

*Lincoln Center Theater production of **Awake and Sing!** (43). Revival of the play by Clifford Odets. André Bishop artistic director, Bernard Gersten executive producer, at the Belasco Theatre. Opened April 17, 2006.

Ralph Berger	Pablo Schreiber	Schlosser	Peter Kybart
Myron Berger	Jonathan Hadary	Moe Axelrod	Mark Ruffalo
Hennie Berger	Lauren Ambrose	Uncle Morty	Ned Eisenberg
Jacob	Ben Gazzara	Sam Feinschreiber	Richard Topol
Bessie Berger	Zoë Wanamaker		

Understudies: Messrs. Hadary, Eisenberg—Tony Campisi; Messrs. Gazzara, Kybart—Stan Lachow; Ms. Ambrose—Annie Purcell; Mr. Schreiber—Charles Socarides; Messrs. Ruffalo, Topol—Ed Vassallo; Ms. Wanamaker—Lori Wilner.

Directed by Bartlett Sher; scenery, Michael Yeargan; costumes, Catherine Zuber; lighting, Christopher Akerlind; sound, Peter John Still and Marc Salzberg; casting, Daniel Swee; stage manager, Robert Bennett; press, Philip Rinaldi, Barbara Carroll.

Time: The mid-1930s. Place: An apartment in the Bronx, New York City. Presented in three parts.

A Jewish family struggles with grinding poverty and the omnipresent sense that their position on the margins of American society might become worse at any moment. A 1934–35 *Best Plays* choice, the original Broadway production opened at the Belasco Theatre (2/19/1935–7/20/1935; 184 performances). After a seven-week hiatus, the production reopened at the Belasco (9/9–28/1935; 24 performances). *Best Plays* has listed this production in its List of Best Plays for many years with a total that was incorrect by one performance—it has been corrected to 208 performances. The original Group Theatre production included direction by Harold Clurman with performances by Luther Adler, Stella Adler, J. Edward Bromberg, Morris Carnovsky, John Garfield, Sanford Meisner and other notables. The 2005–06 production was the fourth Broadway revival. It received 2006 Tony Awards for best revival of a play and best costume design of a play (Ms. Zuber).

*Three Days of Rain (49). Revival of the play by Richard Greenberg. Produced by Marc Platt, David Stone, the Shubert Organization, at the Bernard B. Jacobs Theatre. Opened April 19, 2006.

Walker; Ned	Paul Rudd	Pip; Theo	Bradley Cooper
Nan; Lina	Julia Roberts		

Understudies: Messrs. Rudd, Cooper—Michael Dempsey. Ms. Roberts—Michelle Federer.

The deluge: Paul Rudd and Julia Roberts in Three Days of Rain. *Photo: Joan Marcus*

Directed by Joe Mantello; scenery and costumes, Santo Loquasto; lighting, Paul Gallo; sound and music, David Van Tieghem; rain, Jauchem and Meeh; hair, Lydell Quiyou; production stage manager, William Joseph Barnes; press, the Publicity Office, Bob Fennell, Marc Thibodeau, Candi Adams, Michael S. Borowski.

Time: 1995; 1960. Place: A loft in downtown Manhattan; the same, years earlier. Presented in two parts.

The passions of their parents create an uneasy legacy for three young people seeking peace from the past. First presentation of record was given at South Coast Repertory, Costa Mesa, California (3/9–4/6/1997). First New York presentation of record was given at Manhattan Theatre Club (11/11/1997–1/4/1998; 32 performances).

*Roundabout Theatre Company production of **The Threepenny Opera** (48). Revival of the musical with book and lyrics by Bertolt Brecht; music by Kurt Weill; translation by Wallace Shawn; based on Elisabeth Hauptmann's German translation of John Gay's *The Beggar's Opera.* Todd Haimes artistic director, Harold Wolpert managing director, Julia C. Levy executive director, at Studio 54. Opened April 20, 2006.

Jenny	Cyndi Lauper	Beggar; Beatrice	Brian Butterick
Smith	John Herrera	Filch	Carlos Leon
Walter; Betty	Maureen Moore	Mrs. Peachum	Ana Gasteyer
Jimmy; Dolly	Brooke Sunny Moriber	Polly Peachum	Nellie McKay
Rev. Kimball; Eunice	Terry Burrell	Jacob	Adam Alexi-Malle
Robert	Romain Frugé	Eddie	Kevin Rennard
Vixen	Deborah Lew	Tiger Brown	Christopher Innvar
Matthew	David Cale	Bruno; Molly	Christopher Kenney
Macheath	Alan Cumming	Harry; Velma	Lucas Steele
Mr. Peachum	Jim Dale	Lucy Brown	Brian Charles Rooney

Ensemble: Maureen Moore, Brooke Sunny Moriber, Terry Burrell, Romain Frugé, Deborah Lew, Brian Butterick, Carlos Leon, Adam Alexi-Malle, Kevin Rennard, Christopher Kenney, Lucas Steele.

Orchestra: Kevin Stites conductor; Paul Raiman associate conductor, harmonium, celeste, piano; Charles duChateau cello, accordion; Greg Utzig guitar, Hawaiian guitar, banjo, mandolin; Richard Sarpola string bass; Eddie Salkin, Roger Rosenberg reeds; Tim Schadt, Matt Peterson trumpet; Mike Christianson tenor trombone; Charles Descarfino percussion, drums.

Understudies: Mr. Cumming—Romain Frugé; Ms. Lauper—Maureen Moore; Ms. McKay—Brooke Sunny Moriber; Ms. Gasteyer—Terry Burrell; Mr. Dale—David Cale; Mr. Rooney—Lucas Steele; Mr. Leon—Adam Alexi-Malle; Mr. Innvar—John Herrera.

Swings: Nehal Joshi, Valisia Lekae Little.

Directed by Scott Elliott; choreography, Aszure Barton; scenery, Derek McLane; costumes, Isaac Mizrahi; lighting, Jason Lyons; sound, Ken Travis; wigs and hair, Paul Huntley; orchestrations, Mr. Weill; music direction, Mr. Stites; music coordination, John Miller; casting, Jim Carnahan; production stage manager, Peter Hanson; press, Boneau/Bryan-Brown, Adrian Bryan-Brown, Matt Polk, Jessica Johnson.

Presented in two parts.

Corruption is so rampant among the bourgeois in England that one cannot tell the "true" criminals without a score card. The first Broadway presentation of record opened at the Empire Theatre (4/13–22/1933; 12 performances). The long-running Off Broadway version at Theatre de Lys (now the Lucille Lortel) first opened in 1954 (3/10–5/30/1954; 96 performances) but was forced by the vagaries of theater booking to take a 15-month hiatus. The production reopened in 1955 at the same theatre (9/20/1955–12/17/1961; 2,611 total performances). Its seven-year run gives it eighth place on the *Best Plays* Long Runs Off Broadway list. Despite the status of the 1955 "return engagement" as an Off Broadway production, it was nominated in two competitive categories for Tony Awards. Lotte Lenya (Mrs. Kurt Weill) received the 1956 Tony Award for best featured actress in a musical, her co-star Scott Merrill did not win in the featured actor in a musical category—that honoree was Russ Brown for *Damn Yankees*. Producers Carmen Capalbo

Innocence betrayed: Christopher Innvar, Nellie McKay and Alan Cumming in The Threepenny Opera. *Photo: Joan Marcus*

and Stanley Chase, however, were given 1956 Special Tony Awards for their work. *Best Plays* conferred a special citation on the 1975–76 Broadway production, which opened at Lincoln Center Theater's Vivian Beaumont (5/1/1976–1/23/1977; 307 performances). The 2005–06 production was the fourth Broadway revival.

ACT I

Overture .... Orchestra
Prologue
"Song of the Extraordinary Crimes of Mac the Knife" .... Jenny, Company
Scene 1: Wardrobe Department of Peachum's Begging Business
    "Peachum's Morning Hymn" .... Mr. Peachum
    "The 'Rather Than" Song" .... Mr. and Mrs. Peachum
Scene 2: An Empty Stable
    "Wedding Song" .... Matthew, Gang
    "Pirate Jenny" .... Polly
    "The Army Song" .... Macheath, Tiger, Polly, Gang
    "Wedding Song" (Reprise) .... Matthew, Gang
    "Love Song" .... Macheath, Polly
Scene 3: Peachum's Wardrobe Department
    "The 'No' Song" .... Polly
    "Certain Things Make Our Life Impossible" .... Mr. Peachum, Mrs. Peachum, Polly
    Scene 4: The Stable
    "Goodbye" .... Macheath
    "Polly's Song" .... Polly

ACT II

Interlude: A Street
    "The Bailad of the Overwhelming Power of Sex" .... Mrs. Peachum
Scene 5: A Brothel in Turnbridge
    "The Ballad of the Pimp" .... Macheath, Jenny

Biker guy: Richard Griffiths in The History Boys. *Photo: Joan Marcus*

Scene 6: The Prison of the Old Bailey
"The Ballad of the Happy Life" .... Macheath
"The Jealousy Duet" .... Lucy, Polly
"How Do Humans Live?" .... Mac, Mrs. Peachum, Company
Scene 7: Peachum's Wardrobe Department
"The Ballad of the Overwhelming Power of Sex" (Reprise) .... Mrs. Peachum
"The Song of Inadequacy of Human Striving" .... Mr. Peachum
"The Song of Inadequacy of Human Striving" (Reprise) .... Mr. Peachum
"Solomon Song" .... Jenny
Scene 8: Lucy Brown's Bedroom, an Attic in the Old Bailey
"Lucy's Aria" .... Lucy
Scene 9: The Death Cell
"Cry from the Grave" .... Macheath
"The Ballad in Which Macheath Asks Everyone's Forgiveness" .... Macheath
"Finale" .... Company

*The History Boys (44). By Alan Bennett. Produced by Boyett Ostar Productions, Roger Berlind, Debra Black, Eric Falkenstein, Roy Furman, Jam Theatricals, Stephanie P. McClelland, Judith Resnick, Scott Rudin, Jon Avnet/Ralph Guild, Dede Harris/Morton Swinsky, in association with the National Theatre (UK), at the Broadhurst Theatre. Opened April 23, 2006.

The Boys
Akthar .... Sacha Dhawan
Crowther .... Samuel Anderson
Dakin .... Dominic Cooper
Lockwood .... Andrew Knott
Posner .... Samuel Barnett
Rudge .... Russell Tovey
Scripps..................................... Jamie Parker
Timms .... James Corden

The Teachers
Headmaster .... Clive Merrison
Mrs. Lintott .... Frances de la Tour
Hector .... Richard Griffiths
Irwin .... Stephen Campbell Moore
TV Director .... Bill Buell
Make-up Lady .... Pippa Pearthree

Other Boys: LeRoy McClain, Alex Tonetta, Jeffrey Withers.

Understudies: Messrs. Griffiths, Merrison—Bill Buell; Messrs. Cooper, Tovey, Dhawan—LeRoy McClain; Ms. de la Tour—Pippa Pearthree; Messrs. Barnett, Parker, Corden, Buell—Alex Tonetta; Messrs. Moore, Anderson, Knott—Jeffrey Withers.

Directed by Nicholas Hytner; scenery and costumes, Bob Crowley; lighting, Mark Henderson; sound, Colin Pink; music, Richard Sisson; video, Ben Taylor; production stage manager, Michael J. Passaro; press, Boneau/Bryan-Brown, Adrian Bryan-Brown, Jim Byk, Juliana Hannett.

Time: The mid 1980s. Place: English high school in the north of England. Presented in two parts.

An aging advocate for liberal education in conflict with a results-oriented headmaster behaves inappropriately with his young charges and loses more than an academic battle. A 2005–06 *Best Plays* choice (see essay by Charles McNulty in this volume). This production received 2006 Tony Awards for best play, best actor in a play (Mr. Griffiths), best featured actress in a play (Ms. de la Tour), best direction of a play (Mr. Hytner), best scenic design of a play (Mr. Crowley) and best lighting design of a play (Mr. Henderson). First presentation of record was given at the National's Lyttelton Theatre in London (5/18–4/26/2005). The production also toured Australia and the UK before its Broadway opening.

Lestat (39). Musical with book by Linda Woolverton; music by Elton John; lyrics by Bernie Taupin; based on The Vampire Chronicles series by Anne Rice. Produced by Warner Bros. Theatre Ventures at the Palace Theatre. Opened April 25, 2006. (Closed May 28, 2006)

Lestat .... Hugh Panaro
Gabrielle .... Carolee Carmello
Armand .... Drew Sarich

Louis .... Jim Stanek
Nicolas.. Roderick Hill
Marius... Michael Genet

Claudia	Allison Fischer	Marquis; Laurent	Will Swenson
Magnus	Joseph Dellger	Beautiful Woman	Megan Reinking

Ensemble: Rachel Coloff, Nikki Renée Daniels, Joseph Dellger, Colleen Fitzpatrick, Patrick Mellen, Chris Peluso, Dominique Plaisant, Megan Reinking, Will Swenson, Tommar Wilson.

Orchestra: Brad Haak conductor; Andy Grobengieser associate conductor, keyboard 2; Thad Wheeler assistant conductor, percussion; Martin Agee concertmaster, violin; Natalie Cenova Cummins, Cecelia Hobbs Gardner violin; Maxine L. Roach viola; Stephanie L. Cummins, Chungsun Kim cello; Chuck Wilson flute, clarinet; Lynne A. Cohen oboe, English horn; Chris Komer, Bradley C. Gemeinhardt horns; Matt Ingman trombone, euphonium; Jason DeBord keyboard 1; Jose Simbulan keyboard 3; Bruce Uchitel guitar; Brian Hamm bass; Dave Ratajczak percussion, drums.

Understudies: Mr. Panaro—Drew Sarich, Will Swenson; Ms. Carmello—Rachel Coloff, Colleen Fitzpatrick; Mr. Sarich—Sean MacLaughlin, Will Swenson; Mr. Hill—Chris Peluso, Tommar Wilson; Mr. Stanek—Chris Peluso, Tommar Wilson; Mr. Genet—Joseph Dellger, Steve Wilson.

Swings: Sean MacLaughlin, Sarah Solie, Steve Wilson.

Directed by Robert Jess Roth; choreography, Matt West; scenery, Derek McLane; costumes, Susan Hilferty; lighting, Kenneth Posner; sound, Jonathan Deans; projections, Howard Werner; wigs and hair, Tom Watson; fight direction, Rick Sordelet; orchestrations, Steve Margoshes, Guy Babylon and Bruce Coughlin; music supervision, Mr. Babylon; music direction, Mr. Haak; music coordination, John Miller; vocal arrangements, Todd Ellison; casting, Jay Binder and Mark Brandon; production stage manager, Bonnie L. Becker; press, Barlow-Hartman Public Relations, John Barlow, Michael Hartman, Wayne Wolfe, Andrew Snyder.

Presented in two parts.

Vampires find that eternal life is not all that it seems. First presentation of record was given at San Francisco's Curran Theatre (1/8–29/2006).

ACT I	ACT II
"From the Dead"	"Welcome to the New World"
"Beautiful Boy"	"Embrace It"
"In Paris"	"I Want More"
"The Thirst"	"I'll Never Have That Chance"
"Right Before My Eyes"	"Sail Me Away"
"Make Me As You Are"	"To Kill Your Kind"
"To Live Like This"	"Embrace it" (Reprise)
"Morality Play"	"After All This Time"
"The Crimson Kiss"	"Finale"

The Wedding Singer (40). Musical with book by Chad Beguelin and Tim Herlihy; music by Matthew Sklar; lyrics by Mr. Beguelin; based on the New Line Cinema film by Tim Herlihy. Produced by Margo Lion, New Line Cinema, the Araca Group, Roy Furman, Douglas L. Meyer, James D. Stern, Rick Steiner/Staton Bell Osher Mayerson Group, Jam Theatricals, in association with Jujamcyn Theaters and Jay Furman, Michael Gill, Lawrence Horowitz, Rhoda Mayerson, Marisa Sechrest, Gary Winnick, Dancap Productions, Inc., Élan V. McAllister/Allan S. Gordon/Adam Epstein, at the Al Hirschfeld Theatre. Opened April 27, 2006.

Robbie Hart	Stephen Lynch	Glen Guglia	Richard H. Blake
Sammy	Matthew Saldivar	Rosie	Rita Gardner
George	Kevin Cahoon	Linda	Felicia Finley
Julia Sullivan	Laura Benanti	Angie	Adinah Alexander
Holly	Amy Spanger		

Impersonators: Tracee Beazer, Cara Cooper, Peter Kapetan, J. Elaine Marcos, T. Oliver Reid, Christina Sivrich, Matthew Stocke.

Ensemble: Adinah Alexander, Matt Allen, Tracee Beazer, Cara Cooper, Ashley Amber Haase, Nicolette Hart, David Josefsberg, Peter Kapetan, Spencer Liff, J. Elaine Marcos, T. Oliver Reid, Christina Sivrich, Matthew Stocke, Eric LaJuan Summers.

Orchestra: James Sampliner conductor, keyboard; John Samorian associate conductor, keyboard; Irio O'Farrill, Matthew Saldivar bass; Larry Saltzman, Stephen Lynch, John Putnam, Gary Sieger guitar; Clifford Lyons, Jack Bashkow reeds; Trevor Neumann trumpet; Jon Werking keyboard; James Saporito percussion; Warren Odze drums.

Standby: Ms. Benanti—Tina Maddigan.

Understudies: Mr. Lynch—Matthew Stocke; Ms. Spanger—Cara Cooper; Messrs. Cahoon, Blake—Kevin Kern; Mr. Saldivar—David Josefsberg; Ms. Finley—Nicolette Hart; Ms. Gardner—Christina Sivrich.

Swings: Angelique Ilo, Kevin Kern, Joanne Manning, Michael McGurk.

Directed by John Rando; choreography, Rob Ashford; scenery, Scott Pask; costumes, Gregory Gale; lighting, Brian MacDevitt; sound, Peter Hylenski; hair, David Brian Brown; orchestrations, Irwin Fisch; dance music arrangements, David Chase; music direction, Mr. Sampliner; music coordination, John Miller; executive producer, Mark Kaufman; casting, Bernard Telsey Casting; production stage manager, Rolt Smith; press, Richard Kornberg and Associates, Richard Kornberg, Don Summa, Carrie Friedman.

Time: 1985. Place: Ridgefield, NJ. Presented in two parts.

A brokenhearted wedding singer finds true love in the wilds of suburban New Jersey. First presentation of record was given at Seattle's 5th Avenue Theatre (2/9–19/2006).

ACT I

Scene 1: Reception Hall
"It's Your Wedding Day" .... Robbie, Company
"Someday" .... Julia
Scene 2: The Loading Dock
Scene 3: Robbie's Bedroom
"Someday" (Reprise) .... Robbie, Rosie
Scene 4: Reception Hall
"A Note From Linda" .... Linda
Scene 5: The Restaurant
"Pop" .... Holly, Julia, Angie, Company
Scene 6: Robbie's Bedroom
"Somebody Kill Me" .... Robbie
(Adam Sandler, Tim Herlihy)
"A Note From Grandma" .... Rosie
Scene 7: Reception Hall
"Casualty of Love" .... Robbie, Company
Scene 8: The Loading Dock
"Come Out of the Dumpster" .... Julia, Robbie
Scene 9: Reception Hall
"Today You Are a Man" .... Robbie, Sammy, George
"George's Prayer" .... George
Scene 10: The Mall
"Not That Kind of Thing" .... Robbie, Julia, Company
Scene 10: Holly's Closet/The Club
"Saturday Night in the City" .... Holly, Company

ACT II

Scene 1: Glen's Office
"All About the Green" .... Glen, Robbie, Company
Scene 2: Reception Hall
"Right in Front of Your Eyes" .... Holly, Sammy
Scene 3: Rosie's Porch
Scene 4: The Bar
"Single" .... Sammy, Robbie, George, Ricky, Blum, Men
Scene 5: Julia's Bedroom
"If I Told You" .... Robbie, Julia
Scnee 6: Robbie's Bedroom
"Let Me Come Home" .... Linda
Scene 7: Reception Hall
"If I Told You" (Reprise) .... Robbie, Julia

"Move That Thang" .... Rosie, George
Scene 8: White House Wedding Chapel, Las Vegas
  "Grow Old With You" .... Robbie, Julia
                          (Adam Sandler, Tim Herlihy)
Scene 9: Reception Hall
  "It's Your Wedding Day" (Finale) .... Company

*Hot Feet (36). Musical with book by Heru Ptah; music and lyrics by Maurice White. Produced by Transamerica, Rudy Durand, in association with Kalimba Entertainment, Inc., at the Hilton Theatre. Opened April 30, 2006.

Louie .... Allen Hidalgo	Anthony .... Michael Balderrama
Emma .... Samantha Pollino;	Victor .... Keith David
Sarah Livingston (alt.)	Naomi .... Wynonna Smith
Kalimba .... Vivian Nixon	Rahim .... Daryl Spiers
Mom .... Ann Duquesnay	

Ensemble: Kevin Aubin, Gerrard Carter, Dionne Figgins, Ramón Flowers, Karla Puno Garcia, Nakia Henry, Duane Lee Holland, Iquail S. Johnson, Dominique Kelley, Steve Konopelski, Sumie Maeda, Jon-Paul Mateo, Vasthy Mompoint, Tera-Lee Pollin, Monique Smith, Daryl Spiers, Felicity Stiverson, Hollie E. Wright.

Band Vocalists: Brent Carter, Keith Anthony Fluitt, Theresa Thomason.

Band: Jeffrey Klitz conductor, synthesizer; Andy Ezrin associate conductor, synthesizer; Keith Robinson, Bernd Schoenhart guitar; Artie C. Reynolds III electric bass, bass synthesizer; Dave Keyes synthesizer; Don Downs, David Trigg trumpet; Keith O'Quinn trombone; Scott Kreitzer saxophone; Errol Crusher Bennett percussion; Brian Dunne drums.

Standbys: Mr. David—Adrian Bailey; Ms. Duquesnay—Sandra Reaves-Phillips; Mr. Hidalgo—Caesar Samayoa; Ms. Pollino—Sarah Livingston.

Understudies: Ms. Nixon—Dionne Figgins; Mr. Balderrama—Daryl Spiers; Ms. Smith—Nakia Henry; Mr. Spiers—Jon-Paul Mateo.

Band Vocalists Swings: Marvel J. Allen, John A. James.

Directed and choreographed by Maurice Hines; scenery, James Noone; costumes, Paul Tazewell; lighting, Clifton Taylor; sound, Acme Sound Partners; hair, Qodi Armstrong; orchestrations and arrangments, Bill Meyers; music direction, Mr. Klitz; music coordination, John Miller; associate producers, Meir Asher, Eli Cohen, Plymer Global Holdings, Godley Morris Group; casting, Stuart Howard, Amy Schecter, Paul Hardt; production stage manager, Michael E. Harrod; press, Springer Associates, Gary Springer, Joe Trentacosta, Michelle Moretta, D'Arcy Drollinger.

Time: Present. Place: New York City. Presented in two parts.

Updating of *The Red Shoes* that probes the price a dancer is willing to pay to live in her work. First presentation of record was given at the National Theatre, Washington, DC (3/21–4/9/2006).

ACT I

Overture .... Band
"In the Stone" .... Band
"Rock That"/"Boogie Wonderland" .... Band, Brent Carter
"When I Dance" .... Band, Theresa Thomason
"Dearest Heart" .... Mom, Kalimba
"September" .... Band, Brent Carter
"Turn It Into Something Good" .... Band, Brent Carter
"Ponta de Areia" .... Band
"Thinking of You" .... Band, Brent Carter
"Mighty, Mighty" .... Band, Brent Carter
"Serpentine Fire" .... Band, Brent Carter
"Fantasy" .... Band, Keith Anthony Fluitt, Theresa Thomason

ACT II

"Louie's Welcome" .... Louie
"Getaway" .... Band, Brent Carter

"Dirty" .... Band, Brent Carter
"After the Love Has Gone" .... Band, Brent Carter
"Can't Hide Love" .... Victor
"You Don't Know" .... Mom, Victor
"Kali" .... Mom
Hot Feet Ballet
   Ballet Intro .... Band
   "Hot Feet" .... Louie
   "Let Your Feelings Show" .... Band, Brent Carter, Keith Anthony Fluitt
   "System of Survival" .... Band, Brent Carter, Keith Anthony Fluitt
   "Saturday Night" .... Band, Brent Carter
   "Africano" .... Band
   "Star" .... Band
   "Faces" .... Band
"Kali" (Reprise) .... Mom
"Mega Mix" .... Band
"September" .... Band
"Shining Star" .... Company
"Gratitude" .... Band, Keith Anthony Fluitt

*The Drowsy Chaperone (36). Musical with book by Bob Martin and Don McKellar;
music and lyrics by Lisa Lambert and Greg Morrison. Produced by Kevin McCollum,
Roy Miller, Boyett Ostar Productions, Stephanie P. McClelland, Barbara Freitag, Jill
Furman, at the Marquis Theatre. Opened May 1, 2006.

Man in Chair	Bob Martin	Robert Martin	Troy Britton Johnson
Mrs. Tottendale	Georgia Engel	George	Eddie Korbich
Underling	Edward Hibbert	Feldzieg	Lenny Wolpe

*Star turn: Joey Sorge, Linda Griffin, Angela Pupello, Sutton Foster, Patrick Wetzel, Jennifer
Smith, Lenny Wolpe, Beth Leavel (seated), Jason Kravits and Garth Kravits in* The Drowsy
Chaperone. *Photo: Joan Marcus*

Kitty ....Jennifer Smith
Gangster #1 ....Jason Kravits
Gangster #2 .... Garth Kravits
Aldopho .... Danny Burstein

Janet Van De Graaff.................... Sutton Foster
The Drowsy Chaperone .... Beth Leavel
Trix .... Kecia Lewis-Evans
Super ....Joey Sorge

Ensemble: Linda Griffin, Angela Pupello, Joey Sorge, Patrick Wetzel.

Orchestra: Phil Reno conductor; Lawrence Goldberg associate conductor, keyboard; Edward Joffe, Tom Murray, Tom Christensen, Ron Jannelli reeds; Dave Stahl, Glenn Drewes, Jeremy Miloszewicz trumpet; Steve Armour, Jeff Nelson trombone; Ed Hamilton guitar; Michael Kuennen bass; Matt Perri keyboard; Bill Hayes percussion; Perry Cavari drums.

Understudies: Mr. Martin—Jay Douglas, Patrick Wetzel; Ms. Sutton—Andrea Chamberlain, Angela Pupello; Mr. Johnson—Jay Douglas, Joey Sorge; Ms. Leavel—Stacia Fernandez, Linda Griffin; Ms. Engel—Stacia Fernandez, Linda Griffin; Mr. Burstein—Jay Douglas, Joey Sorge; Mr. Hibbert—Kilty Reidy, Patrick Wetzel; Mr. Wolpe—Jay Douglas, Patrick Wetzel; Ms. Smith—Andrea Chamberlain, Angela Pupello; Mr. Korbich—Kilty Reidy, Patrick Wetzel; Messrs. Kravitses—Kilty Reidy, Joey Sorge; Ms. Lewis-Evans—Stacia Fernandez, Linda Griffin.

Directed and choreographed by Casey Nicholaw; scenery, David Gallo; costumes, Gregg Barnes; lighting, Ken Billington and Brian Monahan; sound, Acme Sound Partners; hair, Josh Marquette; orchestrations, Larry Blank; dance and music arrangements, Glen Kelly; music direction, Mr. Reno; music coordination, John Miller; associate producers, Sonny Everett and Mariano Tolentino Jr.; casting Bernard Telsey Casting; production stage manager, Karen Moore; press, Boneau/Bryan-Brown, Chris Boneau, Joe Perrotta, Heath Schwartz.

Presented without intermission.

An obsessed musical theater fan shares his enthusiasm for a madcap 1920s musical, bringing it to life with commentary as he plays a cast recording on his phonograph. First presentation of record was given at Toronto's George Ignatieff Theatre (7/2/1999). After other runs in Toronto at Theatre Passe Muraille (11/28–12/12/1999) and the Winter Garden Theatre (6/12–7/28/2001), it was featured at the National Alliance for Musical Theatre showcase in New York (10/3–4/2004). There was also a pre-Broadway run at the Center Theatre Group's Ahmanson Theatre in Los Angeles (11/18–12/24/2005). The Broadway production received 2006 Tony Awards for best book of a musical (Mr. Martin and Mr. McKellar), best original score (Ms. Lambert and Mr. Morrison), best featured actress in a musical (Ms. Leavel), best scenic design of a musical (Mr. Gallo) and best costume design of a musical (Mr. Barnes).

MUSICAL NUMBERS

Overture .... Orchestra
"Fancy Dress" .... Company
"Cold Feets" .... Robert, George
"Show Off" ....'............ Janet, Company
"As We Stumble Along" .... Drowsy Chaperone
"I Am Aldolpho" .... Aldolpho, Drowsy Chaperone
"Accident Waiting to Happen" .... Robert, Janet
"Toledo Surprise" .... Gangsters, Feldzieg, Kitty, Aldolpho,
George, Janet, Robert, Underling,
Mrs. Tottendale, Drowsy Chaperone, Company
"Message From a Nightingale" .... Kitty, Gangsters, Aldolpho, Drowsy Chaperone
"Bride's Lament" .... Janet, Company
"Love Is Always Lovely in the End" .... Mrs. Tottendale, Underlineg
"I Do, I Do in the Sky" .... Trix, Company
"As We Stumble Along" (Reprise) .... Company

*The Lieutenant of Inishmore (33). Transfer of the Off Broadway play by Martin McDonagh. Produced by Randall L. Wreghitt, Dede Harris, Atlantic Theater Company, David Lehrer, Harriet Newman Leve and Ron Nicynski, Zavelson Meyrelles Greiner Group, Morton Swinsky and Redfern Goldman Productions, and Ruth Hendel, at the Lyceum Theatre. May 3, 2006.

Davey ....Domhnall Gleeson   Donny .... Peter Gerety

Tweedledum and tweedledee: Domhnall Gleeson and Peter Gerety in The Lieutenant of Inishmore. *Photo: Monique Carboni*

Padraic .... David Wilmot   Christy .... Andrew Connolly
James .... Jeff Binder   Joey .... Dashiell Eaves
Mairead .... Alison Pill   Brendan .... Brian d'Arcy James

Understudies: Messrs. Gerety, Connolly—John Ahlin; Messrs. Wilmot, Eaves, Gleeson, Binder, Connolly—Brian Avers; Ms. Pill—Cristin Milioti.

Directed by Wilson Milam; scenery, Scott Pask; costumes, Theresa Squire; lighting, Michael Chybowski; sound, Obadiah Eaves; fight direction, J. David Brimmer; music, Matt McKenzie; associate producer, Braun-McFarlane Productions; casting, Pat McCorkle; production stage manager, James Harker; press, Boneau/Bryan-Brown, Chris Boneau, Susanne Tighe, Heath Schwartz.

Time: 1993. Place: Island of Inishmore, County Galway. Presented in two parts.

A sadistic Irish revolutionary becomes unhinged when he learns that something bad may have happened to his cat. A 2005–06 *Best Plays* choice (see essay by John Istel in this volume). First presentation of record was given at the Royal Shakespeare Company's Other Place in Stratford-Upon-Avon (4/18–10/12/2001). The RSC then moved the production to the Pit in London's Barbican (12/20/2001–2/23/2002). It went on to a commercial run at the Garrick Theatre (6/26/2002–11/2/2002). See Plays Produced Off Broadway section of this volume.

*Faith Healer (32). Revival of the play by Brian Friel. Produced by Michael Colgan and Sonia Friedman Productions, the Shubert Organization, Robert Bartner, Roger Berlind, Scott Rudin, Spring Sirkin, in association with the Gate Theatre Dublin, at the Booth Theatre. Opened May 4, 2006.

Frank Hardy .... Ralph Fiennes   Teddy .... Ian McDiarmid
Grace Hardy .... Cherry Jones

Standbys: Mr. Fiennes—Patrick Boll; Mr. McDiarmid—Jarlath Conroy; Ms. Jones—Robin Moseley.

Directed by Jonathan Kent; scenery and costumes, Jonathan Fensom; lighting, Mark Henderson; sound, Christopher Cronin; video, Sven Ortel; associate producer, Lauren Doll; casting, Jim

In her cups: Cherry Jones in Faith Healer. *Photo: Joan Marcus*

Carnahan; production stage manager, Jane Grey; press, Barlow-Hartman Public Relations, John Barlow, Michael Hartman, Dennis Crowley, Ryan Ratelle.

Presented in two parts.

Four monologues tell a story of love, art, passion and death from three perspectives. First presentation of record was given at New York's Workshop of the Players Art (WPA) in the company's Fifth Annual New Plays Festival (6/2–9/1976). Long Wharf Theatre in New Haven presented a version of the play in its Monday Night Series (11/22/1976–1/24/1977). A pre-Broadway tryout played Baltimore's Mechanic Theatre (3/13–31/1979) with James Mason, Clarissa Kaye and Donal Donnelly. That production had a brief Broadway run at the Longacre Theatre (4/5/1979–4/22/1979; 20 performances). Mr. McDiarmid received a 2006 Tony Award for best featured actor in a play. The 2005–06 production was the first Broadway revival.

The Caine Mutiny Court-Martial (17) Revival of the play by Herman Wouk. Produced by Jeffrey Richards, Jerry Frankel, Debra Black, Roger Berlind, Ronald Frankel, Terry E. Schnuck, Sheldon Stein, Barry Weisbord, in association with Roy Furman, at the Gerald Schoenfeld Theatre. Opened May 7, 2006. (Closed May 21, 2006)

Lt. Barney Greenwald .... David Schwimmer	Lt. Thomas Keefer .... Geoffrey Nauffts
Lt. Stephen Maryk .... Joe Sikora	SM3 Junius Urban .... Paul David Story
Lt. Com. John Challee .... Tim Daly	Lt. (J.G.) Willis Keith .... Ben Fox
Lt. Com. Philip Queeg .... Zeljko Ivanek	Capt. Randolph Southard .... Murphy Guyer
Captain Blakely .... Terry Beaver	Dr. Forest Lundeen .... Brian Reddy

Dr. Bird .... Tom Nelis   Orderly .... Robert L. Devaney
Stenographer .... Tom Gottlieb

Members of the Court: Peter Bradbury, Michael Quinlan, Brian Russell, Doug Stender.

Party Guests: Denis Butkus, Greg McFadden.

Understudies: Messrs. Devaney, Nelis, Reddy—Brian Russell; Messrs. Beaver, Guyer—Michael Quinlan; Messrs. Story, Fox, Gottlieb—Denis Butkus; Messrs. Sikora, Daly, Nauffts—Robert L. Devaney; Messrs. Ivanek, Daly—Peter Bradbury; Messrs. Beaver, Guyer, Reddy—Doug Stender; Messrs. Bradbury, Quinlan, Russell, Stender, Nauffts, Gottlieb—Greg McFadden; Messrs. Story, Fox, Nelis—Tom Gottlieb.

Directed by Jerry Zaks; scenery, John Lee Beatty; costumes, William Ivey Long; lighting, Paul Gallo; sound, Dan Moses Schreier; casting, Stuart Howard, Amy Schecter and Paul Hardt; production stage manager, Steven Beckler; press, Jeffrey Richards Associates/Irene Gandy, Adam Farabee, Alana Karpoff, Eric Sanders.

Time: February 1945. Place: General Court-Martial Room of the 12th Naval District, San Francisco. Presented in two parts.

Courtroom drama centered on an alleged mutiny aboard a World War II ship. First presentation of record at the Granada Theatre in Santa Barbara, California (10/12/1953) before a tour that culminated in the Broadway opening. A 1953–54 *Best Plays* choice, the original Broadway production opened at this same venue, then known as the Plymouth Theatre (1/20/54–1/22/55; 415 performances). Charles Laughton directed a cast led by Henry Fonda and Lloyd Nolan. Based on Mr. Wouk's best-selling 1951 novel, the play opened several months before the 1954 motion picture starring Humphrey Bogart, Van Johnson, Jose Ferrer and Fred MacMurray. The 2005–06 production was the second Broadway revival.

*Manhattan Theatre Club production of **Shining City** (27). By Conor McPherson. Lynne Meadow artistic director, Barry Grove executive producer, in association with Scott Rudin, Roger Berlind, Debra Black, at the Biltmore Theatre. Opened May 9, 2006.

Defrocked: Brían F. O'Byrne in Shining City.
Photo: Joan Marcus

Ian .... Brían F. O'Byrne   Neasa .... Martha Plimpton
John .... Oliver Platt   Laurence .... Peter Scanavino

Understudies: Messrs. O'Byrne, Scanavino—Chris Genebach; Ms. Plimpton—Fiana Toibin.

Directed by Robert Falls; scenery, Santo Loquasto; costumes, Kaye Voyce; lighting, Christopher Akerlind; sound, Obadiah Eaves; casting, Nancy Piccione and David Caparelliotis; production stage manager, Barclay Stiff; press, Boneau/Bryan-Brown, Chris Boneau, Jim Byk, Aaron Meier, Heath Schwartz.

Time: Present. Place: An office in Dublin. Presented without intermission.

A former priest, now a therapist, helps a man deal with disabling guilt even as the therapist encounters his own demons. A 2005–06 *Best Plays* choice (see essay by David Cote in this volume). First presentation of record was given at London's Royal Court Theatre (6/9–8/7/2004) before a Dublin Theatre Festival run at the Gate Theatre (9/28–10/9/2004).

African idol: Jenn Gambatese and Josh Strickland in Tarzan. *Photo: Joan Marcus*

*****Tarzan** (25). Musical with book by David Henry Hwang; music and lyrics by Phil Collins; based on *Tarzan of the Apes* by Edgar Rice Burroughs and the Disney film *Tarzan*. Produced by Disney Theatrical Productions, under the direction of Thomas Schumacher, at the Richard Rodgers Theatre. Opened May 10, 2006.

Kerchak .... Shuler Hensley   Professor Porter .... Tim Jerome
Kala .... Merle Dandridge   Mr. Clayton .... Donnie Keshawarz
Young Tarzan .... Daniel Manche;   Snipes .... Horace V. Rogers
                                              Alex Rutherford   Ribbon Dancer .... Kara Madrid
Terk .... Chester Gregory II   Lead Vocals .... Horace V. Rogers
Tarzan .... Josh Strickland   Moth .... Andy Pellick
Jane Porter .... Jenn Gambatese

Ensemble: Marcus Bellamy, Celina Carvajal, Dwayne Clark, Kearran Giovanni, Michael Hollick, Kara Madrid, Kevin Massey, Anastacia McCleskey, Rika Okamoto, Marlyn Ortiz, John Elliott Oyzon, Andy Pellick, Stefan Raulston, Horace V. Rogers, Sean Samuels, Niki Scalera.

Orchestra: Jim Abbott conductor, keyboard 1; Ethan Popp associate conductor, keyboard 2; Martyn Axe keyboard 3; Jeanne LeBlanc cello; Hugh Mason bass; JJ McGeehan guitar; Charles Pillow reeds; Anders Boström flute; Anthony Kadleck trumpet; Bruce Eidem trombone; Theresa MacDonnell, French horn; Roger Squitero, Javier Diaz percussion; Gary Seligson drums.

Standby: Messrs. Hensley, Jerome—Darrin Baker.

Understudies: Mr. Strickland—Joshua Kobak, Kevin Massey; Ms. Gambatese—Celina Carvajal, Niki Scalera; Mr. Hensley—Michael Hollick, Horace V. Rogers; Ms. Dandridge—Kearran Giovanni, Natalie Silverlieb; Mr. Gregory—Dwayne Clark, Nick Sanchez; Mr. Keshawarz—Michael Hollick, Joshua Kobak; Mr. Jerome—Michael Hollick.

Swings: Veronica deSoyza, Joshua Kobak, Whitney Osentoski, Angela Phillips, Nick Sanchez, Natalie Silverlieb, JD Aubrey Smith, Rachel Stern.

Directed by Bob Crowley; choreography, Meryl Tankard; scenery and costumes, Mr. Crowley; lighting, Natasha Katz; sound, John Shivers; flying, Pichón Baldinu; hair, David Brian Brown; special creatures, Ivo Coveney; soundscape, Lon Bender; fight direction, Rick Sordelet; orchestrations, Doug Besterman; vocal arrangements, Paul Bogaev; dance arrangements, music direction, Mr. Abbott; music coordination, Michael Keller; associate producer, Marshall B. Purdy; casting, Bernard Telsey Casting; production stage manager, Clifford Schwartz; press, Boneau/Bryan-Brown, Chris Boneau, Jim Byk, Matt Polk, Juliana Hannett.

Presented in two parts.

Child reared by apes grows into his humanity and falls in love with a woman.

ACT I

"Two Worlds" .... Voice of Tarzan, Company
"You'll Be in My Heart" .... Kala, Company
"Jungle Funk" .... Instrumental
"Who Better Than Me?" .... Terk, Young Tarzan
"No Other Way" .... Kerchak
"I Need to Know" .... Young Tarzan
"Son of Man" .... Terk, Tarzan, Company
"Son of Man" (Reprise) .... Terk, Tarzan, Company
"Sure As Sun Turns to Moon" .... Kalia, Kerchak
"Waiting for This Moment" .... Jane, Company
"Different" .... Tarzan

ACT II

"Trashin' the Camp" .... Terk, Company
"Like No Man I've Ever Seen" .... Jane, Porter
"Strangers Like Me" .... Tarzan, Jane, Company
"For the First Time" .... Jane, Tarzan
"Who Better Than Me?" (Reprise) .... Terk, Tarzan
"Everything That I Am" .... Voice of Young Tarzan,
Tarzan, Kala, Company
"You'll Be in My Heart" (Reprise) .... Tarzan, Kala
"Sure As Sun Turns to Moon" (Reprise) .... Kala
"Two Worlds" (Finale) .... Company

PLAYS PRODUCED OFF BROADWAY
○ ○ ○ ○ ○

FOR THE PURPOSES of *Best Plays* listing, the term "Off Broadway" signifies a show that opened for general audiences in a Manhattan theater seating 499 or fewer and 1) employed an Equity cast, 2) planned a regular schedule of 8 performances a week in an open-ended run (7 a week for solo shows and some other exceptions) and 3) offered itself to public comment by critics after a designated opening performance.

Figures in parentheses following a play's title give the number of performances from the press-opening date. These numbers do not include previews or extra nonprofit performances. Performance interruptions for cast changes and other breaks have been taken into account. Performance numbers are figured in consultation with press representatives and company managements.

Plays marked with an asterisk (*) were still in a projected run on June 1, 2006. The number of performances is figured from press opening through May 31, 2006.

In a listing of a show's numbers—dances, sketches, musical scenes, etc.—the titles of songs are identified wherever possible by their appearance in quotation marks (").

HOLDOVERS FROM PREVIOUS SEASONS

OFF BROADWAY SHOWS that were running on June 1, 2005 are listed below. More detailed information about them appears in previous *Best Plays* volumes of appropriate date. Important cast changes since opening night are recorded in the Cast Replacements section in this volume.

*Perfect Crime (7,772). By Warren Manzi. Opened October 16, 1987.

*Blue Man Group (Tubes) (7,619). Performance piece by and with Blue Man Group. Opened November 17, 1991.

*Stomp (5,149). Percussion performance piece created by Luke Cresswell and Steve McNicholas. Opened February 27, 1994.

*I Love You, You're Perfect, Now Change (4,089). Musical revue with book and lyrics by Joe DiPietro; music by Jimmy Roberts. Opened August 1, 1996.

*Naked Boys Singing! (2,398). Musical revue conceived by Robert Schrock; written by various authors. Opened July 22, 1999.

The Donkey Show (1,488). Musical conceived and created by Randy Weiner and Diane Paulus; adapted from William Shakespeare's *A Midsummer Night's Dream*. Opened August 12, 1999. (Closed July 16, 2005)

Menopause: The Musical (1,724). Musical revue with book and lyrics by Jeanie Linders; music by various popular artists. Opened April 4, 2002. (Closed May 14, 2006)

York Theatre Company production of **The Musical of Musicals–The Musical** (512). Musical with book by Eric Rockwell and Joanne Bogart; music by Mr. Rockwell; lyrics by Ms. Bogart. Opened December 16, 2003. Production hiatus January 25–June 10, 2004 and October 2–February 10, 2005. Transferred to Dodger Stages for run beginning February 10, 2005. (Closed November 13, 2005)

Cookin' (632). Transfer of the Off Off Broadway performance piece by Seung Whan Song. Opened March 7, 2004. (Closed August 7, 2005)

*__Slava's Snowshow__ (721). By Slava Polunin. Opened September 8, 2004.

*__Jewtopia__ (671). By Bryan Fogel and Sam Wolfson. Opened October 21, 2004.

*__Forbidden Broadway: Special Victims Unit__ (508). Musical revue by Gerard Alessandrini. Opened December 16, 2004. Production hiatus May 29–June 24, 2005 and March 27, 2006 through the end of the 2005–06 season. Re-opening scheduled for June 9, 2006.

Thom Pain (based on nothing) (382). Solo performance piece by Will Eno. Opened February 1, 2005. (Closed December 31, 2005)

Picon Pie (121). Play with music by Rose Leiman Goldemberg. Opened February 17, 2005. (Closed June 2, 2005)

*__Altar Boyz__ (521). Transfer of the Off Off Broadway musical with book by Kevin Del Aguila; music and lyrics by Gary Adler and Michael Patrick Walker; conceived by Marc Kessler and Ken Davenport. Opened March 1, 2005.

Woman Before a Glass (109). Solo performance piece by Lanie Robertson. Opened March 10, 2005. (Closed June 12, 2005)

Orson's Shadow (337). By Austin Pendleton; conceived by Judith Auberjonois. Opened March 13, 2005. (Closed December 31, 2005)

Beast on the Moon (103). By Richard Kalinoski. Opened April 27, 2005. (Closed July 24, 2005)

New York Theatre Workshop production of **Score** (34). Solo performance piece by Jocelyn Clarke, in association with the SITI Company; based on the writings of Leonard Bernstein. Opened May 1, 2005. (Closed June 9, 2005)

York Theatre Company production of **Captain Louie** (46). Musical with book by Anthony Stein; music and lyrics by Stephen Schwartz; based on *The Trip* by Ezra Jack Keats. James Morgan producing artistic director, in association with Meridee Stein, Pam Koslow, Kurt Peterson, at the Theatre at St. Peter's. Opened May 8, 2005. (Closed June 12, 2005)

Trolls (70). Musical with book and lyrics by Bill Dyer; music by Dick DeBenedictis. Opened May 19, 2005. (Closed July 17, 2005)

New York Theatre Workshop production of **Songs From an Unmade Bed** (20). Solo musical performance piece with lyrics by Mark Campbell; music by Debra Barsha, Mark Bennett, Peter Foley, Jenny Giering, Peter Golub, Jake Heggie, Stephen Hoffman, Lance Horne, Gihieh Lee, Steve Marzullo, Brendan Milburn, Chris Miller, Greg Pliska, Duncan Sheik, Kim D. Sherman, Jeffrey Stock, Joseph Thalken. Opened May 24, 2005. (Closed June 19, 2005)

Playwrights Horizons production of **BFE** (16). By Julia Cho. Opened May 31, 2005. (Closed June 12, 2005)

PLAYS PRODUCED JUNE 1, 2005–MAY 31, 2006

Lazer Vaudeville (86). Transfer of Off Off Broadway vaudeville. Produced by Lazer Vaudeville, Inc., at the Lamb's Theatre. Opened June 9, 2005. (Closed August 21, 2005)

Performed by Carter Brown, Cindy Marvell, Nicholas Flair.

Directed by Mr. Brown; choreography, Ms. Marvell; scenery, Maia Robbins-Zust; costumes, Jennifer Johanos; music, Jesse Manno and Max Morath; laser design, Cory Simpson; music direction, Mr. Manno; production stage manager, Seth Allshouse; press, Keith Sherman and Associates, Keith Sherman, Scott Klein.

Presented in two parts.

Touring company transfer after the demolition of the John Houseman Theatre of a vaudeville centering on juggling, rope spinning and other acts of theatrical magic.

Manuscript (73). By Paul Grellong. Produced by Daryl Roth and Scott Rudin at the Daryl Roth Theatre. Opened June 12, 2005. (Closed August 14, 2005)

Chris Ferrando ....Jeffrey Carlson
Elizabeth Hawkins .... Marin Ireland
David Lewis .... Pablo Schreiber

Understudies: Messrs. Carlson, Schreiber—Gene Farber; Ms. Ireland—Russell Arden Koplin.

Directed by Bob Balaban; scenery, David Swayze; costumes, Sara Tosetti; lighting, David Weiner; sound, Peter Fitzgerald; production stage manager, Donald Fried; press, Pete Sanders Group, Pete Sanders, Shane Brown.

Time: Two evenings in the December. Place: The bedroom of a Brooklyn townhouse. Presented without intermission.

College students with literary aspirations (and pretensions) cross one another in pursuit of fame and money. First presentation of record was given at the Cape Cod Theatre Project in Falmouth, Massachusetts, with Anna Paquin as Elizabeth (07/10/2003).

Roundabout Theatre Company production of **The Paris Letter** (65). By Jon Robin Baitz. Todd Haimes artistic director, Harold Wolpert managing director, Julia C. Levy executive director, in the Laura Pels Theatre at the Harold and Miriam Steinberg Center for Theatre. Opened June 12, 2005. (Closed August 7, 2005)

Burt Sarris;
Young Anton .... Jason Butler Harner
Sandy Sonnenberg;
Dr. Moritz Schiffman .... Ron Rifkin
Anton Kilgallen .... John Glover
Katie Arlen;
Lillian Sonnenberg .... Michele Pawk
Sam Arlen;
Young Sandy .... Daniel Eric Gold
Waiter .... Christopher Czyz

Directed by Doug Hughes; scenery, John Lee Beatty; costumes, Catherine Zuber; lighting, Peter Kaczorowski; sound and music, David Van Tieghem; production stage manager, Tripp Phillips; press, Boneau/Bryan-Brown, Adrian Bryan-Brown, Joe Perrotta, Jessica Johnson.

Presented in two parts.

Sexual attraction, repression and gratification overpower lives also driven by money, angst and occasional desperation. First presentation of record was given at the Center Theatre Group's Kirk Douglas Theatre in Los Angeles (12/12/2004–1/2/2005).

Brits Off Broadway and **Stephen Joseph Theatre** production of **Private Fears in Public Places** (23). By Alan Ayckbourn. Opened June 14, 2005. (Closed July 3, 2006)

Nicola .... Melanie Gutteridge
Stewart .... Paul Kemp
Ambrose .... Adrian McCloughlin
Charlotte .... Alexandra Mathie

Vive la différence! *John Glover, Michele Pawk and Ron Rifkin in* The Paris Letter. *Photo: Joan Marcus*

Imogen .... Sarah Moyle   Dan .... Paul Thornley
    Directed by Mr. Ayckbourn; scenery, Pip Leckenby; costumes, Christine Wall; lighting, Mick Hughes; music, John Pattison; stage manager, Jenny Deady.
    Presented without intermission.
    Six contemporary Londoners lead lives of quiet (and comic) desperation.

The Culture Project production of **Border/Clash: A Litany of Desires** (54). Solo performance piece by Staceyann Chin. Allen Buchman artistic director, in assocation with Ira Pittelman, at 45 Bleecker Street. Opened June 16, 2005. (Closed August 7, 2005)
    Performed by Ms. Chin
    Directed by Rob Urbinati; scenery and lighting, Garin Marschall; sound, Emily Wright; press, Origlio Public Relations, Catie Monck.
    Presented without intermission.
    Autobiographical tale of a young woman negotiating the boundaries of family, identity and sexuality. First presentation of record was given at the Culture Project's Women Center Stage (8/5–21/2004).

*Drumstruck (400). By Warren Lieberman and Kathy-Jo Ross. Produced by Drum Cafe, Dodger Theatricals and Visual Sprint, in association with Globility, at Dodger Stages. Opened June 16, 2005.
    Performed by Nicholas Africa Djanie, Ayanda, Sebone Dzwanyudzwanyu Rangata, Enock Bafana Mahlangu, Tiny, Richard Carter, Nomvula Gerashe, Thema Kubheka, Ronal Thabo Medupe, Molutsi Mogami, Molebeledi Sponch Mogapi.
    Directed by Gregory Thompson; scenery, Neil Patel; lighting, Jeff Croiter; sound, Tom Morse; production stage manager, Bernita Robinson; press, Boneau/Bryan-Brown, Adrian Bryan-Brown, Susanne Tighe, Heath Schwartz.

Presented without intermission.

Audience and performers interactively explore the resonant power of drumming (a drum is placed at every seat). First presentation of record was given in 1997 at Mr. Lieberman's cafe in Johannesburg, South Africa.

Brooklyn Academy of Music presentation of the **Royal Shakespeare Company** production of **Hecuba** (10). Revival of the play by Euripides; adapted by Tony Harrison. Alan H. Fishman chairman of the board, Karen Brooks Hopkins president, Joseph V. Melillo executive producer, at the Howard Gilman Opera House. Opened June 18, 2005. (Closed June 26, 2005)

Polydorus	Matthew Douglas	Talthybius	Alan Dobie
Hecuba	Vanessa Redgrave	Hecuba's servant	Judith Paris
Polyxena	Lydia Leonard	Agamemnon	Malcolm Tierney
Odysseus; Polymestor	Darrell D'Silva		

Sons of Polymestor: John Dominici, Christopher Madden, Otto Pippenger.

Chorus: Charlotte Allam, Jane Arden, Rosalie Craig, Maisie Dimbleby, Aileen Gonsalves, Lisa McNaught, Michele Moran, Sasha Oakley, Katherine O'Shea, Judith Paris, Sarah Quist, Natalie Turner-Jones.

Directed by Mr. Harrison; choreography, Heather Habens; scenery and costumes, Es Devlin; lighting, Adam Silverman; sound, Fergus O'Hare; music, Mick Sands; music direction, Bruce O'Neil; production stage manager, Laura Deards; press, Sandy Sawotka, Fatima Kafele, Eva Chien, Tamara McCaw, Jennifer Lam.

Presented without intermission.

Modern adaptation of Euripides drawing parallels to current wars and warriors. First presentation of record of this version was given at London's Albery Theatre (4/7–5/7/2005). The production was directed by Laurence Boswell who was replaced by Mr. Harrison before the US tour that began in the Kennedy Center's Eisenhower Theater (5/21–6/12/2005).

Second Stage Theatre production of **Birdie Blue** (29). By Cheryl L. West. Carole Rothman artistic director, Timothy J. McClimon executive director. Opened June 23, 2005. (Closed July 17, 2005)

Birdie	S. Epatha Merkerson	Bam; others	Billy Porter
Jackson	Charles Weldon		

Directed by Seret Scott; scenery, Anna Louizos; costumes, Emilio Sosa; lighting, Donald Holder; sound, Obadiah Eaves; production stage manager, Lisa J. Snodgrass; press, Richard Kornberg and Associates, Richard Kornberg, Tom D'Ambrosio.

Presented without intermission.

An upbeat African-American woman recalls life's many struggles and often downbeat results. First presentation of record was given at the Williamstown Theatre Festival in Massachusetts (7/10–21/2002).

Fatal Attraction: A Greek Tragedy (56). By Alana McNair and Kate Wilkinson. Produced by Gorilla Productions at the East 13th Street Theatre. Opened July 10, 2006. (Closed August 27, 2005)

Chorus 2	Nick Arens	Ellen Hamilton Latzen	Aaron Haskell
Chorus 3	Sergio Lobito	Michael Douglas	Corey Feldman
Chorus 4	Kellie Arens	Anne Archer	Kate Wilkinson
Chorus 1	Ebony A. Cross	Glenn Close	Alana McNair

Directed by Timothy Haskell; choreography, Rebeca Ramirez; scenery, Paul Smithyman; costumes, Wendy Yang; lighting, Tyler Micoleau; sound, Vincent Olivieri; fight direction, Rod Kinter; production stage manager, Denyse Owens.

Presented without intermission.

Spoof of the 1987 film starring Glenn Close and Michael Douglas.

The Public Theater production of **As You Like It** (5). Revival of the play by William Shakespeare. Oskar Eustis artistic director, Mara Manus executive director, at the Delacorte Theater. Opened July 12, 2005. (Closed July 17, 2005)

Oliver .... Al Espinosa	Lords .... Dale Ho, Reynaldo Valentin
Orlando .... James Waterston	1st Lord .... John G. Preston
Adam .... Herb Foster	Amiens;
Dennis .... Alec Beard	Sir Oliver Martext .... Bob Stillman
Charles; William .... Gregory Derelian	Boy .... Danny Fetter
Celia .... Jennifer Ikeda	Corin .... Helmar Augustus Cooper
Rosalind .... Lynn Collins	Silvius .... Michael Esper
Touchstone .... Richard Thomas	Jaques .... Brian Bedford
Le Beau .... Philip Kerr	Audrey .... Vanessa Aspillaga
Duke Frederick;	Phoebe .... Jennifer Dundas
Senior .... David Cromwell	Jaques de Boys .... Enver Gjokaj

Ensemble: Alec Beard, Kristen Bush, Jordan Dean, Jocelyn Greene, Brian Henderson, Andre Holland, Chad Hoeppner, Steve Kazee.

Directed by Mark Lamos; choreography, Sean Curran; scenery, Riccardo Hernández; costumes, Candice Donnelly; lighting, Peter Kaczorowski; sound, Acme Sound Partners; music, William Finn and Vadim Feichtner; fight direction, Rick Sordelet; production stage manager, Michael McGoff; press, Arlene R. Kriv, Elizabeth Wehrle.

Presented in two parts.

Pastoral comedy with gender confusions, unjustly deposed royalty and meditations on life in the country. Charles Boyce notes that the first presentation of the play is believed to have been for the Globe Theatre's first season in the autumn of 1599, but that there is no record of an early

Forest fools: Richard Thomas and Brian Bedford in As You Like It. *Photo: Michal Daniel*

performance. A 1723 version known as *Love in a Forest* was adapted by Charles Johnson from several Shakespearean sources. First presentation of record in this country was given at New York's John Street Theatre (7/14/1786).

New York Theatre Workshop production of **Oedipus at Palm Springs** (31). By the Five Lesbian Brothers. James C. Nicola artistic director, Lynn Moffat managing director. Opened August 3, 2005. (Closed August 28, 2005)

Joni	Babs Davy	Prin	Dominique Dibbell
Con	Lisa Kron	Terri	Peg Healey
Fran	Maureen Angelos		

Directed by Leigh Silverman; scenery, David Korins; costumes, Miranda Hoffman; lighting, Mary Louise Geiger; sound and music, John Gromada; production stage manager, Martha Donaldson; press, Richard Kornberg and Associates, Richard Kornberg, Don Summa.

Time: The present. Place: A Palm Springs resort. Presented without intermission.

A domestic comedy with two lesbian couples at its core finds characters confronting relational ennui before darker themes surrounding a primal taboo arise. First presentation of record was given at the Out on the Edge Festival by Boston's Theater Offensive (10/22–23/2004).

The One-Man Star Wars Trilogy (122). Solo performance piece by Charles Ross. Produced by Dan Roche, in association with Carolyn Rossi Copeland Productions, at the Lamb's Theatre. Opened August 9, 2005. Production hiatus November 1–22, 2005 and December 19–26, 2005. (Closed December 31, 2005)

Performed by Mr. Ross.

Directed by TJ Dawe; lighting, Mike Schaldmose; production stage manager, Christine Fisichella; press, Keith Sherman and Associates, Keith Sherman, Scott Klein.

Presented without intermission.

Solo actor performs an abridged version of *Star Wars* films. First presentation of record was given by the Toronto International Fringe Festival at the Helen Gardiner Phelan Playhouse (7/3–14/2002).

Once Around the Sun (66). Musical with book by Kellie Overbey; music and lyrics by Robert Morris, Steven Morris and Joe Shane. Produced by Sibling Entertainment and URL Productions, in association with Maffei Productions, at the Zipper Theater. Opened August 11, 2005. (Closed October 7, 2005)

Kevin	Asa Somers	Richie	Wes Little
Skye; Fred	Caren Lyn Manuel	Lane	John Hickok
Ray; Waldo	Kevin Mambo	Nona	Maya Days
Dave; Guy	Jesse Lenat		

Orchestra: Henry Aronson conductor, keyboard; Gillian Berkowitz assistant conductor, keyboard; Chris Biesterfeldt, Tony Di Lullo guitar; Steve Count bass; Wes Little drums; Frank Pagano percussion.

Directed by Jace Alexander; choreography, Taro Alexander; scenery, Beowulf Boritt; costumes, Daniel Lawson; lighting, Jason Lyons; sound, T. Richard Fitzgerald and Carl Casella; orchestrations, David Spinozza; musical direction, Mr. Aronson; production stage manager, Renee Rimland; press, Keith Sherman.

Presented in two parts.

Musical essay on the dark heart of the popular music business.

MUSICAL NUMBERS

"It's All Music"
"First Dance"
"Life Is What You Make of It"
"You're My Lullaby"
"Let Go"

"And That's Your Life"
"Fool Like Me"
"Once Around the Sun"
"Lucky Day"
"G-I-R-L"

"Missing You, My Friend"   "Love and Live On"
"Something Sentimental"   "Just Another Year"

Joy (49). By John Fisher. Produced by Sean Mackey, Eva Price, Ben Rimalower at the Actors' Playhouse. Opened August 14, 2005. (Closed September 25, 2005)

Corey	Ken Barnett	Elsa	Brooke Sunny Moriber
Darryl	Michael Busillo	Gabriel	Christopher Sloan
Christian	Ben Curtis	Paul	Paul Whitthorne
Kegan	January LaVoy		

Directed by Mr. Rimalower; choreography, James Deforte; scenery, Wilson Chin; costumes, David Kaley; lighting, Ben Stanton; sound, Zach Williamson; music direction, Mark Hartman; executive producer, Phillip D. Gibson; production stage manager, Jennifer Noterman; press, Shaffer-Coyle Public Relations, Jeremy Shaffer, Bill Coyle.

Presented in two parts.

Comedy about love and neurosis in the gay and lesbian life. The first presentation of record was given at UC Berkeley in 1994 under the title *The Joy of Gay Sex* before a commercial run in San Francisco. Prior to the 2005–06 production, there was a run at New York's Producers Club (2/2–20/2005) under the original title.

Sides: The Fear Is Real (72). Transfer of the Off Off Broadway play by Sekiya Billman, Jane Cho, Paul H. Juhn, Peter Kim, Hoon Lee, Eileen Rivera and Rodney To. Produced by Mr. Miyagi's Theatre Company, in association with the Culture Project and REL2 Productions, at 45 Bleecker. Opened August 25, 2005. (Closed October 30, 2005)

Sunny Kenai'Apuni; others	Sekiya Billman	Pete Suh; others	Peter Kim
Tracy Cheung; others	Jane Cho	Johnny Fantastiko; others	Hoon Lee
Chip Kim; others	Paul H. Juhn	Danbury Brackenbury III; others	Rodney To

Directed by Anne Kauffman; scenery, David Korins; costumes, Elizabeth Flauto; lighting, John-Paul Szczepanski; sound and video, Jamie McElhinney; production stage manager, Daryn Brown.

Presented without intermission.

The agonies of the audition process as performed by actors often given short shrift in the casting process. First presentation of record was given by the Ma-Yi Theater Company at P.S. 122 in New York (4/9–5/1/2005).

The Public Theater production of **Two Gentlemen of Verona** (13). Revival of the musical with book by John Guare and Mel Shapiro; music by Galt MacDermot; lyrics by Mr. Guare; adapted from the play by William Shakespeare. Oskar Eustis artistic director, Mara Manus executive director, at the Delacorte Theater. Opened August 28, 2005. (Closed September 11, 2005)

Vissi D'Amore Boy; Thurio	Don Stephenson	Vissi D'Amore Girl	Kate Chapman
Speed	John Cariani	Antonio	Richard Ruiz
Valentine	Norm Lewis	Duke of Milan	Mel Johnson Jr.
Proteus	Oscar Isaac	Silvia	Renée Elise Goldsberry
Julia	Rosario Dawson	Eglamour	Paolo Montalban
Lucetta	Megan Lawrence	Milkmaid	Danielle Lee Greaves
Launce	David Costabile	Crab	Buster

Ensemble: Tracee Beazer, Bridget Berger, Kate Chapman, Shakiem Evans, Danielle Lee Greaves, Joanne Javien, Raymond J. Lee, Dequina Moore, Maurice Murphy, Richard Ruiz, Stacey Sargeant, Amber Stone, Will Swenson, JD Webster, Noah Weisberg.

Orchestra: Kimberly Grigsby conductor, keyboard; Allen Won woodwinds; Christian Jaudes, Elaine Burt trumpet; Wayne Goodman trombone; Steve Bargonetti guitar, mandolin; Wilbur Bascomb bass; Joseph Cardello percussion, Brian Brake drums.

Far out: Renée Elise Goldsberry in Two Gentlemen of Verona. *Photo: Michal Daniel*

Understudies: Messrs. Isaac, Montalban—Will Swenson; Mr. Lewis—JD Webster; Ms. Dawson—Bridget Berger; Ms. Lawrence—Kate Chapman; Ms. Goldsberry—Dequina Moore; Messrs. Johnson, Costabile, Stephenson—Richard Ruiz; Mr. Cariani—Noah Weisberg.

Swings: Christine DiGialloanardo, Rubén Flores.

Directed and choreographed by Kathleen Marshall; scenery, Riccardo Hernández; costumes, Martin Pakledinaz; lighting, Peter Kaczorowski; sound, Acme Sound Partners; music direction, Ms. Grigsby; music supervision, Rob Fisher; music coordination, Seymour Red Press; associate producers, Peter DuBois, Steven Tabakin, Heidi Griffiths; casting, Jordan Thaler and Ms. Griffiths; production stage manager, Lori Lundquist; press, Arlene R. Kriv, Elizabeth Wehrle.

Presented in two parts.

An ethnically diverse musical updating of a romantic Shakespearean comedy with friendship and betrayal at its core. According to Charles Boyce, although the play was surely performed in the 16th century, the first presentation of record was given in 1762 by David Garrick in an adaptation. First presentation of record in this country was given at New York's Park Theatre with Charles Kean as Valentine (10/6/1846). Kean's wife, the former Ellen Tree, played Julia. First presentation of record of the Guare-Shapiro-MacDermot version was given at the Delacorte Theater in Central Park (7/22–8/12/1971; 14 performances), before a Broadway run at the St. James Theatre (12/1/1971–5/20/1973; 614 performances). For many years *Best Plays* counted these two productions—one Off Broadway, the other on—as a single entity for the purpose of recording long runs. With this volume, we correct the Long Runs on Broadway list to correctly reflect the number of performances for the Broadway run, which also required an adjustment upwards by one performance. Inconsistent exceptions were formerly made for counting the first performance date of certain Off Broadway productions—particularly in the nonprofit arena. Occasionally the number was counted from the first public performance, other times from the first press performance. The first press performance for the original Off Broadway run of *Two Gentlemen of Verona* was July 27, 1971, not July 22. It is now the editorial policy of *Best Plays* to count performances only from the press date, if known. The original Broadway production received 1972 Tony Awards for best musical and best book (Messrs. Guare and Shapiro).

ACT I

"Love, Is That You?" .... Vissi D'Amore Boy
"Summer, Summer" .... Company
"I Love My Father" .... Company
"That's a Very Interesting Question" .... Proteus, Valentine
"I'd Like to Be a Rose" .... Proteus, Valentine, Company
"Thou, Julia, Thou Hast Metamorphosed Me" .... Proteus
"Symphony" .... Proteus, Company
"I Am Not Interested in Love" .... Julia
"Love, Is That You?" (Reprise) .... Vissi D'Amore Boy and Girl
"Thou, Proteus, Thou Hast Metamorphosed Me" .... Julia, Company
"What Does a Lover Pack?" .... Julia, Proteus, Company
"Pearls" .... Launce
"I Love My Father" (Reprise) .... Proteus, Company
"Two Gentlemen of Verona" .... Julia, Lucetta, Women
"Follow the Rainbow" .... Valentine, Speed, Proteus,
                                                                                       Launce, Julia, Lucretia
"Where's North?" .... Valentine, Speed, Duke of Milan,
                                                                                       Silvia, Thurio, Company
"Bring All the Boys Back Home" .... Duke of Milan, Company
"Who Is Silvia?" .... Valentine
"Love's Revenge" .... Valentine
"To Whom It May Concern Me" .... Silvia, Valentine
"Night Letter" .... Silvia, Valentine
"Love's Revenge" (Reprise) .... Valentine, Proteus, Speed, Launce
"Calla Lily Lady" .... Proteus

ACT II

"Land of Betrayal" .... Lucetta
"Thurio's Samba" .... Thurio, Duke of Milan, Company
"Hot Lover" .... Launce, Speed
"What a Nice Idea" .... Julia, Lucetta
"Who is Silvia?" (Reprise) .... Proteus, Company
"Love Me" .... Silvia, Company
"Eglamour" .... Eglamour, Silvia
"Kidnapped" .... Julia, Lucetta, Duke of Milan,
                                                                                       Proteus, Thurio, Company
"Eglamour" (Reprise) .... Silvia, Eglamour
"Mansion" .... Valentine
"What's a Nice Girl Like Her" .... Proteus
"Don't Have the Baby" .... Lucetta, Speed, Launce, Julia
"Love, Is That You?" (Reprise) .... Thurio, Lucetta
"Milkmaid" .... Launce, Milkmaid
"I Love My Father" (Reprise) .... Silvia, Valentine, Julia, Proteus
"Love Has Driven Me Sane" .... Company

New York Theatre Workshop production of **Spirit** (29). By Improbable (Julian Crouch, Phelim McDermott, Lee Simpson, Guy Dartnell, Arlene Audergon). James C. Nicola artistic director, Lynn Moffat managing director. Opened September 15, 2005. (Closed October 9, 2005)

Performed by Guy Dartnell, Phelim McDermott, Lee Simpson.

Directed by Mr. Crouch and Ms. Audergon; scenery, Mr. Crouch, Graeme Gilmour, Rob Thirtle and Helen Maguire; lighting, Colin Grenfell; sound, Andrew Paine; press, Richard Kornberg and Associates, Richard Kornberg, Don Summa.

Presented without intermission.

Nonlinear narrative exploring the nature of conflict using live actors, puppetry, miniature models and other visual imagery. First presentation of record was given at the Tron Theatre in

Glasgow (5/10/2000). The production later opened at the Royal Court Theatre's Jerwood Theatre (3/16–4/7/2001).

Dr. Sex (23). Musical with book by Larry Bortniker and Sally Deeting; music and lyrics by Mr. Bortniker. Produced by Richard Ericson and Greg Young in the Peter Norton Space. Opened September 21, 2005. (Closed October 9, 2005)

Alfred C. Kinsey	Brian Noonan	Jack; Edgar Stevens	Benjie Randall
Miss Baxter; others	Linda Cameron	George; Messenger	Jared Bradshaw
Dean Howell; others	David Edwards	Daphne; Brenda	Christy Faber
Clara Kinsey	Jennifer Simard	Phoebe	Colleen Hawks
Wally	Christopher Corts		

Directed by Greg Hirsch; choreography, Mark Esposito; scenery, Rob Bissinger; costumes, John Carver Sullivan; lighting, Richard Winkler; sound, Michael Ward and Tony Smolenski IV; orchestrations, Larry Hochman, David Siegel and Ned Ginsburg; dance-music arrangements, Sam Davis; music supervision and vocal arrangements, Patrick Vaccariello; press, David Gersten and Associates.

Presented in two parts.

Comic musical focusing on the life and work of sex researcher, Alfred C. Kinsey. First presentation of record given at Chicago's Bailiwick Repertory Theatre (9/5/2003). The production received seven citations from the Joseph Jefferson Awards Committee at the 2004 Citation Wing ceremony. By the time of the Off Broadway opening, Pamela Hunt's name had been removed as director and replaced by Mr. Hirsch as "production supervisor."

Playwrights Horizons production of **Fran's Bed** (17). By James Lapine. Tim Sanford artistic director, Leslie Marcus managing director, William Russo general manager. Opened September 25, 2005. (Closed October 9, 2005)

Fran	Mia Farrow	Birdie	Julia Stiles
Vicky	Heather Burns	Lynne; Doctor	Marcia DeBonis
Dolly	Brenda Pressley	Eddie; Doctor	Jonathan Walker
Hank	Harris Yulin		

Directed by Mr. Lapine; scenery, Derek McLane (based on a design by Douglas Stein); costumes, Susan Hilferty; lighting, David Lander; sound and music, Fitz Patton; projections, Elaine J. McCarthy; casting, Alaine Alldaffer, James Calleri and Cindy Tolan; production stage manager, Scott Taylor Rollison; press, the Publicity Office, Bob Fennell, Marc Thibodeau, Michael S. Borowski, Candi Adams.

Time: The present and the past. Place: Arizona and Michigan. Presented without intermission.

Meditation on end-of-life issues and the fragility of human consciousness. First presentation of record was given at the Long Wharf Theatre in New Haven, Connecticut (10/29–11/25/2003).

The Great American Trailer Park Musical (80). Musical with book by Betsy Kelso; music and lyrics by David Nehls. Produced by Jean Doumanian, Jeffrey Richards, Rick Steiner/Osher Staton Bell Group, in association with Janet Pailet, at Dodger Stages. Opened September 27, 2005. (Closed December 4, 2005)

Betty	Linda Hart	Jeannie	Kaitlin Hopkins
Linoleum	Marya Grandy	Pippi	Orfeh
Pickles	Leslie Kritzer	Duke	Wayne Wilcox
Norbert	Shuler Hensley		

Directed by Ms. Kelso; choreography, Sergio Trujillo; scenery, Derek McLane; costumes, Markas Henry; lighting, Donald Holder; sound, Peter Fitzgerald; hair and wigs, Josh Marquette; music direction, Mr. Nehls; production stage manager, Richard C. Rauscher; press, Irene Gandy.

Presented without intermission.

Sketch-driven musical celebration of trailer-park culture. First presentation of record was given at Theatre Three as part of the New York Musical Theatre Festival (9/28/2004–10/3/2004; 7 performances).

In the Wings (22). By Stewart F. Lane. Produced by Bonnie Comley and Stellar Productions International at the Promenade Theatre. Opened September 28, 2005. (Closed October 16, 2005)

Melinda	Lisa Datz	Nicky	Brian Henderson
Steve	Josh Prince	Bernardo	Peter Scolari
Martha	Marilyn Sokol		

Directed by Jeremy Dobrish; scenery, William Barclay; costumes, Mattie Ullrich; lighting, Phil Monat; sound, Jill BC DuBoff; music, Michael Garin; press, Keith Sherman and Associates, Brett Oberman.

Show business tale about love, betrayal and broken dreams.

Cycling Past the Matterhorn (45). By Deborah Grimberg. Produced by Farm Avenue Productions and Joseph Smith. Opened September 29, 2005. (Closed November 6, 2005)

Esther	Shirley Knight	Doug	Ben Fox
Amy	Carrie Preston	Joanne	Nina Jacques
Anita	Brenda Wehle		

Directed by Eleanor Holdridge; scenery, Beowulf Boritt; costumes, Kiki Smith; lighting, Les Dickert; sound and music, Scott Killian; casting, Carrie Gardner; production stage manager, Wesley Apfel; press, Shaffer-Coyle Public Relations, Bill Coyle, Jeremy Shaffer.

Presented in two parts.

A British mother going blind engages with her quirky daughter as the elder becomes more dependent upon the younger.

Slut (51). Musical with book and lyrics by Ben H. Winters; music and lyrics by Stephen Sislen. Produced by Dena Hammerstein, Pam Pariseau and James Hammerstein Productions at the American Theatre of Actors. Opened October 1, 2005. (Closed November 13, 2005)

Adam	Andy Karl	Janey	Amanda Watkins
Yesterday's News;		J-Dogg;	
Veronica	Mary Faber	Buddy Pendleton	David Josefsberg
Doug; others	Kevin Pariseau	Dan	Jim Stanek
Lilly; Janey's Mother	Harriett D. Foy	Delia	Jenn Colella

Directed by Gordon Greenberg; choreography, Warren Carlyle; scenery, Beowulf Boritt; costumes, Anne Kennedy; lighting, Jane Cox; sound, Peter Hylenski; music direction, Eric Svejcar; production stage manager, Sara Jaramillo; press, Bill Evans and Associates, Jim Randolph.

Presented in two parts.

Musical centering on the vagaries of casual sex among the 20-something set. First presentation of record was given at the New York International Fringe Festival (8/18/2003).

A Woman of Will (9). Solo performance piece with book by Amanda McBroom and Joel Silberman; music by Mr. Silberman, Ms. McBroom and Michele Brourman; lyrics by Ms. McBroom. Produced by Jack and Julie Nadel and David A. Braun at the Daryl Roth Theatre. Opened October 2, 2005. (Closed October 9, 2005)

Kate McNeill .... Amanda McBroom

Voiceovers: George Ball, Patrick Cassidy, Jim Dale, André De Shields, Alix Korey, Jay Rogers.

Directed by Mr. Silberman; choreography, Thommie Walsh; scenery and projections, Trefoni Michael Rizzi; costumes, Tobin Ost; sound, Lewis Mead; music direction, Sam Davis; orchestrations, Larry Hochman; music coordination, Michael Keller; production stage manager, Jane Pole; press, Shaffer-Coyle Public Relations.

Presented without intermission.

A lyricist with writer's block struggles for the right words in a lonely hotel room.

MUSICAL NUMBERS

"Cleveland"
"Words"
"Tomorrow Was Born Tonight"
"The Bitch Is Out"
"Ophelia"
"Stand Up"
"Suddenly Love"
"Lady Macbeth Sings the Blues"

"In His Hands"
"The Hard-to-Be-a-Fairy Blues"
"True to My Heart"
"Is It Love"
"Hello"
"The Road Not Taken"
"I Choose to Love"

Five Course Love (70). Musical with book, music and lyrics by Gregg Coffin. Produced by Geva Theatre Center (Mark Cuddy artistic director) and Five Course Love Company, LLC, at the Minetta Lane Theatre. Opened October 16, 2005. (Closed December 31, 2005)

Barbie; others ....Heather Ayers
Matt; others ....John Bolton

Dean; others ....Jeff Gurner

Offstage Singers: Erin Maguire, Billy Sharpe.

Orchestra: Fred Tessler conductor, keyboards; Carl Haan keyboards; Taylor Price guitar, bass; Steve McKeown percussion.

Understudies: Ms. Ayers—Erin Maguire; Messrs. Bolton, Gurner—Billy Sharpe.

Directed by Emma Griffin; choreography, Mindy Cooper; scenery and costumes, G.W. Mercier; lighting, Mark Barton; sound, Robert Kaplowitz; hair, Bettie O. Rogers; orchestrations and arrangements, David Labman; music direction, Mr. Tessler; casting, Paul Fouquet and Elissa Myers; production stage manager, Martha Donaldson; press, Origlio Public Relations, Tony Origlio, Kip Vanderbilt, Philip Carrubba.

Time: Now. Place: Five different restaurants. Presented without intermission.

Love stories told in a variety of restaurant vignettes. First presentation of record was given at the Geva Theatre Center in Rochester, New York (6/16/2004–7/11/2004).

Matt's Car
"A Very Single Man" .... Matt
Dean's Old-Fashioned All-American Down-Home Bar-B-Que Texas Eats
"Dean's Old-Fashioned All-American Dow-Home Bar-B-Que Texas Eats" ....Dean
"Jumpin' the Gun" .... Barbie, Matt
"I Loved You When I Thought Your Name Was Ken" ....Barbie
"Morning Light" .... Dean, Matt
Trattoria Pericolo
"If Nicky Knew" .... Sofia, Carlo, Gino
"Give Me This Night" .... Gino, Sofia
"Nicky Knows" .... Sofia, Carlo, Gino
Dear Schlupfwinkel Speiseplatz
"Shetler-Lied" .... Heimlich
"'No' Is a Word I Don't Fear" .... Gretchen
"Der Bunsen-Kratzentanz" .... Klaus, Heimlich, Gretchen
"Risk Love" .... Klaus, Heimlich
"Gretchen's Lament" .... Gretchen
Ernesto's Cantina
"The Ballad of Guillermo" .... Ernesto, Guillermo
"Come Be My Love" .... Rosalinda, Guillermo
"Pick Me" .... Ernesto, Guillermo
"The Blue Flame" .... Ernesto, Kitty
The Star-Lite Diner
"True Love at the Star-Lite Tonight" .... Clutch, Kitty, Pops
"It's a Mystery" .... Clutch, Kitty
"Medley" ....Pops, Dean, Gino, Heimlich, Guillermo
"Love Looking Back at Me" .... Kitty

Second Stage Theatre production of **A Soldier's Play** (48). Revival of the play by Charles Fuller. Carole Rothman artistic director, Timothy J. McClimon executive director. Opened October 17, 2005. (Closed November 27, 2005)

Pvt. Tony Smalls .... Teagle F. Bougere
Pvt. C.J. Memphis .... Mike Colter
Capt. Richard Davenport .... Taye Diggs
Cpl. Bernard Cobb .... Nelsan Ellis
Capt. Wilcox .... Joe Forbrich
Pvt. James Wilkie .... Michael Genet

Cpl. Ellis .... Royce Johnson
TSgt. Vernon C. Waters .... James McDaniel
PFC Melvin Peterson .... Anthony Mackie
Pvt. Louis Henson .... Dorian Missick
Capt. Charles Taylor .... Steve Pasquale
Lt. Byrd .... Joaquín Pérez-Campbell

Directed by Jo Bonney; scenery, Neil Patel; costumes, David Zinn; lighting, David Weiner; sound, Fitz Patton; fight direction, Rick Sordelet; casting, Tara Rubin Casting; production stage manager, C. Randall White; press, Richard Kornberg and Associates, Richard Kornberg, Tom D'Ambrosio.

Time: 1944. Place: US Army post in Louisiana. Presented in two parts.

An African-American officer in the US Army investigates the murder of an African-American sergeant hated by African-American soldiers stationed in Louisiana. A 1981–82 *Best Plays* choice, the first presentation of record was given by the Negro Ensemble Company at the Lucille Lortel Theatre (11/20/1981–1/2/1983; 468 performances). That production featured Adolph Caesar, Charles Brown, Denzel Washington, Samuel L. Jackson and Peter Friedman. Mr. Fuller received the 1982 Pulitzer Prize in Drama.

Lincoln Center Theater production of **Third** (64). By Wendy Wasserstein. André Bishop artistic director, Bernard Gersten executive producer, in the Mitzi E. Newhouse Theater. Opened October 24, 2005. (Closed December 18, 2005)

Boomer crisis: Charles Durning, Dianne Wiest and Gaby Hoffman in Third. *Photo: Joan Marcus*

Laurie Jameson .... Dianne Wiest   Jack Jameson .... Charles Durning
Woodson Bull III .... Jason Ritter   Nancy Gordon .... Amy Aquino
Emily Imbrie .... Gaby Hoffmann

Recorded voices: William Cain, Josh Heine, Stefanie Nava, Caitlin O'Connell.

Understudies: Mses. Wiest, Aquino—Caitlin O'Connell; Ms. Hoffman—Stefanie Nava; Mr. Ritter—Josh Heine; Mr. Durning—William Cain.

Directed by Daniel Sullivan; scenery, Thomas Lynch; costumes, Jennifer von Mayrhauser; lighting, Pat Collins; sound, Scott Stauffer; music, Robert Waldman; casting, Daniel Swee; stage manager, Roy Harris; press, Philip Rinaldi, Barbara Carroll.

Time: Academic year 2002–03. Place: A small New England college. Presented in two parts.

A professor at a small, elite college faces the large and small indignities of life in middle age. A 2005–06 *Best Plays* choice (see essay by Anne Cattaneo in this volume). First presentation of record was given by Theater J in Washington, DC (1/8/2004–2/15/2004).

Playwrights Horizons production of **Manic Flight Reaction** (25). By Sarah Schulman. Tim Sanford artistic director, Leslie Marcus managing director, William Russo general manager. Opened October 30, 2005. (Closed November 20, 2005)

Grace .... Jessica Collins   Albert .... Austin Lysy
Susan .... Angel Desai   Marge .... Deirdre O'Connell
Luke .... Michael Esper   Cookie; Claire .... Molly Price

Directed by Trip Cullman; scenery, Louisa Thompson; costumes, Jenny Mannis; lighting, Paul Whitaker; sound, Fitz Patton and Harris Skibell; casting, Alaine Alldaffer and James Calleri; production stage manager, Marion Friedman; press, the Publicity Office, Bob Fennell, Marc Thibodeau, Michael S. Borowski, Candi Adams.

Secret friendship: Deirdre O'Connell and Molly Price in Manic Flight Reaction. *Photo: Joan Marcus*

Time: The present. Place: Outside Urbana, Illinois. Presented in two parts.

Distracted academic with a sexual secret finds herself in a tabloid-inspired political scandal.

The Public Theater production of **See What I Wanna See** (41). Musical by Michael John LaChiusa; based on the stories of Ryunosuke Akutagawa. Oskar Eustis artistic director, Mara Manus executive director, in the Anspacher Theater. Opened October 30, 2005. (Closed December 4, 2005)

Kesa and Morito—Part 1

Kesa .... Idina Menzel	Morito .... Marc Kudisch

R Shomon

Janitor .... Henry Stram	Husband .... Marc Kudisch
Thief ....Aaron Lohr	Medium .... Mary Testa
Wife ....Idina Menzel	

Kesa and Morito—Part 2

Morito ....Marc Kudisch	Kesa .... Idina Menzel

Gloryday

Priest .... Henry Stram	Actress .... Idina Menzel
Aunt Monica .... Mary Testa	Reporter ....Aaron Lohr
CPA ....Marc Kudisch	

Orchestra: Chris Fenwick conductor, piano; Todd Groves reed 1; John Winder reed 2; Mark Vanderpoel bass; Diana Herold, Mark Sherman percussion; Norbert Goldberg drums.

Directed by Ted Sperling; choreography, Jonathan Butterell; scenery, Thomas Lynch; costumes, Elizabeth Caitlin Ward; lighting, Christopher Akerlind; sound, Acme Sound Partners; orchestrations, Bruce Coughlin; music direction, Mr. Fenwick; music coordinator, Seymour Red Press; associate producers, Peter DuBois, Mandy Hackett and Steven Tabakin; casting, Jordan Thaler and Heidi Griffiths; production stage manager, Heather Cousens; press, Arlene R. Kriv, Elizabeth Wehrle.

Time: Medieval era; 1951; the present. Place: Japan; New York City. Presented in two parts.

Song cycle that takes the relative merits of storytelling into account as it spins tales of violation, betrayal and redemption. First presentation of record was given at the Williamstown Theatre Festival in Massachusetts under the title *R Shomon* (7/21/2004–8/1/2004; 14 performances).

MUSICAL NUMBERS

Kesa and Morito
  "Kesa"

R Shomon
The Janitor's Statement
The Thief's Statement
  "She Looked At Me"
  "See What I Wanna See"
  "Big Money"
  "The Park"/"You'll Go Away With Me"
  "Best Not to Get Involved"
The Wife's Statement
  "Louie"

The Medium and Husband's Statement
  "You'll Go Away With Me" (Quartet)
  "No More"
  "Simple as This"
The Janitor's Statement
  "Light in the East"
Finale

Kesa and Morito
Morito

Gloryday
  "Confession"/"Last Year"
  "The Greatest Practical Joke"
  "First Message"
  "Central Park"
  "Second Message"
  "Coffee"

  "Gloryday"
  "Curiosity"/"Prayer"
  "Third Message"/"Feed the Lions"
  "There Will Be a Miracle"
  "Rising Up"
Finale

Captain Louie (16). Transfer of the musical with book by Anthony Stein; music and lyrics by Stephen Schwartz; based on the book *The Trip* by Ezra Jack Keats. Produced by Meridee Stein, Kurt Peterson, Bob Reich at the Little Shubert Theatre. Opened October 31, 2005. (Closed November 13, 2005)

Louie	Douglas Fabian	Ziggy	Paul Pontrelli
Amy; Broom	Sara Kapner	Archie	Ricky Smith
Roberta; Mouse	Katelyn Pippy	Julio	Ronny Mercedes

Directed by Ms. Stein; choreography, Joshua Bergasse; scenery, Jeff Subik; costumes, Elizabeth Flauto; sound, Shannon Slaton; music direction, Ray Fellman; press, the Publicity Office, Marc Thibodeau.

Presented without intermission.

Family-oriented musical based on a 1978 picture book that celebrated an imaginative life. First presentation of record was given by New York's First All Children's Theatre with the same creative team (12/2–12/4/1983). The 2005–06 transfer is a restaging of the York Theatre Company production (5/8–6/12/2005; 46 performances). See Holdovers From Previous Seasons at the beginning of this section.

A Mother, a Daughter and a Gun (30). By Barra Grant. Produced by Brian Reilly and Nelle Nugent at Dodger Stages. Opened November 1, 2005. (Closed November 27, 2005)

Jess	Veanne Cox	Juan	Mario Campanaro
Beatrice	Olympia Dukakis	Paul	David Bishins
Eleanor; Cheryl	Stephanie Kurtzuba	Alvin	George S. Irving
Fran	Laura Heisler	David	Matthew Greer
Bob; Stefan	Daniel Pearce		

Directed by Jonathan Lynn; scenery, Jesse Poleshuck; costumes, David C. Woolard; lighting, Beverly Emmons; sound, T. Richard Fitzgerald and Carl Casella; hair and wigs, Paul Huntley; production stage manager, Donald Fried.

Presented in two parts.

Mother and daughter spar verbally over failings in life with a deadly weapon close at hand. First presentation of record was given at the Helen Hayes Theatre in Nyack, New York (9/23–10/9/2005).

Bingo (92). Musical with book by Michael Heitzman and Ilene Reid; music and lyrics by Mr. Heitzman, Ms. Reid and David Holcenberg. Produced by Aruba Productions and Buddy and Sally Productions at St. Luke's Theatre. Opened November 7, 2005. (Closed February 12, 2006)

Vern	Liz McCartney	Sam; Frank	Patrick Ryan Sullivan
Patsy	Janet Metz	Bernice; Marilyn	Klea Blackhurst
Honey	Liz Larsen	Alison	Beth Malone
Minnie	Chevi Colton		

Orchestra: Steven Bishop conductor, keyboard; Bill Stanley keyboard; Aaron Russell percussion.

Understudies: Ms. Blackhurst—Debra Cardona; Mr. Sullivan—Michael Pemberton; Mses. Larsen, Malone, Metz, Colton—J.B. Wing.

Directed by Thomas Caruso; choreography, Lisa Stevens; scenery, Eric Renschler; costumes, Carol Brys; lighting, John Viesta; sound, Lewis Mead; musical orchestrations and direction, Mr. Bishop; casting, Dave Clemmons Casting; production stage manager, Gregory Covert; press, Shaffer-Coyle Public Relations, Jeremy Shaffer, Bill Coyle.

Presented without intermission.

Interactive musical on the pleasures and pitfalls of bingo. First presentation of record was given at the Hermosa Beach Playhouse in California (4/23–5/6/2001).

MUSICAL NUMBERS

"Girls Night Out"   "Anyone Can Play Bingo"

"I Still Believe in You"
"I've Made Up My Mind"
"Under My Wing"
"Gentleman Caller"
"The Birth of Bingo"
"Ratched's Lament"
"Anyone Can Play Bingo" (Reprise)

"Swell"
"Gentleman Caller" (Reprise)
"I Still Believe in You" (Reprise)
"B4"
"I've Made Up My Mind"
"Girls Night Out" (Finale)

Almost Heaven: Songs of John Denver (61). Musical revue based on the songs and autobiography of Mr. Denver. Produced by Harold Thau, in association with Lexie Potamkin, R.H. and Ann Crossland, Lawrence J. Winnerman, Robert Courson, at the Promenade Theatre. Opened November 9, 2005. (Closed December 31, 2005)

Performed by Jennifer Allen, Terry Burrell, Valisia Lekae Little, Lee Morgan, Jim Newman, Nicholas Rodriguez.

Musicians: Chris Biesterfeldt guitar, Steve Count bass, Bob Green fiddle, mandolin, acoustic guitar, Frank Pagano percussion.

Directed by Randal Myler; scenery, Kelly Tighe; costumes, Tobin Ost; lighting, Don Darnutzer; sound, Lewis Mead; projections, Jan Hartley; orchestrations and vocal arrangments, Jeff Waxman; music direction, Charlie Alterman; music coordination, John Miller; production stage manager, Jane Pole; press, Shaffer-Coyle Public Relations, Jeremy Shaffer, Bill Coyle.

Presented in two parts.

Songs and stories from the life of a popular musician. An earlier version with Peter Glazer credited as writer, adapter and director was first presented by the Denver Center Theatre Company in Colorado (3/28–4/27/2002).

ACT I

"All of My Memories" .... Jim, Lee, Company
"For Bobbie" .... Nicholas, Lee, Jim
"Rhymes and Reasons" .... Valisia
"Draft Dodger Rag" .... Lee
"I Wish I Could've Been There" .... Jim, Company
"Take Me Home, Country Roads" .... Jennifer, Company
"Fly Away" .... Terry
"I Guess He'd Rather Be in Colorado" .... Terry, Jennifer, Valisia
"Rocky Mountain High" .... Lee, Company
"Matthew" .... Jim
"Let Us Begin (What Are We Making Weapons For?)" .... Nicholas, Terry
"Calypso" .... Nicholas, Company

ACT II

"This Old Guitar" .... Lee, Jim
"Thank God I'm a Country Boy" .... Jim
"Grandma's Feather Bed" .... Company
"Annie's Song" .... Jennifer
"Goodbye Again" .... Jim, Jennifer
"How Can I Leave You Again" .... Lee, Terry
"Back Home Again" .... Nicholas, Valisia
"Leaving on a Jet Plane" .... Terry, Company
"For You" .... Nicholas
"I'm Sorry" .... Jennifer
"Sunshine on My Shoulders" .... Valisia, Company
"Looking for Space" .... Jim
"Wild Montana Skies" .... Jennifer, Terry, Valisia
"Songs Of" .... Lee, Company
"Poems, Prayers and Promises" .... Terry, Jim, Company
"Yellowstone" .... Company

The Ark (8). Musical with book and lyrics by Michael McLean and Kevin Kelly; music by Mr. McLean. Produced by Erik Orton and Karen Walter Goodwin, in association with D. Keith and Suzanne Ross Jr., at 37 Arts. Opened November 14, 2005. (Closed November 20, 2005)

Martha	Marie-France Arcilla	Eliza	Annie Golden
Ham	D.B. Bonds	Sariah	Jacquelyn Piro
Shem	Justin Brill	Japheth	Rob Sutton
Egyptus	Janeece Aisha Freeman	Noah	Adrian Zmed

Directed and choreographed by Ray Roderick; scenery, Beowulf Boritt; costumes, Lisa L. Zinni; lighting, Eric T. Haugen; sound, Ryan Powers; orchestrations and arrangements, Joseph Baker; production stage manager, Bryan Landrine; press, Keith Sherman and Associates.

Presented in two parts.

The travails of the biblical Noah and his family told in musical form. First presentation of record was given at the Village Theatre in Issaquah, Washington (3/13–4/20/2003).

ACT I

"What a Sight" .... Elira, Sariah, Japheth, Shem, Martha
"Ship Without an Ocean" .... Noah, Eliza, Sariah, Japheth, Shem, Martha
"More Than I Asked For" .... Ham, Egyptus
"Noah's Prayer" .... Noah, Eliza, Egyptus, Sariah, Japheth, Shem, Martha
"Whenever He Needs a Miracle" .... Ham
"It Takes Two" .... Noah, Eliza
"Lift Me Up" .... Company
"Rain Song #1" .... Eliza
"You Cannot Be a Beauty Queen Forever" .... Sariah
"Rain Song #2" .... Egyptus
"Rain Song #3" .... Sariah
"I Got a Man Who Loves Me" .... Martha
"I Got a Man Who Loves Me" (Reprise) .... Martha, Sariah
"Oh, Yeah" .... Japheth, Shem, Ham
"Rain Song #4" .... Company
"Song of Praise" .... Company
"Why Can't We?" .... Egyptus, Company

ACT II

"Couple of Questions" .... Company
"Couple of Questions" (Reprise) .... Egyptus
"In a Perfect World" .... Egyptus, Noah, Ham
"Eliza's Breakdown"/"Hold On" .... Eliza, Noah
"Dinner" .... Ham, Eliza, Sariah, Martha, Shem, Egyptus, Japheth
"You Must Believe in Miracles #1" .... Egyptus
"You Must Believe in Miracles #2" .... Egyptus, Sherri, Martha
"You Must Believe in Miracles #3" .... Egyptus, Japheth, Sariah
"You Must Believe in Miracles #4" .... Egyptus, Company
"So Much More Than I Asked For" (Reprise) .... Ham, Egyptus
"Lift Me Up"/"Hold On" (Reprise) .... Noah, Ham, Company
"I Thought I Was Alone" .... Ham
"Lift Me Up" (Reprise) .... Company
"Song of Praise" (Reprise) .... Company

New York Theatre Workshop production of **Bach at Leipzig** (38). By Itamar Moses. James C. Nicola artistic director, Lynn Moffat managing director. Opened November 14, 2005. (Closed December 18, 2005)

German idol: Boyd Gaines, Jeffrey Carlson, Michael Emerson and Richard Easton in Bach at Leipzig. *Photo: Carol Rosegg*

Johann F. Fasch .... Boyd Gaines
Georg B. Schott .... Michael Emerson
Georg Lenck .... Reg Rogers
Georg F. Kaufmann .... Richard Easton

Johann M. Steindorff .... Jeffrey Carlson
Johann C. Graupner .... Andrew Weems
Greatest Organist
  in Germany .... Jonathan Donahue

Directed by Pam MacKinnon; scenery, David Zinn; costumes, Mathew J. LeFebvre; lighting, David Lander; sound, John Gromada; fight direction, Felix Ivanov; production stage manager, C.A. Clark; press, Richard Kornberg and Associates, Richard Kornberg, Don Summa.

Time: 1722. Place: Leipzig, Germany. Presented in two parts.

Comic competition among musicians who vie for the position of organmaster of Leipzig's Thomaskirche (St. Thomas Church). First presentation of record was given at the Hangar Theatre in Ithaca, New York (7/24–8/3/2002).

Hilda (32). By Marie NDiaye; translated by Erika Rundle. Produced by the Laura Pels International Foundation at 59E59 Theaters. Opened November 15, 2005. (Closed December 11, 2005)

Mrs. Lemarchand .... Ellen Karas
Frank .... Michael Earle

Corinne .... Brandy Burre

Directed by Carey Perloff; scenery, Donald Eastman; costumes, David F. Draper; lighting, Nancy Schertler; sound, Cliff Caruthers; music, David Lang; press, Karen Greco Entertainment, Karen Greco.

Presented without intermission.

First presentation of record was given at Théâtre de l'Atelier in Paris (2/2002). First presentation of record of Ms. Rundle's translation was given at the American Conservatory Theater in San Francisco (2/1–26/2005).

The Culture Project production of **RFK** (117). Solo performance piece by Jack Holmes. Allen Buchman artistic director, in assocation with Winship Cook, Arleen Sorkin, Martin Davich, at 45 Bleecker Street. Opened November 15, 2005. (Closed February 26, 2006)

Robert F. Kennedy .... Mr. Holmes

Directed by Larry Moss; scenery, Neil Patel; lighting, David Weiner; sound, Philip Lojo; production stage manager, Greg Hirsch; press, Origlio Public Relations, Tony Origlio, Catie Monck.

Presented without intermission.

Solo performance piece on the life and times of a legendary US politician. First presentation of record was given under the title *The Awful Grace of God: A Portrait of Robert F. Kennedy* at the Court Theatre in Los Angeles (7/21–8/29/2004).

The Public Theater production of **The Ruby Sunrise** (20). By Rinne Groff. Oskar Eustis artistic director, Mara Manus executive director, in Martinson Hall. Opened November 16, 2005. (Closed December 4, 2005)

Ruby; Elizabeth Hunter .... Marin Ireland	Tad Rose .... Jason Butler Harner
Henry; Paul Benjamin .... Patch Darragh	Lulu .... Maggie Siff
Lois; Ethel Reed .... Anne Scurria	Suzie Tyrone .... Audra Blaser
Martin Marcus .... Richard Masur	

Ensemble: Ron Brice, Eric Martin Brown, Christine DiGiallonardo, Vaneik Echeverria, Jocelyn Greene, Peter McCain, Chad Smith, Eric Thorne.

Directed by Oskar Eustis; scenery, Eugene Lee; costumes, Deborah Newhall; lighting, Deb Sullivan; sound, Bray Poor; associate producers, Peter DuBois and Mandy Hackett; casting, Jordan Thaler and Heidi Griffiths; production stage manager, Buzz Cohen; press, Arlene R. Kriv, Elizabeth Wehrle.

Beautiful dreamer: Marin Ireland and Patch Darragh in The Ruby Sunrise. *Photo: Michal Daniel*

Time: 1927; 1952. Place: Rural Indiana; New York City. Presented in two parts.

A female inventor battles conventional expectations as she attempts to harness technology and create what will become known as television. First presentation of record was given at the Humana Festival of New American Plays in Louisville, Kentucky (3/20–4/4/2004).

Roundabout Theatre Company production of **Mr. Marmalade** (79). By Noah Haidle. Todd Haimes artistic director, Harold Wolpert managing director, Julia C. Levy executive director, in the Laura Pels Theatre at the Harold and Miriam Steinberg Center for Theatre. Opened November 20, 2005. (Closed January 29, 2006)

Lucy .... Mamie Gummer	Bradley .... David Costabile
Mr. Marmalade .... Michael C. Hall	George; others .... Michael Chernus
Sookie; others .... Virginia Louise Smith	Larry .... Pablo Schreiber

Understudies: Ms. Gummer—Julie Jesneck; Ms. Smith—Frances Mercanti-Anthony; Messrs. Hall, Costabile—Alex Cranmer; Messrs. Schreiber, Chernus—Quincy Dunn-Baker.

Directed by Michael Greif; scenery, Allen Moyer; costumes, Constance Hoffman; lighting, Kevin Adams; sound, Walter Trarbach and Tony Smolenski IV; music, Michael Friedman; casting, Mele Nagler; production stage manager, Lori M. Doyle; press, Boneau/Bryan-Brown, Adrian Bryan-Brown, Joe Perrotta, Jessica Johnson, Matt Polk.

Time: The present. Place: A New Jersey living room. Presented without intermission.

Comic tale of a neglected girl who employs adult fantasies to fill the void left by her mother's frequent absences. First presentation of record was given at South Coast Repertory in Costa Mesa, California (4/30–5/16/2004).

Playwrights Horizons production of **Miss Witherspoon** (40). By Christopher Durang. Tim Sanford artistic director, Leslie Marcus managing director, William Russo general manager, in association with McCarter Theatre. Opened November 29, 2005. (Closed January 1, 2006)

Veronica .... Kristine Nielsen	Father 1 and 2; others .... Jeremy Shamos
Maryamma .... Mahira Kakkar	Teacher; Woman in a Hat .... Lynda Gravátt
Mother 1 and 2 .... Colleen Werthmann	

Directed by Emily Mann; scenery, David Korins; costumes, Jess Goldstein; lighting, Jeff Croiter; sound, Darron L. West; casting, Alaine Alldaffer and James Calleri; production stage manager, Alison Cote; press, the Publicity Office; Bob Fennell, Marc Thibodeau, Michael S. Borowski, Candi Adams.

Time: Recent past; foreseeable future. Place: Earth; not Earth. Presented without intermission.

Dark comedy in which an anxious woman faces crisis after existential crisis as she reincarnates again and again. First presentation of record was given at the McCarter Theatre in Princeton, New Jersey (9/16–10/16/2005).

Peter Pan (37). Revival of the musical with book by James Barrie; music by Moose Charlap and Jule Styne; lyrics by Carolyn Leigh, Betty Comden and Adolph Green. Produced by McCoy Rigby Entertainment, the Nederlander Organization and La Mirada Theatre for the Performing Arts, in association with Albert Nocciolino, Larry Payton, Lynn Singleton, Bronsand Music, Inc., in the Theater at Madison Square Garden. Opened December 1, 2005. (Closed December 30, 2005)

Mrs. Darling .... Tracy Lore	Peter Pan .... Cathy Rigby
Wendy Darling .... Elisa Sagardia	Curly .... Jordan Bass
John Darling .... Gavin Leatherwood	First Twin .... Sarah Marie Jenkins
Michael Darling .... Abigail Taylor,	Second Twin .... Theresa McCoy
Victoria Wood	Slightly .... Omar D. Brancato
Liza .... Lauren Masiello	Tootles .... Tiffany Barrett
Nana .... Jonathan Warren	Mr. Smee .... Patrick Richwood
Mr. Darling .... James Clow	Cecco .... Tony Spinosa

Old soul: Jeremy Shamos, Kristine Nielsen and Colleen Werthmann in Miss Witherspoon. *Photo: Joan Marcus*

Gentleman Starkey .... Noel Douglas Orput
Noodler .... Nathan Balser
Bill Jukes .... Jonathan Warren
Captain Hook .... James Clow
Crocodile .... Tony Spinosa,
                                                        Luis Villabon
Tiger Lily .... Lauren Masiello
Mermaids .... Tiffany Helland,
                                                        Tracy Lore
Wendy (Adult) .... Tracy Lore
Jane .... Theresa McCoy

Pirates and Indians: Nathan Balser, Tim Fournier, Seth Hampton, Tiffany Helland, Luis Villabon, Tony Spinosa, Jonathan Warren, John B. Williford.

Touring Orchestra: Craig Barna conductor; Bruce Barnes associate conductor, keyboard 1; Flint Hawes keyboard 2; Stephen Purdy keyboard 3; Richard Henry Grant percussion, drums.

Local Orchestra: Sean Carney violin; Roger Shell cello; Phil Chester flute, piccolo, baritone sax; Shelley Woodworth flute, oboe, English horn; Bill Meade clarinet, bass clarinet, tenor sax; Chris Jaudes trumpet, piccolo trumpet; Elaine Burt, Joe Reardon trumpet; Jason Ingram trombone; Tom Charlap bass, Grace Paradise harp.

Understudies: Ms. Rigby—Gail Bianchi; Mr. Clow—Noel Douglas Orput; Ms. Lore—Tiffany Helland; Mr. Richwood—Cameron Henderson, John B. Williford; Ms. Sagardia—Tiffany Barrett, Theresa McCoy; Mr. Leatherwood—Tiffany Barrett, Gail Bianchi; Ms. Masiello—Tiffany Helland, Sarah Marie Jenkins; Mses. Jenkins, McCoy—Gail Bianchi; Ms. McCoy—Tiffany Barrett; Mr. Brancato—Jordan Bass, Luis Villabon; Ms. Barrett—Gail Bianchi, Luis Villabon; Mr. Bass—Luis Villabon; Mr. Orput—Nathan Balser; Mr. Balser—Cameron Henderson; Messrs. Warren, Spinosa, Villabon—Cameron Henderson, John B. Williford.

Swings: Gail Bianchi, Cameron Henderson.

Directed by Glenn Casale; choreography, Patti Colombo; scenery, John Iacovelli; costumes, Shigeru Yaji; lighting, Tom Ruzika; sound, Julie Ferrin; flying, Paul Rubin; wigs and hair, Monica Sabedra; orchestrations, musical direction, Mr. Barna; casting, Julia Flores; production stage manager, Michael McEowen; press, Anita Dloniak and Associates, Melissa A. Rodes.

Presented in two parts.

Musical version of Mr. Barrie's play about a magical boy who won't grow up. First presentation of record was given in a four-week run at the Curran Theatre in San Francisco (7/19/1954) before a soldout run at the Philharmonic Auditorium in Los Angeles (8/17–10/9/1954). The original Broadway run at the Winter Garden Theatre (10/20/1954–2/26/1955; 152 performances) was planned as a limited-run precursor to a national tour. The Broadway success led to a two-hour NBC television broadcast viewed in an estimated 20 million homes (3/7/1955). Mary Martin and Cyril Ritchard received 1955 Tony Awards for best actress in a musical and best featured actor in a musical. There have been five Broadway revivals of the musical, four of them with Ms. Rigby in the lead role.

ACT I

Scene 1: The Nursery of the Darling Residence
"Tender Shepherd" .... Mrs. Darling, Wendy, John, Michael
"I Gotta Crow" .... Peter
"Neverland" .... Peter
"I'm Flying" .... Peter, Wendy, John, Michael

ACT II

Scene 1: Neverland
"Pirate March" .... Hook, Pirates
"A Princely Scheme" .... Hook, Pirates
"Indians!" .... Tiger Lily, Indians
"Wendy" .... Peter, Boys
"I Won't Grow Up" .... Peter, Wendy, Boys
"Another Princely Scheme" .... Hook, Pirates
Scene 2: Marooner's Rock
Scene 3: The Home Underground
"Ugg-a-Wugg" .... Peter, Tiger Lily, Wendy, Boys, Indians
"Distant Melody" .... Wendy, Peter

ACT III

Scene 1: The Pirate Ship
"Hook's Waltz" .... Hook, Pirates
"I Gotta Crow" (Reprise) .... Peter, Company
Scene 2: The Nursery of the Darling Residence
"Tender Shepherd" (Reprise) .... Wendy, John, Michael
"I Won't Grow Up" (Reprise) .... Darling Family, Lost Boys
Scene 3: The Nursery Many Years Later
"Neverland" (Reprise) .... Peter

Apparition (39). By Anne Washburn. Produced by Apparition Off Broadway, LLC, at the Connelly Theater. Opened December 4, 2005. (Closed January 7, 2006)

Performed by Maria Dizzia, Emily Donahoe, David Andrew McMahon, Garrett Neergaard, T. Ryder Smith.

Directed by Les Waters; scenery, Andromache Chalfant; costumes, Christal Weatherly; lighting, Jane Cox; sound, Darron L. West; stage manager, Elizabeth Moreau; press, Shaffer-Coyle Public Relations, Jeremy Shaffer, Adriana Douzos.

Presented without intermission.

Spooky vignettes designed to make the spine tingle. First presentation of record was given at Chashama (11/7–23/2003).

Rope (24). Revival of the play by Patrick Hamilton. Produced by Drama Dept., True Love Productions, Highbrow Entertainment and Zipper Theater at the Zipper Theater. Opened December 4, 2005. (Closed December 23, 2005)

Brandon	Sam Trammell	Kenneth Raglan	John Lavelle
Granillo	Chandler Williams	Leila	Ginifer King
Sabot	Christopher Duva	Sir Johnstone Kentley	Neil Vipond

Mrs. Debenham .... Lois Markle   Rupert Cadell .... Zak Orth

Directed by David Warren; scenery, James Youmans; lighting, Jeff Croiter; costumes, Gregory Cale; sound, Kai Harada; fight direction, Rick Sordelet; production stage manager, Adam Grosswirth.

Presented in three parts.

Two young men kill a third for the thrill of it and spend the rest of the evening entertaining guests as the dead body lies unseen in an onstage trunk. The play was inspired by the 1924 Leopold and Loeb murder case. First presentation of record was given by the Repertory Players at the Strand Theatre in London (3/3/1929). It later began a continuing run at the Ambassador's Theatre in London under the auspices of Reginald Denham (4/25/1929). First presentation of record in New York was a Lee Shubert transfer of the British production. It was retitled twice before opening—first as *Complex* and then as *Rope's End*—at the Theatre Masque (9/19–12/14/1929; 100 performances). Near the end of its run, the Broadway production departed the Masque (today known as the John Golden Theatre) and moved to Maxine Elliott's Theatre for one week (12/2–7/1929). *Rope's End* then returned for a final week in the Masque (12/9–14/1929). The renaming of the play occurred due to a 1928 *Rope* by David Wallace and T.S. Stribling that had played briefly at the Biltmore Theatre.

Manhattan Theatre Club production of **The Other Side** (48). By Ariel Dorfman. Lynne Meadow artistic director, Barry Grove executive producer, at City Center Stage I. Opened December 6, 2005. (Closed January 15, 2006)

Atom Roma .... John Cullum   Levana Julak .... Rosemary Harris
Guard .... Gene Farber

Understudies: Mr. Cullum—Bev Appleton; Ms. Harris—Darrie Lawrence; Mr. Farber—Chris Genebach.

Directed by Blanka Zizka; scenery, Beowulf Boritt; costumes, Linda Cho; lighting, Russell H. Champa; sound, Scott Killian; casting, Nancy Piccione and David Caparelliotis; production stage manager, James Fitzsimmons; press, Boneau/Bryan-Brown, Chris Boneau, Jim Byk, Aaron Meier.

Presented without intermission.

At the cessation of war, a couple finds that their heritages force them to be separated under the terms of the negotiated peace. First presentation of record was given at the New National Theatre, Tokyo (4/12–28/2004).

Dog Sees God: Confessions of a Teenage Blockhead (86). By Bert V. Royal. Produced by Dede Harris, Martian Entertainment, in association with Sharon Karmazin/Michelle Schneider/Morton Swinsky, at Century Center for the Performing Arts. Opened December 15, 2005. (Closed February 20, 2006)

CB .... Eddie Kaye Thomas   Beethoven .... Logan Marshall-Green
CB's Sister .... America Ferrera   Tricia .... Kelli Garner
Van .... Keith Nobbs   Marcy .... Ari Graynor
Matt .... Ian Somerhalder   Van's Sister .... Eliza Dushku

Directed by Trip Cullman; scenery, David Korins; costumes, Jenny Mannis; lighting, Brian MacDevitt; sound, Darron L. West; wigs and hair, Erin Kennedy Lunsford; production stage manager, Lori Ann Zepp; press, Sam Rudy Media Relations.

Presented without intermission.

Characters from the *Peanuts* comic strip face existential crises in their teen years. First presentation of record was given at Soho Playhouse under the auspices of the New York International Fringe Festival (8/14–9/19/2004). The date in the preceding sentence takes into account an extension following the Fringe run.

New York Gilbert and Sullivan Players production of **HMS Pinafore** (4). Revival of the operetta with book by W.S. Gilbert; music by Arthur Sullivan. Albert Bergeret artistic director, at City Center. Opened January 6, 2006. (Closed January 15, 2006)

Sir Joseph Porter .... Stephen Quint   The Captain .... Keith Jurosko

The Captain (alt.) .... Richard Holmes   Ralph Rackstraw .... Andrew MacPhail
Little Buttercup .... Angela Smith
    Direction and scenery by Mr. Bergeret; costumes, Gail J. Wofford; lighting, Sally Small; musical direction, Mr. Bergeret; press, Cromarty and Company, Peter Cromarty.
    Presented in two parts.
    A sailor loves the captain's daughter, but nothing is simple where the upper class is concerned. First presentation of record was given at London's Opera Comique (5/28/1878).

New York Gilbert and Sullivan Players production of **The Mikado** (5). Revival of the operetta with book by W.S. Gilbert; music by Arthur Sullivan. Albert Bergeret artistic director, at City Center. Opened January 7, 2006. (Closed January 14, 2006)

The Mikado .... Keith Jurosko   Ko-Ko .... Stephen O'Brien
Yum-Yum .... Laurelyn Watson   Pooh-Bah .... Louis Dall'Ava
Nanki-Poo .... Michael Scott Harris
    Direction and scenery by Mr. Bergeret; costumes, Gail J. Wofford; lighting, Sally Small; musical direction, Mr. Bergeret; press, Cromarty and Company, Peter Cromarty.
    Presented in two parts.
    Star-crossed love and mistaken identity played in a fantasy Japan. First presentation of record was given at London's Savoy Theatre (3/14/1885).

Second Stage Theatre production of **The Little Dog Laughed** (56). By Douglas Carter Beane. Carole Rothman artistic director, Timothy J. McClimon executive director. Opened January 9, 2006. (Closed February 26, 2006)

Alex ....Johnny Galecki   Ellen .... Zoe Lister-Jones
Mitchell .... Neal Huff   Diane .... Julie White
    Directed by Scott Ellis; scenery, Allen Moyer; costumes, Jeff Mahshie; lighting, Donald Holder; sound and music, Lewis Flinn; production stage manager, Linda Marvel; press, Richard Kornberg and Associates, Richard Kornberg, Tom D'Ambrosio, Don Summa, Carrie Friedman.
    Presented in two parts.
    Show business comedy about a male movie star attempting to cloak his homosexuality in a sudden marriage and baby. A truncated version titled *He Meaning Him* was given as part of the Downtown Plays festival under the auspices of the Drama Dept. (10/21–31/2004).

Manhattan Theatre Club production of **Beauty of the Father** (48). By Nilo Cruz. Lynne Meadow artistic director; Barry Grove executive producer, at City Center Stage II. Opened January 10, 2006. (Closed February 19, 2006)

Emiliano .... Ritchie Coster   Karim .... Pedro Pascal
Federico Garcia Lorca .... Oscar Isaac   Marina .... Elizabeth Rodriguez
Paquita .... Priscilla Lopez
    Understudies: Messrs. Isaac, Pascal—Joaquin Torres; Mses. Rodriguez, Lopez—Marina Squerciati.
    Directed by Michael Greif; scenery, Mark Wendland; costumes, Miranda Hoffman; lighting, James F. Ingalls; sound, Darron L. West; production stage manager, Barclay Stiff; press, Boneau/ Bryan-Brown, Chris Boneau, Jim Byk, Aaron Meier.
    Presented in two parts.
    Lyric drama centering on the reunion of a father and his adult daughter with whom he competes for the affections of a young man. First presentation of record was given as a joint production of the New Theatre in Coral Gables, Florida (1/3/2004), and the Seattle Repertory Theatre (4/28/2004).

Almost, Maine (38). By John Cariani. Produced by Jack Thomas, Bulldog Theatricals and Bruce Payne, in association with Kathy Hogg, Andrew Polk and Haviland Stillwell, at the Daryl Roth Theater. Opened January 12, 2006. (Closed February 12, 2006)

Guess who: Julie White and Neal Huff in The Little Dog Laughed. *Photo: Joan Marcus*

Pete; others	Todd Cerveris	Sandrine;others	Miriam Shor
East; others	Justin Hagan	Ginette; others	Finnerty Steeves

Directed by Gabriel Barre; scenery, James Youmans; costumes, Pamela Scofield; lighting, Jeff Croiter; sound, Tony Smolenski IV and Walter Trarbach; music, Julian Fleisher; production stage manager, Karyn Meek; press, Pete Sanders Group, Pete Sanders, Glenna Freedman.

Presented in two parts.

Collection of vignettes on the topic of love lost and found. First presentation of record was given under the auspices of the Cape Cod Theatre Project at the Community Hall in Woods Hole, Massachusetts (7/2002).

Lenny Bruce: In His Own Words (26). Solo performance piece by Joan Worth and Alan Sacks; based on Mr. Bruce's work. Produced by Marvin Worth Productions at the Zipper Theater. Opened February 1, 2006. (Closed February 25, 2006)

Performed by Jason Fisher.

Directed by Ms. Worth and Mr. Sacks.

Presented without intermission.

An actor performs the comic routines (and commentary) of Mr. Bruce. First presentation of record was given Saturday evenings at M Bar in Hollywood, California (10/22–12/17/2005).

Confessions of a Mormon Boy (81). Solo performance piece by Steven Fales. Produced by MB at Soho Playhouse. Opened February 5, 2006. (Closed April 16, 2006)

Performed by Mr. Fales.

Directed by Jack Hofsiss; scenery and lighting, Tim Saternow; costumes, Ellis Tillman; sound, Robert Kaplowitz; production stage manager, Charles M. Turner III; press, Shaffer-Coyle Public Relations, Jeremy Shaffer, Bill Coyle.

Presented without intermission.

An excommunicated Mormon tells of life before and after acceptance of his homosexuality. First presentation of record was given in Salt Lake City (11/2001).

New York City Center Encores! presentation of **Kismet** (5). Concert version of the musical with book by Charles Lederer and Luther Davis; music and lyrics by Robert Wright and George Forrest; based on the play by Edward Knoblock; concert adaptation by David Ives. Jack Viertel artistic director, at City Center. Opened February 9, 2006. (Closed February 12, 2006)

Hajj	Brian Stokes Mitchell	Wazir of Police	Danny Rutigliano
Lalume	Marin Mazzie	Chief Policeman	Michael X. Martin
Marsinah	Marcy Harriell	Jawan	Tom Aldredge
Caliph	Danny Gurwin	Nedeb; Princess	Elizabeth Parkinson
Omar Khayyam	Randall Duk Kim		

Ensemble: Rachelle Rak, Venus Hall, Liza Bugarin, Michelle Camaya, Sumie Maeda, Christine Arand, Michael Balderrama, Dennis Blackwell, Jane Brockman, Marcus Choi, Christine Clemmons-McCune, Scott Dispensa, Tony Falcon, Keith Kuhl, Jay Lusteck, Frank Mastrone, Andre McRae, Justin Lee Miller, Marcus Nance, Nina Negri, Robyn Payne, Joe Aaron Reid, Roland Rusinek, Tim Salamandyk, Jennifer Savelli, Larry Beale Small, Laura Yen Solito, Scott Watanabe.

Directed by Lonny Price; choreography, Sergio Trujillo; scenery, John Lee Beatty; costumes, Tracy Christensen; lighting, Kevin Adams; sound, Dan Moses Schreier; orchestrations, Arthur Kay; music direction, Paul Gemignani; music coordination, Seymour Red Press; production stage manager, Tripp Phillips.

Desire denied: Priscilla Lopez and Ritchie Coster in Beauty of the Father. *Photo: Joan Marcus*

Hostel hooker: Christopher Denham and Lisa Joyce in Red Light Winter. *Photo: Paul Kolnik*

Musical tale that toys with stereotypes of the mystical Middle East. First presentation of record was given in Los Angeles at the Civic Light Opera (8/17/1953). The original Broadway production opened at the Ziegfeld Theatre with Alfred Drake as Hajj and Richard Kiley as the Caliph (12/3/1953–4/23/1955; 583 performances). The production received 1954 Tony Awards for best musical, best actor in a musical (Mr. Drake) and musical conductor (Louis Adrian).

MUSICAL NUMBERS

"Sands of Time"
"Rhymes Have I"
"Fate"
"Bazaar of the Caravans"
"Not Since Nineveh"
"Baubles, Bangles and Beads"
"Stranger in Paradise"
"He's in Love!"

"Gesticulate"
"Night of My Nights"
"Was I Wazir?"
"Rahadlakum"
"And This Is My Beloved"
"The Olive Tree"
"Ceremonial of the Caliph's Diwan"

*Red Light Winter (128). By Adam Rapp. Produced by Scott Rudin/Paramount Pictures, Robyn Goodman, Roger Berlind, Stuart Thompson, in association with the Steppenwolf Theatre Company, at the Barrow Street Theatre. Opened February 9, 2006.

Matt .... Christopher Denham   Christina .... Lisa Joyce
Davis .... Gary Wilmes

Standbys: Messrs. Denham, Wilmes—Jason Fleitz; Ms. Joyce—Monica West.

Directed by Mr. Rapp; scenery, Todd Rosenthal; costumes, Michelle Tesdall; lighting, Keith Parham; sound, Eric Shim; associate producers, Ruth Hendel and Stephen Kocis; casting, Erica Daniels and David Caparelliotis; production stage manager, Richard A. Hodge; press, Boneau/Bryan-Brown, Chris Boneau, Jim Byk, Juliana Hannett, Matt Ross.

Time: The present. Place: Amsterdam; New York City. Presented in two parts.

An awkward writer falls in love with a prostitute who loves only the writer's abusive friend. A 2005–06 *Best Plays* choice (see essay by Chris Jones in this volume). First presentation of record was given at the Steppenwolf Theatre Company in Chicago (5/30/2005).

New York Theatre Workshop production of **The Seven** (31). Musical with music and lyrics by Will Power; additional music by Will Hammond and Justin Ellington; adapted from Aeschylus's *Seven Against Thebes*. James C. Nicola artistic director, Lynn Moffat managing director, in association with the Public Theater, at New York Theatre Workshop. Opened February 12, 2006. (Closed March 12, 2006)

Oedipus, Laius .... Edwin Lee Gibson	Right Hand .... Tom Nelis
Eteocles .... Benton Greene	Tydeus .... Flaco Navaja
Polynices .... Jamyl Dobson	

Ensemble: Amber Efe, Charles Turner, Postell Pringle, Pearl Sun, Shawtane Monroe Bowen, Uzo Aduba, Manuel Herrera.

Directed by Jo Bonney; choreography, Bill T. Jones; scenery, Richard Hoover; costumes, Emilio Sosa; lighting, David Weiner; sound, Darron L. West; projections, Kelly Bray, Reese Hicks, Richard Hoover, Frank Luna and Robi Silvestri; music direction, Daryl Waters; production stage manager, Wendy Ouellette; press, Richard Kornberg and Associates, Richard Kornberg, Don Summa.

Presented in two parts.

Hip-hop musical fusing the poetry of Aeschylus's *Seven Against Thebes* with a postmodern sensibility.

York Theatre Company production of **Fanny Hill** (32). Musical with book, music and lyrics by Ed Dixon; based on the novel by John Cleland. James Morgan producing artistic director, at the Theatre at St. Peter's. Opened February 14, 2006. (Closed March 12, 2006)

Fanny Hill .... Nancy Anderson	Mrs. Brown .... Patti Allison
Phoebe Davis .... Christianne Tisdale	Charles Waneigh .... Tony Yazbeck

Ensemble: Emily Skinner, Gina Ferrall, David Cromwell, Adam Monley, Michael J. Farina.

Orchestra: Tara Chambers cello; Jeff Nichols reed; Stanley Tucker piano, keyboard.

Directed by James Brennan; scenery and costumes, Michael Bottari and Ronald Case; lighting, Phil Monat; wigs, Gerard Kelly; orchestrations, Nick DeGregorio; music direction, Mr. Tucker; production stage manager, Jack McDowell; press, Shaffer-Coyle Public Relations, Bill Coyle.

Presented in two parts.

An innocent girl, corrupted by society's cruelties, becomes a prostitute. First presentation of record was given at Goodspeed Musicals in Chester, Connecticut (8/5–8/29/1999).

ACT I

Overture .... Orchestra, Fanny
"Lancashire" .... Company
"On the Road" .... Company
"Seeing London" .... Company
"Going to Mrs. Brown's" .... Mrs. Brown
"House of Joy" .... Cousins, Mrs. Brown
"Croft's Serenade" .... Croft, Fanny
"Welcome to London" .... Martha, Fanny
"Sailor's Song" .... Sailors, Charles
"The Most Heavenly Creature" .... Charles, Robbers
"I Have Never Been So Happy" .... Charles, Fanny
"Marriage Song" .... Charles, Fanny
"Phoebe's Song" .... Phoebe, Esther, Martha
"The Weeping Song" .... Fanny, Company

ACT II

Entr'acte	Mrs. Brown, Esther, Phoebe, Martha, Sailor
"The Card Game"	Mrs. Brown, Esther, Phoebe, Martha
"Tea Service"	Mrs. Brown, Cousins
"Honor Lost"	Fanny
"A Little House in the Country"	Fanny, Company
"My Only Love"	Fanny, Charles
"Every Man in London"	Mrs. Brown
"Big"	Fanny, Will
"I Came To London"	Fanny
"Goodbye"	Fanny, Company
"Storm"	Fanny, Charles, Company
Finale	Company

I Love You Because (111). Musical with book and lyrics by Ryan Cunningham; music by Joshua Salzman. Produced by Jennifer Maloney, Fred M. Caruso, Robert Cuillo, GFour Productions, at the Village Theatre. Opened February 14, 2006. (Closed May 21, 2006)

Austin Bennet	Colin Hanlon	Diana Bingley	Stephanie D'Abruzzo
Jeff Bennet	David A. Austin	NYC Man	Jordan Leeds
Marcy Fitzwilliams	Farah Alvin	NYC Woman	Courtney Balan

Orchestra: Brad Russel bass; Fred Dechristofaro reeds; Jana Zielonka, Brian Cimmet keyboard; Sean Dolan percussion, drums.

Understudies: Ms. Alvin—Courtney Balan; Msers. Austin, Hanlon, Leeds—Barrett Hall; Mses. Alvin, Balan, D'Abruzzo—Jaclyn Huberman.

Directed by Daniel Kutner; choreography, Christopher Gattelli; scenery, Beowulf Boritt and Jo Winiarski; costumes, Millie B. Hiibel; lighting, Jeff Croiter; sound, Tony Smolenski IV and Walter Trarbach; orchestrations, Larry Hochman; music direction, Jana Zielonka; production stage manager, Brian Meister; press, Shaffer-Coyle Public Relations, Adriana Douzos, Jeremy Shaffer.

Presented in two parts.

Gender-reversed updating of Jane Austen's *Pride and Prejudice*. First presentation of record was a staged reading given at the East 13th Street Theatre (7/2005).

ACT I

"Another Saturday Night in New York"	Austin, Jeff, Diana, NYC Man, NYC Woman
"Oh What a Difference"	Jeff, Austin
"The Actuary Song"	Diana, Marcy
"But I Don't Want to Talk About Her"	Austin, Marcy
"Coffee"	Austin, Marcy
"The Perfect Romance"	NYC Man, NYC Woman
"Because of You"	Marcy, Austin
"We're Just Friends"	Diana, Jeff
"Maybe We Just Made Love"	Austin
"Just Not Now"	Marcy
"I Love You Because"	Company

ACT II

"Alone"	Marcy, NYC Man , NYC Woman
"That's What's Gonna Happen"	Jeff, Austin, NYC Man
"Even Though"	Marcy
"But I Do"	Austin, Diana, Jeff, Marcy
"What Do We Do It For?"	NYC Man, NYC Woman
"Marcy's Yours"	Diana, Jeff, Austin
"Goodbye"	Austin

Indoor/Outdoor (31). By Kenny Finkle. Produced by Margo Lion, Hal Luftig, Daryl Roth, in association with Lily Hung, at the DR2. Opened February 22, 2006. (Closed March 19, 2006)

Oscar; others	Mario Campanaro	Samantha	Emily Cass McDonnell
Shuman	Brian Hutchison	Matilda; others	Keira Naughton

Directed by Daniel Goldstein; scenery, David Korins; costumes, Michael Krass; lighting, Ben Stanton; sound, Walter Trarbach and Tony Smolenski IV; production stage manager, Brian Maschka.

Presented without intermission.

Love and longing explored by cats—performed by humans—and their human friends. First presentation of record was given at the Hangar Theatre in Ithaca, New York (7/21–31/2004).

Atlantic Theater Company production of **The Lieutenant of Inishmore** (48). By Martin McDonagh. Neil Pepe artistic director, Andrew D. Hamingson; in association with Randall L. Wreghitt and Dede Harris. Opened February 27, 2006. (Closed April 9, 2006)

Davey	Domhnall Gleeson	Mairead	Kerry Condon
Donny	Peter Gerety	Christy	Andrew Connolly
Padraic	David Wilmot	Joey	Dashiell Eaves
James	Jeff Binder	Brendan	Brian d'Arcy James

Directed by Wilson Milam; scenery, Scott Pask; costumes, Theresa Squire; lighting, Michael Chybowski; sound, Obadiah Eaves; music, Matt McKenzie; fight direction, J. David Brimmer; production stage manager, James Harker; press, Boneau/Bryan-Brown, Chris Boneau, Susanne Tighe, Heath Schwartz.

Time: 1993. Place: Island of Inishmore, County Galway. Presented in two parts.

A sadistic Irish revolutionary becomes unhinged when he learns that something bad may have happened to his cat. A 2005–06 *Best Plays* choice (see essay by John Istel in this volume). First presentation of record was given at the Royal Shakespeare Company's Other Place in

Trigger happy: Brian d'Arcy James, Andrew Connolly and Dashiell Eaves in The Lieutenant of Inishmore. *Photo: Monique Carboni*

Semper Fi: Chris Chalk, Stephen Lang and Chris Bauer in Defiance. *Photo: Joan Marcus*

Stratford-Upon-Avon (4/18–10/12/2001). The RSC then moved the production to the Pit in London's Barbican (12/20/2001–2/23/2002). It went on to a commercial run at the Garrick Theatre (6/26/2002–11/2/2002). See Plays Produced on Broadway section of this volume.

*Manhattan Theatre Club** production of **Defiance** (107). By John Patrick Shanley. Lynne Meadow artistic director, Barry Grove executive producer, at City Center Stage I. Opened February 28, 2006.

Chaplain White	Chris Bauer	Lt. Col. Littlefield	Stephen Lang
Capt. Lee King	Chris Chalk	Gunnery Sgt.	Trevor Long
Margaret Littlefield	Margaret Colin	PFC Evan Davis	Jeremy Strong

Understudies: Mr. Chalk—Royce Johnson; Messrs. Lang, Bauer, Long—Christopher McHale; Mr. Strong—Trevor Oswalt; Ms. Colin–Rita Rehn.

Directed by Doug Hughes; scenery, John Lee Beatty; costumes, Catherine Zuber; lighting, Pat Collins; sound and music, David Van Tieghem; casting, Nancy Piccione and David Caparelliotis; production stage manager, James Fitzsimmons; press, Boneau/Bryan-Brown, Chris Boneau, Jim Byk, Aaron Meier, Heath Schwartz.

Time: Spring 1971. Place: Camp Lejeune, North Carolina. Presented without intermission.

An African-American Captain in the US Marines finds himself pitted against his commanding officer, creating a moral dilemma for the junior officer.

Brooklyn Academy of Music presentation of the **Sydney Theatre Company** production of **Hedda Gabler** (26). Revival of the play by Henrik Ibsen; adapted by Andrew Upton. Alan H. Fishman chairman of the board, Karen Brooks Hopkins president, Joseph V. Melillo executive producer, in the BAM Harvey Theater. Opened March 1, 2006. (Closed March 26, 2006)

Julle Tesman	Julie Hamilton	Berte	Annie Byron

Daddy's girl: Cate Blanchett in Hedda Gabler. *Photo: Heidrun Löhr*

Jorgen Tesman	Anthony Weigh	Judge Brack	Hugo Weaving
Hedda Gabler	Cate Blanchett	Ejlert Lovborg	Aden Young
Thea Elvsted	Justine Clarke		

Directed by Robyn Nevin; scenery, Fiona Crombie; costumes, Kristian Fredrikson; lighting, Nick Schlieper; sound, Paul Charlier; music, Alan John; stage manager, Mary Macrae; press, Sandy Sawotka, Fatima Kafele, Eva Chien, Tamara McCaw, Jennifer Lam.

Presented in two parts.

Mr. Ibsen's tale of an unhappy housewife who seeks vicarious thrills as she attempts to influence the destiny of others. The 2005–06 production was first presented at Sydney Theatre Company's Wharf 1 Theatre (7/27/2004). First English language production of record in New York was given at the Fifth Avenue Theatre (3/30/1898). Elizabeth Robins played the title role. First presentation of record was given at the Hoftheater in Munich (1/31/1891).

Lincoln Center Theater production of **Bernarda Alba** (40). Musical with music and lyrics by Michael John LaChiusa; based on *The House of Bernarda Alba* by Federico Garcia Lorca. André Bishop artistic director, Bernard Gersten executive producer, at the Mitzi E. Newhouse Theater. Opened March 6, 2006. (Closed April 9, 2006)

Bernarda Alba	Phylicia Rashad	Adela	Nikki M. James
Angustias	Saundra Santiago	Maria Josepha	Yolande Bavan
Magdalena	Judith Blazer	Poncia	Candy Buckley
Amelia	Sally Murphy	Young Maid	Laura Shoop
Martirio	Daphne Rubin-Vega	Servant; Prudencia	Nancy Ticotin

Orchestra: Deborah Abramson conductor, synthesizer; Larry Spivak associate conductor, percussion; Joseph Gottesman viola; Benjamin Wyatt, Katie Schlaikjer cello; Raymond Kilday bass; Stephen Benson guitar; Sarah Davol woodwinds; Jennifer Hoult harp.

Understudies: Ms. Rashad—Cheryl Alexander; Mses. Bavan, Buckley—Bertilla Baker; Mses. Santiago, Blazer, Ticotin—Stephanie Pope Caffey; Mses. Murphy, Rubin-Vega—Betsy Morgan; Mses. James, Shoop—Diane Veronica Phelan.

Directed and choreographed by Graciela Daniele; scenery, Christopher Barreca; costumes, Toni-Leslie James; lighting, Stephen Strawbridge; sound, Scott Stauffer; orchestrations, Michael Starobin; music direction, Ms. Abramson; music coordination, Seymour Red Press; casting, Cindy Tolan; production stage manager, Jennifer Rae Moore; press, Philip Rinaldi, Barbara Carroll.

Time: 1930s. Place: A Spanish rural village. Presented without intermission.

Musical adaptation of Mr. Garcia Lorca's play about the matriarch of a family of women who attempts to keep her household from boiling into emotional chaos. First US presentation of record of *The House of Bernarda Alba* was given by John Houseman's Pelican Productions at the Coronet Theatre in West Hollywood, California (11/13–12/7/1947). First Broadway presentation of record of the play was given at the ANTA Playhouse—now the August Wilson Theatre (1/7–1/20/1951; 17 performances).

ACT I

Prologue .... Poncia, Women
"The Funeral" .... Bernarda, Women
"On the Day That I Marry"/"Prayer" .... Young Maid, Bernarda, Poncia, Servant
"Love, Let Me Sing You" .... Amelia, Martirio, Magdalena, Adela, Servant
"Let Me Go to the Sea" .... Maria Josepha, Women

ACT II

"Magdalena" .... Magdalena
"Angustias" .... Angustias
"Amelia" .... Amelia
"Martirio" .... Martirio
"Adela" .... Adela
"I Will Dream of What I Saw" .... Women
"Thirty Odd Years" .... Poncia
"Limbrada's Daughter" .... Bernarda, Women

ACT III

"One Moorish Girl" .... Young Maid, Servant, Poncia
"The Smallest Stream" .... Bernarda
"The Stallion" .... Daughters
"Lullaby" .... Maria Josepha
"Open the Door" .... Adela, Women
Finale .... Bernarda

Playwrights Horizons production of **Grey Gardens** (63). Musical with book by Doug Wright; music by Scott Frankel; lyrics by Michael Korie; based on the film *Grey Gardens* by David Maysles, Albert Maysles, Ellen Hovde, Muffie Meyer and Susan Froemke. Tim Sanford artistic director, Leslie Marcus managing director, William Russo general manager. Opened March 7, 2006. (Closed April 30, 2006)

Prologue (1973)

Edith Bouvier Beale .... Mary Louise Wilson		"Little" Edie Beale .... Christine Ebersole

Act I (1941)

Edith Bouvier Beale .... Christine Ebersole	Lee Bouvier .... Audrey Twitchell
George Gould Strong .... Bob Stillman	"Little" Edie Beale .... Sara Gettelfinger
Brooks Sr. .... Michael Potts	Joseph P. Kennedy Jr. .... Matt Cavenaugh
Jacqueline Bouvier .... Sarah Hyland	J.V. "Major" Bouvier .... John McMartin

Act II (1973)

Edith Bouvier Beale .... Mary Louise Wilson	Jerry .... Matt Cavenaugh
"Little" Edie Beale .... Christine Ebersole	Norman Vincent Peale .... John McMartin
Brooks Jr. .... Michael Potts	

Orchestra: Lawrence Yurman conductor; Karl Mansfield associate conductor, synthesizer; Eric DeGioia violin; Anik Oulianine cello; Bill Sloat acoustic bass; Ken Hitchcock, Tom Murray reeds;

Cat people: Christine Ebersole and Mary Louise Wilson in Grey Gardens. *Photo: Joan Marcus*

Jeremy Miloszewicz trumpet, flugelhorn; Patrick Pridemore, French horn; Tim McLafferty percussion, drums.

Directed by Michael Greif; choreography, Jeff Calhoun; scenery, Allen Moyer; costumes, William Ivey Long; lighting, Peter Kaczorowski; sound, Brian Ronan; projections, Wendall K. Harrington; wigs and hair, Paul Huntley; orchestrations, Bruce Coughlin; music direction, Mr. Yurman; music coordination, John Miller; casting, Alaine Alldaffer, James Calleri and Alan Filderman; production stage manager, Judith Schoenfeld; press, the Publicity Office, Bob Fennell, Marc Thibodeau, Michael S. Borowski, Candi Adams.

Time: 1941; 1973. Place: Grey Gardens, East Hampton, New York. Presented in two parts.

Musical based on the imagined early life of a pair of former society dames and the reality of their later lives as depicted in a cult-hit documentary film. A 2005–06 *Best Plays* choice (see essay by Michael Feingold in this volume).

PROLOGUE (1973)

"Toyland" .... Edith

ACT I (1943)

"The Five-Fifteen" .... Edith, Gould, Brooks, Jackie, Lee
"Body Beautiful Beale" .... Gould, Edith, Brooks, Edie,
Jackie, Lee, Joe
"Mother, Darling" .... Edie, Edith, Gould
"Better Fall Out of Love" .... Joe, Edie
"Being Bouvier" .... Major, Brooks, Jackie, Lee, Edie
"Hominy Grits" .... Edith, Gould, Jackie, Lee
"Peas in a Pod" .... Edie, Edith
"Drift Away" .... Gould, Edith
"The Five-Fifteen" (Reprise) .... Edith
"Tomorrow's Woman" .... Edie, Jackie, Lee
"Daddy's Girl" .... Edie

"The Telegram" .... Edie, Edith
"Being Bouvier" (Reprise) .... Major, Jackie, Lee
"Will You" .... Edith

ACT II (1973)

"The Revolutionary Costume for Today" .... Edie
"The Cake I Had" .... Edith
"Entering Grey Gardens" .... Company
"The House We Live In" .... Edie, Company
"Jerry Likes My Corn" .... Edith, Edie
"Around the World" .... Edie
"Will You?" (Reprise) .... Edie
"Choose to Be Happy" .... Norman Vincent Peale, Company
"Around the World" (Reprise) .... Edie
"Another Winter in a Summer Town" .... Edie, Edith
"Peas in a Pod" (Reprise) .... Edith, Edie

Family Secrets (39). Revival of the solo performance piece by Sherry Glaser and Greg Howells. Produced by Harriet Newman Leve, in association with Dan Markley, Mike Skipper and Bisno/Shapiro/Finewill Entertainment, at 37 Arts. Opened March 8, 2006. (Closed April 9, 2006)

Performed by Ms. Glaser.

Directed by Bob Balaban; scenery, Rob Odorisio; lighting, John-Paul Szczepanski; sound, Ryan Powers; production stage manager, Pamela Edington; press, Barlow-Hartman Public Relations, John Barlow, Michael Hartman, Leslie Baden.

Presented without intermission.

First presentation of record was given at the Improv in San Francisco (5/23/1991) after originating in San Diego. First New York presentation of record was given at the Westside Theatre (10/6/1993–1/1/1995; 458 performances).

The Public Theater production of **Measure for Pleasure** (23). By David Grimm. Oskar Eustis artistic director, Mara Manus executive director, in the Anspacher Theater. Opened March 8, 2006. (Closed March 26, 2006)

Will Blunt	Michael Stuhlbarg	Dame Stickle	Susan Blommaert
Sir Peter Lustforth	Wayne Knight	Hermione Goode	Emily Swallow
Captain Dick Dashwood	Saxon Palmer	Footmen	Frederick Hamilton,
Molly Tawdry	Euan Morton		Ryan Tresser
Lady Vanity Lustforth	Suzanne Bertish		

Directed by Peter DuBois; scenery, Alexander Dodge; costumes, Anita Yavich; lighting, Christopher Akerlind; sound, Walter Trarbach and Tony Smolenski IV; music, Peter Golub; associate producers, Mr. DuBois and Mandy Hackett; casting, Jordan Thaler and Heidi Griffiths; production stage manager, Jane Pole; press, Arlene R. Kriv, Elizabeth Wehrle.

Time: 1751, the season of Lent. Place: The city and country. Presented in two parts.

Restoration-style sex farce encouraging all manner of libidinous activity. Developed at the Sundance Theatre Institute (7/11–31/2005).

Irish Repertory Theatre production of **George M. Cohan Tonight!** (77). Solo performance piece with book by Chip Deffaa; music and lyrics by Mr. Cohan. Charlotte Moore artistic director, Ciarán O'Reilly producing director. Opened March 9, 2006. (Closed May 14, 2006)

Performed by Jon Peterson.

Musicians: Vince Giordano bass, Rob Garcia drums.

Directed by Mr. Deffaa; scenery, James Morgan; costumes, David Toser; lighting, Mary Jo Dondlinger; arrangements, Mr. Deffaa, Sterling Price-McKinney, D.J. Bradley and Broc Hempel; music direction, Mr. Price-McKinney; stage manager, Rachel S. McCutchen.

Presented without intermission.

Musical celebration of the life and work of Mr. Cohan, who was a two-time honoree of the *Best Plays* series.

MUSICAL NUMBERS

"Hello, Broadway!"
  "Give My Regards to Broadway"
"The Man Who Owns Broadway"
"Night Time"
"Musical Moon"
"Ireland: My Land of Dreams"
"I'm Saving Up to Buy a Home for Mother"
"Josephine"
  "Oh, You Wonderful Girl"
"The Dancing Master"
"Until My Luck Comes Rolling Along"
"The Hinkey Dee"
"Harrigan"
"You Won't Do Any Business
  If You Haven't Got a Band"
"My Father Told Me"
"I Was Born in Virginia"
"Forty-Five Minutes From Broadway"
"I'm Awfully Strong for You"
"Oh! You Beautiful Girl"
  "I Want the World to Know

"Goodbye Flo"
"I Want to Hear a Yankee Doodle Tune"
"The Fatal Curse of Drink"
"The Yankee Doodle Boy"
"Mary's a Grand Old Name"
"You're a Grand Old Flag"
"Over There"
"Sweet Popularity"
  "I'm a Popular Man"
"Drink With Me"
  "Did Ya Ever Have One of Those Days"
"I Love Everyone in the Wide Wide World"
  "I'm True to Them All
"All-American Sweetheart"
"Josephine" (Reprise)
"I Won't Be an Actor No More
"Life's a Funny Proposition"
"All Aboard for Broadway"
  "Give My Regards to Broadway"

Sidd (13). Musical with book and lyrics by Andrew Frank; music and lyrics by Doug Silver; based on *Siddhartha* by Hermann Hesse. Produced by Always on the Way at Dodger Stages. Opened March 15, 2006. (Closed March 26, 2006)

Sidd	Manu Narayan	Lead Mystic; others	Nicole Lewis
Valerie; others	Marie-France Arcilla	Buddha; others	Arthur W. Marks
Willie; others	Dann Fink	Father; others	Gerry McIntyre
Mala; others	Natalie Cortez		

Directed by Mr. Frank; choreography, Fran Kirmser Sharma; scenery, Maruti Evans; costumes, Michael Bevins; lighting, Chris Dallos; sound, Andrew Bellware; orchestrations, Mr. Silver and Ned Paul Ginsburg; music direction, Mr. Ginsburg; executive producer, Ms. Sharma; associate producer, Joel Schonfeld; production stage manager, Kate Hefel.

Presented in two parts.

A well known spiritual quest set to music.

ACT I

"Bravest of All" .... Company
"You Will Do Great Things" .... Father, Townspeople
"Valerie's Decision" .... Valerie
"Standing and Waiting" .... Father, Sidd
"The Map Song" .... Sidd, Valerie
"Let it Go" .... Mystics
"Two Villagers" .... Villagers
"Borders" .... Sidd, Valerie, Mystics
"Buddha's Song" .... Buddha
"Everybody Needs Something" .... Willie, Sidd
"Happy Shop" .... Mala, Dancers
"That's Business" .... Willie, Sidd, Swami
"Teach Me How to Move" .... Sidd, Mala
Finale .... Company

ACT II

Roundabout Theatre Company production of **Entertaining Mr. Sloane** (77). Revival of the play by Joe Orton. Todd Haimes artistic director, Harold Wolpert managing director, Julia C. Levy executive director, in the Laura Pels Theatre at the Harold and Miriam Steinberg Center for Theatre. Opened March 16, 2006. (Closed May 21, 2006)

Kath .... Jan Maxwell   Kemp .... Richard Easton
Sloane .... Chris Carmack   Ed .... Alec Baldwin

Directed by Scott Ellis; scenery, Allen Moyer; costumes, Michael Krass; lighting, Kenneth Posner; sound, John Gromada; wigs and hair, Paul Huntley; fight direction, Rick Sordelet; casting, Mele Nagler; production stage manager, Diane DiVita; press, Boneau/Bryan-Brown, Adrian Bryan-Brown, Joe Perrotta, Jessica Johnson.

Sibling rivalry: Chris Carmack, Alec Baldwin and Jan Maxwell in Entertaining Mr. Sloane. *Photo: Joan Marcus*

Understudies: Mr. Baldwin—Tony Carlin; Mr. Easton—Philip LeStrange; Mr. Carmack—Richard Short; Ms. Maxwell—Barbara Sims.

Time: September; early March. Place: Outside London.

Presented in two parts.

Brother and sister are seedy rivals for the sexual attentions of a less-than-innocent young man. First presentation of record was given at the New Arts Theatre Club in London (5/6/1964). First New York presentation of record was given at Broadway's Lyceum Theatre (10/12–23/1965; 13 performances).

The Property Known as Garland (68). By Billy Van Zandt. Produced by Barry Krost, in association with Sally V. Winters, Mark Fleming and Jane Milmore, at Actors' Playhouse. Opened March 23, 2006. (Closed May 21, 2006)

Judy Garland .... Adrienne Barbeau   Ed .... Kerby Joe Grubb

Directed by Glenn Casale; scenery, Charlie Smith; costumes, Cynthia Nordstrom; lighting, Richard Winkler; sound, Jill BC DuBoff; stage manager, Tom Schilling.

Time: 1969. Place: Copenhagen. Presented without intermission.

Backstage tale of Ms. Garland's struggles with life on the evening of her final concert performance.

*Jacques Brel Is Alive and Well and Living in Paris (74). Revival of the musical revue with book and English lyrics by Eric Blau and Mort Shuman; music and lyrics by Jacques Brel. Produced by Dan Whitten, Bob and Rhonda Silver and Ken Grossman, in association with Tiger Theatricals, at the Zipper Theater. Opened March 27, 2006.

Performed by Robert Cuccioli, Natascia Diaz, Rodney Hicks, Gay Marshall.

Musicians: Eric Svejcar piano, accordion, guitar; Steve Gilewski bass; Brad Carbone percussion.

Directed by Gordon Greenberg; choreography, Mark Dendy; scenery, Robert Bissinger; costumes, Mattie Ullrich; lighting, Jeff Croiter; sound, Peter Fitzgerald; music direction, Mr. Svejcar; associate producer, Kathleen Brochin; casting, Cindi Rush; production stage manager, Sara Jaramillo; press, Origlio Public Relations, Tony Origlio.

Presented in two parts.

Songs of love, loss and the failures of existence inspired by Mr. Brel's commentaries on life and by his withdrawal from concert performance. First presentation of record was given at the Village Gate (1/22/1968–7/2/1972; 1,847 performances). Transferred to Broadway's Royale Theatre for a brief run (9/15–10/28/1972; 51 performances). The 1968–72 Off Broadway production is ranked 15th on the *Best Plays* Long Runs Off Broadway list as of 5/31/2006. A later revival played at the Astor Place Theater (5/17–9/1/1974; 125 performances).

MUSICAL NUMBERS

"Le Diable (Ca Va)"
"If We Only Have Love"
"Alone (Seul)"
"I Loved (J'Aimais)"
"Jackie (La Chanson de Jacky)"
"My Childhood"
"Madeleine"
"Bachelor's Dance"
"Fanette (La Fanette)"
"The Desperate Ones"
"Timid Frieda (Les Timides)"
"The Statue (La Statue)"
"Sons Of (Fils de)"

"Amsterdam"
"The Bulls (Les Toros)"
"Brussels (Bruxelles)"
"The Middle Class (Les Bourgeois)"
"Old Folks (Les Vieux)"
"Funeral Tango (Le Tango Funbre)"
"My Death"
"Marieke"
"Next (Au Suivant)"
"No, Love, You're Not Alone"
"Carousel (La Valse Mille Temps)"
"If We Only Have Love"

The God Committee (38). By Mark St. Germain. Produced by Carolyn Rossi Copeland, in association with Robert Stillman, at the Lamb's Theatre. Opened March 29, 2006. (Closed April 30, 2006)

Dr. Keira Bank	Maha Chehlaoui	Dominick Piero	Ron Orbach
Dr. Alex Gorman	Peter Jay Fernandez	Nurse Nella Larkin	Brenda Thomas
Fr. Charles Dunbar	Gerrit Graham	Dr. Ann Ross	Amy Van Nostrand
Dr. Jack Klee	Larry Keith		

Directed by Kevin Moriarty; scenery, Beowulf Boritt; costumes, David Murin; lighting, Tyler Micoleau; sound, Robert Kaplowitz; production stage manager, Marc Eardley; press, Keith Sherman and Associates, Brett Oberman.

Presented without intermission.

When an organ becomes available for transplant, a committee convenes to decide who will be the beneficiary. First presentation of record was given at the Barrington Stage Company in Sheffield, Massachusetts (7/22/2004).

Primary Stages production of **A Safe Harbor for Elizabeth Bishop** (33). Solo performance piece by Marta Góes; translated by Mario Góes, Julia Beirao and Amy Irving. Casey Childs executive producer, Andrew Leynse artistic director, in association with Mahega Productions, at 59E59 Theaters. Opened March 30, 2006. (Closed April 30, 2006)

Performed by Ms. Irving.

Directed by Richard Jay-Alexander; scenery, Jeff Cowie; costumes, Ilona Somogyi; lighting, Russell H. Champa; sound and music, Fitz Patton; wigs, Paul Huntley; projections, Zachary Borovay; production stage manager, Darcy Stephens; press, Origlio Public Relations, Philip Carrubba.

Presented without intermission.

An American poet seeks refuge in the love of other women in this biographical monodrama. First presentation of record was given in São Paulo, Brazil (6/2001) under the title *A Port for Elizabeth Bishop*. First US presentation of record was given by New York Stage and Film Company at Vassar College's Powerhouse Theater in Poughkeepsie, New York (6/23–7/3/2004).

New York City Center Encores! presentation of **70, Girls, 70** (5). Concert version of the musical with book by Fred Ebb and Norman L. Martin; music by John Kander; lyrics by Mr. Ebb; adapted by Joe Masteroff from *Breath of Spring*, a play by Peter Coke; concert adaptation by David Thompson. Jack Viertel artistic director, at City Center. Opened March 30, 2006. (Closed April 2, 2006)

Fritzi Clews	Mary Jo Catlett	Harry Hardwick	George S. Irving
Gert Appleby	Carole Cook	Lorraine	Lalan Parrott
Walter Hatfield	Bob Dishy	Eddie	Mark Price
Ida Dodd	Olympia Dukakis	Sadie	Charlotte Rae
Melba Jones	Tina Fabrique	Mr. McIlhenny	Carleton Carpenter
Eunice Miller	Anita Gillette		

Directed and choreographed by Kathleen Marshall; scenery, John Lee Beatty; costumes, William Ivey Long; lighting, Peter Kaczorowski; sound, Brian Ronan; orchestrations, Don Walker; music direction, Paul Gemignani; music coordination, Seymour Red Press; production stage manager, Tripp Phillips.

Presented in two parts.

A group of retired theatrical troupers plot to steal furs in order to enhance their lifestyles. First presentation of record was given at the Forrest Theatre in Philadelphia (3/1971). First Broadway presentation of record was given at the Broadhurst Theatre (4/15–5/15/1971; 35 performances). First presentation of record of Mr. Coke's *Breath of Spring*—a comedy in which a retired British military officer and a coterie of his female friends get involved in criminal capers—was given at the Cambridge Theatre in London (3/26/1958). Mr. Coke's play was made into the 1960 film *Make Mine Mink*, starring Terry-Thomas and Billie Whitelaw.

MUSICAL NUMBERS

"Old Folks"
"Broadway, My Street"
"The Caper"
"Coffee in a Cardboard Cup"
"You and I, Love"
"Do We?"
"Hit It, Lorraine"

"See the Light"
"Boom Ditty Boom"
"Believe"
"Go Visit"
"70, Girls, 70"
"The Elephant Song"
"Yes"

Playwrights Horizons production of **Pen** (16). By David Marshall Grant. Tim Sanford artistic director, Leslie Marcus managing director, William Russo general manager. Opened April 2, 2006. (Closed April 16, 2006)

Jerry .... Reed Birney   Helen .... J. Smith-Cameron
Matt .... Dan McCabe

    Directed by Will Frears; scenery, Robin Vest; costumes, Jenny Mannis; lighting, Matthew Richards; sound, Obadiah Eaves; casting, Alaine Alldaffer and James Calleri; production stage manager, Carmen I. Abrazado; press, the Publicity Office, Bob Fennell, Marc Thibodeau, Michael S. Borowski, Candi Adams.

    Time: 1969. Place: Long Island. Presented in two parts.

    Divorced parents battle for influence over their teenage son in a dramatic comedy set in a middle-class household where the mother is confined to a wheelchair.

*Sandra Bernhard: Everything Bad and Beautiful (57). Solo performance piece by Ms. Bernhard. Produced by Daryl Roth and the Nederlander Company at the Daryl Roth Theatre. Opened April 5, 2006.

    Performed by Ms. Bernhard and the Rebellious Jezebels.

Guilt trip? Dan McCabe and J. Smith-Cameron in Pen. *Photo: Carol Rosegg*

Directed by Ms. Bernhard; scenery, David Swayze; lighting, Ben Stanton; sound, Walter Trarbach and Tony Smolenski IV; music direction; LaFrae Sci; press, Pete Sanders Group, Shane Marshall Brown, Pete Sanders.

Presented without intermission.

Ms. Bernhard's acerbic performance of musical numbers interspersed with ironic commentaries on the nature of celebrity and show business. First presentation of record was given at the Silent Movie Theatre in Los Angeles (3/9–27/2005).

Second Stage Theatre production of **Show People** (29). By Paul Weitz. Carole Rothman artistic director, Ellen Richard interim executive director. Opened April 6, 2006. (Closed April 30, 2006)

Tom	Ty Burrell	Marnie	Debra Monk
Natalie	Judy Greer	Jerry	Lawrence Pressman

Directed by Peter Askin; scenery, Heidi Ettinger; costumes, Jeff Mahshie; lighting, Jeff Croiter; sound and music, Lewis Flinn; casting, Tara Rubin Casting; production stage manager, Rachel J. Perlman; press, Richard Kornberg and Associates, Richard Kornberg, Tom D'Ambrosio, Don Summa, Carrie Friedman.

Time: The present. Place: Montauk. Presented in two parts.

Comedy in which a computer software developer hires a pair of actors to pretend they are his parents in order to impress his new girlfriend.

*Tryst (63). By Karoline Leach. Produced by Morton Wolkowitz, Suite and Barbara Freitag at the Promenade Theatre. Opened April 6, 2006.

George Love	Maxwell Caulfield	Adelaide Pinchin	Amelia Campbell

Directed by Joe Brancato; scenery, David Korins; costumes, Alejo Vietti; lighting, Jeff Nellis; sound, Johanna Doty; wigs and hair, Paul Huntley; production stage manager, David H. Lurie; press, Cromarty and Company, Peter Cromarty.

Presented in two parts.

Edwardian romance that applies twists to a tale about a handsome conman and an aging woman of means.

Los Big Names (41). Solo performance piece by Marga Gomez. Produced by Jonathan Reinis, in association with Puerto Rican Traveling Theatre (Miriam Colón Valle founder and producer) and Jamie Cesa, at the 47th Street Theatre. Opened April 9, 2006. (Closed May 14, 2006)

Performed by Ms. Gomez.

Directed by David Schweizer; scenery, lighting and projections, Alexander V. Nichols; sound, Mark O'Brien; associate producers, Adam Friedson, David Friedson, Melvin Honowitz, Eva Price; production stage manager, Scott Pegg; press, Cromarty and Company, Peter Cromarty.

Presented without intermission.

A woman tells stories about being raised by Latino performers and their impact on her development. First presentation of record was given in Washington, D.C. at the Kennedy Center's Film Theater (3/25–4/18/2004).

Manhattan Theatre Club production of **Based on a Totally True Story** (56). By Roberto Aguirre-Sacasa. Lynne Meadow artistic director, Barry Grove executive producer, at City Center Stage II. Opened April 11, 2006. (Closed May 28, 2006)

Ethan Keene	Carson Elrod	Michael Sullivan	Pedro Pascal
Tyler; others	Erik Heger	Ethan's Dad	Michael Tucker
Mary Ellen	Kristine Nielsen		

Understudies: Mr. Tucker—Mitchell Greenberg; Ms. Nielsen—Linda Marie Larson; Messrs. Elrod, Heger, Pascal—Carter Roy.

California crazy: Kristine Nielsen and Carson Elrod in Based on a Totally True Story. *Photo: Joan Marcus*

Directed by Michael Bush; scenery, Anna Louizos; costumes, Linda Cho; lighting, Traci Klainer; sound, Ryan Rumery; casting, Nancy Piccione and David Caparelliotis; production stage manager, Gail Eve Malatesta; press, Boneau/Bryan-Brown, Chris Boneau, Jim Byk, Aaron Meier, Heath Schwartz.

Time: The present. Place: New York, Philadelphia and Los Angeles. Presented in two parts.

Comedy about a writer of superhero comics who attempts to balance the demands of work, family, relationship and being a gay man in his 20s.

Brooklyn Academy of Music presentation of the **National Theatre of Bergen** and the **Norwegian Theatre of Oslo** production of **Peer Gynt** (5). Revival of the play by Henrik Ibsen; adapted by Robert Wilson. Alan H. Fishman chairman of the board, Karen Brooks Hopkins president, Joseph V. Melillo executive producer, at the Howard Gilman Opera House. Opened April 11, 2006. (Closed April 16, 2006)

Peer (young man)	Henrik Rafaelsen	Ase	Wenche Medboe
Peer (grown man)	Endre Hellestveit	Solveig	Kjersti Sandal
Peer (old man)	Sverre Bentzen	Anitra	Gjertrud Jynge

Directed by Robert Wilson and Ann-Christin Rommen; scenery and lighting, Mr. Wilson; costumes, Jacques Reynaud; music, Michael Galasso; production stage manager, Per Berg-Nilsen; press, Sandy Sawotka, Fatima Kafele, Eva Chien, Tamara McCaw, Jennifer Lam.

Presented in two parts.

Mr. Wilson's unique take on Mr. Ibsen's sprawling morality tale. First New York presentation of record of the play by Mr. Ibsen was given as a recital in Norwegian by Ole Bang at the Manhattan Theatre (1/12/1905). First presentation of record in English was given at the Grand Opera House in Chicago (10/29–12/1/1906) with Richard Mansfield in the title role. First presentation of record on Broadway was given at the New Amsterdam Theatre (2/25–3/23/1907).

On the Line (16). By Joe Roland. Produced by Mike Nichols, Jill Furman and Boyett Ostar Productions, in association with Jill Neuberger, at the Cherry Lane Theatre. Opened April 11, 2006. (Closed April 23, 2006)

Dev .... Joe Roland   Jimmy .... John Zibell
Mikey .... David Prete

Directed by Peter Sampieri; scenery, Michael McGarty; costumes, Robin L. McGee; lighting, Brian Lilienthal; sound, Peter Sasha Hurowitz; production stage manager, Jennifer Rogers; press, Pete Sanders Group, Glenna Freedman.

Presented in two parts.

Three working-class pals face the growing divide between the powerful and the powerless in contemporary America.

*****The Public Theater** production of **Stuff Happens** (56). By David Hare. Oskar Eustis artistic director, Mara Manus executive director, in the Newman Theater. Opened April 13, 2006.

Hans Blix; others .... George Bartenieff
Donald Rumsfeld .... Jeffrey DeMunn
George Tenet; others .... Glenn Fleshler
Dick Cheney .... Zach Grenier
Palestinian Academic;
    others .... Lameece Issaq
Colin Powell .... Peter Francis James
Tony Blair .... Byron Jennings
David Manning; others .... Ken Marks
Paul Wolfowitz; others .... David Pittu
Condoleezza Rice .... Gloria Reuben
George W. Bush .... Jay O. Sanders
Alastair Campbell; others .... Thomas Schall
Jonathan Powell; others .... Armand Schultz
Angry Journalist; others .... Robert Sella
Labour Politician;others .... Brenda Wehle
Iraqi Exile; others .... Waleed F. Zuaiter

Directed by Daniel Sullivan; scenery, Riccardo Hernández; costumes, Jess Goldstein; lighting, Pat Collins; sound and music, Dan Moses Schreier; casting, Jordan Thaler and Heidi Griffiths; associate producers, Peter DuBois and Mandy Hackett; production stage manager, James Latus; press, Arlene R. Kriv, Elizabeth Wehrle.

Presented in two parts.

Reconstruction of the conversations—including personal and political dramas—among the principals involved in the decision to invade Iraq in 2003. A 2005–06 *Best Plays* choice (see essay by Misha Berson in this volume). First presentation of record was given at the National Theatre's Olivier Theatre in London (9/10–11/6/2004). First US production of record was given at the Mark Taper Forum in Los Angeles (6/5–7/17/2005).

Brooklyn Academy of Music presentation of the **Theatre Royal Bath/Peter Hall Company** production **The Importance of Being Earnest** (28). Revival of the play by Oscar Wilde. Alan H. Fishman chairman of the board, Karen Brooks Hopkins president, Joseph V. Melillo executive producer, in the BAM Harvey Theater. Opened April 18, 2006. (Closed May 14, 2006)

Lady Bracknell .... Lynn Redgrave
Lane .... James A. Stephens
Algernon Moncrieff .... Robert Petkoff
Jack Worthing .... James Waterston
Gwendolen Fairfax .... Bianca Amato
Miss Prism .... Miriam Margolyes
Cecily Cardew .... Charlotte Parry
Rev. Canon Chasuble .... Terence Rigby
Merriman .... Geddeth Smith
Footman .... Greg Felden

Directed by Peter Hall; scenery, costumes and lighting, Kevin and Trish Rigdon; sound, Rob Milburn and Michael Bodeen; production stage manager, John McNamara; press, Sandy Sawotka, Fatima Kafele, Eva Chien, Tamara McCaw, Jennifer Lam.

Presented in two parts.

Complications arise when a man of uncertain parentage wishes to wed a young lady of breeding in this farce interlaced with Mr. Wilde's epigrammatic dialogue. First presentation of record was given at the St. James Theatre in London (2/14/1895). First presentation of record in the US was given at the Empire Theatre in New York (4/22–5/1/1895; 12 performances) with

Henry Miller as Jack Worthing. The two productions bookended the conclusion of Mr. Wilde's unsuccessful suit against the Marquis of Queensberry for libel and the playwright's subsequent imprisonment for his behavior with young men.

York Theatre Company production of **A Fine and Private Place** (29). Musical with book and lyrics by Erik Haagensen; music by Richard Isen; lyrics by Mr. Haagensen; based on the novel by Peter S. Beagle. James Morgan artistic director, at the Theatre at St. Peter's. Opened April 27, 2006. (Closed May 21, 2006)

Jonathan Rebeck	Joseph Kolinski	Laura Durand	Christiane Noll
Raven	Gabriel Barre	Gertrude Klapper	Evalyn Baron
Michael Morgan	Glenn Seven Allen	Campos	Larri Rebega

Orchestra: Milton Granger piano; David Wolfson keyboard; Suzy Perelman violin; Alan Brady reeds; Barbara Merjan percussion.

Directed by Mr. Barre; scenery, James Morgan; costumes, Pamela Scofield; lighting, Jeff Croiter; sound, Eric Miller; projections, Scott DelaCruz; orchestrations, Mr. Isen; music direction, Mr. Granger; production stage manager, Allison Deutsch.

Presented in two parts.

Musical fantasy set in a cemetery among the living and the dead. First attempted as a dramatic work by Joseph L. Mankiewicz, based on Mr. Beagle's 1960 novel, before Jay Thompson (*Once Upon a Mattress*) began work on a version under the auspices of Kermit Bloomgarden. The version by Messrs. Haagensen and Isen is unrelated to those early attempts. First presentation of record was given at the Goodspeed-at-Chester in Connecticut (8/3–20/1989). A later version was given by the American Stage Company at the Becton Theater on the campus of Fairleigh Dickinson University in Teaneck, New Jersey (1/24–2/18/1990).

ACT I

Prologue	Rebeck
"I'm Not Going Gently"	Michael
"Much More Alive"	Rebeck
"You Know What I Mean"	Klapper
"A Fine and Private Place"	Laura, Michael
"As Long as I Can"	Michael, Laura
"Stop Kidding Yourself"	Rebeck, Klapper
"The Telepathetique"	Michael, Laura
"What Did You Expect?"	Laura
"Let Me Explain"	Michael
"It's None of My Business"	Klapper, Rebeck
Quartet	Michael, Laura, Rebeck. Klapper

ACT II

"What Should I Do?"	Klapper, Laura, Rebeck, Michael
"Close Your Eyes"	Laura
"Argument"	Rebeck, Klapper
"No One Ever Knows"	Klapper
"Because of Them All"	Michael, Laura
"Much More Alive" (Reprise)	Rebeck
"Do Something"	Laura, Michael, Rebeck
"How Can I Leave Here?"	Rebeck

*All Dolled Up (26). By Bobby Spillane. Produced by Colin Quinn and Working Stiff Productions at the Acorn Theatre. Opened May 7, 2006.

Sally	Michael Basile	Vince; Tom	John F. O'Donohue
Frankie; others	Tomm Bauer	John	Rocco Parente
Newswomen	Jennifer Blood	Joey; Bartender	Christo Parenti
Patti	Jamie Bonelli	Karen; Jody	Alyssa Truppelli
Ricky	Matt Gallagher		

Directed by Susan Campanaro; scenery, Kenny McDonough and Chris Wiggins; lighting, Tim Stephenson and Dana Giangrande, sound and music, Alex Jost; video, Billy Delace; Shaffer-Coyle Public Relations, Bill Coyle.

Presented without intermission.

Comedy about a mobster who finds his true calling as a cross-dresser.

New York City Center Encores! presentation of **Of Thee I Sing** (6). Concert version of the musical with book by George S. Kaufman and Morrie Ryskind; music and lyrics by George and Ira Gershwin; concert adaptation by David Ives. Jack Viertel artistic director, at City Center. Opened May 11, 2006. (Closed May 15, 2006)

John P. Wintergreen .... Victor Garber	French Ambassador .... David Pittu
Mary Turner .... Jennifer Laura Thompson	Senator Lyons .... Jonathan Freeman
Alexander Throttlebottom .... Jefferson Mays	Senator Jones .... Erick Devine
Matthew Arnold Fulton ...... Michael Mulheren	Sam Jenkins .... Jeffry Denman
Louis Lippman .... Lewis J. Stadlen	Diana Devereaux .... Jenny Powers
Francis X. Gilhooley .. .. Wayne Duvall	Miss Benson .... Mara Davi

Ensemble: Eric Michael Gillett, David Baum, Sara Edwards, Patty Goble, Blythe Gruda, Holly Holcomb, Todd A. Horman, Drew Humphrey, Fred Inkley, Cara Kjellman, Ian Knauer, Todd Lattimore, Mark Ledbetter, Jay Lusteck, Raymond Jaramillo McLeod, Marcus Nance, Nina Negri, Shannon Marie O'Bryan, Greg Stone, Kelly Sullivan, Jacqueline Thompson, Anna A. White.

Directed by John Rando; choreography, Randy Skinner; scenery, John Lee Beatty; costumes, Toni-Leslie James; lighting, Paul Miller; sound, Dan Moses Schreier; music direction, Paul Gemignani; music coordination, Seymour Red Press; production stage manager, Tripp Phillips; press, Helene Davis Public Relations.

Presented in two parts.

Musical satire on the nature of national political campaigns that resonates to this day. A 1931–32 *Best Plays* choice, the first presentation of record was given at Boston's Majestic Theatre (12/8/1931). First Broadway presentation of record was given at the Music Box (12/26/1931–1/14/1933; 441 performances). It was the first musical to win the Pulitzer Prize in Drama (1932). There have been two Broadway revivals: one in 1933, the other in 1952.

MUSICAL NUMBERS

"Wintergreen for President"
"Who Is the Lucky Girl To Be?"
"The Dimple on My Knee"
"Because, Because"
"As the Chairman of the Committee"
"How Beautiful"
"Never Was There a Girl So Fair"
"Some Girls Can Bake a Pie"
"Love Is Sweeping the Country"
"Of Thee I Sing"
"I Was the Most Beautiful Blossom"

"Hello, Good Morning"
"Who Cares?"
"Garcon, S'il Vous Plait"
"The Illegitimate Daughter"
"We'll Impeach Him"
"The (Senatorial) Roll Call"
"Jilted"
"Who Could Ask For Anything More?"
"Posterity (Is Just Around the Corner)"
"Trumpeter, Blow Your (Golden) Horn"

*Annulla (14). Revival of the solo performance piece by Emily Mann. Produced by Edmund Gaynes and West End Artists Company at St. Luke's Theatre. Opened May 14, 2006.

Annulla .... Eileen De Felitta   Voice of Emily .... Neva Small

Directed by Pamela Hall; scenery, Josh Iacovelli, costumes, Elizabeth Flores; lighting, Kimberly Jade Tompkins; press, David Gersten and Associates.

Time: 1974. Place: London.

A Jewish survivor of Nazi Germany tells an unseen interviewer her tale of pretending to be Aryan in order to stay alive. First presentation of record was given at the Guthrie Theater's Guthrie Two venue (3/16/1977) under the title *Annulla Allen: The Autobiography of a Survivor* in a production directed by Ms. Mann. First New York presentation of record was given at the New Theatre of Brooklyn (10/27–11/20/1988; 20 performances) under the title *Annulla, an Autobiography* with Ms. Mann as the director and Linda Hunt in the title role.

*New York Theatre Workshop presentation of the **United States Theatre Project** production of **columbinus** (10). By Stephen Karam and PJ Paparelli; additional material by Josh Barrett, Sean McNall, Karl Miller, Michael Milligan, Will Rogers. James C. Nicola artistic director, Lynn Moffat managing director. Opened May 22, 2006.

Dylan Klebold .... Will Rogers   Erik Harris .... Karl Miller

Ensemble: Anna Camp, Joaquín Pérez-Campbell, James Flanagan, Carmen M. Herlihy, Nicole Lowrance, Mr. Miller, Keith Nobbs, Bobby Steggert.

Directed by Mr. Paparelli; scenery, Tony Cisek; costumes, Miranda Hoffman; lighting, Dan Covey; sound, Martin Desjardins; projections, JJ Kaczynski; fight direction, Scott Barrow; dramaturg, Patricia Hersch; production stage manager, Amy McCraney; press, Richard Kornberg and Associates, Don Summa, Richard Kornberg.

Presented in two parts.

Documentary drama based on the killing spree committed by two high school students in Littleton, Colorado. First presentation of record was given as a developmental work in the Downstairs Series at the Arena Stage in Washington, DC (4/12/2003). A staged reading followed at the Curious Theatre Company in Denver (3/1/2004). First fully staged presentation of record was given by the Round House Theatre in its Silver Spring, Maryland venue (3/7–4/10/2005).

CAST REPLACEMENTS
AND TOURING COMPANIES

○ ○ ○ ○ ○

Compiled by Paul Hardt

THE FOLLOWING IS a list of the major cast replacements of record in productions that opened during the current and in previous seasons, and other New York shows that were on a first-class tour in 2005–06.

The name of each major role is listed in *italics* beneath the title of the play in the first column. In the second column directly opposite appears the name of the actor who created the role in the original New York production (whose opening date appears in *italics* at the top of the column). Indented immediately beneath the original actor's name are the names of subsequent New York replacements—with the date of replacement when available.

The third column gives information about first-class touring companies. When there is more than one roadshow company, #1, #2, etc., appear before the name of the performer who created the role in each company (and the city and date of each company's first performance appears in *italics* at the top of the column). Subsequent replacements are also listed beneath names in the same manner as the New York companies, with dates when available.

ALTAR BOYZ

New York 3/1/05

Matthew	Scott Porter
	James Royce Edwards 2/9/06
	John Celaya 4/3/06
Mark	Tyler Maynard
	Danny Calvert 7/12/05
	Tyler Maynard 1/9/06
	Zach Hannah
Luke	Andy Karl
	James Royce Edwards
	Andrew C. Call 2/9/06
Abraham	David Josefsberg
	Dennis Moench
Juan	Ryan Duncan
	Nick Sanchez
	Clyde Alves
	Ryan Duncan 5/1/06

AVENUE Q

	New York 7/31/03	*Las Vegas 2/15/05* *Closed 5/28/06*
Princeton; Rod	John Tartaglia Barrett Foa 2/1/05	#1 John Tartaglia #2 Jonathan Root
Brian	Jordan Gelber	#1 Nicholas Kohn #2 Cole Porter
Kate Monster; Lucy	Stephanie D'Abruzzo Mary Faber 12/26/05	#1 Brynn O'Malley #2 Kelli Sawyer
Nicky; Trekkie	Rick Lyon Christian Anderson 7/5/05 Rick Lyon 5/2/06	#1 Rick Lyon #2 David Benoit
Christmas Eve	Ann Harada Ann Sanders 10/26/04 Ann Harada 1/25/05	#1 Angela Ai #2 Natalie Gray
Gary Coleman	Natalie Venetia Belcon	#1 Tonya Dixon #2 Haneefah Wood

BEAUTY AND THE BEAST

	New York 4/18/94
Beast	Terrence Mann Jeff McCarthy Chuck Wagner James Barbour Steve Blanchard Jeff McCarthy 2/17/04 Steve Blanchard 4/13/04
Belle	Susan Egan Sarah Uriarte Berry Christianne Tisdale Kerry Butler Deborah Gibson Kim Huber Toni Braxton Andrea McArdle Sarah Litzsinger Jamie-Lynn Sigler Sarah Litzsinger 2/11/03 Megan McGinnis 4/15/03 Christy Carlson Romano 2/17/04 Brooke Tansley 9/14/04 Ashley Brown 9/20/05 Sarah Litzsinger 5/30/06
Lefou	Kenny Raskin Harrison Beal Jamie Torcellini Jeffrey Schecter Jay Brian Winnick 11/12/99 Gerard McIsaac Brad Aspel Steve Lavner Aldrin Gonzalez

Gaston	Burke Moses
	Marc Kudisch
	Steve Blanchard
	Patrick Ryan Sullivan
	Christopher Sieber
	Chris Hoch 12/10/02
	Grant Norman
Maurice	Tom Bosley
	MacIntyre Dixon
	Tom Bosley
	Kurt Knudson
	Timothy Jerome
	JB Adams 11/12/99
	Jamie Ross
Cogsworth	Heath Lamberts
	Peter Bartlett
	Robert Gibby Brand
	John Christopher Jones
	Jeff Brooks 11/12/99
	Christopher Duva
Lumiere	Gary Beach
	Lee Roy Reams
	Patrick Quinn
	Gary Beach
	Meshach Taylor
	Patrick Page
	Paul Schoeffler
	Patrick Page
	Bryan Batt
	Rob Lorey 5/7/02
	David DeVries
	Peter Flynn
	Jacob Young 5/9/05
Babette	Stacey Logan
	Pamela Winslow
	Leslie Castay
	Pam Klinger
	Louisa Kendrick
	Pam Klinger
	Meredith Inglesby
Mrs. Potts	Beth Fowler
	Cass Morgan
	Beth Fowler
	Barbara Marineau 11/12/99
	Beth Fowler
	Cass Morgan
	Alma Cuervo 2/17/04
	Jeanne Lehman

LA CAGE AUX FOLLES

New York 11/9/04

Albin	Gary Beach
Georges	Daniel Davis

	John Hillner 3/28/05 Robert Goulet 4/15/05
Jean-Michel	Gavin Creel
Anne Dindon	Angela Gaylor
Jacob	Michael Benjamin Washington
Edouard Dindon	Michael Mulheren
Mme. Dindon	Linda Balgord
Jacqueline	Ruth Williamson
Francis	John Shuman

CHICAGO

	New York 11/14/96	*Washington, DC 6/10/03*
Roxie Hart	Ann Reinking	Bianca Marroquin
	Marilu Henner	Paige Davis
	Karen Ziemba	Bianca Marroquin
	Belle Calaway	
	Charlotte d'Amboise	
	Sandy Duncan 8/12/99	
	Belle Calaway 1/18/00	
	Charlotte d'Amboise 3/24/00	
	Belle Calaway	
	Nana Visitor	
	Petra Nielsen 10/8/01	
	Nana Visitor 11/19/01	
	Belle Calaway 1/13/02	
	Denise Van Outen 3/18/02	
	Belle Calaway 4/22/02	
	Amy Spanger 8/6/02	
	Belle Calaway	
	Tracy Shayne 4/15/03	
	Melanie Griffith 7/11/03	
	Charlotte d'Amboise 10/7/03	
	Bianca Marroquin 12/15/03	
	Gretchen Mol 1/5/04	
	Charlotte d'Amboise 3/1/04	
	Tracy Shayne	
	Charlotte d'Amboise	
Velma Kelly	Bebe Neuwirth	Brenda Braxton
	Nancy Hess	Reva Rice 12/30/03
	Ute Lemper	Terra C. MacLeod
	Bebe Neuwirth	
	Ruthie Henshall 5/25/99	
	Mamie Duncan-Gibbs 10/26/99	
	Bebe Neuwirth 1/18/00	
	Donna Marie Asbury 3/23/00	
	Sharon Lawrence 4/11/00	
	Vicki Lewis	
	Jasmine Guy	
	Bebe Neuwirth	
	Donna Marie Asbury	
	Deidre Goodwin	
	Vicki Lewis	
	Deidre Goodwin 6/29/01	

Anna Montanaro 7/9/01
Deidre Goodwin 9/14/01
Donna Marie Asbury
Roxane Carrasco 1/13/02
Deidre Goodwin 3/18/02
Stephanie Pope
Roxane Carrasco
Caroline O'Connor 11/8/02
Brenda Braxton 3/3/03
Deidre Goodwin 6/24/03
Reva Rice 10/7/03
Brenda Braxton 1/1/04
Pia Dowes 4/8/04
Brenda Braxton 5/16/04
Terra C. MacLeod 7/27/04
Donna Marie Asbury 2/14/05
Brenda Braxton 2/21/05
Luba Mason 6/28/05
Brenda Braxton
Robin Givens

Billy Flynn

James Naughton
Gregory Jbara
Hinton Battle
Alan Thicke
Michael Berresse
Brent Barrett
Robert Urich 1/11/00
Clarke Peters 2/1/00
Brent Barrett 2/15/00
Chuck Cooper
Brent Barrett 7/2/01
Chuck Cooper 8/27/01
George Hamilton 11/12/01
Eric Jordan Young 1/18/02
Ron Raines 3/26/02
George Hamilton 5/21/02
Michael C. Hall 8/8/02
Destan Owens
Taye Diggs
Billy Zane 11/8/02
Kevin Richardson 1/20/03
Clarke Peters
Gregory Harrison
Brent Barrett 6/2/03
Patrick Swayze 12/15/03
James Naughton 01/05/04
Norm Lewis 2/2/04
Christopher Sieber 3/23/04
Tom Wopat 5/16/04
Christopher Seiber 6/17/04
Marti Pellow 8/3/04
Wayne Brady 9/7/04
Tom Wopat 12/7/04
Brent Barrett 1/4/05
Christopher McDonald 7/1/05
Huey Lewis 11/18/05
John O'Hurley 1/16/06

Gregory Harrison
Patrick Swayze 12/30/03
Tom Wopat 1/27/04
Gregory Harrison
Obba Babatundé
Tom Wopat
Obba Babatundé
John O'Hurley
Greg Evigan

Amos Hart	Joel Grey	Ray Bokhour
	Ernie Sabella	P.J. Benjamin
	Tom McGowan	Kevin Carolyn
	P.J. Benjamin	Ron Orbach
	Ernie Sabella 11/23/99	
	P.J. Benjamin	
	Tom McGowan	
	P.J. Benjamin	
	Ray Bokhour 7/30/01	
	P.J. Benjamin 8/13/01	
	Rob Bartlett	
	P.J. Benjamin 3/3/03	
	Ray Bokhour	
	P.J. Benjamin	
Matron	Marcia Lewis	Roz Ryan
	Roz Ryan	Marcia Lewis 8/4/03
	Marcia Lewis	Carol Woods 9/23/03
	Roz Ryan	Roz Ryan
	Marcia Lewis	Carol Woods
	Roz Ryan	Patti LaBelle
	Marcia Lewis	Carol Woods
	Jennifer Holliday 6/18/01	Camille Saviola
	Marcia Lewis 8/27/01	
	Roz Ryan 11/16/01	
	Michele Pawk 1/14/02	
	Alix Korey 3/4/02	
	B.J. Crosby 3/3/03	
	Angie Stone 4/15/03	
	Camille Saviola 6/10/03	
	Debbie Gravitte 12/15/03	
	Roz Ryan 3/15/04	
	Carol Woods	
	Roz Ryan	
	Anne L. Nathan 9/13/04	
	Carol Woods 1/31/05	
	Anne L. Nathan 2/21/05	
	Mary Testa	
	Carol Woods	
	Debra Monk	
Mary Sunshine	D. Sabella	R. Bean
	J. Loeffelholz	
	R. Bean	
	A. Saunders	
	J. Maldonado	
	R. Bean	
	A. Saunders 1/2/02	
	R. Bean 1/14/02	
	M. Agnes	
	D. Sabella 3/24/03	
	R. Bean 5/17/04	
	R. Lowe	

DIRTY ROTTEN SCOUNDRELS

New York 3/3/05

Lawrence Jameson	John Lithgow

Jonathan Pryce 1/17/05
Keith Carradine

Freddy Benson   Norbert Leo Butz
                           Brian d'Arcy James

Christine Colgate   Sherie René Scott
                           Rachel York 2/7/06
                           Sherie René Scott 6/20/06

Muriel Eubanks   Joanna Gleason
                           Lucie Arnaz

Jolene Oakes   Sara Gettelfinger
                           Mylinda Hull 1/17/05
                           Sara Gettelfinger

Andre Thibault   Gregory Jbara

DOG SEES GOD

New York 12/15/05
Closed 2/20/06

Van's Sister   Eliza Dushku
                           Melissa Picarello

CB's Sister   America Ferrera
                           Karen DiConcetto

Tricia   Kelli Garner

Marcy   Ari Graynor

Beethoven   Logan Marshall-Green

Van   Keith Nobbs

Matt   Ian Somerhalder
                           Colby Chambers

CB   Eddie Kaye Thomas

DOUBT, A PARABLE

New York 3/31/05

Sister Aloysius   Cherry Jones
                           Eileen Atkins 1/17/06

Father Flynn   Brían F. O'Byrne
                           Ron Eldard 1/11/06

Sister James   Heather Goldenhersh
                           Jena Malone 1/11/06

Mrs. Muller   Adriane Lenox

FIDDLER ON THE ROOF

New York 2/26/04
Closed 1/8/06

Tevye   Alfred Molina
                           Harvey Fierstein 1/4/05

Golde   Randy Graff
                           Andrea Martin 1/4/05
                           Rosie O'Donnell 9/18/05

Yente	Nancy Opel
Tzeitel	Sally Murphy
Hodel	Laura Michelle Kelly
	Laura Shoop 6/11/04
Chava	Tricia Paoluccio
Motel	John Cariani
	Peter Matthew Smith 3/15/05
	Michael Therriault
Perchik	Robert Petkoff
	Paul Anthony Stewart 2/15/05
Fyedka	David Ayers
	Patrick Heusinger 1/4/05

HAIRSPRAY

	New York 8/15/02	Baltimore 9/17/03
Tracy Turnblad	Marissa Jaret Winokur	#1 Carly Jibson
	Kathy Brier 8/12/03	Keala Settle 4/13/04
	Carly Jibson 5/4/04	#2 Katrina Rose Dideriksen
	Marissa Jaret Winokur 6/8/05	
	Shannon Durig	
Edna Turnblad	Harvey Fierstein	#1 Bruce Vilanch
	Michael McKean 5/4/04	John Pinette
	Bruce Vilanch	JP Dougherty
	John Pinette 9/6/05	#2 Harvey Fierstein
	Blake Hammond	Paul Vogt 5/1/06
Wilbur Turnblad	Dick Latessa	#1 Todd Susman
	Peter Scolari	Stephen DeRosa
	Todd Susman	Jim J. Bullock
	Stephen DeRosa 9/6/05	#2 Dick Latessa
		Eddie Mekka 5/1/06
Amber Von Tussle	Laura Bell Bundy	#1 Jordan Ballard
	Tracy Jai Edwards 7/14/03	Worth Williams
	Jordan Ballard	Tara Macri
	Becky Gulsvig	#2 Katherine Leonard
Velma Von Tussle	Linda Hart	#1 Susan Cella
	Barbara Walsh 7/14/03	Susan Henley
	Leah Hocking	#2 Susan Anton
	Liz Larsen	
	Leah Hocking 3/13/06	
	Isabel Keating 6/6/06	
Link Larkin	Matthew Morrison	#1 Austin Miller
	Richard H. Blake 1/13/04	Serge Kushnier
	Andrew Rannells	Aaron Tveit
		#2 Austin Miller
Motormouth Maybelle	Mary Bond Davis	#1 Charlotte Crossley
	Darlene Love	#2 Fran Jaye
Seaweed	Corey Reynolds	#1 Terron Brooks
	Chester Gregory II 7/14/03	Alan Mingo Jr.
	Tevin Campbell 12/13/05	#2 Terry Lavell
Penny Pingleton	Kerry Butler	#1 Sandra DeNise
	Jennifer Gambatese 6/15/04	Chandra Lee Schwartz

Brooke Tansley 4/11/04   Melissa Larsen
Jennifer Gambatese 6/15/04   Cassie Levy
Tracy Miller   #2 Chandra Lee Schwartz
Diana DeGarmo 2/7/06

Corny Collins   Clarke Thorell   #1 Troy Britton Johnson
Jonathan Dokuchitz 1/13/04   Paul McQuillan
                                #2 Kevin Spirtas

Little Inez   Danelle Eugenia Wilson   #1 Kianna Underwood
Aja Maria Johnson 7/19/03   Kahliah Fatima Rivers
Nia Imani Soyemi   #2 Shannon Antalan

I LOVE YOU, YOU'RE PERFECT, NOW CHANGE

Man #1   Jordan Leeds
Danny Burstein 10/01/96
Adam Grupper 8/22/97
Gary Imhoff 2/09/98
Adam Grupper 4/01/98
Jordan Leeds 3/17/99
Bob Walton 10/27/00
Jordan Leeds 1/30/01
Darrin Baker 1/29/02
Danny Burstein 4/12/02
Jordan Leeds 6/03/02
Will Erat 12/20/05
Ron Bohmer 3/20/06

Man #2   Robert Roznowski
Kevin Pariseau 5/25/98
Adam Hunter 4/20/01
Sean Arbuckle 9/23/02
Frank Baiocchi 2/17/03
Colin Stokes 10/10/03
Jamie LaVerdiere
Adam Arian

Woman #1   Jennifer Simard
Erin Leigh Peck 5/25/98
Kelly Anne Clark 1/10/00
Andrea Chamberlain 3/13/00
Lori Hammel 11/04/00
Andrea Chamberlain 1/29/01
Amanda Watkins 8/24/01
Karyn Quackenbush 1/02/02
Marissa Burgoyne 8/09/02
Andrea Chamberlain 12/17/02
Karyn Quackenbush 2/17/03
Sandy Rustin 6/13/03
Andrea Chamberlain 11/19/04
Jordan Ballard
Jodie Langel

Woman #2   Melissa Weil
Cheryl Stern 2/16/98
Mylinda Hull 9/17/00
Melissa Weil 2/09/01
Evy O'Rourke 3/13/01
Marylee Graffeo 6/11/01

Cheryl Stern 1/18/02
Marylee Graffeo 3/11/02
Janet Metz 4/26/02
Anne Bobby 12/17/02
Janet Metz 3/03/03
Anne Bobby 5/23/05

THE LIGHT IN THE PIAZZA

New York 4/18/05

Margaret Johnson	Victoria Clark
Clara Johnson	Kelli O'Hara
	Jennifer Hughes 12/3/05
	Katie Clarke 12/16/05
Fabrizio Naccarelli	Matthew Morrison
	Aaron Lazar 9/2/05
Signor Naccarelli	Mark Harelik
	Chris Sarandon 9/13/05
Signora Naccarelli	Patti Cohenour
Franca Naccarelli	Sarah Uriarte Berry
Giuseppe Naccarelli	Michael Berresse
Roy Johnson	Beau Gravitte

THE LION KING

New York 11/13/97   *#1 Gazelle Company*
#2 Cheetah Company

Rafiki	Tsidii Le Loka	#1 Futhi Mhlongo
	Thuli Dumakude 11/11/98	Phindile Mkhize
	Sheila Gibbs	#2 Thandazile A. Soni
	Nomvula Dlamini	Gugwana Dlamini
	Tshidi Manye	
Mufasa	Samuel E. Wright	#1 Alton Fitzgerald White
	Alton Fitzgerald White	Thomas Corey Robinson
		L. Steven Taylor
		#2 Rufus Bonds Jr.
		Nathaniel Stampley
Sarabi	Gina Breedlove	#1 Jean Michelle Grier
	Meena T. Jahi 8/4/98	Lashanda Reese-Fletcher
	Denise Marie Williams	#2 Marvette Williams
	Meena T. Jahi	
	Robyn Payne	
	Jean Michelle Grier	
Zazu	Geoff Hoyle	#1 Jeffrey Binder
	Bill Bowers 10/21/98	Mark Cameron Pow
	Robert Dorfman	#2 Derek Hasenstab
	Tony Freeman	Timothy McGeever
	Adam Stein	
	Jeffrey Binder	
Scar	John Vickery	#1 Patrick Page
	Tom Hewitt 10/21/98	Dan Donohue
	Derek Smith	#2 Larry Yando
	Patrick Page	Kevin Gray

	Derek Smith	
	Patrick Page	
Banzai	Stanley Wayne Mathis	#1 James Brown-Orleans
	Keith Bennett 9/30/98	#2 Melvin Abston
	Leonard Joseph	Rudy Roberson
	Curtiss I'Cook	
	Rodrick Covington	
	Benjamin Sterling Cannon	
Shenzi	Tracy Nicole Chapman	#1 Jacquelyn Renae Hodges
	Vanessa S. Jones	Kimberly Hebert Gregory
	Lana Gordon	Jayne Trinette
	Marlayna Sims	#2 Shaullanda Lacombe
	Bonita J. Hamilton	Danielle Lee Greaves
Ed	Kevin Cahoon	#1 Wayne Pyle
	Jeff Skowron 10/21/98	#2 Brian Sills
	Jeff Gurner	Robbie Swift
	Timothy Gulan	
	Thom Christopher Warren	
	Enrique Segura	
Timon	Max Casella	#1 John Plumpis
	Danny Rutigliano 6/16/98	#2 Benjamin Clost
	John E. Brady	Adam Hunter
	Danny Rutigliano	Damian Baldet
Pumbaa	Tom Alan Robbins	#1 Ben Lipitz
		#2 Bob Amaral
		Phil Fiorini
Simba	Jason Raize	#1 Alan Mingo Jr.
	Christopher Jackson	S.J. Hannah
	Josh Tower	#2 Brandon Victor Dixon
		Brandon Louis
		Wallace Smith
Nala	Heather Headley	#1 Kissy Simmons
	Mary Randle 7/7/98	Lisa Nicole Wilkerson
	Heather Headley 12/8/98	Adrienne Muller
	Bashirrah Creswell	Chauntee Schuler
	Sharon L. Young	#2 Adia Ginneh Dobbins
	Renée Elise Goldsberry	Ta'rea Campbell
	Kissy Simmons	

MAMMA MIA!

	New York 10/18/01	*#1 US Tour*
		#2 Las Vegas
Donna Sheridan	Louise Pitre	#1 Dee Hoty
	Dee Hoty 10/22/03	Laurie Wells
	Carolee Carmello 10/20/04	#2 Tina Walsh
	Michele Pawk 10/19/05	Jacqueline Holland
	Corinne Melancon	Carol Linnea Johnson
Sophie Sheridan	Tina Maddigan	#1 Chilina Kennedy
	Jenny Fellner 10/22/03	Carrie Manolakos
	Sara Kramer 10/20/04	#2 Jill Paice
	Carey Anderson 10/19/05	Suzie Jacobsen Balser
		Kelly Anise Daniells
Tanya	Karen Mason	#1 Cynthia Sophiea
	Jeanine Morick	Lisa Mandel

	Tamara Bernier	#2 Karole Foreman
	Judy McLane 10/20/04	Reyna Von Vett
		Vicki Van Tassel
Rosie	Judy Kaye	#1 Rosalyn Rahn Kerins
	Harriett D. Foy	Laura Ware
	Liz McCartney 10/20/04	#2 Jennifer Perry
	Olga Merediz 10/19/2005	Kristine Zbornik
		Robin Baxter
Sky	Joe Machota	#1 P.J. Griffith
	Aaron Staton	Corey Greenan
	Andy Kelso 10/19/05	#2 Victor Wallace
		Patrick Sarb
Sam Carmichael	David W. Keeley	#1 Gary Lynch
	John Hillner	Sean Allan Krill
	David W. Keeley	#2 Nick Cokas
	John Hillner	Lewis Cleale
	Daniel McDonald 10/20/04	Rick Negron
	John Dossett 10/19/05	
Harry Bright	Dean Nolen	#1 Michael DeVries
	Richard Binsley	Ian Simpson
	Michael Winther	#2 Michael Piontek
	David Beach 10/20/04	Andy Taylor
Bill Austin	Ken Marks	#1 Craig Bennett
	Adam LeFevre	Milo Shandel
	Mark L. Montgomery	#2 Mark Leydorf
		Patrick Gallo
		Jefferson Slinkard

THE PHANTOM OF THE OPERA

	New York 1/26/88	*National Tour*
The Phantom	Michael Crawford	Franc D'Ambrosio
	Thomas James O'Leary	Brad Little
	Hugh Panaro 2/1/99	Ted Keegan
	Howard McGillin 8/23/99	Brad Little
	Brad Little	Ted Keegan
	Howard McGillin	Brad Little
	Hugh Panaro 4/14/03	Gary Mauer
	Howard McGillin 12/22/03	John Cudia
	Hugh Panaro 1/5/04	
Christine Daaé	Sarah Brightman	Tracy Shane
	Sandra Joseph 1/29/98	Kimilee Bryant
	Adrienne McEwan 8/2/99	Amy Jo Arrington
	Sarah Pfisterer 1/17/00	Rebecca Pitcher
	Sandra Joseph 10/30/00	Kathy Voytko
	Sarah Pfisterer 8/6/01	Julie Hanson
	Elizabeth Southard 3/25/02	Rebecca Pitcher
	Lisa Vroman 4/22/02	Lisa Vroman
	Sandra Joseph 6/10/03	Rebecca Pitcher
		Marie Danvers
		Jennifer Hope Wills
Christine Daaé (alt.)	Patti Cohenour	Tamra Hayden
	Adrienne McEwan	Marie Danvers
	Sarah Pfisterer	Megan Starr-Levitt
	Adrienne McEwan	Marni Raab

Lisa Vroman 10/30/00   Elizabeth Southard
Adrienne McEwan 7/9/01   Sarah Lawrence
Julie Hanson 9/20/03

Raoul   Steve Barton   Ciaran Sheehan
Gary Mauer 4/19/99   Jason Pebworth 1/29/97
Jim Weitzer 4/23/01   Jim Weitzer
Michael Shawn Lewis 11/2/01 Jason Pebworth 7/22/98
John Cudia 4/7/03   Richard Todd Adams 3/31/99
Jim Weitzer 10/3/03   Jim Weitzer 1/12/00
John Cudia 12/21/03   John Cudia
Tim Martin Gleason 5/27/05   Tim Martin Gleason
Jim Weitzer
Adam Monley

THE PRODUCERS

| | *New York 4/19/01* | *#1 Max Company* |
| | | *#2 Leo Company* |

Max Bialystock   Nathan Lane   #1 Lewis J. Stadlen
Henry Goodman 3/19/02   Jason Alexander 4/21/03
Brad Oscar 4/16/02   Lewis J. Stadlen 1/6/04
Lewis J. Stadlen   #2 Bob Amaral
Fred Applegate 10/7/03
Nathan Lane 12/31/03
Brad Oscar 4/6/04
Richard Kind 1/11/05
Brad Oscar
John Treacy Egan 10/25/05

Leo Bloom   Matthew Broderick   #1 Don Stephenson
Steven Weber 3/19/02   Martin Short 4/21/03
Roger Bart 12/17/02   Alan Ruck 1/6/04
Don Stephenson 5/20/03   #2 Andy Taylor
Matthew Broderick 12/31/03
Roger Bart 4/6/04
Hunter Foster 6/13/04
Alan Ruck 1/11/05
Hunter Foster
Roger Bart 5/15/06

Ulla   Cady Huffman   #1 Angie L. Schworer
Sarah Cornell 8/5/03   Charley Izabella King 1/6/04
Angie L. Schworer 11/4/03   #2 Ida Leigh Curtis

Roger De Bris   Gary Beach   #1 Lee Roy Reams
John Treacy Egan   Gary Beach
Gary Beach 10/7/03   Lee Roy Reams 1/6/04
Jonathan Freeman 8/31/04   #2 Stuart Marland
Gary Beach 9/6/05
Lee Roy Reams

Carmen Ghia   Roger Bart   #1 Jeff Hyslop
Sam Harris 7/2/02   Michael Paternostro
Brad Musgrove 12/17/02   Josh Prince
Brooks Ashmanskas 8/31/04   Harry Bouvy
Jai Rodriguez 11/1/05   #2 Rich Affanato
Brad Musgrove

Franz Liebkind   Brad Oscar   #1 Bill Nolte
John Treacy Egan   Fred Applegate
Peter Samuel   #2 Bill Nolte

John Treacy Egan
Bill Nolte

RENT

New York 4/29/96

Roger Davis

Adam Pascal
  Norbert Leo Butz
  Richard H. Blake (alt.)
  Manley Pope 6/1/02
  Sebastian Arcelus 12/30/02
  Ryan Link 9/8/03
  Jeremy Kushnier 11/14/03
  Carey Shields 1/18/05
  Tim Howar

Mark Cohen

Anthony Rapp
  Jim Poulos
  Trey Ellett 5/15/00
  Matt Caplan 6/1/02
  Joey Fatone 8/5/02
  Matt Caplan 12/23/02
  Drew Lachey 9/10/04
  Matt Caplan 3/14/04

Tom Collins

Jesse L. Martin
  Michael McElroy
  Rufus Bonds Jr. 9/7/99
  Alan Mingo Jr. 4/10/00
  Mark Leroy Jackson 1/15/01
  Mark Richard Ford 2/3/02
  Destan Owens 8/16/04
  Mark Richard Ford 12/20/04
  Destan Owens

Benjamin Coffin III

Taye Diggs
  Jacques C. Smith
  Stu James 3/13/00
  D'Monroe
  Stu James 11/29/04
  D'Monroe

Joanne Jefferson

Fredi Walker
  Gwen Stewart
  Alia León
  Kenna J. Ramsey
  Danielle Lee Greaves 10/4/99
  Natalie Venetia Belcon 10/2/00
  Myiia Watson-Davis 6/1/02
  Merle Dandridge 10/28/02
  Kenna J. Ramsey 3/03/03
  Merle Dandridge
  Nicole Lewis

Angel Schunard

Wilson Jermaine Heredia
  Wilson Cruz
  Shaun Earl
  Jose Llana
  Jai Rodriguez
  Andy Señor 1/31/00
  Jai Rodriguez 3/10/02

Andy Señor 2/17/03
Jai Rodriguez 7/05/04
Andy Señor 7/19/04
Jai Rodriguez 8/2/04
Justin Johnson 8/16/04
Andy Señor 3/15/04
Justin Johnson

Mimi Marquez   Daphne Rubin-Vega
Marcy Harriell 4/5/97
Krysten Cummings
Maya Days
Loraine Velez 2/28/00
Karmine Alers 6/1/02
Krystal L. Washington 5/15/03
Melanie Brown 4/19/04
Krystal L. Washington 8/23/04
Jamie Lee Kirchner

Maureen Johnson   Idina Menzel
Sherie René Scott
Kristen Lee Kelly
Tamara Podemski
Cristina Fadale 10/4/99
Maggie Benjamin 6/1/02
Cristina Fadale 10/28/02
Maggie Benjamin
Melanie Brown
Maggie Benjamin 4/19/04
Kelly Karbacz 7/19/04
Maggie Benjamin
Ava Gaudet

SPAMALOT

	New York 3/17/05	*Boston 3/7/06*
King Arthur	Tim Curry Simon Russell Beale 12/20/05 Harry Groener 4/25/06	Michael Siberry
Lady of the Lake	Sara Ramirez Lauren Kennedy 12/20/05	Pia C. Glenn
Sir Dennis Galahad	Christopher Sieber	Bradley Dean
Sir Robin	David Hyde Pierce Martin Moran 4/4/06	David Turner
Sir Lancelot	Hank Azaria Alan Tudyk 8/6/05 Hank Azaria 12/2/05 Steve Kazee 4/4/06	Richard Holmes
Patsy	Michael McGrath	Jeff Dumas
Sir Bedevere	Steve Rosen	Christopher Gurr

SWEET CHARITY

New York 5/4/05
Closed 12/31/05

Charity Hope Valentine	Christina Applegate
Oscar Lindquist	Denis O'Hare
Herman	Ernie Sabella
	Rob Bartlett 6/11/05
	Wayne Knight 9/20/05
	Ernie Sabella 11/22/05
Helene	Kyra Da Costa
	Kearran Giovanni
Nickie	Janine LaManna
	Mylinda Hull 11/1/05
Vittorio Vidal	Paul Schoeffler

THE 25TH ANNUAL PUTNAM COUNTY SPELLING BEE

New York 5/2/05

William Barfee	Dan Fogler
	Josh Gad 1/31/06
Marcy Park	Deborah S. Craig
Leaf Coneybear	Jesse Tyler Ferguson
Rona Lisa Peretti	Lisa Howard
Olive Ostrovsky	Celia Keenan-Bolger
Mitch Mahoney	Derrick Baskin
Chip Tolentino	Jose Llana
Douglas Panch	Jay Reiss
	Greg Stuhr 10/27/06
Logainne S.	Sarah Saltzberg

WICKED

	New York 10/30/03	*#1 Toronto 3/9/05*
		#2 Chicago 7/13/05
Glinda	Kristin Chenoweth	#1 Kendra Kassebaum
	Jennifer Laura Thompson 7/20/04	#2 Kate Reinders
	Megan Hilty 5/31/04	Stacie Morgain Lewis
	Kate Reinders 5/30/05	
Elphaba	Idina Menzel	#1 Stephanie J. Block
	Eden Espinosa 6/15/04	Julia Murney 3/8/06
	Idina Menzel 7/6/04	#2 Ana Gasteyer
	Shoshana Bean 1/11/05	Kristy Cates 1/24/05
	Eden Espinosa 1/10/06	
Wizard of Oz	Joel Grey	#1 David Garrison
	George Hearn 7/20/04	P.J. Benjamin 3/8/06
	Ben Vereen 5/31/05	#2 Gene Weygandt
	David Garrison 4/4/06	
Madame Morrible	Carole Shelley	#1 Carol Kane
	Rue McClanahan 5/31/05	Carole Shelley
	Carol Kane	Alma Cuervo
		#2 Rondi Reed
		Carole Shelley
Fiyero	Norbert Leo Butz 12/21/04	#1 Derrick Williams

	Taye Diggs 1/18/05	Sebastian Arcelus 3/8/06
	Norbert Leo Butz 1/20/05	#2 Kristopher Cusick
	Joey McIntyre 7/20/04	
	David Ayers 1/11/05	
	Derrick Williams 1/10/06	
Boq	Christopher Fitzgerald	#1 Logan Lipton
	Randy Harrison 6/22/04	Kirk McDonald
	Christopher Fitzgerald 7/27/04	#2 Telly Leung
	Robb Sapp 1/4/05	Adam Flemming
	Jeffrey Kuhn 1/11/05	
	Robb Sapp	
Dr. Dillamond	William Youmans	#1 Timothy Britten Parker
	Sean McCourt	K. Todd Freeman
		#2 Steven Skybell
		Timothy Britten Parker
Nessarose	Michelle Federer	#1 Jenna Leigh Green
	Cristy Candler 1/10/06	Jennifer Waldman 3/8/06
	Jenna Leigh Green 3/14/06	#2 Heidi Kettenring

FIRST-CLASS NATIONAL TOURS

BOMBAY DREAMS

Costa Mesa, 2/21/06
Closed 10/1/06

Akaash	Sachin Bhatt
Rani	Sandra Allen
Priya	Reshma Shetty
Vikram	Deep Katdare
Sweetie	Aneesh Sheth
Kitty DaSouza	Christine Toy Johnson
Madan	Suresh John
Shanti; Mumtaaz	Marie Kelly

THE BOYFRIEND

East Haddam, CT 7/8/05
Closed 3/5/06

Hortense	Bethe B. Austin
Maisie	Andrea Chamberlain
Percival Browne	Paul Carlin
Lord Brockhurst	Drew Eshelman
Lady Brockhurst	Darcy Pulliam
Polly	Jessica Grové
Bobby Van Husen	Rich Faugno
	Eric Daniel Santagata
Tony Brockhurst	Sean Palmer
Mme. Dubonnet	Nancy Hess

DR. DOLITTLE

Pittsburgh 8/2/05

Dr. Dolittle	Tom Hewitt
	Tommy Tune 1/17/06
Emma Fairfax	Nancy Anderson
	Dee Hoty 1/17/06
Albert Blossom	Ed Dixon
	Joel Blum 1/17/06
Polynesia	Susan J. Jacks
	Sarah Stiles

EVITA

Boston 11/02/04
Closed 2/12/06

Eva Peron	Kathy Voytko
	Sarah Litzsinger 10/27/05
Juan Peron	Philip Hernandez
Che	Bradley Dean
	Keith Byron Kirk
Mistress	Kate Manning
	Heidi Dean
Magaldi	Gabriel Burrafato
	Andrew Ragone 10/10/05

JOSEPH AND THE AMAZING TECHNICOLOR DREAMCOAT

Milwaukee 9/6/05
Closed 7/30/06

Joseph	Patrick Cassidy
Narrator	Amy Adams
	Natalie Hill
	Amy Adams
Potiphar; Jacob	Nicholas F. Saverine
Pharoah; Levi	Todd DuBail

LITTLE SHOP OF HORRORS

Los Angeles
Opened 8/29/04

Seymour	Anthony Rapp
	Jonathan Rayson
	Joe Farrell 11/15/05
	Jim Poulos
Audrey	Tari Kelly
	Liz Pearce 11/15/05
Mr. Mushnik	Lenny Wolpe
	Ray De Mattis
	Lenny Wolpe
	Darin DePaul

| *Orin; et al.* | James Moye |
| | Daniel C. Levine 11/15/05 |

LITTLE WOMEN

	San Diego 9/2/05
Jo March	Kate Fisher
Marmee March	Maureen McGovern
Meg March	Renee Brna
Amy March	Gwen Hollander
Beth March	Autumn Hurlbert
Aunt March	Louisa Flaningam
Laurie	Stephen Patterson

LES MISÉRABLES

	Atlanta 9/9/03
Jean Valjean	Randal Keith
Javert	James Clow
	Joseph Mahowald
	Stephen Tewksbury
	Robert Hunt
Fantine	Tonya Dixon
	Joan Almedilla
Eponine	Ma-Anne Dionisio
	Melissa Lyons
Cosette	Amanda Huddleston
	Leslie Henstock
Marius	Josh Young
	Adam Jacobs
	Daniel Bogart
Enjolras	John-Andrew Clark
	Michael Halling
	Victor Wallace
Thénardier	Michael Kostroff
	David McDonald
	David Benoit
	Norman Large
Madame Thénardier	Cindy Benson
	Jennifer Butt

THE SEASON OFF
OFF BROADWAY

THE SEASON OFF OFF BROADWAY

○ ○ ○ ○ ○ *By John Istel* ○ ○ ○ ○ ○

L AST SEASON, THIS ESSAY focused on how Off Off Broadway as a category, contrary to its name, is no longer a phenomenon of geography. Although at its inception some 40 years ago, anything worth seeing OOB could be had within 10 or 20 blocks of Washington Square Park, that real estate has become too precious to harbor the low-budget experiments and creations of noncommercial theater and performance artists. Nothing could illustrate this state of affairs more clearly than two key moments at the May 2006 Obie Awards, the 51st ceremony produced by *The Village Voice.*

For the first time in its half-century of history, the event was held at New York University's swanky new Skirball Center. Co-host Eric Bogosian, the ascerbic one-time downtown monologuist now a television regular on *Law and Order: Criminal Intent*, was impressed. "I've never used a teleprompter before," he commented as he looked around the plush, high-tech venue—the kind in which OOB artists rarely produce. He tried half-jokingly to reassure everyone, "We're still downtown." As Christine Ebersole said after winning for her performance in *Grey Gardens*, "Y'all went uptown—I don't see any empty beer bottles around." And Dana Ivey, after winning an award for her knockout turn as the title character in Irish Repertory Theatre's revival of *Mrs. Warren's Profession,* said, "I'm overwhelmed by the fanciness of this all."

John Clancy, certainly deserved his award for sustained excellence of direction, considering just the past season. He helmed *Goner*, by former *Voice* editor Brian Parks; *screwmachine/eyecandy*, a new play by C.J. Hopkins, one of OOB's most promising playwrights; *Fat Boy*, an adaptation of Alfred Jarry's *Ubu Roi*; and *Cincinnati,* a revival of the Don Nigro play for Neurofest. No one has done more for creating a geography of OOB than Clancy and Present Company. During the 1990s, he and other intrepid directors such as Aaron Beall, had set up storefront performance spaces in the Lower East Side. Then Clancy helped found the New York International Fringe Festival, which creates an annual August carnival of Off Off Broadway spirit when hundreds of shows sprout like weeds over the gentrifying real estate south of Houston Street. At the Obies, Clancy decried the dangers and begged the audience to "stay downtown" if only aesthetically, since it may not be possible physically. "We're losing Stanton Street. We're losing downtown."

By the middle of the event, *Voice* critic Michael Feingold couldn't take the constant critique by the attendees who, deluded by the amenities, thought the event was occurring 40 blocks north of Washington Square Park, instead of beside it. He told the audience, "It doesn't matter where we are geographically. Off Broadway is a state of mind. It's wherever we gather." Indeed, he thereby made explicit the fact of the OOB diaspora, where the theatrical aesthetic and artistic energy once found in neighboring venues during the movement's nascent years in the 1960s and 1970s, only reunites during such events. Award ceremonies—the number of which seems to increase each season—and the many different theater festivals that New York hosts, have become ersatz theater communities, mobile Left Banks of bohemianism.

Mass Appeal

MAKE NO MISTAKE, HOWEVER: the infinite variety of OOB productions, from the epic to the epicurean, the mammoth to the miniscule, form the crucial and mysterious dark matter of New York theater's universe. While Broadway productions are increasingly populated by stars of film and television, and increasingly commercial (and expensive) Off Broadway shows garner more visibility, OOB's sheer mass threatens to overwhelm any writer trying to examine its black hole-like gravitational pull.

The OOB season was just getting started in July 2005 when French director Ariane Mnouchkine's staging of a sprawling allegorical spectacle on immigration and refugees, *Le Dernier Caravansérail (Odyssées)* rolled into town for the Lincoln Center Festival. The six-hour, two-part Théâtre du Soleil production employed a 75-member ensemble and a special stage in Damrosch Park. It relied on a script compiled from diaries, reports and interviews with refugees—and it was performed in a dozen or so languages. One day earlier, a much different, though more typical OOB production opened at the 64-seat Access Theater on the fourth floor of an industrial building below Canal Street: Blue Coyote's 65-minute satire *Busted Jesus Comix* by David Johnston, one of OOB's more accomplished playwrights. Inspired by America's only obscenity case involving a comic-book artist, the play featured cartoonish cardboard-cutout design elements and 10 actors.

Although from opposite ends of the spectrum in their superficialities, both of these productions shine a floodlight on the one resource that OOB has always had in abundance: theatrical imagination. Both shows infuse the act of theater with a sense that it can delight in artifice as it also mirrors the darker side of reality. Although many of these theatrical features—such as the use of puppetry or suggestive scenic designs—are seen more often on Broadway today, for OOB productions, imagination and creativity are never optional.

Has the term "Off Off Broadway" outlived its usefulness?

Back to the Future

ALTHOUGH THE OBIE AWARD ceremony is the oldest devoted exclusively to Off Broadway and Off Off Broadway theater, OOB work from the 2005–06 season was recognized by the Drama Desk, the Lucille Lortels and the Outer Critics' Circle, among others. But even these events, like the Obies, seem increasingly "uptown." To rectify the situation, the equivalent of the People's Choice Awards, the New York Innovative Theatre Awards, or New York IT Awards, were introduced. At the first award ceremony in 2005, playwright Kirk Wood Bromley suggested ditching the "Off Off Broadway" handle and replacing it with "Indie Theater." No longer tied to geography or Equity contract, Indie Theater could be found anywhere as long as it embodied a certain aesthetic. As Bromley wrote for the Indie Theater website (www.indietheater.org/why.htm):

> I'm describing "artist-driven" theater, as opposed to "producer-driven" theater. That which, at every point in its development, answers the question, "What do we do here?," with the answer, "Whatever the artists want," NOT with "Whatever the producer wants." Theater that has as its sole goal the creation of something satisfying to the involved artists' sensibilities, not the creation of something gratifying to the involved producers' financial portfolio and its various budgetary outlays and speculations. Theater that is done to please the audience as the artist imagines it, not as the producer imagines it[. . . .]

One way of translating this might be to look at the art world. Independent artists create their work in studios and display it on their walls or in small gallery spaces. Neighborhood studio tours are another way that artists and audiences are peripatetically united. Similarly, the most innovative and independent theater artists working Off Off Broadway display their work where they can—in galleries, coffee shops, laundromats and all manner of abandoned industrial spaces. Broadway and large nonprofit theaters are museums of theater, where producer-curators display anything that has bubbled to the top and may draw large audiences.

Bromley's use of the term "indie theater"—was subsequently picked up by critic Martin Denton, who created the website and publishes annual anthologies of what he considers the best OOB plays—clearly harks to film and music. Both media, now digital and available via the internet, have been democratized. While traditional means of distribution—radio and movie houses—have fallen into the hands of fewer and fewer large corporations, the internet has given independent filmmakers and musicians their own opportunity to find larger audiences. Unlike film and music, however, theater is by definition a live art resisting digitization. Instead, OOB producers must enhance the visibility of their shows by size and packaging, organizing varied offerings under all manner of themes. We're witnessing the festivalization of theater in the OOB community.

Festivals of Lights

PACKAGING WORKS TOGETHER CREATES enough mass to penetrate the media and help attract the audiences that all artists want. The grandparent of this marketing and artmaking strategy is the Brooklyn Academy of Music's fall classic Next Wave Festival. The 2005–06 edition was the institution's 23rd autumnal event. Often, as others have noted, the artists presented are from the "last wave" in the 1960s and 1970s: Philip Glass, Robert Wilson, Lee Breuer, Pina Bausch, to name a few of the most prominent and regular. This season, such names were notably absent. Instead, BAM co-commissioned *Shelter*, a collaboration between Ridge Theater and Bang on a Can Festival founders Michael Gordon, Julia Wolfe and David Lang. Under Obie Award-winner Bob McGrath's direction, and accompanied by Bill Morrison's film and Laurie Olinder's projections, the multimedia work tried, with mixed results, to investigate the notion of "home" and "homelessness"—which due to the recent spate of hurricanes, flooding and tsunamis, seems to exist only at the whim of nature. Another Obie winner, Marianne Weems's Builders Association (*Alladeen*), along with dbox, presented *Super Vision*. The Builders Association works with a high-tech bag of theatrical tricks similar to McGrath and company, only the technology is the point. In *Super Vision*, three storylines—involving a Ugandan traveler, a Sri Lankan woman and a suburban American family—are intercut to explore issues of "identity theft" and, indeed, the very nature of identity in our digital age.

Edward Hall's Propeller company, an all-male ensemble from England devoted to invigorating productions of Shakespeare returned to BAM with a much-lauded production of *The Winter's Tale*. The company's inspired stagecraft, in which the ensemble moves imaginative but spare scenic pieces while creating a lush sound design, embodies the OOB can-do spirit with tremendous grace and sophistication.

British playwright Sarah Kane, whose edgy, poetic scripts may have been more popularized by their creator's suicide than by their productions, received her second mounting in Brooklyn within a year of *4:48 Psychosis* (under the title *4.48 Psychose*), her last and most despondent play. The previous season, it was seen at St. Ann's Warehouse, the performance venue near the Brooklyn Bridge, but the BAM presentation was a French version of the script, directed by Claude Régy and performed without intermission by film star Isabelle Huppert. Glued to a single spot onstage, Huppert barely moved in the 100-odd minutes that it took to recite Kane's raging, lyrical piece, creating a chilly and challenging experience for audiences not, perhaps, unlike the first productions of Samuel Beckett seen downtown.

Aside from the large-scale dance and theater spectacles mounted by BAM and Lincoln Center, other festivals relied on a variety of productions that required single actors, tiny ensembles, spare stagings and theatrical imagination. It is not that the American Living Room festival or Couchworks @ Chashama—where Mat Smart's one-act *Music for a High Ceiling* was particularly well regarded—feel under produced; their antitheatrical titles, help to lower expectations for technical wizardry while making audiences feel at home. American Living Room's 16th summer slate of nearly two-dozen offerings used video, dance, film and sound to tackle the theme of America's "Carousel of Progress." There were immigrant tales such as Michael Lew's *Yit, Ngay (One, Two)* about four Chinese sisters—two born in China, two in the US—performed by a single actress; and Saviana Stanescu's *Aurolac Blues*, about two Romani boys dreaming of making it to America. More exotic work, an international multimedia solo piece performed by the Icelandic actress Palina Jonsdottir in *The Secret Face*, for instance, could also be found.

Across the river in Williamsburg, Brooklyn, the enterprising Brick Theater followed up last season's Hell Festival with one centered on "Moral Values." One of the most spectacular performances, given the resources, was Ian Hill's *World Gone Wrong*, which used a score of actors to perform a script composed of snippets of classic film noir and quotes from various Bush administration officials. Two of the more interesting solo shows included *Mahamudra* by Chris Harcum, a self-referential nightmare involving a hostile theater critic; and the provocatively titled *My Year of Porn*, written and performed by journalist and comedian Cole Kazdin, which describes the hilarious but soul-draining experience of shooting a documentary about the sex-film industry. Kazdin subsequently performed her irreverent show at the Magnet Theater.

Other gatherings of like-minded writers, actors and theater artists could be found in the latest iterations of Ensemble Studio Theatre's OctoberFest and One-Act Play Festival; the annual Young Playwrights Festival, which showcases work by dramatists under the age of 18; the New York Musical Theatre Festival, one of the few devoted to America's premier theatrical art form; the Midtown International Theatre Festival; and Soho Think Tank's summer Ice Factory, a compendium of aesthetically diverse works by emerging and established "downtown" artists, which is one of the best. The last kicked off its 13th edition with an ecstatically received production from Canada's SaBooge Theatre. Marilyn Stasio in *Variety,* for one, called it "mind-altering." The Victorian-era story about a boy who lived under water, performed in a Jacques LeCoq-influenced style, won a summer festival citation for "overall production and technical achievement" from Talkin' Broadway. As a symbol of the OOB community, few productions could have as many interconnections as the eight-time Obie Award-winning Foundry Theatre's *Major Bang, or: How I Learned to Stop Worrying and Love the Dirty Bomb,* a self-described "suspense comedy with magic." Inspired by *Dr. Strangelove*—and the true story of a Boy Scout who built a nuclear reactor to earn a merit badge—Kirk Lynn's script was performed by Wooster Group member Steve Cuiffo and Radiohole co-founder Maggie Hoffman. The two actors played a host of characters, including a conservative preacher. R.C. Baker in the *Voice* wrote, "In 75 minutes, the pair make a case for laughter trumping fundamentalism." It received its New York premiere at St. Ann's Warehouse in Brooklyn, as part of the Public Theater's Under the Radar festival celebrating the Public's 50th anniversary. Ben Brantley in *The New York Times* called *Major Bang* "a disarming political cabaret" and was charmed by the insouciant show's insistence on battling fear and paranoia in post-September 11 New York with humor and imagination. As with other innovative productions, *Major Bang* subsequently toured the country.

The largest and least manageable event—in other words, the festival most symbolic of Off Off Broadway as a community—has become the New

York International Fringe Festival, which completed its seventh summer in 2005. It bills itself as "the largest multiarts festival in North America." Although bigger doesn't always mean better, how could one possibly stand to choose between the titles of the four pieces that won Fringe awards for outstanding solo shows: *The Miss Education of Jenna Bush*, *Bridezilla Strikes Back!*, *Jesus in Montana*, and *Surviving David?* Produced in dozens of primarily downtown venues during the month of August, this behemoth offers a little bit of everything. Unlike the Ice Factory and larger festivals, the Fringe is uncurated. Its motto might as well be: excess is best.

Usual Suspects, Unusual Plays

EVEN WITHOUT THEATER FESTIVALS, OOB would be abuzz with activity. There are presenters such as Theater for the New City and La MaMa ETC which, bless them, continue to give homes to a myriad of companies, international and domestic. Then there are the small, hardy stalwarts that have the ability to mount seasons and (egads!) even sell subscriptions. These include Ensemble Studio Theatre, Classic Stage Company, Manhattan Class Company (MCC Theater), Primary Stages, Atlantic Theater Company, Irish Repertory Theatre, Signature Theatre Company, and Vineyard Theatre, among others.

At least three new works of particular note arose from this group last season. The quirky musical about writing musicals, aptly named *[title of show]* charmed critics, was extended three times, and won Obie Awards for librettist Hunter Bell, composer and lyricist Jeff Bowen and director Michael Berresse. It was deftly produced by Vineyard, a company steaming into the middle of its third decade, which, under the direction, of Doug Aibel regularly presents new plays and small chamber musicals in its subterranean space just off Union Square. *[title of show]*'s two main characters are (not coincidentally) named Hunter and Jeff. The tandem is under tremendous pressure to write a musical for a contest deadline. Based on their reality as struggling musical-theater collaborators—Bowen and Bell rushed *[title of show]* for the New York Musical Theatre Festival—the piece is filled with in-jokes and an encyclopedic collection of musical-theater references presented in a bare-bones physical production.

Primary Stages and Atlantic Theater Company both presented Best Plays represented by longer essays in this book. Primary Stages's bit of prescience was in producing *In the Continuum*, a piece written and performed by Danai Gurira and Nikkole Salter, two African-American women who met while students in New York University's graduate acting program.

Originally two solo pieces the combined works centered on the effects of HIV/AIDS on black women from opposite ends of the globe: Gurira's was set in her homeland of Zimbabwe, Salter mined her experience in Southern California. Both pieces interweave a variety of characters to trace the cost of the scourge on their respective communities. Directed by Robert O'Hara, the production went on to a commercial run at the Perry Street Theatre and has since toured Africa and the US.

Atlantic presented the original voice of Yale Drama School playwright Rolin Jones, thanks to a recommendation from playwright and mentor Lynn Nottage. Jones's *The Intelligent Design of Jenny Chow* won an Obie and was one of the most effervescent comedies of the season—in which an agoraphobic teenage genius creates a robot of herself as a conduit to the outside world.

Few companies embody the OOB spirit as much as the Flea Theater. It has become one of downtown's most fecund and idiosyncratic hatcheries of new work even as it completes its first decade of existence. Director James Simpson employs a resident acting company called "the Bats"; offers work to the likes of Sigourney Weaver (his wife), Bebe Neuwirth and John Lithgow; and presents new plays by relatively new writers. The Flea's mission statement reads in part:

> Noninstitutional and resolutely noncommercial, The Flea embodies the spirit of adventure and experiment that has defined Off Off Broadway since its inception. [. . .] Part playground, part laboratory and part training ground, we have been home to established artists taking new risks, emerging artists developing their ideas and mid-career artists building sustained audiences.

At the end of last season, A.R. Gurney took his latest "new risk" with the Flea (following *Mrs. Farnsworth* and *O Jerusalem*) by offering *Screen Play,* his third political fantasy-satire in response to the Bush era. This one's about a future when the House Un-American Activities Committee has returned and liberals fleeing to Canada have revivified once moribund border cities like the author's hometown of Buffalo. *Screen Play*'s characters are coy takeoffs on those made famous in *Casablanca*. As the 2005–06 season got underway, offerings that embodied the variety of Flea's work included choreographer and dancer Sarah East Johnson's troupe LAVA, which offered *(w)HOLE*, a multimedia piece about the history of the earth and women's place in it; and *Ashley Montana Goes Ashore in the Caicos . . . or: What Am I Doing Here?,* a play by award-winning journalist Roger Rosenblatt that featured actors more often seen on Broadway: Bebe Neuwirth and Jeffrey DeMunn; Gip Hoppe's *Mercy on the Doorstep*, a mother-stepdaughter black comedy; and an encore presentation of Brenda Currin in *Sister and Miss Lexie*, an adaptation of Eudora Welty short stories that Currin has performed for 25 years.

Re-Mixes and Revivals

THE INTELLIGENT DESIGN OF JENNY CHOW wasn't the only OOB show featuring a robot. In *Heddatron*, produced by Les Freres Corbusier (the same folks who brought us *A Very Merry Unauthorized Children's Scientology Pageant)* the program listed a "Robot Design" credit along with the usual set, lights, costumes and sound. The credit belongs to Botmatrix (Cindy Jeffers and Meredith Finkelstein). The show, produced at HERE Arts Center, mixed five robots with live actors, including the fearless Carolyn Baeumler as a housewife kidnapped by robots and forced to perform as Hedda over and over. Under the direction of Alex Timbers, who had dreamt of such a *Hedda* for years, Elizabeth Meriwether's script epitomized the extent to which creativity and imagination can totally reconfigure the reality of a classic from the dramatic canon—and suggest new directions for the future.

Theatre for a New Audience's season was bookended by two notable productions. Its opener, *Measure for Measure*, featured a guest appearance by British actor Mark Rylance, recently disengaged from Shakespeare's Globe in London; and the New York premiere of Howard Brenton's *Sore Throats* (1979) starring Laila Robins and Bill Camp as a married couple in a Strindbergian power struggle. (A 1985 presentation by New York Theatre Workshop was not a fully staged production.)

There were plenty of heady revivals, where directorial intelligence and design savvy allowed good acting to resuscitate a few linchpins of dramatic literature. Brian Kulick, settling in as artistic director of Classic Stage Company, offered a vivid *Hamlet* with Michael Cumpsty in the title role. Kulick and long-time scenic collaborator Mark Wendland created a visually surprising environment in which the audience stood uncomfortably onstage as the lights went down. The battlement scene that begins the play took place by flashlight as Elsinore's watchmen scurried around, among the audience, trying to catch the ghost. This effectively spooky start, strangely ended when the lights rose after the scene, and the audience members casually took their seats. The play proceeded in fairly straightforward fashion. While clearly too old to play the melancholy university student, Cumpsty managed to convey the character's tightrope walk between anguished grief and antic madness.

The same 13th Street black box also played host to director David Herskovits, whose Target Margin company has followed CSC's mission, though often tending toward the underrepresented in revivals. Herskovits stamps each production with his Foreman-esque insistence on drawing attention to the artificiality of everything onstage. He's particularly obsessed with *Faust*, and earlier had produced each part separately. In December 2005, Target Margin presented Goethe's *Helena* at the Ohio Theatre as an appetizer to the *Faust* that ended the season at CSC. The latter was a two-part, six-hour version of Goethe's classic in a translation by Douglas Langworthy. Herskovits doesn't literally use a company, but many of the same actors return to every production. Will Badgett did; turning Faust into a mystical, tormented, but earthbound soul. And critics were particularly enamored of David Greenspan's Mephisto.

What CSC does for pre-20th century classics, Signature Theatre has done for 20th century playwrights. The 2005–06 season may have been one of its best, thanks to the venerable stage actress Lois Smith, who topped even her memorable Ma Joad in *The Grapes of Wrath* (1990) with her performance in Horton Foote's *The Trip to Bountiful*. John Guare's *Landscape of the Body* followed and received equally rapturous reviews. When Smith accepted her Obie Award she may have best expressed the bottom line for all OOB theater artists: "We were there with audiences happy to be there—and that's as good as it gets."

Obviously, no critic could catch more than a third of the work offered OOB, and that feat would require seeing six shows a week. But thanks to the incredible variety of work, nowhere in the world do theatergoers have as many riches to choose from as they do Off Off Broadway, wherever that state of mind may be. And for audiences, that's as good as it gets.

PLAYS PRODUCED OFF OFF BROADWAY AND ADDITIONAL NYC PRESENTATIONS

○ ○ ○ ○ ○

Compiled by Vivian Cary Jenkins

BELOW IS A broad sampling of 2005–06 Off Off Broadway productions in New York. There is no definitive "Off Off Broadway" area or qualification. To try to define or regiment it would be untrue to its fluid, often exploratory purpose. This listing of hundreds of works produced by scores of OOB groups is as inclusive as reliable sources allow. This section pertains to professional theater in New York that is covered by neither Broadway nor full Off Broadway contracts.

The more active and established producing groups are identified in **bold face type**, in alphabetical order, with artistic policies and the names of its leaders given whenever possible. Each group's 2005–06 schedule, with emphasis on new plays, is listed with play titles in CAPITAL LETTERS. Often these are works-in-progress with changing scripts, casts and directors, sometimes without an engagement of record (but an opening or early performance date is included when available).

Many of these Off Off Broadway groups have long since outgrown a merely experimental status and offer programs that are the equal—and in many cases the superior—of anything in the New York theater. These listings include special contractual arrangements such as the showcase code, letters of agreement (allowing for longer runs and higher admission prices than usual) and, closer to the edge of commercial theater, so-called "mini-contracts." In the list below, available data has been compiled from press representatives, company managers and publications of record.

A large selection of developing groups and other shows that made appearances Off Off Broadway during the season under review appears under the "Miscellaneous" heading at the end of this listing. Festival listings include samples of the schedules offered and are sometimes limited to the title and author of the work listed to allow for the inclusion of more works.

Atlantic Theater Company. Produces new plays and reinterpretations of classics with an artistic voice that reflects today's society. Neil Pepe artistic director.

> THE CHERRY ORCHARD. By Anton Chekhov; adapted by Tom Donaghy. June 15, 2005. Directed by Scott Zigler; scenery, Scott Pask and Orit Jacoby Carroll; costumes, Theresa Squire; lighting, Howard Werner; sound and music, Fitz Patton; wigs and hair, Robert-Charles Vallance; stage manager, Jennifer Grutza. With Brooke Adams, Larry Bryggman, Scott Foley,

269

Death grip: Eunice Wong and Julienne Hanzelka Kim in Rolin Jones's The Intelligent Design of Jenny Chow. *Photo: Carol Rosegg*

Alvin Epstein, Peter Maloney, Mary McCann, Todd Weeks, Isiah Whitlock Jr., Laura Breckenridge, Pepper Binkley, Erin Gann, Diana Ruppe, Dan Domingues.

THE INTELLIGENT DESIGN OF JENNY CHOW. By Rolin Jones. September 19, 2005. Directed by Jackson Gay; scenery, Takeshi Kata; costumes, Jenny Mannis; lighting, Tyler Micoleau; sound, Daniel Baker; music, Matthew Suttor; stage manager, Robyn Henry. With Remy Auberjonois, Michael Cullen, Linda Gehringer, Julienne Hanzelka Kim, Ryan King, Eunice Wong. A 2005–06 Best Plays choice (see essay by Charles Wright in this volume).

CELEBRATION and THE ROOM. By Harold Pinter. December 5, 2005. Directed by Neil Pepe; scenery, Walt Spangler; costumes, Ilona Somogyi; lighting, David Weiner; sound, Obadiah Eaves; fight direction, Rick Sordelet; stage manager, Darcy Stephens. With (*The Room*) Thomas Jay Ryan, Mary Beth Peil, Peter Maloney, Kate Blumberg, David Pittu, Earle Hyman; (*Celebration*) David Pittu, Patrick Breen, Betsy Aidem, Thomas Jay Ryan, Carolyn McCormick, Brennan Brown, Kate Blumberg, Philip Goodwin, Christa Scott-Reed.

Brooklyn Academy of Music Next Wave Festival. Since 1983, this annual festival has presented hundreds of performing arts events, including dozens of world premieres. Featuring leading international artists, it is one of the world's largest contemporary performing arts festivals. Alan H. Fishman chairman of the board, Karen Brooks Hopkins president, Joseph V. Melillo executive producer.

TALL HORSE. By Khephra Burns. October 4, 2005. Directed by Marthinus Basson; choreography, Koffi Kôkô; scenery and costumes, Adrian Kohler; lighting, Wesley France; video, Jaco Bouwer; puppetry, Yaya Coulibaly and Mr. Kohler; press, Sandy Sawotka, Fatima Kafele, Eva Chien, Tamara McCaw, Jennifer Lam.

EMILIA GALOTTI. By Gotthold Ephraim Lessing. October 12, 2005. Directed by Michael Thalheimer; scenery and costumes, Olaf Altmann; music based on "Yumei's Theme" by Shigeru Umebayashi, Bert Wrede.

4.48 PSYCHOSE. By Sarah Kane. October 19, 2005. Directed by Claude Régy; scenery, Daniel Jeanneteau; costumes, Ann Williams; lighting, Dominique Bruguière; sound, Philippe Cachia. With Isabelle Huppert, Gérard Watkins.

THE WINTER'S TALE. Revival of the play by William Shakespeare. November 2, 2005. Directed by Edward Hall; scenery, Michael Pavelka; lighting, Ben Ormerod. With Propeller Company. Presented in association with Watermill Theatre (UK).

BRIGHT ABYSS. By James Thiérrée. November 9, 2005. Directed by Mr. Thiérrée; costumes, Victoria Thiérrée and Cidalia Da Costa; lighting, Jérôme Sabre; sound, Thomas Delot. With Niklas Ek, Thiago Martins, Uma Ysamat, Raphaelle Boitel, Mr. Thiérrée. Presented in association with La Compagnie du Hanneton.

SHELTER. Music-theater piece with book by Deborah Artman; music by Michael Gordon, David Lang and Julia Wolfe. November 16, 2005. Directed by Bob McGrath; scenery, Jim Findlay; costumes, Ruth Pongstaphone; lighting, Matt Frey; sound, Norbert Ommer; projections, Laurie Olinder; film, Bill Morrison. With musikFabrik and trio mediæval. Presented in association with Ridge Theater.

SUPER VISION. By the Builders Association, dbox, Charles d'Autrement, Matthew Bannister, Dan Dobson, James Gibbs, Constance De Jong, Tanya Selvaratnam, Marianne Weems. November 29, 2005. Directed by Ms. Weems; scenery and costumes, Stewart Laing; lighting, Jennifer Tipton and Allen Hahn; sound and music, Mr. Dobson.

Classic Stage Company. Reinventing and revitalizing the classics for contemporary audiences. Brian Kulick artistic director, Jessica R. Jenen executive director.

HAMLET. Revival of the play by William Shakespeare. November 13, 2005. Directed by Brian Kulick; scenery, Mark Wendland; costumes, Oana Botez-Ban; lighting, Brian H. Scott; sound, Jorge Muelle; stage manager, Melissa M. Spengler. With Michael Cumpsty, Caroline Lagerfelt, Robert Dorfman, Kellie Overbey, Herb Foster, Graham Winton, Jon DeVries, Karl Kenzler, Jason Ma.

FRAGMENT. By Kelly Copper; adapted from the works of Sophocles and Euripides. March 26, 2006. Directed by Pavol Liska; scenery, Peter Nigrini; costumes, Oana Botez-Ban; lighting, Tim Cryan; sound, Kristin Worrall. With Juliana Francis, Tony Torn, Zachary Oberzan.

FAUST, PARTS I AND II. By Johann Wolfgang von Goethe; translated by Douglas Langworthy. April 30, 2006. Directed by David Herskovits; scenery, Carol Bailey; costumes, Kaye Voyce; lighting, Lenore Doxsee; sound, John Collins; music, Katie Down and John King. With Will Badgett, Aysan Celik, Daphne Gaines, David Greenspan, George Hannah, Lian-Marie Holmes, Ty Jones, E.C. Kelly, Wayne Alon Scott, Eunice Wong. Presented in association with Target Margin Theater.

Ensemble Studio Theatre. Membership organization of playwrights, actors, directors and designers dedicated to supporting individual theater artists and developing new works. Stages more than 300 projects each season, ranging from readings to fully mounted productions. Curt Dempster artistic director.

MARATHON 2005 (SERIES B). June 1–19, 2005.
HOME. By David Mamet. Directed by Curt Dempster. CRAZY EIGHTS. By David Linday-Abaire. Directed by Brian Mertes. ERROS. By Cherie Vogelstein. Directed by Jamie Richards.

MARATHON 2005 (SERIES C). June 14–26, 2005.
THE ONE-ARMED MAN. By Horton Foote. Directed by Harris Yulin. GRYZK. By Kate Long. Directed by Evan Bergman. YOUR CALL IS IMPORTANT. By Craig Lucas. Directed by William Carden. THE UNWRITTEN SONG. By Romulus Linney; based on *The Unwritten Song* by Willard R. Task. Directed by Carlos Armesto.

OCTOBERFEST 2005. October 14–30, 2005.
VANISHING POINT. Musical with book by Liv Cummings and Rob Hartman; music by Mr. Hartman; lyrics by Ms. Cummings and Mr. Hartman. PROGRESS IN FLYING. By Lynn Rosen.

CRIMINAL CONVERSATION. By Susan Haar. GLUE. By Richard Hinojosa. ROSEMARY WITH GINGER. By Ed Baker. HERO AND VILLAIN. By M. Ardito. BULLETPROOF and TOAST OF THE TOWN. By Brian Sheridan. FANNY. By Julie Leedes. NATURAL SELECTION. By Leslie Lyles. MONKEY'S UNCLE. By Matthew Wells. YUMEE AND JACK. By Bill Bozzone. THE BLUE SKY BOYS. By Deborah Brevoort. SEREIA. By Sonya Martin. AIRBORN. By Rob Ackerman. PARADISE VILLAGE. By Larry Bloom. TINY BUBBLES. By Richard Willett. AT THE STARLITE MOTEL. By Jacqueline Heinze. MY SECRET LANGUAGE OF WISHES. By Cori Thomas. MIND GAMES. By Patrick Bonvitacola. ABU GHRAIB TRIPTYCH. By Peter Maloney. CAZ AND DIANE. Conrad Bromberg. THE BAD SON. By David Zellnick. MISS CORPUS. By Clay McLeod Chapman. CARNIVAL. By Carl Capotorto. AMERICAN DREAMERS. By Jay Veduccio. BIRTHMARKS–ACT II. By Leslie Peterson Caputo. JE REGRETTE TOUT. By Jeanne Darst. DEMON AT THE DOOR. By Kate Long. STONE BABY SOLITARE. By Keith Byron Kirk. THE EFFECTS OF MAKEOVERS. By Maria Gabriele. DAYGLO. By Randee Smith. THE GOOD STENO. By Leah Kornfeld Friedman and Paul Ben-Victor. HONEYMOON HOTEL. By Amy Fox. THE FAMILY WAY. By Kathryn Grant. DAY AT THE PARK. By Peter Marsh. INTERCOURSE IN THE MORNING. By Arthur Giron. UNLOVABLE. By Troy Hill.

KLONSKY AND SCHWARTZ. By Romulus Linney. December 5, 2005. Directed by Jamie Richards; scenery and lighting, Maruti Evans; costumes, Amela Baksic; sound, Graham Johnson; fight direction, Ian Unterman. With Chris Ceraso, Bill Wise.

THICKER THAN WATER 2006. January 30–February 18, 2006.
HUNGRY. By Amy Herzog. Directed by Christine Farrell. With Erin McMonagle, Lucia Brizzi, Rebecca Pace.

HENRIETTA HERMALINE'S FALL FROM GREAT HEIGHTS. By Maggie Smith. Directed by Abigail Zealey Bess. With Nicol Zanzarella-Giacalone, Denny Bess, Brendan McMahon.

A BITTER TASTE. By Kevin Christopher Snipes. Directed by RJ Tolan. With Peter O'Connor, Haskell King, Paul Clark.

THE TRAVELING LADY. By Horton Foote. March 3, 2006. Directed by Marion Castleberry; scenery, Maruti Evans; costumes, Maggie Lee-Burdorff; lighting, Jason Jeunnette; sound, Graham Johnson; stage manager, Angrette McCloskey. With Lynn Cohen, Stan Denman, Frank Girardeau, Margot White, Carol Goodheart, Rochelle Oliver, Alice McLane, Jamie Bennett, Matthew Conlon, Quincy Confoy. Presented in association with Baylor University.

RELATIVITY. By Cassandra Medley. April 30, 2006. Directed by Talvin Wilks. With Starla Benford, Anthony Crane, Elain Graham, Petronia Paley, Kim Sullivan, Melanie Nicholls-King.

MARATHON 2006 (SERIES A). May 23–June 10, 2006.
BREAKFAST AND BED. By Amy Fox. Directed by Abigail Zealey-Bess. THE OTHER WOMAN. By David Ives. Directed by Walter Bobbie. DAVY AND STU. By Anton Dudley. Directed by Jordan Young. NOT ALL KOREAN GIRLS CAN FLY. By Lloyd Suh. Directed by RJ Tolan.

MARATHON 2006 (SERIES B). May 30–June 19, 2006.
BONE CHINA. By David Mamet. Directed by Curt Dempster. 100 MOST BEAUTIFUL NAMES OF TODD. By Julia Cho. Directed by Jamie Richards. ON THE SPORADIC. By James Ryan. Directed by Charles Richter. INTERMISSION. By Will Eno. Directed by Michael Sexton.

The Flea Theater. Formed to present distinctive, cutting-edge work that raises the standards of Off Off Broadway. Jim Simpson artistic director, Carol Ostrow producing director.

BOOCOCK'S HOUSE OF BASEBALL. Solo performance piece by Paul Boocock. June 30, 2005. Directed by Mary Catherine Burke. With Mr. Boocock.

HALF LIFE. By Robert Moulthrop. September 9, 2005. Directed by Teresa K. Pond; scenery, Dana Liebowitz; costumes, Mimi Maxmen; lighting, Julie Duro; sound, Timothy Owen Mazur; dramaturg, Vincent Marano; stage manager, Eliza Johnson. With Anna Chlumsky, Cynthia Foster, Michele Fulves, Mark Lynch, Cameron Hughes.

ASHLEY MONTANA GOES ASHORE IN THE CAICOS . . . OR: WHAT AM I DOING HERE? By Roger Rosenblatt. October 20, 2005. Directed by Jim Simpson. With Bebe Neuwirth, Jenn Harris, Jeffrey DeMunn, James Waterston.

SISTER AND MISS LEXIE. By David Kaplan and Brenda Currin; based on the works of Eudora Welty. November 13, 2005. Directed by Mr. Kaplan; scenery, Mr. Kaplan and Sue Rees; costumes, Ellen Pittman Stockbridge; lighting, Megan Tracy; stage manager, Gwendolyn Gilliam. With Ms.Currin, Ayako Morino.

(W)HOLE. By Sarah East Johnson, Sini Anderson and Capital B. January 12, 2006. Directed by Ms. Johnson; costumes, Liz Prince; lighting, Chloe Brown; music, Steven Hamilton; video, Heather Delaney. With Natalie Agee, Diana Y. Greiner, Molly Chanoff, Ms. Johnson, Eugenia Chiappe, Rebecca Stronger.

BACK OF THE THROAT. By Yussef El Guindi. February 2, 2006. Directed by Jim Simpson; choreography, Mimi Quillin; scenery, Michael Goldsheft; costumes, Erin Elizabeth Murphy; lighting, Benjamin C. Tevelow; stage manager, Lindsay Stares. With Adeel Akhtar, Bandar Albuliwi, Jamie Effros, Jason Guy, Erin Roth.

THE MAG-7: SEVEN ONE-ACT PLAYS. By Louis Cancelmi (*The Handlers*), Graham Gordy (*Waning Poetic*), John Kim (*Orange Alert*), Heather MacDonald (*Waiting*), Itamar Moses (*Untitled Short Play*), Hugh Murtagh (*A Twist So Shocking You'll Have to See It to Believe It*) and Deirdre O'Connor (*Penicillin*). February 16, 2006. Directed by Glynis Rigby (*The Handlers*), Jonathan Bernstein (*Waning Poetic*), Kerry Whigham (*Orange Alert*), Julia Gibson (*Waiting*), Michelle Tattenbaum (*Untitled Short Play*), and Dave Dalton (*Penicillin*); scenery,

Third degree: Adeel Akhtar and Jamie Effros in Yussef El Guindi's Back of the Throat. *Photo: Max Ruby*

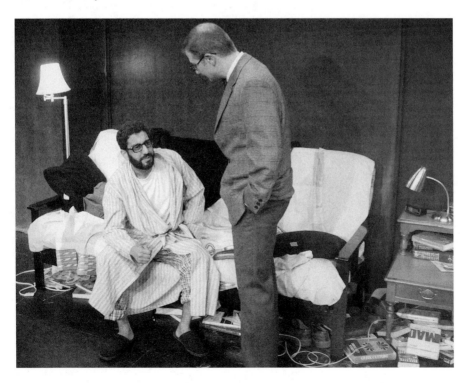

Faye Armon; costumes, Daphne Javitch; lighting, Benjamin C. Tevelow; sound, Brittany O'Neill; stage manager, Rhonda Picou. With Gideon Banner, Michael Crane, Bill Cwikowski, Tim Cummings, Tom Riis Farrell, Kelly Hutchinson, Erik Jensen, Abbie Killeen, James McMenamin, Erin McMonagle, Nancy McNulty, Eric Miller, and Sam Breslin Wright. Presented in association with Naked Angels.

MERCY ON THE DOORSTEP. By Gip Hoppe. March 23, 2006. Directed by Jim Simpson; choreography, Mimi Quillin; scenery, Susan Zeeman Rogers; costumes, Erin Elizabeth Murphy and Nathalie Ferrier; lighting, Kevin Hardy; sound, Rick Arnoldi; stage manager, Jennifer Noterman. With Laura Esterman, Jenn Harris, Mark Rosenthal.

Intar. Identifies, develops and presents the talents of gifted Hispanic-American theater artists and multicultural visual artists. Eduardo Machado artistic director.

KISSING FIDEL. By Eduardo Machado. September 20, 2005. Directed by Michael John Garcés; scenery, Mikiko Suzuki; costumes, Meghan E. Healey; lighting, Paul Whitaker; sound, David M. Lawson; stage manager, Michael Alifanz. With Javier Rivera; Karen Kondazian, Judith Delgado, Lazaro Perez, Bryant Mason and Andres Munar.

TIGHT EMBRACE. By Jorge Ignacio Cortinas. December 6, 2005. Directed by Lisa Peterson; scenery, Mikiko Suzuki; costumes, Meghan E. Healey; lighting, Paul Whitaker; sound, David M. Lawson; stage manager, Michael Alifanz. With Mia Katigbak, Zabryna Guevara, Robert M. Jimenez, Andres Munar, Marisa Echeverria.

POINTS OF DEPARTURE. By Michael John Garcés. March 21, 2006. Directed by Ron Daniels; scenery, Mikiko Suzuki; costumes, Meghan E. Healey; lighting, Paul Whitaker; sound, David M. Lawson; music, Cristian Amigo; stage manager, Michael Alifanz. With David Anzuelo, Sandra Delgado, Marisa Echeverria, Mateo Gomez, Alfredo Narciso, Antonio Suarez.

Irish Repertory Theatre. Brings works by Irish and Irish-American playwrights to a wider audience and develops new works focusing on a wide range of cultural experience. Charlotte Moore artistic director, Ciarán O'Reilly producing director.

PHILADELPHIA, HERE I COME. By Brian Friel. July 21, 2005. Directed by Ciarán O'Reilly; scenery, David Raphel; costumes, David Toser; lighting, Brian Nason; sound, Murmod, Inc. With Paddy Croft, Michael Fitzgerald, James Kennedy, Edwin C. Owens, James Stevens, Tessa Klein, Gil Rogers, Helena Carroll, John Leighton, Geddeth Smith, Tim Ruddy, Joe Berlangero, Darren Connolly, Leo Leyden.

BEOWULF. Musical by Lenny Pickett and Lindsey Turner; adapted from the ancient epic. October 16, 2005. Directed by Charlotte Moore; scenery, Akira Yoshimura; costumes, Randall Klein; lighting, Brian Nason; sound, Zachary Williamson; puppetry, Bob Flanagan; stage manager, Pamela Brusoski. With Richard Barth, Edwin Cahill, David Garry, Bill Daelin Gross, John Halbach, Jay Lusteck, Shaun R. Parry, Jack Wadell.

MRS. WARREN'S PROFESSION. Revival of the play by George Bernard Shaw. December 18, 2005. Directed by Charlotte Moore; scenery, Dan Kuchar; costumes, David Toser; lighting, Mary Jo Dondlinger; sound, Murmod, Inc.; stage manager, Rebecca Goldstein-Glaze. With Dana Ivey, Laura Odeh, David Staller, Sam Tsoutsouvas, Kevin Colllins, Kenneth Garner.

YOU DON'T HAVE TO BE IRISH. Solo performance piece by Malachy McCourt. January 17, 2006. With Mr. McCourt.

NEW WORKS READING SERIES. January 27–April 28, 2006.
FROM THESE GREEN HEIGHTS. By Dermot Bolger. With Elizabeth Canavan, Lynn Cohen, Ronald Cohen, Stevie Ray Dallimore, Leslie Lyles, Katie Wetherhead.

RAGTOWN. By Jayme McGhan. With Todd Cerveris, Catherine Curtain, Kevin Geer, Roxanne Hope, Greg Keller, Sam Kitchin, Nicole Lowrance, James McMenamin.

DEFENDER OF THE FAITH. By Stuart Carolan. With Colby Chambers, Luke Kirby, David Lansbury, Michael O'Keefe, David Rasche.

MIND THE WAY. By Ann Deignan. With Rob Campbell, Maria Dizzia, Chris McGarry, Dee Pelletier, Jesse Pennington.

THE FIELD. By John B. Keane. May 9, 2006. Directed by Ciarán O'Reilly; scenery, Charles Corcoran; costumes, Martha Hally; lighting, Jason Lyons; sound, Zachary Williamson; fight direction, Rick Sordelet; stage manager, Elis C. Arroyo. With Craig Baldwin, Orlagh Cassidy, Malachy Cleary, Paddy Croft, Karen Lynn Gorney, Chandler Williams, Brian Henderson, Ken Jennings, Laurence Lowry, Marty Maguire, Paul Nugent, John O'Creagh, Tim Ruddy.

Jean Cocteau Repertory. Founded by Eve Adamson in 1971, the company is dedicated to the production of classic theater. David Fuller and Ernest Johns artistic directors. Re-formed as Egopo/Cocteau Ensemble. Lane Savadove artistic director.

THE MAIDS. By Jean Genet; translated by Bernard Frechtman. July 15, 2005. Directed by Ernest Johns; scenery, Roman Tatarowicz; costumes, Nicole Frachiseur; lighting, Richard Dunham; stage manager, Allison R. Smith. With Ramona Floyd, Kate Holland, Amanda Jones.

MOTHER COURAGE. Revival of the play by Bertolt Brecht; translated by Marc Blitzstein; music by Paul Dessau. September 4, 2005. Directed by David Fuller; scenery, Roman Tatarowicz; costumes, Viviane Galloway; lighting, Giles Hogya; dramaturg, Ryan Mark Weible; stage manager, Andrea Cibelli. With Lorinda Lisitza, Sara Jeanne Asselin, Danaher Dempsey, Seth Duerr, Angus Hepburn, Lynn Marie Macy, Tim McDonough, Mickey Ryan, Taylor Wilcox.

MEDEA. Revival of the play by Euripides; translated by Joseph Goodrich. October 30, 2005. Directed by Ernest Johns; scenery and lighting, David Kniep; costumes, Nicole Frachiseur; stage manager, Allen Hale. With Ramona Floyd, Pascal Beauboeuf, Angus Hepburn, Elsie James, Lynn Marie Macy, Mickey Ryan, Taylor Wilcox.

CANDIDA. By George Bernard Shaw. December 28, 2005. Directed by Michael Halberstam; scenery, Brian Sidney Bembridge; costumes, Sean Sullivan; lighting, Joel Moritz; sound, Josh Schmidt; stage manager, Allen Hale. With Amanda Jones, David Tillistrand, Angus Hepburn, Danaher Dempsey, Seth Duerr, Kate Holland.

THE MISER. Revival of the play by Molière; translated by Charles Heron Wall. February 26, 2006. Directed by Dan Zisson; costumes, Timmy Church; lighting, Rich Dunham; stage manager, Allen Hale. With Angus Hepburn, Seth Duerr, Albert Aeed, Leah Bonvissuto, Craig Brown, Melanie Hopkins, Lorinda Lisitza, Margarita Martinez, Timothy McDonough, Mickey Ryan, Taylor Wilcox.

THE MAIDS X 2. Revision of the play by Jean Genet. March 31, 2006. Directed by Lane Savadove; scenery, Nick Lopez and Mr. Savadove; costumes, Mattie Olson; lighting, Mr. Lopez; stage manager, Ed Farrell. With J.J. Brennan, Alejandra Cejudo, Leah Loftin, Mr. Lopez, Kevin V. Smith, Taylor Wilcox.

SUCKER FISH MESSIAH. By Ryan Michael Teller. May 12, 2006. Directed by Taylor Brooks; scenery, Matthew Allar; lighting, Evan O'Brient; stage manager, Amanda Kadrmas. With Melanie Hopkins, Shannon Jones, Darren Ryan, Jennifer Sanders.

La MaMa Experimental Theatre Club (ETC). A workshop for experimental theater of all kinds. Ellen Stewart founder and director.

THREE SISTERS. Revival of the play by Anton Chekhov; translated by Arthur Adair. June 16, 2005. Directed by Mr. Adair; choreography, Michael Baldwin; scenery and lighting, Mr. Adair; costumes, Karen Anselm; stage manager, Carla Bosnjak. With Ben Pirtle, Michele Cuomo, Caesar Del Treco, Alana DiMaria, Sara Elsen, Jason Grechanik, Chris Oden, Rick Redondo, Andrew Rothkin, Jessica Marie Smith, Joseph Sousa, Pierre van der Spuy, Liza Bryn, Wendy Callard-Booz, Joe McGee.

THE WHORE OF SHERIDAN SQUARE. By Michael Baron. June 16, 2005. Directed by Mr. Baron; scenery, Erminio Pinque; costumes, Lora LaVon; lighting, Brian J. Lilienthal. With Ken Barnett, Doug Brandt, Harris Doran, Ginger Eckert, Vanessa Hidary, Eric McNaughton.

WHY HANNA'S SKIRT WON'T STAY DOWN. By Tom Eyen. October 7, 2005. Directed by George Ferencz; scenery, Gian Marco LoForte; lighting, Jeff Tapper; sound, Tim Schellenbaum. With Helen Hanft, Christopher Zorker.

SAINT OEDIPUS. By Piotr Tomaszuk. October 16, 2005. Directed by Mr. Tomaszuk; scenery, Jan Zavarsky; costumes, Eva Farkasova; lighting, Mr. Tomaszuk; music, Piotr Nazaruk. With Edyta Lukaszewicz-Lisowska, Rafal Gasowski.

HAMLET. Revival of the play by William Shakespeare; adapted by Kanako Hiyama. November 3, 2005. Directed by Ms. Hiyama; scenery, Ryo Onodera; costumes, Ms. Hiyama. With Joseph C. Yeargain; Erin Treadway, Brendan Bradley, Ivo Velon, Tony Naumovski, Roger Dale Stude, David Gochfeld, Morteza Tavakoli, Neimah Djourabchi.

MAMI WATA. By Prisca Ouya. December 1, 2005. Directed by Ms. Ouya; choreographed by Ms. Ouya and Kiazi Malonga. With Ms. Ouya, Karisma Jones, Ronee Mattingly, Beti Garcia, Rashida Ngouamba, Adea, Chaney Pollard, Alexis Doster, Kimann Johnson, Fontaine Traore, Stephane Goudjo, Amber Canty, Shaina Stephen, Indiria Carr, Anne Andre, Isacc Kataly, Martin Vejarano, Coster Massamba, Meredith Wright.

MAJOR BARBARA. Revival of the play by George Bernard Shaw. January 12, 2006. Directed by Brooke O'Harra; scenery, Peter Ksander and Justin Townsend; music, Brendan Connelly. With Heidi Schreck, Tina Shepard, Mike Mikos, David Brooks, Bob Jaffe, Tatiana Pavela, Johnny Klein, Nadia Scherazade Mahdi, Tom Lipinski, Rosemary Quinn, Laryssa Husiak, Derrick Karg.

DELICIOUS RIVERS. By Ellen Maddow. January 15, 2006. Directed by Paul Zimet; choreography, Karinne Keithley; scenery, Nic Ularu; costumes, Kiki Smith; lighting, Carol Mullins. With Gary Brownlee, Kimberly Gambino, Jan Leslie Harding, Cortez Nance Jr., Mary Shultz, Jay Smith, Chris Wells, Taylor Bergren-Chrisman, Mark Kaczmarczyk, Sam Kulik.

HARVEST. By Manjula Padmanabhan. January 19, 2006. Directed by Benjamin Mosse; scenery, Lee Savage; costumes, Chloe Chapin; lighting, Scott Bolman; video, Matt Bockelman. With Zina Anaplioti, Diksha Basu, Sam Chase, Rupak Ginn, Naheed Khan, Christianna Nelson, Debargo Sanyal, Jeffrey Withers.

THE EMPEROR JONES. Revival of the play by Eugene O'Neill. February 2, 2006. Directed by Arthur Adair; scenery and lighting, Mr. Adair; costumes, Wendy Meiling Yang. With Xander Gaines, Sheila Dabney, Brian P. Glover.

DEATH AND THE PLOUGHMAN. By Johannes von Saaz; adapted by Peter Case. February 9, 2006. Directed by Mr. Case. With Rob Howard, Robert Yang, Elli Stefanidi, Bridget Clark, Storm Garner.

ODCHODZI (PASSING AWAY). By Leszek Madzik; based on the work of Tadeusz Rosewicz. February 16, 2006. Directed by Mr. Madzik. With Janusz Buchoski, Przemyslaw Dudek, Urszula Dudziak, Jaroslaw Figura, Liwia Madzik, Monika Michalowicz, Justyna Niezgoda, Tomasz Pluta, Tomasz Wentland, Bartlomiej Witek, Tomasz Zoltak.

THE LAST NIGHT OF SALOME. By Emanuele Vacchetto. March 2, 2006. Directed by Maria Luisa Bigai; sound and music, Alessandro Molinari. With Lidia Biondi, Carla Cassola.

TRILOGY. *Helen, Queen of Sparta. Odyssey: The Homecoming. Iphigenia.* By Theodora Skipitares; based on stories of the Trojan War. March 16, 2006. Directed and designed by Ms. Skipitares; music by Arnold Dreyblatt, Tim Schellenbaum, Yukio Tsuji; puppetry, Cecilia Schiller and Ms. Skipitares. With Carolyn Goelzer, Nicky Paraiso.

MUSTARD. By Mitchell Polin. April 28, 2006. Directed by Mr. Polin; choreography by Michael Burke and Mr. Polin; lighting, Blu; music and video, Tungsten74. With Kimberly Brandt, Jessie Richardson, Mr. Burke, Ben Horner, Kristopher Kling; Philly.

SUNDOWN. By Watoku Ueno. April 28, 2006. Directed by Mr. Ueno; costumes, Luba Kierkosz; projections, Makoto Takeuchi; music, Storm Garner. With Nick Bosco, Jhon Chou, Yuriko Hoshina, Ai Kiyono, Yoshiro Kono, Kazue Tani, Robert Torigoe.

SISTER. By Mario Fratti. May 18, 2006. Directed by Pamela Billig; scenery, Eugene Brogyányi. With Eleanor Ruth, Russell Stevens, Brian Voelcker, Shân Willis.

HERAKLES VIA PHAEDRA. By Ellen Stewart; based on the ancient stories. May 22, 2006. Directed by Ms. Stewart; choreography by Renouard Gee, Bharata Natyam, Kamala Cesar and Shigeko Suga; scenery, Jun Maeda; sound, Tim Schellenbaum; music, Genji Ito, Michael Sirotta, Heather Paauwe, Elizabeth Swados, Ms. Stewart; projections, Jeffrey Issac. With Brian Glover, Peter Case, Eugene the Poogene, Mr. Gee, Allison Hiroto, Benjamin Marcantoni, JT Netterville, Chris Wild, Ms. Paauwe, David Sawyer, Ben Sher, Yukio Tsuji.

Lincoln Center Festival 2005. An annual international summer arts festival offering classic and contemporary work. Nigel Redden director.

I LA GALIGO. By Rhoda Grauer; adapted from from the Indonesian epic *Sureq Galigo*. July 13, 2006. Directed by Robert Wilson and Ann-Christin Rommen; choreography, Restu I. Kusumaningrum; scenery, Mr. Wilson; costumes, Joachim Herzog; lighting, A.J. Weissbard; music, Rahayu Supanggah. With Kadek Tegeh Okta WM, Ascafeony Daengtanang Maladjong, Sri Qadariatin, M. Gentille Andi Lolo.

LE DERNIER CARAVANSÉRAIL (ODYSSÉES). *Part 1: Le Fleuve Cruel (The Cruel River)*. By Théâtre du Soleil; music by Jean-Jacques Lemêtre. July 17, 2005. Directed by Ariane Mnouchkine. LE DERNIER CARAVANSÉRAIL (ODYSSÉES). *Part 2: Origines et destins (Origins and Destinies)*. By Théâtre du Soleil; music by Jean-Jacques Lemêtre. July 17, 2005. Directed by Ariane Mnouchkine.

ARLECCHINO, SERVANT OF TWO MASTERS. By Carlo Goldoni. July 20, 2005. Directed by Giorgio Strehler; scenery, Ezio Frigerio; costumes, Franca Squarciapino; lighting, Gerardo Modico. With Ferrruccio Soleri, Giorgio Bongiovanni, Paolo Calabresi, Pia Lanciotti, Sara Zoia, Enrico Bonavera.

MY LIFE AS A FAIRY TALE. Musical with book by Erik Ehn; music and lyrics by Stephin Merritt; based on the life and fairy tales of Hans Christian Anderson. July 27, 2005. Directed by Chen Shi-Zheng; scenery, Walt Spangler; costumes, Elizabeth Caitlin Ward; lighting, Christopher Akerlind; sound, David Meschter and Mr. Merritt; video and projections, Peter Flaherty; stage manager, Lisa Iacucci. With Fiona Shaw, Blair Brown, Mia Maestro, Qian Yi, Mary Lou Rosato.

MODERN NOH PLAYS: SOTOBA KOMACHI AND YOROBOSHI. By Yukio Mishima. July 28, 2005.Directed by Yukio Ninagawa; choreography by Uran Hirosaki; scenery, Kaoru Kanomori and Tsukasa Nakagoshi; costumes, Lily Komine; lighting, Tamotsu Harada; sound, Masahiro Inoue. With (*Sotoba Komachi*) Haruhiko Jo, Yo Takahashi, Eiichi Seike, Yukio Tsukamoto, Masato Shinkawa, Yutaka Suzuki, Makoto Tamura, Tadashi Okada, Takeshi Inomo, Yuki Tsukikawa, Takuma Harada, Shiro Tsubouchi, Mikio Shimizu; (*Yoroboshi*) Tatsuya Fujiwara, Mari Natsuki, Tetsuro Sagawa, Machiko Washio, Mikio Shimizu, Tomoko Jinbo.

AMERICAN SONGBOOK. In its eighth season, devoted to popular American songs, singers and songwriters. Season included:

ORPHEUS AND EURIDICE. By Ricky Ian Gordon. October 5, 2005. Directed and choreographed by Doug Varone; scenery, Allen Moyer; costumes, Jane Greenwood; lighting, Robert Wierzel; stage manager, Tricia Toliver. With Elizabeth Futral, Todd Palmer, Mr. Varone, Melvin Chen, John Beasant III, Daniel Charon, Natalie Desch, Adriane Fang, Stephanie Liapis, Michael Sean Marye, Catherine Miller, Eddie Taketa.

BRIAN STOKES MITCHELL. Solo performance. January 12, 2006.

ANDY BEY. Solo performance. January 13, 2006.

DEBORAH VOIGT. Solo performance. January 25, 2006.

IT'S ONLY LIFE: THE SONGS OF JOHN BUCCHINO. Concert performance. January 27, 2006. Directed by Daisy Prince. With Brooks Ashmanskas, Andrea Burns, Gavin Creel, Jessica Molaskey, Billy Porter, Mr. Bucchino.

MY GUY CY: LILL' CELEBRATES CY COLEMAN. Concert performance. February 7, 2006. With Lillias White.

THE MUSIC THAT MAKES ME DANCE: A JULIE STYNE SONGBOOK. Concert performance. February 8, 2006. With Eric Comstock.

HOW CAN I KEEP FROM SINGING? Solo concert performance. February 10, 2006. With Victoria Clark.

THE LOSER'S LOUNGE TRIBUTE TO BURT BACHARACH. Concert performance. February 11, 2006. Music direction Joe McGinty.

JAMES, GREG AND KEIRA: THE NAUGHTON FAMILY. Concert performance. February 23, 2006.

GO THE DISTANCE: THE LYRICS OF DAVID ZIPPEL. Concert performance February 24, 2006. With Brent Barrett, Barbara Cook, Jenny Fellner, Jason Graae, Brian d'Arcy James, Anne Letscher, Sally Mayes, Lindsay Mendez, Donna Murphy.

BERNADETTE PETERS IN CONCERT. May 1, 2006.

Mabou Mines. Established in 1970, the company creates new works based on original and existing texts. The current artistic directorate includes Julie Archer, Lee Breuer, Sharon Fogarty, Ruth Maleczech, Frederick Neumann and Terry O'Reilly.

RED BEADS. By Mabou Mines; poem by Lee Breuer; music by Ushio Torikai; based on a story by Polina Klimovitskaya. September 20, 2005. Directed by Mr. Breuer; puppetry, Basil Twist; costumes, Meganne George; lighting, Jennifer Tipton and M.L. Geiger; sound, Ken Travis; projections, Julie Archer; flying, Foy. With Clove Galilee, Rob Besserer, Ruth Maleczech.

SUITE RESIDENT ARTISTS 2006. February 3–27, 2006.
FISS IT, LITTLE OL' BROTHER MAN ANGEL. Solo performance piece by Jana Haimsohn. TIERRA DEL FUEGO. By Henry Guzman. LOSING MYSELF. Choreographed by Erica Rebollar; sound, Charlie Campagna. THE LOST BOX OF UTOPIA. By Jill Campbell. Directed by Mark Parees. BEAUTIFUL DAY. By A. Rey Pamatmat. RUS. By James Scruggs. Directed by Kristin Marting. LI, THE LAST KING. By Julie Landau. Directed by Lu Yu. The Spider Operas. Created by Elizabeth Swados and Taylor Mac. GEO-WEB AND HER SHADOW. By Leonora Loeb.

MCC Theater. Dedicated to the promotion of emerging writers, actors, directors and theatrical designers. Robert LuPone and Bernard Telsey artistic directors, William Cantler associate artistic director, John G. Schultz executive director.

ASSISTED LOVING. By Bob Morris. September 26, 2005. Directed by Josh Hecht. With Mr. Morris.

COLDER THAN HERE. By Laura Wade. September 28, 2005. Directed by Abigail Morris; scenery, Jeff Cowie; costumes, Candice Donnelly; lighting, Michael Chybowski; sound, John Leonard; projections, Brian H. Kim; production stage manaer, Amy McCraney. With Judith Light, Brian Murray, Sarah Paulson, Lily Rabe.

THE WOODEN BREEKS. By Glen Berger. February 21, 2006. Directed by Trip Cullman; scenery, Beowulf Boritt; costumes, Anita Yavich; lighting, Paul Whitaker; sound and music, Fitz Patton; fight direction, Rick Sordelet; stage manager, Hannah Cohen. With Louis Cancelmi, Veanne Cox, Maria Dizzia, Jaymie Dornan, Ron Cephas Jones, Steve Mellor, Ana Reeder, Adam Rothenberg, T. Ryder Smith.

Mint Theater Company. Committed to bringing new vitality to worthy but neglected plays. Jonathan Bank artistic director.

THE SKIN GAME. By John Galsworthy. July 10, 2005. Directed by Eleanor Reissa; scenery, Vicki R. Davis; costumes, Tracy Christensen; lighting, Traci Klainer; sound, Bruce Ellman; stage manager, Amber Wedin. With Nick Berg Barnes, Denis Butkus, Monique Fowler, James Gale, Leo Kittay, Diana LaMar, Nicole Lowrance, Pat Nesbit, Carl Palmer, Stephen Rowe, John C. Vennema, Richard Waddingham.

IVANOV. By Anton Chekhov; translated by Paul Schmidt. August 2, 2005. Directed by Jonathan Bank; scenery, Sarah Lambert; costumes, Elly van Horne; lighting, Stephen Petrilli; sound, Jane Shaw; stage manager, Jason Hindelang. With Michi Barall, Joel de la Fuente, Mel Duane Gionson, Keiko Green, Deepti Gupta, Mia Katigbak, Daniel Dae Kim, C.S. Lee,

Orville Mendoza, Stephen Park, Rochele Tillman, Virginia Wing. Presented in association with the National Asian-American Theatre Company.

WALKING DOWN BROADWAY. By Dawn Powell. September 25, 2005. Directed by Steven Williford; scenery, Roger Hanna; costumes, Brenda Turpin; lighting, Stephen Petrilli. With Christine Albright, Denis Butkus, Antony Hagopian, Carol Halstead, Amanda Jones, Emily Moment, Stacy Parker, Ben Roberts, Cherene Snow, Sammy Tunis.

SOLDIER'S WIFE. By Rose Franken. February 23, 2006. Directed by Eleanor Reissa; scenery, Nathan Neverin; costumes, Clint Ramos; lighting, Josh Bradford; sound, Elizabeth Rhodes; stage manager, Karen Hergesheimer. With Judith Hawking, Jordan Lage, Kate Levy, Angela Pierce, Michael Polak.

New Dramatists. An organization devoted to playwrights. Members may use the facilities for projects ranging from private readings of their material to public scripts-in-hand readings. Listed below are readings open to the public during the season under review. Todd London artistic director, Joel K. Ruark executive director.

New Playwright Welcome. September 12, 2005. DANCE OF THE HOLY GHOSTS: A PLAY ON MEMORY. By Marcus Gardley. Directed by Mr. Gardley. With Paul Butler, Muhammad Cunningham. PERFECT EVENING. By Daniel Reitz. Directed by Hal Brooks. With Johanna Day, Daniel Talbott, Tim Ransom. CRADLE OF MAN. By Melanie Marnich. Directed by Loretta Greco. With Lynn Cohen, Isabel Keating, Michael Laurence, Tim Ransom. SCARCITY. By Lucy Thurber. Directed by Brian Mertes. With Chris Kipiniak, Linda Larson, Bill Camp, Jan Leslie Harding, Samantha Soule, Daniel Talbott. SOUTH ST. BERNARD STREET. By Quiara Alegría Hudes. Directed by Ms. Hudes. With Stephanie Beatriz.

STANLEY. By Lisa D'Amour. September 15, 2005. With Todd D'Amour.

THE PUBLIC. By Caridad Svich; adapted from Federico Garcia Lorca. September 22, 2005. Directed by Michael John Garcés. With Stephen Webber, Chris Wells, Yul Vazquez, Ray Rizzo, Carlo Alban, Eisa Davis, Jennifer Morris, Andres Munar, Piter Marek, Eunice Wong.

CANDOR. By Daniel Reitz. September 26, 2005. Directed by Mr. Reitz. With Marc Aden Gray, Rashaad Ernesto Green, Simon Kendall, Kristina Valada-Viars, Ed Vassallo, Maria Dizzia, Haskell King, Daniel Talbott, Deirdre O'Connell, Laura Heisler.

REDEMPTION. By Brooke Berman. October 3, 2005. Directed by Orla O'Loughlin. With Polly Lee, Maria Dizzia, Zakiyyah Alexander, Lucas Papaelias, Simon Kendall.

THE NECKLACE: EPISODE II. By Paul Zimet; music by Peter Gordon. October 14, 2005. Directed by Mr. Zimet. With David Brooks, Mary Bacon, Polly Lee, John Daggett, Gary Brownlee, Tina Shepard, Larry Block, Ellen Maddow.

MARFA LIGHTS. By Octavio Solis. October 18, 2005. Directed by Randy White. With Alfredo Narciso, Paolo Andino, Jono Hustis, Maria Dizzia, Haskell King, Carla Briscoe, Christina Kirk, L. Pontius.

GULF VIEW DRIVE. By Arlene Hutton. October 20, 2005. Directed by Eric Nightengale. With Alexandra Geis, Greg Steinbruner, Ruth Nightengale, Jean Taylor, Lori Wolter.

LEMKIN'S HOUSE. By Catherine Filloux. October 21, 2005. Directed by Jean Randich. With John Daggett, Ed Vassallo, Michael Potts, Connie Winston, Mercedes Herrero.

PANIC. By Joseph Goodrich. October 27, 2005. Directed by Nick Faust. With Erik Liberman, Maria Dizzia, Molly Powell, Matthew Lewis, Jenny Sterlin.

THE 5000 FINGERS OF DR. T. By Karen Hartman. October 27, 2005. Directed by Susan H. Schulman. With Brent Barrett, Kaitlin Hopkins, Shuler Hensley, Noah Galvin, Jenny Fellner, Amy McAlexander, Joy Lynn Matthews, Blake Ewing, Trent Kendall, Erick Devine, Lila Coogan.

DANCE OF THE HOLY GHOSTS: A PLAY ON MEMORY. By Marcus Gardley. November 7, 2005. Directed by Liz Diamond. With Roger Robinson, Sterling Brown, Harriett D. Foy, Pascale Armand, Kelly McCreary, Stephen Conrad Moore, Gordon Carver.

THE VISITOR. By Carol Mack. November 8, 2005. Directed by Marcy Arlin. With Bill Phillips, Jonathan Smith, Christian Baskous, Ralph Pochoda, Chris Henry Coffey, Dan Matisa, Frank Hentschker, Renata Hinrichs.

GRACELESS. By Michael John Garcés. November 10, 2005. Directed by Loy Arcenas. With Carolyn Baeumler, Ritchie Petrocelli, Lori McNally, Gardiner Comfort, Kenajuan Bentley, Laurence Lau.

DELICIOUS RIVERS. By Ellen Maddow. November 10, 2005. Directed by Paul Zimet. With Jan Leslie Harding, Lori Tan Chinn, Ron Bagden, Charles Parnell, David Brooks, Mary Schultz, Gary Brownlee, Robert Osborne, Taylor Bergren-Chrisman, Steve Parker.

SOFA: ENCHANTED EVENING. By Sherry Kramer. November 15, 2005. Directed by Melissa Kievman. With Ms. Kramer.

EPHEMERIS. By Dominic Taylor. November 17, 2005. Directed by Mr. Taylor. With Roger Robinson, Brienin Nequa Bryant, Chris Wells.

FIX UP. By Kwame Kwei-Armah. November 17, 2005. Directed by Clinton Turner Davis. With Paul Butler, Craig Alan Edwards, Eric Leroy Harvey, Connie Winston, Yvette Ganier.

DEAD MAN'S CELL PHONE. By Sarah Ruhl. November 18, 2005. Directed by Ms. Ruhl. With Randy Danson, Robert Dorfman, Polly Noonan, Boris McGiver, Carla Harting, Aysan Celik, Emily Morse.

INFINITUDE. By Sung Rno. November 21, 2005. Directed by Victor Maog. With Aaron Yoo, Laura Kai Chen, Paul H. Juhn, Cristofer Jean, Hana Moon, C.S. Lee.

BRER CLARE, OR LIFE AMONG THE MIGHTY. By Lonnie Carter. December 15, 2005. Directed by Loy Arcenas. With Michael Potts, Danyon Davis, Michael John Garcés, Mercedes Herrero, April Matthis, Jennifer Morris, Tanya Selvaratnam, KJ Sanchez.

THE FRAIL MAN. By Anthony Crowley. January 24, 2006. Directed by Hal Brooks. With Jonno Roberts, Meg MacCary, Mike Hodge, Geraldine Librandi, Daniel Pearce, Jon Krupp, Jennifer Gibbs, Piter Marek.

TOUGH TITTY. By Oni Faida Lampley. January 31, 2006. Directed by Charles Randolph-Wright. With Quincy Tyler Bernstine, Peter Jay Fernandez, Michelle Hurst, Christine Toy Johnson, Antoinette LaVecchia, Shona Tucker, Jon Krupp.

A STORY ABOUT A GIRL. By Jackie Reingold. February 7, 2006. Directed by Ms. Reingold. With Megan Ofsowitz, Haskell King, Andrew Weems, Tamilla Woodard, Erik Liberman, Karen Kandel.

ONE BIG LIE. By Liz Duffy Adams; music by David Rhodes. March 4, 2006. Directed by KJ Sanchez. With Matthew Dellapina, Roxane Carrasco, Antoinette LaVecchia, Piter Marek, Kathryn Morath, Jill Anna Ponasik, Chris Wells, Stephanie Beatriz, Mingzhao Zhou, Sam Smith, Joe Sargent.

VERBATIM. By Caridad Svich. March 17, 2006. Directed by Michael Sexton. With Polly Lee, Florencia Lozano, Alfredo Narciso.

THE MOST BEAUTIFUL LULLABY YOU'VE EVER HEARD. By Greg Romero. March 31, 2006. Directed by Jasson Minadakis. With Blake Delong, Natalie Wheeler, Ian Galloway.

THE VIRGIN WITH 10,000 ARROWS. By Jason Tremblay. April 1, 2006. Directed by Robbie McCauley. With Hal Fickett, Charles Parnell, Rashaad Ernesto Green, Alfredo Narciso, Stephanie Beatriz, April Matthis, Ron Bagden.

ORGANIZING ABRAHAM LINCOLN. By Lonnie Carter and Rich Klimmer. April 22, 2006. Directed by Brian Mertes. With Vanessa Aspillaga, Danyon Davis, Ron Domingo, Charles H. Hyman, Orville Mendoza, Zoe Perry, Ron Riley, Tanya Selvaratnam, Keith Randolph Smith, Matthew Stadelmann, Ruttina Wesley.

DRIP. By Christina Anderson. May 2, 2006. Directed by Liesl Tommy. With Tamilla Woodard, Jordan Mahome, Edward O'Blenis, Nikki E. Walker, Keli Garrett, Tinashe Kajese.

GUERNICA. By Kristoffer Diaz. May 3, 2006. Directed by Tlaloc Rivas. With Vanessa Aspillaga, Alfredo Narciso, Stephanie Beatriz.

OPHELIA THREE. By Aya Ogawa. May 4, 2006. With Melissa Mathes, Saori Tsukada, Ikuko Ikari, Aaron Mostkoff Unger, Connie Hall, Peter Lettre, Alanna Medlock, Ana Carolina, Jenny Emerson, Drae Campbell, Pablo Ribot.

MARE'S NEST. By Joseph Goodrich. May 5, 2006. Directed by Nick Faust. With Brenda Thomas, Tinashe Kajese, Richard Riehle, Charles Hyman, Erik Liberman, Walker Jones.

THIS JOAN. By Gary Sunshine. May 9, 2006. With Mary Fogarty, Ronald Cohen, Charlotte Colavin, Charles Hyman, Phyllis Somerville, Nora Chester, Irma St. Paule.

THE MOST DECORATED MAN IN TOWN. By Mark Druck. May 11, 2006. Directed by Leslie Lee. With Heather Massie, Zina Less, Alison Floyd, Robert Pemberton, Tamara Grady, Bret Dykes, Carol Ann Foley, Charles Regan, Taylor Treadway.

STEP ASIDE. By Barry Jay Kaplan; music by Kim Sherman. May 25, 2006. Directed by Kyle Fabel. With Oni Faida Lampley, Peter Jay Fernandez, Jumel Rodriquez, Stacey Linnartz, Amirh Rosario Van, Bavish Patel.

New Federal Theatre. Dedicated to integrating minorities into the mainstream of American theater through the training of artists and the presentation of plays by minorities and women. Woodie King Jr. producing director.

PAUL ROBESON. By Phillip Hayes Dean. November 20, 2005. Directed by Shauneille Perry. With Kevin Maynor, Cary Gant.

REAL BLACK MEN DON'T SIT CROSS-LEGGED ON THE FLOOR (A COLLAGE IN BLUES). By Malik. February 2, 2006. Directed by Passion; sound, Sean O'Halloran. With Chet Anekwe, Jerome Preston Bates, D.K. Bowser, Gerard William Catus, Arthur French, Nyasha Hatendi, Stanley Wayne Mathis, Charles Reuben.

CHAMPION. By David Paladino. April 12, 2006. Directed by Tommy Redmond Hicks; scenery, Tony Davidson; costumes, Anita Davis; sound, Sean O'Halloran. With Ski (Cutty) Carr, Mr. Paladino. Presented in association with Black Spectrum Theatre.

THE STUTTERING PREACHER. By Levy Lee Simon. April 12, 2006. Directed by Woodie King Jr.; scenery, Tony Davidson; costumes, Anita Davis; sound, Sean O'Halloran. With Joyce Sylvester, Mr. Simon. Presented in association with Black Spectrum Theatre.

The New Group. Provides an artistic home for fresh acting, writing and design talent. Committed to cultivating a young and diverse theatergoing audience. Scott Elliott artistic director, Geoffrey Rich executive director.

ABIGAIL'S PARTY. By Mike Leigh. December 1, 2005. Directed by Scott Elliott; scenery, Derek McLane; costumes, Eric Becker; lighting, Jason Lyons; sound, Ken Travis; stage manager, Fran Rubenstein. With Max Baker, Lisa Emery, Darren Goldstein, Elizabeth Jasicki, Jennifer Jason Leigh.

THE MUSIC TEACHER. By Wallace Shawn; music by Allen Shawn. March 6, 2006. Directed by Tom Cairns; choreography, David Neumann; scenery, Mr. Cairns; costumes, Kaye Voyce; lighting, Matt Frey; sound, Shane Rettig; music direction, Timothy Long; stage manager, Cat Domiano. With Ross Benoliel, Marc Blum, Elisa Cordova, Jason Forbach, Wayne Hobbs, Lauren Jelencovich, Kristin Knutson, Stefanie Nava, Kellie Overbey, Jeffrey Picón, Rebecca Robbins, Kathryn Skemp, Bobby Steggert, Kristina Valada-Viars, Sarah Wolfson.

A SPALDING GRAY MATTER. Solo performance piece by Michael Brandt. Directed by Ian Morgan; scenery, Peter R. Feuchtwanger; costumes, Kristine Koury; lighting, Jason Lyons; sound, Matt Sherwin; stage manager, Stephanie Gatton. With Mr. Brandt.

Pan Asian Repertory Theatre. Introducing Asian-American theater to the general public with the aim of deepening appreciation and understanding of Asian-American cultural heritage. Tisa Chang artistic director.

CAMBODIA AGONISTES. Revival of the musical with book and lyrics by Ernest Abuba; music by Louis Stewart. November 2, 2005. Directed and choreographed by Tisa Chang; scenery, Kaori Akazawa; costumes, Carol Ann Pelletier; lighting, Victor En Yu Tan; music direction, Jack Jarrett; masks, Tom Lee. With Lydia Gaston, Ron Nakahara, John Baray, Ariel Estrada, Rebecca Lee Lerman, Virginia Wing, Derek Wong, Sam-Oeun Tes.

PAN ASIAN FESTIVAL OF NEW WORKS. May 3–28, 2006.
RECOLLECTIONS. By Kendra Ware. ELEVATOR SEX. By Lan Tran. ABC (AMERICAN BORN CHINESE). By John Quincy Lee. 38TH PARALLELS. By Terry Park.

Performance Space 122. Provides artists of a wide range of experience a chance to develop work and find an audience. Vallejo Gantner artistic director.

FROM DAKOTA. Performance piece by Colin Gee and Shane Belles. September 7, 2005. With Erin Gee, Mr. Gee.

FORGET ME NOT. By Praxis (Brainard Carey and Delia Bajo). September 7, 2005. Directed by Praxis. With Mr. Carey, Ms. Bajo, Perry Ojeda, Cady Zuckerman, Susie Abraham, Bret Mantyk, Shara Ashley Zeiger, Evan Shafran, Sarah Armstrong, Racheline Maltese, Ryan Hill, Jun Kim.

CHRISTINA OLSON: AMERICAN MODEL. Solo performance piece by Tamar Rogoff. September 21, 2005. Directed and choreographed by Ms. Rogoff; costumes, Liz Prince; lighting, David Ferri; video, Harvey Wang and Andrew Baker; music, Rachel's. With Claire Danes.

PASTORALIA. By George Saunders; adapted by Yehuda Duenyas. September 25, 2005. Directed by Mr. Duenyas; scenery, Michael Casselli; costumes, Kirstin Tobiassen; lighting, Ben Kato; sound, Jody Elff. With Ryan Bronz, Aimee McCormick, James Stanley, Jesse Hawley, Richard Ferone, Alissa Ford, Dmitri Freidenberg, Peter Lettre.

MURDER. By Hanoch Levin; adapted by Michael Weiselberg; translated by Kurt Beals and Liel Golan. October 15, 2005. Directed by Mr. Weiselberg; scenery, David Esler; costumes, Katherine Lake; lighting, Martin E. Vreeland; sound, Christopher Rummel. With Nathalya Bey, Kyrian Friedenberg, Yafit Hallely, Brandon Jones, Sarah Matthay, Eric Miller, Elizabeth Ruelas, Gina Shmukler, Jarrad Skinner, Gilbert Vela, Bradley Wells, Jerry Zellers, Rochelle Zimmerman.

PROPHET. By Thomas Bradshaw. November 30, 2005. Directed by Mr. Bradshaw; scenery, James Stanley; costumes, Iracel Rivero; lighting, Ben Kato; music, Lois Dilivio. With Peter McCabe, Dirk Smile, Detra Payne, Jason Grant, Hilary Ketchum, Paula Ehrenberg, Jerry Zellers.

'TWAS THE NIGHT BEFORE THE TWELVE DAYS OF A NUTRCRACKER CHRISTMAS CAROL. By Ken Nintzel. December 15, 2005. Directed and designed by Mr. Kintzel; choreography, Johanna Meyer. With Doug Allen, Darren Anderson, Chuck Blasius, Michael Casselli, Andrew Dinwiddie, Bill Donovan, Eric Dyer, Leigh Garrett, Jesse Hawley, Matt Kalman, Kiyoko Kashiwagi, Beth Kurkjian, Amy Larimer, Ms. Meyer, David Neumann, Beth Portnoy, Jenny Seastone Stern, Orion Taraban, Croft Vaughn, Richard Foreman.

NO GREAT SOCIETY. By Elevator Repair Service. February 2, 2006. Directed by John Collins. With Susie Sokol, Ben Williams.

THE MONEY CONVERSATION. By Sara Juli. February 15, 2006. Directed by Chris Ajemian; costumes, Roxana Ramseur; lighting, Owen Hughes. With Ms. Juli.

A PARSIFAL. By Susan Sontag. February 23, 2006. Directed by John Jahnke; choreography, Hillary Spector; scenery, Michael Casselli; costumes, Ramona Ponce, Pilar Limosner and Hillary Moore; lighting, Shaun Fillion; sound, Kristin Worrall. With Okwui Okpokwasili, Black-Eyed Susan, Gardiner Comfort, Andrew Schneider, Kathryn Gracey, Matthew Bondy.

SINNER. By Ben Payne. March 15, 2006. Directed by Liam Steel and Rob Tannion; lighting, Ian Scott; video, Matt Spencer. With Ben Wright, Mr. Steel.

RED TIDE BLOOMING. By Taylor Mac. April 13, 2006. Directed by Mr. Mac; choreography, Julie Atlas Muz; scenery, Derek Little; costumes, Steven Menendez; lighting, Garin Marschall; puppetry, Basil Twist. With Todd D'Amour, Bridget Everett, James Tigger Ferguson, Laryssa Husiak, Stacie Karpen, Bianca Leigh, Mr. Mac, Dirty Martini, Steven Menendez, Ruby Lynn Reyner, Suzi Takahashi, Layard Thompson.

Ecstasy and agony: Nathan Lane and Marian Seldes in Terrence McNally's Dedication or the Stuff of Dreams. *Photo: James Leynse*

ABSENCE AND PRESENCE. Solo performance piece by Andrew Dawson. April 27, 2006. Lighting and sound, Steven Mark Smith; music, Joby Talbot, With Mr. Dawson.

AT SAID. By Gary Winter. May 15, 2006. Directed by Tim Farrell; scenery, Sue Rees; costumes, Meghan E. Healey; lighting, Andre Hill; sound, Jody Elff; stage manager, Danielle Monica Long. With Lia Aprile, Gilbert Cruz, Marisa Echeverria, Vedant Gokhale, Anita Hollander.

CLEANSING THE SENSES. Solo performance piece by Peter Rose. May 18, 2006. Lighting, Katrina Maurer; sound, Bruce Steinberg and Sarah Nerboso. With Mr. Rose.

LEFTOVER STORIES TO TELL: A TRIBUTE TO SPALDING GRAY. By Kathleen Russo and Lucy Sexton. May 31, 2006. Directed by Mses. Russo and Sexton. With Jonathan Ames, Hazelle Goodman, Ain Gordon, Bob Holman, James Urbaniak, Olympia Dukakis, David Strathairn, Steve Buscemi, Aidan Quinn, Fisher Stevens, Debra Winger, Joel Grey.

Primary Stages. Dedicated to new American plays. Casey Childs executive producer, Andrew Leynse artistic director.

DEDICATION OR THE STUFF OF DREAMS. By Terrence McNally. August 18, 2005. Directed by Michael Morris; scenery, Narelle Sissons; costumes, Laura Crow; lighting, Jeff Croiter; sound and music, Lindsay Jones; fight direction, B.H. Barry; stage manager, Emily N. Wells. With Nathan Lane, Michael Countryman, Alison Fraser, Darren Pettie, R.E. Rodgers, Marian Seldes, Miriam Shor.

IN THE CONTINUUM. By Danai Gurira and Nikkole Salter. October 2, 2005. Directed by Robert O'Hara; costumes, Sarah Hillard; lighting, Jim French; sound, Lindsay Jones; stage manager, Kate Hefel. With Mses. Gurira, Salter. A 2005–06 *Best Plays* choice (see essay by Anne Marie Welsh in this volume). Transferred to Perry Street Theatre (11/18/2005).

THE RIGHT KIND OF PEOPLE. By Charles Grodin. February 9, 2006. Directed by Chris Smith; scenery, Annie Smart; costumes, Jenny Mannis; lighting, Russell H. Champa; sound, Fabian Obispo; stage manager, Emily N. Wells. With Doris Belack, Stephen Bradbury, Fred Burrell, Mitchell Greenberg, Keith Jochim, Katherine Leask, Edwin C. Owens, Robert Stanton, Evan Thompson, John C. Vennema. The playwright replaced Mr. Owens during the final week of the run.

The Public Theater. Schedule of special projects, in addition to its regular Off Broadway productions. Oskar Eustis artistic director, Mara Manus executive director.

New Works Now! Festival of New Play Readings.
THE END OF IT ALL. By Cusi Cram. September 9, 2005. Directed by Margaret Whitton. LOVE CHILD. By Luther Goins. September 19, 2005. Directed by Billy Porter. LIFE, LOVE AND E.B.I.T.D.A. By Anuvab Pal. September 11, 2005. Directed by John Dias. AUTOBIOGRAPHY OF A TERORIST. By Saïd Sayrafiezadeh. September 11. 2005. Directed by Anne Kauffman. DURANGO. By Julia Cho. September 12, 2005. Directed by Chay Yew. KINGDOM. By Aaron Jafferis and Ian Williams. September 13, 2005. Directed by Michael John Garcés. STOCKHOLM BROOKLYN. By Desmond Hall. September 14, 2005. Directed by Mr. Hall. ALL WE CAN HANDLE. By Andrew Dainoff. September 15, 2005. Directed by

Facing facts: Nikkole Salter and Danai Gurira in their play, In the Continuum. Photo: James Leynse

Alex Lippard. PARIS COMMUNE. By Steven Cosson and Michael Friedman. September 16, 2005. Directed by Mr. Cosson. THE POOR ITCH. By John Belluso. September 17, 2005. Directed by Lisa Peterson. UNTITLED. By Sunil Kuruvilla. September 18, 2005. Directed by Liz Diamond. RANTS. By Eric Bogosian, Lea DeLaria, Florencia Lozano, Billy Porter, Jennifer Miller, Pamela Sneed, Mike Daisey. September 18, 2005.

New Work Then! Festival of Play Readings. September 2–October 3, 2005.
TOP GIRLS. By Caryl Churchill. September 23, 2005. FOR COLORED GIRLS WHO HAVE CONSIDERED SUICIDE WHEN THE RAINBOW IS ENUF. By Ntozake Shange. September 24, 2005. CURSE OF THE STARVING CLASS. By Sam Shepard. September 24, 2005. F.O.B. By David Henry Hwang. September 25, 2005. A MOVIE STAR HAS TO STAR IN BLACK AND WHITE. By Adrienne Kennedy. September 25, 2005. Directed by Estelle Parsons. The Colored Museum. By George C. Wolfe. September 29, 2005. Directed by Mr. Wolfe. THE MARRIAGE OF BETTE AND BOO. By Christopher Durang. September 30, 2005. Directed by Jerry Zaks. SHORT EYES. By Miguel Piñero. Directed by John Ortiz. October 1, 2005. THE BASIC TRAINING OF PAVLO HUMMEL. By David Rabe. October 2, 2005. MISS MARGARIDA'S WAY: TRAGICOMIC MONOLOGUE FOR AN IMPETUOUS WOMAN. By Roberto Athayde. October 3, 2005. With Estelle Parsons.

JACKIE HOFFMAN: CHANUKAH AT JOE'S PUB. Solo performance piece by Jackie Hoffman. December 5, 2005. Directed by Michael Schiralli; lighting, Mr. Schiralli; music direction, Bobby Peaco. With Ms. Hoffman, David Rakoff and Mr. Peaco.

Under the Radar 2006. January 19–23, 2006.
SHADOWS. Solo performance piece by William Yang. January 20, 2006. With Mr. Yang; in the Public Theater's Newman Theater (Australia). REHEARSAL.HAMLET. By Cia dos Atores. With Cesar Augusto, Maria Galli, Maria Garcia, Fernando Eiras, Marcel Olinto, Felipe Rocha; in the Public Theater's LuEsther Hall (Brazil). BIG 2ND EPISODE (SHOW/BUSINESS). By Superamas; in the Public Theater's Newman Theater (France/Austria). FIVE STREAMS. By Ibrahim Quaishi. Choreography, Parul Shah; music, Paul D. Miller; at the Asia Society (South Asia). KOMMER. By Kassys. With Mischa van Dullemen, Ton Heijligers, Jan Kostwinder, Rienus Krul, Saskia Meulendijks, Esther Snelder; in the Public Theater's Newman Theater (The Netherlands). AMAJUBA: LIKE DOVES WE RISE. By Yael Farber. Directed by Ms. Farber; at 651 Arts (South Africa). MY ARM. Solo performance piece by Tim Crouch. Performed by Mr. Crouch; in the Public Theater's LuEsther Hall (United Kingdom). THE SEVEN. By Will Power; at New York Theatre Workshop (United States). (See Plays Produced Off Broadway section of this volume.) THE END OF REALITY. By Richard Maxwell. Directed by Mr. Maxwell; with Thomas Bradshaw, Alex Delinois, James Fletcher, Marcia Hidalgo, Shannon Kennedy, Brian Mendes; at the Kitchen (United States). MAJOR BANG, OR: HOW I LEARNED TO STOP WORRYING AND LOVE THE DIRTY BOMB. By Steve Cuiffo, Kirk Lynn and Melanie Joseph. Directed by Paul Lazar. With Mr. Cuiffo, Maggie Hoffman; at St. Ann's Warehouse, presented in association with the Foundry (United States). THE MYTH CYCLE: AHRAIHSAK. By Rubén Polendo. Directed by Mr. Polendo; at the Clemente Soto Velez Cultural Center, presented in association with Theater Mitu (United States). ¡EL CONQUISTADOR! By Thaddeus Phillips, Tatiana Mallarino and Victor Mallarino; at New York Theatre Workshop (United States/Colombia).

Puerto Rican Traveling Theatre. Professional company presenting English and Spanish productions of Puerto Rican and Hispanic playwrights, emphasizing subjects of relevance today. Miriam Colón Valle founder and producer.

2006 Workshop Productions. May 11–28, 2006.
THE LAST OF BERNARDA. By Oscar A. Colón. May 11, 2006. Directed by Sturgis Warner. PHOMPH!!! By Fred Crecca. May 18, 2006. Directed by Mary Keefe. THREE MEN ON A BASE. May 25, 2006. By María Elena Torres. Directed by Shawn Rozsa.

Signature Theatre Company. Dedicated to the exploration of one playwright's body of work over the course of a single season. The season under review marked the first part of a 15th anniversary celebration featuring the work of playwrights previously celebrated by the company. James Houghton artistic director.

THE TRIP TO BOUNTIFUL. By Horton Foote. December 4, 2005. Directed by Harris Yulin; scenery, E. David Cosier; costumes, Martin Pakledinaz; lighting, John McKernon; sound, Fitz Patton; stage manager, Cole Bonenberger. With Lois Smith, Hallie Foote, Devon Abner, Meghan Andrews, Gene Jones, Sam Kitchin, Frank Girardeau, Jim Demarse.

LANDSCAPE OF THE BODY. By John Guare. April 16, 2006. Directed by Michael Greif; scenery, Allen Moyer; costumes, Miranda Hoffman; lighting, Howell Binkley; sound, Brett R. Jarvis; fight direction, Rick Sordelet; stage manager, Cole Bonenberger. With Lili Taylor, Sherie René Scott, Jonathan Fried, Brian Sgambati, Paul Sparks, Stephen Scott Scarpulla, Paul Iacono, Jill Shackner, Colby Minifie, Bernard White.

Soho Rep. Dedicated to the development and production of exuberant, unconventional new plays. Sarah Benson and Daniel Aukin artistic directors, Alexandra Conley executive director.

PENINSULA. By Madelyn Kent. January 14, 2006. Directed by Ms. Kent; scenery, Narelle Sissons; costumes, Theresa Squire; lighting, Matt Frey; sound, Kenta Nagai; stage manager, Ryan Parow. With Louis Cancelmi, David Chandler, Tim Cummings, Curzon Dobell, Marielle Heller.

NOT CLOWN. By Steve Moore and Carlos Treviño. March 18, 2006. Directed by Mr. Treviño; scenery, Mr. Treviño; costumes, Allison Stelly; lighting, Natalie George; sound, Robert Pierson; stage manager, Ms. George. With Robert Deike, Elizabeth Doss, Lee Eddy, Matt Hislope, Josh Meyer, Robert Pierson, Mark Stewart, Rommel Sulit.

Theater for the New City. Developmental theater and new experimental works. Crystal Field executive director.

REN AH, REN (YOU, O YOU HUMANS). By Joanna Chan; based on a novel by Dai HouYing. June 2, 2005. Directed by Ms. Chan; scenery, Peter Spack; costumes, Harrison Xu; lighting, Dana Sterling. With Arthur Kwan, Dinh Q. Doan, Vivian Chiu, Erik Strongbowe, Jo Mei, Kathleen Kwan, John We, Nelson Ando.

THE REAL INSPECTOR HOUND. By Tom Stoppard. July 13, 2005. Directed by Ron Jones; scenery and lighting, Jason Sturm. Mary Theresa Archbold, Erin Clancy, Lawrence Merritt, Laurel Sanborn, Todd Schmidt, Anthony Scott, Frank Senger, Kenneth Stewart, Nicholas Viselli.

DESERT SUNRISE. By Misha Shulman. September 29, 2005. Directed by Mr. Shulman; scenery, Celia Owens; lighting, Itai Erdal. With Aubrey Levy, Haythem Noor, Alice Borman, Yifat Sharabi, Morteza Tavakoli, Bhavani Lee.

FEAR ITSELF (SECRETS OF THE WHITE HOUSE). By Jean-Claude van Itallie. December 10, 2005. Directed by George Ferencz; costumes, Sally Lesser; lighting, Federico Restrepo; stage manager, Tashika Futch. With Rene Andersen, Timothy Doyle, Joe Gioco, Eric Goss, Leslie Ann Hendricks, Jason Howard, Susan Patrick, Ken Perlstein, Roland Sanchez, Mr. van Itallie, Jenne Vath.

THE ART OF LOVE. By Robert Kornfeld. January 12, 2006. Directed by Tom Thornton; scenery, Mark Marcante; lighting, Alex M.; sound, Elliot Lanes. With Laura Lockwood, Stephen Francis, Dawn Jamieson, Doug Stone, Clyde Kelley, Samantha Payne, Nina Covalesky.

TROUBLE. By Michael Smith. January 12, 2006. Directed by Mr. Smith; scenery, DONALD L. BROOKS; costumes, Patti Dodd. With Kathryn Chilson, Jimmy Camicia, Alfred St. John Smith, Renato R. Biribin, Dino Roscigno, Joshua Levine.

FOLLIES OF GRANDEUR. By Ross MacLean. February 2, 2006. Directed by Mark Finley; scenery, Michael Muccio; lighting, Igor Goldin. With Daryl Brown, Melissa Center, Brian Hoover, Kevin Kelleher, Jolie Meshbesher, Mary Louise Mooney, Bobbi Owens, McGregor Wright, Jennifer Dominguez.

REPUBLIC OF IQRA. By Bina Sharif. February 23, 2006. Directed by Ms. Sharif; scenery, Aesha Jatoi; lighting, Alex Bartenieff. With Marie Therese Abou-Daoud, Wendy Callard-Booz,

Robert Freedman, Aliza Hedges, Nathan J. Schorr, Kevin Mitchell Martin, Haythem Noor, Ms. Sharif, Pierre O'Farrell.

RUE. By August Schulenburg. March 3, 2006. Directed by Kelly O'Donnell; scenery, Jared Klein; costumes, Jessa-Raye Court; lighting, Mr. Klein and Rebecca Marzalek-Kelly; sound, Matt Given; music, Michelle O'Connor; fight direction, Owen Timoney. With Rachel Bauder, Ian Bedford, Kacy Christensen, Tiffany Clementi, Jessica Conrad, David Crommett, Liz Dailey, Will Ditterline, Candice Holdorf, Joseph Mathers, Ms. O'Connor, Jason Paradine, Colleen Raney, Mr. Schulenburg, Rodman Spilling, Isaiah Tanenbaum, Victor Truro, Adina Verson, Laura Walczak, Gregory Waller, Cotton Wright.

LONG TIME PASSING. By Barbara Kahn. March 9, 2006. Directed by Ms. Kahn; scenery, Mark Marcante; costumes, Carla Gant; lighting, David Ullman; music, Alicia Svigals. With Evan Bass, Karla Bruning, Alexandra Gutierrez, Maria Hansen, Brian Morvant, Matthew Rappaport, Erin Leigh Schmoyer, Steph Van Vlack.

WHAT DO I KNOW ABOUT WAR? Solo performance piece by Margo Lee Sherman. March 9, 2006. With Ms. Sherman.

SUCK SALE AND OTHER INDULGENCES. By Evan Laurence. May 4, 2006. Directed by Mr. Laurence. With Dan Almekinder, Lindsay Brill, Andie Cartwright, Wendy Charles, Tanya Everett, Mr. Laurence, David F. Slone.

Theatre for a New Audience. Founded in 1979, the company's mission is to energize the performance and study of Shakespeare and classic drama. Jeffrey Horowitz founding artistic director, Dorothy Ryan managing director.

MEASURE FOR MEASURE. Revival of the play by William Shakespeare. December 22, 2005. Directed by John Dove; scenery and costumes, Jennifer Tiramani; lighting, Stan Pressner; music, Claire van Kampen. With Mark Rylance, Liam Brennan, David Sturzaker, Edward Hogg, Michael Brown, Peter Shorey, Colin Hurley, Bill Stewart, Terry McGinity, Roger Watkins, Thomas Padden, Roger McKern, John Dougall, David Hartley. Presented in association with St. Ann's Warehouse, 2Luck Concepts and Shakespeare's Globe Theatre.

ALL'S WELL THAT ENDS WELL. Revival of the play by William Shakespeare. February 12, 2006. Directed by Darko Tresnjak; scenery, David P. Gordon; costumes, Linda Cho; lighting, Rui Rita; sound, Aural Fixation; dramaturg, Michael Feingold; stage manager, Renee Lutz. With Laurie Kennedy, Lucas Hall, Tom Bloom, Kate Forbes, Gordon Stanley, Adam Stein, George Morfogen, Thomas Michael Hammond, Paul Niebanck, John Christopher Jones, Lisa Velten, Price Waldman, Myra Lucretia Taylor, Nicole Lowrance.

SORE THROATS. By Howard Brenton. April 30, 2006. Directed by Evan Yionoulis; scenery, Adam Stockhausen; costumes, Katherine Roth; lighting, Donald Holder; sound and music, Mike Yionoulis; fight direction, J. David Brimmer; stage manager, Linda Marvel. With Laila Robins, Bill Camp, Meredith Zinner.

Vineyard Theatre. The company is committed to nurturing the work of developing playwrights and composers, while providing established artists with a supportive environment in which to experiment, take risks, and grow. Douglas Aibel artistic director, Jennifer Garvey-Blackwell executive director.

MIRACLE BROTHERS. Musical by Kirsten Childs. September 18, 2005. Directed by Tina Landau; choreography, Mark Dendy; scenery, G.W. Mercier; costumes, Anita Yavich; lighting, Scott Zielinski; sound, Brett R. Jarvis; projections, Jan Hartley; fight direction, Rick Sordelet; stage manager, Bret Torbeck. With Kerry Butler, Cheryl Freeman, Jay Goede, Anika Larsen, Nicole Leach, Tyler Maynard, Devin Richards, Darrell Moultrie, Clifton Oliver, Karen Olivo, Gregory Treco, William Youmans.

[TITLE OF SHOW]. Musical with book by Hunter Bell; music and lyrics by Jeff Bowen. February 26, 2006. Directed and choreographed by Michael Berresse; scenery, Neil Patel; costumes, Chase Tyler; lighting, Ken Billington and Jason Kantrowitz; sound, Acme Sound Partners; music direction, Larry Pressgrove; stage manager, Martha Donaldson. With Messrs. Bell and Bowen, Susan Blackwell, Heidi Blickenstaff.

Women's Project. Nurtures, develops and produces plays written and directed by women. Julia Miles founder, Loretta Greco producing artistic director, Julie Crosby managing director.

Women's Work. November 7–17, 2005.

YELLOW. By Cybele Pascal. Directed by Lisa Rohte. IMAGINARY FRIENDS. By Karen Hartman, Laura Flanagan, Chris Wells. BECHNYA. By Saviana Stanescu. THE RICH SILK OF IT. By Deb Margolin. GOING AFTER ALICE. By Megan Mostyn-Brown. Directed by Meredith McDonough. KILLING WOMEN. By Marisa Wegrzyn. Directed by Elyse Singer. LAS MENINAS. By Lynn Nottage. Directed by Kate Whoriskey. STILL LIFE. By Emily Mann. Directed by Tamsen Wolff. VICTORIA MARTIN: MATH QUEEN. By Kate Walat. Directed by Loretta Greco.

JUMP/CUT. By Neena Beber. February 1, 2006. Directed by Leigh Silverman; scenery, Narelle Sissons; costumes, Miranda Hoffman; lighting, M.L. Geiger; sound, Jill BC DuBoff; stage manager, Leigh Boone. With Luke Kirby, Michi Barall, Thomas Sadoski.

THE CATARACT. By Lisa D'Amour. April 2, 2006. Directed by Katie Pearl; scenery, Rachel Hauck; costumes, Sarah Beers; lighting, Sarah Sidman; sound, Daniel Baker; stage manager, Leigh Boone. With Vanessa Aspillaga, Barnaby Carpenter, Tug Coker, Kelly McAndrew.

The Wooster Group. Ensemble of artists collaborating on the development and production of theatre pieces that respond to the evolving culture. Elizabeth LeCompte director.

POOR THEATER. By the Wooster Group; based on the work of Jerzy Grotowski, William Forsythe and Max Ernst. September 23, 2005. Directed by Elizabeth LeCompte; scenery, Ruud van den Akker; lighting, Jennifer Tipton; sound, Geoff Abbas and John Collins; video, J. Reid Farrington, Ken Kobland and Christopher Kondek. With Ari Fliakos, Sheena See, Scott Shepherd, Kate Valk.

THE EMPEROR JONES. By Eugene O'Neill. March 1, 2006. Directed by Elizabeth LeCompte; scenery, Jim Clayburgh; costumes, the Wooster Group; lighting, Jennifer Tipton; sound, John Collins and Geoff Abbas; music, David Linton; video, Christopher Kondek; stage manager, Teresa Hartmann. With Kate Valk, Scott Shepherd, Ari Fliakos.

York Theatre Company. Dedicated to the development of small-scale musicals, to the rediscovery of underappreciated musicals from the past and to serving the community through educational initiatives. James Morgan artistic director.

Musicals in Mufti. October 21–December 16, 2005.

I CAN GET IT FOR YOU WHOLESALE. Musical with book by Jerome Weidman; music and lyrics by Harold Rome. October 21, 2005. Directed by Richard Sabellico; with Chris Hoch, Rena Strober, Jodi Stevens, Jonathan Hammond, Andrea Burns, Josh Prince, Anne Torsiglieri, Stuart Zagnit, Christopher Totten, Jana Robbins.

THE GREAT BIG RADIO SHOW! Musical with book by Philip Glassborow and Nick McIvor; music and lyrics by Mr. Glassborow. October 28, 2005. Directed by David Glenn Armstrong; music direction, Ken Clifton. With Tyler Maynard, Nancy Anderson, Lynne Wintersteller, David Staller and Seth Rudetsky.

IS THERE LIFE AFTER HIGH SCHOOL? Musical with book by Jeffrey Kindley; music and lyrics by Craig Carnelia; based on the book by Ralph Keyes. November 4, 2005. Directed by Mr. Carnelia; music direction Bryan Perri. With Stephanie Bast, Jed Cohen, Jeffrey Doornbos, Chris Fuller, Stacie Morgain Lewis, Garrett Long, Holly Davis, Greg Roderick and Caesar Samayoa.

THEDA BARA AND THE FRONTIER RABBI. Musical with book and lyrics by Jeff Hochhauser; music and lyrics by Bob Johnston. December 2, 2005. Directed by Lynne Taylor-Corbett. With Fred Berman, Patrick Boll, Jonathan Brody, Alison Cimmet, Lois Hart, Alicia Irving, Susan J. Jacks, Tom Lucca, Allen Lewis Rickman, Rena Strober.

MISS LIBERTY. Musical with book by Robert E. Sherwood; music and lyrics by Irving Berlin. December 9, 2005. Directed by Michael Montel. With Jerry Christakos, Erick Devine, David Garry, Nikki James, Julie Kotarides, David Larsen, Patricia O'Connell, Fred Rose, Roland Rusinek, Deborah Jean Templin, Tom Treadwell, Nick Verina, Carla Woods.

MIRETTE. Musical with book by Elizabeth Diggs; music by Harvey Schmidt; lyrics by Tom Jones; based on the book *Mirette on the Hire Wire* by Emily Arnold McCully. December 16, 2005. Directed by Drew Scott Harris; music direction, Matt Castle. With Susan Cella, Robert Cuccioli, Ed Dixon, Davis Duffield, Joyce Franz, Patti Murin, Anthony Santelmo, Kelly Sullivan, Maggie Watts.

Developmental Reading Series. May 9–25, 2006.
ETHAN FROME: AN AMERICAN ROMANCE. Musical with book by Michael Ruby; music and lyrics by Adam Gwon; based on the work of Edith Wharton. May 9, 2006. KISS A MAD DOG. Musical by P.J. Barry. May 22, 2006. GONE TO TEXAS. Musical with book by Steve Warren; music by Tom Masinter; lyrics by June Rachelson-Ospa. May 25, 2006

MISCELLANEOUS

In the listing of 2005–06 Off Off Broadway productions below, the names of the producing groups, theater venues or festivals appear in CAPITAL LETTERS and the titles of the works in *italics*.

ABINGDON THEATRE COMPANY. *Evensong* by Mary Gage. July 28, 2005. Directed by Lewis Magruder; with Ruby Holbrook. *In the Arms of Baby Jesus* by Michèle Raper Rittenhouse. September 9, 2005. Directed by Carole Mansley; with Brian Gianci, Joseph LaRocca, Patti Mariano. *Walking in Memphis*. Solo performance piece by Jonathan Adam Ross. November 27, 2005. Directed by Chantal Pavageuz; with Mr. Ross. *Fool for Love* by Sam Shepard. December 8, 2005. Directed by Christopher Martin; with Marc Menchaca, Michelle David, Laurence Cantor, Ben Wiggins. *Tape* by Stephen Belber. January 19, 2006. Directed by David Newer; with Jayson Gladstone, Ben Schmoll, Randa Karambelas. *Men of Clay* by Jeff Cohen. April 2, 2006. Directed by Mr. Cohen; with Matthew Arkin, Steve Rattazzi, Danton Stone, Daniel Ahearn, Victor Barbella, Gabrielle Maisels. *My Deah* by John Epperson. April 21, 2006. Directed by Mark Waldrop; with Bryan Batt, Phillip Clark, Lori Gardner, Michael Hunsaker, Geoffrey Molloy, Nancy Opel, Jay Rogers, Kevin Townley.

ACCESS THEATER. *Busted Jesus Comix* by David Johnston. July 16, 2005. Directed by Gary Shrader; with Bruce Barton, Michael Bell, Paul Caiola, R. Jane Casserly, Brian Fuqua, Vince Gatton, Tracey Gilbert, John Koprowski, David Lapkin, Joseph C. Yeargain. *Murdering Marlowe* by Charles Marowitz. October 11, 2005. Directed by Jason King Jones; with Jeremy Beazlie, Bryan Cogman, Nicholas Coleman, Patrick Hallahan, Cedric Hayman, Caralyn Kozlowski, Tim McGeever, Mandy Olsen, Glenn Peters. *The Supporting Cast* by George Furth. December 1, 2005. With Rod Cassavale, Laura Baldassare, Stephanie Schwartz, Bridget Trama, Ashley Eichhorn. *Fits and Starts: The Sacred Heart* by Caroline Cheatwood. January 13, 2006. Directed by Tania Inessa Kirkman; with Jenni Tooley, Patrick Dall'Occhio, Lenni Benicaso, Ken Matthews, Thomas Hoyt Godfrey, Vince Phillip. *Paradise* by David Foley. February 6, 2006. Directed by Gary Shrader; with Nathalie Altman, Bruce Barton, Michael Bell, Robert Buckwalter, Tracey Gilbert, John Koprowski, Tom Ligon, Jonna McElrath, Lana Marks, Joseph Melendez, Gregory Northrop, Brandon Wolcott. *A Lie of the Mind* by Sam Shepard. January 27, 2006. Directed by Alex Correia; with Guil Fisher, Getchie Argetsinger, Pam Tate, Wendy Brantley, Gina DeMayo, Doug Goodenough, Kevin Kaine, Scott Laska. *The Palooka* by Brandon Ramos. March 2, 2006. Directed by Jeffrey Lawhorn; with Doug Friedman, Chris George, Gerry Goodstein, Stephen A. Kuhel, Geoff Schmith, Karen Stanion, John O'Creagh, Ford Winter. *Port Authority Throw Down* by Mike Batistick. April 5, 2006. Directed by Connie Grappo; with James Murray Jackson, Annie McNamara, Debargo Sanyal, Aladdin Ullah. *Pains of Youth* by Ferdinand Bruckner. May 6, 2006. Directed by Charles Wilson and Michael Fitzgerald; with Sheila Carrasco, Amy Ewing, Kari Floberg, Josh Heine, Donna Lazar, Mick Lauer, Michael Newman.

THE ACTORS COMPANY THEATRE (TACT). *Watch on the Rhine* by Lillian Hellman. October 15, 2005. Directed by Scott Alan Evans; with Kyle Fabel, Cynthia Harris, Darrie Lawrence, Francesca

DiMauro, Margaret Nichols, Terry Layman, Leah Morales, Sean Moran, Daniel Oreskes, Travis Walters. *Both Your Houses* by Maxwell Anderson. March 11, 2006. Directed by Michael Pressman. With Kyle Fabel, Richard Ferrone, Darrie Lawrence, James Murtaugh, James Prendergast, Scott Schafer, Jenn Thompson, Anthony Crane, Curzon Dobell, Tara Falk, Terry Layman, Tuck Milligan.

ALTERED STAGES. *The Caterers* by Jonathan Leaf. October 10, 2005. Directed by Jose Zayas; with Judith Hawking, Ian Blackman, Peter Reznikoff, Brian Wallace. FULLY PACT. November 10-20, 2005. *The Exciting Life* by Anthony Pennino. Directed by Don Jordan; with Tom Walker, Timothy J. Cox, Tanya Moberly, Paul Romanello. *Theory of Heaven* by Patrick Kennedy. Directed by Elizabeth London; with Baz Snider, Julie Sharbutt, Greg LoProto. *Issues* by Danna Call. Directed by Maryna Harrison; with Manon Halliburton, Amy Bizjak, Amy Dickenson, Kenny Wade Marshall, Ebbe Bassey. *Train of Thought* by Craig Pospisil. Directed by Chris Maring; with Michael Rhodes, Missy Hall, Nancy Wu. *Tragedy (A Comedy)* by Stuart D'Ver. Directed by Jody O'Neil; with Gerry Goodstein, Aaron Simms, Mary Murphy, Julie Berndt. *Vermouth and Chicken* by P. Seth Bauer. Directed by Jorelle Aronovitch; with Katharine Clark Gray, Roy Havrilack, Kathy Gail MacGowan, Steven Pelton, Jane Petrov. *Oh, Mr. Cadhole!* Musical with book by Lisa Ferber; music by Robert Firpo-Cappiello; lyrics by Ms. Ferber. Directed by Chris Windom; with Kevin Draine, Lisa Barnes, Ivanna Cullinan, Tom Kelly, Devon Hawkes Ludlow, Eric C. Bailey, Marci Occhino, Alyssa Simon. *The Dickens* by Michael Scott-Price. December 1. 2005. Directed by Jaime Robert Carrillo; with Brian Shaer, Rich Renner, Johanna Bon, Shaka Malik, Jorge Luis. *Shortly After Takeoff* by Stuart Warmflash. March 11, 2006. Directed by Mr. Warmflash; with Patricia Kalember, Tobias Segal, Lucy McMichael, Anthony Bagnetto, Adelia Saunders, Bruce Mohat. *Cupid and Psyche* by Joseph Fisher. April 10, 2006. Directed by Alex Lippard; with Jeannie Dalton, Nick Cearley, Stephanie Janssen, Jonathan Todd Ross, Kim Schultz, Johnny Sparks, Richard Sterne, Lanette Ware. *Down the Road* by Lee Blessing. May 18, 2006. Directed by Malini Singh McDonald; with Lawrence Hoffman, Mary Lynch, Ian M. McDonald.

AMERICAN PLACE THEATRE. *To Nineveh: A Modern Miracle Play* by Bekah Brunstetter. October 28, 2005. Directed by Isaac Byrne; with Paul Fears, Jared Culverhouse, David Carr-Berry, Julian James, Andaye Hill, Brian Schlanger, Ellen David, Roy Miller.

AMERICAN THEATRE OF ACTORS. *An Ideal Husband* by Oscar Wilde. August 31, 2005. Directed by Robert Francis Perillo; with Trevor St. John, Christian Cohn, Christina Apathy, Kevin Cramer, Carolyn DeMerice, Robert Haufrecht, Lian-Marie Holmes, Lynne McCollough, Hal Smith-Reynolds. *Balm in Gilead* by Lanford Wilson. October 27, 2005. Directed by Eric Nightengale; with Anna Chlumsky, Victoria Malvagano, Diego Ajuz, Jeremy Brena, Louis Reyes Cardenas, Sabrina C. Cataudella, John Gazzale, Trey Gibbons, Jerzy Gwiazdowski, Elizabeth June, Jeff Keilhotz, David Lamberton, Luke Leonard, Michael LoPorto, Ruben Luque, Victoria Malvagano, Diane Mashburn, Joe B. McCarthy, Chiara Montallo, Roderick Nash, Luca Pierucci, Francisco Solorzano, Jennie West, Christopher Whalen. *The War at Dawn* by Eric Alter. October 11, 2005. Directred by Rodney E. Reyes; with Miguel Emir, Morgan Parker, Hayden Roush, Sonia Tatninov. *Anomal.* Solo performance piece by Ehud Segev; with additional material by Carl Kissin. January 2, 2006. Directed by Glory Bowen; with Mr. Segev. *Buried Child* by Sam Shepard. January 27, 2006. Directed by Cyndy A. Marion; with Rod Sweitzer, Bill Rowley, Karen Gibson, David Look, Chris Stetson, Ginger Kroll, David Elyha. *Good Enough to be True* by Raphael Bob-Wakesberg. March 3, 2006. Directed by Kielsen Baker; with Jake Alexander, Ali Skye Bennet, Siobhan Doherty, Matt Lockwood. *Sickle* by Sophia Romma. April 6, 2006. Directed by Leslie Lee; with Heather Massie, Malcolm Madera, Emily Mitchell, Ralpha Petrarca, Stu Richel, Matt Zehnder, Pernell Walker. *A Jew Grows in Brooklyn* by Jake Ehrenreich. April 10, 2006. Directed by Jon Huberth; with Mr. Ehrenreich, Todd Isler, Zvi Klein, Dave Solomon, Elysa Sunshine.

AQUILA THEATRE COMPANY. *Twelfth Night.* Revival of the play by William Shakespeare. June 17, 2005. Directed by Peter Meineck and Robert Richmond; with Anthony Cochrane, Kenn Sabberton, Lisa Carter, Louis Butelli, Lindsay Rae Taylor, Andrew Schwartz, Lincoln Hudson, Natasha Piletich. *The Invisible Man* by H.G. Wells. October 27, 2005. Choreographed by Doug Varone; with Anthony Cochrane, Robert Richmond, Peggy Baker, John Beasant, Daniel Charon, Natalie Desch, Adriane Fang, Larry Hahn, Stephanie Liapis, Catherine Miller, Eddie Taketa.

ARCLIGHT. *Richard and Anne* by Maxwell Anderson. June 2, 2005. Directed by Anthony Nelson; with Kyle T. Jones, Lauren Marie Jones, Devon Jackson, Zina Anaplioti, Lindsey Anderson, Lucas Beck, Catherine Campbell, Jay Chafin, Rachel Evans, Ian Forrester, Zachary Green, Kim Katzberg,

Nicholas Uber Leonard, Charles McAteer, Aubyn Philabaum, Macadam Smith, Max Shulman, Nicholas Ward, Sarah Jane Eigerman. *Apartment 3A* by Jeff Daniels. January 23, 2006. Directed by Valentina Fratti; with Amy Landecker, Jonathan Teague Cook, J. Austin Eyer, Arian Moayed, Joseph Collins. *Nora* by Ingmar Berman; adapted from *A Doll House* by Henrik Ibsen. February 23, 2006. Directed by Pamela Moller Kareman; with Sarah Bennett, Tyne Firmin, Carey Macaleer, Troy Myers, John Tyrell. *Freak Winds* by Marshall Napier. March 28, 2006. Directed by Mr. Napier; with Mr. Napier, Tamara Lovatt-Smith, Damian de Montemas.

ARS NOVA. *Holy Cross Sucks.* Solo performance piece by Rob Nash. November 9, 2005. Directed by Jeff Calhoun; with Mr. Nash. *Letting Go of God.* Solo performance piece by Julia Sweeney. November 10, 2005. With Ms. Sweeney. *25 Questions for a Jewish Mother* by Kate Moira Ryan and Judy Gold. January 25, 2006. Directed by Karen Kohlhaas; with Ms. Gold. *Ann E. Wrecksick and the Odyssey of the Bulimic Orphans* by Scott Allgauer and Damon Intrabartolo; music and lyrics by Mr. Intrabartolo. Directed by Kristin Hanggi. *Neal Medlyn Loves You. For Real.* by Mr. Medlyn. April 25, 2006. Directed by Virginia Scott; with Mr. Medlyn.

AXIS COMPANY. *Hospital 2005* by Randy Sharp; with Wren Arthur, David Alutanski, Brian Barnhart, David Crabb, George Demas, Joe Fuer, Valerie Hallier, Jason Kaufman, Laurie Kilmartin, Sue Ann Molinell, Edgar Oliver, Marc Palmieri, Margo Passalaqua, Sayra Player, Jim Sterling, Christopher Swift, Ian Tooley. *Seven in One Blow, Or The Brave Little Kid* by Axis Company. December 2, 2005. Directed by Randy Sharp; with Brian Barnhart, David Crabb, Joe Fuer, Laurie Kilmartin, Sue Ann Molinell, Edgar Oliver, Marc Palmieri, Margo Passalaqua, Abigail Savage, Jim Sterling, Deborah Harry.

BANK STREET THEATRE. *Edward II* by Bertolt Brecht. September 8, 2005. Directed by Gabriel Shanks; with Willie LeVasseur, Noshir Dalal, Janice Herndon, Frank Blocker, Joshua Marmer, Josh Billig, Oscar Castillo, John Dohrmann, Christian Felix, R.J. Foster, Avi Glickstein, J. Damian Houston, Jeffrey James Keyes, Shannon Maddox, Christopher McAllister, Matthew Trumbull. *The Bubble* by Frank J. Avella. September 29, 2005. With Joe Pistone, Guenia Lemos, Wind Klaison, Marie Lazzaro, Tom Patterson, Justin D. Quackenbush, Brian Townes. *Greener* by Frank J. Avella. February 16, 2006. Directed by Mr. Avella; with Joe Pistone, Patrick Allen, Lisa Marie Gargione, Wind Klaison, Nicholas Lazzaro, Nick Matthews, Jennifer Nehila, Justin D. Quackenbush.

THE BARROW GROUP (TBG). *Name Day* by Jovanka Bach. June 1, 2005. Directed by Marcy Arlin; with Mikel Sarah Lambert, Laryssa Lauret, Bob Adrian, Michael Baisley, Elaine Smith, Tibor Feldman, Victor Steinbach, Charles Randall, Anastasia Barnes. *Driving on the Left Side* by Amy Merrill. June 30, 2005. Directed by Florante Galvez; with Sharon Tsahai King, Jennifer McCabe, Paul Navarra, Postell Pringle. THE READING SERIES. September 9–December 2, 2005. *Spine* by Bill C. Davis. *Exits and Entrances* by Athol Fugard. *Permanent Collection* by Thomas Gibbons. *Cloaca* by Maria Goos. *The Glass Jaw* by Jane Shepard. *The Gift of the Gorgon* by Peter Shaffer.

BLUE HERON ARTS CENTER. *Trailerville* by John Dufresne. June 5, 2005. Directed by Wayne Maugans; with Ann Hillary, Ron Faber, Peter Waldren, Michele Ammon, Christian Kohn, Miles Purinton, Erik Kever Ryle, Greta Sleeper, Lenore Zann. *Lunch at Armegeddon* by Richard Lay. September 15, 2005. Directed by Simcha Borenstein; with J. Garrett Glaser, Erin Kate Howard, Steve Kasprzak, Arlene Love, Pierre O'Farrell. *The Marilyn Tapes.* Solo performance piece by Lenore Zann. October 9, 2005. Directed by David Raleigh; with Ms. Zann. *Bartleby, the Scrivener* by R.L. Lane; based on the novel by Herman Melville. November 6, 2005. Directed by Alessandro Fabrizi; with Gerry Bamman, Marco Quaglia, Jeff Burchfield, Sterling Coyne, Hunter Gilmore, Robert Grossman, Christian Haines, Brian Linden.

BOOMERANG THEATRE COMPANY. *The Two Gentlemen of Verona.* Revival of the play by William Shakespeare. June 18, 2005. Directed by Kate Ross; with Jeremy Beck, Mac Brydon, Patrick Connolly, Benjamin Ellis Fine, Henry Martone, Ron McClary, Dennis McNitt, Peter Morr, Jessica Myhr, Sharon Paige, Sara Thigpen, Bill Weeden. *Artist Descending a Staircase* by Tom Stoppard. October 10, 2005. Directed by John Hurley; with Ronald Cohen, Tom Knutson, Mary Murphy, Michael Poignand, Ed Schultz, Joe Whelski, Aaron Michael Zook.

BRIDGE THEATRE COMPANY. *Making Marilyn* by Ken Cameron. November 30, 2005. Directed by Robin A. Paterson; with Ashlie Atkinson, Patrick Costello, Robin Mervin, Reyna DeCourcy, Devin Scott. *Laundry and Bourbon* and *Lone Star* by James McLure. February 12, 2006. Directed by Janice Goldberg; with Ellen Dolan, Jason Fraser, Avi Glickstein, Dustin Olson, Robin Suzukawa,

Jennifer Lane Williams. *Zarathustra Said Some Things, No?* by Trevor Ferguson. April 25, 2006. Directed by Robin A. Paterson; with Lina Roessler, Brett Watson.

CAP 21 THEATER. THE BARBARA WOLFF MONDAY NIGHT READING SERIES. October 17– December 5, 2005. *Blithe Spirit* by Noël Coward. Directed by Evalyn Baron. *Pages*. Musical with book by Josh Halloway; music by Will Van Dyke; lyrics by Messrs. Halloway and Van Dyke. Directed by Larry Arancio. *Lady Alice*. Musical with book by Diane Seymour; music by Steven Schoenberg; lyrics Ms. Seymour. Directed by David Loud. *The Classics Professor* by John Pielmeier. Directed by Clayton Phillips. *The 60s Project*. Musical by Janet Brenner. November 9, 2005. Directed by Richard Maltby Jr.; with Cameron Adams, Jeb Brown, Mark Bush, Dwayne Clark, J.D. Goldblatt, Steven Goldsmith, Kevin Hale, Rodney Hicks, Claire Karpen, Chad Kimball, Anika Larsen, Megan Lewis, Amy McAlexander, Jason Poole, Lois Robbins, Marlayna Syms, Idara Victor, Max von Essen, Andi Whaley, Angela Williams. *Goddess Wheel*. Musical with book by Matty Selman; music by Galt MacDermot; lyrics by Mr. Selman. November 30, 2005. Directed by Frank Ventura. *Radiant Baby* by Stuart Ross; music by Debra Barsha; lyrics by Ira Gasman, Mr. Ross and Ms. Barsha; based on *Keith Haring: The Authorized Biography* by John Gruen. March 1, 2006. Directed by Frank Ventura. *Starmites*. Musical with book by Stuart Ross and Barry Keating; music and lyrics by Mr. Keating. March 29, 2006. Directed by Mr. Keating and Jeremy Quinn; with Jenna Bracciale, Kaitlyn Bardley, Laraisha Burnette, Dawn Cantwell, Adam Cochran, Brittany Cornelius, Miko Deleon, Kelly Felthous, J. Sebastian Greene, Kera Halbersleben, Courtney Hammond, Jonathan Heilman, Leigh Jones, Ryan David Lamont, Evan Jay Newman, Kevin Santos, Mackenzie Sherburne, Ryan Worsing.

CENTER STAGE, NY. *The Bigger Man* by Sam Marks. July 2, 2005. Directed by Louis Moreno; with Mark Alhadeff, Barnaby Carpenter, Sharon Freedman, Greg Keller, Molly Pearson. *Toughing Slumaria* by Janeen Stevens. October 29, 2005. Directed by Barry Gomolka; with Scott Van Tuyl, Ali Squitieri, Maire-Rose Pike, Chudney Sykes, Jahnavi Rennison, Barbara Miluski, Lane Wray, Stephanie English, Erin Fogel, Manny Liyes, Ray Wasik. *Crave* by Sarah Kane. February 22, 2006. Directed by Justin Quinn Pelegano; with Heidi Armbruster, Michael Chmiel, Ryan Farley, Julie Fitzpatrick. *Baby Girl* by Edith Freni. March 12, 2006. Directed by Padraic Lillis; with Curran Connor, Sarah Hayon, Chris Kipiniak, Trisha LaFache, Andrew Stewart-Jones, John Summerour. *Living Dead in Denmark* by Qui Nguyen. May 4, 2006. Directed by Robert Ross Parker; with Noshir Dalal, Jason Liebman, Maggie Macdonald, Tom Myers, Melissa Paladino, Jason Schumacher, Maureen Sebastian, Andrea Marie Smith, Temar Underwood, Amy Kim Waschke.

CHASHAMA. COUCHWORKS. An evening of seven short plays. By Rachel Axler, Evan Cabnet, Marcus Gardley, Adam Knight, Adam Rapp, Theresa Rebeck, Mat Smart. *The Collection* by Christina Masciotti. October 13, 2005. Directed by Ms. Masciotti; with John Hagan, Jimmie James, Anna Kohler. *Wounds to the Face* by Howard Barker. April 26, 2006. Directed by Katie McGehee; with Ashley Bell, Jessie Barr, Jonathan Clem, Josh Gelb, Tom Hennes, Craig Jorczak, Francesca Choy Kee, Georgia X. Lifsher, James Malley, Grace McClean, David Morris, Justin Nestor, Nicole Pacent, Dan Pfau, Steve Smith, Theo Stockman, Lindsay Wolf. *Clocks and Whistles* by Samuel Adamson. May 9 2006. Directed by Talya Klein; with Meghan Andrews, Christopher Randolph, Catherine Eaton, Jerzy Gwiazdowski, David Mawhinney.

CHERRY LANE THEATRE. *Dottie Hope* by Laurie Sanderson. June 8, 2005. Directed by Courtney Munch; with Ms. Sanderson. *Please Stop Talking* by Sam Froman. October 13, 2005. Directed by Erwin Maas; with Heather Hollingsworth, Bridgett Ane Lawrence, Leah Lawrence. *Bhutan* by Daisy Foote. November 8, 2005. Directed by Evan Yionoulis; with Amy Redford, Sarah Lord, Tasha Lawrence, Jedadiah Schultz. *Huck and Holden* by Rajiv Joseph. January 17, 2006. Directed by Giovanna Sardelli; with Cherise Boothe, Nick Choski, Arjun Gupta, LeRoy McClain, Nilaja Sun. *Black Girl, You've Been Gentrified* by Nichole R. Thompson-Adams. February 3, 2006. With Ms. Thompson-Adams. MENTOR PROJECT 2006. March 13–May 6, 2006. Schedule included: *Lascivious Something* by Sheila Callaghan; mentored by Michael Weller. Directed by Suzanne Agins; with Charles Borland, Jessi Campbell, Christina Lind, Danielle Skraastad. *Hoodoo Love* by Katon Hall; mentored by Lynn Nottage. Directed by Lucie Tiberghien; with Eric Abrams, Marjorie Johnson, Angela Lewis, Postell Pringle. *Girl* by Megan Mostyn-Brown; mentored by Theresa Rebeck. Directed by Josh Hecht. *On the Line* by Joe Roland. April 11, 2006. Directed by Peter Sampieri; with David Prete, Mr. Roland, John Zibell. *All That Fall* by Samuel Beckett. May 24, 2006. Directed by John Sowie; with Helen Calthorpe, Rand Mitchell.

THE CHOCOLATE FACTORY. *The Gut Girls* by Sarah Daniels. July 17, 2005. Directed by Michaela Goldhaber; with Soraya Broukhim, Twinkle Burke, Rodrigo Chazaro, Beth Wren Elliott, Tiffany Green, Janine Kyanko, Irene McDonnell, Kila Packett, Tracy Perez, Brandt Reiter. *Gun Play* by Brian Rogers. January 12, 2006. Directed by Mr. Rogers; with Kanako Hiyama, Mikeah Ernest Jennings, Sheila Lewandowski, Elizabeth Ward, Paula Wilson.

CLASSICAL THEATRE OF HARLEM. *Medea* by Euripides; adapted by Alfred Preisser. September 23, 2005. Directed by Mr. Preisser; with Earle Hyman, April Thompson, Lawrence Winslow, Shamika Cotton, Lorey Hayes, Zora Howard, Zainab Jah. *Funnyhouse of a Negro* by Adrienne Kennedy. January 11, 2006. Directed by Bernie Allen; with Suzette Gunn, Alice Spivak, Trish McCall, Monica Stith, Danny Camiel, Leopold Lowe, Kellie McCants. *Ain't Supposed to Die a Natural Death*. Musical with book, music and lyrics by Melvin Van Peebles. April 14, 2006. Directed by Alfred Preisser; with Mo Brown, Tracy Jack, Charles Rueben, Willie Teacher, Glen Turner. *Waiting for Godot* by Samuel Beckett. May 18, 2006. Directed by Christopher McElroen; with Wendell Pierce, J. Kyle Manzay.

CLEMENTE SOTO VELEZ CULTURAL CENTER (CSV). *Limitless Joy* by Josh Fox. September 11, 2005. Directed by Mr. Fox; with Peter Schmitz, Beth Griffith, Pablo Ribot, Jonathan Green, Anne Robinson, Nick Konow, Beau Alluili. *Cheeks* by Guillermo Gentile. November 11, 2005. With Michael Camacho, Jesse Soursourian, Louis Vuolo. *Fountain of Youth* by Noemi de la Puente. March 3, 2006. Directed by Mike Smith Rivera and Mateo Gomez; with Ms. de la Puente. *Bloody Mary: A Comedy of Tragic Proportions* by Rachel Shukert. April 28, 2006. Directed by Stephen Brackett; with Jeff Addiss, Adam Arian, James Caldwell, Sam Forman, Edi Gathegi, Colin Gilroy, Chris Hale, Van Hansis, Jo Hudson, Madeline Maby, Evan Shafran, Kristin Slaysman, Danielle Streisand, Allison Tigard, Ian Unterman, Reginald Veneziano, Audrey Lynn Weston, Raina Wildenberg.

CONNELLY THEATRE. *Kicker* by Robert Simonson. June 9, 2005. Directed by Brendan Hughes; with Jonathan Fielding, Juliet Gowing, Dalane Mason, Lordon Napoli, Matt Pepper, James Lloyd Reynolds. *The Breadwinner* by W. Somerset Maugham. September 9, 2005. Directed by Carl Forsman; with Joe Delafield, Jennifer Van Dyck, Jack Gilpin, Virginia Kull, Margaret Laney, Robert Emmet Lunney, Alicia Roper, David Standish. *Normal*. Musical with book by Yvonne Adrian; music by Tom Kochan; lyrics by Cheryl Stern. October 30, 2005. Directed by Jack Cummings III; with Barbara Walsh, Adam Heller, Erin Leigh Peck, Nicholas Belton, Nancy Johnston, Toni DiBuono, Shannon Polly. *Norman and Beatrice* by Barbara Hammond. February 5, 2006. Directed by David Travis; with Graeme Malcolm, Jane Nichols. *Children of a Lesser God* by Mark Medoff. March 18, 2006. Directed by Blake Lawrence; with Alexandria Walles, Jeffry Denman, Ian Blackman, Guthrie Nutter, Lee Roy Rogers, Tami Lee Santimyer, Makela Spielman.

THE CULTURE PROJECT. *Karla* by Steve Earle. October 23, 2005. Directed by Bruce Kronenberg; with Jodie Markell, Linda Marie Larson, E. Jason Liebrecht, Jenny Maguire, Jeremy Schwartz. *Guardians* by Peter Morris. April 11, 2006. Directed by Jason Moore; with Katherine Moennig, Lee Pace. *The Mistakes Madeline Made* by Elizabeth Meriwether. April 23, 2006. Directed by Evan Cabnet; with Ian Brenna, Laura Heisler, Brian Henderson, Thomas Sadoski, Colleen Werthmann. *Trout Stanley* by Claudia Dey. May 22, 2006. Directed by Jen Wineman; with Kelly McAndrew, Erika Rolfsrud, Warren Sulatycky.

DR2. *Not a Genuine Black Man* by Brian Copeland. May 17, 2006. Directed by Bob Balaban; with Mr. Copeland.

EAST 13TH STREET THEATRE. *The Ladies of the Corridor* by Dorothy Parker and Arnaud d'Usseau. September 9, 2005. Directed by Dan Wackerman; with Kelly AuCoin, Ron Badgen, Hal Blankenship, Patrick Boyd, Peggy Cowles, Jo Ann Cunningham, Dawn Evans, Libby George, Susan Jeffries, Andy Phelan, Carolyn Seiff, Susan Varon, Domenica Cameron-Scorese.

EDGE THEATER COMPANY. *Living Room in Africa* by Bathsheba Doran. March 22, 2006. Directed by Carolyn Cantor; with Marsha Stephanie Blake, Guy Boyd, Rob Campbell, Michael Chernus, Ana Reeder, Maduka Steady.

EMERGING ARTISTS THEATRE COMPANY. EATFEST. March 7–26, 2006. Schedule included: *My Sister the Cow* by Gregory Fletcher. Directed by Paul Adams; with Amy Bizjak, Jason Hare, Lue McWilliams. *Blackout* by Vladimir Maicovski. Directed by Paul Adams; with Danny Mullock, Maureen

Sebastian. *Star Train* by Susan Merson. Directed by Melissa Atteberry; with Ryan Hilliard, Yvonne Roen, Jarret Summers. *A Perfectly Normal Family Dinner* by Matthew J. Hanson. Directed by Deb Guston; with Ron Bopst, Jack Herholdt, Irene Longshore, Christine Mosere, Matt Stapleton. *The Secret of Our Success* by Staci Swedeen. Directed by Derek Jamison; with Patrick Arnheim, AJ Handegard, Aimee Howard. *Nagasaki* by Kevin Brofsky. Directed by Kel Haney; with Irene Glezos, Steven Hauck. *Mr. Company* by Marc Castle. Directed by Max Montel; with Deb Annelino, Christopher Borg, Sarah Dacey Charles. *What We Talk About* by Emily Mitchell. Directed by Ian Streicher; with Blanche Cholet, Betty Hudson, Vivian Meisner, Jenny Mitchell. *The Test* by Caitlin Mitchell. Directed by Chris Maring; with Brian Louis Hoffman, Kyle T. Jones, Maya Rosewood, Kelly Scanlon. *Mom, Stoned* by Bekah Brunstetter. Directed by Kevin Dodd; with Michele Fulves, Stacy Mayer, Rhoda Pauley.

59E59. BRITS OFF BROADWAY. *Faster* by Stephen Brown. June 12, 2005. Directed by Guy Rettalack; with Will Adamsdale, Chris Branch, Victoria Moseley, Tim Phillips, Ferdy Roberts. *Jackson's Way* by Will Adamsdale. June 12, 2005. With Mr. Adamsdale. *Unsuspecting Susan* by Stewart Permutt. June 19, 2005. Directed by Lisa Forrell; with Celia Imrie. *Daph!* by Le Wilhelm. August 3, 2005. Directed by Merry Beamer; with Tracy Newirth. *Crestfall* by Mark O'Rowe. October 6, 2005. Directed by George C. Heslin; with Fiana Toibin, Mari Howells, Barbara J. Spence. *His Royal Hipness Lord Buckley in the Zam Zam Room* by Jake Broder. November 30, 2005. Directed by Phillip Breen; with Mr. Broder. *This Way That Way* by Mark Lonergan. December 18, 2005. Directed by Mr. Lonergan; with Joel Jeske, Ryan Kasprzak. *The Park Avenue Whirl*. With Daryl Sherman, Vince Giordano, Marion Cowings, Alexander Cowings, Dave Brown, Brad Shigeta, Dan Block, Mark Lopeman, Mark McCarron, John Gill. *Give Up! Start Over!* by Jessica Almasy. January 10, 2006. Directed by Rachel Chavkin; with Ms. Almasy, Jake Margolin, Josh Heine, Tim Peper, Frank Boyd, Kristen Sieh. *Ping Pong Diplomacy* by Joe Basque. January 13, 2006. Directed by David Kilder; with Kim Donover, Christopher Graham, Jerzy Gwiazdowski, Jesse Hooker, Jeffrey Nauman, David Shih, Constance Wu, Robert Wu. *Havana Bourgeois* by Carlos Lacamara. January 19, 2006. Directed by Jocelyn Sawyer; with Alexander Alito, George Bass, Ursula Cataan, Rashaad Ernesto Green, James Martinez, Selena Nelson, Thom Rivera, Jaime Sanchez. *(I Am) Nobody's Lunch* by Steven Cosson. January 19, 2006. Directed by Mr. Cosson; with Quincy Tyler Bernstine, Matthew Dellapina, Brad Heberlee, Daoud Heidami, Caitlin Miller, Jennifer R. Morris. *Clean Alternatives* by Brian Dykstra. February 15, 2006. Directed by Margarett Perry; with Mr. Dykstra, Mark Boyett, Sue-Anne Morrow. *Retzach* by Hanoch Levin; translated by Liat Glick, Shauna Kanter, Tzahi Moshkovitz. February 16, 2006. Directed by Ms. Kanter; with Gili Getz, Christel Halliburton, Sarah Imes, Amy Kovalchick, Simon MacLean, Joe Mancuso, Stephen Medwid, Tony Naumovski, Chris Paolucci, Raj Pannu, Andrew Russell, Emily Shapiro, Hadar Shemesh, Jelena Stupljanin, Arley Tapirian, Morteza Tavokoli. *Walk the Mountain* by Jude Narita. March 19, 2006. Directed by Darling Narita; with Jude Narita. *Fahrenheit 451* by Ray Bradbury. March 21, 2006. Directed by Joe Tantalo; with Ken King, Gregory Konow, Gracy Kaye, Cyrus Roxas, Kristen Rozanski, Mike Roche, Sam Whitten, Katherine Boynton, Jessica Rider, Teal Wicks.

FLORENCE GOULD HALL. *Silk Stockings*. Musical with book by George S. Kaufman, Leueen MacGrath, Abe Burrows; music and lyrics by Cole Porter. September 11, 2005. Directed by Ian Marshall Fisher; choreography, Donald Saddler; music direction, Lawrence Yurman; with Valerie Cutko, Wally Dunn, Daniel Gerroll, Liz Larsen, Robert Ari, Meghann Babo, Ryan Brunton, Sarahjean Davenport, Ray Demattis, Philip Deyesso, Bill Galarno, Bryan Kenneth, Jean McCormick, Ann Rothenberg, Jeffery Stern, Peter Van Wagner. *Liaison Transatlantique: Letters of Simone de Beauvoir to Nelson Algren*. Solo performance piece by Fabrice Rozie. September 30, 2005. Directed by Sandrine Dumas; with Marie-France Pisier. *Bye Bye Birdie*. Musical with book by Michael Stewart; music by Charles Strouse; lyrics by Lee Adams. March 26, 2006. Directed by Daniel Harris; with Ngozi Anyanwu, Michael Baldwin, Thomas Honeck, Ali Martin, Bo Ranney, Jennifer Veltre Smith, Jacob Thompson, T. Rich Jones.

45TH STREET THEATRE. *Merrily We Roll Along*. Musical with book by George Furth; music and lyrics by Stephen Sondheim. July 15, 2005. Directed by Steve Velardi; with James Archer, Jason Beaubien, Holden Berryman, Charles Bonnin, Kelley Calpin, Felicity Claire, Robert J. Cross, Angela Donovan, Jason Alan Edward, Meredith Ellis, Laurice Alicia Farrell, Kristen Florio, Jenny Gattone, Joshua William Gelb, Heather Gladis, Eoghan Broderick Greely, Anna Kirkland, Chazmond J. Peacock, Mr. Velardi, Lisa Villalobos. *Suicide, Anyone?* by John Patrick. October 5, 2005. Directed by Jeffrey Davolt; with George Antonopoulos, Victor Barella, Gregory Patrick Jackson, Lara Anne Slife. *The High Life*. Musical with book by Michael Kanin and Fay Kanin; music by Arthur Schwartz; lyrics by Howard Dietz. October 18, 2005. Directed by Thomas Mills; with Paul Green, Doug Shapiro, Roger Rifkin, Barbara McCulloh, Jenni Barber, Deborah Jean Templin, Dennis Holland. *Good News*. Musical with book by Lawrence Schwab and B.G. DeSylva; music by Rya Henderson; lyrics by Mr. DeSylva and Lew Brown. November 1, 2005. Directed by Thomas Mills; with Adam MacDonald, Jonathan Osborne, Noel Molinelli, Dana Zihlman, Adam Shonkwiler, Annie Ramsey, Ryan Dunkin, Roger Rifkin, Tad Wilson, Selby Brown, Leo Ash Evens, Katy Frame, Ben Franklin, Missy Matherne, Patrick Maubert, Erik McEwen, Emily Mixon, Sandie Rosa. ONE FESTIVAL. November 16–20, 2005. *Creation* by Lucas Caleb Rooney. Directed by Orlando Patoboy; with Mr. Rooney. *Jazz Desert* by Rebecca Hart. *Accidental Pervert* by Andrew Goffman. Directed by Charles Messina. *Soul to Keep* by Joyia Bradley. Directed by Joanne Zipay. *Wild Rice* by Scarlett Lam. With Ms. Lam. *I Need a Guy Who Blinks* by Janine Squillari. With Ms. Squillari. *Pentecostal Wisconsin* by Ryan Paulson. Directed by Virginia Scott; with Mr. Paulson. *Grown Ups* by Jules Feiffer. January 12, 2006. Directed by Frank Blake; with David Berent, Kelly Ann Moore, Lawrence Frank, Joy Keaton, Kate Tellers, Cai Tanikawa Oglesby. *Soul Searching*. Musical with book, music and lyrics by Matt Okin; music and lyrics by Avi Kunstler. January 21, 2006. Directed by Mr. Okin; with Robyn Brausa, Susan Erenberg, Russell Feder, Aaron Grant, Andrew Hubbard, Amanda Hunt, Danielle Faith Leonard, Avery Pearson, Max Roll, Stewart Schneck, Melissa Schoenberg, Elizabeth Woodard. *Offspring* by Jimmy Barden. March 3, 2006. Directed by Stacy Wring; with Maryam Myika Day, Brad Holbrook, Janice Marie, Hisham Tawfiq. *Mademoiselle Modiste*. Musical with book and lyrics by Henry Blossom; music by Victor Herbert. March 21, 2006. Directed by Thomas Mills; with Richard Barth, Jennifer Bowles, Caitlin Burke, Maxime Alvarez de Toledo, Heather Dornoff, Francis Dumaurier, Stephanie Fravel, Gary Harger, Bram Heidinger, John F. Herget, Hannah Knowlton, Leila Martin, Erik McEwen, Susan Molloy, Kristine Nevins, Megan Opalinski, Heather Parcells, Roger Rifkin, Ric Ryder, Blake Whyte. DREAD AWAKENING. April 6–23, 2006. *Bloody Mary* by Roberto Aguirre-Sacasa. Directed by Pat Diamond. *Pearls* by Clay McLeod Chapman. Directed by Arin Arbus. *Sleep Mask* by Eric Sanders. Directd by Amanda Charlton. *Treesfall* by Justin Swain. Directed by Jessica Davis-Irons. With Danny Defarri, Robert Funaro, Jenny Gammello, Abe Goldfarb, Meredith Holzman, Christianna Nelson, Joe Plummer, Jedadiah Schultz, Margie Stokley. *The Debate Plays* by Mat Smart. April 8, 2006. Directed by Evan Cabnet, Wes Grantom, Adam Knight; with Jeff Galfer, Chad Goodridge, Garrett Neergaard, Kathleen White. *Oh, Lady! Lady!* Musical with book by P.G. Wodehouse and Guy Bolton; music by Jerome Kern; lyrics by Mr. Wodehouse. April 25, 2006. Directed by Thomas Mills; with Amy Bils, Christopher Corts, John O'Creagh, Elizabeth DeRosa, Maxime Alvarez de Toledo, Katherine Harber, Genevieve Koch, Megan Opalinski, Robyne Parrish, Trip Plymale, George Psomas, Roger Rifkin, Marc Schaffer, Eyal Sherf, Jennifer Winegardner. *Let's Face It*. Musical with book by Dorothy and Herbert Fields; music and lyrics by Cole Porter. May 9, 2006. Directed by Thomas Mills; with Amy Barker, David Beris, Paul Binotto, Steve Brady, Ari Butler, Roseanne Colosi, Donna Coney Island, Ben Franklin, Amy Griffin, Hannah Knowlton, Erik McEwen, Rachel Alexa Norman, Trip Pettigrew, Sandie Rosa, Jessica Scholl, Blake Whyte.

45 BLEECKER. REVELATION READINGS. September 19–December 13, 2005. *Melissa Arctic* by Craig Wright. Directed by Aaron Posner; with Michael Rudko, Kiah Victoria, Kelly AuCoin, Ian Merrill Peakes, Holly Twyford, Erin Weaver, Mark Sullivan, Dori Legg, James Sugg, David Marks, Howard Overshown. *Dido, Queen of Carthage* by Christopher Marlowe. Directed by Joseph Hardy; with Richard Easton. *The Scottish Play* by Lee Blessing. Directed by Jesse Berger; with Mary Stuart Masterson. *Orestes* by Anne Washburn. Directed by Johanna McKeon; with James Urbaniak. *The Maid's Tragedy* by Francis Beaumont and John Fletcher. Directed by Jesse Berger; with Michael Stuhlbarg. *The Man of Mode* by George Etherege. Directed by Kay Matschullat; with Kate Burton, Dana Ivey. *Playhouse Creatures* by April De Angelis. Directed by Kate Whoriskey; with Dana Ivey. *The Broken Heart* by John Ford. Directed by Jef Hall-Flavin; with Robert Cuccioli, Remy Auberjonois, Mia Barron, Philip Goodwin, Michael Rudko, Claire Lautier, Margot White, Raphael Nash Thompson, Sean Arbuckle, Matthew Greer, Eric Hoffman, Sarah Hartmann, Addie Brownlee, Allan Care, Tyler Pierce, Dale Soules, Daniel Harray. *The Atheist's Tragedy* by Cyril Tourneur. Directed by Will Pomerantz; with Sam Tsoutsouvas, Jack Wetherall, Pamela Nyberg, Steven Rattazzi, Mary Bacon, Joel Bernstein, Dylan Greene, Frank Deal, Kenneth Garner, Mikel Sarah Lambert, Chris Kelly, Alvaro Mendoza, Kevin Collins, Aaron Clayton. *The Revenger's Tragedy* by Thomas Middleton; adapted by Jesse Berger. November 28, 2005. Directed by Mr. Berger; with Denis

Butkus, Jason C. Brown, Aaron Clayton, Saudia Davis, Ryan Farley, Ty Jones, Daryl Lathon, Claire Lautier, Paul Niebanck, Chris Oden, Petronia Paley, William Peden, Naomi Peters, Matthew Rauch, Russ Salmon, Daniel Cameron Talbott, Haynes Thigpen, Marc Vietor, Yaegel Welch. *Elliot, a Soldier's Fugue* by Quiara Alegria Hudes. February 4, 2006. Directed by Davis McCallum; with Mateo Gomez, Zabryna Guevara, Armando Riesco, Triney Sandoval.

14TH STREET Y. *My Sweetheart's the Man in the Moon* by Don Nigro. June 16, 2005. Directed by Amy Feinberg; with Mark Pinter, Kit Paquin, Timothy Altmeyer, Annette Hunt, Katerine Dowling. *Two Destinies* by Guile Branco. July 9, 2006. Directed by Emanuelle Villorini; with Mr. Branco, Robert Haufrecht.

GENE FRANKEL THEATRE. *Belly* by Julie Tortorici. September 30, 2005. Directed by Alicia Arinella; with Ms. Tortorici. *Cop-Out* and *The Talking Dog* by John Guare. October 6, 2005. Directed by Ronit Muszkatblit; with Monica Arazi, Kevin T. Collins, Kevin Dwyer, Luis Galli, Nobuo Inubus, Emily Rome Mudd. *A Brilliant Play* by John McEnroe. January 20, 2006. Directed by Maggie McBrien; with Zach Steel, Adam Carpenter, Alexa Kryzaniwsky, Brian Sacca, Paul Kropfl, Ryan Judd, Joey Zvejnieks, Benn Simington, Dan McCarthy, Keenan McCarthy. *Shiloh Rules* by Doris Baizley. March 24, 2006. Directed by Michaela Goldhaber; with Gwen Eyster, Cordis Heard, Janine Kyanko, Judi Lewis Ockler, Samarra, Kate Weiman.

GREENWICH STREET THEATRE. *Nights of Wrath* by Armand Salacrou; translated by David Looseley. June 3, 2005. Directed by Rafael De Mussa; with Alicia Adams, Gary Carlson, James Craft, John Gilligan, Alison Saltz, Ed Suarez, Ruth Kavanagh, Douglas Taurel. *Arcadia* by Tom Stoppard. November 6, 2005. Directed by Zander Teller; with Michael Anderson, Tim Astor, Mac Brydon, Tom Cleary, Micah Freedman, Lori Garrabrant, Rachel Jablin, Jennifer Lima, Shelley McPherson, John McWhorter, Michael O'Brien, Andrew Rein. *Anton* by Pierre van der Spuy. January 11, 2006. Directed by Mr. Van Der Spuy; with Loyita Chapel, Ana Kearin Genske, Jim Heaphy, Lee Kaplan, Kent Langloss, Shelley Phillips, Mr. Van Der Spuy, Jamison Vaughn. *Four Women* by Cheever Tyler. February 5, 2006. Directed by Christopher Carter Sanderson; with Kelly Tuohy, Ninon Rogers, Robin Benson, Debbie Stanislaus. *Exit 13* by Frank Terranova. May 17, 2006. Directed by Mr. Terranova; with Amelia Arena, Nathan Craig, Frankie Ferrara, Clare Ferraro, Beth Krafchik, Mr. Terranova, Craig Thomas Rivela.

HB PLAYWRIGHTS. THE WHITE HOUSE PLAYS. June 7–26, 2006. *Geneva* by Joe Sutton; directed by Sturgis Warner. *In the Lincoln Bedroom* by Laura Shane Cunningham; directed by Amy Wright. *Passion.com* by Catherine Filloux; directed by Deborah Saivetz. *The Last Standing Protester* by Lydia Stryk; directed by Karen Ludwig. *The Third Temple* by Sharr White; directed by Adam Forgash. *The Van Buren Cloak Room* by Adam Kraar; directed by Randy White. *Barbershop* by Quincy Long; directed by Kathleen Dimmick. *Higher Power* by Tug Yougrau; directed by Susan Einhorn. *Punk'd* by Frank Basloe; directed by Randy White. *Purple Hearts* by David Weiner; directed by Andrew Grosso. *Self-Portrait in a Blue Room* by Daniel Reitz; directed by Adam Forgash. *Shards* by Joan Vail Thorne; directed by Sturgis Warner. *The Next Question* by Amy Evans; directed by Paul Weldner. *The American Clock* by Arthur Miller. November 3, 2005. Directed by Austin Pendleton; with David Adams, Sam Antar, Michael Berry, Jim Boerlin, Phillip Bonn, Edward Boroevich, Fabio Costaprado, Ian Darrah, Allen Davison, Barbara Eda-Young, Dorothi Fox, Arthur French, Adam Groves, Daniel Gurian, Duncan Hazzard, Ryen Herrmann, Christian Hogarth, Glynis Hutchinson, Gene Jakupi, Rob Khack, Etienne Novarre, Takumi Mitobe, Dara O'Brien, Tadhg O'Mordha, George Morfogen, Jess Osuna, Kathleen Peirce, Julio Peña, Thomas Pendleton, Amanda Plant, Rob Khack, Hannah Reimann, Richard Rella, Sophia Remolde, David Rosenberg, Judy Rosenblatt, David Shih, Catherine Siracusa, David Sochet, Sean St. John, Susan Stein, Thomas Tagliente, Matthew Tishler, Marisa Viola, Robert Walden.

HERE ARTS CENTER. *Disposable Men* by James Scruggs. Directed by Kristin Marting; with Mr. Scruggs. THE AMERICAN LIVING ROOM. July 20–August 21, 2005. Schedule included: *Aurolac Blues* by Saviana Stanescu. Directed by Nina Hein. *Yit, Ngay (One, Two)* by Michael Lew. Directed by Mr. Lew; with Alix Price. *The Secret Face* by Elisabet Jokulsdottir. Directed by Steinunn Knutsdottir; with Palina Jonsdottir. *Flint, Michigan* by Elizabeth Bourgeois. Directed by Ms. Bourgeois. *Bath Party* by Meital Dohan, Karen Shefler and Ayelet Dekel. August 21, 2005. Directed by Ms. Shefler; with Mses. Dohan, Shefler, Dekel. *Box of Fools* by Joshua Putnam Peskay. August 21, 2005. Directed by Matthew A. Peskay; with Patrick Block, Liz Davito, Ben Jones, Kyle Lange, Jessica Leatherman, Kelly Markus, Marta Mondelli, Mr. Peskay, Jacqueline van Biene. *The Water Station* by Shogo

Ohta. September 7, 2005. Directed by Steve Pearson; with Francile Albright, James Garver, Scott Giguere, Nathan Guisinger, Maile Holck, Robyn Hunt, Tim Johnson, Peter Kyle, Megan McQuillin, Jamie Morgan, Michael Place, Amy Kim Waschke. *Paulsen's Lonely Banquet.* Solo performance piece by John Paulsen. November 26, 2005. Directed by George L. Lewis; with Mr. Paulsen. *Old Clown Wanted* by Matei Visniec; translated by Alison Sinclair. November 29, 2005. Directed by Gregory Fortner. *Heddatron* by Elizabeth Meriwether. February 16, 2006. Directed by Alex Timbers; with Carolyn Baeumler, Sam Forman, Gibson Frazier, Nina Hellman, Ryan Karels, Julie Lake, Daniel Larlham, Spenser Leigh, Michael Schulman, Ian Unterman. *InsideOut* by Jason Pizzarello. February 23, 2006. Directed by Aaron Rhyne; with Maria Teresa Creasey, Maria McConville, Graham Skipper, Steven Stafford. *Phenomenon* by Gordon Cox; music by Lance Horne. March 6, 2006. Directed by Alyse Rothman; with Rebecca Hart, Michael Lopez, Julie Toliver, Michael Urie, Marshall York. *Slipped Disc: A Study of the Upright Walk* by Ingrid Lausund; translated by Henning Bochert. May 3, 2006. Directed by Simone Blattner; with Andrea Ciannavei, Sanjit De Silva, Ron Domingo, Danielle Skraastad, John Summerour. *The Woman Before* by Roland Schimmelpfennig; translated by David Tushingham. May 5, 2006. Directed by Daniel Fish; with Christen Clifford, Cynthia Mace, Ronald Marx, Jeremiah Miller, Diana Ruppe.

IRISH ARTS. *The Blowin of Baile Gall* by Ronan Noone. September 13, 2005. Directed by David Sullivan; with Ato Essandoh, Susan McConnell, Ciaran Crawford, Colin Hamell. *A Night in November* by Marie Jones. March 17, 2006. Directed by Tim Byron Owen; with Marty Maguire.

KRAINE THEATER. *Serenading Louie* by Lanford Wilson. June 19, 2005. Directed by Lisa Mitchell; with Cadence Allen, Erin DePaula, John Samuel Jordan, Nate Rubin. *Adventures of Everywoman* by Jeff Bedillion. July 18, 2005. Directed by Mr. Bedillion; with Stefanie Eris, Lisa McQuade, Danielle Morellino, Jennifer Susi, Margaret Spirito, Maiken Weiss. *Sodom: The Musical.* Musical with book by Kevin Laub; music by Adam David Cohen; lyrics by Mr. Laub. November 8, 2005. Directed by Ben Rimalower; with Jonathan Kaplan, Randy Jones, Brian Munn, Blythe Gruda, Amy Barker, Stanley Bahorek, Matt Owen, David Abeles, Jake Manabat, Ryan Kelly, Stephanie Kovacs, Patrick Gallagher, Galit Sperling. *Crescendo Falls* by Kevin Hammonds. November 21, 2005. Directed by Wes Grantom; with Sean Attebury, Jennifer Boutell, Brooks Braselman, Timothy Dietrich, Kevin Hammonds, Eric Hunt, L. Jay Meyer, Jake Mosser, Jessica West Regan, Lori Ann Strunk, Diane Bilardi, Jennifer Winegardner. *Radio Theatre Presents King Kong* by Dan Bianchi. November 30, 2005. Directed by Mr. Bianchi; with Collin Biddle, Charles Wilson, John Nolan, Donna Heffernan, Jason Grossman. *Goner* by Brian Parks. January 7, 2006. Directed by John Clancy; with David Calvitto; Bill Coelius, Leslie Farrell, Patrick Federic, Jody Lambert, Matt Oberg, Jona Tuck. *Man of the Heart* by Sudipto Chatterjee. April 27, 2006. Directed by Suman Mukherjee; with Mr. Chatterjee. *The Crucible* by Arthur Miller. May 11, 2006. Directed by Melissa Atteberry; with Seth Abrams, Akia, Rey Oliver Bune, Elizabeth Burke, Patrick Egan, Reginald Ferguson, William Greville, Anna Gorman, John Hart, Barbara Lifton, Prentiss Marquis, Jared Mercier, Nic Mevoli, Adam Purvis, Kelly Scanlon, Jenn Schatz, Alessia Siniscalchi, Sarah Sirota, Jarret Summers, Lorraine Thompson, Brian Trybom.

LABYRINTH THEATER COMPANY. *Massacre (Sing to Your Children)* by José Rivera. October 5, 2005. Directed by Kate Whoriskey; with Julian Acosta, Elizabeth Canavan, Ron Cephas Jones, Florencia Lozano, Adrian Martinez, Jason Manuel Olazábal, Matt Saldívar, Sona Tatoyan. THE 2005 BARN SERIES FESTIVAL. December 2–19, 2005. *Intríngulis* by Carlo Alban. *A Small Melodramatic Story* by Stephen Belber. *1+1* by Eric Bogosian. *City of Palms* by Raul Castillo. *Pretty Chin Up* by Andrea Ciannavei. *All the Bad Things* by Cusi Cram. *The Little Flower of East Orange* by Stephen Adly Guirgis. *No Viet Cong Ever Called Me Nigger* by Brett C. Leonard. *Going After Alice* by Megan Mostyn-Brown. *She Talks to Rainbows* by Michael Puzzo. *All the Bad Things* by Cusi Cram. February 15, 2006. Directed by Paula Pizzi; with Vanessa Aspillaga, Jennifer Lauren Grant, Justin Reinsilber, Alexa Scott-Flaherty, Phyllis Somerville, David Zayas.

LARK PLAY DEVELOPMENT CENTER. *The Face of Jizo* by Hisashi Inoue. September 12, 2005. Directed by John C. Eisner; with Olivia Oguma, James Saito. *Jihad Jones and the Kalashnikov Babes* by Yussef El Guindi. September 15, 2005. Directed by Sturgis Warner; with Kristen Cerelli, T. Scott Cunningham, Wayne Schroder, Erica Schroeder, Waleed Zuaiter. *The Misfortune of Our Friends* by Sandi Goff. September 26, 2005. Directed by Steven Williford; with Mark Blum, Kelli Giddish, Matthew Stadelmann, Janet Zarish. *Misterioso-119* by Koffi Kwahule; translated by Chantal Bilodeau. October 27, 2005. Directed by Liesl Tommy. *Barnstormer.* Musical with book by Cheryl

L. Davis; music by Douglas J. Cohen; lyrics by Ms. Davis. November 5, 2005. Directed by Jerry Dixon; with Cheryl Alexander, Erica Ash, Stu James, Andre Montgomery, Ken Prymus, David St. Louis, Gayle Turner. *Vattago* by Ian Cohen. November 17, 2005. Directed by Steven Williford. *Mauritius* by Theresa Rebeck. December 8, 2005. *American Hwangap* by Lloyd Suh. December 15, 2005. Directed by John C. Eisner. *Smart* by Robert Fieldsteel. January 12, 2006. Directed by Linnet Taylor. *Lenin's Shoe* by Saviana Stanescu. February 1, 2006. Directed by Daniella Topol; with Amir Arison, William Carden, Walter Masterson, Florin Penisoara, Jessica Warner, Jennifer Dorr White, Shawn-Caulin Young. *Pleasure and Pain* by Chantal Bilodeau. February 16, 2006. *Breathe* by Javon Johnson. March 15, 2006. Directed by Rajendra Ramoon Maharaj. *Something Else Again* by Brian Dykstra. April 6, 2006. Directed by Margarett Perry.

MANHATTAN REPERTORY THEATRE. *One Good Marriage* by Sean Reycraft. April 11, 2006. Directed by Diana Belshaw; with Justin Conley, Siobhan Power. *Donna's Late-Night Cabaret* by Donna Stearns. May 5, 2006. Directed by Ms. Stearns; with Laura Mae Baker, Joshua David Bishop, Amber Bogdewiecz, Megan Cooper, Hannah Fairchild, Floryn Glass, Clara Barton Green, Joseph Hamel, Jules Hartley, Dawn Jones, Ashley Rebecca King, Jared R. Lopatin, Juliet Markowitz, Aurora Nessly, Jaki Silver, JessAnn Smith, Renee Threattle, Debra Wassum.

MANHATTAN THEATRE SOURCE. *Saint Frances of Hollywood* by Sally Clark. July 13, 2005. Directed by Daryl Boling; with Sarah Ireland, Dave Bachman, Jeff Broitman, Hank Davies, Sharon Fogarty, Fiona Jones, Kendra Kohrt, Jeffrey Plunkett, Michael Shattner, Lex Woutas. *Midnight* by David Epstein. August 12, 2005. Directed by Mr. Epstein; with Dan Patrick Brady, Elizabeth Horn, Gerry Lehane, Jesse Gavin, Rob Armstrong, Jeff Galfer, Douglas Goodrich, Kathleen Wallace, Nicholas Warren-Gray. *Finding Pedro* by James Heatherly, Lisa Gardner. *Screwups* by Justin Warner. November 9, 2005. Directed by Courtney Birch, Michael D. Jackson and Ari Laura Kreith; with Andrea Biggs, Matt Boethin, Ryan Dietz, Virginia Drda, Jason Grossman, Bridget Harvey, Jeff Hiller, Matt Knight, Janine Kyanko, Jill MacLean, Steve Minow, Amy Picar, Adam A. Sullivan. *Coronado* by Dennis Lehane. December 3, 2005. Directed by David Epstein; with Elizabeth Horn, Rebecca Miller, Lance Rubin, Kathleen Wallace, Jason MacDonald, Gerry Lehane, Avery Clark, Dan Patrick Brady, Maggie Bell. *The Mandrake* by Niccolo Machiavelli; translated by Vinnie Marano and Ollie Rasini. January 5, 2006. Directed by Daryl Boling; with Jeffrey Plunkett, Clare Stevenson, Steve Deighan. *Machiavelli* by Richard Vetere. January 12, 2006. Directed by Andrew Frank; with Liza Vann, James Wetzel, Jason Howard, Stephanie Janssen, Chip Phillips, Lex Woutas. *Temple* by Tim Aumiller. February 23, 2006. Directed by Greg Foro; with Audrey Amey, Tom Baran, Tom Macy, Leslie Miller, David Rudd, Joshua Seidner, Shannon Michael Wamser. *Good* by C.P. Taylor. March 15, 2006. Directed by Jennifer Gordon Thomas; with Daryl Boling, Waltrudis Buck, Nat Cassidy, Jason Grossman, Stephanie Kovacs, Danielle Quisenberry, Chip Phillips, G. Ivan Smith, Laura Schwenninger, Jeff Wills.

MA-YI THEATER COMPANY. *No Foreigners Beyond This Point* by Warren Leight. September 17, 2005. Directed by Loy Arcenas; with Laura Kai Chen, Ron Domingo, Wai Ching Ho, Francis Jue, Karen Tsen Lee, Abby Royle, Ean Sheehy, Henry Yuk. *Trial by Water* by Qui Nguyen. March 26, 2006. Directed by John Gould Rubin; with Arthur Acuna, Genevieve DeVeyra, Dinh Q. Doan, Jojo Gonzalez, Karen Tsen Lee, Timothy McCown Reynolds, Jessica Chandlee Smith.

MCGINN/CAZALE. *Swimming in the Shallows* by Adam Bock. June 28, 2005. Directed by Trip Cullman; with Michael Arden, Logan Marshall-Green, Rosemarie DeWitt, Mary Schultz, Murphy Geyer. *The Dear Boy* by Dan O'Brien. August 8, 2005. Directed by Michael John Garcés; with Daniel Gerroll, Dan McCabe, T. Scott Cunningham, Susan Pourfar. *The Nastiest Drink in the World*. Musical with book by Mark Loewenstern; music by John Gregor; lyrics by Mr. Loewenstern. September 10, 2005. Directed by Linda Ames Key; with Julie Brooks, Brooke Hetrick, Michael Huber, Chris Janssen, Dan Kalodny. *Full Bloom* by Suzanne Bradbeer. March 14, 2006. Directed by Linda Ames Key; with Jennifer Blood, Jennifer Dorr White, Jason Furlani, William Jackson Harper, Leeanne Hutchison.

MEDICINE SHOW THEATRE. *Pilgrims* by Jamie Carmichael. July 14, 2005. Directed by Geordie Broadwater; with Rufus Tureen, Emily Young, Eric Murdoch, Catherine Gowl. *The Last Bohemians* by Stelios Manolakakis. September 16, 2005. Directed by Mr. Manolakakis; with Ian Tomaschik, Lucas Steele, Carla Brandberg, Esther Barlow, Stewart Cummings, Ewan Ross, Melissa Silver. *Undercover Lover*. Musical with book by Arnold Weinstein and Frank O'Hara; music by John Gruen; lyrics by Mr. Weinstein and Mr. O'Hara. November 11, 2005. Directed by Barbara Vann;

with Morton Banks, Sarah Engelke, Mark Dempsey, Diana Dunbar, Kirt Harding, Phyllis Sanfiorenzo, Mike Still, Ms. Vann, Monrico Ward, David Weitzer, Andrew York. *Don Juan in Hell* by George Bernard Shaw. February 10, 2006. Directed by Alec Tok; with Mark J. Dempsey, Monica Lynch, Peter Judd, Barbara Vann. *Fire Exit* by V.R. Lang. April 27, 2006. Directed by Barbara Vann; with Morton Banks, Alexander Bilu, Jennifer Cintron, John Crefeld, Mark J. Dempsey, Lora Lee Ecobelli, Julia Granacki, Jason Alan Griffin, Beth Griffin, Amy Kersten, Constantine Montana, Sarah Nuffer, Ms. Vann, Greg Vorob, Joel Bernstein.

MELTING POT THEATER COMPANY. *Terezin.* Musical with book by Peter Ullian; music by Joel Derfner; lyrics by Len Schiff. February 23, 2006. Directed by Jeremy Dobrish; with Danny Gurwin, Zac Halley, David Hibbard, Carolann Page, Donna Vivino, Kathy Voytko, Blake Whyte, Stuart Zagnit. *In This House.* Musical with book by Sarah Schlesinger and Mike Reid; music by Mr. Reid; lyrics by Ms. Schlesinger. April 26, 2006. Directed by Jonathan Bernstein; with George Lee Andrews, Mary Beth Peil, Charlie Pollock.

METROPOLITAN PLAYHOUSE. *The Scarecrow* by Percy MacKaye. October 8, 2005. Directed by Alex Rose; with Avery Clark, Sidney Fortner, Ian Gould, Paul Jackel, Deborah Johnstone, Andy MacDonald, Melissa Miller, Jeff Pagliano, Courtney Sieberling, Shelley Virginia. *The Inheritors* by Susan Glaspell. November 11, 2005. Directed by Yvonne Conybeare; with Sean Dill, David Gentile Fraioli, Peter Judd, David Lally, Tod Mason, Jeff Pagliano, Margaret Loesser Robinson, Matthew Trumbull. *The Melting Pot* by Israel Zangwill. March 3, 2006. Directed by Robert Z. Kalfin; with Paul de Cordova, Christina Demetriou, Page Hearn, Ronnie Newman, Kendall Rileigh, Margaret Loesser Robinson, Daniel Shevlin, Steve Sterner, Suzanne Toren. *Haunted* by Alex Roe. May 6, 2006. Directed by Mr. Roe; with Leith Conybeare, Andrew Firda, Charlotte Hampden, Teresa Kelsey, Greg LoProto, Tod Mason.

MICHAEL WELLER THEATRE. *Revolution Row* by Edward Miller. August 16, 2005. Directed by Aaron Daniel Haber; with Charles Gould, Josh Stein-Sapir. *The Safety Net* by Christopher Kyle. September 22, 2005. Directed by Martha Banda; with Jason Pugatch, Tinashe Kajese, Eva Kaminsky, Maren Perry, Peggy Scott, Mark Setlock. *The Uncertainty Principle* by Bethany Larsen. October 24, 2005. Directed by Julie Fei Fan Balzer; with Anne Ashby, Jennifer Gegan, Tim Intravia, Chris Kloko, Fabio Pires. *Fish Bowl* by Simona Berman and Andrew Thomas Pitkin. January 7, 2006. Directed by Chris Henry; with Katie Apicella, Simona Berman, Mike Borrelli, Jeff Edgerton, Simone Harrison, James Huffman, Pamela Stewart, Victor Verhaeghe, Shevaun Smythe-Hiler, Anna Farkas, Christine Pland, Reiko Yamanaka. *Girl in Heat* by Nelson Avidon. January 27, 2006. Directed by Robert Walden; with Cheryl Leibert, Mr. Avidon. *Impossible Lorca: A Theatrical Hat-Trick* by Federico Garcia Lorca; translated and adapted by Caridad Svich. March 6, 2006. Directed by Melissa Fendell; with Jeanne Harris, Sarah Lemp, Casey McClellan, Jennifer Perrotta, Larry Pontius, Jordan Zolan.

MIDTOWN INTERNATIONAL THEATRE FESTIVAL. July 18–August 7, 2005. Schedule included: *Spit It Out!* by Valerie Smaldone and Amy Coleman. Directed by Sarah Gurfield; with Mses, Coleman, Smaldone, Stephen Bienskie, Andy Bassford, Donna Kelly. *Apathy–The Gen X Musical.* Musical with book and music by Mickey Zetts. Directed by Paul D'Alessandria; with Fiona Choi, Ethan Gomez, Samantha Leigh Josephs, Ryan G. Metzger, Matt Miniea, Duncan Pflaster, Sami Rudnick. *Charles and Diana.* Musical with book and music by Lewis Papier; lyrics by Mary Sullivan Struzi. Directed by Clyde Baldo; with Michael Digioia, Amanda Ladd, Rob Resnick, Kate Greer, Tracy Rosten, Kenneth Garner, Natalie Delena, Kiirsten Kuhi, Amy Russ, Monica Russell, Alan Ostroff. *Feasting on Cardigans* by Mark Eisman. Directed by Amy Henault; with Ian Pfister, Kate Sandberg, Katie Barrett, Andrea Gallo, Tyler Samuel Lee. *Glory Road.* Musical with book and lyrics by Greg Senf; music by Gregory Max. Directed by George Wolf Reily; with Chet Carlin, Beth Chiarelli, Michael Finkelstein, Kristen Hammer, Barbara Litt, Jeannine Otis, Eric Petersen, Jessie Thatcher. *Invisible Child* by Lisa Barri. Directed by Don Johanson; with Ms. Barri. *It's Only a Play* by Terrence McNally. Directed by John Capo; with Yuval David, Frederick Hamilton, Cynthia Henderson, Betty Hudson, Sheila Mart, Charles Marti, Glenn Peters, John Squire. *On the Couch with Nora Armani* by Nora Armani. Directed by François Kergourlay; with Ms. Armani. *Peace Now* by Tom Peterson. Directed by Mr. Peterson; with Michael C. Maronna, Frank Harts, Carter Jackson, Genia Michaela, Cameron Blair, Cameron Peterson, Matthew Decapua, Christian Pedersen, Adrianne Rae-Rodger, Kim Shaw. *Shooting Yourself in the Foot* by Marci Adilman and Jessica Jill Turner. Directed by Melissa Boswell and Jane Steinberg. *Cervix With a Smile.* Solo performance piece with book and lyrics by Elisa DeCarlo; music by Ms. DeCarlo and Ellen Mandel. Directed by Rod

Cassavale; with Ms. DeCarlo. *End Caligula* by Sean Michael Welch. Directed by Stacee Mandeville. *Grieving for Genevieve* by Kathleen Warnock. Directed by Peter Bloch; with Karen Stanion, Susan Barnes Walker, Jo Anne Bonn. *Savior* by Michael R. O'Brien. Directed by Christopher Carter Sanderson; with Jy Murphy, Hilary Howard, Jeff Barry. *Shakespeare Is Dead* by Orran Farmer. Directed by Chris Chaberski; with Chelsea Lagos, Luke Rosen. *Under My Apron* by Debbie Williams. Directed by Ms. Williams; with Ron Williams, Kristen Egan, Jessa Watson, Corey Greenan, Debbie Williams, Kevin Starzynski, Maria Couch. *How to Ride Roller Coasters.* Solo performance piece by Tina Lee. Directed by David Godbey; with Ms. Lee. *Soul to Keep* by Joyia D. Bradley. Directed by Alexandra Lopez; with Ms. Bradley, B.J. Wheeler. *Fell in Love With a Girl* by Samara Siskind. Directed by Ryan Brown; with Amanda Clayton, Meagan Gordon, Mike Kulbeida, Anthony Saracino. *The Goat Song* by Kimberly Patterson. Directed by Jill Jichetti; with Sarah Doudna, Megan Hutten, Ingrid Nuñez, Bryan Ponemon. *Actor. Comedian. Negro.* Solo performance piece by Baron Vaughn. Directed by Mr. Vaughn; with Mr. Vaughn. *Old Words, New Words* by Mary E. Goulet. Directed by Jess L. Kearney Jr.; with Mr. Kearny Jr., Sarah M. Wilson, Danielle Fisk, Laura Heidinger, Corey Jay. *The Baby Is Blue* by Matt Schatz. Directed by S. Caden Hethorn; with Ethan Baum, Ayelet Blumberg, Mark Montgomery, Elizabeth Schmidt. *Good Opinions* by Anne Fizzard. Directed by Katrin Hilbe; with Nicole Taylor, Marc Geller, Stephen Morfesis, Andrew Dawson, Oliver Conant, Kevin Stapleton, Joan Pelzer, Wende O'Reilly. *Passing Time* by Khemali Murray. Directed by Chuck Patterson; with Ms. Murray.

NATIONAL ASIAN AMERICAN THEATER COMPANY (NAATCO). *Cowboy vs. Samurai* by Michael Golamco. November 8, 2005. Directed by Lloyd Suh; with Timothy Davis, Joel de la Fuente, C.S. Lee, Hana Moon.

NEW YORK INTERNATIONAL FRINGE FESTIVAL. August 8–August 28, 2005. Schedule included: *All Consuming* by Clare Nicholls. Directed by Ms. Nicholls. *Ambrosia* by Christine Ashe, Lilli Birdsell, Susan Dalian. Directed by Julie Ariola. *Anaerobic Respiration* by Krista Knight. Directed by Alex Torre. *Ankhst* by Clarinda Karpov. Directed by Jonathan Warman. *Aquarium* by Robin Maguire. Directed by Tim Redmond. *Arias for the Mundane* by James Junio. Directed by Melanie T. Morgan; with Mr. Junio. *As Much As You Can* by Paul Oakley Stovall. Directed by Krissy Vanderwarker. *Beware of Dog* by Melih Cevdet Anday. Directed by Turkar Coker. *Tarot Reading: Love, Sex and Mommy* by Kimberlee Auerbach. Directed by Eric Davis; with Ms. Auerbach. *Thick* by Rick Bland. Directed by Mark Bruce; with Mr. Bruce, Tamara Bick, Ross Mullan. *Silence! The Musical.* Musical with book, music and lyrics by Hunter Bell, Jon Kaplan and Al Kaplan. Directed and choreographed by Christopher Gattelli; with Paul Kandel, Stephen Bienskie, Jenn Harris. *The Last Days of Cleopatra.* Musical with book, music and lyrics by Charles Barnett. Directed by Christopher Gerken; with Anna Roberts, Michael Deleget, Cara Kem, Tom Beckett, E.C. Kelly, Bobby Matoney, Brett Rigby, Valerie Issembert, Christopher LaCroix, Alan Ostroff, Michael Baldwin, Michael Siller, Robin Levine, Anna Lombardi, Michael Frishman. *Movie Geek* by Dylan Dawson. Directed by Andy Donald; with Eric Clem, Mr. Dawson, Josh Halloway, Adam Lustice, Maggie Marion, Shannon Walker. *Bridezilla Strikes Back!* By Cynthia Silver and Kenny Finkle. Directed by Paul Urcioli. *Hercules in High Suburbia* by Mary Fulham; lyrics by Paul Foglino. Directed by Ms. Fulham; with Neal Young, Postell Pringle, Dan Marisa, Dana Vance. *Uncle Sam's Satiric Spectacular* by Greg Allen, Sheila Callaghan, Bridget Carpenter, Eric Coble, Richard Dresser, Hilly Hicks, Michael Friedman. Directed by Wendy McClellan. *Love Sick* by Gabriel McKinley. Directed by Mark Fratello; with Mr. McKinley, Stefanie Frame. *Treaty 321.* Musical with book by Christopher Buckley; music by Stephen L. Murphy; lyrics by Mr. Buckley. Directed by Sam Scalamoni; with Chris Mattthias, Megan Lavner, Bob Barth, Thay Floyd, Glennis McMurray, Derek Travis Collard, Thadd Krueger. *The Salacious Uncle Baldrick* by Sean Kent and Kenan Minkoff. Directed by Matt Coward; with Shaun Kevlin, Christy Pusz, Ryan Cyrus Shams, Alan Mozes, Richard Robichaux, Paige Hutchinson, Josh Perilo, Will Rogers, Brian Philage. *The Banger's Flopera–A Musical Perversion.* Musical with book by Kirk Wood Bromley; music by John Gideon; lyrics by Mr. Bromley. Directed by Ben Yalom.

NEW YORK MUSICAL THEATRE FESTIVAL. September 12–October 2, 2005. Schedule included: *Monica! The Musical.* Musical with book by Daniel J. Blau; music by Adam Blau; lyrics by Mr. Blau. Directed by Casey Hushion. *The Unknown.* Musical with book by Janet Allard and Jean Randich; music by Shane Rettig; lyrics by Mses. Allard, Randich. Directed by Ms. Randich. *The Ballad of Bonnie and Clyde.* Musical with book and lyrics by Michael Aman and Oscar E. Moore;

music by Dana P. Rowe. Directed by Michael Bush; with Sherrié Austin, Deven May. *The Shaggs: Philosophy of the World*. Musical with book and lyrics by Joy Gregory; music and lyrics by Gunnar Madson. Directed by John Langs; with Dana Acheson, Jimmy Bennett, Bill English, Amy Eschman, Peter Friedman, Jamey Hood, Glenn Peters, Tracy Sallows. *Yank!* Musical with book and lyrics by David Zellnik; music by Joseph Zellnik. Directed by Igor Goldin; with Ken Alan, Jeffrey J. Bateman, Jeffry Denman, Joey Dudding, Julie Foldesi, Ivan Hernandez, Daniel Frank Kelley, Doug Kreeger, James Patterson, Tally Sessions. *The Mistress Cycle*. Musical with book and lyrics by Beth Blatt; music by Jenny Giering. Directed by Joe Calarco; with Lynne Wintersteller, Sally Wilfert, Stephanie Bast, Lisa Brescia, Mary Bond Davis. *But I'm a Cheerleader*. Musical with book and lyrics by Bill Augustin; music by Andrew Abrams. Directed by Daniel Goldstein; with Chandra Lee Schwartz, Tom Richter, Erik Lochtefeld, Kelly Karbacz. *Wild Women of Planet Wongo*. Musical with book by Steve Mackes; music by Dave Ogrin; lyrics by Messrs. Budick, Mackes and Ogrin. Directed by Doug Moser; with Alicia Irving, Max Perlman, Daniel C. Levine, Heath Calvert, Tracy Jai Edwards, Beth Curry, Lauren Lebowitz, NRaca, Jessica Barbick. *Planet Crazy*. Musical with book, music and lyrics by Suzy Conn. Directed by Jamibeth Margolis; with Erin Crouch, Kevin Kraft, Christopher Guilmet, William Broderick, Eric John Mahlum, Craig Laurie, Nicky Venditti. *The Tutor*. Musical with book by Maryrose Wood; music by Andrew Gerle; lyrics by Ms. Wood. Directed by Sarah Gurfield, Ray Fellman; with Eric Ankrim, Meredith Bull, Gayton Scott, Richard Pruitt, Rafael Fetta, Lucy Sorensen. *The Big Time*. Musical with book by Douglas Carter Beane; music by Douglas J. Cohen; lyrics by Mr. Cohen. With Debbie Gravitte, David Beach, Raymond Bokhour, Bradley Dean, Joanna Glushak, Jackie Hoffman, Michael McCormick, Patrick Quinn, Sal Viviano. *Nerds*. Musical with book and lyrics by Jordan Allen-Dutton; music by Hal Goldberg. Directed by Andy Goldberg; with William Selby, Anthony Holds, Jessica-Snow Wilson. *Richard Cory*. Musical with book, music and lyrics by Ed Dixon; adapted from a play by A.R. Gurney. Directed by James Brennan; with Catherine Cox, Harris Doran, Cady Huffman, Herndon Lackey, Maureen Moore, Christeena Riggs, John Sloman, Lynne Wintersteller. *You Might As Well Live*. Musical with book and music by Norman Mathews; lyrics by Dorothy Parker. With Karen Mason.

NEW YORK THEATRE WORKSHOP. *Get Lucky*. By Steven Drukman. November 10, 2005. Directed by Lou Jacob; with Remy Auberjonois, Mia Barron, Penny Fuller, Maulik Pancholy.

OHIO THEATRE. *Little Suckers* by Andrew Irons. June 4, 2005. Directed by Jessica Davis-Irons; with Arthur Aulisi, Ryan Bronz, Erin Quinn Purcell, Margie Stokley. *Commedia dell Smartass* by Sonya Sobieski. September 12, 2005. Directed by Jean Randich; with Jessi Campbell, Jesse Hooker, Nurit Monacelli, Debargo Sanyal. *Helena* by Johann Wolfgang von Goethe; translated by Douglas Langworthy. December 1, 2005. Directed by David Herskovits; with Will Badgett, Daphne Gaines, David Greenspan, Nicole Halmos, Lian-Marie Holmes, Wayne Alon Scott, Eunice Wong. *What Then* by Rinne Groff. January 9, 2006. Directed by Hal Brooks; with Andrew Dolan, Meg MacCary, Piter Marek, Merritt Wever. *.22 Caliber Mouth* by Lauren Robert. February 22, 2006. Directed by Diane Paulus; with Ms. Robert, Tim Warmen, Laura Jordan, Ted Brunetti, Paul Oakley Stovall. *Little Willie* by Mark Kassen. April 10, 2006. Directed by John Gould Rubin; with Mr. Kassen, Roxanna Hope. *The Necklace* by Lisa D'Amour, Ellen Maddow, Lizzie Olesker, Paul Zimet. May 6, 2006. Directed by Anne Kauffman and Melissa Kievman; with David Brooks, Gibson Frazier, Ian Holloway, Suli Holum, Jodi Lin, Ellen Maddow, Katie Pearl, Andy Paris, Tina Shepard, Paul Zimet.

ONTOLOGICAL-HYSTERIC THEATRE. *Gravediggers* by Karly Maurer. June 2, 2005. Directed by Ms. Maurer; with Randi Berry, Dimitra Bixby, Nicholas Bixby, Dechelle Damien, Michelle Diaz, Tara Grieco, Benjamin Spradley. *Panel, Animal* by Jason Craig. July 1, 2005. Directed by Mallory Catlett; with Peter Blomquist, Jason Craig, Sarah Engelke, Jessica Jelliffe, Rod Hipskind, Heather Peroni. *La Tempestad* by Larry Loebell. October 13, 2005. Directed by Eric Parness; with Gordon Stanley, Alberto Bonilla, Brian Flegel, Vivia Font, Felipe Javier Gorostiza, Ed Jewett, Lori McNally, Patrick Melville, Ray A. Rodriguez, Frank Tamex, James T. Ware. *The Tempest*. Revival of the play by William Shakespeare; adapted by Victor Maog. October 14, 2005. Directed by Mr. Maog; with Rashaad Ernesto Green, Daniel Larlham, Orlando Pabotoy. *Zomboid!* by Richard Foreman. January 12, 2006. Directed by Mr. Foreman; with Katherine Brook, Temple Crocker, Ben Horner, Caitlin McDonough Thayer, Stephanie Silver.

PEARL THEATRE COMPANY. *The Master Builder* by Henrik Ibsen. October 2, 2005. Directed by Shepard Sobel; with Robin Leslie Brown, Dan Daily, Robert Hock, Sean McNall, Marsha Stephanie Blake, Arthur French, Michele Vazquez. *The Gentleman Dancing-Master* by William Wycherley.

November 20, 2005. Directed by Gus Kaikkonen; with Marsha Stephanie Blake, Robin Leslie Brown, Dan Daily, Sean McNall, Ryland Blackinton, Rachel Botchan, Bradford Cover, John Livingstone Rolle, Heather Girardi, Michele Vazquez. *Hecuba* by Euripides; translated by Janet Lembke and Kenneth J. Reckford. January 5, 2006. Directed by Shepard Sobel; with Joanne Camp. *Measure for Measure*. Revival of the play by William Shakespeare. April 5, 2006. Directed by Beatrice Terry; with Rachel Botchan, Dominic Cuskern, TJ Edwards, Holley Fain, Robert Hock, Kelli Holsopple, Romel Jamison, John Mazurek, Sean McNall, Raphael Peacock, Carol Schultz, Edward Seamon, Ron Simons, Noel Velez. *Mary Stuart* by Friedrich Schiller; translated by Michael Feingold. April 30, 2006. Directed by Eleanor Holdridge; with Joanne Camp, Dominic Cuskern, Beth Dixon, TJ Edwards, Kenric Green, Bryan Hicks, Robert Hock, Sean McNall, Raphael Peacock, Celester Rich, Carol Schultz, Edward Seamon, Noel Velez, Tyler Woods.

PERRY STREET THEATRE. *Treason* by Sallie Bingham. October 23, 2005. Directed by Martin Platt; with Sam Tsoutsouvas, Mary Bacon, Kathleen Early, Rodney Hicks, Shannon Koob, Pamela Nyberg, Lucas Caleb Rooney, Jennifer Sternberg. *In the Continuum* by Danai Gurira and Nikkole Salter. November 18, 2005. Directed by Robert O'Hara; with Mses. Gurira and Salter. *Sake With the Haiku Geisha* by Randall David Cook. March 2, 2006. Directed by Alex Lippard; with David Shih, Geneva Carr, Fiona Gallagher, Angela Lin, Sala Iwamatsu, Ikuma Issac, David Bowers, Jeremy Hollingworth.

PRODUCERS CLUB. *Drummers, Dreams and Family Matters* by Norman Weinstein. November 7, 2005. Directed by Mr. Weinstein; with Deborah Hope, Clyde Kelley, Colleen Kennedy, Alex Kosma, Mary Sheridan, Tom Thornton, George Trahanis. *The Screwtape Letters* by C.S. Lewis; adapted by Nigel Forde. November 9 2005. Directed by Ralph Irizarry; with Steven Wargo, Maria Bellantoni, Kevin O'Bryan, Justin Stoney, David Esteve, Holly Hurley, Paul Parker, Sheila Simmons, David Arthur. *Five Days With Dylan* by Pamela Scott. December 7, 2005. Directed by Nye Heron; with Michael McGuire, Walter DeForest, Darcy Reed, Sandra Cummings, Alicia Frank, Vance Clemente, Edgar Felix, Sultan Mahmud, Rose Courtney, Chris Dugger, Jennifer Neumann, Lisa Marie Reisenweber, Nina Rochelle.

PROSPECT THEATER COMPANY. *The Book of the Dun Cow*. Musical with book by Mark St. Germain; based on the book by Walter Wangerin Jr.; music by Randy Courts; lyrics by Messrs. St. Germain and Courts. February 4, 2006. Directed by Cara Reichel; with Jacob Grigolia-Rosenbaum, Brian Munn, Micah Bucey, Jesse Kearney, Robby Sharpe, Carol Hickey, David Foley Jr., Vanessa June Marshall. *Iron Curtain*. Musical with book by Susan DiLallo; music by Stephen Weiner; lyrics by Peter Mills. April 8, 2006. Directed by Cara Reichel; with Jeff Edgerton, Marcus Neville, Bethe B. Austin, Larry Brustofski, Maria Couch, Jessica Grové, Gordon Stanley, Amber Dow, David S. Miller, Doug Shapiro, Robby Sharpe, Dara Seitzman, Rich Silverstein, Brad York.

RATTLESTICK THEATER. *The Pavilion* by Craig Wright. September 20, 2005. Directed by Lucie Tiberghien; with Stephen Bogardus, Brian d'Arcy James, Jennifer Mudge. *It Goes Without Saying*. Solo performance piece by Bill Bowers. December 10, 2005. Directed by Martha Banta; with Mr. Bowers. *Acts of Mercy: passion-play* by Michael John Garcés. February 16, 2006. Directed by Gia Forakis; with Veronica Cruz, José Febus, Jenny Maguire, Bryant Mason, Andres Munar, Ivan Quintanilla, Tommy Schrider. *Cagelove* by Christopher Denham. May 15, 2006. Directed by Adam Rapp; with Daniel Eric Gold, Gillian Jacobs, Emily Cass McDonnell.

SANFORD MEISNER THEATRE. *Little Mary* by William Leavengood. June 2, 2005. Directed by Jessica Dubzansky; with Ron Orbach, Jeremy Lawrence, Nelson Avidon, Robyn Hatcher, Monica Raymund. *The Roof* by Suzanne Bradbeer. September 15, 2005. Directed by Maggie Low; with Lucas Blondheim, Andrew Lawton, Denise Lute. *Deviant* by A. Rey Pamatmat. October 7, 2005. Directed by Kara-Lynn Vaeni; with Daniel Zaitchik, Courtnie Sauls, Jennifer Lim, Jacob Blumer. *The Northern Quarter* by Alex van Warmerdam; translated by Mr. van Warmerdam and Erwin Maas. January 7, 2006. Directed by Mr. Maas; with Joy Barrett, Michael B. Downing, Adam Gallo, Dave Gueriera, Heather Hollingsworth, Justin G. Krauss, Noah Trepanier, Vincent van der Valk, Matt Walters. *The Ends of the Earth* by Morris Panych. March 17, 2006. Directed by Peter Sanfilippo; with Mary Aufman, Amy Broder, David Jacks, Leslie Loggans, Kelly Miller, Elizabeth Alice Murray.

78TH STREET THEATRE LAB. *The Great American Desert*. Musical with book by Joel Oppenheimer; music by Joe Schlitz and Joe Jung; lyrics by Mr. Oppenheimer. October 3, 2005. Directed by Garrett Ayers; with Brian Frank, Ben Rosenblatt, Erin Gorski, Chris Vandijk, Maurice Doggan, Andrew McLeod, Brian Sell, Emily Moulton, Joe Jung. *The Devil of Delancey Street* by Sharon

Fogarty. October 19, 2005. Directed by Ms. Fogarty; with John Cunningham, Ms. Fogarty, Patti Goettlicher, Jeffrey R. Plunkett, Matthew Porter, Bobbi Owens, Bradley True, Karen Christie-Ward. *Dear Maudie* by Michele Willens. October 30, 2005. Directed by Jamibeth Margolis; with Danielle Carlacci, Allison Brustofski, Kelsey Merritt, Kristen Piacentile, Leanne Cabrera, Hunter Gallagher, Tommy McKiernan, Michael Jacobs, Staci Rudnitsky. *The Last Christmas of Ebenezer Scrooge* by Marvin Kaye. December 1, 2005. With Mr. Kaye, Stacey Jenson, H. Clark Kee, Nancy Temple. *Lemkin's House* by Catherine Filloux. February 9, 2006. Directed by Jean Randich; with John Daggett, Christopher McHale, Christopher Edwards, Constance Winston, Laura Flanagan. *Bluff* by Jeffrey Sweet. March 10, 2006. Directed by Sandy Shinner; with Ean Sheehy, Bill Tatum, Sarah Yorra, Michelle Best, Luke MacCloskey, Kristine Niven. *Mrs. California* by Doris Baizley. March 15, 2006. Directed by Megan R. Willis; with Elizabeth Burke, Heather E. Cunningham, Matilda Downey, David DiLoreto, Jim Kilkenny, India Myone McDonald, Kristen Vaughan, Jack H. Cunningham, Reginald V. Ferguson, Kimberly Greene. *The Amulet* by Peretz Hirshbein. April 13, 2006. Directed by Isaac Butler; with Hanna Cheek, Anita Keal, Daryl Lathon, David Little. *I Will Come Like a Thief* by Trish Harnetiaux. May 13, 2006. Directed by Jude Domski; with Arthur Acuna, Henry Afro-Bradley, JJ Auczkiewicz, Carey Cromelin, Loris Diran, Michael Colby Jones, Corey Tazmania Stieb.

SOHO PLAYHOUSE. *Belly of a Drunken Piano* by Stewart D'Arrietta and John Waters. August 28, 2005. With Mr. D'Arrietta. *Bukowski From Beyond* by Leo Farley and Steve Payne; adapted from the work of Charles Bukowski. October 10, 2005. Directed by Mr. Farley; with Mr. Payne. *Ham Lake* by Sam Rosen and Nat Bennett. April 27, 2006. Directed by Ian Morgan; with Mr. Rosen.

STORM THEATRE. *The Salvage Shop* by Jim Nolan. November 2, 2005. Directed by Peter Dobbins; with Kristen Bush, Karen Eke, Roland Johnson, David Little, Paul Anthony McGrane, Ted McGuinness. *'Tis Pity She's a Whore* by John Ford. October 2, 2005. Directed by Alex Lippard; with Craig Baldwin, Rachel Matthews Black, Craig Braun, Colby Chambers, Sam Chase, Mel Cobb, Helmar Augustus Cooper, Catherine Curtin, Cameron Folmar, Jan Leslie Harding, Mauricio Tafur Salgado, John Douglas Thompson, Betsy Winchester. *The Merchant of Venice*. Revival of the play by William Shakespeare. March 16, 2006. Directed by John Basil; with Robert Chaney, Wendy Chu, Bill Fairbairn, Richard Fay, Deepti Gupta, David Dean Hastings, Jon Hoche, Kara Jackson, Elizabeth Keefe, Damon Kinard, Debra Lewis, Nicole Patrick, Rainard Rachele, Mathew J. Sanders, Graham Stevens, Robert Lee Taylor, Warren Watson.

STUDIO DANTE. *Late Fragment* by Francine Volpe. October 1, 2005. Directed by Michael Imperioli and Zetna Fuentes; with Ken Forman, Dean Harrison, Michael Mosley, Nick Sandow, Jenna Stern. *Cyclone* by Ron Fitzgerald. March 18, 2006. Directed by Brian Mertes; with Michael Cullen, Jeremy Davidson, James Hendricks, Marin Ireland, Hamish Linklater, Lucas Papaelias, Matthew Stadelmann. *Dark Yellow* by Julia Jordan. May 27, 2006. Directed by Nick Sandow; with Tina Benko, Elias Koteas, Max Kaplan.

THEATER BY THE BLIND. *Oedipus* by Sophocles; adapted by Ted Hughes. June 12, 2005. Directed by Ike Schambelan; with George Ashiotis, Melanie Boland, Nicholas Viselli, J.M. McDonough, Pamela Sabaugh. *Hamlet*. Revival of the play by William Shakespeare. May 21, 2006. Directed by Ike Schambelan; with George Ashiotis, Melanie Boland, Nick Cordileone, John Little, Pamela Sabaugh, Nicholas Viselli.

THEATRE AT ST. CLEMENT'S. *Waiting for Godot* by Samuel Beckett. November 16, 2005. Directed by Alan Hruska; with Sam Coppola, Joseph Ragno, Ed Setrakian, Martin Shakar. *The Contrast* by Royall Tyler. April 15, 2006. Directed by Peter Bloch; with Lindsey Andersen, Catie Campbel, Matthew Cowles, Zachary Green, Emily Hartford, Kyle T. Jones, Nicholas Uber Leonard, Jesse May, Rachel Sullivan.

THEATRE ROW THEATRES. THE ACORN. *Einstein's Gift* by Vern Thiessen. October 16, 2005. Directed by Ron Russell; with Shawn Elliott, Aasif Mandvi, James Wallert, Melissa Friedman, Sarah Winkler, Glenn Fleshler, Godfrey L. Simmons Jr., Nilaja Sun. THE BECKETT. *Haymarket* by Zayd Dohm. December 12, 2005. Directed by Stephen Sakowsko; with Morgan Baker, Birgit Huppuch, Judson Jones, Dennis McNitt, Squeaky Moore, D. Zhonzinsky. *India Awaiting* by Anne Marie Cummings. October 23, 2005. Directed by Tyler Marchant; with Maulik Pancholy, Margot White, Naheed Khan, Robert Ian Mackenzie, Patricia Mauceri, Alok Tewari. *Lovely Day* by Leslie Ayvazian. January 22, 2006. Directed by Blair Brown; with Deirdre O'Connell, David Rasche, Javier Picayo.

Didi and Gogo: Sam Coppola and Joseph Ragno in Samuel Beckett's Waiting for Godot. *Photo: Joan Marcus*

No Child by Nilaja Sun. May 10, 2006. Directed by Hal Brooks; with Ms. Sun. THE CLURMAN. *Bag Fulla Money* by Scott Brooks. January 16, 2006. Directed by Sam Viverito; with Diana De La Cruz, Amber Dow, Heather Dilly, Jon Ecklund, Richard Mazda, Stu Richel, Darius Stone, Christopher Wisner, David White. *Transatlantic Liaison* by Fabrice Rozie. March 1, 2006. Directed by John McLean; with Elizabeth Rothan, Matthew S. Tompkins. THE LION. *Julius Caesar.* Revival of the play by William Shakespeare. August 7, 2005. Directed by Beverly Bullock; with Geoffrey Dawe, John Montague, Marcus Dean Fuller, Shari Paige Acker, C. Daniel Barr, Wayne Preston Chambers, Corey Cicci, Eric Conley, Susanna Harris, Peter Herrick, Gretchen Howe, Douglas Clark Johnson, Matt Mercer, Jeff Riebe, Ellen Seltz, Lillian Small, Nicholas Stannard, Jared Waltzer, Melon Wedick. *Jane Ho* by John Pallotta. November 4, 2005. Directed by Arian Blanco; with Mikaela Kafka, Daina Michelle Griffin, Heather Male, A.B. Lugo, Liche Ariza. *Romeo and Juliet.* Revival of the play by William Shakespeare. January 13, 2006. Directed by Beverly Bullock; with Peter Richards, Katherine Kelly Lidz, Peter Herrick, Marca Leigh, Jonathan J. Lidz, Eric Jorgensen, Jared Waltzer, Geoffrey Dawe, Vanessa Elder, Daniel Barr, Michael Ernest Moore, Nicholas Stannard, Sidney Fortner, Eric Conley, Matt Stapleton, James Beaman, Benjamin Rishworth, Douglas Clark Johnson, Gretchen Howe. *Savages* by Anne Nelson. March 9, 2006. Directed by Chris Jorie; with Julie Danao-Salkin, Brett Holland, Jim Howard, James Matthew Ryan. *Prime Time* by Alex De Witt. May 5, 2006. Directed by Fern R. Lopez; with Steve Beauchamp, Vance Bradford, Julia Montgomery Brown, Aquarius Cheers, Ms. De Witt, Dudley F. Findlay Jr., David F. Gandy, Harlin C. Kearsley, Peyton List, Spencer List, Jack Mulcahy. STUDIO THEATRE. *Christine Jorgensen Reveals* by Bradford Louryk. February 16, 2006. Directed by Josh Hecht; with Mr. Louryk, Rob Grace.

THEATRE THREE. *Broken Journey* by Glyn Maxwell. November 12, 2005. Directed by Ted Altschuler; with Craig Smith, Michael Surabian, Elise Stone, Sheila O'Malley, Joe Rayome. *Candy and Dorothy* by David Johnston. January 9, 2006. Directed by Kevin Newbury; with Sloane Shelton, Vince Gatton, Nell Gwynn, Brian Fuqua, Amir Arison. *Wolfpit* by Glyn Maxwell. April 7, 2006. Directed by Robert Hupp; with Craig Smith, Elise Stone, Angela Madden, Jason Crowl, Joe Menino, Jason O'Connell, John Lenartz, Nicole Raphael, Margo Passalaqua.

37 ARTS THEATER. *Billy Connolly Live!* by Billy Connolly. May 11, 2006. With Mr. Connolly. *Lee Evans: Same Planet, Different World* by Lee Evans. May 25, 2006. With Mr. Evans.

TRIAD THEATRE. *The Great Divide* by Charles Messina. June 15, 2005. Directed by Mr. Messina; with Ernie Curcio, Gina Ferranti, Johnny Tammaro, Barbie Insua. *Bush Is Bad: The Musical Cure for the Blue States Blues.* Musical revue by Joshua Rosenblum. September 29, 2005. Directed and choreographed by Gary Slavin; with Kate Baldwin, Neal Mayer, Michael McCoy. *Kabbalah* by Tuvia Tenenbom. November 22, 2005. Directed by Ms. Tenenbom; with Mario Golden, Adam Hayes, Emily Stern, Michael Shimkin, Oliver Conant, Alison Ritchie. *The Accidental Pervert.* Solo performance piece by Andrew Goffman. February 2, 2006. Directed by Charles Messina; with Mr. Goffman. *Her Song.* Musical revue by Brenda and Barry Levitt. February 19, 2006. Directed by Mr. Levitt; with B.J. Crosby, Nina Hennessy, Terri Klausner, Deborah Tranelli. *One Man's War* by Sammy Dallas Bayes. March 11, 2006. Directed by Mr. Bayes; with Ed Bergtold, Jeremy Eric Feldman, James Gagne, Max Hambleton, Daniel Kipler, Aubrey Levy, Mike Marinaccio, Brian Nemiroff, Chris Perry, Scott Seliga, Andrew Smith, Lane Wray.

UNDER ST. MARKS. *Hell Cab* by Will Kern. January 14, 2006. Directed by Akia; with Seth Abrams, David Anthony, Rey Oliver Bune, Elizabeth Burke, Patrick J. Egan, Reginald Ferguson, Crystal Franceschini, Steve Gribben, Josh Hyman, Nic Mevoli, Sahadev Poudel, Adam Purvis, Rob Richardson, Sarah Sirota, Lindsey Smith, Renee Valenti, Nicole Watson, Reagan Wilson. *The Understudies* by Jeff Bedillion. January 13, 2006. Directed by Mr. Bedillion; with Robert Abid, Tomas Bell, Stefanie Eris, Jennifer Susi, Maiken Wiese.

URBAN STAGES. *Marion Bridge* by Daniel MacIvor. October 1, 2005. Directed by Susan Fenichell; with Susan Louise O'Connor, Christa Scott-Reed, Henny Russell. *Safety* by Chris Thorpe. January 23, 2006. Directed by Daisy Walker; with David Wilson Barnes, Katie Firth, Susan Molloy, Jeffrey Clarke. *Bulrusher* by Eisa Davis. March 11, 2006. Directed by Leah C. Gardiner; with Robert Beitzel, Peter Bradbury, Charlotte Colavin, Zabryna Guevara, Guiesseppe Jones, Tinashe Kajese. *Devil Land* by Desi Moreno-Penson. April 14, 2006. Directed by Jose Zayas; with Ms. Moreno-Penson, Paula Ehrenberg, Miguel Sierra. *Nerve* by Adam Szymkowicz. May 21, 2006. Directed by Scott Ebersold; with Susan O'Connor, Travis York.

VILLAGE THEATRE. *Graham Norton: Know All.* Solo performance piece by Graham Norton. October 4, 2005. With Mr. Norton.

WALKERSPACE. *Big Times* by Mia Barron, Maggie Lacey, Danielle Skraastad. June 18, 2005. Directed by Leigh Silverman; with Mses. Barron, Lacey, Skraastad. *Strom Thurmond Is Not a Racist* by Thomas Bradshaw. August 11, 2005. Directed by Eliza Hittman; with James Stanley, Monica Stith, Jerry Zellers. *Einstein's Secret Letters (a love story)* by J.B. Edwards. September 26, 2005. Directed by G. Beaudin; with Marvin Starkman, Memory Contento, Waltrudis Buck, R. Edward Tyler II. *The Girl in the Flammable Skirt* by Aimee Bender; adapted by Bridgette Dunlap. October 15, 2005. Directed by Ms. Dunlap; with Jeff Addiss, Cormac Bluestone, Ryan Canfield, Alexis Grausz, Kathryn Ekblad, Jeff Hughes, Madeleine Maby, Sara Montgomery, Elizabeth Neptune. *The Private Life of the Master Race* by Bertolt Brecht; translated by Binyamin Shalom. April 5, 2006. Directed by James Phillip Gates; with Kristen Barnett, Tracy Hostmeyer, Betty Hudson, David Beck, Nicholas Daniele, Peter Levine, Khris Lewin, Brad Russell. *Bone Portraits* by Deborah Stein. May 5, 2006. Directed by Lear deBessonet; with Mike Crane, Adam Green, Gian-Murray Gianino, Miriam Silverman, Jessi Wortham.

WHITE BIRD PRODUCTIONS. *The Barbie Project.* November 11, 2005. Directed by Michael Schiralli; with Paul Boocock, Redwal Dance Company, the Jones Twins, Janice Lowe, Lorrie Harrison, Cindy Hanson, Kathryn Dickinson.

WINGS THEATRE COMPANY. *The Audition* by Betsy Head. September 7, 2005. Directed by Ms. Head. *Jigsaw* by Jayson McDonald. October 31, 2005. Directed by Mr. McDonald; with Shannon Black, Anthony Crep, Paola Grande, Hanna Hayes, Mark Lawrence, Lil Malinich. *Rachel.* Musical by Lou Green. December 1, 2005. Directed by Scott Peg; with Kay Arnold, James Bormann, Karen Dillie, John Kelly, Susan Jerome, Geany Masai, Leslie Shreve, Mark Silberberg. *Through a Naked Lens* by George Barthel. December 19, 2005. Directed by L.J. Kleeman and Richard Bacon; with

JoHary Ramos, Stephen Smith, Raymond O. Wagner, Laura Beth Wells, Mr. Bacon, Shay Coleman, Tracy Gaillard, Heather Murdock, Joe Pepe, Sheila Shaigany. *Galileo: Father Dearest* by Barbara Bregstein. January 25, 2006. With Jack Drucker, Margot Staub, Warren Katz, Michael Muldoon, Marguerite Moray, JessAnn Smith, Isaac Scranton. *Tiger by the Tail* by Frawley Becker. March 27, 2006. Directed by Jules Ochoa; with Terrence Michael McCrossan, Franklin John Westbrooks, Steven Hauck, Nick Marcotti, Christian Rummel, Matthew Wilkas, Dan Cordle, Susan Burns, Sebastian LaCause. *Cowboys.* Musical with book and lyrics by Clint Jeffries; music by Paul Johnson. April 28, 2006. Directed by Jeffrey Coorick; with Stephen Cabral, Nick Cianfrogna, Jesse Factor, Jennifer Fagundes, Rory Hughes, Brynn Neal, Brian Ogilvie, Jeff Sheets, David Tacheny.

WORKSHOP THEATER COMPANY. *Pineapple and Henry* by Linda Segal Crawley. June 18, 2005. Directed by Scott C. Sickles; with Ellen Dolan, Raymond Alvin, Dee Dee Friedman, Harry Peerce, Frank Piazza, David M. Pincus, Brian Voelcker. *Raisins Not Virgins* by Sharbari Z. Ahmed. September 23, 2005. Directed by Thomas Cote; with Ms. Ahmed, Marc Geller, Anna Itty, Nelson Lugo, Harry Peerce, Anar Vilas. *Stealing Home.* Solo performance piece by Raymond Alvin. September 20, 2005. Directed by Holli Harms; with Mr. Alvin. *Messiah* by Martin Sherman. November 18, 2005. Directed by David Gautschy; with Alexandra Devin, Carrie Edel, Letty Ferrer, Jenny Greeman, Tobi Kanter, Stewart Steinberg, Peter Stoll. *Desire in the Suburbs* by Frederic Glover. January 13, 2006. Directed by Timothy Scott Harris. *Love Me Knots* by Dave Riedy. January 19, 2006. Directed by Holli Harms. *Caseload.* Musical with book by Levy Lee Smith; music and lyrics by Mark Bruckner. April 28, 2006. Directed by Mary Beth Easley; with Ellen Barry, Sandflower Dyson, Brian C. Homer, Erik Kilpatrick, Madeline McCray, Gary Mink, Rob Morgan, Terence Mueller, Darcie Siciliano, Ayanna Siverls.

THE SEASON AROUND
THE UNITED STATES

STEINBERG/AMERICAN THEATRE CRITICS
NEW PLAY AWARD AND CITATIONS
○ ○ ○ ○ ○
A DIRECTORY OF NEW
UNITED STATES PRODUCTIONS

THE AMERICAN THEATRE CRITICS ASSOCIATION (ATCA) is the organization of drama critics in all media throughout the United States. One of the group's stated purposes is "To increase public awareness of the theater as a national resource." To this end, ATCA has annually cited outstanding new plays produced around the US, which were excerpted in our series beginning with the 1976–77 volume. As we continue our policy of celebrating playwrights and playwriting in *Best Plays*, we offer essays on the recipients of the 2006 Harold and Mimi Steinberg/ATCA New Play Award and Citations. The Steinberg/ATCA New Play Award of $25,000 was given to Lee Blessing for his play *A Body of Water*. The Steinberg/ATCA New Play Citations were given to Adam Rapp for *Red Light Winter*—which was also named a Best Play during its Off Broadway run—and August Wilson for *Radio Golf*. Citation honorees receive prizes of $7,500 each.

The ATCA awards are funded by the Harold and Mimi Steinberg Charitable Trust, which supports theater throughout the United States with its charitable giving. The awards were renamed this year, putting the Steinberg family name first, to honor the trust's renewed (and enhanced) commitment to the honors. The Steinberg/ATCA New Play Award and Citations are given in a ceremony at Actors Theatre of Louisville. Essays in the next section—by Dominic P. Papatola (*St. Paul Pioneer Press*) and Christopher Rawson (*Pittsburgh Post-Gazette*)—celebrate the Steinberg/ATCA Citation honorees. An essay by Chris Jones on *Red Light Winter* appears in The Best Plays of 2005–2006 section of this volume.

ATCA's 13th annual M. Elizabeth Osborn Award for a new playwright was voted to Steven Tomlinson for *American Fiesta*, which was produced in 2005 by the State Theatre in Austin, Texas.

The process of selecting these outstanding plays is as follows: any American Theatre Critics Association member may nominate the first full professional production of a finished play (not a reading or an airing as a play-in-progress) that premieres outside New York City during the calendar year under consideration.

Nominated 2005 scripts were studied and discussed by the New Plays Committee chaired by Elizabeth Maupin (*The Orlando Sentinel*). The committee included ATCA members Jonathan Abarbanel (freelance, Chicago), Misha Berson (*The Seattle Times*), Jackie Demaline (*The Cincinnati Enquirer*), Michael Elkin (*Jewish Exponent,* Philadelphia), Bill Gale (Theater New England), Barbara Gross (freelance, Rockville, Maryland), Claudia W. Harris (freelance, Orem, Utah), George Hatza (*Reading Eagle*), Bill Hirschman (*South Florida Sun-Sentinel*), Kevin Nance (*Chicago Sun-Times*) and Wendy Parker (*Village Mill*, Virginia).

Committee members made their choices on the basis of script rather than production. If the timing of nominations and openings prevents some works from being considered in any given year, they may be eligible for consideration the following year if they haven't since moved to New York City.

2006 Steinberg/ATCA New Play Award

A BODY OF WATER

By Lee Blessing

○ ○ ○ ○ ○

Essay by Dominic P. Papatola

> WREN: Try to relax. Just let yourself . . . relax. That's the only way you're going to get through this. And you know what? That's when memories really come anyway, when all the stress melts and we realize it's enough to be, well . . . here—in a lovely room with a lovely view. Memory's friendly, but it's shy. It wants an invitation. It wants to creep back quietly and nestle at out feet. It wants to pretend it's never been gone.

PHYSICALLY, WE'RE MOSTLY made of water. Psychologically, we're mostly made of memories. Both of these core elements are fluid. The past meanders through our consciousness like a river, taking twists and turns for reasons unknown and arbitrary. Both change form when subjected to outside forces. Water can disappear into vapor or freeze so hard you can drive a car on it. Memories color or fade with time, or even reshape in the extremes of stress or pleasure or trauma. In *A Body of Water*, Lee Blessing ponders what happens when our memories are washed away.

As the lights rise, 50-somethings Moss and Avis wake one morning in what seems like paradise. The house is contemporary but refined, gorgeous but not ostentatious, nestled on a bucolic hill somewhere, surrounded by water. Their clothes are expensive and tasteful. If you could smell the coffee in Moss's mug, it would be something expensive and hand-roasted.

But there's trouble in this placid dream house. Just as Moss and Avis are unable to place their setting, or to identify whether the water that surrounds them is lake or river or ocean, they can't place themselves. They don't know their names. They don't know how they're related to each other—if at all. And they have no idea how they came to be where they are.

They're an intelligent pair, obviously accustomed to navigating through difficult situations. The ease of their communication—finishing each other's thoughts and sometimes using the same interjections simultaneously—suggests some kind of long-running relationship. And

311

Clean slate: Edward Herrmann in A Body of Water. *Photo: Michal Daniel*

they're in no immediate danger—the room is comfortable, their closets are stuffed with designer duds and breakfast is on the way. In another situation, this late-middle-age couple in bathrobes might be mistaken for characters in a Noël Coward comedy.

BUT FOOD, CLOTHING and shelter are not enough. Comfort they have but context they lack, and without it, Moss and Avis are adrift, perhaps soon to become unmoored:

> MOSS: Maybe we're just acquaintances. This is just a glitch. We'll be on track any minute. The old chain'll engage and—(*Suddenly*) Maybe I sell houses like this. You could be a prospective buyer.
>
> AVIS: With whom you went to bed?
>
> MOSS: It happens.
>
> AVIS: Wouldn't one of us have a car? (*Her tone changing.*) This is the worst feeling in the world.

High-end real estate aside, Moss and Avis are lodgers in an existential nightmare. It's reminiscent of the antechamber to the Great Beyond in Sartre's *No Exit,* or perhaps the seaside tower in an Ionesco play, which might be retitled, *The Mission-Style Chairs.*

The setting is significant: In the way they speak and the manner in which they conduct themselves, Moss and Avis are clearly the products of privilege. In the Guthrie Theater's world premiere production, Edward Herrmann and Michael Learned mulled a number of possibilities. Perhaps they were terrorists, flown via helicopter to a safe house for debriefing or deprogramming. Perhaps they were man and wife, a theory they test by flashing their robes open to each other, hoping that "birthmarks, scars, a mole pattern" will jog their memories.

But Moss and Avis never seriously consider the possibility that they don't, somehow, deserve to be in this lovely house. Moss's libidinous-realtor

---

There is trouble in this placid dream house.

---

theory notwithstanding, neither ever seriously considers the possibility that they might be interlopers. Or grifters. Or even the caretakers, playing dress-up and spending a naughty night in the master bedroom.

They're nice enough folks, but though it's benign enough, they also have something of an entitlement complex. This attitude sets the context of the play as much as the contemporary furnishings of the house: We're not only undoubtedly in the United States, but situated in part of and time in America where affluence can be taken for granted, where *noblesse* has no *oblige* and where the prevailing culture defines identity by one's possessions rather than one's character.

Does that notion weave somehow into the gestalt of the play? By continually looking outward for ways to define ourselves, have we lost our ability to find ourselves within? Perhaps. When Wren (Michelle O'Neill)—a pretty twenty-something about the right age to be Moss and Avis's daughter—enters the house, she's toting breakfast, familiarity and a hint of menace. She knows who Moss and Avis are (and is perhaps the only one with this certainty—a year after its premiere, Blessing himself confessed only that he's "getting closer" to figuring that out), but she has her own reasons for keeping the information to herself.

We now discover one of the only (apparently) solid facts of the play: Through some combination of circumstance, Moss and Avis have together acquired a syndrome that has rubbed them clean. They wake each morning, naked in bed next to each other, their intelligence intact, their knowledge of things etymological and 911 calls in place but their personal histories utterly blank.

And Wren? The flow of her character has a few possible tributaries:

Maybe she's their attorney, trying to jog back their memories so that they can defend themselves against charges that they murdered their 11-year-old daughter and dumped her body in the water outside. Makes sense—and she's got the grisly morgue photos to prove it.

Maybe she's their caretaker, trying to keep them active and engaged by giving them different stories. That makes sense as well—If this is Moss and Avis's house, they obviously can afford live-in care.

Or maybe she's their daughter who, after years of caring for her parents, has grown weary and periodically a little cruel toward her parents:

> WREN: Do you know what it's like taking care of you every day? Oh, there's a nurse, a male nurse named Ernie. He helps some days. But mostly it's just you and me. And every morning it is *the exact same thing.* Hello . . . who are you? Who am I? Who are *you?* And I

Fog of reality: Michelle O'Neill, Michael Learned and Edward Herrmann in A Body of Water. *Photo: Michal Daniel*

tell you, and you're grateful—and you forget again the next day and get all scared again, so I tell you again. And again. And again. Every day. And sometimes, I lie—yes, I lie. I make up a whole, huge story about a daughter named Robin, 'cause that's what I always wished you'd named me instead of Wren. I work out scenario after scenario, tell you you're physicists or chess champions or revolutionaries or chess champions or—

MOSS: You're lying.

WREN: No. No, *now* I'm telling the truth. And you know what? If you were in my place, facing this situation day after day, you'd do the same damn thing.

And this perhaps makes the most sense of all. It's certainly the explanation on which Blessing spends the most time, and the one to which the audience almost inevitably settles by the time the curtain rings down.

THERE IS A DREADFULNESS in Moss and Avis's situation, and, even if they can't conjure anything of their own pasts from day to day, this looming sense of horror is never far from them. They can pretend to be a "normal" family, perusing the *National Geographic*, doing crossword puzzles and plotting jaunts into town. They can distract themselves with thoughts of moseying into the garden or slinking into the bedroom. They can even create their own elaborate back-stories. But they can't know for sure. And they can't escape themselves.

It's a discomfiting feeling for the characters, to be sure, but also for the audience. Sitting in the theater, we progress through a variety of reactions—intrigue, confusion, perhaps impatience and annoyance. We collectively put on our detective caps, thinking ahead of the action that's in front of us, projecting our own prejudices and values into the futures of the characters. Perhaps intentionally, Blessing allows us the time and space in the play to go a few steps ahead, to work out a likely conclusion for ourselves, helping us to create a sense of anticipation, a yearning to find out if we were "right."

As the play works its way to conclusion—"climax" seems too strong a word for an evening that's so knotty and contemplative—Moss, Avis, Wren and the audience have worked out a few days' worth of scenarios. Each has gone through his or her respective terrors, pangs of guilt, flashes of anger and brief glimmerings of joy for what we can only assume to be the thousandth time.

And then, Blessing pulls the switcheroo on us. What if memory—the thing that holds our identity together—also proves to be our undoing?

It's a tangy proposition, and Blessing presents it casually. Avis is off in the kitchen and, in a quiet moment together, Moss is finally able to put the words and sentiments together in a way that compels Wren to produce a piece of evidence about their lives that's just as explosive and every bit as disturbing as the morgue photos. It's a note, ostensibly written by Avis the day before she drove their car off a cliff in a planned murder-suicide. In it, Avis talks about how her perfect life with Moss was not, in the end, enough. How she didn't trust a lifetime of experiences. So Avis goes snooping, searching for the "truth" about her husband. She uncovers no surprises, no evidence of a secret life. But she does find a journal. Wren hands the note to Moss, who reads:

> MOSS: "Page after page of notes about things I'd said or looks I'd given him or tunes I'd hummed or how I brushed my teeth or redid a room or cooked carrots or—it was endless. An endless parade of small comments, criticizing everything I was or said or did. The journal was titled 'Not Worth Mentioning,' and it was full. The final entry said, 'Time to burn this one.'"

Avis is dead. Moss survived the crash, physically intact but, in a cruelly ironic twist, unable to access those small memories that bedeviled him so.

THERE IS A MOMENT of silence. And then we hear Avis's voice calling cheerily from the kitchen.

> MOSS: For God's sake, don't you see her?
>
> WREN: Of course I see her.

Wren departs. Moss and Avis begin their conversation with the same words that opened the play. Moss is devastated, but that feeling will fade before the next morning. Probably.

In a few lines, the audience will applaud, gather their belongings and depart as well. Unlike Moss, they'll be able to recall what just happened here when they wake up tomorrow. But like their befuddled protagonist, they'll never be quite certain if what they remembered was right.

2006 Steinberg/ATCA New Play Citation

RADIO GOLF

By August Wilson

○ ○ ○ ○ ○

Essay by Christopher Rawson

HARMOND: This is 1997. Things have changed. This is America. This is the land of opportunity. I can be mayor. I can be anything I want.

AT THE END, AUGUST WILSON was doing something new. We've heard this optimism before in his Pittsburgh Cycle, but not from a successful entrepreneur of the black middle class. But in Wilson's 10th play, with the purposefully un-Wilsonian title of *Radio Golf*, he takes as his protagonist Harmond Wilks, college educated, with a plausible chance of being the first black mayor of Pittsburgh.

Directed by Timothy Douglas, *Radio Golf* premiered April 28, 2005, the day after Wilson turned 60, at New Haven's Yale Repertory Theatre—where the first five of Wilson's cycle of plays set in different decades of the 20th century had made their debuts. It showed some awkwardness in dealing with this new subject matter and speech, but it was clearly an August Wilson play, with the familiar conflict between aspiration and a heritage that both oppresses and sustains. By its second production, directed by Kenny Leon for an August 10 opening at the Mark Taper Forum in Los Angeles, Wilson had a finished script, awaiting only sharpening and polishing on the way to its eventual New York debut.

But between New Haven and Los Angeles, fate intervened in the form of liver cancer, diagnosed too late for successful treatment. So Wilson worked on the revision of *Radio Golf* under a sentence of death.

He may have had a premonition. In a lengthy interview in December 2004, he spoke of his upcoming 60th birthday. "At a certain age, you should be prepared to go at any time. [. . .] There's more behind me than ahead. I think of dying every day." A lot of his childhood friends had died, he said. That feeling of mortality deepened when his old friend and producer, Benjamin Mordecai, also just turned 60, died shortly after *Radio Golf* opened.

Reclaiming narratives: Richard Brooks and Anthony Chisholm in Radio Golf *at Yale Repertory Theatre. Photo: Carol Rosegg*

So, two weeks after the Los Angeles opening, with only six weeks to live and with news spreading of his terrible illness, Wilson expressed satisfaction that he had lived to complete his cycle. "I've lived a blessed life," he said. "I'm ready." His death came October 2.

In lamenting his loss, we focus on the creative flood stilled too soon. Wilson had other plays underway, plus a novel, a collection of poems, screenplays and more. But it is best to focus, as he did, on his achievement in bringing all 10 plays to fruition in just 21 years. Already 39 when *Ma Rainey's Black Bottom* reached Broadway in 1984, he worked fast and hard. At least death, which would have come too early no matter when, waited until his grand project was complete.

THE LAST OF THE 10 Pittsburgh Cycle plays to be written, *Radio Golf* also ends the sequence. It is set in 1997 during a confrontation over the economic redevelopment of the Hill District where Wilson grew up and where all the plays but one take place. The conflict between redevelopment and the historical soul of what used to be a vibrant, black-centered city within a city looks both backward and, with prescience, forward: As this is written in 2006, a battle rages over a plan to appropriate the lower Hill for Pittsburgh's first slots casino, a plan eerily reminiscent of the 1950s, when that same area, then the heart of the Hill, was ripped out by a massive urban "renewal" from which it has never recovered.

A similar struggle between economic power and the spiritual health of the community runs through most of the plays. But in *Radio Golf*, along with references to Model Cities, Mellon Bank, black radio stations and federal set-asides, there is a slick modernity that feels eons distant from the doomed 1980s of *King Hedley II* or the feisty 1970s of *Jitney*. For the first

---

At the end, August Wilson was doing something new.

---

time in the Pittsburgh Cycle, we meet the black bourgeoisie in the person of Harmond, whose family made its money in real estate.

It's no surprise to discover that Harmond is the grandson of Caesar Wilks, the slum landlord who, in *Gem of the Ocean*, patrolled black Pittsburgh on behalf of the white mill owners. As Harmond's ambitious wife, Mame, and partner, Roosevelt Hicks, point out, he has had money, education and position handed to him. Now he may be the Democratic choice to run for mayor.

Harmond is also the survivor of twins. Raymond was an idealist, an athletic star who gave up an ivy league scholarship to go to a black college and ended up dying in Vietnam out of a sense of duty. Harmond's plan for high-rise apartments and chain-stores has a strain of idealism, too, but it threatens traditional community values, as when Wal-Mart knocks out a small town's Main Street.

The play is set in the storefront office of Bedford Hills Redevelopment, Inc., an offshoot of Wilks Realty. The entrepreneurial dream is most vigorously expressed by Harmond's friend and partner, Roosevelt:

> ROOSEVELT: [. . .] I'm at the table! There was a time they didn't let any blacks at the table. You opened the door. You shined the shoes. You served the drinks. And they went in the room and made the deal. I'm in the room! Them motherfuckers who bought and traded them railroads . . . how do you think they did it? This is business. This is the way it's done in America. [. . .]

The cautionary counter to this glee comes from Old Joe Barlow, 79, one of Wilson's wise, eccentric elders. He's a living chronicle of seemingly random dates, a street-corner historian, philosopher and guru. "America is a giant slot machine," he says. "You walk up and put in your coin and it spits it back out. [. . .] Is the problem with the quarter or the machine?" Harmond responds:

> HARMOND: If it don't take all the quarters you fix it. [. . .] Some people say you got to tear it down to fix it. Some people say you got to build it up to fix it. Some people say they don't know how to fix it. [. . .]
>
> OLD JOE: I say get a new machine. What you say?
>
> HARMOND: We fixing it. We're going to redevelop this whole area. We'll get the Hill District growing so fast, people from all over will start moving back.

Harmond takes Old Joe's broad metaphor of black powerlessness and applies it specifically to the Hill, expressing confidence approaching hubris in his

Century's end: Rocky Carroll and John Earl Jelks in Radio Golf *at the Mark Taper Forum. Photo: Craig Schwartz*

dream of reversing the diaspora of recent decades. But there is corruption in the system that has tainted even him, and he must come to terms with the past. For Harmond, the central conflict is between his dreams of entrepreneurial and political success and the demands of his heritage, symbolized by a dilapidated mansion at 1839 Wylie Avenue.

THAT MANSION, WHICH IS TO be torn down for the big development, turns out to be Aunt Ester's house, a monument to an ancient legacy of black identity and spirit. Harmond doesn't know this, but we do. In the chronology of the cycle, we last heard of that house in the 1980s play, *King Hedley II*, when Aunt Ester died. We heard about Aunt Ester before that in the 1960s play, *Two Trains Running*, when she gave spiritual succor to a young man named Sterling. We also met Aunt Ester and saw 1839 Wylie Avenue for ourselves in *Gem of the Ocean*, the play set in 1904.

For those who know *Gem*, the names Wilks and Barlow in *Radio Golf* raise expectations, and Harmond's and Old Joe's climactic discovery of their relationship half way through Act II changes their lives. Harmond is the grandson of Caesar, and Old Joe is the son of Citizen Barlow and Caesar's half-sister, Black Mary. It is she who, in *Gem*, agrees to take on her mentor's mantle, becoming the latest Aunt Ester in a line reaching back to 1619, when the first African slaves arrived in Virginia.

The descendents of Caesar and Black Mary—whose names are a dichotomy of worldly and spiritual power—have been connected for years, because Caesar and then his son (Harmond's father) regularly paid the taxes on Black Mary/Ester's house at 1839 Wylie. This is an ironic reversal of the Biblical "render unto Caesar" directive, since it shows Caesar paying tribute in government coin on behalf of the spiritual. But Harmond's father stopped those tax payments in 1985, when Aunt Ester died, and her legacy was quickly forgotten, even by Old Joe. He did name his daughter Black Mary, but apparently neither this Black Mary nor anyone else carried on the Aunt Ester line. That absence in *Radio Golf* marks the loss of the past that lays the Hill open to exploitation.

The central conflict of the play is between Aunt Ester's legacy and bourgeois greed, but its major ongoing action is Harmond's recovery of his own history and its connection to family and community. For those who know *Gem*, that is heartfelt drama enough. But some reviews of the premiere version of *Radio Golf* suggested it did not suffice, and Wilson clearly agreed. So Aunt Ester, who was not even mentioned in the first script, is invoked openly in the second, sharpening the transforming effect of the recovered past on Harmond. It is tempting to believe Wilson might have gone even further down this road in subsequent polishing.

Radio Golf also has another, more theatrical climax involving Sterling Johnson, the young man from *Two Trains Running*, who reappears here 28 years later as an itinerant handyman, joining with Old Joe to call Harmond back to his roots. Sterling memorably attacks Roosevelt:

> STERLING: [. . .] You a Negro. White people will get confused and call you a nigger but they don't know like I know. I know the truth of it. I'm a nigger. Negroes are the worst thing in God's creation. Niggers got style. Negroes got blind-eyetist. A dog knows it's a dog. A cat knows it's a cat. But a Negro don't know he's a Negro. He thinks he's a white man. It's Negroes like you who hold us back.

Wilson has Roosevelt respond memorably:

> ROOSEVELT: [. . .] It's not my fault if your daddy's in jail, your mama's on drugs, your little sister's pregnant and the kids don't have any food 'cause the welfare cut off the money. Roosevelt Hicks ain't holding nobody back. [. . .]

The only other place in the cycle we hear something like Roosevelt's self-defense is in *Gem*, where Caesar indicts black shiftlessness with even greater vigor. Caesar and Roosevelt are as close to black villains as Wilson draws, but he is willing to give them their due, even finding some comedy in Roosevelt's meretricious argument that it is time for blacks to develop their own millionaires by whatever means.

WILL HARMOND ANSWER THE CALL to arms issued by Sterling and Old Joe? Reminding him of the alternative attractions of money, position and power are his partner and wife. Roosevelt is a wonderful portrait of a hungry capitalist, played with zest by James A. Williams in both New Haven and Los Angeles. It is Roosevelt's passion for golf that justifies the play's unusual title. Mame, played by Michele Shay in New Haven and Denise Burse in Los Angeles, wants the good things money can buy and has no respect for landmarks of past struggles. You couldn't pay her to move back to the Hill, no matter how redeveloped. But she doesn't get enough stage time to develop fully or to explain a late scene of marital crisis.

On the other side are Old Joe and Sterling, played in both productions by Anthony Chisholm and John Earl Jelks, key members of the Wilson theater family. Sterling speaks with increasing authority as the play progresses, adapting Old Joe's ramblings into a more pointed challenge. This comes to bear heavily on Harmond, played in New Haven by Richard

Brooks and in Los Angeles by Rocky Carroll. There's a stiffness to Harmond, a predilection for press-release prose. He gradually warms, but I wish he could be stirred sooner to recognize the significance of Aunt Ester's ancient ministry.

Wilson's great flow of language continues, albeit chastened by the contemporary scene. Tellingly, Harmond speaks with Wilson's most persuasive voice only when he awakens to the past. Until then, the most robust language is left to Old Joe and Sterling, although Roosevelt's greed also gives him verbal conviction. The joy he shares with Harmond when their biggest deal comes through turns into a materialist celebration in ironic counterpoint to the "juba" of *Joe Turner's Come and Gone.*

If it's a flaw that *Radio Golf* rewards a knowledge of *Gem*, so be it. You can't create an epic without the audience wanting to savor its interconnections. The Pittsburgh Cycle is itself what it depicts, a search for the prophetic voice that roots the present in the tragic and triumphant past. That voice belongs equally to Aunt Ester and August Wilson.

A DIRECTORY OF NEW UNITED STATES PRODUCTIONS

○ ○ ○ ○ ○

Compiled by Rue E. Canvin

T HIS LISTING INCLUDES professional productions that opened during the June 1, 2005–May 31, 2006 season. Its focus is on new plays—and other productions of note—by a variety of resident companies around the United States. Production information listed here in alphabetical order, by state, was supplied by the 76 producing organizations included. Resident theaters producing new plays and operating under contracts with Actors' Equity Association were queried for this comprehensive directory. Active US theater companies not included in this list may not have presented new (or newly revised) scripts during the year under review or had not responded to our query by July 1, 2006. Productions listed below are world premieres, US premieres, regional premieres, substantial revisions or otherwise worthy of note. Relatively new plays that have received widespread production are not listed here due to space and other considerations. Theaters in the US are encouraged to submit proposed listings of new works, new adaptations and other productions of significant concept or cast to the editor of *The Best Plays Theater Yearbook* series.

ALABAMA

Alabama Shakespeare Festival, Montgomery
Producing artistic director Geoffrey Sherman

Southern Writers' Project. February 3–6, 2006.

GEE'S BEND. By Elyzabeth Gregory Wilder. Direction, Janet Cleveland; lighting, Rebecca Dail; music direction, Brett Rominger; dramaturgy, Evalyn Baron; stage management, Janice Lane.

Sadie Pettway	Cheri Lynne	Nella	Margo Moorer
Alice; Asia	Maura Gale	Macon	James Bowen

THINKING OF YOU. By Peter Hicks. Direction, Nancy Rominger; lighting, Brian Elliott; dramaturgy, Susan Willis; stage management, Trudy L. Paxton-Mass.

Junie Mae Delacroix	Merideth Kaye Clark	Leonard Belle	Timothy Gittings
Celeste Delacroix	Greta Lambert	Arthur Fregonard	Greg Thornton
Sheldon Jennings	Mark Alan Jeter	Sharon Pendegast	Meghan Lisi

FOUR SPIRITS. By Sena Jeter Naslund and Elaine Wood Hughes. Direction, Gary Anderson; lighting, Brian Elliott; dramaturgy, Marlon M. Bailey; stage management, Sara Lee Howell.

Charlotte; Agnes La Fayt ... Georgette Norman	Charles Powers; Mike .... Yohance Myles
T.J. LaFayt; Mr. Bones .... Quinton Cockrell	Lionel Parrish .... Monrico Ward
Gloria Callahan .... Alketa Eboni Witcher	Cat Cartwright .... Jennifer Hunt
Christine Powers .... Kelly Taffe	Stella Silver .... Lauren Bloom
Edmund Powers .... Mikal Webb	Jonathan Green; others .... Doug Rossi

SANCTIFIED. By Javon Johnson; music by Ron Metcalf. Direction, Rajendra Ramoon Maharaj; lighting, Rebecca Dail; dramaturgy, Sybil Roberts; stage management, Kimberly J. First

Thelma .... Kellie Turner	Mister .... Chad Boseman
Bobby .... Drummond Crenshaw	Monique .... Alexis J. Phillips
Sister Jones .... Ramona Dunlap	Jamal .... Glenn Gordon
Sir .... Wayne Pretlow	Pastor .... Will Sims
Sister Sarah .... Clare Bathé	Deacon .... Frederick Strother
Clara .... Ebony Jo-Ann	

ARIZONA

Arizona Theatre Company, Tucson

David Ira Goldstein artistic director, Jessica L. Andrews managing director

PRIDE AND PREJUDICE. By Jane Austen; adapted by Jon Jory. September 16, 2005 (world premiere). Direction, Mr. Jory; choreography, Daniel Pelzig; scenery, Robert A. Dahlstrom; costumes, Michael Krass; lighting, Michael Philippi; sound, Stephen LeGrand; music, Peter Eckstrom; stage management, Glenn Bruner. Presented in association with Atlanta's Alliance Theatre Company and the San Jose Repertory Theatre.

Mr. Bennet .... David Pichette	Mr. Bingley; Fitzwilliam .... Liam Vincent
Lydia Bennet;	Mr. Darcy .... Anthony Marble
Georgiana .... Jennifer Erdmann	Mr. Lucas; others .... Remi Sandri
Elizabeth Bennet .... Julia Dion	Miss Bingley;
Mary Bennet;	Mrs. Gardiner .... Amy Resnick
Charlotte Lucas .... Sarah Roberts	Lt. Wickham .... Joe Knezevich
Jane Bennet .... Krista Hoeppner	Lady Catherine;
Mrs. Bennet .... Peggity Price	Housekeeper .... Pat Nesbit
Kitty Bennet .... Adele Bruni	Dancer; others .... Douglas B. Giorgis

Time: 1813. Place: Hertfordshire, England. Presented in two parts.

SHERLOCK HOLMES: THE FINAL ADVENTURE. By Steven Dietz; based on the 1889 play by William Gillette and Arthur Conan Doyle. March 9, 2006 (world premiere). Direction, David Ira Goldstein; scenery, Bill Forrester; costumes, David Kay Mickelsen; lighting, Dennis Parichy; composer, Roberta Carlson; sound, Brian Jerome Peterson; fight direction, Kenneth Merckx Jr.; stage management, Glenn Bruner. Presented in association with the Pasadena Playhouse.

Doctor Watson .... Victor Talmadge	Madge Larrabee .... Erin Bennett
Sherlock Holmes .... Mark Capri	Sid Prince .... Roberto Guajardo
The King of Bohemia .... Preston Maybank	Professor Moriarty .... Laurence Ballard
James Larrabee .... Kenneth Merckx Jr.	Ensemble .... H. Michael Croner,
Irene Adler .... Libby West	Jonathan Hicks

ARKANSAS

Arkansas Repertory Theatre, Little Rock
Robert Hupp producing artistic director

TOWNS FACING RAILROADS. By Jo McDougall. January 20, 2006 (world premiere). Direction, Eve Adamson; scenery, Mike Nichols; costumes, Olivia Koach; lighting, Matthew Webb; sound, M. Jason Pruzin; stage management, Julie Stemmler.
  Performed by Nancy Eyermann, Joseph Graves, JoAnn Johnson.

THE RETREAT FROM MOSCOW. By William Nicholson. April 14, 2006. Direction, Brad Mooy; scenery, Mike Nichols; costumes, Olivia Koach; lighting, Matthew Webb; sound, M. Jason Pruzin; stage management, Christina Gould.

Edward	Samuel Maupin	Alice	JoAnn Johnson
Jamie	Tom Bateman		

  Time: The present. Place: England. Presented in two parts.

BAD DATES. By Theresa Rebeck. March 3, 2006. Direction, Brad Mooy; scenery and properties; Christina Gould; costumes, Stephanie Crenshaw; lighting, Katharine Lowery; sound, M. Jason Pruzin; stage management, Christine Lomaka.

Haley .... Mary Proctor

CALIFORNIA

American Conservatory Theater, San Francisco
Carey Perloff artistic director, Heather Kitchen managing director

THE OVERCOAT. By Nikolai Gogol; adapted by Morris Panych and Wendy Gorling from the short story. August 31, 2005. Direction, Mr. Panych and Ms. Gorling; scenery, Ken MacDonald; costumes, Nancy Bryant; lighting, Alan Brodie; music, Dmitri Shostakovich; stage management, Jan Hodgson. Presented in association with the Canadian Stage Company, Glynis Henderson Productions and the Bushnell Center for the Performing Arts.

Man	Peter Anderson	Architect	Ryan Hollyman
Office Worker	Victoria Adilman	Sweatshop Worker	Matthew Hunt
Landlady's Mom	Manon Beaudoin	Tenant	Darren Hynes
Inmate	Matt Bois	Secretary	Cyndi Mason
Tailor	Mark Christmann	Head of Firm	Allan Morgan
New girl	Judi Closkey	Architect	Graham Percy
Office Worker	Diana Coatsworth	Inmate	Avi Phillips
Office Worker	Monica Dottor	Office Janitor	Derek Scott
Landlady	Tracey Ferencz	Thug	Sal Scozzari
Architect	Peter Grier	Architect	Courtenay Stevens
Office Management	Colin Heath	Inmate	Brahm Taylor

A NUMBER. By Caryl Churchill. May 3, 2006. Direction, Anna D. Shapiro; scenery, David Korins; costumes, Callie Floor; lighting, Russell H. Champa; sound, Rob Milburn and Michael Bodeen.

Bernard; Michael	Josh Charles	Salter	Bill Smitrovich

Berkeley Repertory Theatre

Tony Taccone artistic director, Susan Medak managing director

FINN IN THE UNDERWORLD. By Jordan Harrison. October 6, 2005 (world premiere). Direction, Les Waters; scenery, David Korins; costumes, Annie Smart; lighting, Matt Frey; sound, Darron L. West; dramaturgy, Scott Horstein; stage management, Kevin Johnson.

Rhoda	Randy Danson	Finn	Clifton Guterman
Gwen	Lorri Holt	Carver	Reed Birney

COMEDY ON THE BRIDGE. By Václav Kliment Klicpera; music by Bohuslav Martinu; adapted by Tony Kushner. November 11, 2005. Direction, Tony Taccone; scenery, Maurice Sendak and Kris Stone; costumes, Robin I. Shane; lighting, Donald Holder; sound, Rob Milburn and Michael Bodeen; stage management, Michael Suenkel. Presented in association with Yale Repertory Theatre.

Liskovite Sentry	Euan Morton	Sykos	Matt Farnsworth
Strokopounkutnik Sentry	Geoff Hoyle	Eva	Angelina Réaux
Popelka	Anjali Bhimani	Professor Ucitelli	William Youmans
Bedronyi	Martin Vidnovic	Captain Ladinsky	Henry DiGiovanni

BRUNDIBÁR. By Adolf Hoffmeister; music by Hans Krasá; adapted by Tony Kushner. November 11, 2005. Direction, Tony Taccone; scenery, Maurice Sendak and Kris Stone; costumes, Robin I. Shane; lighting, Donald Holder; sound, Rob Milburn and Michael Bodeen; stage management, Michael Suenkel. Presented in association with Yale Repertory Theatre.

Pepicek	Aaron Simon Gross	Policeman	Martin Vidnovic
Aninku	Devynn Pedell	Brundibár	Euan Morton
Ice Cream Seller	Henry DiGiovanni	Sparrow	Anjali Bhimani
Baker; Dog	Geoff Hoyle	Cat	Angelina Réaux
Milkman	Matt Farnsworth	Professor Ucitelli	William Youmans

9 PARTS OF DESIRE. By Heather Raffo. January 20, 2006. Direction, Joanna Settle; scenery, Antje Ellermann; costumes, Kasia Walicka Maimone; lighting, Peter West; sound, Obadiah Eaves; stage management, Nicole Dickerson.

Performed by Mozhan Marnò.

ZORRO IN HELL. By Culture Clash. March 23, 2006 (world premiere). Direction, Tony Taccone, scenery, Christopher Acebo; costumes, Christal Weatherly; lighting, Alexander V. Nichols; sound, Robbin E. Broad; fight direction, Dave Maier; dramaturgy, Shirley Fishman; stage management, Kimberly Mark Webb. Presented in association with La Jolla Playhouse.

Clasher	Richard Montoya	Diego; Zorro	Joseph Kamal
Kyle the Bear	Ric Salinas	200-Year-Old Woman	Sharon Lockwood
Don Ringo	Herbert Siguenza	El Musico	Vincent Christopher Montoya

Center Theatre Group, Los Angeles

Gordon Davidson founding artistic director, Michael Ritchie artistic director,
Charles Dillingham managing director

STUFF HAPPENS. By David Hare. June 5, 2005. Direction, Gordon Davidson; scenery, Ming Cho Lee; costumes, Candice Cain; lighting, Christopher Akerlind; sound, Jon

Gottlieb; music, Karl Fredrik Lundeberg; stage management, Mary Michele Miner; in the Mark Taper Forum.

George W. Bush	Keith Carradine	Jack Straw	Francis Guinan
Laura Bush; others	Jane Carr	David Manning	John Vickery
Dick Cheney	Dakin Matthews	Jonathan Powell;	
Donald Rumsfeld	John Michael Higgins	Dominique de Villepin	Stephen Spinella
Colin Powell	Tyrees Allen	Alistair Campbell;	
Condoleezza Rice	Lorraine Toussaint	Robin Cook	Paul Messinger
George Tenet; others	Mitchell Edmonds	Sir Richard Dearlove	John Rafter Lee
Paul Wolfowitz;		Philip Bassett	Jay Harik
Alan Simpson	Kip Gilman	Trevor Macdonald;	
Paul O'Neill; others	James Handy	Kofi Annan	Henry Brown
Dan Bartlett;		M. Gourdault-Montagne	Brian George
Jeremy Greenstock	James Gleason	Hans Blix	Alan Oppenheimer
Tony Blair	Julian Sands	African Official	Inger Tudor
Cherie Blair	Anna Khaja		

RADIO GOLF. By August Wilson. August 10, 2005. Direction, Kenny Leon; scenery, David Gallo; costumes, Susan Hilferty; lighting, Donald Holder; sound, Jon Gottlieb; music, Kathryn Bostic; stage management, Narda E. Alcorn and Mary K. Klinger; in the Mark Taper Forum.

Mame Wilks	Denise Burse	Sterling Johnson	John Earl Jelks
Harmond Wilks	Rocky Carroll	Elder Joseph Barlow	Anthony Chisholm
Roosevelt Hicks	James A. Williams		

Time: 1997. Place: The Hill District in Pittsburgh. Presented in two parts.

Urban renewal? John Earl Jelks, Denise Burse and Rocky Carroll in Radio Golf. *Photo: Craig Schwartz*

ROMANCE. By David Mamet. October 9, 2005. Direction, Neil Pepe; scenery, Robert Brill; costumes, Sarah Edwards; lighting, James F. Ingalls; sound, Obadiah Eaves; fight direction, Rick Sordelet; stage management, Matthew Silver. Presented in association with Atlantic Theater Company; in the Mark Taper Forum.

Prosecutor	Jim Frangione	Bailiff	Steven Hawley
Defendant	Steven Goldstein	Bernard	Noah Bean
Defense Attorney	Ed Begley Jr.	Doctor	Todd Weeks
Judge	Larry Bryggman		

Time: The present. Place: A courtroom. Presented in two parts.

THE DROWSY CHAPERONE. Musical with book by Bob Martin and Don McKellar; music and lyrics by Lisa Lambert and Greg Morrison. November 18, 2005. Direction and choreography by Casey Nicholaw; scenery, David Gallo; costumes, Gregg Barnes; lighting, Ken Billington and Brian Monahan; sound, Acme Sound Partners; orchestrations, Larry Blank; music direction and vocal arrangements, Phil Reno; dance and incidental music arrangements, Glen Kelly; stage management, Karen Moore; in the Ahmanson Theatre.

Man in Chair	Bob Martin	Gangster #1	Jason Kravits
Mrs. Tottendale	Georgia Engel	Gangster #2	Garth Kravits
Underling	Edward Hibbert	Aldolpho	Danny Burstein
Robert	Troy Britton Johnson	Janet	Sutton Foster
George	Eddie Korbich	Drowsy	Beth Leavel
Feldzieg	Lenny Wolpe	Trix	Kecia-Lewis Evans
Kitty	Jennifer Smith		

Ensemble: Linda Griffin, Angela Pupello, Joey Sorge, Patrick Wetzel, Keith A. Bearden, Suzanne Carlton.

Musical numbers included: "Fancy Dress," "Cold Feets," "Best Man for the Job," "Show Off," "As We Stumble Along," "I Am Aldolpho," "Accident Waiting to Happen," "Toledo Surprise," "Message From a Nightingale," "Bride's Lament," "Groom's Reverie," "I Remember Love," "I Do, I Do in the Sky."

Presented without intermission.

LEWIS AND CLARK REACH THE EUPHRATES. By Robert Schenkkan. December 11, 2005 (world premiere). Direction, Gregory Boyd; scenery, Jeff Cowie; costumes, Judith Dolan; lighting, Howell Binkley; music and sound, John Gromada; projections, Marc I. Rosenthal; fight direction, Steve Rankin; dramaturgy, Tom Bryant; stage management, Mary K. Klinger; in the Mark Taper Forum.

William Clark	Jeffrey Nordling	York	Eugene Lee
Meriwether Lewis	James Barbour		

Ensemble: Morgan Rusler, Tess Lina, Randy Oglesby, Tony Amendola, Ruben C. Gonzalez, Ty Mayberry, Roy Abramsohn.

Presented in two parts.

THE CHERRY ORCHARD. By Anton Chekhov; adapted by Martin Sherman. February 12, 2006. Direction, Sean Mathias; scenery, Alexander Dodge; costumes, Catherine Zuber; lighting, James F. Ingalls; sound, Jon Gottlieb; stage management, David S. Franklin; in the Mark Taper Forum.

Ranyevskaya	Annette Bening	Simeonov-Pishchik	Lyle Kanouse
Gaev	Lothaire Bluteau	Firs	Alan Mandell
Yasha	Peter Cambor	Lopakhin	Alfred Molina
Dunyasha	Jennifer Dundas	Anya	Rebecca Mozo
Carlotta	Frances Fisher	Varya	Sarah Paulson
Trofimov	Jason Butler Harner	Yepikhodov	Raphael Sbarge

Ensemble: Tom Costello, Jeanie Hackett, Heidi Johanningmeier, Tom Monsion, Reed Rudy, Don Oscar Smith, Alison Weller, Alexander Zale.

iWITNESS. By Joshua Sobol; adapted by Barry Edelstein. April 9, 2006. Direction, Mr. Edelstein; scenery, Neil Patel; costumes, Robert Blackman; lighting, Russell H. Champa; sound, Jon Gottlieb; projections, Jan Hartley; cinematography, Alice Brooks; dramaturgy, Mike Sablone and Gerald Schwarz, stage management, James T. McDermott; in the Mark Taper Forum.

Franz Jagerstatter	Gareth Saxe	Martin; others	James Joseph O'Neil
Franca	Rebecca Lowman	Hans; others	Seamus Dever
Maria	Christina Burdette	Vice Admiral Arps; others	Joan McMurtrey
Margaret	Katrina Lenk	Schreiber; others	Michael Rudko

Time: Summer 1943. Place: A prison cell on death row in Berlin.

East West Players, Los Angeles
Tim Dang producing artistic director, Trent Steelman managing director

STEW RICE. By Edward Sakamoto. September 7, 2005. Direction, James A. Nakamoto; scenery, Mina Kinukawa; costumes, Ken Takemoto; lighting, Jose Lopez; sound, Miles Ono; projections, Maiko Nezu; stage management, Pat Loeb. Presented in association with Ken Takemoto.

Sharon	Millie Chow	Zippy	Michael Sun Lee
Ruby	Chanel Akiko Hirai	Shima	Shaun Shimoda
Donna	Kaliko Kauahi	Ben	Keo Woolford

Time: 1957–58; 1978. Place: Oahu.

EQUUS. By Peter Shaffer. October 26, 2006. Direction, Tim Dang; scenery, Maiko Nezu; costumes, Annalisa Adams; lighting, Rand Ryan; music, Bryan Yamami; equine movement, Marc Oka; stage management, Anna Woo.

Martin Dysart	George Takei	Dora Strang	Dian Kobayashi
Alan Strang	Trieu D. Tran	Nugget	Wesley John
Nurse	Claudia Choi	Harry Dalton	Nelson Mashita
Hesther Salomon	Jeanne Sakata	Jill Mason	Cheryl Tsai
Frank Strang	Alberto Isaac		

Horses: Cesar Cipriano, Art Hsu, Paul S. Leach, Charles Romaine, Elbert Traister.

Time: 1970s. Place: Rokeby Psychiatric Hospital in Southern England. Presented in two parts.

Laguna Playhouse, Laguna Beach
Andrew Barnicle artistic director, Richard Stein executive director

THE MUSICAL OF MUSICALS—THE MUSICAL! Musical with book by Eric Rockwell and Joanne Bogart; music by Mr. Rockwell; lyrics by Ms. Bogart. July 5, 2005. Direction and choreography, Pamela Hunt; scenery, James Morgan; costumes, John Carver Sullivan; lighting, Mary Jo Dondlinger; sound, David Edwards; music direction, Jeffrey Rockwell; stage management, Nancy Staiger.

Performed by Alli Mauzey, Mary Gordon Murray, Jeffrey Rockwell, Brent Schindele.

BAD DATES. By Theresa Rebeck. September 13, 2005. Direction, Judith Ivey; scenery, Dwight Richard Odle; costumes, Julie Keen; lighting, Paulie Jenkins; sound, David Edwards; stage management, Vernon Willet. Presented in association with Michael Alden.

Haley .... Beth Broderick

MANY HAPPY RETURNS. By Bernard Farrell. November 15, 2005. Direction, Andrew Barnicle; scenery, Dwight Richard Odle; costumes, Julie Keen; lighting, Paulie Jenkins; sound, David Edwards; stage management, Nancy Staiger.

Irene	Susan Duerden	Declan	Brendan Ford
Matty	Nick Ullett	Amanda	Melanie Lora
Arthur	Barry Lynch	Gladys	Robin Pearson Rose

Time: Christmas Eve. Place: A farmhouse not far from Dublin.

THE SLEEPER. By Catherine Butterfield. February 14, 2006. Direction, Andrew Barnicle; scenery, Bruce Goodrich; costumes, Julie Keen; lighting, Paulie Jenkins; sound, David Edwards; stage management, Nancy Staiger.

Gretchen	Amy Tribbey	Therapist; others	Cynthia Beckert
Bill	Tim Meinelschmidt	Anthrax Expert; others	Jeff Marlow
Vivien	Clarinda Ross	Toy Salesman; others	Eric Curtis Johnson
Matthew	Ray DeJohn		

Time: March–May 2002. Place: California.

La Jolla Playhouse

Des McAnuff artistic director, Steven B. Libman managing director

PALM BEACH—THE SCREWBALL MUSICAL. Musical with book by Robert Cary and Benjamin Feldman; music by David Gursky; lyrics by Mr. Cary. June 12, 2005 (world premiere). Direction, Des McAnuff; choreography, Debbie Rosche; scenery, Klara Zieglerova; costumes, Paul Tazewell; lighting, Howell Binkley; sound, Andrew Keister; music direction, Eric Stern; dramaturgy, Shirley Fishman; stage management, Frank Hartenstein.

Jessica	Anastasia Barzee	Tessa 2	Taryn Darr
Lance	Matt Cavenaugh	Character Man	Jay Douglas
Leo	Chris Hoch	Wilton	Ryan Hilliard
Eustacia	Heather Lee	Liz	Erica Piccininni
Jimmy	Noah Racey	Victoria	Amanda Watkins
Max	Clarke Thorell	Ensemble	Spencer Moses,
Bixby	John Alban Coughlan		Ryan Drummond
Tessa 1	Jennifer Evans		

Musical numbers included: "A Family Is a Truly Priceless Thing, "Palm Beach (That's Where I Belong)," "To Serve You," "Lise," "Bachelor Street," "I Still See You/Who, What, Where," "To Be a Proper Servant," "Fly With Me," "The End of the World," "The Happy Hour," "Who Needs Love?," "May the Best Man Win," "I'm Fine," "A Bad Man Is Easy to Find."

THE SCOTTISH PLAY. By Lee Blessing. September 25, 2005 (world premiere). Direction, Melia Bensussen; scenery, Judy Gailen; costumes, Christal Weatherly; lighting, Daniel Kotlowitz; sound, David Remedios; fight direction, Bobby C. King; dramaturgy, Shirley Fishman; stage managment, Linda Marvel.

Jack Bonner	Jere Burns	Maud Meckley	Susan Knight
Alex McConnell	John C. Vennema	Zita Virago	Rebecca Wisocky
Billy Neil	Peter Bartlett	Eden Hunt	Bridget Regan
Fred Oberg	Robert L. Devaney	Path Sanderson	Erik Heger
Pewter Piper	Diana Ruppe	Morgan Bonner	Morgan Hollingsworth

MUCH ADO ABOUT NOTHING. By William Shakespeare; adapted by Robert Richmond. January 20, 2006. Direction, Mr. Richmond; scenery, Peter Meineck and Mr. Richmond; costumes, Megan Bowers; lighting, Mr. Meineck; music, Anthony Cochrane; stage management, Jenny Slattery.

Margaret	Marwa Bernstein	Claudio; Verges	John Lavelle
Beatrice	Jessica Boevers	Hero	Kathryn Merry
Don Juan; others	Louis Butelli	Leonato	Craig Wroe
Benedick	Anthony Cochrane	Don Pedro; Borachio	Kenn Sabberton

ZHIVAGO. Musical with book by Michael Weller; music by Lucy Simon; lyrics by Michael Korie and Amy Powers; based on Boris Pasternak's *Doctor Zhivago*. May 25, 2006. Direction, Des McAnuff; choreography, Sergio Trujillo; scenery, Heidi Ettinger; costumes, David C. Woolard; lighting, Howell Binkley; sound, Steve Canyon Kennedy; orchestrations, Don Sebesky; music direction, Eric Stern; fight direction, Steve Rankin; dramaturgy, Allison Horsley; stage management, Frank Hartenstein.

Yurii A. Zhivago	Ivan Hernandez	Sasha	Bibi Valderrama
Lara Guishar Antipova	Jessica Burrows	Anna Gromeko	Maureen Silliman
Pasha Antipov; Strelnikov	Matt Bogart	Alexander Gromeko	Edward Conery
Tonya Gromeko	Rena Strober	Katerina	Mackenzie Holmes
Viktor Komarovsky	Tom Hewitt		

Ensemble: Dominic Bogart, Sandy Campbell, Ryan Drummond, Mark Emerson, David Carey Foster, Jason Heil, Melissa Hoff, Christopher Kale Jones, Rebecca Kaasa, Melina Kalomas, David McDonald, Spencer Moses, Eduardo Placer, Graham Rowat, Tina Stafford, Nick Ullett, Melissa van der Schyff.

Musical numbers included: "Peace, Bread and Land," "To Light the New Year," "Who Is She?," "Wedding Vows," "It's a Godsend," "When the Music Played," "Watch the Moon," "Forward March for the Tsar," "Now," "Blood on the Snow," "In the Perfect World," "A Man Who Lives Up to His Name," "In This House," "The Hope of the Peasants," "No Mercy At All," "Love Finds You," "Nowhere to Run," "It Comes as No Surprise," "Ashes and Tears," "On the Edge of Time."

Lamb's Players Theatre, Coronado

Robert Smyth producing artistic director, Kerry Meads and Deborah Gilmour Smyth associate artistic directors

COLD COMFORT FARM. By Paul Doust; adapted from the novel by Stella Gibbons. June 10, 2005. Direction, Robert Smyth; scenery, Mike Buckley; costumes, Jeanne Reith; lighting, Nate Parde; sound, Greg Campbell; music, Deborah Gilmour Smyth; stage management, Maria Mangiavellano.

Flora	Sarah Zimmerman	Sneller;Amos	David Cochran Heath
Charles; Seth	Matt Thompson	Elfine	Chrissy Reynolds Vogele
Mr. Neck; Adam	Doren Elias	Urk; Richard	Chris Bresky
Judith	Deborah Gilmour Smyth	Reuben	Patrick J. Duffy
Rennet	Season Duffy	Ada	K.B. Mercer

Time: The early 1930s. Place: Cold Comfort Farm in rural Sussex, England; the lawn of a nearby grand estate.

Magic Theatre, San Francisco

Chris Smith artistic director, David Gluck managing director

LOS BIG NAMES. By Marga Gomez. July 23, 2005. Direction, David Schweizer; scenery and lighting, Alexander Nichols; sound, Mark O'Brien; stage management, Heather Deutsch. Presented in association with Jonathan Reinis Productions and Z Space Studio.

Performed by Marga Gomez.

FAMILY BUTCHERS. By Edna O'Brien. October 2, 2005. Direction, Paul Whitworth; choreography, Marybeth Cavanaugh; scenery, Kate Edmunds; costumes, Todd Roehrman;

lighting, Kurt Landisman; sound, Norman Kern; fight direction, Ken Sonkin; stage management, Risa Aratyr.

Lil	Esther Mulligan	Peg	Patricia Miller
Jamie	Robertson Dean	Carmel	Laura Hope
Gurnet	Ian Scott McGregor	Teddy	Mark Phillips
Emer	Anne Francisco Worden	Helen	Joan Harris-Gelb

Presented in two parts.

THE HOPPER COLLECTION. By Mat Smart. November 25, 2005 (world premiere). Direction, Chris Smith; scenery, Erik Flatmo; costumes, Callie Floor; lighting, Christopher Studley; sound, Yvette Janine Jackson; stage management, Nicole Dickerson.

Marjorie	Julia Brothers	Edward	Zac Jaffee
Daniel	Andy Murray	Sarah; Natalie	Anna Bullard

Presented without intermission.

NERO (ANOTHER GOLDEN ROME). By Steven Sater; music by Duncan Sheik; lyrics by Mr. Sater. February 18, 2006 (world premiere). Direction, Beth F. Milles; scenery, Melpomene Katakalos; costumes, Raquel Barreto; lighting, Russell H. Champa; sound, Norman Kern; music direction, Joshua Raoul Brody; stage management, Karen Runk.

Boccaccio; others	Andrew Hurteau	Agrippa; others	Catherine Smitko
Nero	Drew Hirshfield	Brittanicus; others	Joe Mandragona
Seneca; others	David Cramer	Octavia; others	Sofia Ahmad

MORBIDITY AND MORTALITY. By Courtney Baron. March 4, 2006. Direction, Loretta Greco; scenery, Melpomene Katakalos; lighting, Russell H. Champa; costumes, Alex Jaeger; sound, Norman Kern; dramaturgy, Heather Honnold; stage management, Karen Runk. Presented in association with the Women's Project, New York City.

Carolyn Goldenhersch	Sasha Eden	Michael Goldenhersch	Jonathan Leveck
Dr. Anil Petal	Hari Dhillon		

THE ICE-BREAKER. By David Rambo. March 18, 2006. Direction, Art Manke; scenery, Robert Mark Morgan; costumes, Callie Floor; lighting, Kurt Landisman; sound and music, Steven Cahill.

Sonia	Blake Lindsley	Lawrence	Charles Shaw Robinson

Presented in two parts.

THE LONG CHRISTMAS RIDE HOME. By Paula Vogel. May 13, 2006. Direction, Basil Twist; choreography, Joe Goode; scenery, John Iacovelli; costumes, Todd Roehrman; lighting, Kate Boyd; sound, Norman Kern; stage management, Angela Nostrand.

Stephen	Nick Sholley	Rebecca	Lisa Anne Porter
Female Narrator	Julia Brothers	Claire	Jennifer Clare
Male Narrator	Steve Irish	Shamisen Player	Philip Flavin
Father; Minister	Jess Curtis		

Puppeteers: Parker Leventer, Patrick Miner, Jessica Scott, Kevin Taylor, Patricia Tyler, Christopher W. White.

Marin Theatre Company, Mill Valley

Lee Sankowich artistic director, Gabriella Calicchio managing director

RIVER'S END. Musical with book and lyrics by Cheryl Coons; music by Chuck Larkin. September 13, 2005 (world premiere). Direction, Lee Sankowich; scenery, Giulio Perrone;

costumes, Cassandra Carpenter; lighting, Kurt Landisman; sound, Norman Kern; stage management, Dick Daley.

Bessie One	Molly Bell	Glen Two	Travis Poelle
Bessie Two	Dani Marcus	Georgie	Lucinda Hitchcock Cone
Glen One	John Patrick Moore	Kent	J.D. Nelson

Presented in two parts.

SPLITTIN' THE RAFT. By Scott Kaiser. November 15, 2005 (world premiere). Direction, Danny Scheie; scenery, Kate Boyd; costumes, Todd Roehrman; lighting, Chris Guptill; sound and projections, Erik Pearson; fight direction, Andrew Hurteau; stage management, June Palladino.

Performed by Karen Aldridge, Aldo Billingslea, Mark Farrell, Stacy Ross.

DISPLACED. By Rogelio Martinez. May 16, 2006 (world premiere). Direction, Amy Glazer; scenery, J.B. Wilson; costumes, Fumiko Bielefeldt; lighting, Kurt Landisman; sound, David Molina; stage management, Nicole Dickerson.

Miranda	Jamie Jones	Ana	Maria Grazia Affinito
Serafin	Johnny Moreno	Matt	Darren Bridgett
Amador	Jarion Monroe	Lily	Isabella Ortega

Presented in two parts.

Time: A few years ago. Place: A once-grand hotel in Havana. Presented in two parts.

New Conservatory Theater Center, San Francisco
Ed Decker artistic director

CRUCIFIXION. By Terrence McNally. October 12, 2005. (world premiere). Direction, Ed Decker; scenery, Guilio Cesare Perrone; costumes, Keri Fitch; lighting, Matthew Miller; sound, Ted Crimy; stage management, Jovan Olague.

James Giraud	Colin Stuart	Jackson Master	Javier Galito-Cava
John Giraud	Paul Araguistain	Don Capps	Scott Cox
Genevieve Kaufmann	Camilla Bushovetsky	Alan Lesker	Andrew Nance
Carrie Miller	Cheryl Smith	Schuyler Hawk	Patrick Michael Dukeman
Bethany Orth	Lizzie Calogero	Bernadette Avril	Amanda King
Tom Russo	Bradford Cooreman		

Presented without intermission.

THEATER DISTRICT. By Richard Kramer. February 10, 2006 (world premiere). Direction, Dennis Lickteig; scenery, Scott Wilber; costumes, Keri Fitch; lighting, John Kelly; sound, Joshua McDermott.

Performed by Scott Alexander, Joe Carrig, P.A. Cooley, Sam Garber, Joseph Holmes, Cynthia Myers, George Quick.

Presented without intermission.

The Old Globe, San Diego
Jack O'Brien artistic director, Louis Spisto executive director, Jerry Patch resident artistic director

THE LADY WITH ALL THE ANSWERS. By David Rambo; adapted from the life and letters of Ann Landers. August 11, 2005 (world premiere). Direction, Tom Moore; scenery, Ralph Funicello; costumes, Robert Blackman; lighting, Chris Rynne; sound, Paul Peterson; stage management, David John O'Brien.

Performed by Randy Graff.

Hoofer's tale: Chita Rivera and company in Chita Rivera: The Dancer's Life. *Photo: Craig Schwartz*

CHITA RIVERA: THE DANCER'S LIFE. Musical with book by Terrence McNally; music and lyrics by Lynn Ahrens and Stephen Flaherty. September 22, 2005 (world premiere). Direction and choreography, Graciela Daniele; Jerome Robbins's choreography, Alan Johnson; Bob Fosse's choreography, Tony Stevens; scenery, Loy Arcenas; costumes, Toni-Leslie James; lighting, Jules Fisher and Peggy Eisenhauer; sound, Scott Lehrer; orchestrations, Danny Troob; music direction, Mark Hummel; stage management, Arturo E. Porazzi.

Chita Rivera .... Chita Rivera   Young Chita Rivera .... Liana Ortiz

Ensemble: Richard Amaro, Lloyd Culbreath, Malinda Farrington, Edgard Gallardo, Deidre Goodwin, Richard Montoya, Lainie Sakakura, Alex Sanchez, Allyson Tucker.

Musical numbers included: "Secret o' Life," "Dancing on the Kitchen Floor," Something to Dance About," "I'm Available," "Camille, Claudette, Fifi," "Garbage," "Can-Can," "A Boy Like That," "Dance at the Gym," "Somewhere," "Put on a Happy Face," "Rosie," "Don't 'Ah Ma' Me," "Big Spender," "Nowadays," "More Than You Know," "A Woman the World Has Never Seen," "Class," "Chief Cook and Bottle Washer," "Kiss of the Spider Woman," "Where You Are," "All That Jazz."

Presented in two parts.

THE TIMES THEY ARE A-CHANGIN'. Musical theater piece by Twyla Tharp; music and lyrics by Bob Dylan. February 9, 2006 (world premiere). Direction and choreography, Ms. Tharp; scenery and costumes, Santo Loquasto; lighting, Donald Holder; sound, François Bergeron; orchestrations, Michael Dansicker; music direction, Henry Aronson; stage management, Arthur Gaffin. Presented in association with James L. Nederlander, Terry Allen Kramer, Debra Black and Hal Luftig.

Coyote .... Michael Arden   Cleo .... Jenn Colella
Captain Arab .... Thom Sesma

Ensemble: Marty Lawson, Jason McDole, Jonathan Nosan, Justin Bohon, Albert Guerzon, Sean Stewart, Tamara Levinson.

Musical numbers included: "Blowin' in the Wind," "Country Pie," "Desolation Row," "Dignity," "Don' Think Twice , "It's All Right," "Everything Is Broken," "Forever Young," "Gotta Serve Somebody," "Highway 61 Revisited," "Hurricane," "I Believe in You," "If Not For You," "I'll Be Your Baby Tonight," "Just Like a Woman," "Knockin' on Heaven's Door," "Lay Lady Lay," "Like a Rolling Stone," "Maggie's Farm," "Man Gave Names to All the Animals," Masters of War," "Mr. Tambourine Man," "Not Dark Yet," "On a Night Like This," "Please Mrs. Henry," "Rainy Day Women #12 and 35," "Simple Twist of Fate," "Subterranean Homesick Blues," "Summer Days," "The Times They Are A-Changin'."

Presented without intermission.

A BODY OF WATER. By Lee Blessing. February 16, 2006. Direction, Ethan McSweeny; scenery, Michael Vaughn Sims; costumes, Charlotte Devaux; lighting, York Kennedy; sound and music, Michael Roth; stage management, Diana Moser.

Avis	Sandy Duncan	Wren	Samantha Soule
Moss	Ned Schmidtke		

Presented in two parts.

TRYING. By Joanna McClelland Glass. April 20, 2006. Direction, Richard Seer; scenery, Alan E. Muraoka; costumes, Charlotte Devaux; lighting, Chris Rynne; sound, Paul Peterson; stage management, Esther Emery.

Judge Biddle	Jonathan McMurtry	Sarah Schorr	Christine Marie Brown

Time: November 1967–January 1968. Place: Judge Biddle's office above a garage in Georgetown. Presented in two parts.

THE VIOLET HOUR. By Richard Greenberg. May 25, 2006. Direction, Carolyn Cantor; scenery, David Korins; costumes, Robert Blackman; lighting, Matt Richards, sound, Paul Peterson; stage management, Leila Knox.

Rosamund Plinth	Kristen Bush	John Pace Seavering	Lucas Hall
Gidger	T. Scott Cunningham	Jessie Brewster	Christen Simon
Denis McCleary	Patch Darragh		

Presented in two parts.

San Jose Repertory Theatre
Timothy Near artistic director, David Jobin managing director

EXCEPTIONS TO GRAVITY. By Avner Eisenberg. June 11, 2005. Direction, Mr. Eisenberg; scenery, Nick Nichols; lighting, Selina Young, stage management, Nicole Olson.
Performed by Mr. Eisenberg.

THE HAUNTING OF WINCHESTER. Musical with book and lyrics by Mary Bracken Phillips; music by Craig Bohmler. September 9, 2005 (world premiere). Direction, Michael Butler; choreography, Cassie Beck; scenery, William Bloodgood; costumes, Maggie Morgan; lighting, Jaymi Lee Smith; sound, Jeff Mockus; music direction and orchestrations, Mr. Bohmler; stage management, June Palladino.

Marisa	Lizzi Jones	Soldier	Jesse Quinn VanAntwerp
Jack Kerrigan	Dan Sharkey	Elena	Cassie Beck
Sarah Winchester	Tamra Hayden	Indian Scout	Michael Dalager
Minnie	Carrie Paff	Sheriff	Ren Reynolds
Banker	Mark Farrell	Architect	David Curley
Murieta	Victor Ballesteros		

Musical numbers included: "Marisa's 1st Riddle," " Kerrigan's Curse," "When All of the Loving Is Over," "Dead Men's Vendetta," "Adding On," "Something Is Wrong With This House," "When I Died," "Marisa's 2nd Riddle," "Write Her I Loved Her, "Her Silhouette," "Honest Man," "Perfect Partners," "Whose Thoughts People My Little World," "Good Riddance," "Marisa's 3rd Riddle," "Worst Day Since Yesterday," "Middle of Nowhere," "The Right Wrong Man," "A Peak in Wyoming," "Village on a Hill," "Marisa's 4th Riddle," "Lord, Take This Child."
Presented in two parts.

THE TRICKY PART. By Martin Moran. October 21, 2005. Direction, Seth Barrish; scenery, Paul Steinberg; lighting, Russell H. Champa; stage management, Laxmi Kumaran.
Performed by Mr. Moran.

THE IMMIGRANT. By Mark Harelik. February 3, 2006. Direction, John McCluggage; scenery, Scott Weldin; costumes, B Modern; lighting, Michael Palumbo; sound, Steve Schoenbeck; dramaturgy, Adina Kletter; stage management, Laxmi Kumaran.

Haskell Harelik	Adam Richman	Milton Perry	Dan Hiatt
Ima Perry	Nancy Carlin	Leah Harelik	Anney Giobbe

Time: From 1909 to the present. Place: Various locales in and around Hamilton, a tiny agricultural community in central Texas.

IPHIGENIA AT AULIS. By Euripides; adapted by Don Taylor. May 5, 2006. Direction, Timothy Near; choreography, Krissy Keefer; scenery, Kris Stone; costumes, Anna Oliver; lighting, Lap-Chi Chu; sound, Jeff Mockus; dramaturgy, Adina Kletter; stage management, Laxmi Kumaran.

Agamemnon	Remi Sandri	Clytemnestra	Stacy Ross
Old Man	Jarek Truszczynski	Iphigenia	Sarah Nealis
Menelaus	Andy Murray	Achilles	Craig W. Marker

Greek Chorus: Tina Banchero, Sarah Bush, Lena Gatchalian, Krissy Keefer, Emily Rosenthal.
Time: Then and now. Place: An army encampment at the Bay of Aulis. Presented in two parts.

South Coast Repertory, Costa Mesa
David Emmes producing artistic director, Martin Benson artistic director

DUMB SHOW. By Joe Penhall. October 1, 2005. Direction, David Emmes; scenery and costumes, Angela Balogh Calin; lighting, Tom Ruzika; sound and music, Dennis McCarthy; dramaturgy, Megan Monaghan; stage management, Scott Harrison.

Barry	Micheal McShane	John; Greg	John Rafter Lee
Jane; Liz	Heidi Dippold		

Place: A five-star hotel room in London; a cafe. Presented in two parts.

THE FURTHER ADVENTURES OF HEDDA GABLER. By Jeff Whitty. January 13, 2006 (world premiere). Direction, Bill Rauch; choreography, Art Manke; scenery, Christopher Acebo; costumes, Shigeru Yaji; lighting, Geoff Korf; sound and music, Paul James Prendergast; dramaturgy, Megan Monaghan; stage management, Randall K. Lum.

Hedda Gabler	Susannah Schulman	Woman in Pink; others	Bahni Turpin
George Tesman	Christopher Liam Moore	Patrick; others	Dan Butler
Servant	Kimberly Scott	Steven; others	Patrick Kerr
Neighbor; others	Kate A. Mulligan	Eilert Lovborg; others	Preston Maybank

Presented in two parts.

HITCHCOCK BLONDE. By Terry Johnson. February 11, 2006. Direction, Mr. Johnson; scenery, costumes and video, William Dudley; lighting, Chris Parry; sound and music, Ian Dickinson; fight direction, Martin Noyes; stage management, Jamie A. Tucker.

South Coast Repertory
2005–2006 Season

Listening? Micheal McShane and Heidi Dippold in Dumb Show. *Photo: Henry DiRocco*

Fantasy: Dakin Matthews and Sarah Aldrich in Hitchcock Blonde. *Photo: Ken Howard*

Ancestor: Reg E. Cathey and Larry Gilliard Jr. in Blue Door. *Photo: Henry DiRocco*

Jennifer .... Adriana DeMeo
Alex .... Robin Sachs
Hitch .... Dakin Matthews
 Presented in two parts.

Blonde .... Sarah Aldrich
Husband .... Martin Noyes

MAN FROM NEBRASKA. By Tracy Letts. March 17, 2006. Direction, William Friedkin; scenery, Christopher Barreca; costumes, Nephelie Andonyadis; lighting, Lonnie Rafael Alcaraz; sound, Drew Dalzell; stage management, Randall K. Lum.

Ken Carpenter .... Brian Kerwin
Nancy Carpenter .... Kathy Baker
Reverend Todd .... Ben Livingston
Cammie Carpenter .... Jane A. Johnston
Ashley Kohl .... Susannah Schulman

Pat Monday .... Laura Niemi
Tamyra .... Susan Dalian
Harry Brown .... Julian Stone
Bud Todd .... Hal Landon Jr.

 Time: The present. Place: The outskirts of Lincoln, Nebraska; London, England. Presented in two parts.

THE STUDIO. By Christopher d'Amboise. April 7, 2006 (world premiere). Direction and choreography, Mr. d'Amboise; scenery, Christopher Barreca, costumes, Angela Balogh Calin; lighting, Peter Maradudin; sound, B.C. Keller; music, Karl Fredrik Lundeberg; dramaturgy, Megan Monaghan; stage management, Erin Nelson.

Jackie .... John Todd
Lisa .... Nancy Lemenager

Emil .... Terrence Mann

 Time: The present. Place: New York City. Presented in two parts.

BLUE DOOR. By Tanya Barfield, April 28, 2006 (world premiere). Direction, Leah C. Gardiner; scenery, Dustin O'Neill, costumes, Naila Aladdin Sanders; lighting, Lonnie Rafael Alcaraz; sound, Jill BC DuBoff; dramaturgy, John Glore; stage management, Randall K. Lum.

Simon; others .... Larry Gilliard Jr.

Lewis .... Reg E. Cathey

 Time: 1851–1995. Presented without intermission.

Pacific Playwrights Festival. May 5–7, 2006.

HUMAN ERROR. By Keith Reddin. Direction, Les Waters; dramaturgy, Shirley Fishman.
 Performed by Steven Culp, Richard Doyle, Meg Gibson.

EMPTY SKY. By Sarah Treem. Direction, Bill Rauch; dramaturgy, Megan Monaghan.
 Performed by Ramy Eletreby, Shane Haboucha, Lynn Milgrim, Allan Miller, Khanya Mkhize, Lina Patel, Adam Wylie.

SYSTEM WONDERLAND. By David Wiener. Direction, Art Manke; dramaturgy, Mead Hunter.
 Performed by Nathan Baesel, Shannon Cochran, Brian Kerwin.

THE PIANO TEACHER. By Julia Cho. Direction, Kate Whoriskey; dramaturgy, Scott Horstein.
 Performed by Melody Butiu, Kevin Daniels, Linda Gehringer.

LEITMOTIF. By Victoria Stewart. Direction, Jessica Kubzansky; dramaturgy, John Glore and Megan Monaghan.
 Performed by Amanda Cobb, James A. Johnston, Gareth Williams.

TheatreWorks, Mountain View
Robert Kelley artistic director, Randy Adams managing director

DOLLY WEST'S KITCHEN. By Frank McGuinness. June 18, 2005. Direction, Robert Kelley; scenery, Andrea Bechert; costumes, Fumiko Bielefeldt; lighting, Pamila Gray; sound, Cliff Caruthers; fight direction, Richard Lane; dramaturgy, Vickie Rozell; stage management, Jaimie L. Johnson.

Dolly West	Stacy Ross	Justin West	Jeremy Bobb
Anna Owens	Desirée Matthews	Alec Redding	Mark Phillips
Esther Horgan	Lanie MacEwan	Marco Delavicario	Christian Conn
Rima West	Charlotte Cornwell	Jamie O'Brien	Craig W. Marker
Ned Horgan	Simon Vance		

Time: 1943–45. Place: The West's house in Ireland, near the border with Northern Ireland. Presented in two parts.

HAROLD AND MAUDE: AN INTIMATE MUSICAL. Musical with book and lyrics by Tom Jones; music by Joseph Thalken; based on the screenplay by Colin Higgins. July 23, 2005. Direction, Robert Kelley; choreography, Janet Watson; scenery, Thomas F. Langguth, costumes, Cathleen Edwards; lighting, Steven B. Mannshardt and Z. William Bakal; sound, Steve Schoenbeck; projections, Ethan Hoerneman; music direction, William Liberatore; fight direction, Richard Lane; dramaturgy, Vickie Rozell; stage management, Rebecca Muench. Presented in association with James Cass Rogers and Mildred and Edward Lewis.

Maude	Pamela Myers	Maria; others	Alice Ewing
Harold	Eric Shelley	Priest; others	Daniel Marcus
Mrs. Chasen	Alice Vienneau		

Ensemble: Ricky Altamirano, Ryder Bach, Elana Ron, Elvy Yost.

Musical numbers included: "Dearest Mother, Self, Self, Self," "Woe," "Round and Round (The Cosmic Dance)," "Where Do You Go?," "Rata-Ta-Tat!," "The Road Less Traveled," "Two Sides of a River," "Quartet," "The Real Thing," "Maude's Waltz," "Song in My Pocket," "Montezuma," "Mirror, Mirror," "Harold and Maude," "The Chance to Sing."

BABY TAJ. By Tanya Shaffer. October 1, 2005 (world premiere). Direction, Matt August; choreography, Sheetal Gandhi; scenery, Joe Ragey; costumes, Fumiko Bielefeldt; lighting, Pamila Gray; sound, Cliff Caruthers; music, Rama; dramaturgy, Vickie Rozell; stage management, Rebecca Muench.

Rachel	Lesley Fera	Osho	Oomung Varma
Anjali	Sunita Param	Abhi	Sam Younis
Chandra	Qurrat Ann Kadwani	Abhi's Mother; Mrs. Sharma	Rashmi Rustagi
Sunita	Kavita Matani	Dancer	Rachel Rajput
Arustu	Indrajit Sarkar	Nathan; others	Noel Wood

Ensemble: Anil Margsahayam, Janak Ramachandran, Rishi Shukla.

Time: In the present and sometimes the past. Place: San Francisco; Agra, India. Presented in two parts.

THE CLEAN HOUSE. By Sarah Ruhl. January 21, 2006. Direction, Juliette Carrillo; choreography, Paco Gomes; scenery, Kate Edmunds; costumes, Maggie Morgan; lighting and projections, Steven B. Mannshardt; sound, Cliff Caruthers; puppetry, Lynn Jeffries; dramaturgy, Vickie Rozell, stage management, Rebecca Muench.

Mathilde	Stephanie Beatriz	Man; Charles	Michael Cooke
Lane	Heather Ehlers	Woman; Ana	Olivia Negrón
Virginia	Lucinda Hitchcock Cone		

Time: The present. Place: A metaphysical Connecticut. Presented in two parts.

New Works Festival. April 26–May 7, 2006.

MEZZULAH, 1946. By Michele Lowe. Direction, Leigh Silverman; stage management, Nicole Olson.

Performed by Jessa Brie Berkner, Jackson Davis, Julie Eccles, Jennifer Erdmann, Clayton B. Hodges, Jonathan Leveck, Gillen Morrison, Ryan Oden, Marcie Prohofsky, Ayla Yarkut.

THE DRUNKEN CITY. By Adam Bock. Direction, Kent Nicholson; stage management, Lisa G. Mitchell.

Performed by Cassie Beck, Chad Deverman, Jason Frazier, Lucy Owen, Nicholas Pelczar, Sigrid Sutter.

AMERICAN KLEPTO. By Allison Moore. Direction, Leslie Martinson; stage management, Lisa G. Mitchell.

Performed by Aldo Billingslea, Marissa Keltie, Laurie Schroeder, Mia Tagano, Jenn Wagner, David Zubiria.

ASPHALT BEACH. Musical with book by T.C. Smith and Peter Spears; music and lyrics by Andrew Lippa. Direction, Kent Nicholson; music direction, William Liberatore; stage management, Darlene Miyakawa.

Performed by Molly Bell, Jessica Lynn Carroll, Jessica Coker, Kevin Crook, David Curley, Carly Jibson, Laurie Keith, Elizabeth Palmer, Kristin Stokes, Danielle Thys, Linda Chuan Tsui, Melissa Wolfklain.

EMMA. Musical with book, music and lyrics by Paul Gordon. Direction, Robert Kelley; music direction, David Kreppel; stage manger, Jaimie L. Johnson.

Performed by Noel Anthony, Lianne Marie Dobbs, Suzanne Grodner, Robert Hamm, Brian Herndon, Dani Marcus, Mandy Munnell, Nick Nakashima, Travis Poelle, Halsey Varady, Virginia Wilcox, George Ward.

BIG RED SUN. Musical with book and lyrics by John Jiler; music by Georgia Stitt. Direction, Annette Jolles; music direction, Tom Murray; stage management, Meredith King.

Performed by Robert Brewer, Alison Ewing, Diana Torres Koss, Stephen Pawley, Matthew Sullivan, Colin Thomson, Brian Yates Sharber, Liana Young.

SOMETHING'S WRONG WITH AMANDINE. Musical with book and lyrics by Winter Miller; music and lyrics by Lance Horne. Direction, Josh Hecht; music direction, Brian J. Nash; stage management, Meredith King.

Performed by Robert Brewer, Elizabeth Carter, Alison Ewing, Michael Jenkinson, Kelsey Jessup, Mark D. Messersmith.

COLORADO

Arvada Center, Arvada
Rod Lansberry artistic producer

A PLACE AT FOREST LAWN. By Luke Yankee and James Bontempo; based on a play by Lorees Yerby. October 20, 2005. Direction, Terry Dodd; scenery, Joseph J. Egan; costumes, Nicole M. Harrison-Hoof; lighting, Gail J. Gober; sound, Steve Stevens; stage management, Connie I. Lane.

Clara Olsen	Judy Phelan-Hill	Albert Hogobarth	William Denis
Gertrude Wynant	Patty Mintz Figel	Father Gabriel	Josh Gaffga

Jack Olsen .... Marcus Waterman   Sonny .... Jordan Leigh
    Presented in two parts.

Curious Theatre Company, Denver
Chip Walton producing artistic director

THE DEAD GUY. By Eric Coble. September 3, 2005 (world premiere). Direction, Chip Walton; scenery, Michael Duran; costumes, Emilee Cooper; lighting, Shannon McKinney; sound, Matthew E. Morgan; video, Bryon Matsuno and Todd Webster; stage management, Keith Orell.

Eldon .... Todd Webster   Virgil; others .... Ed Cord
Gina .... Elizabeth Rainer   Roberta; others .... Dee Covington
Dougie .... Bryon Matsuno   Christy; others .... Jessica Austgen

THE WAR ANTHOLOGY. By Will Eno; Tony Kushner; Melissa Lucero McCarl; Bonnie Metzgar; Suzan-Lori Parks; Elaine Romero; Mildred Ruiz; Steven Sapp; Robert Lewis Vaughan; Paula Vogel; and contributing artists. March 11, 2006. (world premiere) Direction, Ms. Metzgar; choreography, David Reuille; scenery, Michael R. Duran; costumes, Ann Louise Piano and Liz Helfrich; lighting, Shannon McKinney; sound, Matthew E. Morgan; video, Brian Freeland; dramaturgy, Patrick Elkins-Zeglarski, Ms. Metzgar, Rebecca Rugg and Laura Tesman; stage management, Lisa Boehm.

BULLY COMPOSITION. By Will Eno.
    Performed by Karen Slack and Erik Sandvold.

THE CLOSEST I'VE BEEN TO WAR. By Paula Vogel.
    Performed by Dee Covington and Step Pearce.

MAKING WHOOPEE. By David Reuille.
    Performed by Dee Covington and Step Pearce.

OLDEST AMERICAN GI. By Bonnie Metzgar.
    Performed by Manuel R. Roybal Sr.

OLD KENTUCKY HOME. Music direction by David Dunbar.
    Performed by the ensemble.

ONE SHOT IN LOTUS POSITION. By Steven Sapp and Mildred Ruiz.
    Performed by GerRee Hinshaw and Tyee Tilghman.

ONLY WE WHO GUARD THE MYSTERY SHALL BE UNHAPPY. By Tony Kushner.
    Performed by Dee Covington and Karen Slack.

THE PLEDGE OF LESIONS. By Melissa Lucero McCarl.
    Performed by the ensemble.

RAIN OF RUIN. By Elaine Romero.
    Performed by GerRee Hinshaw, Peter Trinh and the ensemble.

WEIRD WATER. By Robert Lewis Vaughan.
    Performed by Erik Sandvold and Step Pearce.

WELCOME ME. By Suzan-Lori Parks.
    Performed by Manuel R. Roybal Sr.

Denver Center Theatre Company
Kent Thompson artistic director

JESUS HATES ME. By Wayne Lemon. January 19, 2006 (world premiere). Direction, David McClendon; scenery, Robert Mark Morgan; costumes, Kevin Copenhaver; lighting, Jane Spencer; sound, Iaeden Hovorka; fight direction, Geoffrey Kent; stage management, Erock.

Ethan	Justin Adams	Boone	Craig Pattison
Trane	Marlon Morrison	Lizzy	Chelsey Rives
Annie	Kathleen McCall	Georgie	Michael Keyloun

Presented in two parts.

CONNECTICUT

Eugene O'Neill Theater Center, Waterford
Amy Sullivan executive director

Playwrights Conference, July 1–30, 2005.

ANTEBELLUM. By Robert O'Hara.

CRADLE OF MAN. By Melanie Marnich.

DURANGO. By Julia Cho.

GREAT FALLS. By Lee Blessing.

THE IMPORTANCE OF BEING ORSON. By Jessica Cooke.

NORMAN ROCKWELL KILLED MY FATHER. By Samuel D. Hunter.

REARVIEW MIRROR. By Erick Winick.

THRASH. By Wendy MacLeod.

Direction: Jeremy Cohen, Carl Forsman, Michael John Garcés, Wendy C. Goldberg, Joe Grifasi, Carey Perloff, Lucie Tiberghien, Chay Yew.

Featured artists: Ross Bickell, Mark Blum, Jere Burns, Amanda Cobb, Emily Donahoe, Will Fowler, Michael Gladis, Brad Heberlee, Patrick Husted, Sue Jean Kim, Ryan King, James Hiroyuki Liao, Rey Lucas, Matthew Mabe, David Andrew McMahon, Matthew Rauch, Laila Robins, Anika Noni Rose, James Saito, Jon Norman Schneider, Ariel Shafir, Phyllis Somerville, PJ Sosko, Makela Spielman, Joe Urla, Jonathan Walker, Jess Weixler, Nancy Wolfe, Janet Zarish.

Goodspeed Musicals, East Haddam
Michael P. Price executive director

THE GIRL IN THE FRAME. Musical with book, music and lyrics by Jeremy Desmon. November 3, 2005 (world premiere). Direction, Jeremy Dobrish; choreography, Dan Knechtges; scenery, Steven Capone; costumes, Mattie Ullrich; lighting, Michael Gottlieb; sound, Jay Hilton; music direction, Jana Zielonka; stage management, Nancy Elizabeth Vest.

Alex	Jim Poulos	Evelyn	Allison Spratt
Laney	Heidi Blickenstaff	Tomás	Edward Watts

Musical numbers included: "Dinner at Cenzo's," "Do You Dance, Evelyn?," "That's What Fantasies Are For," "This Isn't Happening," "Enough's Enough," "Pinch Me," "One Big, Happy Family," "What Can You Do?," "Man of Your Dreams," "Picture Perfect."

Presented in two parts.

Hartford Stage, Hartford

Michael R. Wilson artistic director, Jim Ireland managing director

THE LEARNED LADIES OF PARK AVENUE. By David Grimm; adapted from Molière. September 1, 2005 (world premiere). Direction, Michael Wilson; choreography, Hope Clarke; scenery, Tony Straiges; costumes, Martin Pakledinaz; lighting, Rui Rita; sound and music, John Gromada; dramaturgy, Christopher Baker; stage management, Carmelita Becnel.

Betty	Nicole Lowrance	Magda	Natalie Brown
Ramona	Nancy Bell	Phyllis Crystal	Annalee Jefferies
Dicky Mayhew	Zach Shaffer	Upton Gabbitt	David Greenspan
Aunt Sylvia	Pamela Payton-Wright	T.S. Baines; Judge Arbogast	Bill Kux
Uncle Rupert	Nafe Katter	Servants	Elizabeth Capinera, Dan Whelton
Henry Crystal	Tom Bloom		

Time: 1936. Place: The Crystals' Park Avenue penthouse in New York.

FLOYD AND CLEA UNDER THE WESTERN SKY. Musical with book and lyrics by David Cale; music by Mr. Cale and Jonathan Kreisberg. October 19, 2005. Direction, Michael Wilson; scenery, Jeff Cowie, costumes, David C. Woolard, lighting, Rui Rita; sound, Michael Miceli, Andre Pluess and Ray Nardelli; music direction, Mr. Kreisberg; dramaturgy, Christopher Baker; stage management, Ellen Hay. Presented in association with the Goodman Theatre.

Floyd	David Cale	Clea	Sarah Glendening

Musicians: Dylan Schiavone, Jim Heffernan, Joe Fitzgerald.

Time: The recent past and the present. Places: Various locales in Texas, Montana and Los Angeles. Presented without intermission.

Long Wharf Theatre, New Haven

Gordon Edelstein artistic director, Michael Stotts managing director

APHRODISIAC. By Rob Handel. December 7, 2005. Direction, Ken Rus Schmoll; scenery, Sue Rees; costumes, Michelle R. Phillips; lighting, Garin Marshall; sound, Bray Poor; dramaturgy, Beatrice Basso; stage management, Charles M. Turner III.

Avery	Rob Campbell	Monica	Yetta Gottesman
Alma	Jennifer Dundas		

Presented without intermission.

Stamford Center for the Arts

Michael J. Cacace president

SAINT HEAVEN. Musical with book by Martin Casella; music and lyrics by Keith Gordon; based on a story by Steve Lyons. June 3, 2006 (world premiere). Direction, Matt Lenz; scenery, David Korins; costumes, Robin McGee; lighting, Paul Miller; sound, Bill Gagliano; stage management, Jovon E. Shuck.

Thomas Rivers	Darren Ritchie	Pastor Joe Bertram	Chuck Cooper

Eshie Willington .... Montego Glover	Millie Walden .... Cheryl Alexander
Maggie Hartford .... Deborah Gibson	Garrison Martin .... Patrick Ryan Sullivan

Musical numbers included: "No Turning Back," "The Gift," "Breathe In," "Nice Girl," "Love Isn't Easy" "Leave The Rescue to Me," "He Had Not Love," "He Don't Mean to Be so Mean," "Not One Thing Tying Me Down," "Love Me Like You Mean It," "My Father's Son."

Presented in two parts.

Stamford TheatreWorks

Steve Karp producing director, Larry Frenock managing director

NATIONAL PASTIME. By Bryan Harnetiaux. February 2, 2006. Direction, Steve Karp; scenery, Richard Ellis; costumes, Amber Schermann; lighting, Aaron Meadow; sound, Christopher A. Granger; stage management, Margaret E. Hall.

Satchel Paige .... Sedley Oscar Bloomfield	Jackie Robinson .... Leopold Lowe
Pee Wee Reese; Bus Driver .... Tristan Colton	Wendell Smith .... Wiley Moore
Branch Rickey .... Paul Falzone	Dixie Walker; Officer of the Day Justin Nadal
Mallie Robinson .... Patricia R. Floyd	Rachel Isum Robinson .... Toks Olagundoye
Clyde Sukeforth .... Philip Maynard Gardiner	Lylah Barber .... Sydney Stone
Jane Rickey .... Kathleen Huber	Red Barber .... David Van Pelt
Mule .... Floyd Lawrence	

Time: 1962 and earlier. Place: The Baseball Hall of Fame and various location in the US and Cuba.

Westport Country Playhouse

Joanne Woodward and Tazewell Thompson artistic directors, Alison Harris executive director

THE IMMIGRANT. Musical with book by Mark Harelik; music by Steven M. Alper; lyrics by Sarah Knapp. October 29, 2005. Direction, Tazewell Thompson; scenery, Donald Eastman; costumes, Arnulfo Maldonado; lighting, Robert Wierzel; sound, Jill BC DuBoff; music direction, David Gaines.

Haskell Harelik .... Tally Sessions	Milton Perry .... Dale Hensley
Ima Perry .... Beth Fowler	Leah .... Kyra Miller

Musical numbers included: "The Stars," "A Stranger Here," "Simply Free," "Changes," "Travel Light," "Keep Him Safe," "I Don't Want It," "Take the Comforting Hand of Jesus," "Padadooly," "The Sun Comes Up," "Candlesticks," "Shabbos," "Where Would You Be?, ""No Place to Go."

Time: From 1909 to the present. Place: Various locales in and around Hamilton, a tiny agricultural community in central Texas.

DAVID COPPERFIELD. By Charles Dickens; adapted by Giles Havergal. December 3, 2005. Direction, Anne Keefe and Joanne Woodward; scenery, David P. Gordon; costumes, Linda Fisher and Randall E. Klein; lighting, Clifton Taylor; sound and music, Ryan Rumery; stage management, Megan Smith.

David Copperfield 1 .... Mark Shanahan	Emily .... Nicole Lowrance
David Copperfield 2 .... Kieran Campion	Steerforth .... Saxon Palmer
Betsey Trotwood .... Molly Regan	Mr. Micawber .... Simon Jones
Peggotty .... Beth Fowler	Mrs. Micawber .... Allison Mackie
Mrs. Copperfield; Agnes .... Samantha Soule	Uriah Heap .... Tom Beckett
Mr. Murdstone; Creakle .... Sean Cullen	Mr. Wickfield .... Patrick Horgan
Ham .... John Keating	Dora .... Winslow Corbett
Dan .... Bill Buell	

Ensemble: Siena D'Addario, Brendan Geiling, Adam Riegler, Josh King, Betsy Selman.

Presented in two parts.

ON THE VERGE (OR THE GEOGRAPHY OF YEARNING). By Eric Overmyer. March 11, 2006. Direction, Tazewell Thompson; scenery, Donald Eastman; costumes, Carrie Robbins; lighting, Robert Wierzel; sound and music, Fabian Obispo; stage management, Linda Harris. Presented in association with Arena Stage, Washington, DC.

Mary	Laiona Michelle	Grover; others	Tom Becker
Fanny	Molly Wright Stuart	Voice	Christopher Plummer
Alex	Susan Bennett		

    Time: 1888 and forward. Place: Terra Incognita. Presented in two parts.

THURGOOD. By George Stevens Jr. May 11, 2006. Direction, Leonard Foglia; scenery, Allen Moyer; costumes, Jane Greenwood; lighting, Brian Nason; sound, Ryan Rumery; projections, Elaine J. McCarthy; stage management, Marti McIntosh. Presented in association with Boyett Ostar Productions.

Thurgood Marshall ....James Earl Jones
    Presented in two parts.

Yale Repertory Theatre, New Haven
James Bundy artistic director, Victoria Nolan managing director

SAFE IN HELL. By Amy Freed. November 17, 2005. Direction, Mark Wing-Davey; choreography, Peter Pucci; scenery, Leiko Fuseya; costumes, Emily Rebholz; lighting, Gina Scherr; sound, David Budries; dramaturgy, Monica Achen; stage management, Glenn J. Sturgis.

Cotton Mather	Erik Lochtefeld	Abigail	Sofia Gomez
Increase Mather	Graeme Malcolm	Little Mary	Alexis McGuinness
Reverend Doakes	Adam Dannheisser	Maggie Smurt	Katie Barrett
Mrs. Doakes; Mr. Smurt	Welker White	Townsman; others	Jeff Steitzer
Tituba	Myra Lucretia Taylor	Young man	Chad Callaghan
Indian Roger	Sean Dougherty		

    Time: 1692. Place: Boston and Salem. Presented in two parts.

THE PEOPLE NEXT DOOR. By Henry Adam. January 19, 2006. Direction, Evan Yionoulis; scenery, Kanae Heike; costumes, Kate Cusack; lighting, Cat Tate; sound and music, Sharath Patel; fight direction, David DeBesse; dramaturgy, Carla Mastraccio; stage management, Shawn Senavinin.

Nigel	Manu Narayan	Phil	Christopher Innvar
Mrs. McCallum	Marcia Jean Kurtz	Marco	James Miles

    Time: 2003. Place: In and around a London flat. Presented in two parts.

COMEDY ON THE BRIDGE. By Václav Kliment Klicpera; music by Bohuslav Martinu; adapted by Tony Kushner. February 10, 2006. Direction, Tony Taccone; scenery, Maurice Sendak and Kris Stone; costumes, Robin I. Shane; lighting, Donald Holder; sound, Rob Milburn and Michael Bodeen; music direction, Greg Anthony; dramaturgy, Yana Ross; stage management, Michael Suenkel. Presented in association with Berkeley Repertory Theatre and the Yale School of Music.

Liskovite Sentry	Henry DiGiovanni	Sykos	Matt Farnsworth
Strokopounkutnik Sentry	Geoff Hoyle	Eva	Angelina Réaux
Popelka	Anjali Bhimani	Professor Ucitelli	William Youmans
Bedronyi	Martin Vidnovic	Captain Ladinsky	Joe Gallagher

BRUNDIBÁR. By Adolf Hoffmeister; music by Hans Krasá; adapted by Tony Kushner. February 10, 2006. Direction, Tony Taccone; scenery, Maurice Sendak and Kris Stone; costumes, Robin I. Shane; lighting, Donald Holder; sound, Rob Milburn and Michael Bodeen; music direction, Greg Anthony; dramaturgy, Yana Ross; stage management, Michael Suenkel. Presented in association with Berkeley Repertory Theatre and the Yale School of Music.

Pepicek	Aaron Simon Gross	Policeman	Martin Vidnovic
Aninku	Devynn Pedell	Brundibár	Joe Gallagher
Ice Cream Seller	Henry DiGiovanni	Sparrow	Anjali Bhimani
Baker; Dog	Geoff Hoyle	Cat	Angelina Réaux
Milkman	Matt Farnsworth	Professor Ucitelli	William Youmans

DANCE OF THE HOLY GHOSTS: A PLAY ON MEMORY. By Marcus Gardley; music by Scott Davenport Richards. March 23, 2006 (world premiere). Direction, Liz Diamond; choreography, Peter Pucci; scenery, Aleksandra Maslik; costumes, Jennifer Moeller; lighting, Jennifer Tipton; sound, Arielle Edwards; music direction, XY Eli; dramaturgy, Gordon Carver; stage management, Adam Ganderson.

Oscar	Chuck Cooper	Viola; Tanisha	Harriett D. Foy
Mother; others	Pascale Armand	Marcus G.	Brian Henry
Darlene; Princess	La Tonya Borsay	Willie; others	Paul J. Medford

Time: Autumn 2005 and other autumns back to 1955. Place: Oakland, California and Monroe, Louisiana. Presented in two parts.

ALL'S WELL THAT ENDS WELL. By William Shakespeare. April 27, 2006. Direction, James Bundy and Mark Rucker; choreography, John Carrafa; scenery, Zane Pihlstrom; costumes, Mike Floyd; lighting, Matthew Frey; sound, Andrew Nagel; music, Matthew Suttor; music direction, Erika Schroth; fight direction, Rick Sordelet; dramaturgy, Jeff Rogers; stage management, Sarah Bierenbaum.

Countess	Kathleen Chalfant	Second Lord Dumaine	Elliott Villar
Bertram	Nicholas Heck	Rynaldo	Brian O'Neill
Lafew	Helmar Augustus Cooper	Lavatch	Nick Corley
Helena	Dana Green	Duke of Florence	Walton Wilson
Parolles	Richard Robichaux	Widow	Dale Soules
Isbel	Lisa Birnbaum	Mariana	Susannah Schulman
King of France	John Cunningham	Diana	Erin Felgar
First Lord Dumaine	Michael Braun	First Soldier	Christopher Grant

Ensemble: Ayano Kataoka, Gamal J. Palmer, Bryce Pinkham, Tom E. Russell, Amanda Warren. Presented in two parts.

DELAWARE

Delaware Theatre Company, Wilmington
Anne Marie Cammarato producing director

A MURDER, A MYSTERY AND A MARRIAGE: A MARK TWAIN MUSICAL MELODRAMA. Musical with book and lyrics by Aaron Posner; music by James Sugg. April 29, 2006 (world premiere). Direction, Aaron Posner; choreography, Karma Camp; scenery, Tony Cisek; costumes, Kate Turner-Walker; lighting, James Leitner; sound, Matthew M. Nielson; music direction, Jay Ansill; stage management, Cary Louise Gillett. Presented in association with Round House Theatre, Bethesda.

Twain (Narrator) .... Dan Manning	Hugh Gregory .... Ben Dibble
Ma (Sally) Gray .... Sherri L. Edelen	The Stranger .... Scott Greer
Pa(John) Gray .... Anthony Lawton	David Gray .... Thomas Adrian Simpson
Mary Gray .... Erin Weaver	

Musical numbers included: "The Story," "The Curse of John Gray," "Just a Love Song," "When Mary Is Married," "Entre Nous," "Dear, Dear, Deer Lick," "I Miss Hugh," "Ill-Fated Love," "Who Woulda Thought It," "My Mary," "Dark Comes a Risin'," "God's World," "Dirty Deeds of Deer Lick," "God's World Reprise," "The Story Reprise."

Presented in two parts.

DISTRICT OF COLUMBIA

Arena Stage, Washington
Molly Smith artistic director, Stephen Richard executive director

PASSION PLAY, A CYCLE. By Sarah Ruhl. September 8, 2005 (world premiere). Direction, Molly Smith; scenery, Scott Bradley; costumes, Linda Cho; lighting, Joel Moritz; sound and music, Andre Pluess; dramaturgy, Mark Bly; stage management, Amber Dickerson.

Mary 1 .... Kelly Brady	Village Idiot .... Polly Noonan
Queen Elizabeth .... Robert Dorfman	John .... Howard W. Overshown
Director .... Leo Erickson	Carpenter 2 .... Lawrence Redmond
Mary 2 .... Carla Harting	Carpenter 1 .... J. Fred Shiffman
Visiting Friar .... Edward James Hyland	Pontius .... Felix Solis
German Officer .... Karl Miller	Ensemble .... Parker Dixon

Time 1575; 1934; 1970s; 1980s; the present. Place: England; Germany; South Dakota. Presented in three parts.

CUTTIN' UP. By Charles Randolph-Wright; adapted from the book by Craig Marberry. November 10, 2005 (world premiere). Direction, Mr. Wright; scenery, Shaun L. Motley; costumes, Emilio Sosa; lighting, Michael Gilliam; sound, Timothy M. Thompson; dramaturgy, Mark Bly; stage management, Lloyd Davis Jr.

Andre .... Peter Jay Fernandez	Lou .... Carl Cofield
Howard .... Ed Wheeler	Vernon Winfrey .... Bill Grimmette
Rudy .... Psalmayene 24	Kenny .... Mark Damon Johnson
Wheeler Parker .... Duane Boutté	Karen .... Marva Hicks

Time: The present. Place: Washington, DC. Presented in two parts.

Downstairs Readings in the Old Vat Room.

THRASH. By Wendy MacLeod. September 14, 2005. Direction, Ms. MacLeod.
Performed by Bradford William Anderson, Clinton Brandhagen, Sue Jean Kim, Rey Lucas, Sean Pratt, Jason Stiles.

THE BIGGER MAN. By Sam Marks. September 15, 2005. Direction, Rebecca Taichman.
Performed by David Fendig, Ian Lockhart, Tuyet Thi Pham, Andrew Price, Elizabeth Webster.

THE BLUEST EYE. By Toni Morrison; adapted by Lydia Diamond. September 16, 2005. Direction, David Muse.
Performed by Tymberlee Chanel, Aakhu TuahNera Freeman, Gabrielle Goyette, Sherri LaVie Linton, Audra Alise Polk, Fatima Quander, Jefferson A. Russell, Frederick Strother.

THE SEPARATION OF BLOOD. By Bridgette A. Wimberly; based on the correspondence of Charles R. Drew. January 7, 2006. Direction, Molly Smith.

Performed by Destiny Jackson-Evans, Gabrielle Goyette, Bill Grimmette, William T. Newman Jr., Frederick Strother.

THE ST. JAMES INFIRMARY. By Brian Tucker. May 13, 2006. Direction, Jennifer L. Nelson.

Performed by Doug Brown, Jessica Frances Dukes, Deidra LaWan Starnes, Craig Wallace, Jeorge Watson.

Shakespeare Theatre Company, Washington

Michael Kahn artistic director, Nicholas T. Goldsborough managing director

DON JUAN. By Molière; adapted by Stephen Wadsworth. January 29, 2006. Direction, Mr. Wadsworth; choreography, Daniel Pelzig; scenery, Kevin Rupnik; costumes, Anna R. Oliver; lighting, Joan Arhelger; sound, Martin Desjardins; fight direction, Geoffrey Alm; stage management, M. William Shiner.

Prologue Player	Laurence O'Dwyer	Mathurine	Laura Kenny
Gusman	Gilbert Cruz	Sganarelle	Michael Milligan
Pierrot	Burton Curtis	Don Juan	Jeremy Webb
Donna Elvira	Francesca Faridany	Don Carlos	Daniel Harray
Charlotte	Laura Heisler		

Ensemble: Dacyl Acevedo, Jordan Coughtry, Nicholas Urda, Ryan Young.

Presented in two parts

ReDiscovery Series.

HERNANI. By Victor Hugo; adapted by John Strand. February 20, 2006. Direction, Paul Takacs.

Performed by Steven Carpenter, Elliot Dash, Steven Eng, Heidi Harris, Jim Jack, Laura Kenny, Michael Milligan, Pedro Pascal, Ian Merrill Peakes, Nicholas Urda, Ted van Griethuysen.

THE MODERN HUSBAND. By Henry Fielding; adapted by Michael Kahn. April 24, 2006. Direction, David Muse.

Performed by Lise Bruneau, Geraint Wyn Davies, Aubrey Deeker, Blake Ellis, Claire Lautier, Andrew Long, Stephen Patrick Martin, Cameron McNary, Lynn McNutt, Jennifer Mendenhall, Hugh Nees, Patrick Page, Mark Ross, Tonya Beckman Ross, Erik Steele, Nicholas Urda.

THE PERSIANS. By Aeschylus; adapted by Ellen McLaughlin. April 9, 2006. Direction, Ethan McSweeny; choreography, Marcela Lorca; scenery, James Noone; costumes, Jess Goldstein; lighting, Kevin Adams; sound and music, Michael Roth; stage management, M. William Shiner.

Atossa	Helen Carey	Navy	David Sabin
Herald	Scott Parkinson	Justice	Emery Battis
Darius	Ted van Griethuysen	Religion	John Seidman
Xerxes	Erin Gann	Army	David Emerson Toney
Chairman	Don Mayo	Treasury	Floyd King
Interior	John Livingstone Rolle	State	Ed Dixon

Ensemble: Dacyl Acevedo, Jordan Coughtry, Blake Ellis, Stephen Graybill, Nicholas Urda, Ryan Young.

Presented without intermission.

Studio Theatre, Washington
Joy Zinoman founding artistic director, Keith Alan Baker managing director

AUTOBAHN. By Neil LaBute. January 15, 2006. Direction, Erica Gould; scenery and lighting, Colin K. Bills; costumes, Kathleen Geldard. A cycle of short plays, listed here alphabetically: *All Apologies, Autobahn, Bench Seat, Merge, Road Trip, Funny.*
   Performed by Scott Kerns, Veronica del Cerro, Darius Suziedelis, Vanessa Vaughn, Karen Novack, Elizabeth Richards, Jesse Terrill, Paloma Ellis, James Konicek, Cecil E. Baldwin.

Theater J, Washington
Ari Roth artistic director, Patricia Jenson managing director

THE DYBBUK. By S. Ansky; adapted by Hannah Hessel and Paata Tsikurishvili. February 11, 2006. Direction, Mr. Tsikurishvili; choreography, Irina Tsikurishvili; scenery and costumes, Anastasia Ryurikov Simes; lighting, Colin K. Bills; sound, Irakli Kavsadze and Paata Tsikurishvili; stage management, Anna Lane. Presented in association with Synetic Theater.

Leah	Irina Tsikurishvili	Frede	Olena Kushch
Sender	Irakli Kavsadze	Samuel	Nathan Weinberger
Chonnon	Andrew Zox	Aaron	Daniel Eichner
Rabbi Azriel	Joel Reuben Ganz	Groom	Philip Fletcher
Isaac; Solomon	Armand Sindoni	Girl	Meghan Grady
David	Dan Istrate		

   Villagers: Julia Kunina, Geoff Nelson, Michael C. Wilson.
   Presented in two parts.

BAL MASQUE. By Richard Greenberg. April 9, 2006 (world premiere). Direction, John Vreeke; scenery and lighting, Daniel Conway; costumes, Kathleen Geldard; sound, Matt Rowe; stage management, Delia Taylor.

Trey	Jeff Allin	Owen	Cameron McNary
Greer	Brigid Cleary	Joanna	Colleen Delany
Marietta	Maia DeSanti	Russell	Todd Scofield

   Time: 1966. Place: Two New York City apartments and a bench in Central Park. Presented in two parts.

Woolly Mammoth Theatre Company, Washington
Howard Shalwitz artistic director, Kevin Moore managing director

STARVING. By S.M. Shephard-Massat. November 20, 2005 (world premiere). Direction, Seret Scott; scenery, Daniel Ettinger; costumes, Kate Turner-Walker; lighting, Dan Covey; sound and music, Mark Anduss; dramaturgy, Caroline Mandler; stage management, Taryn J. Colberg.

Frieda	Lizan Mitchell	Bettie	Jessica Frances Dukes
Rosetta	Dawn Ursula	Dolsiss	Bethany Butler
Archer	Craig Wallace	Dubiard	Michael Anthony Williams
Felix	Doug Brown	Meeker	J. Paul Nicholas

   Time: Spring 1950. Place: A upscale African-American neighborhood in Atlanta. Presented in two parts.

THE VELVET SKY. By Roberto Aguirre-Sacasa. January 30, 2006 (world premiere). Direction, Rebecca Taichman; scenery, Scott Bradley; costumes, Helen Huang; lighting,

Colin K. Bills; sound and music, Martin Desjardins and Vincent Olivieri; dramaturgy, Elissa Goetschius; stage management, Colleen Martin.

Bethany Palmer	Jeanine Serralles	Woman; others	Dawn Ursula
Warren Palmer	Will Gartshore	Officer Russell; others	Michael Russotto
Andrew Palmer	Matthew Stadelmann	Bathroom Man; others	Rick Foucheux

    Time: The present. Place: Blue Valley; New York City. Presented without intermission.

THE GIGLI CONCERT. By Tom Murphy. April 3, 2006. Direction, Tom Prewitt; scenery, Anne Gibson; costumes, Deb Sivigny; lighting, Lisa L. Ogonowski; sound, Hana Hellers; dramaturgy, Joan K. Andrews and Caroline Mandler; stage management, Taryn J. Colberg.

JPW King	Howard Shalwitz	Mona	Kimberly Schraf
Irish Man	Mitchell Hébert		

    Time: The early 1980s. Place: Dublin. Presented in two parts.

FLORIDA

Caldwell Theatre Company, Boca Raton
Michael Hall artistic director

UNDER THE BED. By Susan Sandler. February 24, 2006 (world premiere). Direction, Michael Hall; scenery, Tim Bennett; costumes, Erin Amico; lighting, Thomas Salzman; sound, M. Anthony Reimer; stage management, Jeffry George.

The Link

Mrs. Katz	Sylvia Kauders	Mrs. Miller	Margery Beddow
Mr. Markowitz	Ben Hammer	The Voice	Kathleen Emrich
Mrs. Pomerantz	Rosemary Prinz		

The Gambling Boat

Selma	Margery Beddow	Miriam	Rosemary Prinz
Abe	Ben Hammer		

The Spot
    Performed by Sylvia Kauders.

Chair Work
    Performed by Margery Beddow.

Under the Bed
    Performed by Ben Hammer.

My Tony
    Performed by Rosemary Prinz.

The Lovely Just So

Sy	Ben Hammer	Mitzi	Margery Beddow

THE IMPRESSIONISTS. By Michael McKeever. April 14, 2006 (world premiere). Direction, Michael Hall; scenery, Tim Bennett; lighting, John D. Hall; costumes, Erin Amico; sound, Steve Shapiro; stage management, Marci A. Glotzer.

Berthe Morisot	Deanna Henson	Edouard Manet	Eric Martin Brown
Camille Pissarro	George Kapetan	Charles Gleyre	Peter Haig
Claude Monet	Terrell Hardcastle	Edma Morisot	Kathryn Lee Johnston
Edgar Degas	Tim Burke	Eugene Manet	Michael Corry
Pierre-Auguste Renoir	Bruce Linser		

    Time: 1860s–1870s. Place: Paris and locations throughout France.

Coconut Grove Playhouse, Coral Gables
Arnold Mittelman producing artistic director

PASSIN' IT ON. Musical with book by Larry Atlas; music and lyrics by Terry Cashman. October 21, 2005 (world premiere). Direction, Jeffrey B. Moss; choreography, Lisa Shriver; scenery, Antje Ellermann; costumes, Ellis Tillman; lighting, Kirk Bookman; sound, Steve Shapiro; music direction, Andrew Wilder; stage management, Heather Dale MacKenzie. Presented in association with Warren Baker and Sally Jacobs.

Teddy	Robert Bartley	Harry	John-Charles Kelly
Mac	Sy Adamowsky	Artie	Joe Ricci
Sig	Len Cariou	Willie	Jordan Bennett
Jo	Julia Haubner	Chip	Michael Flanigan
Madge	Anna McNeely	Rick	Chris-Ian Sanchez
Shep	Frank Anderson		

Time: Spring. Place: Near a ballpark.

Musical numbers included: "Ballplayer," "Opening Day," "Medicine Man," "Third Base Coach," "The Ballad of Herb Score," "The Money Doesn't Matter To Me," "The Babe," "There Must Be Something Inside," "Passin' It On," "Time Traveler, "Rain Delay," "The Seasons in the Sun," "Good Enough to Dream," "Willie, Mickey and The Duke (Talkin' Baseball)."

SOUTHERN COMFORTS. By Kathleen Clark. February 10, 2006 (world premiere). Direction, Leonard Foglia; scenery, Thomas Lynch; costumes, Jane Greenwood; lighting, Brian D. Nason; sound, Steve Shapiro; music, Paul Schwartz; stage management, Heather Dale MacKenzie.

Amanda	Dixie Carter	Gus	Hal Holbrook

Presented without intermission.

SONIA FLEW. By Melinda Lopez. April 21, 2006. Direction, David Ellenstein; scenery, Michael Anania; costumes, Ellis Tillman; lighting, Frances Aronson; sound, Steve Shapiro; stage management, Heather Dale MacKenzie.

Sonia; Marta	Lucie Arnaz	Jen; Young Sonia	Katharine D. Luckinbill
Daniel; Tito	David Brummel	Sam; Orfeo	Robert Grossman
Zak; Jose	Matthew Dellapina	Nina; Pilar	Yetta Gottesman

Time: 2001; 1961. Place: Minneapolis; Havana. Presented in two parts.

Florida Stage, Manalapan
Louis Tyrrell producing director, Nancy Barnett managing director

A MARRIAGE MINUET. By David Wiltse. October 21, 2005 (world premiere). Direction, Wendy C. Goldberg; choreography, Karma Camp; scenery, Kent Goetz; costumes, Anne Kennedy; lighting, Suzanne M. Jones; sound, Matt Briganti Kelly; stage management, James Danford.

Rex	Stephen Schnetzer	Lily	Laura Flanagan
Girl	Autumn Horne	Violet	Kate Levy
Douglas	David Mann		

Time: Present. Place: A New England college town.

EXITS AND ENTRANCES. By Athol Fugard. December 9, 2005. Direction, Stephen Sachs; scenery and lighting, Richard Crowell; costumes, Morgan Lane Tanner and Shon LeBlanc; stage management, Suzanne Clement Jones.

The Playwright	William Dennis Hurley	André	Morlan Higgins

CRADLE OF MAN. By Melanie Marnich. January 27, 2006 (world premiere). Direction, Michael John Garcés; scenery, Jim Kronzer; costumes, Erin Amico; lighting, Suzanne M. Jones; sound, Ryan Rumery; stage management, James Danford.

Mona	Helen-Jean Arthur	Bonnie	Jennifer Mendenhall
Mason	Chris Clavelli	Debra	Elizabeth Rich
Jack	Chamblee Ferguson		

Time: The present. Place: Dar es Salaam, Tanzania.

BEYOND THE RAINBOW. By William Randall Beard. March 17, 2006. Direction, Ron Peluso; scenery, Kate Sutton-Johnson; costumes, Rich Hamson; lighting, Chris Johnson; sound, Matt Briganti Kelly; music, David Lohman and Ron Peluso; music direction, Jimmy Martin; stage management, Suzanne Clement Jones.

Garland	Jody Briskey	Judy	Norah Long
Louis B. Mayer; others	Clark A. Cruikshank	Frank Gumm; others	Peter Moore
Ethel Gumm; others	Cathleen Fuller		

Musical numbers included: "When You're Smiling (The Whole World Smiles With You)," "Jingle Bells," "Judy," "Born in a Trunk," "I Can't Give You Anything But Love,"" "Be a Clown," " "Zing Went the Strings of My Heart," "You Made Me Love You," "We're Off to See The Wizard," "Rock-a-Bye Your Baby with a Dixie Melody," "The Trolley Song," "Do It Again," "How Long Has This Been Going On?," "Who Cares (As Long As You Care for Me)," "That's Entertainment," "Come Rain or Come Shine," "Alone, Together," "They Can't Take That Away From Me," "Get Happy," "After You've Gone," " You Go to My Head," "For Me and My Gal," "Swanee," "Stormy Weather," "The Man That Got Away," "Over the Rainbow," "San Francisco."

Time: April 23, 1961. Place: Carnegie Hall in New York; Judy Garland's memory.

SPLITTING INFINITY. By Jamie Pachino. May 5, 2006. Direction, Louis Tyrrell; scenery and lighting, Richard Crowell; costumes, Suzette Paré, sound, Matt Briganti Kelly; stage management, James Danford.

Young Leigh	Tory Shulman	Robbie March	Brad Barfield
Young Saul	Dustin Sullivan	Saul Lieberman	Stephen Schnetzer
Leigh Sangold	Lisa Bostnar	Mrs. March	Lourelene Snedeker

Time: 1979; 2006. Place: A university office; a hospital room; a synagogue.

Florida Studio Theatre, Sarasota
Richard Hopkins artistic director, Rebecca Langford managing director

ETHEL WATERS: HIS EYE IS ON THE SPARROW. Musical with book, music and lyrics by Larry Parr. October 7, 2005 (world premiere). Direction and choreography, Dennis Courtney; scenery, Nayna Ramey; costumes, Marcella Beckwith; lighting, Martin E. Vreeland; music direction, Michael Sebastian; stage management, Stacy A. Blackburn.

Ethel Waters	Jannie Jones	Ethel Waters	Chaundra Cameron

Musical numbers included: "His Eye Is on the Sparrow," "Masculine Men, Feminine Women," "Frankie and Johnny," "I Don't Dig You Jack," "Sweet Georgia Brown," "The Joint Is Jumpin'," "Little Black Boy," "Old Man Harlem," "Dinah," "Taking a Chance on Love," "Am I Blue?," "Stormy Weather," "Heat Wave," "Cabin in the Sky," "Black and Blue."

New Theatre, Coral Gables
Rafael de Acha artistic director, Eileen Suarez managing director

MADAGASCAR. By JT Rogers. September 9, 2005. Direction and sound, Ricky J. Martinez; scenery, Jesse Dreikosen; lighting, Micheal Foster; stage management, Joseph NeSmith.

| June .... Kathryn Lee Johnston | Nathan .... Bill Schwartz |
| Lillian ....Angie Radosh | |

LADIES AND NOT-SO GENTLE WOMEN. By Alfred Allan Lewis. December 2, 2005 (world premiere). Direction, Rafael de Acha; choreography, Ricky J. Martinez; scenery, Jesse Dreikosen; costumes, Estela Vrancovich; lighting, Eric Nelson; stage management, Caron Grant.

Bessy Marbury .... Kimberly Daniel	Anne Morgan .... Aubrey Shavonn
Elsie de Wolfe .... Patti Gardner	First Actress .... Annemaria Rajala
Anne Vanderbilt .... Lisa Morgan	Second Actress .... Tara Vodihn

PARADISE. By Glyn O'Malley. January 13, 2006. Direction, Ricky J. Martinez; scenery, Jesse Dreikosen; lighting, Micheal Foster; sound, M. Anthony Reimer; stage management, Joseph NeSmith.

Shoshana .... Bridget Connors	Bassam .... Rudy Mungaray
Omar .... Euriamis Losada	Sarah .... Samara Siskind
Fatima .... Beatriz Montanez	

DAY OF RECKONING. By Melody Cooper. February 24, 2006. Direction, Ricky J. Martinez; scenery, Jesse Dreikosen; costumes, Estela Vrancovich; lighting, Patrick Tennant; sound, Nate Rausch; stage management, Joseph NeSmith.

| Lucy Cooper .... Tara Vodihn | Albert Parsons Jr. .... Brandon Morris |
| Albert Parsons .... Keith Cassidy | Lulu Parsons .... Karina Fernandez |

THE SUNKEN LIVING ROOM. By David Caudle. April 6, 2006 (world premiere). Direction, Ryan Rilette; scenery, Jesse Deikosen; lighting, Micheal Foster; sound, Ricardo Mungaray; costumes, K. Blair Brown; stage management, Arianne Pelletier. Presented in association with Southern Rep, New Orleans.

| Wade .... John Magaro | Lynette .... Pamela Roza |
| Chip .... Rudy Mungaray | Tammy..................................... Arianne Ellison |

GEORGIA

Alliance Theatre Company, Atlanta

Susan V. Booth artistic director, Thomas Pechar managing director

TICK, TICK . . . BOOM! Musical with book, music and lyrics by Jonathan Larson. September 14, 2005. Direction and choreography, Kent Gash; scenery, Emily Jean Beck; costumes, Alvin B. Perry; lighting, Liz Lee; sound, Clay Benning; music direction, Michael Fauss; orchestrations, Stephen Oremus; dramaturgy, Freddie Ashley; stage management, lark hackshaw.

| Michael .... Dwayne Clark | Jonathan .... Matthew Scott |
| Susan; Karessa .... Soara-Joye Ross | |

Musical numbers included: "30/90," "Green Green Dress," "Johnny Can't Decide," "Sunday," "No More," "Therapy," "Real Life," "Sugar," "See Her Smile," "Come To Your Senses," "Why," "Louder Than Words."

Time bomb: Matthew Scott in tick, tick . . . BOOM!
Photo: Christopher Oquendo

MOONLIGHT AND MAGNOLIAS. By Ron Hutchinson. September 21, 2005. Direction, Lynne Meadow; scenery, Santo Loquasto; costumes, Jane Greenwood; lighting, Rui Rita; sound, Jason Romney; stage management, Pat A. Flora.

Miss Poppenghul	Tess Malis Kincaid	Ben Hecht	David Pittu
Victor Fleming	Kevin O'Rourke	David O. Selznick	Thomas Sadoski

BLUISH. By Janece Shaffer. February 10, 2006 (world premiere). Direction, Susan V. Booth; scenery, Joseph P. Tilford; costumes, Rachel Anne Healy; lighting, Ken Yunker; sound designer, Obadiah Eaves; dramaturgy, Celise Kalke; stage management, Kate McDoniel.

Lane	Karen Uchida Beyer	Manny	Howard Elfman
Beth	Kati Brazda	Ben	Todd Gearhart
Ilene	Suehyla El-Attar	Lillian	Joyce Reehling

Time: The present. Place: Atlanta. Presented in two parts.

. . . ," SAID SAID. By Kenneth Lin. April 14, 2006 (world premiere). Direction, Sharon Ott; scenery and lighting, Kent Dorsey; costumes, Deborah L. Trout; sound, Stephen LeGrand; fight direction, Jason Armit; dramaturgy, Freddie Ashley; stage management, Robert Allen Wright.

Sarah Said	Jacqueline Antaramian	Guard	David Limbach
Emily	Kate Donadio	Michael Garcet	Victor Slezak
Andre Said	Edward A. Hajj		

Place: The Said residence in Vermont; an Algerian prison cell.

ILLINOIS

About Face Theatre, Chicago
Eric Rosen artistic director, Greg Copeland managing director

LOVING REPEATING: A MUSICAL OF GERTRUDE STEIN. By Frank Galati; based on the writings of Ms. Stein; music by Stephen Flaherty. February 18, 2006. Direction, Mr. Galati; choreography, Liza Gennaro; scenery, Jack Magaw; costumes, Michelle Tidal; lighting, Chris Binder; sound, Rob Milburn and Michael Bodeen; music direction, Thomas Murray; stage management, Jonathan Templeton.

Gertrude Stein .... Cindy Gold   Alice B. Toklas ....Jenny Powers
Young Gertrude .... Christine Mild
   Ensemble: Zach Ford, Cristen Paige, Harriet Nzinga Plumpp, Travis Turner, Bernie Yvon.

Court Theatre, Chicago
Charles Newell artistic director, Dawn J. Helsing executive director

MABOU MINES DOLLHOUSE. By Mabou Mines; adapted from Henrik Ibsen's *A Doll House*; music by Edvard Grieg and Eve Beglarian. December 3, 2005. Direction, Lee Breuer; choreography, Eamonn Farrell, Martha Clarke and Erik Liberman; scenery, Narelle Sissons; costumes, Meganne George; lighting, Mary Louise Geiger; sound, Edward Cosla; puppetry, Jane Catherine Shaw; dramaturgy, Mr. Breuer and Maude Mitchell; stage management, Martin Lechner.

Hollywood mayhem: Thomas Sadoski, Kevin O'Rourke and David Pittu in Moonlight and Magnolias. *Photo: Christopher Oquendo*

Nora Helmer	Maude Mitchell	Emmy Helmer	Hailey Gould,
Torvald Helmer	Mark Povinelli		Lillian Almaguer
Nils Krogstad	Kristopher Medina	Bob Helmer	Sophie Birkedlalen,
Kristine Linde	Honora Fergusson		Eilert Sundt
Dr. Rank	Ricardo Gil	Cameo	Eamonn Farrell,
Helene	Margaret Lancaster		Ilia Dodd Loomis

The Goodman Theatre, Chicago
Robert Falls artistic director, Roche Schulfer executive director

DOLLHOUSE. By Rebecca Gilman; adapted from the play by Henrik Ibsen. June 28, 2005 (world premiere). Direction, Robert Falls; choreography, Randy Duncan; scenery, Robert Brill; costumes, Mara Blumenfeld; lighting, James F. Ingalls; sound and music, Richard Woodbury; stage management, Sascha Connor.

Nora Helmer	Maggie Siff	Max	Ryan Cowhey,
Terry	Anthony Starke		Matthew Gerdisch
Raj Patel	Firdous Bamji	Skyler	Melody Hollis,
Kristine	Elizabeth Rich		Allison Sparrow
Pete	Lance Baker	Marta	Charin Alvarez
Macy	Jordyn Knysz,	Iris	Maritza Cervantes
	Emily Leahy		

BEYOND GLORY. By Stephen Lang; adapted from the book by Larry Smith. September 20, 2005 (world premiere). Direction, Mr. Lang; scenery, Tony Cisek; lighting, Dan Covey; sound, Cecil Averett; music, Robert Kessler and Ethan Neuburg; projections, John Boesche; stage management, Kimberly Osgood.

Performed by Stephen Lang; with the voices of John Bedford, Anne Twomey and Matt Sincell representing armed forces veterans Nicky Daniel Bacon, Vernon J. Baker, Hector Cafferata, John William Finn, Daniel K. Inouye, Lewis L. Millett, Clarence Sasser and James Bond Stockdale.

New Stages Series. November 1–5, 2005.

SIX POSTCARDS. By Lisa Dillman. Direction, Steve Scott. November 1, 2005.

CRIPPLED SISTERS. By Susan Nussbaum. Direction, Karen Kessler. November 2, 2005.

SAM'S COMING. By Kia Corthron. Direction, Henry Godinez. November 3, 2005.

PALMER PARK. By Joanna McClelland Glass. Direction, Chuck Smith. November 4, 2005.

GET WHAT YOU NEED. By Jessica Goldberg. Direction, Carolyn Cantor. November 5, 2005.

VIGILS. By Noah Haidle. Direction, Dexter Bullard. November 6, 2005.

PERICLES. By William Shakespeare. January 17, 2006. Direction, Mary Zimmerman; choreography, Daniel Pelzig; scenery, Daniel Ostling; costumes, Mara Blumenfeld; lighting, T.J. Gerckens; sound, Andre Pluess and Ben Sussman; stage management, Joseph Drummond.

Antiochus	Glenn Fleshler	Escanes	Gary Wingert
Pericles	Ryan Artzberger	Lord of Tyre	Berwick Haynes
Daughter to Antiochus	Laura Scheinbaum	Cleon	Joseph Costa
Thaliard	Dan Kenney	Dionyza	Michelle Shupe
Helicanus	Craig Spidle	Leonine	Evan Zes

1st Fisherman .... Gary Wingert	Marina .... Marguerite Stimpson
2nd Fisherman .... Erik Steele	Pander .... Glenn Fleshler
3rd Fisherman .... Berwick Haynes	Bawd .... Naomi Jacobson
Simonides.. Joel Hatch	Boult .... Jesse J. Perez
Thaisa .... Colleen Delany	Lysimachus .... Erik Steele
Lychorida .... Naomi Jacobson	Diana .... Michelle Shupe
Cerimon... Glory Kissel	

Ensemble: JT Drew, Katherine Foster, Stephen Grush, Bethany Hubbard, Kenneth Z. Kendall, Akili Moore, Meghan Murphy, Dillon Porter, Dan Sanders-Joyce, Laura Scheinbaum, Kevin V. Smith.

THE CLEAN HOUSE. By Sarah Ruhl. April 29, 2006. Direction, Jessica Thebus; choreography, Marla Lampert; scenery, Todd Rosenthal; costumes, Linda Roethke; lighting, James F. Ingalls; sound and music, Andre Pluess and Ben Sussman; dramaturgy, Tanya Palmer; stage management, Joseph Drummond.

Lane .... Mary Beth Fisher	Ana .... Marilyn Dodds Frank
Charles .... Patrick Clear	Mathilde ....Guenia Lemos
Virginia .... Christine Estabrook	

Lookingglass Theatre Company, Chicago
David Catlin artistic director, Rachel E. Kraft executive director

HILLBILLY ANTIGONE. Musical with book, music and lyrics by Rick Sims. June 4, 2005 (world premiere). Direction, Heidi Stillman; choreography, Kirsten Hara; scenery, Daniel Ostling; costumes, Mara Blumenfeld; lighting, Chris Binder; sound, Andre Pluess and Ray Nardelli; music direction, Mr. Sims; stage management, Sara Gmitter.

Grandma .... Cynthia Baker	Zachariah ....Rick Sims
Clayton; Tree; Jesse .... Lawrence E. DiStasi	Creon ....Philip R. Smith
Grace ....Christine Mary Dunford	Jeb.. Andrew White
Antigone .... Mattie Hawkinson	Mama Virginia .... Tracy Walsh
Tubby Gaines; Kenesaw .... Keith Kupferer	Harmon ....Matt Ziegler
Amos .... Chris Mathews	

Steppenwolf Theatre Company, Chicago
Martha Lavey artistic director, David Hawkanson executive director

THE PAIN AND THE ITCH. By Bruce Norris. July 10, 2005 (world premiere). Direction, Anna D. Shapiro; scenery, Daniel Ostling; costumes, Janice Pytel; lighting, James F. Ingalls; sound, Rob Milburn and Michael Bodeen; dramaturgy, Edward Sobel; stage management, Robert H. Satterlee.

Clay ....Zak Orth	Kalina .... Kate Arrington
Kelly .... Mariann Mayberry	Kayla .... Lillian Almaguer,
Cash .... Tracy Letts	Darragh Quinn Dolan
Carol .... Jayne Houdyshell	Mr. Hadid ....James Vincent Meredith

Time: The present. Place: An urban home. Presented in two parts.

AFTER THE QUAKE. By Haruki Murakami; adapted by Frank Galati. October 20, 2005 (world premiere). Direction, Mr. Galati; scenery, James Schuette; costumes, Mara Blumenfeld; lighting, James F. Ingalls; sound and music, Andre Pluess and Ben Sussman; stage management, Malcolm Ewen. Presented in association with the Long Wharf Theatre.

Performed by Tiffany Fujiwara, Jason McDermott, Aiko Nakasone, Andrew Pang, Keong Sim, Hanson Tse, Kayla Tucker, Jeff Wichmann.

Presented without intermission.

THE WELL-APPOINTED ROOM. By Richard Greenberg. January 12, 2006 (world premiere). Direction, Terry Kinney; scenery, Robert Brill; costumes, Laura Bauer; lighting, James F. Ingalls; sound and music, Rob Milburn and Michael Bodeen; stage management, Robert H. Satterlee.

Stewart; Mitchell	Tracy Letts	Mark	Josh Charles
Natalie; Penelope	Amy Morton	Gretchen	Kate Arrington

Time: The first years of the 21st century. Place: New York City. Presented in two parts.

LADY MADELINE. By Mickle Maher; adapted from Edgar Allan Poe's "The Fall of the House of Usher." February 7, 2006 (world premiere). Direction, Jessica Thebus; scenery, Stephanie Nelson; costumes, Tatjana Radisic; lighting, J.R. Lederle; sound and music, Andre Pluess and Ben Sussman; stage management, Deb Styer.

Madeline	Tracy Michelle Arnold	Guest	Kirk Anderson
Roderick	Matthew Krause	Madeline Double	Katie Jeep

Quartet: Lili-Anne Brown, Jess Godwin, Richard Manera, Jonathan Raviv.

Time: 1840. Place: Ancient house.

LOVE SONG. By John Kolvenbach. March 30, 2006 (world premiere). Direction, Austin Pendleton; scenery, Brian Sidney Bembridge; costumes, Rachel Anne Healy; lighting, Michelle Habeck; sound and music, Andre Pluess and Ben Sussman; stage management, Deb Styer.

Beane	Ian Barford	Harry; Waiter	Francis Guinan
Joan	Molly Regan	Molly	Mariann Mayberry

Time: The present. Place: Beane's apartment; Joan and Harry's apartment.

LOVE-LIES-BLEEDING. By Don DeLillo. April 27, 2006 (world premiere). Direction, Amy Morton; scenery, Loy Arcenas; costumes, Nan Cibula-Jenkins; lighting, J.R. Lederle; sound, Josh Schmidt; stage management, Malcolm Ewen.

Alex	John Heard	Toinette	Martha Lavey
Lia	Penelope Walker	Sean	Louis Cancelmi
Alex in extremis	Larry Kucharik		

Time: Within the past six years. Place: A spacious room in an old, remote house.

THE SUNSET LIMITED. By Cormac McCarthy. May 18, 2006 (world premiere). Direction, Sheldon Patinkin; scenery, Scott Neale; costumes, Tatjana Radisic; lighting, Keith Parham; sound, Martha Wegener; stage management, Hilary Martin.

White	Austin Pendleton	Black	Freeman Coffey

Time: Present. Place: A New York subway tenement.

Victory Gardens Theater, Chicago
Dennis Zacek artistic director, Marcelle McVay managing director

SYMMETRY. By David C. Field. June 6, 2005 (world premiere). Direction, Dennis Zacek; scenery, Mary Griswold; costumes, Christine Pascual; lighting, Todd Hensley; sound, Andre Pluess and Ben Sussman; stage management, Tina M. Jach.

Neal Julian	Matt DeCaro	Ecco Sagada	Jennifer Liu
John Slocum	J.J. Johnston	Edmond Lakos	William J. Norris

Myra Julian .... Meg Thalken   Oscar Newman .... Aaron Roman Weiner
 Time: The present. Place: A small university in New Mexico. Presented in two parts.

MEMORY HOUSE. By Kathleen Tolan. September 19, 2005. Direction, Sandy Shinner; scenery, Robert C. Martin; costumes, Lorraine Venberg; lighting, Christopher Ash; sound, Lindsay Jones; stage management, Tina M. Jach.

Katia .... Cassandra Bissell   Maggie .... Taylor Miller
 Time: New Year's Eve. Place: New York City. Presented without intermission.

WHEATLEY. By Lonnie Carter. October 10, 2005 (world premiere). Direction, Sharon Scruggs; scenery, Brian Sidney Bembridge; costumes, Rachel Anne Healy; lighting, Todd Hensley; sound, Mikhail Fiksel; stage management, Danielle S. Boyke.

Phillis Wheatley .... Yetide Badaki   Rev. Cooper; others .... Aaron Todd Douglas
Samson Ossee; others .... Daniel Bryant   Susannah; others .... Ann Joseph
 Time: 1760–84; the present. Place: Boston; London; Bath. Presented in two parts.

HORTENSIA AND THE MUSEUM OF DREAMS. By Nilo Cruz. November 14, 2005. Direction, Diane Rodriguez; scenery, Brian Sidney Bembridge; costumes, Judith Lundberg; lighting, Jesse Klug; sound, Andre Pluess and Rick Sims; stage management, Tina M. Jach.

Luciana .... Alex Meneses   Basilio .... Christopher De Paola
Luca .... Ivan Vega   General Viamonte .... Ricardo Gutierrez
Hortensia .... Cheryl Lynn Bruce   Delita .... Marcela Munoz
Samuel .... Joe Minoso
 Time: January 1998, during the Pope's visit. Place: Cuba.
 Presented in two parts.

I HAVE BEFORE ME A REMARKABLE DOCUMENT GIVEN TO ME BY A YOUNG LADY FROM RWANDA. By Sonja Linden. January 30, 2006. Direction, Andrea J. Dymond; scenery, Mary Griswold; costumes, Debbie Baer; lighting, Jaymi Lee Smith; sound, Victoria DeIorio; stage management, Rita Vreeland.

Juliette .... Yetide Badaki   Simon .... Lance Baker
 Time: 1999, five years after the Rwandan genocide. Place: London.

CRADLE OF MAN. By Melanie Marnich. March 24, 2006. Direction, Sandy Shinner; scenery, Keith Pitts; costumes, Judith Lundberg; lighting, Jacqueline Reid; sound, Andre Pluess; stage management, Tina M. Jach.

Mason .... Sean Cooper   Bonnie .... Jennie Moreau
Jack .... David Eigenberg   Mona .... Peggy Roeder
Debra .... Julie Ganey
 Time: The present. Place: Dar es Salaam, Tanzania.

HALF AND HALF. By James Sherman. May 26, 2006 (world premiere). Direction, Dennis Zacek; scenery, Mary Griswold; costumes, Christine Pascual; lighting, Rita Pietraszek; sound, Andre Pluess; stage management, Tina M. Jach.

Earth Day

Susan .... Laura T. Fisher   Lucy .... Mattie Hawkinson
Stewart .... Joe Dempsey
 Time: April 22, 1970. Place: A kitchen in the Rogers Park area, Chicago.

Anniversary Day

Lucy .... Laura T. Fisher   Katie .... Mattie Hawkinson
Jeremy .... Joe Dempsey
   Time: July 5, 2005. Place: A kitchen in the Rogers Park area, Chicago.

KENTUCKY

Actors Theatre of Louisville

Marc Masterson artistic director, Alexander Speer executive director

30th Anniversary Humana Festival of New American Plays. March 7–April 8, 2006.

SIX YEARS. By Sharr White. March 7, 2006. Direction, Hal Brooks; scenery, Paul Owen; costumes, Catherine F. Norgren; lighting, Tony Penna; sound, Matt Callahan; video, Joanna K. Donehower; fight direction, Cliff Williams III; dramaturgy, Julie Felise Dubiner; stage management, Nancy Pittelman.

Phil Granger .... Michael J. Reilly   Peg Muncie .... Marni Penning
Meredith Granger .... Kelly Mares   Dorothy .... Stephanie Thompson
Tom Wheaton .... Harry Bouvy   Michael Granger .... Isaac Gardner
Jack Muncie .... Frank Deal
   Time: 1949–73. Place: St. Louis; Chicago; Vacaville, California. Presented in two parts.

ACT A LADY. By Jordan Harrison. March 7, 2006. Direction, Anne Kauffman; scenery, Kris Stone; costumes, Lorraine Venberg; lighting, Deb Sullivan; sound, Benjamin Marcum; music, Michael Friedman; dramaturgy, Adrien-Alice Hansel; stage management, Debra Anne Gasper.
   Performed by Cheryl Lynn Bowers, Steven Boyer, Suzanna Hay, Paul O'Brien, Matt Seidman, Sandra Shipley.

   Time: 1927. Place: A very small town in the Midwest. Presented in two parts

THE SCENE. By Theresa Rebeck. March 11, 2006. Direction, Rebecca Taichman; scenery, Paul Owen; costumes, Catherine F. Norgren; lighting, Tony Penna; sound, Matt Callahan; fight direction, Cliff Williams III; dramaturgy, Mervin P. Antonio; stage management, Brady Ellen Poole.

Charlie .... Stephen Barker Turner   Clea .... Anna Camp
Lewis .... David Wilson Barnes   Stella .... Carla Harting
   Time: The present. Place: New York City. Presented in two parts.

NATURAL SELECTION. By Eric Coble. March 16, 2006. Direction, Marc Masterson; scenery, Kris Stone; costumes, Lorraine Venberg; lighting, Deb Sullivan; sound, Martin Desjardins; video, Jason Czaja; fight direction, Mark Mineart; dramaturgy, Julie Felise Dubiner; stage management, Paul Mills Holmes.

Henry Carson .... Jay Russell   Suzie Carson .... Melinda Wade
Ernie Hardaway;   Zhao Martinez .... Javi Mulero
   Mr. Neiberding .... Mark Mineart   Terrance .... Joseph Benjamin Glaser
Yolanda Pastiche; others .... Heather Dilly
   Time: Next week. Place: Orlando and points west. Presented in two parts.

HOTEL CASSIOPEIA. By Charles L. Mee. March 21, 2006. Direction, Anne Bogart; scenery, Neil Patel; costumes, James Schuette; lighting, Brian H. Scott; sound, Darron L. West;

2006
Humana
Festival of New
American Plays

Top to bottom: Michael J. Reilly and Kelly Mares in Six Years; *Steven Boyer and Matt Seidman in* Act a Lady; *Anna Camp in* The Scene. *Photos: Harlan Taylor*

2006
Humana Festival of
New American Plays

Top to bottom: Javi Mulero and Jay Russell in Natural Selection; *Ellen Lauren in* Hotel Cassiopeia; *Rha Goddess in* Low. *Photos: Harlan Taylor*

dramaturgy, Adrien-Alice Hansel; stage management, Elizabeth Moreau. Presented in association with SITI Company.

Joseph	Barney O'Hanlon	Pharmacist	J. Ed Araiza
Waitress	Michi Barall	Allegra	Ellen Lauren
Astronomer	Stephen Webber	Mother	Akiko Aizawa
Herbalist	Leon Ingulsrud		

LOW. By Rha Goddess. March 25, 2006. Direction, Chay Yew; choreography, Rennie Harris; sound and music, Baba Israel, Darrin Ross and Marcel Wierckx; dramaturgy, Mervin P. Antonio; stage management, Sarah Goshman. Presented in association with Divine Dime Entertainment, Sasha Dees for Made in da Shade and MultiArts Projects and Productions.

Lowquesha; others .... Rha Goddess

NEON MIRAGE. By Liz Duffy Adams; Dan Dietz; Rick Hip-Flores; Julie Jensen; Lisa Kron; Tracey Scott Wilson; Chay Yew. March 25, 2006. Direction, Wendy McClellan; scenery, Paul Owen; costumes, John P. White; lighting, Nick Dent; sound, Benjamin Marcum; music direction, Rick Hip-Flores; dramaturgy, Adrien-Alice Hansel; stage management, Megan Schwarz.

Performed by Sarah Augusta, Lauren Bauer, Ashanti Brown, Kim Carpenter, Tom Coiner, Bryan Manley Davis, Lee Dolson, Melissa Dowty, Ben Friesen, Isaac Gardner, Eva Gil, Cindy N. Kawasaki, Keira Keeley, Toby G. Knops, Aaron Alika Patinio, Michael C. Schantz, Robin Grace Thompson, Stephanie Thompson, Elizabeth Truong, Cliff Williams III.

Time: The past, present and future. Place: Las Vegas.

Ten Minute Plays. April 1–2, 2006.

SOVEREIGNTY. By Rolin Jones. Direction, Shirley Serotsky; scenery, Paul Owen; costumes, John P. White and Stacy Squires; lighting, Paul Werner; sound, Benjamin Marcum; dramaturgy, Julie Felise Dubiner; stage management, Debra Anne Gasper.

Mrs. Elsbeth	Heather Dilly	Boy	James B. Seiler Jr.
Mrs. Merriweather	Sandra Shipley	Boy's Father	Matt Seidman

Time: Now. Place: The next town.

THREE GUYS AND A BRENDA. By Adam Bock. Direction, Frank Deal; scenery, Paul Owen; costumes, John P. White and Stacy Squires; lighting, Paul Werner; sound, Benjamin Marcum; dramaturgy, Julie Felise Dubiner; stage management, Debra Anne Gasper.

Joe	Suzanna Hay	Randall	Cheryl Lynn Bowers
Bob	Keira Keeley	Brenda	Sarah Augusta

LISTENERS. By Jane Martin. Direction, Jon Jory; scenery, Paul Owen; costumes, John P. White and Stacy Squires; lighting, Paul Werner; sound, Benjamin Marcum; dramaturgy, Julie Felise Dubiner; stage management, Debra Anne Gasper.

Eleanor	Melinda Wade	Walter	Jay Russell
Ralph	Mark Mineart		

Listeners: Tom Coiner, Lee Dolson, Ben Friesen, Aaron Alika Patinio.

MARYLAND

Center Stage, Baltimore
Irene Lewis artistic director, Michael Ross managing director

ONCE ON THIS ISLAND. Musical with book and lyrics by Lynn Ahrens; music by Stephen Flaherty; based on *My Love, My Love* by Rosa Guy. December 21, 2005. Direction and choreography by Kenneth Lee Roberson; scenery, Neil Patel; costumes, Emilio Sosa; lighting, David Weiner; sound, Garth Hemphill; music direction and orchestrations, Darryl G. Ivey; dramaturgy, Otis Ramsey-Zoe; stage management, Debra Acquavella.

Andrea	Lakisha Anne Bowen	Armand	Erick Pinnick
Erzulie	E. Faye Butler	Agwe	David St. Louis
Asaka	LaVon Fisher	Tonton Julian	C.E. Smith
Daniel Beauxhomme	J.D. Goldblatt	Mama Euralie	Gayle Turner
Ti Moune	Trisha Jeffrey	Little Ti Moune	Heaven Leigh Horton
Papa Ge	Christopher L. Morgan		

Musical numbers included: "Prologue/We Dance," One Small Girl," "Waiting for Life," "And the Gods Heard Her Prayer," "Rain," "Pray," "Forever Yours," "The Sad Tale of the Beauxhommes," "Ti Moune," "Mama Will Provide," "Some Say," "The Human Heart," "Some Girls," "The Ball," "A Part of Us," "Why We Tell the Story."

Place: An island in the French Antilles. Presented without intermission.

THE MURDER OF ISAAC. By Motti Lerner; translated by Anthony Berris. February 9, 2006. Direction, Irene Lewis; choreography, Kenneth Lee Roberson; scenery, Christopher Barreca; costumes, Candice Donnelly; lighting, Mimi Jordan Sherin; sound, David Budries; music, Eric Svejcar; fight direction, J. Allen Suddeth; dramaturgy, Gavin Witt; stage management, Mike Schleifer.

Shulamit	Lise Bruneau	Binder	David Margulies
Talia	Charlotte Cohn	Avi	Chaz Mena
Female Guard	Kelli Danaker	Avner	Tzahi Moskovitz
Lola	Mia Dillon	Yigal	Benjamin Pelteson
Musician	Daniel Feyer	Eliahu	Jeffrey Ware
Yuda	Olek Krupa	Mendel	Gordon Joseph Weiss
Boris	Dan Manning	Natan	Joe Zaloom

Time: 1998, three years after the assassination of Yitzhak Rabin. Place: An Israeli rehabilitation center for victims of Post-Traumatic Stress Disorder. Presented in two parts.

MASSACHUSETTS

Actors' Shakespeare Project, Boston
Benjamin Evett artistic director, Sara Stackhouse executive producer

KING LEAR. By William Shakespeare. October 1, 2005. Direction, Patrick Swanson; scenery and costumes, David R.Gammons; lighting, Ben Pilat; music direction, Bill Barclay; fight direction, Robert Walsh; stage management, Adele Nadine Traub. Presented in association with the Boston University School of Theatre.

King Lear	Alvin Epstein	Cornwall	Michael F. Walker
Kent	Allyn Burrows	Albany; Old Man	William Gardiner
Gloucester	Colin Lane	Goneril	Jeannie Israel
Edmund	Benjamin Evett	Regan	Paula Langton

Cordelia .... Sarah Newhouse	Edgar .... Doug Lockwood
France; others .... Gabriel Levey	Fool .... Ken Cheeseman
Burgundy; Oswald .... Bill Barclay	Curan; others .... Matt Dickson

Presented in two parts.

American Repertory Theatre, Cambridge
Robert Woodruff artistic director, Robert J. Orchard executive director

THE KEENING. By Humberto Dorado; translated by Joe Broderick and Ryan McKittrick. October 16, 2005. Direction, Nicolás Montero; scenery and lighting, Alejandro Luna; costumes, David Reynoso; sound, David Remedios; dramaturgy, Mr. McKittrick; stage management, Peter Braasch Dean.

The Woman .... Marissa Chibas
Presented without intermission.

THREE SISTERS. By Anton Chekhov; adapted by Krystian Lupa; translated by Paul Schmidt. November 30, 2005. Direction and scenery, Mr. Lupa; costumes, Piotr Skiba; lighting, Scott Zielinski; sound, David Remedios; music, Jacek Ostaszewski; video, Zbyszek Bzymek; dramaturgy, Gideon Lester and John Herndon; stage management, Chris De Camillis.

Andrei Prozorov .... Sean Dugan	Chebutykin .... Thomas Derrah
Olga .... Kelly McAndrew	Fedotik .... Patrick Mapel
Natasha .... Julienne Hanzelka Kim	Ferapont .... Jeremy Geidt
Kulygin .... Will LeBow	Solyony .... Chris McKinney
Irina .... Sarah Grace Wilson	Baron Tuzenbach .... Jeff Biehl
Masha .... Molly Ward	Rohde .... Sean Simbro
Vershinin .... Frank Wood	Anfisa .... Mikki Lipsey

Soldiers: Freddy Franklin, Elbert Joseph, Mason Sand.
Presented in two parts.

NO EXIT. By Jean-Paul Sartre; translated by Stuart Gilbert. January 11, 2006. Direction and scenery, Jerry Mouawad; costumes, Rafael Jaen; lighting, Jeff Forbes; sound, David Remedios; dramaturgy, Mark Poklemba; stage management, Darren Brannon.

Valet .... Remo Airaldi	Estelle .... Karen MacDonald
Garcin .... Will LeBow	Inez .... Paula Plum

Presented without intermission.

ORPHEUS X. By Rinde Eckert. March 29, 2006 (world premiere). Direction, Robert Woodruff; scenery, David Zinn and Denise Marika; costumes, Mr. Zinn; lighting, Christopher Akerlind; sound, David Remedios; video, Ms. Marika; dramaturgy, Ryan McKittrick and Shari Perkins; stage management, Peter Braasch Dean.

Orpheus .... Rinde Eckert	John; Persephone .... John Kelly
Eurydice ...., Suzan Hanson	

Musicians: Timothy Feeney, Jeff Lieberman, Blake Newman, Wendy Richman.

THE ISLAND OF SLAVES. By Pierre Marivaux; translated by Gideon Lester. May 17, 2006 (world premiere). Direction, Robert Woodruff; scenery and costumes, David Zinn; lighting, Christopher Akerlind; sound, David Remedios; video, Leah Gelpe; dramaturgy, John Herndon and Mark Poklemba; stage management, Chris De Camillis.

Iphicrate .... John Campion	Euphrosine .... Karen MacDonald
Arlequin .... Remo Airaldi	Cléanthis .... Fiona Gallagher

Trivelin .... Thomas Derrah	Raquel Blake .... Adam Shanahan
Mohogoney Brown .... Freddy Franklin	JuJu Bee .... Airline Inthyrath
Fena Barbitall .... Ryan Carpenter	Landa Plenty .... Santio Cupon

Barrington Stage Company, Sheffield
Julianne Boyd artistic director

FUENTE. By Cusi Cram. July 7, 2005 (world premiere). Direction, Sturgis Warner; scenery, Brian Prather; costumes, Guy Lee Bailey; lighting, D. Benjamin Courtney; dramaturgy, Alexis Greene; stage management, Jamie Thoma.

Adela .... Zabryna Guevara	Omar .... Piter Marek
Soledad .... Lucia Brawley	Blair-Maria .... Jeanine Serralles
Chaparro; Gustavo .... Michael Ray Escamilla	Esteban; Denver .... Paolo Andino

  Place: A southern, desert location. Presented in two parts.

Berkshire Theatre Festival, Stockbridge
Kate Maguire executive director

AMERICAN BUFFALO. By David Mamet. July 29, 2005. Direction, Anders Cato; scenery, Carl Sprague; costumes Olivera Gajic; lighting, Jeff Davis; sound and music, Scott Killian; stage management, Jennifer Cicelsky-George.

Don Dubrow .... Jim Frangione	Teach .... Chris Noth
Bobby .... Sean Nelson	

SOUVENIR: A FANTASIA ON THE LIFE OF FLORENCE FOSTER JENKINS. By Stephen Temperley. August 17, 2005. Direction, Vivian Matalon; scenery, R. Michael Miller; costumes, Tracy Christensen; lighting, Ann G. Wrightson; sound, David Budries; stage management, Jack Gianino.

Cosme McMoon .... Donald Corren	Florence Foster Jenkins .... Judy Kaye

Huntington Theatre Company, Boston
Nicholas Martin artistic director, Michael Maso managing director

CAROL MULRONEY. By Stephen Belber. October 26, 2005 (world premiere). Direction, Lisa Peterson; scenery, Rachel Hauck; costumes, Kristen Glans; lighting, Alexander V. Nichols; sound and music, John Gromada; stage management, David Lurie.

Carol Mulroney .... Ana Reeder	Hutton Mulroney .... Larry Pine
Joan .... Johanna Day	Lesley .... Tim Ransom
Ken Parker .... Reuben Jackson	

  Time: A Friday in autumn; several days later. Place: A city; a rooftop and places nearby. Presented without intermission.

THE HOPPER COLLECTION. By Mat Smart. March 8, 2006. Direction, Daniel Aukin; scenery, Adam Stockhausen; costumes, Kaye Voyce; lighting, Matt Frey; sound, Benjamin Emerson; stage management, Stephen M. Kaus.

Daniel .... Bruce McKenzie	Edward .... Brian Leahy
Marjorie .... Leslie Lyles	Sarah .... Therese Barbato

  Time: A summer evening.

Breaking Ground. Festival of New Play Readings. April 6–9, 2006.

KIND HEARTS AND CORONETS. Musical with book by Robert L. Freedman; music by Steven Lutvak; lyrics by Messrs. Freedman and Lutvak; based on *Kind Hearts and Coronets*, a film by Robert Hame. April 6, 2006. Direction, Mr. Freedman; music direction, Mr. Lutvak.

Performed by Nancy Anderson, Marilyn Caskey, Kate deLima, Kent French, Bill Gross, Jonathan Hadley, Jill Paice, Tregoney Shepherd, Douglas Sills, Price Waldman.

Time: 1902. Place: London.

PERSEPHONE. By Noah Haidle. April 7, 2006. Direction, Justin Waldman.

Performed by Jeremiah Kissel, Mimi Lieber, Jeremy Shamos, Julie White.

Time: 1506; 2006. Place: Florence; New York City.

VOYEURS DE VENUS. By Lydia Diamond. April 8, 2006. Direction, Emma Griffin.

Performed by Jeff Gill, Brad Heberlee, Richard McElvain, Nathaniel McIntyre, Chinasa Ogbuagu, Rachel Rusch, Vincent E. Siders, Tamilla Woodward.

Time: Early 1800s; the present. Place: France; London; Chicago.

PROPERTY. By Valerie Martin. April 8, 2006. Direction, Peter Schneider.

Performed by Teagle Bougere, Amber Gray, Pamela J. Gray, Jason Butler Harner,Will LeBow, Angela Thornton, Michael Weiss.

Time: 1828. Place: A plantation north of New Orleans; in the city of New Orleans.

THE ATHEIST. By Ronan Noone. April 9, 2006, Direction, David Sullivan.

Performed by Campbell Scott.

Time: A few days ago.

MAURITIUS. By Theresa Rebeck. April 9, 2006. Direction, Justin Waldman.

Performed by Michael Aronov, Maria Dizzia, Dominic Fumusa, Laura Latreille.

North Shore Music Theatre, Beverly
Jon Kimbell artistic director, Robert Alpaugh executive director

DAMN YANKEES. Musical with book by George Abbott and Douglas Wallop; music and lyrics by Richard Adler and Jerry Ross; adapted by Joe DiPietro. April 27, 2006. Direction and choreography, Barry Ivan; scenery, Russell Parkman; costumes, Vincent Scassellati; lighting, David Neville; sound, John A. Stone; music direction, Bruce Barnes; stage management, Bethany Ford. Presented in association with the Boston Red Sox.

Meg Boyd	Kay Walbye	Joe Hardy	George Merrick
Joe Boyd	Richard Pruitt	Van Buren	Steve Luker
Applegate	Jim Walton	Gloria Thorpe	Christy Faber
Sister	Becky Barta	Lola	Shannon Lewis
Doris	Mary Callanan	Devil's Handmaiden	Amanda Paulson

Ensemble: Noah Aberlin, Ryan Patrick Binder, David T. Guggino, Craig Kaufman, Kasey Marino, Matthew S. Morgan, Leo Nouhan, Amanda Paulson, Christopher Saunders, Kevin Steele.

Musical numbers included: "Hopeless, Hapless Ballet," "Six Months Out of Every Year," "Goodbye Old Girl," "Heart," "Shoeless Joe," "A Little Brains, A Little Talent," "The Boyd's House," "A Man Doesn't Know," "Whatever Lola Wants Lola Gets," "The Game," "Near to You," "The Good Old Days," "Two Lost Souls."

Presented in two parts.

Williamstown Theatre Festival

Roger Rees artistic director, Deborah Fehr general manager

CREATE FATE. By Etan Frankel. July 13, 2005 (world premiere). Direction, Christopher Ashley; scenery, Michael Carnahan; costumes, David Zinn; lighting, Charles Foster; sound, Nevin Steinberg; stage management, Heather Cousens.

Maria .... Sarah Chalke   Fuller .... John Bedford Lloyd
Nathan .... Michael Chernus
    Presented in two parts.

THE SUGAR SYNDROME. By Lucy Prebble. July 27, 2005. Direction, Maria Mileaf; scenery, Takeshi Kata; costumes, Katherine Roth; lighting, Nicole Pearce; sound, Nick Borisjuk; stage management, David H. Lurie.

Jan .... Betsy Aidem   Tim .... Tim Hopper
Lewis .... Patch Darragh   Gyne Bloke .... Jonathan Kells Phillips
Voice of the Internet .... Erin Felgar   Voice Mail .... Liz Wisan
Davis .... Gaby Hoffmann
    Presented in two parts.

Hero worship: Grant R. Krause, Randall Godwin (rear) and Patrick Michael Kenney in Guest Artist. *Photo: Danna Segrest*

MICHIGAN

Purple Rose Theatre Company, Chelsea
Guy Sanville artistic director, Jeff Daniels executive director

AND THE WINNER IS. By Mitch Albom. July 1, 2005 (world premiere). Direction, Guy Sanville; scenery, Vincent Mountain; lighting, Reid G. Johnson; costumes, Christianne Myers; sound, Quintessa Gallinat; stage management, Michelle DiDomenico.
   Performed by Jerri Doll, Paul Hopper, Sarab Kamoo, Patrick Michael Kenney, Grant R. Krause, Wayne David Parker.

GUEST ARTIST. By Jeff Daniels. January 19, 2006 (world premiere). Direction, Guy Sanville; scenery, Bartley H. Bauer; costumes, Christianne Myers; lighting, Dana White; sound, Quintessa Gallinat; stage management, Katie M. Doral.

Ticket Man	Randall Godwin	His Hero	Grant R. Krause
Young Man	Patrick Michael Kenney		

THE LATE GREAT HENRY BOYLE. By David MacGregor. April 14, 2006. Direction, Guy Sanville; scenery, Daniel C. Walker; costumes, Darcy Elora Hofer; lighting, Dana White; sound, Quintessa Gallinat; stage management, Amy Hickman.

Winslow Saxonhouse	Paul Hopper	Turk Logan	Wayne David Parker
Henry Boyle	John Lepard	Chorus	Randall Godwin
Rachel Vialli	Inga R. Wilson		

   Time: Now and then. Place: In and around Henry Boyle's office at a midwestern university. Presented in two parts.

MINNESOTA

The Guthrie Theater, Minneapolis
Joe Dowling artistic director, Thomas C. Proehl managing director

A BODY OF WATER. By Lee Blessing. June 15, 2005 (world premiere). Direction, Ethan McSweeny; scenery, Michael Vaughn Sims; costumes, Rich Hamson; lighting, Matthew Reinert; music, Michael Roth; dramaturgy, Amy Wegener; stage management, Michaella K. McCoy.

Moss	Edward Herrmann	Wren	Michelle O'Neill
Avis	Michael Learned		

   Presented without intermission.

HIS GIRL FRIDAY. By John Guare; adapted from *The Front Page* by Ben Hecht and Charles MacArthur. July 15, 2005. Direction, Joe Dowling; scenery, John Lee Beatty; costumes, Jess Goldstein; lighting, Brian MacDevitt; sound, Scott W. Edwards; dramaturgy, Carla Steen; stage management, Martha Kulig.

Hildy Johnson	Angela Bassett	Molly Malloy	Kate Eifrig
Walter Burns	Courtney B. Vance	Sweeney	Matthew Amendt
Mayor	Peter Michael Goetz	Mrs. Baldwin	Barbara Bryne
Bruce Baldwin	Karl Kenzler	Buddy "Mac"McCue	Raye Birk
Earl Holub	Kris L. Nelson	Eddie Schwartz	Bill McCallum
Sheriff Hartman	Reginald VelJohnson	Jack Wilson	Bob Davis

Mike Endicott .... Shawn Hamilton   Roy V. Bensinger .... Jim Lichtscheidl
Ernie Kruger .... Terry Hempleman

Ensemble: Byran Clark, Zach Curtis, Wayne A. Evenson, Joel Friedman, Jonas Goslow, Darien Johnson, Andrew Nowak, Mark Rosenwinkel.

Presented in two parts.

THE PEOPLE'S TEMPLE. By Leigh Fondakowski; with Greg Pierotti, Stephen Wangh and Margo Hall. January 13, 2006. Direction, Ms. Fondakowski; scenery, Sarah Lambert; costumes, Gabriel Berry; lighting, Betsy Adams; sound, Jake Rodriguez; music direction, Miche Braden; dramaturgy, Kelli Simpkins and Jo Holcomb; stage management, Cynthia Cahill.

Performed by Will Badgett, Colman Domingo, Margo Hall, Mike Hartman, Lauren Klein, John McAdams, Novella Nelson, Greg Pierotti, Barbara Pitts, Kelli Simpkins, Regina Marie Williams, Michael Winther.

Penumbra Theatre, St. Paul
Lou Bellamy artistic director

GRANDCHILDREN OF THE BUFFALO SOLDIERS. By William S. Yellow Robe Jr. September 23, 2005. Direction, Lou Bellamy; choreography, Patricia Brown, Maggie Erickson and Jason Turner; scenery, Loy Arcenas; costumes, Matthew J. LeFebvre; lighting, Michael Wangen; sound, Martin Gwinup; music direction, Brent Michael Davids; dramaturgy, May Mahala; stage management, Mary K. Winchell. Presented in association with Trinity Repertory Company, Providence, Rhode Island.

Craig Robe .... James Craven   August Jackson .... Maya Washington
Brent Robe .... Jake Hart   Juanita Jones .... Donna Brooks
Elmo Robe .... Freedome Bradley   Kevin Tassel .... Jason Turner
Carol (Sugar) Robe .... George A. Keller   MC Announcer ...... William S. Yellow Robe Jr.
Stevie Jackson .... M. Cochise Anderson

Time: 1885. Place: A reservation in eastern Montana. Presented in two parts

Theatre de la Jeune Lune, Minneapolis
Barbra Berlovitz, Steven Epp, Vincent Gracieux,
Robert Rosen and Dominique Serrand artistic directors;
Steve Richardson producing director

ANTIGONE. By Sophocles; adapted by Robert Rosen, Ben Kernan and Theatre de la Jeune Lune. September 23, 2005. Direction, Mr. Rosen; scenery and lighting, Marcus Dilliard; costumes, Sonya Berlovitz; music direction, Michael Koerner; stage management, Jennifer Eve Schuchert.

Antigone; others .... Barbra Berlovitz   Ismene; others .... Karen Landry
Creon .... Vincent Gracieux

Ensemble: Jason Bohon, Katie Bradley, Maren Bush, Lisa Rafaela Clair, Lisa Marie Fulton, Katie Melby, Becka Ollmann, Simone Perrin, Mike Rasmussen.

THE LITTLE PRINCE. By Antoine de St. Exupery; adapted by Rick Cummins and John Scoullar. November 25, 2005. Direction, Dominique Serrand; scenery, Messrs. Serrand and Steven Epp; lighting, Marcus Dilliard; stage management, Jennifer Eve Schuchert.

Performed by Steven Epp, Max Friedman, Nathan Keepers.

AMERIKA OR THE DISAPPEARANCE. By Gideon Lester, Steven Epp and Dominique Serrand; adapted from the unfinished novel by Franz Kafka. January 21, 2006. Direction, scenery and video by Mr. Serrand; costumes, Sonya Berlovitz; lighting, Marcus Dilliard; sound, David Remedios; stage management, Jennifer Eve Schuchert.

Klara; others	Sarah Agnew	Karl	Nathan Keepers
Mack; others	Stephen Cartmell	Green; Robinson	Luverne Gerald Seifert
Uncle Jacob; others	Steven Epp	Innkeepress; others	Suzanne Warmanen

Ensemble: Shad Cooper, Katrina Hawley, Jennifer J. Phillips.
Musician: Travis Lund.

MEFISTOFELE. By Arrigo Boito; additional music by Hector Berlioz, Franz Liszt, Gustav Mahler, Gioacchino Rossini and Robert Schumann; adapted by Steven Epp and Theatre de la Jeune Lune. March 24, 2006. Direction and scenery, Dominique Serrand; costumes, Sonya Berlovitz; lighting, Marcus Dilliard; music direction, Barbara Brooks; stage management, Jennifer Eve Schuchert.

Lilith	Christina Baldwin	Faust	Doug Scholz-Carlson
Faust	Emmanuel Cadet	Mefistofele	Blixen
Mefistofele	Bradley Greenwald	Lilith's Offspring	Rita Venus
Margherita; Helen	Jennifer Baldwin Peden		

Ensemble: Adena Brumer, Nathan Petersen-Kindem, Corissa White.
Presented without intermission.

MISSOURI

Kansas City Repertory Theatre
Peter Altman producing artistic director, William P. Prenevost managing director

CARTER'S WAY. By Eric Simonson; music by Darrell Leonard. June 8, 2005 (world premiere). Direction, Mr. Simonson; scenery, Neil Patel; costumes, Karin Kopischke; lighting, Michelle Habeck; sound, Barry G. Funderburg; stage management, Chad Zodrow.

Peewee Abernathy	Walter Coppage	Johnny Cozollol	Danny Mastrogiorgio
Marilyn Stokes	Nikki E. Walker	Eunice Fey	Kelly Sullivan
Oriole Carter	Damon Gupton	Jack Thorpe	Gary Neal Johnson
Corky	Dean Vivian		

Musicians: Brian Hunter, George Forbes, Elijah Murray.

Musical numbers included: "Gospel According to Peewee," "Swingin' at the Planet Mars," "Rain from My Eyes," "Right Now," "Long Long Road," "Twisting and Turning," "Take a Chance," "Hip, Hep, Hi, Ho," "Take a Chance," "Low Down and Blue," "In Our Hideaway," "Oh Yeah," "Lullaby, Nightmare," "Steppin' With Marilyn," "Boss Jack's Boogie Woogie," "Peewee's Kansas City," "Blue Johnny," "Oriole's Back," "Carter's Way," "At the Black and Tan," "Lonely Tonight."

Time: 1936. Place: Kansas City, Missouri. Presented in two parts.

The Repertory Theatre of St. Louis
Steven Woolf artistic director, Mark D. Bernstein managing director

MACBETH. By William Shakespeare; adapted by Bruce Longworth. January 19, 2006. Direction, Jeffery Matthews; scenery and costumes, Dorothy Marshall Englis; stage management, Brian Peters.

Macbeth; Bloody Sergeant	Jason Contini	Lady Macbeth; others	Meghan Brown
First Witch; others	Alan Knoll	Third Witch; others	Anna Blair

HENRY IV. By Luigi Pirandello; adapted by Tom Stoppard. February 10, 2006. Direction, Steven Woolf; scenery, Narelle Sissons; costumes, Elizabeth Covey; lighting, Mary Jo Dondlinger; stage management, Glenn Dunn.

Landolf	Alex Burkart	Frida	Lori Prince
Harold	Nathan Lee Burkart	Belcredi	Jerry Vogel
Ordulf	Will Davis	Doctor	John Thomas Waite
Bertold	Matt Timme	Matilda	Susan Wands
Giovanni	Keith Perry	Henry IV	Andrew Long
Di Nolli	Dan Domingues		

Time: Afternoon; four hours later. Place: The throne room of Henry IV of Germany.

NEW JERSEY

Centenary Stage Company, Hackettstown
Carl Wallnau producing director

THE POETRY OF PIZZA. By Deborah Brevoort. February 24, 2006 (world premiere). Direction, Carl Wallnau; scenery and lighting, Will Rothfuss; costumes, Julia Sharp; sound, Matthew Given; stage management, Kimothy Cruse.

Pam Adams	Wendy Peace	Inga Enevold	Michèle LaRue
Sarah Middleton	Katrina Ferguson	Rebar Frie	Eli Ganias
Heino Anderson	Mark Simmons	Soran Saleen	Joseph Pisapia
Olga Oulund	Angela Della Ventura	Ule Enevold	J.C. Hoyt

Time: The present. Place: Copenhagen; the US.

Women's Playwright Series. April 5–April 26, 2006.

THE QUEEN'S TWO BODIES–THE DOUBLE LIFE OF ELIZABETH I. By Jeanne Murray Walker. April 5, 2006. Direction, Margo Whitcomb.
    Performed by Jessica Beltz, Katherine Emmer, Christopher Conant, Will Rothfuss, Jack Moran, Shamira Levy, Osborn Focht, Carly-Jean Booker, Eve-Marie Quinones, Cristina Marie, Danielle Tampier.

GOD, I NEED HER. By YoungSoon Kim. April 12, 2006. Direction, Katelyn Reiter.
    Performed by Will Rothfuss, Becky Engborg, Maria Brodeur, Doug West, Chris Young, Laura Quackenbush, April Dunlop.

CLOWN–A LOVE STORY. By Kristen Dabrowski. April 19, 2006. Direction, Katelyn Reiter.
    Performed by Lea Antolini, John Keller, Leon Hill, Gloria Lamoureux, Marissa La.

BOSSA NOVA. By Kirsten Greenridge. April 26, 2006. Direction, Margo Whitcomb.
    Performed by Marla Teyolia, Christel Halliburton, Andrea Scott, Maria Brodeur, Steven L. Barron, Eve-Marie Quinones, Cristina Marie, Danielle Tampier.

McCarter Theatre, Princeton
Emily Mann artistic director, Jeffrey Woodward managing director

MISS WITHERSPOON. By Christopher Durang. September 16, 2005 (world premiere). Direction, Emily Mann; scenery, David Korins; costumes, Jess Goldstein; lighting, Jeff Croiter; sound, Darron L. West; dramaturgy, Janice Paran; stage management, Alison Cote. Presented in association with Playwrights Horizons, New York City.

Veronica .... Kristine Nielsen	Fathers; others .... Jeremy Shamos
Maryamma .... Mahira Kakkar	Teacher; Woman in a Hat .... Lynda Gravátt
Mothers .... Colleen Werthmann	

Time: Recent past; foreseeable future. Place: Earth; not earth. Presented without intermission.

Readings. October 22, 2005–March 6, 2006.

THE DREAMS OF SARAH BREEDLOVE. By Regina Taylor. October 22, 2005. Direction, Adam Immerwahr.

Performed by Wren T. Brown, Caroline Clay, Lawrence Clayton, LaTanya Richardson Jackson, Novella Nelson, Tiffany Thompson.

PEER GYNT. By Henrik Ibsen; adapted by Will Eno. October 31, 2005. Direction, Jade King Carroll.

Performed by John Ahlin, Blair Brown, Samantha Buck, Ed Jewett, Michael Milligan, James Urbaniak.

RIDICULOUS FRAUD. By Beth Henley. December 5, 2005. Direction, Lisa Peterson.

Performed by Larry Bryggman, Barbara Garrick, Mary Catherine Garrison, John Bedford Lloyd, Daniel London, Reg Rogers, Ali Marsh Weller, Frederick Weller.

THE BLUEST EYE. By Toni Morrison; adapted by Lydia Diamond. January 30, 2006. Direction, Kemati Porter.

Performed by Nora Cole, Lou Ferguson, Harriett D. Foy, Suzette Gunn, Danai Gurira, Adam Immerwahr, Linda Powell, Nikkole Salter, John Douglas Thompson.

IKAMVA. By Janet Neipris. March 6, 2006. Direction, Barbara Rubin.

Performed by Cherise Boothe, Lolita Foster, Ty Jones, Roberta Maxwell, Kathleen McNenny, Cortez Nance, Victor Slezak, Keith Randolph Smith, Myra Lucretia Taylor, Liesl Tommy.

GEM OF THE OCEAN. By August Wilson. October 11, 2005. Direction, Ruben Santiago-Hudson; scenery, Michael Carnahan; costumes, Karen Perry; lighting, Jane Cox; sound, Garth Hemphill; music, Bill Sims Jr.; additional music, Broderick Santiago; stage management, Cheryl Mintz. Presented in association with American Conservatory Theater, San Francisco.

Eli .... Chuck Patterson	Rutherford Selig .... Raynor Scheine
Citizen Barlow .... Russell Hornsby	Solly Two Kings .... John Amos
Aunt Ester .... Phylicia Rashad	Caesar .... Keith Randolph Smith
Black Mary .... Roslyn Ruff	

Time: 1904. Place: The parlor of Aunt Ester's home at 1839 Wylie Avenue in the Hill District of Pittsburgh. Presented in two parts.

A MIDSUMMER NIGHT'S DREAM. By William Shakespeare; music by GrooveLily. March 24, 2006. Direction, Tina Landau; scenery, Louisa Thompson; costumes, Michael Krass; lighting, Scott Zielinski; sound, Michael Bodeen and Rob Milburn; dramaturgy, Douglas Langworthy; stage management, Alison Cote. Presented in association with Paper Mill Playhouse.

Theseus; Oberon .... Jay Goede	Peaseblossom .... Karl Christian
Hippolyta; Titania .... Ellen McLaughlin	Cobweb .... Jesse Nager
Egeus; Peter Quince .... Stephen Payne	Moth .... Ryan Overberg
Lysander .... James Martinez	Mustardseed .... Reginald Holden Jennings
Demetrius .... Will Fowler	Fairies .... Adam Lobato, Christopher Mai
Hermia .... Stacey Sargeant	Nick Bottom.................................. Lea DeLaria
Helena .... Brenda Withers	Francis Flute .... Demond Green
Philostrate; Puck .... Guy Adkins	Tom Snout .... Brendan Milburn

Robin Starveling .... Valerie Vigoda	Snug .... Gene Lewin

Place: A court; a forest; a dreamscape. Presented in two parts.

RIDICULOUS FRAUD. By Beth Henley. May 12, 2006 (world premiere). Direction, Lisa Peterson; scenery, Michael Yeargan; costumes, Jess Goldstein; lighting, Peter Kaczorowski; sound, Martin Desjardins; fight direction, Rick Sordelet; dramaturgy, Janice Paran; stage management, Cheryl Mintz.

Lafcad .... Daniel London	Baites .... Charles Haid
Andrew .... Reg Rogers	Georgia .... Heather Goldenhersh
Willow .... Ali Marsh	Maude .... Barbara Garrick
Kap .... Tim DeKay	Ed .... John Carroll Lynch

Presented in four parts.

New Jersey Repertory Company, Long Branch
Suzanne Barabas artistic director, Gabor Barabas executive producer

TOUR DE FARCE. By Philip LaZebnik and Kingsley Day. January 28, 2006. Direction, James Glossman; scenery, Carrie Mossman; costumes, Patricia E. Doherty; lighting, Jill Nagle; sound, Merek Royce Press; stage management, Rose Riccardi.

Performed by Ames Adamson and Prentiss Benjamin.

Presented in two parts.

Shakespeare Theatre of New Jersey, Madison
Bonnie J. Monte artistic director, Stephen Klein managing director

THE TRIUMPH OF LOVE. By Pierre Marivaux; translated and adapted by Bonnie J. Monte. July 23, 2005. Direction, Craig A. Miller; scenery, Jesse Dreikosen; costumes, Amy Ritchings; lighting, Danielle Almeida Wilson; sound, Mr. Miller; stage management, Christine Whalen.

Dimas .... Brian Cogman	Corine .... Alison Weller
Hermocrate .... Brian Dowd	Agis .... Geoff Wilson
Harlequin .... Greg Jackson	Leontine .... Pamela Vogel
Leonide .... Mandy Olsen	

Presented in one act.

LIFE OF GALILEO. By Bertolt Brecht; translated by John Willett. August 6, 2005. Direction, Joe Discher; scenery, James Wolk; costumes, Brian Russman; lighting, Matthew E. Adelson; sound, Richard M. Dionne; music, Mr. Discher and Jay Leibowitz; stage management, Jana Llynn.

Galileo Galilei .... Sherman Howard	Virginia .... Justine Williams
Andrea Sarti .... Robbie Collier Sublett	Federzoni .... Remy Auberjonois
Signora Sarti .... Derin Altay	Grand Duke .... Kevin Palermo
Ludovico Marsili .... Jeffrey M. Bender	Father Clavius .... Brian Schilb
Priuli .... Robert Hock	Mucius .... Nathan Kaufman
Sagredo .... Bruce Cromer	Cardinal Inquisitor .... Edmond Genest
Doge .... Joe Mancuso	Cardinal Barberini .... Richard Bourg

Ensemble: Patrick Toon, John Heath, Michael Stewart Allen, Michael Rossmy, Jay Leibowitz, Jessica Ires Morris, David Arsenault, Nathan Kaufman, Michael R. Pauley, Victoria Hudziak, Dawn Souza, Sean Hudock.

Presented in two parts.

NEW YORK

Geva Theatre Center, Rochester
Mark Cuddy artistic director, John Quinlivan managing director

THE ROAD HOME: RE-MEMBERING AMERICA. By Marc Wolf. September 24, 2005 (world premiere). Direction, David Schweizer; scenery, Andrew Lieberman; costumes, David Zinn; lighting, Peter West; sound, Robert Kaplowitz; stage management; Kirsten Brannen. Presented in association with the Huntington Theatre Company, Boston.

Performed by Mr. Wolf.

A MARVELOUS PARTY: THE NOEL COWARD CELEBRATION. Musical revue with music and lyrics by Noël Coward. October 15, 2005 (world premiere). Direction, David Ira Goldstein; choreography, Patricia Wilcox; scenery, Bill Forrester; costumes, David Kay Mickelsen; lighting, Todd Hensley; sound, William Pickens; music direction, Carl J. Danielsen; stage management, Frank Cavallo. Presented in association with Northlight Theatre, Chicago.

Performed by Mark Anders, Mr. Danielsen, Anna Lauris.

Musical numbers included: "Together With Music," "London Is a Little Bit of Alright," "London Pride," "The Stately Homes of England," "Any Little Fish," "Chase Me Charlie," "What Ho! Mrs. Brisket," "Would You Like to Stick a Pin in My Balloon?," "Has Anybody Seen Our Ship?," "Matelot," "I Like America," "Mad Dogs and Englishmen," "Mrs. Wentworth-Brewster," "The Coconut Girl," "Mrs. Worthington," "Mad About the Boy," "I've Been to a Marvelous Party," "Why Do the Wrong People Travel?," "Sail Away," "There Are Bad Times Just Around the Corner," "A Room With a View/Dance Little Lady," "Someday I'll Find You," "I'll Follow My Secret Heart," "If Love Were All," "Nina," "Let's Do It," "The Party's Over Now/I'll See You Again."

VIGIL. By Morris Panych. January 14, 2006. Direction, Mark Cuddy; scenery. G.W. Mercier; costumes, Gail Brassard; lighting, Michelle Habeck; sound, William Pickens; music, Scott Killian; stage management, Frank Cavallo.

Grace	Irma St. Paule	Kemp	Raymond Bokhour

Time: Now. Place: Grace's bedroom.

IRON KISSES. By James Still. March 17, 2006 (world premiere). Direction, Stephanie Gilman; scenery, Wilson Chin; costumes, Anne R. Emo; lighting, S. Ryan Schmidt; sound, Daniel Baker; music, Matthew Suttor and the Broken Chord Collective; stage management, Alexandra M. Backus.

Barbara	Mary Bacon	Billy	Jacob Blumer

Time: Now. Place: A small town in the Midwest and San Francisco.

SPLITTING INFINITY. By Jamie Pachino. April 18, 2006 (world premiere). Direction, Mark Cuddy; scenery and costumes, G.W. Mercier; lighting, Ann G. Wrightson; sound, Lindsay Jones; dramaturgy, Marge Betley; stage management, Frank Cavallo.

Young Leigh	Morgan Hallett	Robbie March	Michael Zlabinger
Young Saul	Paul Kropfl	Saul Lieberman	Michael Rupert
Leigh Sangold	Elizabeth Hess	Mrs. March	Deborah Leydig

Time: 1979; 2006. Place: A university office; a hospital room; a synagogue.

OHIO

Cincinnati Playhouse in the Park
Edward Stern producing artistic director, Buzz Ward executive director

COMPANY. Musical with book by George Furth; music and lyrics by Stephen Sondheim. March 18, 2006. Direction and choreography, John Doyle; scenery, David Gallo; costumes, Ann Hould-Ward; lighting, Thomas C. Hase; sound, Andrew Keister; music direction, Mary-Mitchell Campbell; fight direction, Drew Fracher; stage management, Suann Pollock.

Robert	Raúl Esparza	Paul	Robert Cunningham
Joanne	Barbara Walsh	Sarah	Kristin Huffman
Marta	Angel Desai	Susan	Amy Justman
April	Elizabeth Stanley	Amy	Heather Laws
Kathy	Kelly Jeanne Grant	Jenny	Leenya Rideout
Harry	Keith Buterbaugh	David	Fred Rose
Peter	Matt Castle	Larry	Bruce Sabath

Musical numbers included: "Company," "The Little Things You Do Together," "Sorry-Grateful," "You Could Drive a Person Crazy," Have I Got a Girl for You," "Someone is Waiting for You," "Another Hundred People," "Getting Married Today," "Marry Me a Little," "Side By Side/What Would We Do Without You," "Poor Baby," "Barcelona," "The Ladies Who Lunch," "Being Alive."

Presented in two parts.

STONE MY HEART. By Joseph McDonough. April 6, 2006 (world premiere). Direction, Edward Stern; scenery, Joseph P. Tilford; costumes, Claudia Stephens; lighting, Thomas C. Hase; music, Douglas Lowry; stage management, Andrea L. Shell.

Robby	Todd Lawson	Zach	Tim Altmeyer
Terrence	Sean Haberle	Marcus	Kevyn Morrow
Jessica	Lanie MacEwan		

Presented in two parts.

The Cleveland Play House, Cleveland
Michael Bloom artistic director, Dean R. Gladden managing director

I AM MY OWN WIFE. By Doug Wright. November 9, 2005. Direction, Anders Cato; scenery, Hugh Landwehr; costumes, Jeffrey Van Curtis; lighting, Howell Binkley; sound, James C. Swonger; stage management, John Godbout.

Charlotte von Mahlsdorf .... Mark Nelson

Presented without intermission.

WELL. By Lisa Kron. March 8, 2006. Direction, Michael Bloom; scenery, Michael Raiford, costumes, Jennifer Caprio; lighting, David Nancarrow; sound, James C. Swonger; stage management, John Godbout.

Lisa .... Alicia Roper   Ann .... Denny Dillon

Ensemble: Zandy Hartig, Jason Miller, Lelund Durond Thompson, Bailey Varness.

DREAM A LITTLE DREAM: THE NEARLY TRUE STORY OF THE MAMAS AND THE PAPAS. Musical with book by Denny Doherty and Paul Ledoux; music and lyrics by the Mamas and the Papas. April 5, 2006. Direction, Randal Myler; scenery, Vicki Smith; costumes, Kevin Copenhaver; lighting, Don Darnutzer; sound, James C. Swonger; video, Gabreal Franklin; stage management, Corrie E. Purdum.

Performed by Denny Doherty, Lisa MacIsaac, Doris Mason, David Smyth; with musicians Bill Ransom, Kip Reed and Graham Shaw.

Musical numbers included: "The Man Who Wouldn't Sing Along With Mitch," "Wild Women," "500 Miles," "Everybody's Been Talkin'," "Shake It Up Baby (Twist and Shout)," "Creeque Alley," "12:30," "Go Where You Want to Go," "California Dreamin'," "Got A Feelin'," "I Saw Her Again," "In Crowd," "San Francisco (Be Sure to Wear Some Flowers in Your Hair)," "Monday, Monday," "Theme From Peyton Place," "It Can Only Happen in America," "Dream a Little Dream of Me."

CUSTODY OF THE EYES. By Anthony Giardina. May 3, 2006 (world premiere). Direction, Michael Butler; scenery, Russell Parkman; costumes, Charlotte Yetman; sound, James C. Swonger; lighting, Nancy Schertler; stage management, John Godbout.

Riley Rosenthal	Alexander Timothy Biats	Donald Leger	J.R. Horne
Edmond LeBlanc	Joseph Collins	Gary Burger; Ferryman	Mark Mayo
Mrs. Callahan	Paula Duesing	Robert Sullivan	Kenneth Tigar
Sheila Rosenthal	Jan Leslie Harding		

The Next Stage Festival of New Plays. May 5–18, 2006.

THE OBSERVATORY. By Greg Germann. May 5, 2006. Direction, Michael Bloom.
Performed by Sean Haberle, John Hines, Blake Lindsley, Kelly Mares.

THE LUNACY. By Sandra Perlman. May 10, 2006. Direction, Mark Alan Gordon.
Performed by Amanda Duffy, Dan Hammond, Michael Regnier.

SAM AND LUCY. By Brooke Berman. May 11, 2006. Direction, Seth Gordon.
Performed by Thomas Degnan, Bruce MacVittie, Andrew May, Elizabeth Ann Townsend, Melynee Weber.

A WORLD BENEATH. By Neena Beber. May 17, 2006. Direction, Seth Gordon.
Performed by Michael Chernus, Marin Ireland, Dorothy Silver, T. Ryder Smith.

AMERICANS. By Eric Schlosser. May 18, 2006. Direction, Seth Gordon.
Performed by Mark Alan Gordon, Jeff Grover, Charles Kartali, Annie Paul, George Roth, Reuben Silver, Dudley Swetland, Elizabeth Ann Townsend, Tom Woodward.

NIGHT BLOOMERS. By Sarah Morton. May 11, 2006. Direction, Eric Schmiedl; scenery, Russ Borski; lighting, Maureen L. Patterson; costumes, Carolyn Dickey; sound, Richard Ingraham; stage management, Richard Maxell.
Performed by Rachel Applebaum, David Hansen, Samuel Holloway, Nicholas Koesters, Lisa Langford, Teresa McDonough, Courtney Schloss, Nan Wray.

OREGON

Oregon Shakespeare Festival, Ashland
Libby Appel artistic director, Paul Nicholson executive director

GIBRALTAR. By Octavio Solis. July 9, 2005 (world premiere). Direction, Liz Diamond; scenery, Richard L. Hay; costumes, Deborah M. Dryden; lighting, Chris Parry; sound, Jeremy J. Lee; fight direction, John Sipes; dramaturgy, Douglas Langworthy; stage management, Jill Rendall.

Amy	Vilma Silva	Francesca	Dee Maaske
Palo	René Millán	Taylor	U. Jonathan Toppo
Steven	Kevin Kenerly	Sharon	Julie Oda

Jackson .... Bill Geisslinger   Dot .... Judith-Marie Bergan
    Time: The present. Place: Amy's condo overlooking the San Francisco Bay. Presented without intermission.

Portland Center Stage
Chris Coleman artistic director, Edith H. Love managing director

THIS WONDERFUL LIFE. By Steve Murray; with Mark Setlock; adapted from the film *It's A Wonderful Life*. November 29, 2005 (world premiere). Direction, Cliff Fannin Baker; scenery, Dex Edwards; costumes, Jeff Cone; lighting, Daniel Ordower; sound, Jen Raynak; stage management, Mark Tynan.

Performed by Matthew Floyd Miller.

THE INTELLIGENT DESIGN OF JENNY CHOW. By Rolin Jones. February 17, 2006. Direction, Kim Rubinstein; scenery, G.W. Mercier; costumes, Nephelie Andonyadis; lighting, Peter Maradudin; sound, Daniel Baker; music, Matthew Suttor; stage management, Nicole Olson. Presented in association with San Jose Repertory Theatre.

Jennifer Marcus .... Sue Jean Kim   Adele .... Valerie Stevens
Mr. Marcus .... Tim True   Todd .... Craig W. Marker
Preston .... Kevin Rich   Jenny Chow .... Ka-Ling Cheung
    Time: Now. Place: A Southern California suburb. Presented in two parts.

CELEBRITY ROW. By Itamar Moses. March 21, 2006 (world premiere). Direction, Chris Coleman; scenery, Daniel Ostling; costumes, Jeff Cone; lighting, Daniel Ordower; sound, Casi Pacilio; dramaturgy, Mead Hunter; stage management, Mark Tynan.

Maze Carroll .... Leslie Kalarchian   Ted Kaczynski .... Ebbe Roe Smith
Luis Felipe .... Jesse J. Perez   Timothy McVeigh .... Daniel Thomas May
Ramzi Yousef .... Ariel Shafir
    Place: ADX-Florence, a prison in Colorado; elsewhere.

PENNSYLVANIA

Arden Theatre Company, Philadelphia
Terrence J. Nolen producing artistic director, Amy L. Murphy managing director

WINESBURG, OHIO. Musical with book and lyrics by Eric Rosen; music and additional lyrics by Andre Pluess and Ben Sussman; with Jessica Thebus; based on the novel by Sherwood Anderson. October 6, 2005. Direction, Terrence J. Nolen; choreography, Myra Bazell; scenery, Daniel Ostling; costumes, Rosemarie McKelvey; lighting, Dennis Parichy; sound, Jorge Cousineau; music direction, Thomas Murray; stage management, John David Flak.

Young Elizabeth .... Elisa Matthews   Seth Richmond .... Darren Michael Hengst
Writer; Stranger .... Andrew White   Wing Biddlebaum .... William Zielinski
Elizabeth Willard .... Derin Altay   Helen White .... Kim Carson
Tom Willard; Father .... Peter Schmitz   Joe Welling; Man .... Tony Freeman
George Willard .... Brian Hissong   Rev. Hartman .... Ben Dibble
Kate Swift .... Lesley Bevan   Violinist .... Phoebe Silva
Alice Hindman .... Dawn Falato

OPUS. By Michael Hollinger. January 17, 2006 (world premiere). Direction, Terrence J. Nolen; scenery, James Kronzer; costumes, Michael McAleer; lighting, Andrew David Ostrowski; sound, Jorge Cousineau; dramaturgy, Carlyn Aquiline; stage management, Patricia G. Sabato. Presented in association with City Theatre Company, Pittsburgh.

Grace	Erika Cuenca	Dorian	David Whalen
Elliot	Patrick McNulty	Alan	Greg Wood
Carl	Douglas Rees		

Presented without intermission.

InterAct Theatre Company, Philadelphia
Seth Rozin producing artistic director, Melissa Amster managing director

THE FEAST OF THE FLYING COW AND OTHER STORIES OF WAR. By Jeni Mahoney. October 26, 2005 (world premiere). Direction, Seth Rozin; scenery and sound, Jorge Cousineau; costumes, Karen Ledger; lighting, Peter Whinnery; fight direction, John V. Bellomo; dramaturgy, Larry Loebell; stage management, Sara May.

Anya	Emmanuelle Delpech-Ramey	Rosa	Martha Kemper
Audrey	Catharine K. Slusar	Niles	Tom Byrn
Izak	Matt Saunders		

Place: The apartment of Anya and Izak Andonov. Presented in three parts.

AMERICAN SUBLIME. By Patricia Lynch. January 25, 2006 (world premiere). Direction, Seth Rozin; scenery, Marka Suber; costumes, Susan Smythe; lighting and sound, Shannon Zura; dramaturgy, Larry Loebell; stage management, Sara May.

Todd	Steve Hatzai	Guard	Jefferson Haynes
Constance	Hayden Saunier		

Time: Today. Place: A large urban Museum of Art. Presented without intermission.

REINVENTING EDEN. By Seth Rozin. April 12, 2006 (world premiere). Direction, Harriet Power; scenery, Daniel Boylen; costumes, Charlotte Cloe Fox Wind; lighting, Jerold Forsyth; sound, Kevin Francis; stage management, Sara May.

Jonas	Tim Moyer	Lizzie	Nancy Boykin
Paul	Matt Pfeiffer	Robert	Seth Reichgott
Boris	John Morrison	Corey	Kevin Bergen
Jason	Ahren Potratz		

Presented in two parts.

SINCE AFRICA. By Mia McCullough. May 26, 2006. Direction, Paul Meshejian; scenery, Hiroshi Iwasaki; costumes, Karen Ledger; lighting, Peter Whinnery; sound, Chris Colucci.

Diane	Susan Wilder	Ater	Bowman Wright
Reggie	Johnnie Hobbs Jr.	Eve	Lori McNally

Philadelphia Theatre Company
Sara Garonzik producing artistic director, Ada Coppock general manager

ADRIFT IN MACAO. Musical with book and lyrics by Christopher Durang; music by Peter Melnick. October 26, 2005 (world premiere). Direction, Sheryl Kaller; choreography, Christopher Gattelli; scenery, Thomas Lynch; costumes, Willa Kim; lighting, Paul Gallo; sound, Peter Fitzgerald; music direction, Fred Lassen; orchestrations, Michael Starobin; stage management, Rachel Bush.

Lureena	Rachel de Benedet	Corinna	Michele Ragusa
Mitch	David McDonald	Rick	Michael Rupert
Tempura	Orville Mendoza		

Trenchcoat Chorus: Jennie Eisenhower, Michael M. Malone.

Musical numbers included: "In a Foreign City," "Tempura's Song," "Mister McGuffin," "Moon Over Macao," "Mambo Malaysian," "Sparks," "Mitch's Story," "Adrift in Macao," "So Long," "The Chase," "Revelation," "Ticky Ticky, Tocky."

Presented without intermission.

AFTER ASHLEY. By Gina Gionfriddo. February 8, 2006. Direction, Pam MacKinnon; scenery, Kris Stone; costumes, Murell Horton; lighting, John Ambrosone; sound, Jorge Cousineau; dramaturgy, Warren Hoffman; stage management, Rachel Bush.

Alden	Russ Anderson	Roderick	Jonathan Partington
David	Tony Braithwaite	Ashley	Jennifer Rohn
Julie	Tracee Chimo	Justin	Peter Stadlen

Presented in two parts.

INTIMATE APPAREL. By Lynn Nottage. March 17, 2006. Direction, Tim Vasen; scenery, Lee Savage; costumes, Janus Stefanowicz; lighting, Ann G. Wrightson; sound, Jorge Cousineau; music, Robert Maggio; dramaturgy, Warren Hoffman; stage management, Rachel Bush.

Mrs. Dickson	Stephanie Berry	Mr. Marks	Maury Ginsberg
Esther	Rosalyn Coleman	George	Stephen Conrad Moore
Mayme	Eisa Davis	Mrs. Van Buren	Anne Louise Zachry

Time: 1905. Place: Lower Manhattan.

Presented in two parts.

SOME MEN. By Terrence McNally. May 17, 2006 (world premiere). Direction, Philip Himberg; choreography, Sean Curran; scenery, Loy Arcenas; costumes, Jane Greenwood; lighting, David Lander; sound, Fitz Patton; music direction, Don Rebic; dramaturgy, Warren Hoffman; stage management, Phyllis Schray.

Alex; others	Don Amendolia	Carl; others	Malcolm Gets
Peter; others	Brandon Bales	Archie; others	John Glover
Bernie; others	Stephen Bogardus	Piano Man; others	Tom Judson
Dark Sugar; others	Duane Boutté	Diva White; others	Barbara Walsh
Dina Black; others	Suzzanne Douglas	Zach; others	Gregory Wooddell

Presented in two parts.

Pig Iron Theatre, Philadelphia

Gabriel Quinn Bauriedel, Dito van Reigersberg and Dan Rothenberg artistic directors

PAY UP. By Robert Quillen Camp. September 3, 2005 (world premiere). Direction, Dan Rothenberg; choreography, Andrew Simonet; scenery and costumes, Anna Kiraly; lighting, Brian Lilienthal; sound, Mr. Camp; stage management, Sarah Bishop-Stone.

Performed by Aram Aghazarian, Barne Baggett, Gabriel Quinn Bauriedel, Valentina Bove, Corinna Burns, Ben Camp, Dylan Clements, Kali Colton, Jessica Conda, Gayle Da Costa, Morgan Eckert, Makoto Hirano, Kelly Jennings, Johnnie Hobbs III, Evan Jonigkeit, Leonard Kelly, Alyssa Kondracki, Rainey Lacey, Cedric Lilly, Matt Lorenz, Sarah McCarron, Danielle Mebane, Eli Metcalf, Christie Parker, Genevieve Perrier, Amanda Schoonover, Dito van Reigersberg, Phoebe Vacharat, Enrique Villacis-Tappia, Leah Walton.

Presented without intermission.

MISSION TO MERCURY. Musical by the company. February 17, 2006. Direction, Dan Rothenberg; scenery, Hiroshi Iwasaki and Gabriel Quinn Bauriedel; costumes, David R. Gammons and Millie Hiibel; lighting, James Clotfelder; sound, Nick Kourtides; stage management, Carol Laratonda.

Performed by Gabriel Quinn Bauriedel, Dito van Reigersberg, Geoff Sobelle, James Sugg, Christie Parker, Sarah Doherty, Bradford Trojan.

Presented in two parts.

Pittsburgh Public Theater
Ted Pappas artistic and executive director

ROLEPLAY. By Alan Ayckbourn. September 29, 2005. Direction, Ted Pappas; scenery, James Noone; costumes, Martha Louise Bromelmeier; lighting, Kirk Bookman; sound and music, Zach Moore; stage management, Ruth E. Kramer.

Julie-Ann Jobson	Tressa Glover	Derek Jobson	Ross Bickell
Justin Lazenby	Brian Hutchison	Dee Jobson	Cynthia Darlow
Paige Petite	Meredith Zinner	Arabella Lazenby	Jane Summerhays
Micky Rale	Mark Mineart		

Time: One evening in March. Place: A riverside apartment in London's Docklands. Presented in two parts.

New Play Readings. October 17, 2005–April 17, 2006.

HARDBALL. By Victoria Stewart. October 17, 2005. Direction, Kyle W. Brenton.
Performed by Ross Bickell, Holli Hamilton, Rebecca Harris, Amy Landis, Mary Rawson, Ron Seibert.

IN. By Bess Whol. January 23, 2006. Direction, Kyle W. Brenton.

ACCORDION LESSONS. By Reed Martin. March 20, 2006. Direction, Mr. Martin.
Performed by Mr. Martin.

BIRD ISLAND. By Vincent Delany. April 17, 2006. Direction, Ted Pappas.

Prince Music Theater, Philadelphia
Marjorie Samoff producing director

DREAMGIRLS. Musical with book and lyrics by Tom Eyen; music by Henry Krieger. December 9, 2005. Direction, Richard M. Parison Jr., choreography, Mercedes Ellington; scenery and projections, Todd Edward Ivins; costumes, Mark Mariani; lighting, Troy Martin-O'Shia; sound, Nick Kourtides; music direction, Jesse Vargas; stage management, Lori Aghazarian.

Effie	Nova Y. Payton	C.C.	Forrest McClendon
Deena	Chauntee Schuler	Jimmy	Eugene Fleming
Lorrell	CJay Hardy Philip	Marty	Milton Craig Neely
Michele	Vanessa A. Jones	M.C.	James T. Lane
Curtis	Erick Pinnick		

Ensemble: Piper Lindsay Arpan, Enrika Vaughn, Nako Adodoadji, Gillian Burke, Janelle Neal, Ryan C. Haggett, Correy West, Gregg Baker, James Clark, Denver Andre Taylor, Jason J. Michael.

Musical numbers included: "I'm Looking for Something, Baby," "Goin' Downtown," "Takin' the Long Way Home," "Move (You're Steppin' On My Heart)," "Fake Your Way to the Top," "Cadillac Car," "Steppin' to the Bad Side," "Party, Party," "I Want You Baby," "Family," "Dreamgirls,"

"Press Conference," "Only the Beginning," "Heavy," "Drivin' Down the Strip," "It's All Over," "(And I am Telling You) I'm Not Going," "Love Me, Love My Baby," "I Am Changing," "One More Picture Please," "When I First Saw You," "Got to be Good Times," "Ain't No Party," "I Meant You No Harm," "Quintet," "Rap," I Miss You Old Friend," "One Night Only," "I'm Somebody," "Chicago," "How to Say Goodbye (My Love)," "Dreamgirls."

THE PIRATE. Musical with book by David Levy and Zack Manna; music and lyrics, Cole Porter; additional music by Brad Ross; additional lyrics by Messrs. Levy and Manna; based on the film and on the S.N. Behrman play. May 13, 2006 (world premiere). Direction, Richard M. Parison Jr.; choreography, Chase Brock; scenery, Ray Klausen; costumes, Mark Mariani; lighting, Shelley Hicklin; sound, Nick Kourtides; music direction, Steven Freeman; fight direction, Charles Conwell; stage management, Tom Helmer.

Mango Woman .... Cheryl Freeman	Bolo .... Steve Pacek
Manuela Alva .... Andrea Burns	Gumbo .... Julian Brightman
Aunt Ines Alva .... Pamela Myers	Serafin .... Seán Martin Hingston
Lizarda .... Aileen Goldberg	Viceroy .... Albert Innaurato
Don Pedro .... Tom Flynn	Burly Man .... Richard J. Hinds
Trillo .... James T. Lane	

Ensemble: Josie Andrews, Kristina Biddle, Julian Brightman, James Clark, Danielle G. Herbert, Kaitlin Rose Mercurio, Marla Mindelle.

Musical numbers included: "Mack the Black,""Macoco" " All of You," "Port Sebastien," "Nina," "You Do Something to Me," "Play On!," "Most Gentlemen Don't Like Love," "What Is This Thing Called Love," "Voodoo," "I've a Strange New Rhythm in My Heart," "Manuela's Vision." "Love of My Life," "A Fool There Was," "Wake Up and Dream," "I Concentrate on You," "Be a Clown," "Strange New Rhythm in My Heart."

Time: Long ago. Place: A Caribbean island. Presented in two parts.

RHODE ISLAND

Trinity Repertory Company, Providence
Curt Columbus and Amanda Dehnert artistic directors, Edgar Dobie executive director

BOOTS ON THE GROUND. By Laura Kepley and D. Salem Smith. April 19, 2006 (world premiere). Direction, Ms. Kepley; scenery, Beowulf Boritt; costumes, William Lane; lighting, Brian J. Lilienthal; sound, Peter Sasha Hurowitz; video, Jamie McElhinney; stage management, Jennifer Sturch.

"Tom"; others .... Richard Donelly	Jen Rose; others .... Rachael Warren
"Lisa"; others .... Anne Scurria	Christian Neary; others .... Joe Wilson Jr.
Private Deitch; others .... Stephen Thorne	

Presented in two parts.

TEXAS

Alley Theatre, Houston
Gregory Boyd artistic director, Terrence Dwyer managing director

BE MY BABY. By Ken Ludwig. October 5, 2005 (world premiere). Direction, John Rando; scenery, Alexander Dodge; costumes, David C. Woolard; lighting, Donald Holder; sound, John Gromada; stage management, Terry Cranshaw.

Gloria Nance .... Elizabeth Bunch
Maud Kinch .... Dixie Carter
Christy McCall .... Ty Mayberry
John Campbell .... Hal Holbrook
Male Ensemble .... James Black
Female Ensemble .... Robin Moseley

Time: 1963. Place: Scotland; the US. Presented in two acts.

THE PILLOWMAN. By Martin McDonagh. February 1, 2006. Direction, Gregory Boyd; scenery and lighting design, Kevin Rigdon; costumes, Linda Ross; sound and music, John Gromada; fight direction, Brian Byrnes; stage management, Terry Cranshaw.

Tupolski .... John Tyson
Katurian .... Rick Stear
Ariel .... David Rainey
Michal .... Jeffrey Bean
Father .... Chris Hutchison
Mother .... Melissa Pritchett
Girl .... Elizabeth Bunch
Boy .... Kirk Van Sickle

Presented in three parts.

Main Street Theater, Houston
Rebecca Greene Udden artistic director

MARGIN FOR ERROR. By Clare Boothe. November 17, 2005. Direction, Steve Garfinkel; scenery, Boris Kaplun; costumes, Amanda Bezemek; lighting, John Smetak; sound, Matthew Crawford; stage management, Janel J. Badrina.

Otto Horst .... Robert Leeds
Baron von Alvenstor .... Fritz Dickmann
Moe Finkelstein .... Brady Alland
Frieda .... Candice Bruder
Dr. Jennings .... George Brock
Sophie Baumer .... Sara Gaston
Consul Karl Baumer .... Kent Johnson
Thomas Denny .... Robert de los Reyes
Captain Mulrooney .... Tim Palumbo

Time: 1939. Place: The German Consulate in New York. Presented in two parts.

WONDERGIRL. By Rutherford Cravens. February 2, 2006 (world premiere). Direction, Cheryl L. Kaplan; scenery, Ethan Krupp; costumes, Amanda Bezemek; lighting, Kirk Markley; sound, Janel J. Badrina; stage management, John Smetak.

Hal .... David Wald
Jenny .... Shannon Emerick
Dr. Foster .... Celeste Roberts
Dr. Phillips .... George Brock
Nurse l, Grady .... Justin Doran
Nurse 2, Paula .... Erin Kidwell
Dr. Ndando-Sekula .... Victor Udoewa

OUROBOROS. By Tom Jacobson. March 11, 2006. Direction, Robert de los Reyes; scenery, Jodi Bobrovsky; costumes, Amanda Bezemek; lighting, Andrew Ruthven; sound, Craig Seanor; dramaturgy, Ms. Bobrovsky; stage management, John Smetak.

The Nun's Tale and *The Priest's Tale*

Margaret, a nun .... Celeste Roberts
Tor, her friend .... Justin Doran
Philip, a minister .... Fritz Dickmann
Catherine, his wife .... Sara Gaston
Others .... Josh Morrison

Place: Great Italian cities in shuffled order. Played in rotating repertory.

Rude Mechanicals, Austin
Madge Darlington, Lana Lesley, Kirk Lynn, Sarah Richardson and Shawn Sides
producing artistic directors

MATCH-PLAY. By Lana Lesley, Kirk Lynn, Barney O'Hanlon and Shawn Sides; with text by Richard Foreman and Mr. Lynn; based on Deborah Hay's dance *The Match*. September

15, 2005 (world premiere). Direction, the company; scenery, Leilah Stewart; costumes, Laura Cannon; lighting, Brian Scott; sound, Robert S. Fisher; dramaturgy, Amy Miley; stage management, Elizabeth Moreau.

> Performed by Ms. Lesley, Mr. Lynn, Mr. O'Hanlon, Ms. Sides.
> Presented without intermission.

GET YOUR WAR ON. By David Rees; adapted by Lana Lesley, Kirk Lynn and Shawn Sides from the internet comic strip. January 19, 2006 (world premiere). Direction, Shawn Sides; scenery, Leilah Stewart; lighting, Natalie George; sound, Robert S. Fisher; stage management, José Hernández.

> Performed by Ms. Lesley, Jason Liebrecht, Amy Miley, Chad Nichols, Robert Pierson.
> Presented without intermission.

Stage West, Fort Worth
Jerry Russell producing director, Jim Covault artistic director

EMBRACING. By Stan Denman. February 11, 2006 (world premiere). Direction and scenery, Jim Covault; lighting, Michael O'Brien; costumes, Mr. Covault and Peggy Kruger O'Brien; stage management, Ms. O'Brien.

Traci Winslow	Jennifer Knight	Ben Spivey	Jason Thomas Mayfield

PUPPET BOY. By Lee Trull. April 1, 2006 (world premiere). Direction and scenery, Jim Covault; costumes, Mr. Covault and Peggy Kruger O'Brien; lighting, Michael O'Brien; stage management, Ms. O'Brien.

Cricket; Punchinello	Michael Corolla	Cat; Harlequin	Sachin Patel
Official; others	Adam Justin Dietrich	Geppetto; Fire Eater	Jerry Russell
Fox; others	Justin Flowers	Blue Fairy	Dana Schultes
Pinocchio	Jason Thomas Mayfield		

Stages Repertory Theatre, Houston
Kenn McLaughlin producing artistic director

LATE: A COWBOY SONG. By Sarah Ruhl. June 3, 2005 (world premiere). Direction, Rob Bundy; scenery and lighting, Kirk Markley; costumes, Andrea Lauer; music, Michael Ray Escamilla; sound and video, Tim Thomson; stage management, Rebecca Skupin.

Mary	Christine Auten	Crick	Corby Sullivan
Red	Susan O. Koozin		

> Presented in two parts.

WASHINGTON

ACT Theatre, Seattle
Kurt Beattie artistic director, Susan Trapnell managing director

THE UGLY AMERICAN. By Mike Daisey. June 8, 2005 (world premiere). Direction, Jean-Michele Gregory; scenery, Matthew Smucker; lighting, Michael Wellborn; stage management, Jeffrey K. Hanson.

> Performed by Mr. Daisey.

FLIGHT. By Charlayne Woodward. October 20, 2005. Direction, Valerie Curtis-Newton; choreography, Kabby Mitchell III; scenery, Matthew Smucker; costumes, Melanie Taylor Burgess; lighting, Christopher Reay; sound, Dominic CodyKramers; music, Karl Fredrik Lundeberg; stage management, Jeffrey K. Hanson.

Nate	David Brown Jr.	Alma	Tracy Michelle Hughes
Ezra	Johnny Lee Davenport	Oh Beah	Margo Moorer
Mercy	Dawn Frances		

Time: 1858. Place: A plantation near Savannah, Georgia.

THE PILLOWMAN. By Martin McDonagh. March 23, 2006. Direction, Kurt Beattie; scenery, Matthew Smucker; costumes, Marcia Dixcy Jory; lighting, Mary Louise Geiger; sound, Dominic CodyKramers; music, Adam Stern; fight direction, Geoffrey Alm; stage management, Jeffrey K. Hanson.

Tupolski	Denis Arndt	Boy	Joshua Froebe
Father	Ian Bell	Katurian	Matthew Floyd Miller
Girl	Corina Boettger	Michal	Shawn Telford
Mother	Julie Briskman	Ariel	R. Hamilton Wright

Presented in two parts.

Empty Space Theatre, Seattle
Allison Narver artistic director, Melanie Matthews managing director

STUPID KIDS. By John C. Russell; music by Chapstick. June 7, 2005. Direction, Adam Greenfield; choreography, Juliet Waller Pruzan; scenery, Etta Lilienthal; costumes, Heidi Ganser; lighting, L.B. Morse; music direction, Ben McAllister; stage management, Amy Poisson.

Kimberly Willis	Megan Hill	Judy Noonan	Jeanette Maus
Neechee Crawford	Louis Hobson	Jim Stark	Lathrop Walker

FROZEN. By Bryony Lavery. September 21, 2005. Direction, Chay Yew; scenery, John McDermott; costumes, Ron Erickson; lighting, Patti West; sound, Nathan Kahler; stage management, Amy Poisson.

Agnetha	Kate Wisniewski	Ralph	Peter Crook
Nancy	Lori Larsen		

Presented in two parts.

5th Avenue Theatre, Seattle
David Armstrong producing artistic director, Marilynn Sheldon managing director

THE WEDDING SINGER. Musical with book by Chad Beguelin and Tim Herlihy; music by Matthew Sklar; lyrics by Mr. Beguelin; based on the film by Mr. Herlihy. February 9, 2006 (world premiere). Direction, John Rando; choreography, Rob Ashford; scenery, Scott Pask; costumes, Gregory Gale; lighting, Brian MacDevitt; sound, Peter Hylenski; music direction, James Sampliner; stage management, Rolt Smith. Presented in association with the Wedding Singer Company.

Robbie Hart	Stephen Lynch	Holly	Amy Spanger
Sammy	Matthew Saldivar	Glen Guglia	Richard H. Blake
George	Kevin Cahoon	Rosie	Rita Gardner
Julia Sullivan	Laura Benanti	Linda	Felicia Finley

Ensemble: Adinah Alexander, Matt Allen, Tracee Beazer, Cara Cooper, Ashley Amber Haase, Nicolette Hart, Angelique Ilo, David Josefsberg, Peter Kapetan, Kevin Kern, Spencer Liff, J. Elaine Marcos, Michael McGurk, T. Oliver Reid, Christina Sivrich, Matthew Stocke, Eric LaJuan Summers.

Musical numbers included: "It's Your Wedding Day," "Wonder," "Eight Men," "A Note From Linda," "Pop," "Somebody Kill Me," "Casualty of Love," "Come Out of the Dumpster," "Today You Are a Man," "George's Prayer," "Not That Kind of Thing," "Saturday Night in the City," All About the Green," "Single," "If I Told You," "Let Me Come Home," "Move That Thang," "Grow Old With You," "Never Let You Go."

Time: 1980s. Place: New Jersey. Presented in two parts.

Intiman Theatre, Seattle
Bartlett Sher artistic director, Laura Penn managing director

THE THREE SISTERS. By Anton Chehkov; adapted by Craig Lucas. June 17, 2005 (world premiere). Direction, Bartlett Sher; scenery, John McDermott; costumes, Martin Pakledinaz; lighting, Stephen Strawbridge; sound, Stephen LeGrand; stage management, Lisa Ann Chernoff.

Andrey Prozorov	Andrew Weems	Solyony	Rob Estes
Natasha	Kristin Flanders	Chebutykin	Michael Winters
Olga	Judy Kuhn	Fedotik	A. Bryan Humphrey
Masha	Julie Dretzin	Rode	K. Brian Neel
Irina	Alexandra Tavares	Feraport	Jack Clay
Kulygin	Larry Paulsen	Anfisa	Ada McAllister
Vershinin	Jay Goede	Maid	Greta Bloor
Tusenbakh	Sam Catlin		

Presented in two parts.

THE TRICKY PART. By Martin Moran. July 20, 2005. Direction, Seth Barrish; scenery, Paul Steinberg; lighting, Russell H. Champa; stage management, J.R. Welden.

Performed by Mr. Moran

INTIMATE APPAREL. By Lynn Nottage. August 24, 2005. Direction, Jacqueline Moscou; scenery, Carey Wong; costumes, Deb Trout; lighting, Allen Lee Hughes; sound, Peter John Still; stage management, Lisa Ann Chernoff.

Esther	Gwendolyn Mulamba	Mrs. Van Buren	Mari Nelson
Mrs. Dickson	Demene E. Hall	Mr. Marks	Marc Jablon
George Armstrong	Albert Jones	Mayme	Yvette Ganier

Time: 1905. Place: Lower Manhattan. Presented in two parts.

THE GRAPES OF WRATH. By John Steinbeck; adapted by Frank Galati. October 14, 2005. Direction, Linda Hartzell; scenery, Carey Wong; costumes, Catherine Hunt; lighting, Mary Louise Geiger; sound and music, Chris R. Walker; fight direction, Geoffrey Alm; stage management, J.R. Welden.

Jim Casy	Todd Jefferson Moore	Granma	Sharva Maynard
Tom Joad	Erick Kastel	Grampa	Philip Davidson
Muley Graves	Laurence Ballard	Noah	John Bogar
Willy	Shawn Telford	Uncle John	Russell Hodgkinson
Car Salesmen	John Bogar,	Ruthie	Mabel Vautravers
	Josephine Howell,	Winfield	Jake Larson
	Aaron Ousley,	Rose of Sharon	Autumn Dornfeld
	Sharia Pierce	Connie Rivers	Aaron Ousley
Pa	Patrick Husted	Al	Connor Toms
Ma	Beth Dixon	Camp Proprietor	Shawn Telford

Man Going Back	Lance McQueen	Elizabeth Sandry	Josephine Howell
Station Attendant	Sharia Pierce	Al's Girl	Sharia Pierce
Station Owner	Bradford Farwell	Ranch Bookkeeper	Aaron Ousley
Agricultural Officer	Laurence Ballard, Shawn Telford	Ranch Guard	Philip Davidson
		Mrs. Wainright	Sharva Maynard
Mayor of Hooverville	Philip Davidson	Mr. Wainright	Laurence Ballard
Floyd Knowles	Bradford Farwell	Aggie Wainright	Sharia Pierce
Contractor	Laurence Ballard	Man in the Barn	John Bogar
Deputy Sheriff	Shawn Telford	His Son	Christopher Langston
Camp Director	Laurence Ballard	Ensemble	Chelsea Taylor

Time: 1938. Place: Oklahoma; California. Presented in two parts.

Seattle Repertory Theatre

David Esbjornson artistic director, Benjamin Moore managing director

RESTORATION COMEDY. By Amy Freed. December 7, 2005 (world premiere). Direction, Sharon Ott; scenery, Hugh Landwehr; costumes, Anna R. Oliver; lighting, Peter Maradudin; sound, Stephen LeGrand.

Mr. Loveless	Stephen Caffrey	Sly; others	Laurence Ballard
Mr. Worthy	Neil Maffin	Amanda	Caralyn Kozlowski
Snap; Young Fashion	Matthew Schneck	Hillaria, Nurse	Laura Kenny
Sir Novelty Fashion;		Narcissa; others	Bhama Roget
Lord Foppington	Jonathan Freeman	Berinthia	Suzanne Bouchard
Lory; Tailor	Gabriel Baron		

Ensemble: Melissa D. Brown, Rebecca Olson, Garlyn Punao.

Presented in two parts.

9 PARTS OF DESIRE. By Heather Raffo. March 22, 2006. Direction, Joanna Settle; scenery, Antje Ellermann; costumes, Kasia Walicka Maimone; lighting, Peter West; sound, Obadiah Eaves; stage management, Melissa Goldhamer.

Performed by Najla Said.

Women Playwrights Festival. April 20–23, 2006.

THE PORK CHOP WARS. By Laurie Carlos. April 20, 2006. Direction, Valerie Curtis-Newton; dramaturgy, Mame Hunt.

Performed by Timeca Briggs, Tracy Hughes, Felicia Loud, Kibibi Monie, Shontina Vernon, Kevin Warren.

MY WANDERING BOY. By Julie Marie Myatt. April 21, 2006. Direction, David Esbjornson; dramaturgy, Christine Sumption.

Performed by Hazel James Bray, Craig Doescher, Séan G. Griffin, Elizabeth Huddle, Marya Sea Kaminski, Todd Jefferson Moore, Cristine Anne Reynolds, Kevin Tighe, Sarah Wallace, Amber Wolfe.

26 MILES. By Quiara Alegría Hudes. Direction, Sharon Ott; dramaturgy, Christine Sumption.

Performed by Alex Balderrama, John Farrage, Leticia Lopez, Larry Paulsen, Stephanie Timm.

SCOOPING THE DARKNESS EMPTY. By Alva Rogers. April 23, 2006. Direction, Allison Narver; dramaturgy, Mame Hunt.

Performed by Suzanne Bouchard, Alycia Delmore, Craig Doescher, Nick Garrison, Jeanne Paulsen, Tracy Repep, Mike Shapiro, Alexandra Tavares, R. Hamilton Wright.

WISCONSIN

Milwaukee Repertory Theatre
Joseph Hanreddy artistic director

SUEÑO. By José Rivera; adapted from *Life Is a Dream* by Pedro Calderón de la Barca. February 19, 2006. Direction, Joseph Hanreddy; choreography, Ed Burgess; scenery, Michael Frenkel; costumes, Martha Hally; lighting, Thomas C. Hase; sound, Barry G. Funderburg; fight direction, Lee E. Ernst; dramaturgy, Paul Kosidowski; stage management, Leslie Anne Stone.

Basilio	Lee E. Ernst	Astolfo	Ted Deasy
Clarin	Torrey Hanson	Segismundo	Reese Madigan
Servant	James Pickering	Clotaldo	Timothy McCuen Piggee
Rosaura	Lanise Antoine Shelley	Estrella	Heather Prete

FACTS AND
FIGURES

LONG RUNS ON BROADWAY

○ ○ ○ ○ ○

THE FOLLOWING SHOWS have run 500 or more continuous performances in a single production, usually the first, not including previews or extra nonprofit performances, allowing for vacation layoffs and special one-booking engagements, but not including return engagements after a show has gone on tour. In all cases, the numbers were obtained directly from the show's production offices. Where there are title similarities, the production is identified as follows: (p) straight play version, (m) musical version, (r) revival, (tr) transfer.

THROUGH MAY 31, 2006

PLAYS MARKED WITH ASTERISK WERE STILL PLAYING JUNE 1, 2006

Plays	Performances	Plays	Performances
*The Phantom of the Opera	7,649	La Cage aux Folles	1,761
Cats	7,485	Hair	1,750
Les Misérables	6,680	The Wiz	1,672
A Chorus Line	6,137	Born Yesterday	1,642
Oh! Calcutta! (r)	5,959	The Best Little Whorehouse in Texas	1,639
*Beauty and the Beast	4,975	Crazy for You	1,622
*Rent	4,195	Ain't Misbehavin'	1,604
Miss Saigon	4,097	*Hairspray	1,578
*Chicago (m)(r)	3,973	Mary, Mary	1,572
*The Lion King	3,566	Evita	1,567
42nd Street	3,486	The Voice of the Turtle	1,557
Grease	3,388	Jekyll & Hyde	1,543
Fiddler on the Roof	3,242	Barefoot in the Park	1,530
Life With Father	3,224	Brighton Beach Memoirs	1,530
Tobacco Road	3,182	42nd Street (r)	1,524
Hello, Dolly!	2,844	Dreamgirls	1,522
My Fair Lady	2,717	Mame (m)	1,508
Annie	2,377	Grease (r)	1,503
Cabaret (r)	2,377	Same Time, Next Year	1,453
Man of La Mancha	2,328	Arsenic and Old Lace	1,444
Abie's Irish Rose	2,327	The Sound of Music	1,443
Oklahoma!	2,212	Me and My Girl	1,420
*The Producers	2,129	How to Succeed in Business	
Smokey Joe's Cafe	2,036	Without Really Trying	1,417
Pippin	1,944	Hellzapoppin'	1,404
South Pacific	1,925	The Music Man	1,375
*Mamma Mia!	1,920	Funny Girl	1,348
The Magic Show	1,920	Mummenschanz	1,326
Aida	1,852	Movin' Out	1,303
Deathtrap	1,793	Angel Street	1,295
Gemini	1,788	Lightnin'	1,291
Harvey	1,775	Promises, Promises	1,281
Dancin'	1,774	The King and I	1,246

Plays	Performances
The Real Thing	566
Happy Birthday	564
Look Homeward, Angel	564
Morning's at Seven (r)	564
The Glass Menagerie	563
I Do! I Do!	560
Wonderful Town	559
The Last Night of Ballyhoo	557
Rose Marie	557
Strictly Dishonorable	557
Sweeney Todd	557
The Great White Hope	556
A Majority of One	556
The Sisters Rosensweig	556
Sunrise at Campobello	556
Toys in the Attic	556
Jamaica	555
Stop the World—I Want to Get Off	555
Florodora	553
Noises Off	553
Ziegfeld Follies (1943)	553
Dial "M" for Murder	552
Good News	551
Peter Pan (r)	551
How to Succeed in Business Without Really Trying (r)	548
Let's Face It	547
Milk and Honey	543
Within the Law	541
Pal Joey (r)	540
The Sound of Music (r)	540
What Makes Sammy Run?	540
The Sunshine Boys	538
What a Life	538
Crimes of the Heart	535
Damn Yankees (r)	533
The Unsinkable Molly Brown	532
The Red Mill (r)	531

Plays	Performances
Rumors	531
A Raisin in the Sun	530
Godspell (tr)	527
Fences	526
The Solid Gold Cadillac	526
Biloxi Blues	524
Irma La Douce	524
The Boomerang	522
Follies	521
Rosalinda	521
The Best Man	520
Chauve-Souris	520
*Dirty Rotten Scoundrels	518
Blackbirds of 1928	518
The Gin Game	517
Side Man	517
Sunny	517
Victoria Regina	517
Fifth of July	511
Half a Sixpence	511
The Vagabond King	511
The New Moon	509
The World of Suzie Wong	508
The Rothschilds	507
On Your Toes (r)	505
Sugar	505
*Spamalot	504
Shuffle Along	504
Up in Central Park	504
Carmen Jones	503
Saturday Night Fever	502
The Member of the Wedding	501
Panama Hattie	501
Personal Appearance	501
Bird in Hand	500
Room Service	500
Sailor, Beware!	500
Tomorrow the World	500

LONG RUNS OFF BROADWAY

Plays	Performances
The Fantasticks	17,162
*Perfect Crime	7,772
*Tubes	7,619
*Stomp	5,149
Tony 'n' Tina's Wedding	4,914
*I Love You, You're Perfect, Now Change	4,089
Nunsense	3,672
The Threepenny Opera	2,611
De La Guarda	2,473
*Naked Boys Singing!	2,398
Forbidden Broadway 1982–87	2,332
Little Shop of Horrors	2,209
Godspell	2,124

Plays	Performances
Vampire Lesbians of Sodom	2,024
Jacques Brel	1,847
Forever Plaid	1,811
Vanities	1,785
Menopause: The Musical	1,724
You're a Good Man, Charlie Brown	1,597
The Donkey Show	1,488
The Blacks	1,408
The Vagina Monologues	1,381
One Mo' Time	1,372
Grandma Sylvia's Funeral	1,360
Let My People Come	1,327
Late Nite Catechism	1,268
Driving Miss Daisy	1,195

NEW YORK DRAMA CRITICS' CIRCLE
1935–1936 TO 2005–2006

○ ○ ○ ○ ○

LISTED BELOW ARE the New York Drama Critics' Circle Awards from 1935–1936 through 2005–2006 classified as follows: (1) Best American Play, (2) Best Foreign Play, (3) Best Musical, (4) Best, Regardless of Category (this category was established by new voting rules in 1962–63 and did not exist prior to that year).

1935–36 (1) *Winterset*

1936–37 (1) *High Tor*

1937–38 (1) *Of Mice and Men*, (2) *Shadow and Substance*

1938–39 (1) No award, (2) *The White Steed*

1939–40 (1) *The Time of Your Life*

1940–41 (1) *Watch on the Rhine*, (2) *The Corn Is Green*

1941–42 (1) No award, (2) *Blithe Spirit*

1942–43 (1) *The Patriots*

1943–44 (2) *Jacobowsky and the Colonel*

1944–45 (1) *The Glass Menagerie*

1945–46 (3) *Carousel*

1946–47 (1) *All My Sons*, (2) *No Exit*, (3) *Brigadoon*

1947–48 (1) *A Streetcar Named Desire*, (2) *The Winslow Boy*

1948–49 (1) *Death of a Salesman*, (2) *The Madwoman of Chaillot*, (3) *South Pacific*

1949–50 (1) *The Member of the Wedding*, (2) *The Cocktail Party*, (3) *The Consul*

1950–51 (1) *Darkness at Noon*, (2) *The Lady's Not for Burning*, (3) *Guys and Dolls*

1951–52 (1) I *Am a Camera*, (2) *Venus Observed*, (3) *Pal Joey* (Special citation to *Don Juan in Hell*)

1952–53 (1) *Picnic*, (2) *The Love of Four Colonels*, (3) *Wonderful Town*

1953–54 (1) *The Teahouse of the August Moon*, (2) *Ondine*, (3) *The Golden Apple*

1954–55 (1) *Cat on a Hot Tin Roof*, (2) *Witness for the Prosecution*, (3) *The Saint of Bleecker Street*

1955–56 (1) *The Diary of Anne Frank*, (2) *Tiger at the Gates*, (3) *My Fair Lady*

1956–57 (1) *Long Day's Journey Into Night*, (2) *The Waltz of the Toreadors*, (3) *The Most Happy Fella*

1957–58 (1) *Look Homeward, Angel*, (2) *Look Back in Anger*, (3) *The Music Man*

1958–59 (1) *A Raisin in the Sun*, (2) *The Visit*, (3) *La Plume de Ma Tante*

1959–60 (1) *Toys in the Attic*, (2) *Five Finger Exercise*, (3) *Fiorello!*

1960–61 (1) *All the Way Home*, (2) *A Taste of Honey*, (3) *Carnival*

1961–62 (1) *The Night of the Iguana*, (2) *A Man for All Seasons*, (3) *How to Succeed in Business Without Really Trying*

1962–63 (4) *Who's Afraid of Virginia Woolf?* (Special citation to *Beyond the Fringe*)

1963–64 (4) *Luther*, (3) *Hello, Dolly!* (Special citation to *The Trojan Women*)

1964–65 (4) *The Subject Was Roses*, (3) *Fiddler on the Roof*

1965–66 (4) *The Persecution and Assassination of Marat as Performed by the Inmates of the Asylum of Charenton Under the Direction of the Marquis de Sade*, (3) *Man of La Mancha*

1966–67 (4) *The Homecoming*, (3) *Cabaret*

1967–68 (4) *Rosencrantz and Guildenstern Are Dead*, (3) *Your Own Thing*

1968–69 (4) *The Great White Hope*, (3) *1776*

1969–70 (4) *Borstal Boy*, (1) *The Effect of Gamma Rays on Man-in-the-Moon Marigolds*, (3) *Company*

1970–71 (4) *Home*, (1) *The House of Blue Leaves*, (3) *Follies*

1971–72 (4) *That Championship Season*, (2) *The Screens* (3) *Two Gentlemen of Verona* (Special citations to *Sticks and Bones* and *Old Times*)

1972–73 (4) *The Changing Room*, (1) *The Hot l Baltimore*, (3) *A Little Night Music*

1973–74 (4) *The Contractor*, (1) *Short Eyes*, (3) *Candide*

1974–75 (4) *Equus* (1) *The Taking of Miss Janie*, (3) *A Chorus Line*

399

1975–76 (4) *Travesties*, (1) *Streamers*, (3) *Pacific Overtures*

1976–77 (4) *Otherwise Engaged*, (1) *American Buffalo*, (3) *Annie*

1977–78 (4) *Da*, (3) *Ain't Misbehavin'*

1978–79 (4) *The Elephant Man*, (3) *Sweeney Todd, the Demon Barber of Fleet Street*

1979–80 (4) *Talley's Folly*, (2) *Betrayal*, (3) *Evita* (Special citation to Peter Brook's Le Centre International de Créations Théâtrales for its repertory)

1980–81 (4) *A Lesson From Aloes*, (1) *Crimes of the Heart* (Special citations to *Lena Horne: The Lady and Her Music* and the New York Shakespeare Festival production of *The Pirates of Penzance*)

1981–82 (4) *The Life & Adventures of Nicholas Nickleby*, (1) *A Soldier's Play*

1982–83 (4) *Brighton Beach Memoirs*, (2) *Plenty*, (3) *Little Shop of Horrors* (Special citation to Young Playwrights Festival)

1983–84 (4) *The Real Thing*, (1) *Glengarry Glen Ross*, (3) *Sunday in the Park With George* (Special citation to Samuel Beckett for the body of his work)

1984–85 (4) *Ma Rainey's Black Bottom*

1985–86 (4) *A Lie of the Mind*, (2) *Benefactors* (Special citation to *The Search for Signs of Intelligent Life in the Universe*)

1986–87 (4) *Fences*, (2) *Les Liaisons Dangereuses*, (3) *Les Misérables*

1987–88 (4) *Joe Turner's Come and Gone*, (2) *The Road to Mecca*, (3) *Into the Woods*

1988–89 (4) *The Heidi Chronicles*, (2) *Aristocrats* (Special citation to Bill Irwin for *Largely New York*)

1989–90 (4) *The Piano Lesson*, (2) *Privates on Parade*, (3) *City of Angels*

1990–91 (4) *Six Degrees of Separation*, (2) *Our Country's Good*, (3) *The Will Rogers Follies* (Special citation to Eileen Atkins for her portrayal of Virginia Woolf in *A Room of One's Own*)

1991–92 (4) *Dancing at Lughnasa*, (1) *Two Trains Running*

1992–93 (4) *Angels in America: Millennium Approaches*, (2) *Someone Who'll Watch Over Me*, (3) *Kiss of the Spider Woman*

1993–94 (4) *Three Tall Women* (Special citation to Anna Deavere Smith for her unique contribution to theatrical form)

1994–95 (4) *Arcadia*, (1) *Love! Valour! Compassion!* (Special citation to Signature Theatre Company for outstanding artistic achievement)

1995–96 (4) *Seven Guitars*, (2) *Molly Sweeney*, (3) *Rent*

1996–97 (4) *How I Learned to Drive*, (2) *Skylight*, (3) *Violet* (Special citation to *Chicago*)

1997–98 (4) *Art*, (1) *Pride's Crossing*, (3) *The Lion King* (Special citation to the revival production of *Cabaret*)

1998–99 (4) *Wit*, (3) *Parade*, (2) *Closer* (Special citation to David Hare for his contributions to the 1998–99 theater season: *Amy's View*, *Via Dolorosa* and *The Blue Room*)

1999–00 (4) *Jitney*, (3) *James Joyce's The Dead*, (2) *Copenhagen*

2000–01 (4) *The Invention of Love*, (1) *Proof*, (3) *The Producers*

2001–02 (4) *Edward Albee's The Goat, or Who is Sylvia?* (Special citation to Elaine Stritch for *Elaine Stritch at Liberty*)

2002–03 (4) *Take Me Out*, (2) *Talking Heads*, (3) *Hairspray*

2003–04 (4) *Intimate Apparel* (Special citation to Barbara Cook for her contribution to the musical theater)

2004–05 (4) *Doubt, a Parable*, (2) *The Pillowman*

2005–06 (4) *The History Boys*, (3) *The Drowsy Chaperone*

NEW YORK DRAMA CRITICS' CIRCLE VOTING 2005–2006

Adam Feldman (*Time Out New York*), President

AT ITS MAY 11, 2006, meeting the New York Drama Critics' Circle, following the example of the Pulitzer Prize board, declined to honor any American play of the 2005–2006 season. When the first ballot resulted in no clear winner, Alan Bennett's *The History Boys* was chosen as best play on a second ballot, which ranked the first, second and third choices of each voter. *The Drowsy*

Chaperone was voted best musical on a first ballot, though it is worth noting that Clive Barnes of the *New York Post* and Jacques le Sourd of *The Journal News* both voted that no musical award be given.

Of the 19 members of the group, only Richard Zoglin of *Time* was absent and he did not file an absentee ballot. The first play-ballot resulted in the tallies that follow: *The History Boys* 9 (David Cote, *Time Out New York*; Adam Feldman, *Time Out New York*; John Heilpern, *The New York Observer*; Howard Kissel, *Daily News*; Michael Kuchwara, The Associated Press; Jacques le Sourd, *The Journal News*; David Rooney, *Variety*; David Sheward, *Back Stage*; Linda Winer, *Newsday*), *The Lieutenant of Inishmore* 4 (Terry Teachout, *The Wall Street Journal*; Michael Sommers, *The Star-Ledger*; Clive Barnes, *New York Post*; Elysa Gardner, *USA Today*), *In the Continuum* 2 (Michael Feingold, *The Village Voice*; Jeremy McCarter, *New York*), *Primo* 1 (Robert Feldberg, *The Bergen Record*), *Red Light Winter* 1 (Frank Scheck, *The Hollywood Reporter/New York Post*), and *Private Fears in Public Places* 1 (John Simon, Bloomberg.com). The second ballot replicated the previous one in the category of first choices, but *The History Boys* received enough second-rank (Robert Feldberg and John Simon) and third-rank votes (Jeremy McCarter) to put it over the top. In addition to the plays mentioned above from the first round, the second ballot also saw advocacy for John Patrick Shanley's *Defiance*, Ariane Mnouchkine's *Le Dernier Caravansérail (Odyssées)*, Douglas Carter Beane's *The Little Dog Laughed*, David Lindsay-Abaire's *Rabbit Hole*, Conor McPherson's *Shining City*, Howard Brenton's *Sore Throats*, David Hare's *Stuff Happens*, Wendy Wasserstein's *Third* and Karoline Leach's *Tryst*.

In the voting for best musical four contenders emerged: *The Drowsy Chaperone*, *Grey Gardens*, *Jersey Boys* and *See What I Wanna See*. The voting was tallied as follows: *The Drowsy Chaperone* 10 (Adam Feldman, *Time Out New York*; David Cote, *Time Out New York*; David Sheward, *Back Stage*; Frank Scheck, *The Hollywood Reporter/New York Post*; Howard Kissel, *Daily News*; Jeremy McCarter, *New York*; John Heilpern, *The New York Observer*; Michael Kuchwara, The Associated Press; Robert Feldberg, *The Bergen Record*; Terry Teachout, *The Wall Street Journal*), *Grey Gardens* 3 (David Rooney, *Variety*; Elysa Gardner, *USA Today*; Michael Feingold, *The Village Voice*), *Jersey Boys* 2 (John Simon, Bloomberg.com; Michael Sommers, *The Star-Ledger*), *See What I Wanna See* 1 (Linda Winer, *Newsday*).

Honorees received their accolades at an Algonquin cocktail party May 23, 2006.

PULITZER PRIZE WINNERS
1916–1917 TO 2005–2006

1916–17 No award
1917–18 *Why Marry?* by Jesse Lynch Williams
1918–19 No award
1919–20 *Beyond the Horizon* by Eugene O'Neill
1920–21 *Miss Lulu Bett* by Zona Gale
1921–22 *Anna Christie* by Eugene O'Neill
1922–23 *Icebound* by Owen Davis
1923–24 *Hell-Bent fer Heaven* by Hatcher Hughes
1924–25 *They Knew What They Wanted* by Sidney Howard
1925–26 *Craig's Wife* by George Kelly
1926–27 *In Abraham's Bosom* by Paul Green
1927–28 *Strange Interlude* by Eugene O'Neill
1928–29 *Street Scene* by Elmer Rice
1929–30 *The Green Pastures* by Marc Connelly
1930–31 *Alison's House* by Susan Glaspell
1931–32 *Of Thee I Sing* by George S. Kaufman, Morrie Ryskind, Ira and George Gershwin
1932–33 *Both Your Houses* by Maxwell Anderson
1933–34 *Men in White* by Sidney Kingsley
1934–35 *The Old Maid* by Zoe Akins
1935–36 *Idiot's Delight* by Robert E. Sherwood
1936–37 *You Can't Take It With You* by Moss Hart and George S. Kaufman
1937–38 *Our Town* by Thornton Wilder
1938–39 *Abe Lincoln in Illinois* by Robert E. Sherwood
1939–40 *The Time of Your Life* by William Saroyan
1940–41 *There Shall Be No Night* by Robert E. Sherwood
1941–42 No award
1942–43 *The Skin of Our Teeth* by Thornton Wilder
1943–44 No award
1944–45 *Harvey* by Mary Chase
1945–46 *State of the Union* by Howard Lindsay and Russel Crouse
1946–47 No award
1947–48 *A Streetcar Named Desire* by Tennessee Williams
1948–49 *Death of a Salesman* by Arthur Miller
1949–50 *South Pacific* by Richard Rodgers, Oscar Hammerstein II and Joshua Logan
1950–51 No award
1951–52 *The Shrike* by Joseph Kramm
1952–53 *Picnic* by William Inge

1953–54 *The Teahouse of the August Moon* by John Patrick
1954–55 *Cat on a Hot Tin Roof* by Tennessee Williams
1955–56 *The Diary of Anne Frank* by Frances Goodrich and Albert Hackett
1956–57 *Long Day's Journey Into Night* by Eugene O'Neill
1957–58 *Look Homeward, Angel* by Ketti Frings
1958–59 *J.B.* by Archibald MacLeish
1959–60 *Fiorello!* by Jerome Weidman, George Abbott, Sheldon Harnick and Jerry Bock
1960–61 *All the Way Home* by Tad Mosel
1961–62 *How to Succeed in Business Without Really Trying* by Abe Burrows, Willie Gilbert, Jack Weinstock and Frank Loesser
1962–63 No award
1963–64 No award
1964–65 *The Subject Was Roses* by Frank D. Gilroy
1965–66 No award
1966–67 *A Delicate Balance* by Edward Albee
1967–68 No award
1968–69 *The Great White Hope* by Howard Sackler
1969–70 *No Place To Be Somebody* by Charles Gordone
1970–71 *The Effect of Gamma Rays on Man-in-the-Moon Marigolds* by Paul Zindel
1971–72 No award
1972–73 *That Championship Season* by Jason Miller
1973–74 No award
1974–75 *Seascape* by Edward Albee
1975–76 *A Chorus Line* by Michael Bennett, James Kirkwood, Nicholas Dante, Marvin Hamlisch and Edward Kleban
1976–77 *The Shadow Box* by Michael Cristofer
1977–78 *The Gin Game* by D.L. Coburn
1978–79 *Buried Child* by Sam Shepard
1979–80 *Talley's Folly* by Lanford Wilson
1980–81 *Crimes of the Heart* by Beth Henley
1981–82 *A Soldier's Play* by Charles Fuller
1982–83 *'night, Mother* by Marsha Norman
1983–84 *Glengarry Glen Ross* by David Mamet
1984–85 *Sunday in the Park With George* by James Lapine and Stephen Sondheim
1985–86 No award

1986–87 *Fences* by August Wilson
1987–88 *Driving Miss Daisy* by Alfred Uhry
1988–89 *The Heidi Chronicles* by Wendy Wasserstein
1989–90 *The Piano Lesson* by August Wilson
1990–91 *Lost in Yonkers* by Neil Simon
1991–92 *The Kentucky Cycle* by Robert Schenkkan
1992–93 *Angels in America: Millennium Approaches* by Tony Kushner
1993–94 *Three Tall Women* by Edward Albee
1994–95 *The Young Man From Atlanta* by Horton Foote
1995–96 *Rent* by Jonathan Larson

1996–97 No award
1997–98 *How I Learned to Drive* by Paula Vogel
1998–99 *Wit* by Margaret Edson
1999–00 *Dinner With Friends* by Donald Margulies
2000–01 *Proof* by David Auburn
2001–02 *Topdog/Underdog* by Suzan-Lori Parks
2002–03 *Anna in the Tropics* by Nilo Cruz
2003–04 *I Am My Own Wife* by Doug Wright
2004–05 *Doubt, a Parable* by John Patrick Shanley
2005–06 No Award

2006 TONY AWARDS

○ ○ ○ ○ ○

THE AMERICAN THEATRE WING'S 60th annual Tony Awards, named for Antoinette Perry, are presented in recognition of distinguished achievement in the Broadway theater. The League of American Theatres and Producers (Gerald Schoenfeld, chairman; Jed Bernstein, president) and the American Theatre Wing (Sondra Gilman, chairman; Doug Leeds, president; Howard Sherman, executive director) present these awards, founded by the Wing in 1947. Legitimate theater productions opening in 39 eligible Broadway theaters during the present Tony season—May 5, 2005 to May 10, 2006—were considered by the Tony Awards Nominating Committee (appointed by the Tony Awards Administration Committee) for the awards in 24 competitive categories. There was no award given in the new category of Best Performance by an Actor or Actress in a Recreated Role. The 2005–2006 Nominating Committee consisted of Victoria Bailey, Susan Birkenhead, Stephen Bogardus, Edward Burbridge, Ben Cameron, Kirsten Childs, Betty Corwin, Jacqueline Davis, Mercedes Ellington, Nancy Ford, Dana Ivey, Andrew Jackness, Geoffrey Johnson, Robert Kamlot, Todd London, Brian Stokes Mitchell, Jon Nakagawa, Enid Nemy, Lynn Nottage, Gilbert Parker, Jonathan Reynolds, Jac Venza and Franklin Weissberg.

The Tony Awards are voted from the list of nominees by members of the theater and journalism professions: the governing boards of the five theater artists' organizations (Actors' Equity Association, the Dramatists' Guild, the Society of Stage Directors and Choreographers, United Scenic Artists and the Casting Society of America), members of the designated first night theater press, the board of directors of the American Theatre Wing and the membership of the League of American Theatres and Producers. Because of fluctuation in these groups, the size of the Tony electorate varies from year to year. For the 2005–2006 season there were 754 qualified Tony voters.

The 2005–2006 nominees follow, with winners in each category listed in **bold face type**.

PLAY (award goes to both author and producer). *The History Boys* **by Alan Bennett, produced by Boyett Ostar Productions, Roger Berlind, Debra Black, Eric Falkenstein, Roy Furman, Jam Theatricals, Stephanie P. McClelland, Judith Resnick, Scott Rudin, Jon Avnet/Ralph Guild, Dede Harris/Morton Swinsky, The National Theatre of Great Britain**. *The Lieutenant of Inishmore* by Martin McDonagh, produced by Randall L. Wreghitt, Dede Harris, Atlantic Theater Company, David Lehrer, Harriet Newman Leve and Ron Nicynski, Zavelson Meyrelles Greiner Group, Morton Swinsky and Redfern Goldman Productions, Ruth Hendel. *Rabbit Hole* by David Lindsay-Abaire, produced by Manhattan Theatre Club, Lynne Meadow, Barry Grove. *Shining City* by Conor McPherson, produced by Manhattan Theatre Club, Lynne Meadow, Barry Grove, Scott Rudin, Roger Berlind, Debra Black.

MUSICAL (award goes to the producer). *The Color Purple* produced by Oprah Winfrey, Scott Sanders, Roy Furman, Quincy Jones, Creative Battery, Anna Fantaci & Cheryl Lachowicz, Independent Presenters Network, David Lowy, Stephanie P. McClelland, Gary Winnick, Jan Kallish, Nederlander Presentations, Inc., Bob and Harvey Weinstein, Andrew Asnes and Adam Zotovich, Todd Johnson. *The Drowsy Chaperone* produced by Kevin McCollum, Roy Miller, Boyett Ostar Productions, Stephanie P. McClelland, Barbara Freitag, Jill Furman. *Jersey Boys* **produced by Dodger Theatricals, Joseph J. Grano, Pelican Group, Tamara and Kevin Kinsella, Latitude Link, Rick Steiner/Staton Bell Osher Mayerson Group**. *The Wedding Singer* produced by Margo Lion, New Line Cinema, The Araca Group, Roy Furman, Douglas L. Meyer/James D. Stern, Rick Steiner/Staton Bell Osher Mayerson Group, Jam Theatricals, Jujamcyn Theaters, Jay Furman, Michael Gill, Lawrence Horowitz, Rhoda Mayerson, Marisa Sechrest, Gary Winnick, Dancap Productions, Inc., Élan

V. McAllister/Allan S. Gordon/Adam Epstein.

BOOK OF A MUSICAL. Marsha Norman for *The Color Purple*. **Bob Martin** and **Don McKellar** for *The Drowsy Chaperone*. Marshall Brickman and Rick Elice for *Jersey Boys*. Chad Beguelin and Tim Herlihy for *The Wedding Singer*.

ORIGINAL SCORE (music and/or lyrics). Brenda Russell, Allee Willis, Stephen Bray (music and lyrics) for *The Color Purple*. **Lisa Lambert** and **Greg Morrison (music and lyrics)** for *The Drowsy Chaperone*. Matthew Sklar (music) and Chad Beguelin (lyrics) for *The Wedding Singer*. Andrew Lloyd Webber (music) and David Zippel (lyrics) *The Woman in White*.

REVIVAL OF A PLAY (award goes to the producer). *Awake and Sing!* **produced by Lincoln Center Theater, André Bishop, Bernard Gersten**. *The Constant Wife* produced by Roundabout Theatre Company, Todd Haimes, Ellen Richard, Julia C. Levy. *Seascape* produced by Lincoln Center Theater, André Bishop, Bernard Gersten. *Faith Healer* produced by Michael Colgan and Sonia Friedman Productions, The Shubert Organization, Robert Bartner, Roger Berlind, Scott Rudin, Spring Sirkin, Gate Theatre (Dublin).

REVIVAL OF A MUSICAL (award goes to the producer). *The Pajama Game* **produced by Roundabout Theatre Company, Todd Haimes, Harold Wolpert, Julia C. Levy, Jeffrey Richards, James Fuld Jr., Scott Landis**. *Sweeney Todd* produced by Thomas Viertel, Steven Baruch, Marc Routh, Richard Frankel, Ambassador Theatre Group, Adam Kenwright, Tulchin/Bartner/Bagert. *The Threepenny Opera* produced by Roundabout Theatre Company, Todd Haimes, Harold Wolpert, Julia C. Levy.

PERFORMANCE BY A LEADING ACTOR IN A PLAY. Ralph Fiennes in *Faith Healer*, **Richard Griffiths** in *The History Boys*, Zeljko Ivanek in *The Caine Mutiny Court-*

Martial, Oliver Platt in *Shining City*, David Wilmot in *The Lieutenant of Inishmore*.

PERFORMANCE BY A LEADING ACTRESS IN A PLAY. Kate Burton in *The Constant Wife*, Judy Kaye in *Souvenir*, Lisa Kron in *Well*, **Cynthia Nixon** in *Rabbit Hole*, Lynn Redgrave in *The Constant Wife*.

PERFORMANCE BY A LEADING ACTOR IN A MUSICAL. Michael Cerveris in *Sweeney Todd*, Harry Connick Jr. in *The Pajama Game*, Stephen Lynch in *The Wedding Singer*, Bob Martin in *The Drowsy Chaperone*, **John Lloyd Young** in *Jersey Boys*.

PERFORMANCE BY A LEADING ACTRESS IN A MUSICAL. Sutton Foster in *The Drowsy Chaperone*, **LaChanze** in *The Color Purple*, Patti LuPone in *Sweeney Todd*, Kelli O'Hara in *The Pajama Game*, Chita Rivera in *Chita Rivera: The Dancer's Life*.

PERFORMANCE BY A FEATURED ACTOR IN A PLAY. Samuel Barnett in *The History Boys*, Domhnall Gleeson in *The Lieutenant of Inishmore*, **Ian McDiarmid** in *Faith Healer*, Mark Ruffalo in *Awake and Sing!*, Pablo Schreiber in *Awake and Sing!*

PERFORMANCE BY A FEATURED ACTRESS IN A PLAY. Tyne Daly in *Rabbit Hole*, **Frances de la Tour** in *The History Boys*, Jayne Houdyshell in *Well*, Alison Pill in *The Lieutenant of Inishmore*, Zoë Wanamaker in *Awake and Sing!*

PERFORMANCE BY A FEATURED ACTOR IN A MUSICAL. Danny Burstein in *The Drowsy Chaperone*, Jim Dale in *The Threepenny Opera*, Brandon Victor Dixon in *The Color Purple*, Manoel Felciano in *Sweeney Todd*, **Christian Hoff** in *Jersey Boys*.

PERFORMANCE BY A FEATURED ACTRESS IN A MUSICAL. Carolee Carmello in *Lestat*, Felicia P. Fields in *The Color Purple*, Megan Lawrence in *The Pajama Game*, **Beth Leavel** in *The Drowsy Chaperone*, Elisabeth Withers-Mendes in *The Color Purple*.

SCENIC DESIGN OF A PLAY. John Lee Beatty for *Rabbit Hole*, **Bob Crowley** for *The History Boys*, Santo Loquasto for *Three Days of Rain*, Michael Yeargan for *Awake and Sing!*

SCENIC DESIGN OF A MUSICAL. John Lee Beatty for *The Color Purple*, **David Gallo** for *The Drowsy Chaperone*, Derek McLane for *The Pajama Game*, Klara Zieglerova for *Jersey Boys*.

COSTUME DESIGN OF A PLAY. Michael Krass for *The Constant Wife*, Santo Loquasto for *A Touch of the Poet*, **Catherine Zuber** for *Awake and Sing!*, Catherine Zuber for *Seascape*.

COSTUME DESIGN OF A MUSICAL. **Gregg Barnes** for *The Drowsy Chaperone*, Susan Hilferty for *Lestat*, Martin Pakledinaz for *The Pajama Game*, Paul Tazewell for *The Color Purple*.

LIGHTING DESIGN OF A PLAY. Christopher Akerlind for *Awake and Sing!*, Paul Gallo for *Three Days of Rain*, Mark Henderson for *Faith Healer*, **Mark Henderson** for *The History Boys*.

LIGHTING DESIGN OF A MUSICAL. Ken Billington and Brian Monahan for *The Drowsy Chaperone*, **Howell Binkley** for *Jersey Boys*, Natasha Katz for *Tarzan*, Brian MacDevitt for *The Color Purple*.

DIRECTION OF A PLAY. **Nicholas Hytner** for *The History Boys*, Wilson Milam for *The Lieutenant of Inishmore*, Bartlett Sher for *Awake and Sing!*, Daniel Sullivan for *Rabbit Hole*.

DIRECTION OF A MUSICAL. **John Doyle** for *Sweeney Todd*, Kathleen Marshall for *The Pajama Game*, Des McAnuff for *Jersey Boys*, Casey Nicholaw for *The Drowsy Chaperone*.

CHOREOGRAPHY. Rob Ashford for *The Wedding Singer*, Donald Byrd for *The Color Purple*, **Kathleen Marshall** for ***The Pajama Game***, Casey Nicholaw for *The Drowsy Chaperone*.

ORCHESTRATIONS. Larry Blank for *The Drowsy Chaperone*, Dick Lieb and Danny Troob for *The Pajama Game*, Steve Orich for *Jersey Boys*, **Sarah Travis** for ***Sweeney Todd***.

SPECIAL AWARD. **Sarah Jones** for ***Bridge and Tunnel***.

LIFETIME ACHIEVEMENT. **Harold Prince**.

REGIONAL THEATRE TONY AWARD. **Intiman Theatre Company**, Seattle Washington.

TONY AWARD WINNERS, 1947–2006

L ISTED BELOW ARE the Antoinette Perry (Tony) Award winners in the catgories of Best Play and Best Musical from the time these awards were established in 1947 until the present.

1947—No play or musical award
1948—*Mister Roberts*; no musical award
1949—*Death of a Salesman*; *Kiss Me, Kate*
1950—*The Cocktail Party*; *South Pacific*
1951—*The Rose Tattoo*; *Guys and Dolls*
1952—*The Fourposter*; *The King and I*
1953—*The Crucible*; *Wonderful Town*
1954—*The Teahouse of the August Moon*; *Kismet*
1955—*The Desperate Hours*; *The Pajama Game*
1956—*The Diary of Anne Frank*; *Damn Yankees*
1957—*Long Day's Journey Into Night*; *My Fair Lady*
1958—*Sunrise at Campobello*; *The Music Man*
1959—*J.B.*; *Redhead*
1960—*The Miracle Worker*; *Fiorello!* and *The Sound of Music* (tie)
1961—*Becket*; *Bye Bye Birdie*
1962—*A Man for All Seasons*; *How to Succeed in Business Without Really Trying*
1963—*Who's Afraid of Virginia Woolf?*; *A Funny Thing Happened on the Way to the Forum*
1964—*Luther*; *Hello, Dolly!*
1965—*The Subject Was Roses*; *Fiddler on the Roof*
1966—*The Persecution and Assassination of Marat as Performed by the Inmates of the Asylum of Charenton Under the Direction of the Marquis de Sade*; *Man of La Mancha*
1967—*The Homecoming*; *Cabaret*
1968—*Rosencrantz and Guildenstern Are Dead*; *Hallelujah, Baby!*

1969—*The Great White Hope*; *1776*
1970—*Borstal Boy*; *Applause*
1971—*Sleuth*; *Company*
1972—*Sticks and Bones*; *Two Gentlemen of Verona*
1973—*That Championship Season*; *A Little Night Music*
1974—*The River Niger*; *Raisin*
1975—*Equus*; *The Wiz*
1976—*Travesties*; *A Chorus Line*
1977—*The Shadow Box*; *Annie*
1978—*Da*; *Ain't Misbehavin'*
1979—*The Elephant Man*; *Sweeney Todd, the Demon Barber of Fleet Street*
1980—*Children of a Lesser God*; *Evita*
1981—*Amadeus*; *42nd Street*
1982—*The Life & Adventures of Nicholas Nickleby*; *Nine*
1983—*Torch Song Trilogy*; *Cats*
1984—*The Real Thing*; *La Cage aux Folles*
1985—*Biloxi Blues*; *Big River*
1986—*I'm Not Rappaport*; *The Mystery of Edwin Drood*
1987—*Fences*; *Les Misérables*
1988—*M. Butterfly*; *The Phantom of the Opera*
1989—*The Heidi Chronicles*; *Jerome Robbins' Broadway*
1990—*The Grapes of Wrath*; *City of Angels*
1991—*Lost in Yonkers*; *The Will Rogers Follies*
1992—*Dancing at Lughnasa*; *Crazy for You*
1993—*Angels in America, Part I: Millennium Approaches*; *Kiss of the Spider Woman*

1994—*Angels in America, Part II: Perestroika*;
    Passion
1995—*Love! Valour! Compassion!*; *Sunset*
    Boulevard
1996—*Master Class*; *Rent*
1997—*The Last Night of Ballyhoo*; *Titanic*
1998—*Art*; *The Lion King*
1999—*Side Man*; *Fosse*
2000—*Copenhagen*; *Contact*

2001—*Proof*; *The Producers*
2002—*The Goat, or Who is Sylvia*; *Thoroughly*
    Modern Millie
2003—*Take Me Out*; *Hairspray*
2004—*I Am My Own Wife*; *Avenue Q*
2005—*Doubt, a Parable*; *Monty Python's*
    Spamalot
2006—*The History Boys*; *Jersey Boys*

2006 LUCILLE LORTEL AWARDS

○ ○ ○ ○ ○

THE LUCILLE LORTEL AWARDS for outstanding Off Broadway achievement were established in 1985 by a resolution of the League of Off Broadway Theatres and Producers, which administers them and has presented them annually since 1986. Eligible for the 21st annual awards in 2005 were all Off Broadway productions that opened between April 1, 2005 and March 31, 2006.

PLAY. ***The Lieutenant of Inishmore*** by Martin McDonagh.

MUSICAL. ***The Seven***. By Will Power.

REVIVAL. ***The Trip to Bountiful*** by Horton Foote, produced by Signature Theatre Company.

ACTOR (tie). **Christopher Denham** in *Red Light Winter* and **David Wilmot** in *The Lieutenant of Inishmore*.

ACTRESS. **Lois Smith** in *The Trip to Bountiful*.

FEATURED ACTOR. **Charles Durning** in *Third*.

FEATURED ACTRESS. **Hallie Foote** in *The Trip to Bountiful*.

DIRECTION. **Harris Yulin** for *The Trip to Bountiful*.

CHOREOGRAPHY. **Bill T. Jones** for *The Seven*.

SCENERY. **Eugene Lee** for *The Ruby Sunrise*.

COSTUMES. **Eric Becker** for *Abigail's Party*.

LIGHTING. **Aaron Black** for *Funnyhouse of a Negro*.

SOUND. **Darron L. West** for *The Seven*.

BODY OF WORK. **Atlantic Theater Company**.

EDITH OLIVER AWARD. **Betty Corwin**.

LIFETIME ACHIEVEMENT. **Wendy Wasserstein**.

LORTEL AWARD WINNERS 1986–2006

LISTED BELOW ARE the Lucille Lortel Award winners in the categories of Outstanding Play and Outstanding Musical from the time these awards were established until the present.

1986—*Woza Africa!*; no musical award
1987—*The Common Pursuit*; no musical award
1988—No play or musical award
1989—*The Cocktail Hour*; no musical award
1990—No play or musical award
1991—*Aristocrats*; *Falsettoland*
1992—*Lips Together, Teeth Apart*; *And the World Goes 'Round*
1993—*The Destiny of Me*; *Forbidden Broadway*
1994—*Three Tall Women*; *Wings*
1995—*Camping With Henry & Tom*; *Jelly Roll!*
1996—*Molly Sweeney*; *Floyd Collins*
1997—*How I Learned to Drive*; *Violet*

1998—*Gross Indecency*, and *The Beauty Queen of Leenane* (tie); no musical award
1999—*Wit*; no musical award
2000—*Dinner With Friends*; *James Joyce's The Dead*
2001—*Proof*; *Bat Boy: The Musical*
2002—*Metamorphoses*; *Urinetown*
2003—*Take Me Out*; *Avenue Q*
2004—*Bug*; *Caroline, or Change*
2005—*Doubt, a Parable*; *The 25th Annual Putnam County Spelling Bee*
2006—*The Lieutenant of Inishmore*; *The Seven*

HAROLD AND MIMI STEINBERG
NEW PLAY AWARDS AND CITATIONS

○ ○ ○ ○ ○

PRINCIPAL CITATIONS AND AMERICAN THEATRE CRITICS ASSOCIATION NEW PLAY AWARD WINNERS, 1977–2006

The American Theatre Critics Association (ATCA) has cited one or more outstanding new plays in United States theater since the 1976–1977 season. The principal honorees have been honored in *The Best Plays Theater Yearbook* since the first year. In 1986 the ATCA New Play Award was given for the first time, along with a $1,000 prize. The award and citations were renamed the American Theatre Critics/Steinberg New Play Award and Citations in 2000 when the Harold and Mimi Steinberg Charitable Trust committed $25,000 per year to the honors. Beginning with the 2006 honors, the awards were renamed the **Harold and Mimi Steinberg/American Theatre Critics Association New Play Award and Citations** to reflect an increased financial commitment of $40,000 per year from the Trust. (See essays on the 2006 Steinberg/ATCA honorees in the Season Around the United States section of this volume.) The award dates were renumbered beginning with the 2000–2001 volume to correctly reflect the year in which ATCA conferred the honor.

New Play Citations (1977–1985)

1977—*And the Soul Shall Dance* by Wakako Yamauchi
1978—*Getting Out* by Marsha Norman
1979—*Loose Ends* by Michael Weller
1980—*Custer* by Robert E. Ingham

1981—*Chekhov in Yalta* by John Driver and Jeffrey Haddow
1982—*Talking With* by Jane Martin
1983—*Closely Related* by Bruce MacDonald
1984—*Wasted* by Fred Gamel
1985—*Scheherazade* by Marisha Chamberlain

NEW PLAY AWARD (1986–1999)

1986—*Fences* by August Wilson
1987—*A Walk in the Woods* by Lee Blessing
1988—*Heathen Valley* by Romulus Linney
1989—*The Piano Lesson* by August Wilson
1990—*2* by Romulus Linney
1991—*Two Trains Running* by August Wilson
1992—*Could I Have This Dance?* by Doug Haverty
1993—*Children of Paradise: Shooting a Dream* by Steven Epp, Felicity Jones,
    Dominique Serrand and Paul Walsh
1994—*Keely and Du* by Jane Martin
1995—*The Nanjing Race* by Reggie Cheong-Leen
1996—*Amazing Grace* by Michael Cristofer
1997—*Jack and Jill* by Jane Martin
1998—*The Cider House Rules, Part II* by Peter Parnell
1999—*Book of Days* by Lanford Wilson.

ATCA/STEINBERG NEW PLAY AWARD AND CITATIONS

2000—*Oo-Bla-Dee* by Regina Taylor
    Citation: *Compleat Female Stage Beauty* by Jeffrey Hatcher
    Citation: *Syncopation* by Allan Knee
2001—*Anton in Show Business* by Jane Martin
    Citation: *Big Love* by Charles L. Mee
    Citation: *King Hedley II* by August Wilson
2002—*The Carpetbagger's Children* by Horton Foote
    Citation: *The Action Against Sol Schumann* by Jeffrey Sweet
    Citation: *Joe and Betty* by Murray Mednick
2003—*Anna in the Tropics* by Nilo Cruz
    Citation: *Recent Tragic Events* by Craig Wright
    Citation: *Resurrection Blues* by Arthur Miller
2004—*Intimate Apparel* by Lynn Nottage
    Citation: *Gem of the Ocean* by August Wilson
    Citation: *The Love Song of J. Robert Oppenheimer* by Carson Kreitzer
2005—*Singing Forest* by Craig Lucas
    Citation: *After Ashley* by Gina Gionfriddo
    Citation: *The Clean House* by Sarah Ruhl

HAROLD AND MIMI STEINBERG/ATCA NEW PLAY AWARD AND CITATIONS

2006—*A Body of Water* by Lee Blessing
    Citation: *Radio Golf* by August Wilson
    Citation: *Red Light Winter* by Adam Rapp

ADDITIONAL PRIZES AND AWARDS 2005–2006

THE FOLLOWING IS a list of major awards for achievement in the theater this season. The names of honorees appear in **bold type**.

2004–2005 GEORGE JEAN NATHAN AWARD. For dramatic criticism. **Raymond Knapp**.

25TH ANNUAL WILLIAM INGE THEATRE FESTIVAL AWARD. For distinguished achievement in American theater. **Honored past recipients**. Otis Guernsey New Voices Award: **Melanie Marnich**.

2006 M. ELIZABETH OSBORN AWARD. Presented by the American Theatre Critics Association to an emerging playwright. **Steven Tomlinson** for *American Fiesta*.

28TH ANNUAL KENNEDY CENTER HONORS. For distinguished achievement by individuals who have made significant contributions to American culture through the arts. **Tony Bennett**, **Suzanne Farrell**, **Julie Harris**, **Robert Redford**, **Tina Turner**.

2005 NATIONAL MEDALS OF THE ARTS. For individuals and organizations who have made outstanding contributions to the excellence, growth, support and availability of the arts in the United States, selected by the President from nominees presented by the National Endowment. **Louis Auchincloss**, **James DePreist**, **Pasquito D'Rivera**, **Robert Duvall**, **Leonard Garment**, **Ollie Johnston**, **Wynton Marsalis**, **Dolly Parton**, **Pennsylvania Academy of the Fine Arts**, **Tina Ramirez**.

2006 DRAMATISTS' GUILD AWARDS. Elizabeth Hull–Kate Warriner Award: **Adam Guettel** and **Craig Lucas** for *The Light in the Piazza*. Frederick Loewe Award for Dramatic Composition: **Harvey Schmidt**. Flora Roberts Award: **Robert Waldman**. Lifetime Achievement: **August Wilson**.

2006 HENRY HEWES DESIGN AWARDS (formerly American Theatre Wing Design Awards). For design originating in the US, selected by a committee comprising Jeffrey Eric Jenkins (chairman), Tish Dace, Michael Feingold, Glenda Frank, Mario Fratti, Randy Gener, Henry Hewes and Joan Ungaro. Scenic design: **Allen Moyer** for *Grey Gardens*. Costume design: **Anita Yavich** for *Measure for Pleasure*. Lighting design: **Howell Binkley** for *Jersey Boys*. Notable effects: **Ruppert Bohle** for the projection design of *Cathay: Three Tales From China*; **Stephen Kaplin** and **Wang Bo** for the puppetry design of *Cathay: Three Tales From China*.

28TH ANNUAL SUSAN SMITH BLACKBURN PRIZE. For women who have written works of outstanding quality for the English-speaking theater. **Amelia Bullmore** for *Mammals* and **Elizabeth Kuti** for *The Sugar Wife*.

2005 GEORGE FREEDLEY MEMORIAL AWARD. Recognizing the year's outstanding book in the area of live performance, given by the Theatre Library Association. ***Charlotte: Being a True Account of an Actress's Flamboyant Adventures in Eighteenth-Century London's Wild and Wicked Theatrical World*** by **Kathryn Shevelow**. Special jury prize: ***Susan Glaspell: Her Life and Times*** by **Linda Ben-Zvi**. Distinguished service in performing arts librarianship (three awards): Maryann Chach; Mary C. Henderson; Madeline Fitzgerald Matz.

61ST ANNUAL CLARENCE DERWENT AWARDS. Given to a female and a male performer by Actors' Equity Association based on New York work that demonstrates promise. **Felicia P. Fields** and **Jason Ritter**.

2006 RICHARD RODGERS AWARDS. For productions and staged readings of musicals in nonprofit theaters, administered by the American Academy of Arts and Letters and selected by a jury including Stephen Sondheim (chairman), Lynn Ahrens, John Guare, Sheldon Harnick, Jeanine Tesori and John Weidman. Production award: *Grey Gardens* by **Scott Frankel, Michael Korie** and **Doug Wright**. Staged reading awards: *The Yellow Wood* by Michelle Elliott and **Danny Larsen**; *True Fans* by **Chris Miller, Bill Rosenfield** and **Nathan Tysen**.

72nd ANNUAL DRAMA LEAGUE AWARDS. For distinguished achievement in the American theater. Play: *The History Boys*. Musical: *Jersey Boys*. Revival of a play: *Awake and Sing!* Revival of a musical: *Sweeney Todd*. Performance: **Christine Ebersole** in *Grey Gardens*.

2006 GEORGE OPPENHEIMER AWARD. To the best new American playwright, presented by *Newsday*. **Elizabeth Meriwether** for *Heddatron*.

2006 NEW DRAMATISTS LIFETIME ACHIEVEMENT AWARD. To an individual who has made an outstanding artistic contribution to the American theater. **Chita Rivera**.

2006 *THEATRE WORLD* AWARDS. For outstanding debut performers in Broadway or Off Broadway theater during the 2005–2006 season, selected by a committee including Peter Filichia, Harry Haun, Frank Scheck, Matthew Murray, Michael Sommers, Douglas Watt and Linda Winer. **Harry Connick Jr.** for *The Pajama Game*; **Felicia P. Fields** for *The Color Purple*; **Maria Friedman** for *The Woman in White*; **Richard Griffiths** for *The History Boys*; **Mamie Gummer** for *Mr. Marmalade*; **Jayne Houdyshell** for *Well*; **Bob Martin** for *The Drowsy Chaperone*; **Ian McDiarmid** for *Faith Healer*; **Nellie McKay** for *The Threepenny Opera*; **David Wilmot** for *The Lieutenant of Inishmore*;

Elisabeth Withers-Mendes for *The Color Purple*, **John Lloyd Young** for *Jersey Boys*.

50TH ANNUAL DRAMA DESK AWARDS. For outstanding achievement in the 2005–2006 season, voted by an association of New York drama reporters, editors and critics from nominations made by a committee. New play: *The History Boys*. New musical: *The Drowsy Chaperone*. Revival of a play: *Awake and Sing!* Revival of a musical: *Sweeney Todd*. Book of a musical: **Bob Martin** and **Don McKellar** for *The Drowsy Chaperone*. Music: **Lisa Lambert** and **Greg Morrison** for *The Drowsy Chaperone*. Lyrics: **Lisa Lambert** and **Greg Morrison** for *The Drowsy Chaperone*. Actor in a play: **Richard Griffiths** in *The History Boys*. Actress in a play: **Lois Smith** in *The Trip to Bountiful*. Featured actor in a play: **Samuel Barnett** in *The History Boys*. Featured actress in a play: **Frances de la Tour** in *The History Boys*. Actor in a musical: **John Lloyd Young** in *Jersey Boys*. Actress in a musical: **Christine Ebersole** in *Grey Gardens*. Featured actor in a musical: **Jim Dale** in *The Threepenny Opera*. Featured actress in a musical: **Beth Leavel** in *The Drowsy Chaperone*. Solo performance: **Antony Sher** in *Primo*. Director of a play: **Nicholas Hytner** for *The History Boys*. Director of a musical: **John Doyle** for *Sweeney Todd*. Choreography: **Kathleen Marshall** for *The Pajama Game*. Orchestrations: **Sarah Travis** for *Sweeney Todd*. Scene design of a play: **Michael Yeargan** for *Awake and Sing!* Scene design of a musical: **David Gallo** for *The Drowsy Chaperone*. Costume design: **Gregg Barnes** for *The Drowsy Chaperone*. Lighting design: **Richard G. Jones** for *Sweeney Todd*. Sound design: **Steve Canyon Kennedy** for *Jersey Boys*. Unique Theatrical Experience: *Christine Jorgensen Reveals*. Career achievement: **Horton Foote**. Ensemble performance: The casts of *Stuff Happens* and *Awake and Sing!* Special awards: **BMI/Lehman Engel Musical Theatre Workshop, York Theatre Company** and **Sh-K-Boom Ghostlight Records**.

56TH ANNUAL OUTER CRITICS' CIRCLE AWARDS. For outstanding achievement in the 2005–2006 season, voted by critics on out-of-town periodicals and media. Broadway play: *The History Boys*. Off Broadway play: *Stuff Happens*. Revival of a play: *Awake and Sing!* Actor in a play: **Gabriel Byrne** in *A Touch of the Poet*. Actress in a play: **Lois Smith** in *The Trip to Bountiful*. Featured actor in a play: **Richard Griffiths** in *The History Boys*. Featured actress in a play: **Frances de la Tour** in *The History Boys*. Director of a play: **Nicholas Hytner** for *The History Boys*. Broadway musical: *Jersey Boys*. Score: **Lisa Lambert** and **Greg Morrison** for *The Drowsy Chaperone*. Off-Broadway musical: *Grey Gardens*. Revival of a musical: *Sweeney Todd*. Actor in a musical: **John Lloyd Young** in *Jersey Boys*. Actress in a musical: **Christine Ebersole** in *Grey Gardens*. Featured actor in a musical: **Jim Dale** in *The Threepenny Opera*. Featured actress in a musical: **Beth Leavel** in *The Drowsy Chaperone*. Director of a musical: **John Doyle** for *Sweeney Todd*. Choreography: **Kathleen Marshall** for *The Pajama Game*. Scenic design: **David Gallo** for *The Drowsy Chaperone*. Costume design: **Gregg Barnes** for *The Drowsy Chaperone*. Lighting design: **Howell Binkley** for *Jersey Boys*. Solo performance: **Antony Sher** in *Primo*. John Gassner Playwriting Award: **Danai Gurira** and **Nikkole Salter** for *In the Continuum*.

51st ANNUAL *VILLAGE VOICE* OBIE AWARDS. For outstanding achievement in Off and Off Off Broadway theater. Performance: **Michael Cumpsty** in *Hamlet*; **Christine Ebersole** in *Grey Gardens*; **Ari Fliakos** in *Poor Theater: A Series of Simulacra*; **Edwin Lee Gibson** in *The Seven*; **Peter Francis James** in *Stuff Happens*; **Byron Jennings** in *Stuff Happens*; **Marin Ireland** in *Cyclone*; **Dana Ivey** in *Mrs. Warren's Profession*; **Meg MacCary** in *What Then*; **S. Epatha Merkerson** in *Birdie Blue*; **Euan Morton** in *Measure for Pleasure*; **Sherie René Scott** in *Landscape of the Body*; **Scott Shepherd** in *Poor Theater: A Series of Simulacra*; **Lois Smith** in *The Trip to Bountiful*; **Julie White** in *The Little Dog Laughed*; **Gary Wilmes** in *Red Light Winter*; **Reed Birney** for sustained excellence. Direction: **Daniel Sullivan** for *Stuff Happens*; **John Clancy** for sustained excellence. Playwriting: **Rolin Jones** for *The Intelligent Design of Jenny Chow*; **Martin McDonagh** for *The Lieutenant of Inishmore*. Design: **The National Theater of the United States of America** for *Abacus Black Strikes Now! The Rampant Justice of Abacus Black*; **Allen Moyer** for sustained excellence; **Anita Yavich** for sustained excellence.

Special Citations: **Hunter Bell**, **Michael Berresse**, **Jeff Bowen** for *[title of show]*; **Ricky Ian Gordon**, **Jane Moss**, **Jon Nakagawa**, **Doug Varone** for *Orpheus and Eurydice*; **Danai Gurira**, **Robert O'Hara**, **Nikkole Salter** for *In the Continuum*; **Adam Rapp** for *Red Light Winter*. Ross Wetzsteon Award: **Soho Repertory Theatre**. Lifetime Achievement: **Eric Bentley**. Grants: **Billie Holiday Theatre**, **Edge Theater Company**, **Red Bull Theatre**. Emerging Playwright Grants: **Neena Beber**; **Rinne Groff**.

16TH ANNUAL CONNECTICUT CRITICS' CIRCLE AWARDS. For outstanding achievement in Connecticut theater during the 2005–2006 season. Production of a play: **Long Wharf Theatre** for *Underneath the Lintel*. Production of a musical: **Downtown Cabaret Theatre** for *Sweet Charity*. Actress in a play: **Lynda Gravátt** in *A Raisin in the Sun*. Actor in a play: **Mark Nelson** in *Underneath the Lintel*. Actress in a musical: **Ernestine Jackson** in *Lady Day at Emerson's Bar and Grill*. Actor in a musical: **R. Bruce Connelly** in *A Funny Thing Happened on the Way to the Forum*. Direction of a play: **Eric Ting** for *Underneath the Lintel*. Direction of a musical: **Owen Thompson** for *The Mikado*. Choreography: **Scott Thompson** for *Sweet Charity*. Scene design: **Tony Straiges** for *The Learned Ladies of Park Avenue*. Lighting design: **Clifton Taylor** for *Journey's End*. Costume design: **Linda Fisher** and **Randall E. Klein** for *David Copperfield*. Sound design: **Arielle Edwards** for *dance of the holy ghosts*. Ensemble performance: **Curtis Billings, Mike Boland, Leon Addison Brown, Natalie Brown, Kevin Cutts, Robert Hannon Davis, Susan Fay, William Jay Marshall, Chandler Parker** and **Erica Tazel** in *The Exonerated*.

Roadshow: **Hartford Stage** for *2 Pianos 4 Hands*. Debut award: **Glenn Lawrence** in *Li'l Abner*. Tom Killen Memorial Award: **The Connecticut Commission on Culture and Tourism**.

24th ANNUAL ELLIOT NORTON AWARDS. For outstanding contribution to the theater in Boston, voted by a Boston Theater Critics Association Selection Committee comprising Terry Byrne, Carolyn Clay, Iris Fanger, Joyce Kulhawik, Jon Lehman, Bill Marx, Ed Siegel and Caldwell Titcomb. Sustained Excellence: **Spiro Veloudos**. Productions—Musical: *On the Twentieth Century* produced by Overture Productions; Visiting company: *Monty Python's Spamalot* produced by Broadway in Boston; Large resident company: *Olly's Prison* produced by American Repertory Theatre; Midsized resident company: *Five by Tenn* produced by SpeakEasy Stage Company; Small resident company: *Arcadia* produced by Publick Theatre; Local fringe company: *P.S. Page Me Later* produced by Alarm Clock Theatre Company. Solo performance: **Jefferson Mays** in *I Am My Own Wife*, Broadway in Boston. Actor—Large company: **Bill Camp** in *Olly's Prison*, American Repertory Theatre. Actor—Midsized company: **Allyn Burrows** in *The Homecoming*, Merrimack Repertory Theatre; *King Lear*, Actors' Shakespeare Project; *Five by Tenn*, SpeakEasy Stage Company. Actress—Large company: **Karen MacDonald** in *Olly's Prison* and *No Exit*, American Repertory Theatre. Actress—Midsized company: **Sandra Shipley** in *Long Day's Journey Into Night*, Gloucester Stage Company. Director—Large company: **Brian McEleney** for *Hamlet*, Trinity Repertory

Company. Director—Small-to-midsized company: **Scott Edmiston** for *Five by Tenn*, SpeakEasy Stage Company. Design: **Janie E. Howland** for *Urinetown*, Lyric Stage Company; *True West*, New Repertory Theatre; *Five by Tenn*, SpeakEasy Stage Company; *Talley's Folly*, Lyric Stage Company. Special citation: **Boston Conservatory** for musical theater training. Guest of Honor: **William Finn**.

22ND ANNUAL HELEN HAYES AWARDS. In recognition of excellence in Washington, D.C., theater, presented by the Washington Theatre Awards Society.

Resident productions—Play (tie): *Take Me Out* produced by The Studio Theatre; *The Clean House* produced by Woolly Mammoth Theatre Company. Musical: *Urinetown* produced by Signature Theatre (Virginia). Lead actress, musical (tie): **Erin Driscoll** in *Urinetown*, Signature Theatre (Virginia); **Meg Gillentine** in *Damn Yankees*, Arena Stage. Lead actor, musical (tie): **Will Gartshore** in *Urinetown*, Signature Theatre (Virginia); **Michael McElroy** in *Big River: The Adventures of Huckleberry Finn*, Ford's Theatre. Lead actress, play: **Eunice Wong** in *The Intelligent Design of Jenny Chow*, The Studio Theatre. Lead actor, play (tie): **Rick Foucheux** in *Take Me Out*, The Studio Theatre; **Patrick Page** in *Othello*, Shakespeare Theatre Company. Supporting actress, musical: **Jenna Sokolowski** in *Urinetown*, Signature Theatre (Virginia). Supporting actor, musical: **Stephen F. Schmidt** in *Urinetown*, Signature Theatre (Virginia). Supporting actress, play: **Franca Barchiesi** in *The Clean House*, Woolly Mammoth Theatre Company. Supporting actor, play: **Bruce R. Nelson** in *The Violet Hour*, Rep Stage. Director, play: **Joy Zinoman** for *A Number*, The Studio Theatre. Director, musical: **Joe Calarco** for *Urinetown*, Signature Theatre (Virginia). Scenic design: **Simon Higlett** for *Lady Windermere's Fan*, Shakespeare Theatre Company. Costume design: **Robert Perdziola** for *Lady Windermere's Fan*, Shakespeare Theatre Company. Lighting design: **Charlie Morrison** for *The Tempest*, Shakespeare Theatre Company. Sound design: **Martin Desjardins** for *columbinus*, Round House Theatre, Perseverance Theatre and United States Theatre Project. Choreography: **Karma Camp** for *Urinetown*, Signature Theatre (Virginia). Musical direction: **Jay Crowder** for *Urinetown*, Signature Theatre (Virginia).

Non-resident productions—Production: *I Am My Own Wife* produced by The National Theatre. Lead actress: **Stephanie J. Block** in *Wicked,* The Kennedy Center. Lead actor: **Jefferson Mays** in *I Am My Own Wife,* The National Theatre.

Charles MacArthur Award for outstanding new play: *Starving* by **S.M. Shephard-Massat**, Woolly Mammoth Theatre Company.

37TH ANNUAL JOSEPH JEFFERSON AWARDS. For achievement in Chicago theater during the 2004–2005 season, given by the Jefferson Awards Committee in 26 competitive categories. Thirty producing organizations were nominated for various awards; 13 different companies were honored. Marriott Theatre led all companies with six awards. Porchlight Music Theatre Chicago followed closely with five; Congo Square Theatre Company, Steppenwolf Theatre Company and The Goodman Theatre were each thrice honored. Porchlight Music Theatre Chicago's production of *Sweeney Todd* led all productions with four awards, 19 others received at least one award. The awards ceremony was held November 7, 2005 at Drury Lane Theatre Water Tower Place in Chicago.

Resident productions—New work (tie): *Red Light Winter* by **Adam Rapp**, Steppenwolf Theatre Company; *The Pain and the Itch* by **Bruce Norris**, Steppenwolf Theatre Company. New Adaptation (tie): *Dollhouse* by **Rebecca Gilman**, The Goodman Theatre; *1984* by **Andrew White**, Lookingglass Theatre Company. Play: *Seven Guitars* produced by Congo Square Theatre Company. Musical: *Beauty and the Beast* produced

by Marriott Theatre. Director, play: **Derrick Sanders** for *Seven Guitars*, Congo Square Theatre Company. Director, musical: **Marc Robin** for *Beauty and the Beast*, Marriott Theatre. Ensemble: *Seven Guitars*, Congo Square Theatre Company. Director, revue: **Marc Robin**, *Swing!*, Marriott Theatre. Actor in a principal role, play: **Jefferson Mays** in *I Am My Own Wife*, The Goodman Theatre. Actress in a principal role, play: **Barbara E. Robertson** in *Who's Afraid of Virginia Woolf?*, Court Theatre. Actor in a supporting role, play: **Tom Aulino** in *Take Me Out*, About Face Theatre. Actress in a supporting role, play: **Jayne Houdyshell** in *The Pain and the Itch*, Steppenwolf Theatre Company. Actor in a principal role, musical: **Michael Aaron Lindner** in *Sweeney Todd*, Porchlight Music Theatre Chicago. Actress in a principal role, musical: **Rebecca Finnegan** in *Sweeney Todd*, Porchlight Music Theatre Chicago. Actor in a supporting role, musical: **Peter Pohlhammer** in *Sweeney Todd*, Porchlight Music Theatre Chicago. Actress in a supporting role, musical: **Renee Matthews** in *The Full Monty*, Drury Lane Theatre Water Tower Place. Actor in a revue: **"Mississippi" Charles Bevel** in *It Ain't Nothin' but the Blues*, Northlight Theatre. Actress in a revue: **Rebecca Finnegan** in *Closer Than Ever*, Porchlight Music Theatre Chicago. Scenic design: **Scott Bradley** for *Silk*, The Goodman Theatre. Costume design: **Nancy Missimi** for *Beauty and the Beast*, Marriott Theatre. Lighting design: **Michael Rourke** for *Kabuki Lady Macbeth*, Chicago Shakespeare Theater. Sound design: **Lindsay Jones** for *Kid-Simple*, American Theater Company. Choreography: **Mark Stuart Eckstein, Beverly Durand** and **Marc Robin** for *Swing!*, Marriott Theatre. Musical direction: **Eugene Dizon** for *Sweeney Todd*, Porchlight Music Theatre Chicago. Original incidental music: **Andre Pluess** and **Ben Sussman** for *Red Herring*, Northlight Theatre. Special achievement: **John Boesche** for *Sunset Boulevard* (projection design), Marriott Theatre; **Sylvia Hernandez-DiStasi** for

Lookingglass Alice (circus choreography), Lookingglass Theatre Company and Actors Gymnasium.

33RD ANNUAL JOSEPH JEFFERSON CITATIONS WING AWARDS. For outstanding achievement in professional productions during the 2005–2006 season of Chicago area theaters not operating under union contracts. Production, play: *The Kentucky Cycle, Parts 1 and 2*, produced by Infamous Commonwealth Theatre. Production, musical: *Kiss of the Spider Woman*, produced by Bailiwick Repertory Theatre. Ensemble: *The Kentucky Cycle, Parts 1 and 2*, produced by Infamous Commonwealth Theatre. Director, play (tie): **Jason Kae** and **Genevieve Thompson** for *The Kentucky Cycle, Parts 1 and 2*, Infamous Commonwealth Theatre; **Jonathan Wilson** for *Two Trains Running*, Pegasus Players. Director, musical or revue: **Susan Finque** for *Kiss of the Spider Woman*, Bailiwick Repertory Theatre. New work (tie): *Fellow Travellers* by **Margaret Lewis**, Stage Left Theatre; *The Masrayana* by **William C. Kovacsik**, Prop Thtr and Rasaka Theatre Company. New work, musical: *Queen Lucia* by **Christina Calvit** and **George Howe**, Lifeline Theatre. New adaptation (tie): *Three Sisters* by **Curt Columbus**, Strawdog Theatre Company; *Johnny Tremain* by **John Hildreth**, Lifeline Theatre. Actress in a principal role, play (tie): **Donna McGough** in *Death of a Salesman*, The Hypocrites; **Rebekah Ward-Hays** in *The Skin of Our Teeth*, BackStage Theatre Company. Actress in a principal role, musical: **Monique Whittington** in *Josephine Tonight!*, Theatre Building Chicago. Actor in a principal role, play (tie): **Paul D'Addorio** in *Hurlyburly*, The Gift Theatre Company; **Jürgen Hooper** in *What's Wrong With Angry?*, Circle Theatre; **Paul Noble** in *True West*, The Hypocrites; **Alfred H. Wilson** in *Two Trains Running*, Pegasus Players. Actor in a principal role, musical (tie): **Ryan Lanning** in *Kiss of the Spider Woman*, Bailiwick Repertory Theatre; **Stan Q. Wash** in *Kiss of the Spider Woman*, Bailiwick Repertory Theatre. Actress in a supporting role, play: **Millie Hurley Spencer** in *Dancing at Lughnasa*, Raven Theatre Company. Actress in a supporting role, musical or revue: **Danielle Brothers** in *A Jacques Brel Revue: Songs of Love and War*, Theo Ubique Theatre Company and Michael James. Actor in a supporting role, play (tie): **Eric Hoffman** in *Loose Knit*, The Actors Workshop Theatre; **Rian Jairell** in *The Kentucky Cycle, Parts 1 and 2*, Infamous Commonwealth Theatre. Actor in a supporting role, musical: **Stephen Feder** in *I Sing!*, White Horse Theatre Company. Scenic design (tie): **Brian Sidney Bembridge** for *Three Sisters*, Strawdog Theatre Company; **Jack Magaw** for *Two Trains Running*, Pegasus Players. Costume design (tie): **Laura M. Dana** for *Seascape*, Signal Ensemble Theatre; **Alison Siple** for *Time and the Conways*, Griffin Theatre Company. Lighting design: **Jared Moore** for *Kiss of the Spider Woman*, Bailiwick Repertory Theatre. Sound design: **Mikhail Fiksel** and **Michael Griggs** for *Angels in America, Part One: Millennium Approaches*, The Hypocrites and Bailiwick Repertory Theatre. Projection design: **Mike Tutaj** for *Martin Furey's Shot*, TimeLine Theatre Company. Choreography: **Brenda Didier** for *Kiss of the Spider Woman*, Bailiwick Repertory Theatre. Fight choreography: **Geoff Coates**, *The Talisman Ring*, Lifeline Theatre. Original incidental music: **Nikhil Trivedi** for *The Masrayana*, Prop Thtr and Rasaka Theatre Company. Musical direction (tie): **Kevin O'Donnell** for *Valentine Victorious*, The House Theatre of Chicago; **Robert Ollis** for *Kiss of the Spider Woman*, Bailiwick Repertory Theatre.

THE THEATER HALL OF FAME

○ ○ ○ ○ ○

THE THEATER HALL OF FAME was created in 1971 to honor those who have made outstanding contributions to the American theater in a career spanning at least 25 years. Honorees are elected annually by members of the American Theatre Critics Association, members of the Theater Hall of Fame and theater historians. Names of those elected in 2005 and inducted January 30, 2006 appear in *bold italics*.

George Abbott	Ethel Barrymore	Peter Brook
Maude Adams	John Barrymore	John Mason Brown
Viola Adams	Lionel Barrymore	Robert Brustein
Jacob Adler	Howard Bay	Billie Burke
Stella Adler	Nora Bayes	Abe Burrows
Edward Albee	John Lee Beatty	Richard Burton
Theoni V. Aldredge	Julian Beck	Mrs. Patrick Campbell
Ira Aldridge	Samuel Beckett	Zoe Caldwell
Jane Alexander	Brian Bedford	Eddie Cantor
Mary Alice	S.N. Behrman	Len Cariou
Winthrop Ames	Barbara Bel Geddes	Morris Carnovsky
Judith Anderson	Norman Bel Geddes	Mrs. Leslie Carter
Maxwell Anderson	David Belasco	Gower Champion
Robert Anderson	Michael Bennett	Frank Chanfrau
Julie Andrews	Richard Bennett	Carol Channing
Margaret Anglin	Robert Russell Bennett	Stockard Channing
Jean Anouilh	Eric Bentley	Ruth Chatterton
Harold Arlen	Irving Berlin	Paddy Chayefsky
George Arliss	Sarah Bernhardt	Anton Chekhov
Boris Aronson	Leonard Bernstein	Ina Claire
Adele Astaire	Earl Blackwell	Bobby Clark
Fred Astaire	Kermit Bloomgarden	Harold Clurman
Eileen Atkins	Jerry Bock	Lee J. Cobb
Brooks Atkinson	Ray Bolger	Richard L. Coe
Lauren Bacall	Edwin Booth	George M. Cohan
Pearl Bailey	Junius Brutus Booth	Alexander H. Cohen
George Balanchine	Shirley Booth	Jack Cole
William Ball	Philip Bosco	Cy Coleman
Anne Bancroft	Dion Boucicault	Constance Collier
Tallulah Bankhead	Alice Brady	Alvin Colt
Richard Barr	Bertolt Brecht	Betty Comden
Philip Barry	Fanny Brice	Marc Connelly

Barbara Cook
Katharine Cornell
Noel Coward
Jane Cowl
Lotta Crabtree
Cheryl Crawford
Hume Cronyn
Rachel Crothers
Russel Crouse
Charlotte Cushman
Jean Dalrymple
Augustin Daly
Graciela Daniele
E.L. Davenport
Gordon Davidson
Ossie Davis
Ruby Dee
Alfred de Liagre Jr.
Agnes de Mille
Colleen Dewhurst
Howard Dietz
Dudley Digges
Melvyn Douglas
Eddie Dowling
Alfred Drake
Marie Dressler
John Drew
Mrs. John Drew
William Dunlap
Mildred Dunnock
Charles Durning
Eleanora Duse
Jeanne Eagels
Fred Ebb
Ben Edwards
Florence Eldridge
Lehman Engel
Maurice Evans
Abe Feder
Jose Ferrer
Cy Feuer

Zelda Fichandler
Dorothy Fields
Herbert Fields
Lewis Fields
W.C. Fields
Jules Fisher
Minnie Maddern Fiske
Clyde Fitch
Geraldine Fitzgerald
Henry Fonda
Lynn Fontanne
Horton Foote
Edwin Forrest
Bob Fosse
Rudolf Friml
Charles Frohman
Robert Fryer
Athol Fugard
John Gassner
Larry Gelbart
Peter Gennaro
Grace George
George Gershwin
Ira Gershwin
Bernard Gersten
William Gibson
John Gielgud
W.S. Gilbert
Jack Gilford
William Gillette
Charles Gilpin
Lillian Gish
Susan Glaspell
John Golden
Max Gordon
Ruth Gordon
Adolph Green
Paul Green
Charlotte Greenwood
Jane Greenwood
Joel Grey

Tammy Grimes
George Grizzard
John Guare
Otis L. Guernsey Jr.
A.R. Gurney
Tyrone Guthrie
Uta Hagen
Peter Hall
Lewis Hallam
T. Edward Hambleton
Oscar Hammerstein II
Walter Hampden
Otto Harbach
E.Y. Harburg
Sheldon Harnick
Edward Harrigan
Jed Harris
Julie Harris
Rosemary Harris
Sam H. Harris
Rex Harrison
Kitty Carlisle Hart
Lorenz Hart
Moss Hart
Tony Hart
June Havoc
Helen Hayes
Leland Hayward
Ben Hecht
Eileen Heckart
Theresa Helburn
Lillian Hellman
Katharine Hepburn
Victor Herbert
Jerry Herman
James A. Herne
Henry Hewes
Gregory Hines
Al Hirschfeld
Raymond Hitchcock
Hal Holbrook

Celeste Holm

Hanya Holm

Arthur Hopkins

De Wolf Hopper

John Houseman

Eugene Howard

Leslie Howard

Sidney Howard

Willie Howard

Barnard Hughes

Henry Hull

Josephine Hull

Walter Huston

Earle Hyman

Henrik Ibsen

William Inge

Bernard B. Jacobs

Elsie Janis

Joseph Jefferson

Al Jolson

James Earl Jones

Margo Jones

Robert Edmond Jones

Tom Jones

Jon Jory

Raul Julia

Madeline Kahn

John Kander

Garson Kanin

George S. Kaufman

Danny Kaye

Elia Kazan

Gene Kelly

George Kelly

Fanny Kemble

Jerome Kern

Walter Kerr

Michael Kidd

Richard Kiley

Sidney Kingsley

Kevin Kline

Florence Klotz

Joseph Wood Krutch

Bert Lahr

Burton Lane

Frank Langella

Lawrence Langner

Lillie Langtry

Angela Lansbury

Charles Laughton

Arthur Laurents

Gertrude Lawrence

Jerome Lawrence

Eva Le Gallienne

Canada Lee

Ming Cho Lee

Robert E. Lee

Lotte Lenya

Alan Jay Lerner

Sam Levene

Robert Lewis

Beatrice Lillie

Howard Lindsay

John Lithgow

Frank Loesser

Frederick Loewe

Joshua Logan

William Ivey Long

Santo Loquasto

Pauline Lord

Lucille Lortel

Dorothy Loudon

Alfred Lunt

Charles MacArthur

Steele MacKaye

Judith Malina

David Mamet

Rouben Mamoulian

Richard Mansfield

Robert B. Mantell

Fredric March

Nancy Marchand

Julia Marlowe

Ernest H. Martin

Mary Martin

Raymond Massey

Elizabeth Ireland McCann

Ian McKellen

Siobhan McKenna

Terrence McNally

Helen Menken

Burgess Meredith

Ethel Merman

David Merrick

Jo Mielziner

Arthur Miller

Marilyn Miller

Liza Minnelli

Helena Modjeska

Ferenc Molnar

Lola Montez

Victor Moore

Robert Morse

Zero Mostel

Anna Cora Mowatt

Paul Muni

Brian Murray

Tharon Musser

George Jean Nathan

Mildred Natwick

Alla Nazimova

Patricia Neal

James M. Nederlander

Mike Nichols

Elliot Norton

Sean O'Casey

Clifford Odets

Donald Oenslager

Laurence Olivier

Eugene O'Neill

Jerry Orbach

Geraldine Page

Joseph Papp

ESTELLE PARSONS

OSGOOD PERKINS

BERNADETTE PETERS

MOLLY PICON

HAROLD PINTER

LUIGI PIRANDELLO

CHRISTOPHER PLUMMER

COLE PORTER

ROBERT PRESTON

HAROLD PRINCE

JOSE QUINTERO

ELLIS RABB

JOHN RAITT

TONY RANDALL

MICHAEL REDGRAVE

VANESSA REDGRAVE

ADA REHAN

ELMER RICE

LLOYD RICHARDS

RALPH RICHARDSON

CHITA RIVERA

JASON ROBARDS

JEROME ROBBINS

PAUL ROBESON

RICHARD RODGERS

WILL ROGERS

SIGMUND ROMBERG

HAROLD ROME

BILLY ROSE

LILLIAN RUSSELL

DONALD SADDLER

GENE SAKS

DIANA SANDS

WILLIAM SAROYAN

JOSEPH SCHILDKRAUT

HARVEY SCHMIDT

ALAN SCHNEIDER

GERALD SCHOENFELD

ARTHUR SCHWARTZ

MAURICE SCHWARTZ

GEORGE C. SCOTT

MARIAN SELDES

IRENE SHARAFF

GEORGE BERNARD SHAW

SAM SHEPARD

ROBERT E. SHERWOOD

J.J. SHUBERT

LEE SHUBERT

HERMAN SHUMLIN

NEIL SIMON

LEE SIMONSON

EDMUND SIMPSON

OTIS SKINNER

MAGGIE SMITH

OLIVER SMITH

STEPHEN SONDHEIM

E.H. SOTHERN

KIM STANLEY

JEAN STAPLETON

MAUREEN STAPLETON

FRANCES STERNHAGEN

ROGER L. STEVENS

ISABELLE STEVENSON

ELLEN STEWART

DOROTHY STICKNEY

FRED STONE

PETER STONE

TOM STOPPARD

LEE STRASBERG

AUGUST STRINDBERG

ELAINE STRITCH

CHARLES STROUSE

JULE STYNE

MARGARET SULLAVAN

ARTHUR SULLIVAN

JESSICA TANDY

LAURETTE TAYLOR

ELLEN TERRY

SADA THOMPSON

CLEON THROCKMORTON

TOMMY TUNE

GWEN VERDON

ROBIN WAGNER

NANCY WALKER

ELI WALLACH

JAMES WALLACK

LESTER WALLACK

TONY WALTON

DOUGLAS TURNER WARD

DAVID WARFIELD

ETHEL WATERS

CLIFTON WEBB

JOSEPH WEBER

MARGARET WEBSTER

KURT WEILL

ORSON WELLES

MAE WEST

ROBERT WHITEHEAD

RICHARD WILBUR

OSCAR WILDE

THORNTON WILDER

BERT WILLIAMS

TENNESSEE WILLIAMS

LANFORD WILSON

P.G. WODEHOUSE

PEGGY WOOD

ALEXANDER WOOLLCOTT

IRENE WORTH

TERESA WRIGHT

ED WYNN

VINCENT YOUMANS

STARK YOUNG

FLORENZ ZIEGFELD

PATRICIA ZIPPRODT

THE THEATER HALL OF FAME
FOUNDERS AWARD

ESTABLISHED IN 1993 in honor of Earl Blackwell, James M. Nederlander, Gerard Oestreicher and Arnold Weissberger, The Theater Hall of Fame Founders Award is voted by the Hall's board of directors to an individual for his or her outstanding contribution to the theater.

1993 JAMES M. NEDERLANDER	1998 EDWARD COLTON	2002 NO AWARD
1994 KITTY CARLISLE HART	1999 NO AWARD	2003 PRICE BERKLEY
1995 HARVEY SABINSON	2000 GERARD OESTREICHER	2004 NO AWARD
1996 HENRY HEWES	2000 ARNOLD WEISSBERGER	2005 *DONALD SEAWELL*
1997 OTIS L. GUERNSEY JR.	2001 TOM DILLON	

MARGO JONES
CITIZEN OF THE THEATER MEDAL

PRESENTED ANNUALLY TO a citizen of the theater who has made a lifetime commitment to theater in the United States and has demonstrated an understanding and affirmation of the craft of playwriting.

1961 LUCILLE LORTEL	1970 JOSEPH PAPP	1988 NO AWARD
1962 MICHAEL ELLIS	1971 ZELDA FICHANDLER	1989 MARGARET GOHEEN
1963 JUDITH R. MARECHAL	1972 JULES IRVING	1990 RICHARD COE
GEORGE SAVAGE	1973 DOUGLAS TURNER	1991 OTIS L. GUERNSEY JR.
1964 RICHARD BARR,	WARD	1992 ABBOT VAN NOSTRAND
EDWARD ALBEE	1974 PAUL WEIDNER	1993 HENRY HEWES
CLINTON WILDER	1975 ROBERT KALFIN	1994 JANE ALEXANDER
RICHARD A. DUPREY	1976 GORDON DAVIDSON	1995 ROBERT WHITEHEAD
1965 WYNN HANDMAN	1977 MARSHALL W. MASON	1996 AL HIRSCHFELD
MARSTON BALCH	1978 JON JORY	1997 GEORGE C. WHITE
1966 JON JORY	1979 ELLEN STEWART	1998 JAMES HOUGHTON
ARTHUR BALLET	1980 JOHN CLARK DONAHUE	1999 GEORGE KEATHLEY
1967 PAUL BAKER	1981 LYNNE MEADOW	2000 EILEEN HECKART
GEORGE C. WHITE	1982 ANDRE BISHOP	2001 MEL GUSSOW
1968 DAVEY MARLIN-JONES	1983 BILL BUSHNELL	2002 EMILIE S. KILGORE
1968 ELLEN STEWART	1984 GREGORY MOSHER	2003 NO AWARD
1969 ADRIAN HALL	1985 JOHN LION	2004 CHRISTOPHER DURANG
EDWARD PARONE	1986 LLOYD RICHARDS	MARSHA NORMAN
1969 GORDON DAVIDSON	1987 GERALD CHAPMAN	2005 NO AWARD

MUSICAL THEATRE HALL OF FAME

THIS ORGANIZATION WAS established at New York University on November 10, 1993.

HAROLD ARLEN

IRVING BERLIN

LEONARD BERNSTEIN

EUBIE BLAKE

ABE BURROWS

GEORGE M. COHAN

DOROTHY FIELDS

GEORGE GERSHWIN

IRA GERSHWIN

OSCAR HAMMERSTEIN II

E.Y. HARBURG

LARRY HART

JEROME KERN

BURTON LANE

ALAN JAY LERNER

FRANK LOESSER

FREDERICK LOEWE

COLE PORTER

ETHEL MERMAN

JEROME ROBBINS

RICHARD RODGERS

HAROLD ROME

IN MEMORIAM
JUNE 2005–MAY 2006
○ ○ ○ ○ ○

PERFORMERS

Adams, Don (82) – September 25, 2005
Askin, Leon (97) – June 3, 2005
Bel Geddes, Barbara (82) – August 8, 2005
Billington, Michael (63) – June 3, 2005
Bishop, Ed (72) – June 8, 2005
Bochner, Lloyd (81) – October 29, 2005
Bova, Joseph (81) – March 21, 2006
Brando, Jocelyn (86) – November 25, 2005
Bright, Richard (68) – February 18, 2006
Browning, Susan (65) – April 23, 2006
Carmines, Al (69) – August 11, 2005
Carson, Jean (82) – November 2, 2005
Carter, Janette (82) – January 22, 2006
Colvin, Jack (71) – December 1, 2005
Cummings, Constance (95) – November 23, 2005
Davila, Raul (74) – January 2, 2006
DeAngelis, Richard (73) – December 28, 2005
Denver, Bob (70) – September 2, 2005
Diener, Joan (76) – May 13, 2006
Dunne, Amanda Duff (92) – April 6, 2006
Eastham, Richard (89) – July 10, 2005
Elcar, Dana (77) – June 6, 2005
Fiedler, John (80) – June 25, 2005
Fitzgerald, Geraldine (91) – July 17, 2005
Ford, Phil (85) – June 15, 2005
Forsythe, Henderson (88) – April 17, 2006
Flon, Suzanne (87) – June 15, 2005
Franciosa, Anthony (77) – January 19, 2006
Getz, Ileen (44) – August 4, 2005
Gleason, Paul (67) – May 27, 2006
Gleason, William (76) – August 25, 2005
Gorshin, Frank (71) – May 17, 2005
Grant Timoney, Simone (44) – November 2, 2005
Gruskiewicz, Paula (47) – December 31, 2005
Hamilton, Peter (90) – January 31, 2006
Harms, Carl (94) – August 11, 2005
Harpel, Larry (55) – October 15, 2005
Kankel, Vlasta Dryak (94) – March 8, 2006

Kosslyn, Jack (84) – June 24, 2005
Jackson, Mary (95) – December 10, 2005
Johnston, Justine (84) – January 13, 2005
Langford, Frances (92) – July 11, 2005
Lawrence, Marc (95) – November 28, 2005
Lawrence, Paula (89) – October 29, 2005
Laybourne, Ottilie Kruger (78) – May 12, 2005
Lewis, Al (95) – February 3, 2006
Lomond, Britt (80) – March 22, 2006
Lopez, Marga (81) – July 4, 2005
Maybach, Christiane (74) – April 12, 2006
McCallister, Lon (82) – June 11, 2005
McCormick, Pat (78) – July 29, 2005
McGavin, Darren (83) – February 25, 2006
McGrory, Matthew (32) – August 9, 2005
Meacham, Anne (80) – January 12, 2006
Meyler, Fintan Ann (75) – July 23, 2005
Moffo, Anna (73) – March 9, 2006
Moore, Constance (84) – September 16, 2005
Nicholas, Fayard (91) – January 24, 2006
Nillo, David (89) – September 28, 2005
Nilsson, Birgit (87) – December 25, 2005
North, Sheree (72) – November 4, 2005
Nye, Louis (92) – October 9, 2005
Owens, Buck (76) – March 25, 2006
Parker, Jean (90) – November 30, 2005
Payn, Graham (87) – November 4, 2005
Penn, Chris (40) – January 24, 2006
Peters, Brock (78) – August 23, 2005
Pickett, Wilson (64) – January 19, 2006
Pitney, Gene (65) – April 5, 2006
Pryor, Richard (65) – December 10, 2005
Rainey, Ford (96) – July 25, 2005
Rice, Bill (74) – January 23, 2006
Russell, Nipsey (80) – October 2, 2005
Schiavelli, Vincent (57) – December 26, 2005
Seitz, John (67) – July 4, 2005
Shearer, Moira (80) – January 31, 2006
Smith, Jane Lawrence (90) – August 5, 2005
Smith, Lane (69) – June 13, 2005

Spencer, John (58) – December 16, 2005
Sperber, Wendie Jo (47) – November 29, 2005
Stapleton, Maureen (80) – March 13, 2006
Sterling, Robert (88) – May 30, 2006
Stewart, Don (70) – January 9, 2006
Stuarti, Enzo (86) – December 16, 2005
Tyler, Beverly (78) – November 23, 2005
Thayer, Lorna (86) – June 4, 2005
Thomas, Frankie (85) – May 11, 2006
Vale, Michael (83) – December 24, 2005
Vandross, Luther (54) – July 1, 2005
Wallace, George D. (88) – July 22, 2005
Ware, Herta (88) – August 15, 2005
White, Charles (87) – June 20, 2005
Winters, Shelley (83) – January 14, 2006

PRODUCERS, DIRECTORS, CHOREOGRAPHERS

Adams, Tony (52) – October 22, 2005
Bakhuyzen, Willem van de Sande (47) – September 27, 2005
Crawford, Dan (62) – July 13, 2005
Dunham, Katherine (96) – May 21, 2006
Feuer, Cy (95) – May 17, 2006
Fleischer, Richard (89) – March 25, 2006
Garinei, Pietro (87) – May 9, 2006
Hambleton, T. Edward (94) – December 17, 2005
Hansen, Tom (80) – April 27, 2006
MacNair, Susan (65) – August 31, 2005
Papich, Stephen (80) – December 16, 2005
Rosenfield, Maurice (91) – October 30, 2005
Simon, Danny (86) – July 26, 2005
Tulchin, Ted (79) – December 19, 2005
Vogel, Frederic B. (late 70s) – November 29, 2005

COMPOSERS, LYRICISTS, SONGWRITERS

Hughes, Dickson (82) – June 18, 2005
Knight, Baker (72) – October 12, 2005

Murphy, Lyle "Spud" (96) – August 5, 2005
Perito, Nick (81) – August 3, 2005
Wright, Robert (90) – July 27, 2005

PLAYWRIGHTS

Allen, Jay Presson (84) – May 1, 2006
Belluso, John (36) – February 10, 2006
Fry, Christopher (97) – June 30, 2005
Halasz, Peter (62) – March 9, 2006
Holland, Endesha Ida Mae (61) – January 25, 2006
Wasserstein, Wendy (55) – January 30, 2005
Wilson, August (60) – October 2, 2005

MUSICIANS

Brown, Clarence Gatemouth (81) – September 10, 2005
Gibson, Michael (60) – July 15, 2005
Griffin, Chris (89) – June 18, 2005
Henderson, Skitch (87) – November 1, 2005
Horn, Shirley (71) – October 20, 2005
Kimball, Narvin (97) – March 17, 2006
Rawls, Lou (72) – January 6, 2006
Sandor, Gyorgy (93) – December 9, 2005

OTHER NOTABLES

Brooks, Donald (77) – August 1, 2005
    Costume designer
Evans, G. Blakemore (93) – December 23, 2005
    Shakespeare scholar
Goodman, Frank (89) – February 3, 2006
    Press representative
Harmon, Lewis (94) – August 14, 2005
    Press representative and producer
Hirschhorn, Joel (67) – September 17, 2005
    Critic and Academy Award-winning songwriter
Hunt, Betty Lee (85) – October 11, 2005
    Press representative and producer
Oscard, Fifi (85) – November 12, 2005
    Literary and talent agent

THE BEST PLAYS AND MAJOR PRIZEWINNERS
1894–2006

○ ○ ○ ○ ○

L ISTED IN ALPHABETICAL order below are all works selected as Best Plays in previous volumes of the *Best Plays Theater Yearbook* series, except for the seasons of 1996–97 through 1999–2000. During those excluded seasons, *Best Plays* honored only major prizewinners and those who received special *Best Plays* citations. Opposite each title is given the volume in which the play is honored, its opening date and its total number of performances. Two separate opening-date and performance-number entries signify two separate engagements when the original production transferred. Plays marked with an asterisk (*) were still playing June 1, 2006 and their numbers of performances were figured through May 31, 2006. Adaptors and translators are indicated by (ad) and (tr), the symbols (b), (m) and (l) stand for the author of the book, music and lyrics in the case of musicals and (c) signifies the credit for the show's conception, (i) for its inspiration. Entries identified as 94–99, 99–09 and 09–19 are late–19th and early–20th century plays from one of the retrospective volumes. 94–95, 95–96, 96–97, 97–98, 98–99 and 99–00 are late–20th century plays.

PLAY	VOLUME	OPENED	PERFS
ABE LINCOLN IN ILLINOIS—Robert E. Sherwood	38–39	Oct. 15, 1938	472
ABRAHAM LINCOLN—John Drinkwater	19–20	Dec. 15, 1919	193
ACCENT ON YOUTH—Samson Raphaelson	34–35	Dec. 25, 1934	229
ADAM AND EVA—Guy Bolton, George Middleton	19–20	Sept. 13, 1919	312
ADAPTATION—Elaine May; and			
NEXT—Terrence McNally	68–69	Feb. 10, 1969	707
AFFAIRS OF STATE—Louis Verneuil	50–51	Sept. 25, 1950	610
AFTER ASHLEY—Gina Gionfriddo	04–05	Feb. 28, 2005	35
AFTER THE FALL—Arthur Miller	63–64	Jan. 23, 1964	208
AFTER THE RAIN—John Bowen	67–68	Oct. 9, 1967	64
AFTER-PLAY—Anne Meara	94–95	Jan. 31, 1995	400
AGNES OF GOD—John Pielmeier	81–82	Mar. 30, 1982	599
AH, WILDERNESS!—Eugene O'Neill	33–34	Oct. 2, 1933	289
AIN'T SUPPOSED TO DIE A NATURAL DEATH—(b, m, l)			
Melvin Van Peebles	71–72	Oct. 20, 1971	325
ALIEN CORN—Sidney Howard	32–33	Feb. 20, 1933	98
Alison's House—Susan Glaspell	30–31	Dec. 1, 1930	41
ALL MY SONS—Arthur Miller	46–47	Jan. 29, 1947	328
ALL IN THE TIMING—David Ives	93–94	Feb. 17, 1994	526
ALL OVER TOWN—Murray Schisgal	74–75	Dec. 29, 1974	233
ALL THE WAY HOME—Tad Mosel, based on			
James Agee's novel *A Death in the Family*	60–61	Nov. 30, 1960	333
ALLEGRO—(b, l) Oscar Hammerstein II,			
(m) Richard Rodgers	47–48	Oct. 10, 1947	315

CONTRIBUTORS TO *BEST PLAYS*

○ ○ ○ ○ ○

Misha Berson is the theater critic for *The Seattle Times*, a post she has held since 1992. She is a regular contributor to *American Theatre*, has taught at the University of Washington, San Francisco State University and the USC/Annenberg NEA Theatre Critics Institute. She is also a frequent commentator for public radio on KUOW-FM. Berson is the author of several books on theater including *The San Francisco Stage* and *Between Worlds: Contemporary Asian-American Plays*. She was a fellow in the National Arts Journalism Program at Columbia University.

Rue E. Canvin worked at the *New York Herald Tribune*, first as a secretary in the advertising department and then as an editorial assistant in the drama department for 15 years where she worked with the editors and the arts critics until the demise of the newspaper in 1966. She also worked at the *World Journal Tribune* until it closed in 1967. Canvin has served as an assistant editor of *The Best Plays Theater Yearbook* series since 1963. She has also transcribed taped interviews for the Dramatists Guild and Authors League.

Anne Cattaneo is the dramaturg of Lincoln Center Theater and head of the Lincoln Center Theater Directors' Lab. A past president of Literary Managers and Dramaturgs of the Americas, she is the recipient of LMDA's first Lessing Award for lifetime achievement in dramaturgy. She has worked widely as a dramaturg on classical plays with directors such as Jack O'Brien, Mark Lamos and Robert Falls. During the late 1970s, she commissioned plays by Wendy Wasserstein (*Isn't It Romantic*), Mustapha Matura (*Meetings*) and Christopher Durang (*Beyond Therapy*) for the Phoenix Theater. For the Acting Company, she created *Orchards*, an evening of plays adapted from Chekhov stories, and *Love's Fire*, responses to Shakespeare sonnets by Wendy Wasserstein and other playwrights. Her translations of German playwrights include Bertolt Brecht's *Galileo* and Botho Strauss's *Big and Little*. She is currently on the faculty at Juilliard.

David Cote is the theater editor and chief drama critic for *Time Out New York*. He has also written for *The New York Times*, *The New York Sun* and *Opera News*. Cote is a member of the New York Drama Critics' Circle and appears as a contributing critic on NY1's *On Stage*. His books include *Wicked: The Grimmerie*, about the Broadway musical *Wicked*, and a similar book about *Jersey Boys*. Cote is also the public dramaturg for Montclair State University's groundbreaking Peak Performance series. In a past life, he was a downtown actor and director, performing in works by Richard Foreman and many others. He is a 1992 graduate of Bard College. His blog appears at http://histriomastix.typepad.com.

Michael Feingold is chief theater critic for *The Village Voice*, New York's weekly newspaper, where his work over the past 35 years has made him a finalist for the Pulitzer Prize in Criticism and a winner of the prestigious George Jean Nathan Award. He has also worked as a playwright, director and dramaturg, and has translated more than 50 plays and operas from various foreign languages. His translations of the music-theater works of Bertolt Brecht and Kurt Weill are the standard ones in use all over the English-speaking world. He currently works as Literary Adviser to New York's Theatre for a New Audience.

Paul Hardt of Stuart Howard Associates works in casting for theatre, television and film. His casting credits include the national tours of *LEGENDS!* starring Joan Collins and Linda Evans, *On Golden Pond* starring Tom Bosley and Michael Learned, *The Who's Tommy* and *Leader of the Pack*. Stuart Howard Associates cast *I Love You, You're Perfect, Now Change*, *On Golden Pond* starring James Earl Jones and Leslie Uggams, *The Caine Mutiny Court-Martial*, *Hot Feet* and the American casting for *A Moon for the Misbegotten*.

John Istel has edited and contributed to a variety of performing arts, general interest and reference publications over the last 20 years including *American Theatre*, *The Atlantic*, *Back Stage*, *Contemporary Playwrights*, *Elle*, *Mother Jones*, *Newsday*, *New York*, *Stagebill* and *The Village Voice*. He has taught at New York University, Medgar Evers College and currently teaches English at Manhattan Theatre Lab High School, a New Visions school, which he helped create in partnership with Roundabout Theatre Company.

Jeffrey Eric Jenkins began editing *The Best Plays Theater Yearbook* series in 2001. Before joining *Best Plays* he served as theater critic, contributor and editor for a wide variety of publications. Since 1998, he has taught in the Department of Drama at New York University's Tisch School of the Arts. Jenkins has also taught at Carnegie Mellon University, the University of Washington, and SUNY–Stony Brook. He received degrees in drama and theater arts from Carnegie Mellon University and San Francisco State University, and he has directed more than two dozen productions in professional and educational theaters across the United States. Jenkins is a former chairman of the American Theatre Critics Association. He now serves on the boards of the Theater Hall of Fame and the American Theatre Wing, for which he chairs the Henry Hewes Design Awards and the Grants and Scholarships Committee.

Vivian Cary Jenkins spent more than twenty years as a healthcare executive and teacher before focusing on editorial work for *The Best Plays Theater Yearbook* series. Prior to her career in healthcare, she was a dancer and a Peace Corps volunteer in Honduras.

Chris Jones is the theater critic for the *Chicago Tribune*. For many years, he has reported on the Broadway road and Midwest theater for *Variety*.

Robert Kamp is the owner of I Can Do That Productions, Inc., a graphic design company in New York City. Prior to starting his own business, Kamp worked for several arts and entertainment publications including *Stagebill* and *City Guide Magazine*. Kamp designed the *Best Plays* logo, and has worked on the book's photos and graphic images since the 2000–2001 edition.

Charles McNulty is the chief theater critic of *The Los Angeles Times*. Before joining the *Times*, he was the theater editor of *The Village Voice*, chairman of the Obie Awards and head of Brooklyn College's program in graduate dramaturgy and theater criticism. A long time theater critic for the *Voice*, he was a member of the Obie Award panel for a decade. His writing has appeared in *The New York Times*, *Variety*, *Modern Drama*, *American Theatre* and *Theater*. He serves on the advisory board of Literary Managers and Dramaturgs of the Americas (LMDA). He received his DFA in dramaturgy and dramatic criticism from the Yale School of Drama. He lives in West Hollywood with his partner, Alex Press, their two cats and one dog.

Dominic P. Papatola has been the theater critic of the *St. Paul Pioneer Press* since 1999. He earned his journalism degree from the University of Minnesota and has written about theater for newspapers from Duluth, Minnesota to New Orleans, Louisiana. He was a juror for the 2003 Pulitzer Prize in Drama, and chaired the American Theatre Critics Association from 2005 to 2007. He teaches criticism at the National Endowment for the Arts Institute, the Eugene O'Neill Theater Center and other locales throughout the country.

Christopher Rawson has been theater critic and theater editor at the *Pittsburgh Post-Gazette* since 1983. Along with local reviews, features, news and columns, he reviews in New York, London and Canada. His BA came from Harvard, his PhD from the University of Washington and his love of theater from his father, actor Richard Hart. He has taught English literature at the University of Pittsburgh since 1968, where his subjects now include Shakespeare and August Wilson. A former chairman of the American Theatre Critics Association, he serves the Theater Hall of Fame as coordinator of the selection process.

Michael Sommers writes reviews, features and news about the New York stage for *The Star-Ledger* of New Jersey and other Newhouse Newspapers publications. During his 25-year career in New York, he has also been an editor of *Back Stage* and *Theatre Crafts* magazine. He has served three terms as President of the New York Drama Critics' Circle and is a longtime judge for the Clarence Derwent and Theatre World Awards.

Anne Marie Welsh has been theater critic for the *San Diego Union-Tribune* since 1997. Welsh earned her MA and PhD degrees in English and drama from the University of Rochester. In 1976, she joined the staff of the *Washington Star* where she was dance critic and backup theater critic until the paper's demise. Welsh came to the *San Diego Union* in 1983 serving as the paper's dance critic, second-chair theater critic and arts reporter before assuming her current post. She co-edited *The Longman Anthology of Modern and Contemporary Drama: A Global Perspective* and co-authored *Shakespeare: Script, Stage and Screen*. She has served on the jury for the Pulitzer Prize in drama and is a member of the *Best Plays* editorial board. She is also the proud mother of three sons.

Charles Wright has contributed essays to six editions of *The Best Plays Theater Yearbook*. His writing has appeared in *Biography Magazine* (for which he was a columnist), *The New Yorker*, *Stagebill* and TheaterMania.com, among other publications. As a business affairs executive at A&E Television Networks, Wright has been involved in hundreds of hours of nonfiction programming, including *Jesus Camp*, produced by A&E IndieFilms, released by Magnolia Pictures, and nominated for a 2007 Academy Award as Best Documentary Feature. A native of Tennessee and longtime resident of New York City, Wright holds degrees from Vanderbilt, Oxford, and the University of Pennsylvania.

Index

Play titles appear in bold. Asterisks (*) mark titles shortened for the index.
Page numbers in italic indicate essay citations.
Page numbers in bold italic indicate Broadway and Off Broadway listings.
Nouns or numbers in parentheses delineate different entities with similar names.